Valuing Your Privately Held Business

The Art & Science of Establishing Your Company's Worth

REVISED EDITION

IRVING L. BLACKMAN

 IRWIN
Professional Publishing®
Burr Ridge, Illinois
New York, New York

ISBN 1-55738-897-0

Printed in the United States of America

BB

1 2 3 4 5 6 7 8 9 0

To Mom and Dad

Mom would have "qvelled."

Dad would have been proud.

Contents

PREFACE

If there is an area in the field of taxation where uncertainty is the hallmark, it is the area of valuation of an interest in a closely held business.

Valuation causes frustration to accountants, who are used to adding and subtracting precise numbers and coming up with results that produce sheets that are in balance. It also frustrates lawyers, who are used to finding cases in point that, when taken in series, produce a brief that neatly proves their client's case. Probably the most frustrated of all is the closely held business owner; uncertainty reigns supreme, and often the financial life of a business and a family hangs in the balance.

Every company to be valued has its own set of facts and circumstances, and each valuation is unique, different from every other valuation. Two companies in the same business with almost identical numbers can have significantly different values because of just one fact difference. No set of general rules or volumes of books can bring out the importance of unique facts.

The valuation process is an art, not a science, but just as art has its discipline, so too does valuation. The discipline lies mainly in approaches and techniques, rather than in some magic formula or an all-too-easy reference to market prices of so-called comparable businesses that are publicly traded. The inquiry is not only on how to select the right approach, but also on how to attain the desired results for the business owners, their families, and sometimes their heirs.

As you read this book, bear in mind that a valuation is *always*:

1. as of a particular *point in time—A difference of only a few months in the valuation date can introduce (or eliminate) a fact of crucial significance. Events affecting the perceived value of the business, such as the loss or gain of a major client, can occur overnight. Fluctuating interest rates affecting the cost of capital can enhance or detract from a business' worth if its capital needs are great.*

2. for a particular *purpose—The value of a business may vary significantly depending upon the purpose of the valuation. If the valuation is for estate tax purposes, the taxpayer's goal is to come up with a low value. If the valuation is for loan security purposes, the taxpayer's goal is to come up with a high value. Accordingly, different valuation methods often are used to come*

up with different valuation amounts to fit the specific purpose of the taxpayer even though the same business is being valued. But one thing is certain: significant variations between the "different valuation amounts" means an incorrect method or valuation theory was used.

Any valuation must begin with this question: What is the purpose of the valuation? Is it for a purchase? Sale? Or is the valuation for tax purposes? A buyer's or a seller's estimation of value naturally will be prejudiced. A similar prejudice is present for tax purposes. Why? Because in that instance all mistakes are paid to an imaginary buyer—the IRS.

This book demonstrates these fundamentals:

1. How to value a specific business for a specific purpose.

2. How to control valuation results with the IRS dictating adverse tax consequences.

3. How to plan a valuation to accomplish lifetime planning as well as estate planning.

The following definition of valuation should be kept in mind throughout the book: *A valuation is a determination of the value of the business on a certain date for a specific purpose.*

However, regardless of the specific purpose, there is also an ultimate purpose to any valuation, which is also the ultimate purpose of this book: to serve the ends of the closely held business owner. Because, if you attain financial success, chances are the Internal Revenue Service will wind up with more of your dollars than you or your family will. Our forebearers fought a war to stop double taxation. Yet, success forces you *to pay taxes on taxes.* You pay tax when you make it; your estate pays tax when you transfer it to your heirs. New and changing tax laws—supercharged by inflation—continue to shave your share: the IRS gets more; you get less. Yes! And it gets worse with every change of overly complex tax laws that increase the tax on success.

In almost every field, the average American is capable of probing, pushing, thinking, and being creative, but not so in the tax field. As taxpayers, most Americans become paralyzed. The ability to save taxes under this nation's scheme of things is more an art than a science. Both Congress and the Internal Revenue Service are aligned toward the same end. It is the job of Congress to enact new tax provisions and at the same time close existing loopholes. The Internal Revenue Service has the unpopular but necessary task of overseeing every aspect of the tax law, carrying out the congressional intent. The match-up is one-sided: the Average American against the System (of laws, regulations, rulings, and cases engineered and maintained by Congress and the IRS).

Over the years, a void has developed between Taxpayers (who need to understand and solve tax problems) and Tax Advisors (who must bring their knowledge to bear on their clients' tax needs).

This book fills the void in the area of valuing a privately held business.

This book has been long overdue. As far as I know it is the first book of its kind in two respects.

First, it puts in one place sample real-life/real business valuations, IRS rulings, and court cases.

Second, it tells it like it is. It discusses and explains the theory of valuation and the various methods, but it also shows how, for real businesses, in real life, between real buyers and sellers, the price at which a business will change hands is determined. This method brings the appraiser as close to the true value of the business as possible. Only a real sale between a real buyer and a real seller could produce a more accurate price (valuation).

It is hoped that this book will be relished by every American Taxpayer who has accumulated enough wealth to possibly feel the sting of the Estate Tax Collector. It is also hoped that tax advisors will find this work not only a how-to book but also a valuable research tool.

At any time while you're reading the book or after you finish reading it, you may find you have a question or need professional help, then—

Call me!	*Fax me!*	*Write me!*
312-207-1040	312-207-1066	300 S. Riverside Plaza
		Chicago, IL 60606

Irving L. Blackman, C.P.A., J.D.
Partner, Blackman Kallick Bartelstein
Certified Public Accountants
Chicago, Illinois

ACKNOWLEDGMENTS

This book became a reality because of my life's two loves: my wife and my profession—accounting. Somehow the excitement that began over a quarter of a century ago still seems as real as yesterday: taking the CPA exam, getting married, and receiving the news—"You passed!" More important, the excitement is still there: the daily, quick-paced challenge of the profession and the pleasant life at home. Oh, no! Don't think for a moment that the two never conflict or that each doesn't present a never-ending parade of perplexing problems in the life style of the average practicing accountant/family man. Practicing in perfect harmony at my two loves, of office and of home, is still an art to be mastered. The married man who is lucky enough to enjoy his profession truly is doubly blessed . . . for in my opinion that is impossible without the right gal. One who knows just how and when to encourage, baby, applaud, and constructively criticize, and who possesses the other attributes necessary to keep her professional husband and family buoyed up and on course. My wife is such a gal—thanks, Sallie!

PART I

SECTION A

FUNDAMENTALS OF VALUATION

CHAPTER 1

VALUATION, FUTURE EXPECTATION, AND UNCERTAINTY

HOW BUSINESSES CHANGE HANDS IN REAL LIFE VS. A TAX VALUATION

When a business is sold in real life, two people—a real seller and a real buyer—negotiate and hammer out a real price. If the two parties can't agree on value, the seller will simply walk away and look for another buyer.

When you try to value that same business—the one you would have sold in the real world—for tax purposes, the entire perspective changes. It's almost like walking behind the mirror in "Alice in Wonderland." Indeed, things do get "curiouser and curiouser." Now we must deal with how to evaluate a *real business* that is to be sold by an *imaginary seller* (who may be alive or dead, and if dead, represented by his or her heirs or an executor) who will sell to an *imaginary buyer*. And guess what our simple mission is? All we have to do is come up with a *"real" price* to be used for tax purposes—a price that was determined in an *imaginary deal* that was made by *imaginary people*.

Crazy as it sounds, that's the way it is. Every business owner, whether he likes it or not, must some day face up to the fact that he will have to value his business for sale or for tax purposes. It can be done voluntarily during life, or it will be done in an involuntary situation, after death, by the IRS. The only "out" is to sell your business in a real transaction during your life. For most closely held business owners, selling doesn't make sense for many reasons. The most common reason is that the typical owner wants to transfer his business to the next generation.

If you want to win the business valuation tax game, this book is for you. Keep reading—you (or your family) will save BIG DOLLARS.

Or maybe you want to sell your business—or buy another business. How do you determine the price to ask or pay? Keep reading.

5

The value of a business stems from

1. the value of its operating and nonoperating assets, and

2. the return on investment those assets can generate.

Ultimately, if the business's operations continually generate a large negative cash flow or net loss, an owner must liquidate. He cannot sell it as a going concern that might require a determination of value; the best he/she could do is a sale at liquidation value. However, the anticipated monetary benefits that a business can generate through its operations as a going concern are what determines the value of the business in the buyer's mind. A business is only one of many places buyers can invest their money, and is an alternative they won't pursue if they can find a higher return on investment elsewhere.

The principle that underlies the valuation of a closely held business is the same principle that underlies the valuation of any investment. *Businesses are valuable not because of what they have done but because of what they are capable of doing.* It is the future expectation of the rate of return that a business can generate that determines its value.

VALUATION IN GENERAL

The valuation of an investment is based upon investors' calculation and expectation of approximately what return on investment they will garner at some point in the future. This is true whether the investment is a commodities futures contract bought in the morning and sold that afternoon, a long-term bond held for decades, or an operating business. This principle—future expectations of return on investment—is the foundation of valuation. Buyers determine the value of a commodity—how much they want to pay for it today—based on the rate of return on investment they think the commodity will make for them over a future period of time.

The next few paragraphs and examples are simplistic. Yet they are extremely important as a base on which this book builds in later chapters.

The *rate of return* of an investment is the percentage earned on the amount of money invested. The higher the percentage, the higher the rate of return. The higher the rate of return on an investment in a commodity, the more valuable it is, and the higher the price an investor is willing to pay for it. The lower the rate of return, the lower the price an investor will pay. For the moment, assume the investment has no risk.

Example

Two ten-year bonds each have a face value of $1,000. The average rate of interest, or market rate, paid by such bonds is 10 percent. However, the one bond pays 5 percent interest, while the other pays 15 percent. An investor would be willing to pay more than $1,000 for the bond yielding 15 percent, and less than $1,000 for the bond yielding 5 percent. The amount of money over the face value of the 15 percent bond that the investor would pay is called bond *premium*. The amount below face value that an investor would pay for the 5 percent bond is called bond *discount*. In this case, to at least equal the 10 percent market rate, the 15 percent bond would sell for a premium of $1,561.58, and the 5 percent bond at a discount of $691.26.

The price of a closely held business is determined in much the same manner. It is the future earning power of the business that determines its worth to a buyer and sets the price he/she is willing to pay. Again, only for the moment, assume no risk and that the earning power of the business is the only factor being considered.

Example

Suppose a business has a book value of $1 million, and over the past five years has returned 20 percent on the owner's investment. A buyer would be willing to pay a premium over that book value because he/she highly values the sustained, proven earning power of the business. Suppose instead, however, that an identical business with the same book value has returned only 2 percent over a five-year period. A seller would have to be willing to discount the value of the business in order to price it the right way to lure the cash for the sale out of a willing buyer's pockets.

The purpose of this book is to illustrate how a buyer or a seller, a taxpayer or the IRS, or a borrower or a lender, arrives at the right premium or discount when valuing a business. If one keeps the basic principle of valuation firmly in mind—future expectation of return on investment—the process becomes one of fine-tuning the price of the business using as many factors as desired or necessary to fit the specific purpose of the valuation.

Anyone endeavoring upon a valuation should also heed these two aphoristic cliches: "One person's sorrow is another's pain," and "Nothing is etched in stone." Why?

1. Any valuation usually has two adversaries valuing a business for diametrically opposite purposes. A fact that one party puts great stock in may seem inconsequential to another.

2. Valuations are also ephemeral. Locked into a certain point in time, and wedded to a specific purpose, the myopic vision of their makers, with the passage of time, usually makes valuations as useless as yesterday's newspapers.

The combination of these two factors makes valuation more of an art than a precise science.

THE IMPACT OF TAX RATES ON VALUATION

The Tax Reform Act of 1986 did many things. The Omnibus Budget Reconciliation Act of 1990 followed suit. However, for valuation purposes, both laws did one important thing—lower tax rates significantly.

How do lower tax rates (assuming risk—along with all other facts—remains constant) affect the value of a business? Since taxes levied on income will be lower, after-tax profits will be higher. Result: a higher return on investment. And it is a basic principal of valuation: The higher the return on investment, the more valuable the underlying asset—in this case, the entire business—producing that return.

The higher-value theory holds in only two possible circumstances: (1) if the business is a successful moneymaker, the premium (see the two preceding examples) should be higher. (2) On the other hand, a business that is losing money should trade hands at a slightly smaller discount (again, see examples).

For many reasons: VIVA LOWER TAX RATES!

UNCERTAINTY IN VALUATION

Welcome to the world of uncertainty. It is uncertainty that makes any valuation at best an unreliable indicator of future worth. The following are some of the uncertainties that professional appraisers face in most valuation situations:

■   They are uncertain about when, if ever, the owner will sell the business.

■   They are uncertain about how long the owner will live.

■   They are uncertain if business will get better or worse, be it a specific business, industry, or the economy in general.

■   They are uncertain about the rate of inflation.

■   They are uncertain about what estate tax bracket the owner will be in when he/she dies.

The uncertainties are as infinite and indeterminable as life itself. With death comes certainty: at that point, the moment of truth for valuation purposes arrives. All that then remains to be done is to apply the appropriate estate tax bracket to the final valuation.

All business owners, whether they like it or not, must someday face the fact that they will have to value their business for tax purposes. They can do it voluntarily during life, or the **IRS** will do it for them in an involuntary situation, after they die. The only "out" is to sell the business in a real transaction while they are alive.

For some business owners, selling doesn't make sense. In particular, if the business owner wants to transfer the business to the next generation or if he/she wants to keep on working until retirement or death, selling is not generally a reasonable option. Chapter 2 illustrates reasons for closely held business owners to undertake periodic valuations, even if they want to keep their businesses. The uncertainty that surrounds future expectations demands that the closely held business owner be prepared to meet any and all contingencies.

CHAPTER 2

WHY VALUATION IS A MUST: SPECIFIC PURPOSES FOR VALUING THE CLOSELY HELD BUSINESS

THE CLOSELY HELD CORPORATION: A DEFINITION

This book concerns itself with the closely held business. Although a closely held business can be any one of many entities (such as partnership, sole proprietorship, joint venture, and so on), this book focuses its attention on the *closely held corporation*. The same valuation principles applicable to closely held corporations, *mutatis mutandi*, can be applied to unincorporated closely held businesses such as sole proprietorships, partnerships, or joint ventures. An IRS valuation ruling (Rev. Rul. 65-192, 1965-2 C.B. 259, 260) specifically states that its valuation principles are applicable to closely held businesses of whatever legal form.

The IRS defines a closely held corporation as follows:

> a corporation whose market quotations are either unavailable or of such scarcity that they do not reflect the fair market value.
> (Rev. Rul. 59-60, 1959-1 C.B. 237)

> a corporation . . . the shareholders of which are owned by a relatively limited number of stockholders. Often the entire stock issue is held by one family. The result of this situation is that little, if any, trading in the shares takes place. There is, therefore, no established market for the stock, and such sales as occur

at irregular intervals seldom reflect all the elements of a representative transaction as defined by the term "fair market value."
(Rev. Rul. 59-60, 1959-1 C.B. 237)

As the following list and explanations illustrate, failure to incorporate may severely limit financial and tax-planning opportunities of the business owner. The idea is clear: in most cases, a business owner who hasn't incorporated should.

A REAL-LIFE HORROR STORY THAT DIDN'T HAVE TO HAPPEN

A simple transfer plan, which included a business valuation provision, could have avoided this family tragedy.

I hate stories like this. Thousands and thousands of dollars wasted on a bitter court trial. Members of a one-time happy family split into warring factions. Looking back, I can see how easy it would have been to avoid all the trouble. And now, I hope that by telling you the story, you won't let the same thing happen to you.

Here's the story. Two brothers owned their west coast business 50/50 and had worked together for years to build it to $25 million in annual sales. Let's call them Joe and Brad. Joe and his wife Mary had two sons who were valuable employees in the business.

Time after time, I counseled them to execute a buy-sell agreement. Every time I brought it up, one of them—usually Joe—would apologize for putting it off and promised to do something about it real soon. But they never got it done. Before they had it drawn up—you guessed it—Joe died. Joe's will named his brother Brad the co-executor and trustee along with a local bank. Joe's entire estate, which consisted mainly of the stock in the company, was left to a trust with his wife Mary as the sole beneficiary.

The executors asked me to value the company for estate tax purposes. Then, before Brad negotiated for the company to buy the stock from Joe's estate, he resigned as co-executor to avoid any conflict of interest. Once the company redeemed (bought) Joe's stock, Brad would become the sole shareholder. I was asked to do an update of the stock valuation for the sole purpose of setting a price for the redemption.

Everyone involved in the negotiations was represented by their own attorneys. This included the widow Mary, the bank as executor and trustee, the corporation and Brad. After many phone conferences, a deal was struck and the appropriate documents were signed.

Then Mary had second thoughts. She got a new lawyer and filed a suit to set aside the redemption agreement on the grounds that the price was too low and that there were conflicts of interest. Even though her sons sided with their uncle Brad, Mary was determined to go through with the trial.

The bank asked me to testify as an expert witness about the stock valuation. As it turned out, my valuation was upheld 100%, but that hardly seems to matter now. On the day I testified, there were eight lawyers in the courtroom and four other expert witnesses. The total cost was astronomical and Joe's estate paid most of the bill. Worst of all, the family isn't talking anymore. And none of it would have happened if Joe and Brad had signed a buy/sell agreement fixing the rights and duties of all the parties.

Don't let it happen to you. Even a transfer plan that isn't perfect will head off a lot of lawyers' costs and, more importantly, family anguish.

WHY PERIODIC VALUATIONS ARE A MUST

Without reliable knowledge of the value of the business, an owner cannot

1. Plan effectively to minimize *estate taxes* by

    a. Having shares redeemed by the corporation (a *redemption* is when a corporation buys its own stock from one or more of its shareholders) at the least tax cost (see Chapter 14)

    b. Planning a *recapitalization* to freeze the value of the business for estate purposes (see Chapter 11)

    c. Selling shares to an *ESOP* (Employee Stock Ownership Plan) as a tax-wise means of transferring the business to a third party (see Chapter 13)

    d. Negotiating proper *buy-and-sell stock agreements* (see Chapter 10)

    e. Developing a *gift program* of business property (see Chapter 15)

2. Negotiate realistically for possible *sale* or *merger*

3. *Spin-off* part of the business for cash-flow, regulatory, or operational purposes

4. Reach an equitable property settlement in a *divorce* that properly divides the closely held business between husband and wife

5. Obtain *financing* using the closely held business as collateral

6. Buy out dissident minority shareholders

7. Restructure the capital makeup of the company in a tax-free *reorganization*

8. Make tax-deductible *charitable contributions* of the closely held corporation's stock

There are a multitude of other reasons for valuing a business. Following are some of the more important reasons:

1. *Reorganization of a Troubled Business*

    Often, a tooling/machining or manufacturing business finds itself cash poor and unable to meet current obligations, yet projects a profitable future. A restructuring of its capital may make it more attractive for financing short-term as well as long-term obligations to reassure creditors that the business will pay its liabilities. The company will be valued based on the projections and its new capital structure.

2. *Obtaining Financing*

    A lender is more apt to furnish capital funds to a business if that business can demonstrate that it possesses valuable assets, whether operating or intangible, and that it also generates substantial revenue and profit from those assets. Valuations that show these factors over and above what is shown on the business' financial statements can make obtaining financing easier.

3. *Buy-Out of Dissident Minority Shareholders*

    Most states have laws that protect the interests of minority shareholders. Often, articles of incorporation provide for contingent buy-outs of minority interests. Valuations of such minority interests that fairly reflect value minimize costly court battles that impose a financial drain on the operations of the business and often cast a cloud of uncertainty over the business' future.

4. *Litigation*

Unfortunately, valuations due to litigation are costly, but necessary, to each of the warring litigants. One bit of advice: Get the best valuation expert who will accept your case. You'll save in the long run.

In each of the various valuation purposes listed, the relationship of the parties, the objectives to be accomplished, and a host of other factors might cause the fair market value to fluctuate. Much depends on the eye of the beholder. Honest, competent people have different ideas of the fair market value of the same business.

The theoretical goal in any valuation is precision. Yet, the true goal is to value the business within a range. The narrower the range, the better.

MINIMIZING ESTATE TAXES

The Fiction of the Estate Tax

Of all the reasons for valuing a closely held business, defeating the estate tax is probably the most important. Valuing a business for purchase or sale is straightforward: a real seller and a real buyer hammer out the price and terms. When you try to value that same business for tax purposes, the entire perspective changes.

This is the estate tax valuation challenge: a *real business* must be valued. It will be sold by an *imaginary seller* (who may be alive or dead, and if dead, represented by heirs or an executor) to an *imaginary buyer*. This fiction is employed to arrive at a "*real price*" to be used for tax purposes—a price that was determined in an *imaginary deal* made by *imaginary people*.

How Estate Tax Can Destroy a Closely Held Business

What follows illustrates what can happen to a closely held business that is not armed with the correct valuation.

Take for example a real business worth more than $500,000, and still growing in value. This book is must reading for the business owner who might own all or a portion of such a business when he dies. Why? Because when he dies, the IRS becomes his partner.

It's an old cliche, but here it has meaning: there are only two sure things in life—death and taxes. The IRS has found a way to combine the two into the estate tax that can rob business owners, their families, and business associates of everything the business owners worked hard for during their lives.

How much the IRS can posthumously tax the deceased owner depends on two factors: *how much* the person is worth when he/she dies, and *when* the person dies.

The Economic Recovery Tax Act of 1981 (ERTA) changed the rules of the game, lowering tax rates and raising the amount exempt from tax. ERTA increased the uni-credit that was being phased in over a six-year period. The following schedule shows the period, amount of credit, amount of the estate exempted from tax, and the maximum and lowest rates.

Year	Amount of Uni-credit	Amount of Estate Exempt from Tax	Maximum Rate	Lowest Rate
1982	$ 62,800	$225,000	65%	32%
1983	79,300	275,000	60	34
1984	96,300	325,000	55	34
1985	121,800	400,000	55	34
1986	155,800	500,000	55	37
1987 and after	192,800	600,000	55	37

Under ERTA, the closely held business owner gets a big break: The "Amount of Uni-credit" protects the "Amount of Estate Exempt from Tax." For example, death since 1987 means the first $600,000 of an estate escapes tax. Then the IRS starts to get its share.

Here's an example. If you are the owner of a small, closely held business, fill in your own numbers to get an idea of what fate could await you.

Example

Right now the owner of the closely held business is alive and the business is worth $500,000. The future prospects of the business are good enough that the business probably will be worth more by the time the owner dies. All things being equal, inflation and business growth are likely to kick the value into seven figures. How much will the tax be? Assume the owner has other property worth $600,000 on the day he/she dies and that his/her spouse is also dead. The schedule shows the federal estate tax bite:

If the business is worth	The estate tax will be
$ 500,000	$ 194,000
1,000,000	408,000
1,500,000	637,000
2,000,000	886,000
2,500,000	1,151,000*

*Plus 53% of the excess over $2.5 million, increasing to 55% in 1993 and thereafter.

These figures illustrate the potential size of the valuation problem in the estate tax context. The obvious question is "Where will the money come from to pay the tax?" Unfortunately, the money is often just not there.

Because the potential tax stakes are so high, placing a value on an owner's interest (usually stock) in a closely held business (usually a corporation) often leads to serious conflict with the Internal Revenue Service. The IRS is the closely held business owner's adversary. Valuation is sort of a game—a game without clearly defined rules. The score is kept in dollars—*the closely held business owner's dollars*. Unlike the publicly traded stock, whose value is published in the daily newspapers, the value of closely held stock must be individually determined. All too often such determinations run as follows:

by the IRS . . . .   much higher than the value reported by the taxpayer, arrived at by comparing the business to comparable businesses whose stock is publicly traded

by the taxpayer . . . . .   much lower than the value claimed by the IRS agents

by the courts . . . .   somewhere in between, arrived at by weighing various factors that concern the business

The schedule following the preceding example gives an idea of the size of the tax payments that may hinge on the outcome of a dispute with the IRS. Professional fees for the fight are high. Result? Business liquidations (at sacrifice prices) sometimes become necessary to pay estate taxes, because a deceased owner failed to foresee the high value that the IRS could successfully claim for his/her closely held stock.

The most common reason for this unfortunate occurrence is inadequate planning concerning a valuation of the company's stock. For the most independent business people, their business will be the biggest asset in their estate. If the IRS wins a valuation battle, the business loses. Everything the closely held business owner worked a lifetime to build might have to be dismantled overnight to pay taxes.

How to Beat the Estate Tax: Planning Tools

The estate tax is a transfer tax. It is levied on the closely held business owner's property that is transferred to their heirs and to those they wish to receive it when they die. Transferring a closely held business at the least tax cost could be the subject of another book altogether, yet it and valuation of the business are inextricably intertwined.

There are three common types of tax-disaster problems in the business-transfer area; they result from the following things:

1. the transfer not being done because the founder doesn't know how to solve the particular transfer problem, which compounds as the potential tax cost continues to mount

2. procrastination

3. the transfer being made, but being made unwisely from a tax standpoint, and the owner, business, or family being clobbered taxwise

Never fear. The government-transfer-tax-machine can be beat.

A variety of tax-saving transfer-of-ownership techniques have been used by "sophisticated business people" for generations. Their use has been limited to those fortunate few who have been able to translate their objectives and applicable tax law into a workable transfer plan. The sooner the plan is put into effect, the greater the tax savings.

In most cases, planning the transfer of a closely held corporation means freezing the owner's estate. A good transfer plan is part of an overall estate plan that attempts to get the asset-freezing process into place as soon as possible. If you can cut wealth off before it accumulates, serious tax problems can be avoided.

Asset freezing is really a generic term for describing the various methods that have been designed to limit the estate tax value of a closely held business:

1. transferring future growth,

2. providing the owner a flow of income during life, and

3. keeping control of the business in the owner for as long as he/she lives.

These methods involve both transfer and valuation. An asset freeze simply seeks to achieve all (or almost all) of the owner's specific objectives. The freeze is usually the most important part of a transfer plan. Following is a list of popular tools employed in asset freezing.

Redemption.   A redemption occurs when a shareholder sells stock back to the corporation. The corporation is said to "redeem" the stock. The proceeds from the sale are treated as dividends to the shareholder, unless

1. the number of shares redeemed is disproportionate to the number of shares held by the shareholder,

2. the redemption terminates the shareholder's entire interest in the corporation,

3. the redemption is not substantially equivalent to a dividend, or

4. the redemption is made to a noncorporate shareholder in partial liquidation.

If the redemption falls into any of these four categories, it is treated as a sale or exchange. Then any property or cash received by the shareholder that results in a profit is taxed as a capital gain.

Here is a typical redemption scenario: The owners' children own a small number of shares, which they purchased from their parents, or received as a gift. The parents sell the balance of their shares to the corporation. The selling of all the parents' shares qualifies under the second exception just mentioned. It is a complete termination of their interest in the corporation.

This method accomplishes the freeze—the children own 100 percent of the future growth. However, there are some drawbacks: the parents must still pay tax on the profit, and the corporation cannot deduct the payments. Not only are the parents out of control, but the tax rules prohibit them from working for the corporation for ten years. If they do, the capital gain may turn into ordinary income—a tax disaster.

Example

In *L. V. Seda* (82 TC 484), a husband and wife who were the sole shareholders in a family corporation had all their stock in the company redeemed, and at the same time, resigned all of their positions as directors and officers of the company. Their son became the sole shareholder. Unfortunately, at the request of the son, the father continued to work for the company as a salaried advisor at $1,000 a month salary.

That continued advisory capacity was enough to constitute an "interest in the corporation" that turned the father's capital gain into ordinary income.

What this case illustrates is that redemptions, although effective tools for freezing the owner's interests in a corporation by removing it, carry with them disadvantages for the closely held business owner who desires to continue working in the business or who wants to nurture the next generation of owners. The owner has to choose: capital gain (not much of an advantage after tax reform) and no control, or ordinary income and a majority shareholder position. This and other tax pitfalls of redemption are discussed in detail in Chapter 14.

Recapitalization.   Prior to 1987, recapitalizations (recaps) were the direct routes to the promised land for freezing the value of family businesses. Everybody did it. The IRS got fed up. The Congress got fed up. Congress changed the law. Recaps were dead and buried.

But wait. Small business complained. Trade associations complained. Tax practitioners complained. Congress heard. Congress listened. Congress changed the law again in late 1990. Recaps are back. Hurrah! Yes? Well, yes as a technical matter. But as a practical matter, they may as well still be dead and buried.

Let's explore the world of recaps. Suppose Joe Owner owns 100 percent of the common stock of Success Co. In December 1991, he exchanged it for 100 percent of all the new common stock and all the new preferred stock of Success Co. Joe has Success Co. appraised. The appraiser values the total company at $1,000,000, the preferred stock at $900,000 and the common at $100,000. That exchange of the old common for the new common and preferred stock is called a "recapitalization." Joe keeps the preferred stock; his two sons—who are active in the business—receive the common stock from Joe as a gift.

Now then, let's make two assumptions: First, Joe does everything right and the recap works (even the IRS agrees); second, Joe messes up and the IRS says (and is right), "the recap doesn't work."

Okay, the first assumption: Suppose the preferred stock is cumulative and pays a 10 percent dividend. Success Co. pays the 10 percent dividend of $90,000 ($900,000 times 10 percent) to Joe every year, until Joe dies in the year 2015 (25 years after the recap). Success Co. is worth $10,900,000 on the day Joe dies. What is the value of the preferred stock in Joe's estate? A measly $900,000. Great! The IRS just got shortchanged on the estate tax that would have been owed on $10 million (the value of the common stock)—a savings of about $5.5 million (assuming the estate tax rates don't change). Good move, Joe.

Now, let's take a look at the second assumption. Somehow, Joe made a mistake; for example, the preferred stock was noncumulative and Success Co. never paid Joe a dime in dividends. The IRS will ignore the attempted recap. Joe dies on the same day as in the first assumption in the year 2015 and Success Co. is worth the same $10.9 million. This time the entire $10.9 million will be taxable in Joe's estate.

The technical tax reasons as to why Joe succeeded in the first case and failed in the second are beyond the scope of this book. But just understand one key point: Unless you think your corporation is about to skyrocket in value (say, double in value or more in the next five years), a recap is not for you.

To make the recap work, you must not only follow the recap rules, but you must also have your total corporation valued. The preferred stock must also be valued. The value of the preferred stock is subtracted from the value of the total corporation; and the difference is considered the value of the common stock.

The rules are a complex maze. Make sure to talk to an expert as to why or why not a recap is in your family business' best interest.

Employee Stock Ownership Plans (ESOPs). If the owner cannot or does not want to transfer the corporation to family members, an ESOP might be the answer. ESOPs can be used to facilitate the transfer of a closely held corporation to nonfamily buyers or the company's employees by creating a market for its shares. Best of all, it lets the owner take cash out of the corporation at capital gains rates or defer the gain by reinvesting the ESOP distribution in domestic common stocks.

An ESOP is a *qualified defined contribution plan*, which is similar to a typical profit-sharing plan but is designed to invest primarily in the employer's stock or securities. Technically, an ESOP can be either a stock bonus plan or a combination stock bonus and money purchase pension plan.

Here's an overview of a common method of operating an ESOP.

1.   An Employee Stock Ownership Trust (ESOT) is established by the employer.

2.   The ESOT invests in the employer's stock or securities. The ESOT can acquire the employer's stock from

  a.   the stockholder of the employer corporation,
  b.   the employer corporation, or
  c.   both.

3.   It can get the cash for the purchase either

  a.   by a direct deductible contribution from the employer, or
  b.   by borrowing the money from a bank.

4.   Subsequent contributions to the ESOT, which are used to pay off principal and interest on funds borrowed to purchase employer stock, are deductible by the employer corporation as made.

The ESOT, with all the rights and benefits of a shareholder, holds the stock for the benefit of participating employees. The stock is distributed to the participants when they are eligible to receive it—upon retirement, disability, or death. Usually, the ESOT or the corporation repurchases the distributed stock from the employees. This flow of stock "to, from, and back" to the trust or corporation, combined with very favorable tax breaks applicable to ESOPs, makes the ESOP an interesting planning tool.

These and other aspects of ESOPs, including valuation of closely held stock sold to an ESOP, are discussed in detail in Chapter 13.

Buy-Sell Agreements. A typical buy-sell agreement is

1.   a contract between shareholders of a closely held corporation (or between the share-holders and the corporation itself), in which the parties agree

2.   that any shareholder transferring corporation stock—because of death, disability, gift, bankruptcy, or any other reason—must sell or transfer the shares

3.   to the other shareholders (or the corporation) at a specified price and on specified terms.

If the agreement is structured properly, the agreed price will be honored by the courts as the correct valuation of the deceased's closely held stock for estate tax purposes. The courts have held that for estate tax purposes the IRS is bound to honor the price specified in the buy-sell agreement, if the following conditions are met:

1. The price of the shares fixed in the buy-sell agreement have been arrived at according to some reasonable valuation method.

2. The agreement has a *bona fide* business purpose and is not, in the IRS' words, "a device to pass the decedent's shares to the natural objects of his/her bounty for less than adequate and full consideration"; in other words, the agreement is not a testamentary device used to defeat the estate tax. This issue is raised by the IRS when the parties to the agreement are related.

3. The estate of the deceased is legally bound to sell the shares to the parties specified in the agreement after the shareholder's death.

4. The parties to the agreement cannot dispose of their stock in their lifetime unless the other parties have a right of first refusal.

If careful drafting does not satisfy the above requirements, the IRS is free to use its own valuation method to arrive at what is usually a higher value for the stock (Reg. 20.2031-2(h); *Estate of O.B. Littick*, 31 TC 181).

Here is an example of how the IRS attacks a buy-sell agreement. Recently, it agreed to the result of the 17-year-old *Littick* case, but disagreed with its reasoning. In *Littick*, three brothers, one of whom had terminal cancer, were sole shareholders of a family corporation. They executed a buy-sell agreement that provided a selling price for the stock of $200,000, even though the agreement stipulated it had a fair market value (FMV) of more than $250,000. The terminally ill brother died shortly thereafter.

The IRS claimed the agreement was a testamentary device, demanding the decedent's stock be included in his estate at FMV. The court upheld the business purpose of the agreement, which was to keep control of the business in the family, and honored the set price. Why? Even though one brother was terminally ill, it was possible that the healthy brothers could die before him.

After brooding for 17 years over its defeat, the IRS is attempting to do with the gift tax what is couldn't do using the estate tax. It now says that the terminally ill brother's shortened life expectancy made his promise to sell worth more than the promise of his brothers. Therefore, there was an immediate gift. Nonsense!

(The factors just mentioned, as well as other IRS methods of attacking the valuation price in buy-sell agreements, are discussed in detail in Chapter 10.)

Gifts of Closely Held Stock to Family Members. A program of gifting closely held stock can transfer stock worth up to $10,000 ($20,000 if the donor's spouse consents to the gift) annually to each donee (family members, and so on) without paying gift tax. Such gifts save estate taxes in two ways: the value of the stock will not be subject to the estate tax when the donor dies, and any appreciation in the stock after the gift is made also escapes estate tax.

That portion of an annual gift over $10,000 ($20,000 if married) will be included in the donor's estate. The use of a gift program that passes IRS muster is discussed in Chapter 15.

SALE, PURCHASE, OR MERGER

Sale or Purchase

The sale or purchase of a closely held business calls for the application of the appraisal techniques described in detail in this book as well as the utilization of a competent, professional appraiser. Those techniques are the meat of this book.

Merger

Most states allow corporations to merge. A not uncommon scenario involves the merger of a closely held corporation into a publicly held corporation, or the merger of two closely held corporations. The shareholders of the former corporation usually exchange their shares for shares of the surviving corporation. Valuation of these shares is important for tax purposes and for protecting and satisfying minority shareholder rights.

State law usually provides that shareholders of the corporation that would cease to exist after the merger have a right to a court hearing to determine whether the price offered for their stock by the surviving corporation is adequate. That hearing usually turns into a battle of valuation experts, not unlike psychiatrists testifying as to sanity of a defendant in a criminal trial; the difference is that the value of the closely held corporation's stock, not a defendant's state of mind, is the bone of contention.

SPIN-OFF OF THE CLOSELY HELD BUSINESS

Most closely held corporations don't have subsidiaries, but those that do may find it necessary to spin-off (sell) the subsidiary for reasons such as these:

1. compliance with government agency regulations (SEC, IRS, FTC, and so on)

2. infusion of working capital into the parent closely held business

3. resolving disputes between shareholders regarding the operations and objective of the business

Usually, shareholders of the parent company receive the subsidiary's stock for a set price. The transaction can be tax free if it is for a legitimate business purpose of the parent company. Whether tax free or not, valuation is necessary to justify the selling price and may be necessary to determine the basis of the stock of the new corporation.

DIVORCE PROPERTY SETTLEMENT

Divorce, in and of itself, can be an unpleasant experience. If one or both of the divorcing spouses are owners of a closely held business, reaching a property settlement can be extremely difficult.

Suppose, for example, that one spouse knows that the other has depreciated the business' assets heavily at an accelerated rate or has depressed income by use of excessive entertainment expense deductions. That spouse will be reluctant, and rightly so, to accept any valuation that does not make appropriate adjustment for these factors.

The property settlement usually ends up with one spouse transferring stock in the corporation to the other. Valuation of the stock is the cornerstone to reaching a settlement. The parties relying upon the valuation are in conflict, often bitter. This can make valuation very difficult.

The Transfer Tax Problem for Pre-July 19, 1984 Transfers

The transfer tax problem that plagued closely held business owners going through a divorce before enactment of the Tax Reform Act of 1984 (TRA) is a real mess.

Example

Mr. Entrepreneur owned 100 percent of the stock of a substantial business. His tax basis was $200,000. Mr. Entrepreneur transferred 25 percent of the stock, with a value of $550,000, to Ms. Entrepreneur as part of a property settlement pursuant to a divorce decree entered into before July 18, 1984. Mr. Entrepreneur suffered a taxable gain (technically, a capital gain) of $500,000 ($550,000 less $50,000—25 percent x $200,000— of basis).

Not only did Mr. Entrepreneur get hung for a current tax on the transfer, but Ms. Entrepreneur shares in the future growth of the business. Often this future-growth result can be avoided by recapitalizing the business and transferring preferred (non-growth) stock, instead of common stock, to the spouse.

The Transfer Problem Shifts for Post-July 18, 1984 Transfers

TRA provides that no gain or loss is recognized to either spouse on the transfer of property between them incidental to divorce. The transferee spouse takes a carryover basis in the transferred property. The transfer problem is shifted from the shoulders of the spouse transferring the property to the shoulders of the spouse receiving it.

Example

Consider the same facts as the previous example, except that Mr. Entrepreneur transfers the stock to Ms. Entrepreneur pursuant to a divorce decree entered into after July 18, 1984. Mr. Entrepreneur recognizes no gain or loss. He is able to take appreciated property and use its fair market value to fulfill his divorce obligations with no adverse tax consequences. Ms. Entrepreneur, however, steps into Mr. Entrepreneur's shoes as owner of the transferred property, and is stuck with his low basis. If she sells the stock she will be the one who suffers a taxable capital gain of $500,000.

Frequently, the net result is that the dispute over valuation ends up in court, with both parties spending money on attorneys' and accountants' fees that they should be dividing between themselves instead. Periodic valuations made before the divorce can narrow the range of disputed value between the parties and make a settlement easier to reach.

Careful planning is essential. A valuation that satisfies both parties makes sharing the transfer tax burden easier in settlement negotiations.

OBTAINING FINANCING

A lender is more apt to furnish capital funds to a business if that business can demonstrate that it possesses valuable assets and that it also generates substantial revenue and profit from those assets. Valuations that show these factors over and above what is shown on the business' financial statements can make obtaining financing easier.

BUY-OUT OF DISSIDENT MINORITY SHAREHOLDERS

Most states have laws that protect the interests of minority shareholders. Often, articles of incorporation provide for contingent buy-outs of minority interests. Valuations of such minority interests that fairly reflect value minimize costly court battles that can drain a business's finances and often cast a cloud of uncertainty over its future.

Valuation of minority interests usually must be discounted for lack of marketability. Such discounting is discussed in Chapter 9.

REORGANIZATION OF A TROUBLED BUSINESS

Often, a closely held corporation finds itself cash-poor and unable to meet current obligations, yet projects a profitable future. A restructuring of capital may make a business more attractive for financing short-term as well as long-term obligations, and so reassure creditors that the business will pay its liabilities.

First the business is valued on a debt-free or reduced debt basis; then the reorganization creates a capital structure that allows the business to survive so the creditors have a better chance of receiving all or part of the amount due to them. This approach can be voluntary or made by a bankruptcy court.

CHARITABLE CONTRIBUTIONS

If a closely held corporation or its shareholders make charitable contributions of the corporation's stock, the donor is entitled to a deduction. Under current law, the deduction is limited to 10 percent of a corporation's taxable income for such contributions, while shareholders are allowed to deduct up to 50 percent of their incomes. Contributions that exceed these limitations can be carried forward to future tax years, according to specific rules. The exact amount allowable as a deduction depends on the value of the shares contributed. Not surprisingly, the IRS has taken a keen interest in the valuation of such contributed shares.

CHAPTER 3

THE LEGAL APPROACH TO VALUATION

FAIR MARKET VALUE

The concept of *fair market value* is mostly a legal device used by the courts and the IRS to settle valuation disputes in estate and gift tax matters. It has little use between a real seller and real buyer who are hammering out the sale price of a real business. The price arrived at in such situations is what the seller will accept and the buyer is willing to pay. That price can vary depending on the buyer and the seller. The process of valuation—using discounts and premiums—described in Chapter 1 is what really happens in the sale and purchase of a business.

However, valuations are made for many purposes other than buying and selling a business, as demonstrated in Chapter 2. The courts and the IRS frequently get involved in valuations, and what they consider to be fair market value in those situations is of paramount importance.

IRS Definition of Fair Market Value

In every valuation matter before the IRS, the meaning of "fair market value" is at center stage and is used to decide the issue. For purposes of estate tax (Regulations 20.2031-1(b)) and gift tax (Regulations 25.2512-1), fair market value is defined this way:

> The price at which the property would change hands between a willing buyer and a willing seller when the former is not under any compulsion to buy and the latter is not under any compulsion to sell, both parties having reasonable knowledge of relevant facts.

This definition is universally accepted in federal taxation. Regulation 1-1001(a) states, "fair market value is a question of fact, but only in rare and extraordinary cases will property be considered to have no fair market value." As Chapter 4 illustrates, fair market value, value, or the price of a closely held business is a determination based on particular facts and circumstances.

Judicial Definition of Fair Market Value

The term "fair market value" has been defined by the courts as "the price which property will bring when it is offered for sale by one who is willing but is not obligated to sell it, and is bought by one who is willing or desires to purchase but is not compelled to do so" (*H.H.Marshman.* 279 F.2d 27.).

Uncertainty of Fair Market Value

As a practical matter, it is impossible to pinpoint the exact price two parties would arrive at in an actual transaction. This is particularly true when a major block of stock is involved, because the price agreed upon is normally determined through a bargaining process. In addition to the underlying economics of the company and its industry, the bargaining skill and the individual circumstances of the two parties also affect the actual price. These highly subjective considerations make a valuation study by an independent analyst imprecise, at best.

The key question is this: Who has the advantage when the uncontested fact is that fair market value is a matter of uncertainty, floating on a wavy sea of opinion—the IRS or the taxpayers? I maintain the advantage is clearly on the taxpayers' side—provided they know what they are doing.

Many sections of the Internal Revenue Code refer to fair market value (it is mentioned 173 times), but neither these sections nor the applicable regulations give any precise definition. Most practitioners assume that the definition for estate and gift tax purposes is universally applicable. So far this assumption has proved correct.

Fair Market Value as It Really Is

In 1928 the court (in *James Couzens*, 11 B.T.A. 1040) really said it like it is:

> It has been said that value is a price at which a willing seller and a willing buyer would agree to trade if they both were aware of the facts. Recognizing all the facts in existence, and from them attempting reasonably to predict those to come, being neither unduly skeptical nor unduly optimistic, we sought to determine what an intelligent and reasonable seller and an intelligent and reasonable buyer would in their fairly mercenary interest have been most likely to agree upon as a price for the property in question.

In the real world, when valuing the stocks of closely held corporations for federal tax purposes, instead of a mythical willing seller and a mythical willing buyer, we have as traditional adversaries a real taxpayer (or the taxpayer's heirs or donees) and the "unreal" IRS. The many litigated cases and the more numerous compromise settlements clearly show each adversary considers the other anything but willing and reasonable.

VALUATION AS THE IRS SEES IT

How the Valuation Tax Game Is Played

In every valuation of a business for tax purposes, the IRS is looking over the taxpayer's shoulder, scouting out the taxpayer as a potential opponent. The way to win the valuation game is to know in advance what the IRS is looking for and how it plays the valuation game.

There are three sources the IRS looks to for guidance in order to best the taxpayer at the game:

1. the Internal Revenue Code,

2. IRS regulations, and

3. rulings.

The referees overseeing the conflict between the IRS and taxpayers are the courts: Tax Court (which also has a small claims division), U.S. District Courts, U.S. Appellate Courts, and the U.S. Supreme Court.

According to information published yearly in the IRS *Statistics of Information Bulletin*, past practice has shown that the higher in the court system a taxpayer goes, the smaller the taxpayer's chance of winning the game.

A Small Business Administration study (SBA Market Research Summary No. 124, April 1963) summarizes the results of cases involving estate tax valuations of closely owned businesses as follows:

1. The IRS usually employs whatever approach to "fair market value" that results in the highest value and, as a result, yields the highest tax liability. The study cautions that the cases may not be wholly representative, since it is the extreme cases that most likely end up in court.

2. There was a strong tendency for the IRS to adopt a rigid formula approach to valuation that considered the enterprise in a vacuum. Market condition studies were rarely undertaken unless the IRS was forced to defend its position in court.

3. Taxpayers usually contended for unrealistically low valuation, as might be expected. However, some cases were lost by default because taxpayers were inadequately prepared to justify their own valuation figures.

4. The courts afforded taxpayers protection by making the IRS justify its valuations with thorough expert testimony and documentation.

5. The final valuation amount reached by the courts in their decisions tended to compromise between the higher figure of the IRS and the lower figure of the taxpayer. This tendency is an incentive for both the IRS and the taxpayer to present an extreme initial valuation.

6. Often, the decision in a case turned not on the merits of the accuracy of contending valuations and their methods but on legalistic procedural and evidentiary rules that prevented the court from considering facts that would result in a fully formed decision.

When reading the following sections of this chapter, which contain statutory and regulatory provisions concerning valuation, take notice of the concept of comparing similar businesses engaged in similar industries as useful guides at arriving at the value of a closely held business. These "comparable" companies, or comparables, can be closely held or publicly traded. You can see the ease of using a publicly traded comparable by turning to the page of *The Wall Street Journal* that contains the market price of the stock selected.

As will be posited in Chapter 6 the use of comparables, although appropriate in some instances, can be deceptively easy for the IRS but is usually disastrous for the closely held business owner.

Estate Tax Code Section

Section 2031(b) of the Code, covering valuation for estate tax purposes of unlisted securities, provides the following:

> In the case of stock and securities of a corporation the value of which, by reason of their not being listed on an exchange and by reason of the absence of sales thereof, cannot be determined with reference to bid and asked prices or with reference to sales prices, the value thereof shall be determined by taking into consideration, in addition to all other factors, *the value of stock or securities of corporations engaged in the same or a similar line of business which are listed on an exchange.* [Author's italics.]

Estate Tax Regulations

The estate tax regulations (Reg. 20.2031.2-(f)) provide in part

> Where selling prices or bid and asked prices are unavailable. If . . . actual sales prices and bona fide bid and asked prices are lacking, then the fair market value is to be determined by taking the following factors into consideration:
>
> 1.   In the case of corporate or other bonds, the soundness of the security, the interest yield, the date of maturity, and other relevant factors; and
>
> 2.   In the case of shares of stock, the company's net worth, prospective earnings power and dividend-paying capacity, and other relevant factors.

> Some of the "other relevant factors" referred to in subparagraphs (1) and (2) of this paragraph are: the good will of the business; the economic outlook in the particular industry and its management; the degree of control of the business represented by the block of stock to be valued; and *the values of securities of corporations engaged in the same or similar lines of business which are listed on a stock exchange.* However, the weight to be accorded such comparisons or any other evidentiary factors considered in the determination of a value depends upon the facts of each case. Complete financial and other data upon which the valuation is based should be submitted with the return, including copies of reports of any examinations of the company made by accountants, engineers, or any technical experts as of or near the applicable valuation date.

The Genesis of Valuation, ARM 34: The Rigid Formula Approach

The IRS first tried to set valuation criteria by issuing Appeals and Review Memorandum (ARM) 34 in 1920. The theory of the ARM 34 was that a business is expected to earn a normal profit on its tangible assets and that any actual profit greater than normal profit must be attributed to intangible assets. ARM 34 thus distinguished between tangible and intangible assets and attributed a set value to each.

This was done by use of a rigid formula. The IRS considered normal profit to be an 8 to 10 percent return on the net book value of tangible assets, a 15 to 20 percent return on intangibles.

Example

If a business with $2 million in tangible assets earned $250,000 a year and its normal profit (according to the IRS) was $160,000 (8 percent of $2 million), then $90,000 ($250,000 minus $160,000) was its profit on intangible assets. The $90,000 profit on intangible assets was capitalized at 15 percent (100 percent divided by 15 percent = 6.66̲6̲), this produced $600,000(6.66̲6̲ x $90,000), the value of the intangible assets. The $600,000 in intangible assets was then added to the $2 million in tangible assets to produce a total value of $2.6 million.

The Arm 34 method is disarmingly simple. Using it, valuation is made without considering any peculiar facts or circumstances concerning the business.

Because of this lack of knowledge about the individual business, the computation of valuation is in fact made in a vacuum. This caused ARM 34 to be hotly contested by taxpayers. Among other faults, ARM 34 did not account for discrepancies in book value and fair market value of operational assets; it did not distinguish between capital-intensive and labor-intensive businesses; it arbitrarily assigned the same rate of return to all businesses, regardless of industry and regardless of nature (such as disparities between retail, wholesale, and manufacturing concerns).

Because of these shortcomings, ARM 34 finally was limited in its use (Rev. Rul. 65-192, 1965-2 C.B. 259).

The Most Important IRS Ruling

Recognizing that simplistic formulas do not work, in 1959 the IRS issued Revenue Ruling 59-60, 1959-1 C.B. 237 (see Appendix B for the full text). This is now the most significant legal guideline in valuations. At least, it is the place to start in determining the value of a business.

Revenue Ruling 59-60's Approach to Valuation. Revenue Ruling 59-60's basic approach is set forth as follows:

.01. A determination of fair market value, being a question of fact, will depend upon the circumstances in each case. No formula can be devised that will be generally applicable to the multitude of different valuation issues arising in estate and gift tax cases. Often, an appraiser will find wide differences of opinion as to the fair market value of a particular stock. In resolving such differences, he should maintain a reasonable attitude in recognition of the fact that valuation is not an exact science. A sound valuation will be based upon all the relevant facts, but the elements of common sense, informed judgment, and reasonableness must enter into the process of weighing those facts and determining their aggregate significance.

.02. The fair market value of specific shares of stock will vary as general economic conditions change from "normal" to "boom" or "depression," that is, according to the degree of optimism or pessimism with which the investing public regards the future at the required date of appraisal. Uncertainty as to the stability or the continuity of future income from a property decreases its value by increasing the risk of loss of earnings and value in the future. The value of shares of stock of a company with very uncertain future prospects is highly speculative. The appraiser must exercise his judgment as to the degree of risk attached to the business of the corporation which issued the stock, but that judgment just be related to all of the other factors affecting value.

.03. Valuation of securities is, in essence, a prophesy as to the future and must be based on facts available at the required date of appraisal. As a generalization, the prices of stocks which are traded in volume in a free and active market by informed persons best reflect the consensus of the investing public as to what the future holds for the corporations and industries represented. When a stock is closely held, is traded infrequently, or is traded in an erratic market, some other measure of value must be used. *In many instances, the next best measure may be found in the prices at which the stocks of companies engaged in the same or similar line of business are selling in a free and open market.* [Author's italics.]

The Many Factors of Valuation.   The last few pages illustrate the IRS' emphasis on the fact that to value a closely held corporation it is necessary to consider the value of stock or securities of corporations engaged in the same or a similar line of business, which are listed on an exchange, *in addition to considering all other factors.* To consider "all other factors" is an endless task. One of the most important aids in determining what those "other factors" are is Revenue Ruling 59-60.

Revenue Ruling 59-60 lists eight factors to consider in valuing a closely held business:

1.   the nature of the business and the history of the enterprise from its inception

2.   the economic outlook in general, and the condition and outlook of the specific industry in particular

3.   the book value of the stock and the financial condition of the business

4.   the earnings capacity of the company

5.   the dividend-paying capacity

6.   whether the enterprise has goodwill or other intangible value

7.   sales of the stock and the size of the block to be valued

8.   the market price of stocks of corporations engaged in the same or similar line of business having their stock actively traded in a free and open market, either on an exchange or over-the-counter

Revenue Ruling 59-69 emphasizes that the eight factors do not necessarily have equal weight and that determination of value is a matter of *judgment* and *common sense* to be arrived at after *consideration of all factors.*

Expanded Application of Revenue Ruling 59-60.   Revenue Ruling 59-60 by its express terms limits the factors it creates to valuations for estate and gift tax purposes. However, Revenue Ruling 65-192, 1965-2 C.B. 259 states

.01   The general approach, methods, and factors outlined in Revenue Ruling 59-60 are equally applicable to valuations of corporate stocks for income and other tax purposes as well as for estate and gift tax purposes. *They apply also to problems involving the determination of the fair market value of business interests of any type, including partnerships, proprietorships, and so on* and of intangible assets for all tax purposes. [Author's italics.]

Although this book deals solely with the incorporated closely held business, as far as the IRS is concerned the same principles involved in valuing a closely held corporation are equally applicable to unincorporated businesses of whatever form.

Some Comments on the Factors

Nature and History of the Business.   The nature of the business is usually the starting point of a valuation. The characteristics of the enterprise and the specific industry within which it operates and competes must be established.

A detailed study of the history of the corporation is needed to enable the appraiser to form an opinion of the degree or risk involved in the enterprise. This factor covers a broad area involving degrees of stability, growth, and diversity of operations, plus analyses and information that will reflect the general nature of the business: its risks, its hazards, and its ability to withstand adverse economic swings.

Nonrecurring items should be discounted, since value has a close relation to future expectancy.

The Economic Outlook in General and the Condition of the Business.   Determination of fair market value must include consideration of the outlook of the economy in general as well as the particular industry.

Usually, this determination begins with an examination of financial data and comparison of earnings. In addition, several questions should be asked: Would the public be an eager investor in the company? Is it a one-person company? Will future management be able to take over in the event of the death or retirement of a key person? Will the loss of key personnel be offset by insurance? Will the market for the company's products grow, decline, or remain stable? Will the general economy sustain the company's future?

Often the figures of the company itself tell a complete economic story. Consider the earnings of three different companies, all with the same total earnings in the past five years:

	Down, Inc.	Yo-Yo, Inc.	Up, Inc.
1987	$ 30,000	$ 20,000	$ 15,000
1988	24,000	24,000	17,000
1989	20,000	18,000	20,000
1990	16,000	22,000	23,000
1991	10,000	16,000	25,000
TOTALS	$100,000	$100,000	$100,000

Obviously the appraiser must consider the earnings pattern in any valuation. One way of computing the ultimate value while still placing primary emphasis on later years is to utilize a weighted average. The most common method of making the computation for Down, Inc. is as follows:

1987	$30,000	x	1	=	$ 30,000
1988	24,000	x	2	=	48,000
1989	20,000	x	3	=	60,000
1990	16,000	x	4	=	64,000
1991	10,000	x	5	=	50,000
TOTALS			15		$252,000

$252,000 ÷ 15 = $16,800 (weighted average earnings)

The exact weighting to be used is flexible. For example, the appraiser might have used a weighting of 1,1,2,3,3, or 1,1,2,3,4 or any number of other combinations.

Sometimes a weighted average does not give the best results. Remember, it is only one of the many methods that can be used to emphasize recent events.

Competition is always a key issue. At the valuation date, the company's current and past performance compared to its competitors should be determined. The competitive trend, the impact on profits, and the ability to overcome the competition must be examined.

The Gallo Case: The IRS Strikes Out

A good example of what a court will look at concerning the nature and history of a business, the outlook of the specific industry in particular, and the effect that consideration has on the final valuation decision is provided in *Estate of Mark M. Gallo* (TCM 1985-363).

In that case, the Tax Court was called upon to value the shares of stock of a holding company closely held by Ernest and Julio Gallo and their families, whose principal asset was all the stock of the well-known Gallo Winery. The shares were part of the estate of a grandson of Julio Gallo, and comprised less than 1 percent of all the issued and outstanding stock of the holding company. The year of the valuation was 1978.

The court reviewed both the state of the U.S. wine industry, including its relation to the worldwide industry, and Gallo's position in that industry in 1978. It summarized that position as follows:

> In sum, although Gallo remained the largest wine producer in the United States, with a market almost double that of the second largest producer, its performance in the years immediately preceding the valuation date and its prospects for the future were not bright as its record prior to 1972. Gallo experienced a substantial decline in its total market share and weakness in its traditional areas of strength. In light of its image as a quantity producer of inexpensive wines, Gallo appeared ill-equipped to take advantage of emerging trends in the industry.

The court went on to reject the valuation of the IRS' expert appraiser because, among other things, he ignored the historical trend within the wine industry.

> The emerging consumer preference for higher price wines with perceived higher quality was apparent as of the valuation date, as was Gallo's actual past and expected future inability to exploit this trend. Because of these and other factors mentioned in our findings, Gallo's earnings exhibited a sharp down-

ward trend after 1972. By virtually any measure of investment merit, Gallo was significantly less attractive on the valuation date than in 1972.

The *Gallo* case was not decided upon this factor alone. But it does illustrate that a valuation that ignores the nature and the history of the business and the industry it operates within, reaches its conclusions in a factual vacuum, and does so at its peril.

Book Value (Net Value) and Financial Condition. Often, the computation of book value is an essential starting point for determining fair market value of stock of a closely held corporation. Generally, book value is acquisition cost (less accumulated depreciation) minus liabilities. It is also referred to as owner's equity. The courts have held that book value, although one of many factors of valuation, is not related to other factors such as earning power, fair market value, or even liquidation value. In *Nellie I. Brown*, (25 TCM 498-1966), the Tax Court stressed this fact in rejecting an IRS' expert witness appraisal that relied solely on book value.

What the courts have used book value for can be illustrated in *Albert L. Luce, Jr.*, (ClmsCt, 84-1 USTC 13,549). Book value is floor value. The courts are reluctant to let any valuation fall below book value. In *Luce*, controlling shareholders of a closely held manufacturing company gave stock to their children and to trusts for the benefit of their children. For gift tax purposes, the shareholders gave the stock a value below book value. In the ensuing court case, the shareholders' expert witness attempted to justify the lower-than-book value by using the capitalization of earnings method and a minority discount.

The court rejected that approach and held book value to be at least one of the proper indicators of worth for the business for the following reasons:

> If a company's net worth consists of substantial write-ups of intangible value acquired in mergers and corporate acquisitions, if it has paid inflated prices for its assets, or if its machinery and equipment are obsolete, and it has been consistently unable to obtain a fair return on investment, then the fair market value of the company may be understandably less than book value. But the undisputed evidence here is that as of the valuation date Blue Bird's [the closely held company at issue] ownership had been in the same family since it was organized, its net worth was not inflated by any substantial tangible value, and its plant and equipment were in good condition and enabled it to be a dominant company in its industry. Moreover, Mr. Shelton's [the expert witness] own computations showed that the company's returns on its tangible net worth ranged between 16.1 and 28.4 percent, with an average of 19.2 percent, over the preceding 5 years, returns far in excess of those earned in the closest comparable industries Mr. Shelton could find. A seller could hardly have been expected to be willing to accept 25 percent less for the company than the cost of duplicating the net depreciated tangible assets alone, without regard to its value as a going concern with goodwill, qualified personnel, an established national distributor's organization and high earning capacity; and a hypothetical buyer could hardly have expected that he could obtain it for that price. In such circumstances, it is reasonable to conclude that book value is at least a floor under fair market value, which an appraiser may not properly ignore.

Book value alone, however, is a poor indicator of value. The court in *Luce* and other courts, only requires that book value not be discarded and that a highly profitable going concern dare not attempt to dip below it. The values of assets and liabilities on a corporation's books do not necessarily reflect fair market values. For example, the value of plant and equipment, which is carried on the books at cost less depreciation, may be inaccurate because an accelerated method of depreciation was employed or because inflation and other market factors make the assets much more valuable than the book figures.

Remember, balance sheets are almost always stated at cost. For example, land carried on the books at cost for a number of years probably has a fair market value due to appreciation—in real value, inflation, or both. For valuation purposes, the balance sheet should be adjusted to reflect the higher value of the land, providing a more realistic worth of the company.

The importance of book value as a measure of fair market value also depends upon the nature of the enterprise. It is considered by the courts as a poor measure for operating companies where earnings and dividend-paying capacity are the most relevant criterion:

> Book value is a factor to be considered, still it is not a reliable measure of fair market value. I am certain the investor is inclined to give earning power and dividend prospects much more weight in appraising the worth of any security. What the buyer is acquiring are the profits and dividends which the business will provide in the future (*Bader* v. *U.S.*, 172 F.Supp. 833 (D.C.Ill. 1959)). A prospective buyer would give some consideration to the book value of $145 a share. He would realize, however, that the company was a going concern, and that, even if it was assumed that the book value could be realized upon the liquidation of the corporation, there was not indication that it was to be liquidated. (*Mathilde B. Hooper, Admnx.*, 41 B.T.A. 114 at 119, acq. and nonacq. 1942-1 C.B. 9, 24).

However, the IRS takes book value as a good indicator of the value of investment and real estate holding companies where the underlying value of the assets closely approximates the worth of the corporation. It states that "computing the book value per share of stock, assets of the investment type should be revalued on the basis of their market price and the book value adjusted accordingly" (Rev. Rul. 59-60, 1959-1 C.B. 237).

Assets not essential to the operation of the business should be identified by an examination of current and past balance sheets. Management should be consulted to identify nonoperating assets that cannot be segregated by looking at the financial statements. These assets may add to or detract from the stock's value, depending on their separate value and earning power. Nonoperating assets must be revalued at current market prices for publicly traded securities or fair market value for other nonoperating assets. The value of the nonoperating assets should be added to the value determined for the operating assets. In effect, two valuations must be made: one for the nonoperating assets and another for the operating assets. The sum of these two values yields the fair market value of the whole.

A valuation analysis should include comparative annual balance sheets and profit and loss statements for at least five years before the valuation date.

Earnings Capacity. Potential future income of the closely held corporation is a prime factor affecting its value. According to Revenue Ruling 59-60, *earnings should be the most important valuation factor when appraising an operating company.*

For an operating company, earnings are usually the most important factor in valuation (*Kline* v. *Commissioner*, 13 F2d 742-1942), but the use of historical earnings may be misleading and must be adjusted for trends and nonrecurring items.

For an investment company, the fair market value of underlying assets is usually more important than earnings (*William Hamm, Jr.*, 325 F2d 934-1964).

As stated by Judge Learned Hand in an early valuation case:

> Everyone knows that the value of the shares in a commercial or manufacturing
> company chiefly depends on what it will earn.
> (*Borg* v. *International Silver*, 11 F.2d 147, 152, CA-2, 1925).

In other words, as stated in Chapter 1, it is essential to keep in mind the central theme of this book: A willing buyer will pay a willing seller a price for a closely held business determined by a valuation based upon the expected future earnings power or capacity of that business.

Revenue Ruling 59-60 states: "Prior earnings records usually are the most reliable guide as to future expectancy." You should examine detailed income statements, preferably for five or more years.

Previous years' earnings are not simply averaged. In most cases, they are weighted with the most recent earnings years under consideration being given the highest importance. This applies whether the trend is an increasing or a decreasing one. "If, for instance, a record of progressively increasing or decreasing net income is found, then greater weight may be accorded the most recent years' profits in estimating earning" (Rev. Rul. 59-60, 1959-1 C.B. 237).

Once the weighted figure is reached, it should be capitalized at an appropriate rate to reach a final valuation (see Chapter 7).

An excellent example of the weighting process necessitated by an earnings trend took place in *Central Trust Co.* v. *U.S.*, 305 F.2d 393 (for the full text, see page 385). There the court took a favorable earnings trend and gave earnings from the five most recent fiscal years a weighting of 5,4,3,2,1, respectively, with 5 for the most recent year.

Analysis of gross income by product line, major deductions from operations, net income, and taxes, will enable you to form opinions regarding future profitability and value of the business. Additional information regarding nonrecurring expenses, officers' salaries, depreciation methods, substantial rental expense, and historical trends with regard to sales, costs, and new income would be discovered through this analysis. Nonrecurring items may require adjustments to reflect normal or fair earnings, and distortions—caused by erroneous or inconsistent practices—must be "normalized." Generally, past earnings experience is indicative of future expected earnings, but reliance on past history, without regard to present trends in both the company and the industry, is not likely to produce a realistic valuation.

The IRS in its *IRS Valuation Guide for Income, Estate, and Gift Taxes: IRS Appeals Officer Valuation Training Guide* has this to say about earnings capacity:

> The earnings of the business have been held by many valuation authorities to be the essence of fair market value. Certainly, investors have a primary concern with the earning power inherent in the securities they are buying or selling.
>
> One of the most frequently used indicators of earning power of a business is the income statement. We have to analyze the income statement to understand the operating results of the company. Usually income statements for a five-year period are obtained for comparison purposes.
>
> Trends in net sales, operating expenses, various classes of expenses or income and net profit should be noted because this will indicate the company's progress in the period preceding the valuation date.

Any valuation based on earnings capacity must be based on the actual historical earnings of the company to be valued. It must not be based on what the company should be earning if not for extraordinary conditions. For example, in *E.J.Fehrs*, (556 F.2d 1019), a gift tax case, the IRS attempted to have the stock of a closely held company engaged in the heavy road and industrial equipment business valued without regard to a poor earnings record. The IRS, instead, wanted to substitute the historical earnings record for the industry, which was higher than the business being valued. This would have resulted in a higher valuation and consequently, higher gift tax. The court stopped the government in its tracks, citing the following problem with this approach:

> the fact that the expert entirely avoided the use of Rental's [the company at issue] own earnings as a basis for the application of the earnings multiplier in favor of a reconstructed earnings base derived wholly from the profitability levels of companies other than Rental. This, as the court sees it, is an approach that proceeds not by comparison but by substitution and, in the last analysis, represents the valuation of a non-existent company.

To be sure, prospective earnings are important in the determination of share price. However, a valuation that completely disregards the recognized importance of actual earnings as a factor in the assessment of future expectations must rest on something more than the naked speculation that a dramatic change in corporate fortunes would follow from a change in corporate management.

Dividend-Paying Capacity.   This is seldom a significant factor since the stockholders in control of a closely held business usually pay little or no dividends. The capacity to pay dividends rather than the actual dividend payout history is what counts.

> Primary consideration should be given to the dividend-paying capacity of the company rather than to the dividends paid in the past. Recognition must be given to the necessity of retaining a reasonable portion of profits in a company to meet competition. Dividend-paying capacity is a factor that must be considered in an appraisal, but dividends paid in the past may not have any relation to dividend-paying capacity. Specifically, the dividends paid by a closely held family company may be measured by the income needs of the stockholders or by their desire to avoid taxes on dividend receipts, instead of by ability of the company to pay dividends. Where an actual or effective controlling interest in a corporation is to be valued, the dividend factor is not a material element, since the payment of such dividends is discretionary with the controlling stockholders. The individual or group in control can substitute salaries and bonuses for dividends, thus reducing net income and understating the dividend-paying capacity of the company. Dividends are less reliable criteria of fair market value than other applicable factors.
> (Rev. Rul. 59-60, 1959-1 C.B. 237).

Once that dividend-paying capacity is determined, it is capitalized in a manner similar to that for earnings. However, remember that dividend-paying capacity capitalization rates will be lower than those for earnings simply because dividends come from earnings, and corporations rarely pay out all their earnings as dividends.

Although not as important as earnings, failure to take dividend-paying capacity into account can be and has been reason for the courts to disregard a valuation (*Louis* v. *U.S.*, 369 F.2d 263, CA-7, 1966).

Goodwill and Other Intangibles. Goodwill stems from various factors, the most significant of which is favored or "excess" earnings capacity. According to Revenue Ruling 59-60:

> In the final analysis, goodwill is based upon earning capacity. The presence of goodwill and its value, therefore, rests upon the excess of net earnings over and above a fair return on the net tangible assets. While the element of goodwill may be based primarily on earnings, such factors as the prestige and renown of the business, the ownership of a trade or brand name, and a record of successful operations over a prolonged period in a particular locality, also may furnish support for the inclusion of intangible value . . .

In other words, the presence and value of goodwill depends on the measure of any unusually high earnings and rate of return the company enjoys. It may also be the result of a patent, an unusually acceptable product, an outstanding distribution or sales system, a location that attracts customers, and so on. While it usually is not accorded a separate value, goodwill is part of the earnings capacity and indicates a more valuable company.

Goodwill is not a factor in the valuation of an investment company.

Normally, the analysis of a business considering the other factors outlined in this book encompasses both the valuation of goodwill and other intangibles.

In many cases, the intangible value of a business, including goodwill, cannot be determined without reference to the tangible assets of the business. Such a case, Revenue Ruling 68-609, 1968-2 C.B. 327 (see Part IIIA), provides that the formula approach of ARM 34, as restated, should be used. This revenue ruling is must reading. It provides authority for a valuation approach that in practice has proven to be the best method of making the valuation when no other method is capable of getting the job done right. Note, however, that despite its prevalent use, the IRS believes it should be used only as a last resort. (See Chapter 8 for a more detailed discussion of goodwill valuation.)

Sales of Stock and the Size of the Block to be Valued. Prior sales of stock are said to be the best evidence of value if the sales were close in time to the valuation date and under comparable circumstances (*Louis* v. *U.S.* 369 F.2d 263). There is no exact period of time at which a valuation becomes outdated. The main factor in determining the weight a representative sale should be given depends primarily on the change, if any, in the financial condition of the business since the date of the representative sale.

There are other factors besides proximity in time that are looked at. Here is what Revenue Ruling 59-60 has to say:

> Sales of stock of a closely held corporation should be carefully investigated to determine whether they represent transactions at arm's length. Forced or distress sales do not ordinarily reflect fair market value, and isolated sales in small amounts do not necessarily control as the measure of value. This is especially true in the valuation of the controlling interest in a corporation. Since, in the case of the closely held stocks, no prevailing market prices are available, there is no basis for making an adjustment for blockage. Those stocks should be valued after a consideration of all the evidence affecting the fair market value. The size of the block of stock is a relevant factor to be considered. Although a minority interest in an unlisted corporation's stock is more difficult to sell than a similar block of listed stock, control of a corpora-

tion, either actual or in effect, representing an added element of value, may justify a higher value for a specific block of stock.

The closer the size of the representative sale is to the block of stock to be valued, the more likely the representative sale value will be accepted as controlling. In *Estate of Vandenhoek* (4 T.C. 125, 1944), the Tax Court disregarded previous small lot sales of stock in valuing a much larger block.

A nother factor given close scrutiny is whether the representative sale was reached at arm's length. Sales between family members especially are suspect, and are given little weight by most courts (*Estate of Anderson*. 31 T.C.M. 502, 1972).

However, in *Estate of Kaye* v. *Comm'r* (32 T.C.M. 1270, 1973), a sale of stock from a business associate of the decedent to the decedent's daughter two years after the decedent's death was held by the court to be representative of the value of the stock in the decedent's estate. This was because the estate presented three expert witnesses who defended the value while the IRS smugly rested upon its assertion of a higher value with no proof.

Here's a case where the court relied heavily on the sale of stock (*First National Bank of Fort Smith*. 85-2 USTC 13,627 DC-Ark.). A block of stock representing a 28 percent interest in a privately held corporation was the subject of this valuation dispute. Both sides used the traditional factors of valuation, yet the court gave great weight to the price paid for a block of stock representing only a 2 percent interest. The sale was made 16 months before the death of the decedent.

The court noted that the size of the blocks were different, but it felt the difference was not substantial. Even though the court did not use the sales price as the sole criterion, it held that the price was determined objectively, and that it could be used to measure other evidence of value.

Here is a checklist of factors that determine the weight given to a previous representative sale:

1.   the proximity of the sale to the valuation date,

2.   the amount of the disparity between the number of shares sold and the number of shares to be valued,

3.   the motives surrounding the sale other than those aimed at arriving at a fair price, and

4.   the amount of any intervening change in the economic or financial condition of the business and the environment from the sale date to the valuation date.

The buyer of a closely held business almost always wants 100 percent of the stock or none at all. Generally, even a controlling interest—if substantially less than all the stock—will sell at a discount below the price for 100 percent of the stock. A minority interest would be discounted even more (see Chapter 9).

Weighing the Factors: The Central Trust Case

The most instructive case to study to get an idea of how a court might use the factors of Revenue Ruling 59-60 in reaching its valuation decision can be found in *Central Trust Co.* v. *U.S.* (305 F.2d 393; Ct. Cls., 1962). The following summary is provided (see page 385 for the full text) to illustrate that step-by-step process.

Facts. In 1954, a member of the board of directors of a closely held manufacturer of cans for food packaging gifted over 70,000 shares of stock in the company to various trusts for the benefit of his children. He died the next year. The executors of his estate first valued the shares at $10 per share and later amended that valuation to $7.50 for estate tax purposes. The IRS contended a value of $24 per share.

The court made the following findings of additional facts:

Nature of the business. Heekin (the company at issue) was a well-established can manufacturer. It had two main product lines: packer cans for shelved canned foods, and larger general line cans used for housewares, for picnic containers, and by institutions for bulk food storage. Annual sales were $17 million. Its main manufacturing facilities were housed in a multi-story plant. It also had four other, smaller facilities. The family members of the decedent were the controlling shareholders, with 79 members owning 71 percent of all outstanding stock.

Business relations. Heekin had six steady major customers accounting for over half its business. It was perfectly situated in the Ohio River Valley, which minimized transportation costs. At the time of the valuation, the canning industry, in general, was experiencing record demand.

Competitive Industry. Heekin was in an industry dominated by two mammoth corporations: American Can and Continental Can. They controlled over 75 percent of the canning market. Heekin accounted for less than 1 percent of the same market. Prices in the industry were set by the two giants, leaving Heekin at their mercy. As a result, Heekin secured and retained its customers by giving better personal service and a quality product.

Age of Equipment. The court highlighted the age and inefficiency of Heekin's plant and equipment as its main problem. It noted that Heekin had been unable to retool and keep up with the technological advancements in canning instituted by the two giant competitors because Heekin lacked the capital for a large-scale modernization program. As a result, Heekin's productivity was 300 cans per minute compared to 400–500 for the rest of the industry. However, this productivity disadvantage existed only in its packer can production. It was competitive with the two giants and the rest of the industry concerning manufacture of the larger general line cans.

Past Sales of Heekin Stock. Trading activity in Heekin stock was infrequent. Sales that did take place were struck at $7.50 per share and made to employees and friends of the Heekin family.

Estate's Expert Witness' Testimony. The Estate's first expert witness reached a valuation based on the following:

Past sales. Although made at the $7.50 per share value, the expert felt the past sales were too limited, and therefore consideration of the other factors listed in Revenue Ruling 59-60 was in order.

Book value. The company's balance sheet produced a book value of $33 per share. Because of the inefficiency and age of the company's plant and equipment, this was reduced by half to $16.60.

Earnings. Using income statements from the past three years, an average earnings per share of $1.77 was found, and was capitalized at a P/E ratio of 6 to 1, yielding a $10.62 per share value. However, recognizing the importance of earnings in valuation of an operating company, that figure was given double weight, resulting in a $21.24 per share value.

Dividend yield. Using a per annum dividend of 50 cents over the last three years, it was assumed that an investor would look for a 7 percent yield. This resulted in a $7.14 value per share.

Here is the result:

Book Value	
$33.20 x .50 x weighted average of 1	$16.60
Earnings	
$1.77 x 6 x weighted average of 2	21.24
Dividends	
$0.50 dividend by .07 x weighted average of 1	7.14
Past sales	
$7.50 x weighed average of 1	7.50
Total all factors	$52.48
Dividend by weighed average total of 5	10.50
Less 25 percent lack of marketability	2.62
Final per share value	7.88

The estate presented two other expert witnesses who used the same formula. Here is the most interesting result: They reached final valuation figures of $9.37 and $11.41 per share. Why the difference? Each made different assumptions. For example, the discount for lack of marketability (see Chapter 9) given by the three witnesses was 25, 5, and 20 percent, respectively. The weight given each of the four factors was different for each witness. Each used a slightly differing book value, and so on and so on. In other words, they differed on the quantitative aspects of the factors but were in approximate agreement as to their qualitative merits as belonging in the valuation process. Each expert juggled the numbers differently.

Court's Criticism of Estate's Witness' Testimony. The court had a field day, criticizing the valuation approach of the estate's witnesses on seven points:

1. The prior stock sales were too insignificant to warrant the weight given them.

2. Financial data used by the experts came from periods after the valuation date, and would have been unavailable to a prospective purchaser.

3. The third witness' data excluded financial data for the year before the valuation date.

4. Adjustments were not made in calculating the company's earnings for excessive income from government contracts as a result of the Korean War.

5. No allowances were made for detecting trends in historical earnings by giving greater weight to most recent earnings.

6.   Despite the fact that earnings are the most important valuation factor to consider for a manufacturing company such as Heekin, two of the experts gave equal weight to earning power and dividend yield:

> Some investors may indeed depend upon dividends. In their own investment programs, they may therefore stress yield and even compare common stocks with bonds or other forms of investment to obtain the greatest yields. However, others, for various reasons, may care little about dividends and may invest in common stocks for the primary purpose of seeking capital appreciation. All investors, however, are primarily concerned with earnings, which are normally a prerequisite to dividends. In addition, the declaration of dividends is sometimes simply a matter of the policy of a particular company. It may bear no relation to dividend-paying capacity. Many investors actually prefer companies paying little or no dividends and which reinvest their earnings, for that may be the key to future growth and capital appreciation.

7.   The experts took too great a discount for lack of marketability. The costs of creating a market for a block of the well-established company's shares should be closer to 12 percent (see Chapter 9).

Whether the court's criticisms are valid is not the point. What is important is to note the issues raised and the manner in which the court attacks them. The issues are such that reasonable people could differ over their solutions. These issues are common to most valuation cases, and an appraiser must be prepared to meet them head on. Needless to say, the court made it clear that it felt the valuation figures of the estate's witnesses were understated.

Ultimately, the court in *Central Trust* used the comparative approach, i.e., used comparable publicly traded companies, to reach an approximate value for the closely held manufacturing company. Since we have not discussed comparables in detail yet, the rest of the *Central Trust* case is reserved for Chapter 6 which discusses the proper use of comparables in detail.

VALUATION AS THE COURTS SEE IT: A SURVEY OF FACTORS DECIDING VALUATION CASES

The *Central Trust* case, which is the subject of an in-depth survey, is just one in the over 300 cases brought before various courts concerning valuations of closely held businesses. The particular facts in that case dictated what valuation approaches were appropriate to use.

However, aside from the assumption that particular facts dictate particular approaches, much can be learned from surveying the various factors that entered into many court decisions over a period from 1945–1984. The following is a list of 30 factors and the number of times in 327 closely held business cases that each factor entered into the court's valuation decision. The raw numbers of the following table can be found in the excellent compendium on valuation cases: *Federal Tax Valuation Digest: Business Enterprises and Business Interests*, 1984 edition (John A. Bishop and Morton Mark Lee, Standard Research Consultants, Published By Warren, Gorham & Lamont, Boston).

As can be seen from the numbers, the eight factors listed in Revenue Ruling 59-60 predominate the courts' thinking.

If a factor was used in a case, it does not necessarily mean it was controlling. In many instances it was disregarded. What the survey shows, as does the *Central Trust* example, is what factors are considered, even if only for strawman purposes.

Valuation Factor	Number of Times Considered by Courts in Their Decisions
1. Historical earnings	139
2. Earning power	66
3. Capitalization of average earnings	24
4. Price/earnings ratio	30
5. Dividends paid or yield	68
6. Dividend-paying capacity	31
7. Book value	115
8. Tangible assets	85
9. Net working capital	21
10. Potential value	14
11. Replacement costs	4
12. Growth of net worth	17
13. Dividend arrearages	3
14. Nature of business	89
15. Position of industry	18
16. Character and quality of management	38
17. Sale of stock (or lack thereof)	165
18. Blockage	38
19. Restrictions	76
20. Marketability	69
21. Controlling interest	21
22. Minority interest	61
23. Comparative companies	37
24. Economic conditions	23
25. Stock market conditions	12
26. Goodwill	11
27. Cost of doing business	4
28. Expert testimony	130
29. Intent of liquidation	12
30. Lack of evidence	85

Like a golfer deciding which is the best club to use for an approach shot to the green, the factors are a smorgasbord from which valuation opponents and the courts can pick and choose in order to bolster their valuation decisions. As in the case of a golfer, it is not so much the club used as it is the skillful swing employed that makes a good shot. So too it is the skill of the appraiser, using the valuation factors to the best advantage, that counts.

How Should You Deal with the Many Factors in Practice?

Your appraiser will look at most of the factors discussed in this book. Sometimes special factors peculiar to your particular business or the exact time of the valuation will come into play. You should have answers that help move your valuation number in the direction that best serves your purposes—up or down. But be realistic. Up or down means within a narrow range that is a value you believe is right. Never, but never, value toward a predetermined number. Remember, the other side will have an opinion (and probably their own expert) too.

CHAPTER 4

BLENDING IN THE FACTS

FACT, NOT LAW, DETERMINES VALUE

Valuation experience dictates that each company to be valued has its own set of facts and circumstances, and each valuation is different from every other valuation. Two companies in similar lines of business with almost identical numbers can have quite different values because of one significant fact difference. No set of textbook rules can bring out the importance of unique facts.

Every valuation must commence with an examination of the balance sheet and operating statement; care must be taken to recognize that both are nothing but sets of numbers. It is important to distinguish between numbers and facts. Numbers represent historical earnings, margins, return on equity, book value, and so on. Numbers are precise and, if correct, are tough to argue—either for or against.

On the other hand, facts are the reason behind the numbers. Facts are not self-evident from a mere reading of the numbers. Facts have to be dug out, verified, assessed, and often discarded for lack of weight. Facts are found everywhere, and the search for them must go everywhere.

Numbers can have a fatal attraction in the valuation process because by their nature they are self-quantifying. Being wholly mathematical, numbers lend themselves all too easily by arithmetic process to translation into the valuation figure, which is also a number. Numbers are easy to work with, but to produce easy answers or quick answers is not to produce sound answers.

The objective of every valuation is to blend the numbers and the facts into a cohesive justification of a business's worth. In order to succeed, facts must be organized toward that end. The methods for doing so follow.

Special Considerations of Specific Industries

A good way to start is to step back for a moment. Look at your industry (the forest) as a whole. Then you can better see the particular segment (the trees) in which you operate. This will allow you to get a better look at how your individual business (your tree) fits into the picture! As the entire forest can be ravaged by fire, storm and disease, so can your industry be ravaged by outside forces. Sometimes only a limited area of the forest (like a certain market area or niche) is totally destroyed or severely damaged. Forests grow back. So do businesses. But in the meantime, the value all but disappears.

Simply put, a healthy tree in a diseased forest has limited value. So does a thriving business in a sick economy. Let's face it, almost every industry has been, is today, and probably always will be like the sphere on a yo-yo—going up and down. Sometimes the market forces doing the pulling and pushing are easy to identify: the national economy; competition—local, national, and international; inflation; the local economy; and growth or shrinking of your market area. These will do for starters. No doubt you can add to the list for your particular business or market niche.

It's a fact. Any one of these market forces can either skyrocket the value of your business or stuff your life's work down a tube overnight. Sometimes these market forces work in tandem to create overnight millionaires (seldom) or instant bankruptcies (more often than should be the case). It is the job of the appraiser to identify two aspects of these market forces. First, if market forces are currently affecting your industry, market niche, or individual business, is the impact positive or negative? How much will it affect your business? For how long? Second and much tougher, if identifiable market forces are not affecting your business now, what is the likelihood of these forces striking in the foreseeable future?

This chapter will help you identify some of the forces (often called "factors")—market and otherwise—that might affect the value of a specific business in a specific industry. If I have some thoughts on what can be done to mitigate negative forces or enhance positive forces, I'll put in my two cents worth.

"Specific" and "Unique" Apply to Every Business

Every business has its own peculiarities. The first order of business to valuing a business is to accumulate the facts and data as discussed in Chapters 4 and 7. This must be done no matter what type of business is being valued. Then you must get very specific by accumulating information relating to the unique factors that apply to the business being valued in the specific industry in which the business operates.

Now let's take a look at the specific factors you should consider today to help make your business more valuable tomorrow.

Foreign Competition

Competition is a way of life. The usual stuff, local or national against U.S. competitors, is bad enough—more businesses making the same or similar products and forever selling for less. But today, foreign competition comes in at least four scary forms:

1. Cheaper labor

2. Foreign government subsidies

3. Dumping

4. Technological advances

It is imperative that you be aware of how foreign competition affects your business. A good appraiser will have a number of questions to ask you about this subject.

Product-Life and Service-Life Cycle

Depending on where you read it or the nature of the study, products and services had an average life of about 35 years in the years immediately before and after World War II. Today, the average life cycle is in the five- to seven-year range. Some products are literally here today and gone tomorrow.

Comment

You should have a long-range plan and/or a strategic plan. I'm not talking about a plan in your head, but a written plan that deals with all facets of the problem. The plan should deal with such points as how to extend the life of your products or services, add new ones, and diversification.

Technology

The question here is how your business measures up to what the existing competition is doing and the predictable developing competition. Assess this situation. Get the numbers and scenarios down on paper. In many cases, it will help to have a professional who knows how to pump the data into a computer and develop "what if" projections based upon the assumptions that give your best, most likely, and worst scenarios.

Remember, past performance (no matter how successful) is not worth a "tinker's damn" if your old methods and technology are a step or more behind the times.

The Value of the U.S. Dollar Against Foreign Currency

I have never seen the problem stated better—before or since—than in the June 1986 issue of *The Financial Forecast Letter* (discussing the last three months of 1985 and the first three months of 1986):

> "The U.S. market became even more *price competitive* as low-priced goods poured in from Korea, Taiwan, Brazil, and Mexico. In the U.S. itself, more and more *producers gave up hope of competing and made arrangements to import foreign parts and products*, for sale under their own name. Meanwhile, restrictions imposed by other nations (including Canada) *kept us from exporting much more*, even with a cheap dollar. The result? A continued erosion of U.S. manufacturing companies."

This foreign currency force can be a joy or a nightmare and has given us a seesaw ride. It brings uncertainty. Uncertainty reduces the value of a business. Keep watching. The ride will most certainly continue during the 1990s and, most likely, beyond.

Growth of Your Business in Your Industry

Profitable growth is the goal of almost every business. Does this growth (profitable) make your business more valuable? Certainly! But not always. Why? Well, cash is king. Most businesses that grow, and maintain or increase the rate of profit, can take cash out of the business. Hail the king—cash. And the business, as a result, is worth more (usually a larger multiple) than a business that does not generate cash.

But careful. For example, most wholesale businesses generate more inventory and receivables, instead of cash, as they grow. As a result, value tends to grow more in terms of increased net worth rather than a multiple of earnings. Often the valuation methods are combined to determine the value of such a business. Make sure you recognize the problem if it applies to your industry.

Growth, or Lack Thereof, of Your Industry Taken as a Whole

Watch out, if your industry has matured (the need for your product or services has become flat or may even be shrinking). Bigger market share means taking business away from a competitor, not a new customer starting to buy from your industry. History tells us competition will stiffen, margins shrink and profits tougher to maintain. Such businesses are now worth less than when the industry market as a whole was expanding. Sure, a buyer will be interested in past profits, but he will discount them somewhat as you look into the future together and try to determine the value of the business in terms of "what will the future profit be."

Your Position in the Marketplace

Consumers—both businesses and individuals—require goods and services. As simplistic as it sounds, it is imperative that you monitor the economic winds. The general demand for goods and services in good economic times causes almost all businesses to be more profitable during such periods. Simple! And everyone knows it. So what.

Unless your business is going against the tide, your business is worth more in good times than in bad.

A Money-Making and Tax-Saving Hint

For those of you who will someday sell your business rather than transfer it to a family member, get your business valued and sell it in good times. DO NOT SELL AT THE BOTTOM OF THE CYCLE.

On the other hand, it makes more sense to transfer your business to your family in bad times. When the current value is low, you can beat the tax collector legitimately.

THE FACT-GATHERING PROCESS: A CHECKLIST

Balance Sheet

To arrive at "adjusted book value," examine the balance sheet in detail.

Inventory. Question the quality of the inventory; a portion of it is almost always bad. Is it LIFO or FIFO? A LIFO inventory may have one value for going-concern purposes (requiring an adjustment to arrive at adjusted book value) and another value for liquidation purposes.

1. *Size.* If too large in relation to sales, the cost of carrying it is an undue burden on profits.

2. *Obsolescence.* If your inventory contains items that are outmoded, or for which there is no likelihood of sale, they must be written off.

3. *Location.* If inventory is stored at off-plant sites, handling costs are higher, and this may be a signal that the plant is not large enough for current operations.

4. *Number of Suppliers.*   It is disadvantageous to be in a position where there is only one supplier for an important component. Where there are several suppliers, it could pay to use only one (saving the others as back-up).

5. *Size of Purchases.*   To the extent possible, supplies should be purchased in quantities large enough to warrant a quantity discount. Limitations on this are the size of the warehouse and the cost of carrying a large inventory.

Receivables.   Review the aging and the quality of receivables. Failure to write off bad debts means equity and earnings are overstated.

Assets Not Essential of the Operations of the Business.   Assets (such as securities or real estate) that are not used in the operation of the business or will not be used in future expansion should be valued separately at fair market value. The value determined for these assets should be added as a separate item to the value of the operating portion of the business. Operating earnings also should be adjusted upward or downward because of profits or losses attributable to such nonessential assets.

Real Estate.   If any real estate used in the operations of the business has been on the books for a long period of time, the depreciated value probably is well under market value. Remember that the operating portion of the business may have little or no value, or be substantially reduced, because of the location of the real estate (if, for example, customers can get to the business only with great difficulty). At other times the real estate could be the whole ballgame (if, for example, a retail business owns a building in the highest traffic area in town; but what if the building is about to be taken by eminent domain?).

Your Plant Facilities.   Most businesses—for example, tooling/machining or manufacturing business—cannot maintain the "best" competitive cost reduction disciplines in an inadequate facility (building[s]).

1. *Building Condition.*   While a new building probably will be more efficiently laid out, cheaper to maintain and heat, and helpful in getting and retaining employees, an old building is not automatically a white elephant. Space that was properly constructed 40 years ago and adequately maintained may be just as good as comparable space only one year old.

2. *Building Layout.*   Such things as heating and air conditioning equipment, illumination, and cosmetics can easily be improved. But there is no cure for inadequate ceiling height, load bearing walls or columns that are in the way of an improved layout or floor plan. Location of the loading dock is crucial; if it is centralized, the distance from all work stations is the same, and the operation is usually more efficient.

3. *Growth.*   Some businesses require increased volume (sales) to meet certain objectives. If the current building footage cannot handle any increased volume and there is no way to expand the present building or add another building, face the music. Your business will have to be moved (or the growth plans abandoned). This costs money. The value of your business, which can realistically attain projected growth and increased profits, is greater. That's true. But the increased value, due to anticipated growth, must be reduced by the cost of the anticipated move.

Don't forget to factor in the increased rental cost. Or if the present facilities are owned, make the appropriate adjustment for the sale of the old facility and the purchase (or rental) of the new facility.

Tangible Personal Depreciable Property. Should tangible personal depreciable property be adjusted to fair market value (usually called *appraisal value* at this initial stage)? If it is a nonoperating asset or an asset no longer to be used in operations, the answer is clearly "Yes!" But if the asset is used in operations, the answer usually must await further probing. Logically, increasing the value of the asset requires an upward adjustment of future depreciation. The increased appraisal value raises the ultimate fair market value, while the increased depreciation lowers future book profits and the ultimate value—one works against the other. Similar reasoning says that if a particular piece of equipment is worth more right now, future earnings will be reduced because of the increased cost of replacing that equipment when it wears out or becomes obsolete—more circular reasoning.

Quite often, even though tangible personal property is worth substantially more than book value, no adjustment is made for valuation purposes. The problem, if applicable, should be recognized in the appraisal report.

Equipment as an Operating Asset

1. *Age.* Many types of basic machinery (lathes, grinders, punch presses) will last for years and work just as well as they did when new.

2. *Technological Obsolescence.* A punch press with a capacity of 30 strokes per minute, whether new or old, is perfectly adequate for short-run production, but for longer runs a newer press with a stroke capacity to meet competition is essential.

3. *Condition.* Physical inspection will reveal current operating condition. Examination of repair and maintenance expense will give a better idea of how well machines hold up under prolonged use.

4. *Replacement Needs.* Examination of recent expenditures for replacement or new equipment will enable a forecast to be made of equipment needs in the near future. If a plant is on two or three shifts rather than one, equipment needs will accelerate. Remember, new equipment almost always costs more than the old equipment being replaced.

Nature and Efficiency of All Assets. The nature, and efficiency of the company's assets will dictate its sales, earnings, and dividends capacity. Assets used efficiently, but with additional capacity, suggest the potential for growth without substantial spending: a positive valuation factor. If the assets are operating at, or close to, full capacity, further growth may dictate additional spending and financing: a negative factor.

Leasehold Improvements. On liquidation leasehold improvements are usually worth nothing; for a going concern, book value usually is used. However, if the improvements are valuable and can be removed, or if the increased value can be utilized over a long-term lease, this asset would be restated at fair market value.

Loans to Shareholders. Are loans to shareholders collectible or worthless? Do they bear interest, and if so at what rate?

Loans from Shareholders.   Are loans from shareholders debt or equity? When in doubt, the appraiser should get written confirmation from the shareholder. Is accrued interest substantial? How would someone purchasing the assets and assuming the liabilities treat this apparent liability?

A Word About Some Assets You Can't Touch—Intangibles

Customers.   A business with only one or two customers is at their mercy, not only for profit but for orders. A better situation exists where no customer takes more than 10 percent—the lower, the better—of sales.

Important

Businesses with few customers (or with many customers but one or more customers who are responsible for a large percentage of the volume—and, as a result, much of the profit) are worth less than a business that has many customers. Why? The loss of one or even a handful of the top customers will only put a small dent in sales and profits.

Receivables.   A large amount of receivables in relation to sales indicates that some customers are slow in paying for goods. Bad debt experience should be checked. Inquiry should be made as to whether any customers should be abandoned. Appropriate adjustments must be made for any anticipated sales losses due to customers being dropped.

Other Intangible Assets.   Determine the special value for patents, trademarks, secret processes and formulas, or the like.

An interesting intangible asset for many labor intensive businesses is the ability to add a second or third shift to handle increased production requirements. If you are running three full shifts now, you simply don't have this asset.

In general, each intangible asset should be separately considered and either eliminated (because it has no intrinsic value) or adjusted to appraisal value as circumstances require.

Goodwill, on the other hand, is an intangible asset with its own peculiar colors and must not be dealt with like the intangible assets discussed above. See Chapter 8.

Operating Statement

When using any valuation approach involving earnings, the operating statement must be analyzed. Appropriate adjustments (increasing or decreasing profit as enumerated below) must be made for each year of operations being considered. (Remember that valuation is an attempt to predict the earning potential of an operating business.) To some degree, future earnings can be given a sharper focus by examining past earnings, as adjusted.

Salaries of Owners.   If salaries are excessive, earnings are understated; the reverse is true if salaries are too low. But this part of the valuation process shouldn't stop with salaries. All of the owner's fringe benefits must be examined to determine whether they are excessive.

Depreciation.   If accelerated depreciation methods are used, earnings may be understated, but the opposite will be true when acceleration runs out. Additional and immediate requirements for capital expenditures might have greater impact than past or anticipated future depreciation.

LIFO Reserve. Adjust to FIFO basis. When inventory is increased by the amount of the LIFO reserve, it must be done by only the after-tax amount on the balance sheet. Cost of sales and gross profit must also be adjusted for the before-tax difference for each year of operations considered, while net profits must be adjusted for the after-tax difference.

Extraordinary Items. Sale of land, equipment, or a division may generate a profit or loss, the effect of which should be eliminated, since this does not represent normal business operations.

Unusual Year. A year of abnormally high profit or loss should be excluded unless other circumstances indicate a recurring trend.

Nonoperating Assets. Exclude income and expense from portfolios, rental real estate, and so on, if it is not part of normal operations.

Earnings Trends. If earnings are erratic, average them; if rising or falling, you may want to weight the later years, but you should investigate the reasons for the changes. Consider the effect of such items as annual union wage increase on projected earnings.

Employee Benefit Contribution. If the company is to be sold to a buyer who has a benefit plan different from the seller's plan, adjust earnings up or down as required. Other employee benefits, of which there is an ever-growing list in the eyes of the IRS, must also be considered. The main goal of the benefit inquiry is to determine if the total benefit package is excessive, normal, or low.

Income Taxes. Adjustments to each income and expense item should be aggregated and an appropriate adjustment to income taxes must be made.

Intangibles. Some factors exercise either a positive or negative effect on the value of goodwill. They are these:

- Favorable location
- Reputation for service or special skills of the owner or employees
- Discount prices
- Majority of sales coming from only a few customers
- Failure of business to keep up with changing market conditions
- Occupancy of a location vital to success not assured by lease or ownership
- Dependence on personality or special skills of an individual who will not be available after the business is acquired (if the owner goes, so does the goodwill)

The first two items on the list are positive; the others are negative.

Other intangible assets, if they do exist, should be valued separately from the goodwill. They include these:

- Customer lists

- Covenant not to compete
- Licenses, to be transferred, restricted as to number by local ordinance
- Contracts that give a special advantage (for example, supply or price)
- Patents
- Trademark

Determine the Answers to the Following Questions:

1. If the company is a corporation:
   a. Have dividends been paid? When and how much?
   b. Does the corporation pay directors' fees? How much and how often?

2. Are there any outstanding loans to/from the company from the shareholders and/or partners? Do these transactions represent valid obligations of the borrower?

3. Have there been any extraordinary items in the last five years that would account for an unusual fluctuation in earnings (i.e., fire, flood, gain on sale of nonoperating assets, bankruptcy of an old major competitor or entry of new major competitor(s) into the market area)?

4. How does the company determine bad debts? Are there any bad debts that need to be written off?

5. Who has legal ownership of the major operating assets, usually land and building? If the assets are in individuals' names as opposed to the company's name, what are the future plans for these assets? Does the company have an airtight long-term lease?

6. What is the depreciation policy of the company for tax purposes and for reporting purposes? Is there any equipment carried at zero cost or at a cost significantly lower than replacement cost? Conversely, is any relatively new equipment carried at a high cost, yet is really obsolete? What new equipment, and at what cost, is necessary to maintain present operating efficiency? Improved (attainable) efficiency? Anticipated growth?

7. What is the exact valuation date? What are the objectives of the client?

8. Has the business ever been valued before? (If so, obtain a copy.)

Here is a Basic List of Documents and Data to Gather:

1. Tax returns for the company for the last five years.

2. Financial statements for the last five years (both income statements and balance sheets).

3. Detail of company's ownership:
   a. Partnership-partners—capital and profits interest and cost basis of their interest. Get copies of all partnership agreements.
   b. Corporation-shareholders—stockholdings and cost basis of their stock. Get copies of all stockholder agreements.

4. Detail of officers' compensation for the preceding five years and the percentage of time the officers devoted to the business.

5. Current real estate appraisals.

6. Copies of significant long-term agreements such as franchise agreements, leases of major assets, etc.

7. Information on the existing economic conditions of the area/industry such as publications of the local Chamber of Commerce.

8. Volume of sales by location if more than one unit.

9. Projections prepared for the next year, or, if available, for as many years as done.

10. A copy of the company's long-range plan or strategic plan.

Hint

Use the checklists every time you value your business. Add points to the list as required. However, using checklists does not automatically produce answers. Often, for any given case, only one or two points on the checklist may be relevant. When a bell rings, research and evaluate the relevant point thoroughly.

Other Points to Ponder/Questions to Ask

Loss of Key Personnel. Is there backup management? Can key people be replaced? What would be the impact on business if one or more key people were lost? Will life insurance solve the problem until new people can be trained?

Present Plant. Is the present plant condemned? Is it adequate for near-term, or will it have to be enlarged or replaced? Is the lease about to expire? How will the cost of these affect future earnings? Can the business survive a move?

State of Industry. If the state of the industry is static, what is the possibility of future growth for the company? What is the impact of present governmental regulations or the likelihood of new or changed regulations? Will necessary raw material be in short supply and put the company out of business? Or cause profits to skyrocket because the company has a source? Or could it be the other way around, with the market being flooded by an oversupply, killing profit margins?

Competitive Position. If your company is one of many similar operations in the area, what is the outlook for growth, sales, and profits?

Cash Flow. Will business requirements outrun your cash flow because of—

1. Inability to pay debt?

2. Needed capital investments?

3. Inflation?

4. Inability to obtain additional financing? for growth? increasing inventory or accounts receivable?

Market Area.   Is your market area growing? Shrinking? Do you get an adequate rate of growth when the market area grows?

Location.   What is your proximity to major highways and arterial streets? Other needed types of transportation? Is ingress and egress for vehicles—yours and customers—easy? Can physical layout be improved? Are major repairs required? Now? To accommodate growth? At what cost? Can your labor force get to your plant easily? Are more of the right kind of employees available if you grow? Is parking adequate?

Neighborhood.   Is the area going downhill? Enough to drive off customers? Make it difficult to hire employees? Are expenses increasing for repairs (from vandalism) and watch service?

Note

Sometimes a current move, in spite of the unwelcome costs, makes more sense in the long run than staying put for short-term savings.

Basic Costs.   Can you maintain warehouse and delivery costs at their present level? Are they likely to increase? Decrease? What about utility costs? Labor costs? Unionization?

Real Estate.   Must the real estate be part of the package to be sold? Can you lease it to the buyer? At what rental? Is the real estate likely to appreciate?

Vendors.   Are your vendors likely to stay in business? Meet your inventory requirements? Increase prices? Change your terms?

Environmental Problems

Have you touched all bases? Legal? Appropriate, ground, engineering, and operational studies?

Note

Environmental problems can kill a sale. Liability can break a corporation and, in some cases, attach to stockholders. For tax purposes, the value of a business can be legitimately driven down. But the danger is so great here, you must pay attention to economics first. Taxes are in second place.

The list and the questions could go on forever. The key is to learn to ask the right questions under the particular facts and circumstances when a real-life business must be valued. The best bet—hire someone who knows and understands your industry. He'll know the right questions to ask.

Hint

This checklist should be used every time a business is valued. Also use it when a valuation is updated. Add points to the list as required. However, using checklists does not automatically produce answers. For any given case, only one or two points on the checklist may be relevant—when a bell rings, research and evaluate the relevant point thoroughly.

EXAMPLES: HOW FACTS DETERMINE VALUE

The following real-life examples were deliberately selected to illustrate the importance of going beyond the mere numbers that appear on the balance sheet and the operating statement. In each case, the numbers alone would have indicated a different value, which in some cases would have been dramatically different.

Example 1

A retail sporting goods store had in its most recent five-year period doubled its sales and earnings. These facts gave the initial impression that the company was doing better than average and should sell at a premium. This impression was erroneous. In each year the store space had expanded, yet sales per square foot were unchanged from year one to year five. The owner had to double his investment to double his sales and earnings. A buyer would have had to increase his investment beyond what he paid at the valuation date if he wished to increase his sales and earnings. This fact negated the impression that the historic five-year growth would continue automatically in the hands of a buyer. A premium was not warranted.

Example 2

A manufacturing concern had a steady five-year earnings record that justified a $1.5 million value. However, a potential buyer inspected the company's plant and found severe physical deterioration. The plant manager admitted that the building was condemned and that the company was actively searching for and planned to buy a new, more expensive plant elsewhere. The net cost for such a move was figured at $500,000. Despite the proven earnings record, what buyer would be willing to pay the $1.5 million knowing that another $500,000 outlay would be required to move the facility?

Example 3

A decedent held the stock of a corporation that owned a small parcel of land on which it operated a restaurant business. The decedent also held the beneficial interest in a land trust that owned a large parking lot adjacent to and leased by the restaurant. One person (a real estate appraiser) valued the parking lot at $70,000. Another person looked at the numbers for the restaurant and valued the restaurant at $400,000. By simple addition, the value of the two holdings equaled $470,000. Subsequently, it was pointed out that the restaurant was worth $400,000 only if the parking lot was available. If no parking lot had been available, the restaurant would be out of business and worth only salvage value. The IRS accepted the no-value-to-the-parking-lot approach and agreed to a $400,000 value for the two holdings.

Example 4

A decedent had been a member of a very small group that had for years owned and operated a successful company. When the lawyers, accountants, and advisors prepared to value the decedent's interest in the corporation, it was under the assumption that the decedent's 60 percent interest was represented by common stock.

Suddenly, someone remembered that the decedent did not own common stock but a voting trust certificate entitling the holder to receive 60 percent of the common stock upon expiration of the voting trust some eight years after date of death. A holder of a voting trust certificate has no voice in running the corporation; this power resides in the voting trustee. Despite the nominal representation of 60 percent control, the voting trust certificate holder has no more voice in management than the holder of a minority interest. This argument was made to the IRS and resulted in a 25 percent discount from the full value of 60 percent of the stock of the corporation.

The most important valuation factor in this example had nothing to do with the numbers but rather with the discovery of the precise nature of the interest in the company held by the decedent.

Example 5

A multiple-store retailer wanted to transfer the future growth of his business to his two sons. Both were active in the business. The business was being evaluated to support a recapitalization. For various reasons the 65 percent owner/founder wanted to have a larger value than what appeared from the usual facts. The other 35 percent was owned by the two sons.

Fortunately, the business rented a number of stores that had very favorable leases. Most of the leases had a number of years (from three to seven years) remaining. The rents were significantly lower than the current market rents.

When a lease has a remaining term at a rent below market, this difference has value (leasehold interest), which is a separately identifiable intangible asset and should not be included with goodwill. Usually, the value of a leasehold interest can be computed by capitalizing, at an appropriate rate for commercial real estate, the annual difference between market rent and actual rent over the remaining term of the lease.

EXAMPLE:	Market Rent	$20,000
	Less Actual Rent	14,000
	Annual Difference	$ 6,000

The present value factor at 10 percent for four years (the remaining term of the lease) is 3.170. Therefore the value of the leasehold interest is $19,020 (3.170 x $6,000).

The value of the business was increased by almost $200,000 because of the value of the leases. Each lease was valued separately.

A Real-Life Example That Should Hit Home

I can think of no better way to end this chapter than with a real-life example. The following letter was sent to me by a new valuation client. As you read it, you will see point after point that affects the valuation of this particular business, and how many of the points probably apply to your closely held business. The letter is an exact quote. All words that might identify the owner or the business, or that do not affect the valuation, are omitted. All words in parentheses were added to help clarify the words omitted.

> The Company was founded twenty-five years ago . . . In January 19__ . . . all (companies) were rolled into one S Corporation. The reason behind this move at the time was to relieve the exposure to an accumulation of earnings tax, and to try to move more assets out of the Corporation for estate planning.

> The . . . sole stockholder is now (60) years old, married with four children . . . The third child is expected (to) enter the family business in about two years. The three daughters . . . show no interest in joining the business . . . wife has never been active in the business.

The Company seems to be wallowing in mediocrity since . . . the late seventies.

In spite of all the above, the Company consistently shows a bottom line profit each year with no sales growth. Operating profits are realized mainly because the Corporation has a) no debt service cost, b) little or no depreciation expenses as most of the equipment has been fully depreciated, c) building is owned by Corporation, completely paid, so no rental expense is charged against income. Interest from accumulated earnings further enhanced the bottom line, particularly during periods of high interest rates.

. . . reluctance to plow more money into the business for new equipment and expanded facilities can probably be laid to the uncertainty of management succession and the lack of a burning desire for any greater personal income than he (the owner) already enjoys.

. . . Any minority interest in the Corporation . . . son acquired through gift or stock option should have a restriction that the Company has the right to repurchase it at the fair market value if he leaves the Company or dies.

CHAPTER 5

THE EIGHT MAJOR APPROACHES TO VALUATION

It has been said that the number of different valuation approaches in existence at any point in time can be determined by multiplying all the appraisers in the world by the number of businesses to be valued.

Years of practice and experience have shown the following eight approaches as the most common valuation approaches:

1. comparative values of similar going concerns

2. reproduction or replacement value

3. present value of the cash flow

4. liquidation approach

5. book value

6. factor approach (often called a formula approach)

7. earnings approach

8. combinations and variations

Observation: At this point, it should be observed that basically there are only two approaches to valuation—the liquidation approach and the earnings approach. All other approaches are combinations.

Which is best? Which should be used and when? Actually there is no pat answer. Often an approach that is just right under one set of circumstances would give ridiculous results if the facts were changed slightly.

COMPARATIVE VALUES OF SIMILAR GOING CONCERNS

One widely used method of valuing closely held corporations entails an examination of comparable publicly held companies and the prices of actual transactions of such companies' securities on or near the valuation date.

The search for comparable companies might begin with *industry classification*. In theory, companies in the same industry share similar markets, and the potential for sales and earnings growth is usually dependent upon the characteristics of the growth rates of these markets. In addition, companies in the same industry are often affected by common operating (production and supply) characteristics. Upon reviewing all those public firms in the same industry classification, adjustments are made for *size, diversity, growth, stability, leverage, dividends,* and other factors.

This method is based on the observation that during any relatively short period of time the relative sales prices of the public common stocks within a given industry generally can be related to the stock of a closely held company. Somehow the relative investment characteristics of these larger, publicly traded corporations and the closely held corporations are supposed to be alike. As explained in Chapter 6 this is, more often than not, an incorrect supposition.

With rare exceptions, the comparative method does not make sense, for any but the very largest of closely held companies. It is difficult (and more often impossible) to find truly comparable companies; however, some large unlisted companies approach the comparability requirements of their listed counterparts (see Chapter 6).

REPRODUCTION OR REPLACEMENT VALUE

The reproduction or replacement value approach is based on the amount of money it would take to replace or reproduce the facilities and systems of the business being valued, by going into the marketplace and obtaining replacement assets. This method is used for insurance purposes. Also, if the seller has unique property that is what the buyer really wants in terms of a physical plant that is operating, this method may be the first choice.

PRESENT VALUE OF THE CASH FLOW

The present value of the cash flow approach is concerned with the present value of the future cash flow of the business adjusted for the time value of money and the business and economic risks. The theory is that the future cash flow represents the recovery of the investment and the receipt of income produced by such investment. This method contains the following factors:

1. The expected growth rates in sales and earnings projected to a selected date on which the stock may be sold.

2. The time period between the valuation date and the sale date.

3. The dividend payout of the company (as it is or potentially could be).

4. An expected price-earning ratio or liquidation value at the end of the time frame. A perpetual dividend stream also could be used.

5. A rate of return investors might seek given their expectations of the four preceding factors, less a discount for the risk of not having such expectations realized.

Cash flow is assumed to be a more valid criterion of value than "book or accounting" profits. Only cash or cash equivalents can be used for reinvestment purposes.

This method (also called the *Discounted Cash Flow Approach* or *Investment Approach*) is often used for nontax purposes to arrive at a comparable price at which to establish an exchange ratio; or in certain other circumstances—for example, a merger. The most significant factor to keep in mind is that this method is based entirely on estimated future earnings and cash flow.

Example

Suppose a rational investor decides the risk for the business she wants to buy merits a 15 percent return. She assumes an annual cash return of $10,000 a year for ten years and a liquidation value of $100,000.

The value today (right now), called the "present value," is $74,840. The following schedule shows how the investor would arrive at this value.

Year	Annual Cash	+	Liquidation Value	=	Total Cash	x	Discount Factor (15%)	Present Value
1	$10,000				$ 10,000		.869	$ 8,690
2	$10,000				$ 10,000		.756	$ 7,560
3	$10,000				$ 10,000		.657	$ 6,570
4	$10,000				$ 10,000		.571	$ 5,710
5	$10,000				$ 10,000		.497	$ 4,970
6	$10,000				$ 10,000		.432	$ 4,320
7	$10,000				$ 10,000		.375	$ 3,750
8	$10,000				$ 10,000		.326	$ 3,260
9	$10,000				$ 10,000		.284	$ 2,840
10	$10,000		$100,000		$110,000		.247	$27,170
Total Present Value								$74,840

The mechanics of the preceding schedule are simple. If an investor had $8,690 on the first day of year one and it earned 15 percent for a full year ($1,310) she would have $10,000 at the end of the year ($8,690 plus $1,310), and so on.

LIQUIDATION APPROACH

Investment companies usually are valued on a liquidation basis. If an operating company has nonoperating assets, such assets should be segregated for valuation purposes. The operating assets and the income produced by such assets must be valued separately.

As a practical matter, every business is worth at least *liquidation value*. If the operating assets—particularly fixed assets—are left in place to be used in a continuing business, then the package has a minimum value at or near *reproduction or replacement* cost less depreciation. Replacement cost, unless the property is unique, means fair market value.

Liquidation value of a going business can be tricky: Costs, expenses, and losses must be estimated for selling the inventory, collecting receivables, terminating employees, selling assets as no longer needed, and a host of other winding-down activities.

BOOK VALUE

Among other names, the book value approach to valuation is called *net tangible asset value* or *adjusted book value.*

Tangible book value is obtained by reference to the business' most recent balance sheet. In essence, it is the net book value of the business: total assets minus total liabilities, with adjustments made for intangibles such as goodwill.

Adjusted book value is based on making the necessary adjustments to book value for such factors as economic depreciation of plant and equipment, appreciation of land and other real estate values, and understated or overstated inventories due to accounting method.

Typically, little or no judgment is required to value assets using this approach. If required, each asset on the balance sheet should be restated at fair market value. (See the Tangible Personal Depreciable Property item on the fact-gathering process checklist in Chapter 4 for an exception for depreciable personal property used in an operating business.)

Such a valuation can be accomplished mechanically by completing a schedule similar to the following:

Steps for Determination of Adjusted Book Value

1. Start with book value. $ _____
2. Add (or subtract) the necessary figure to arrive at line 3.   _____
3. Appraisal or fair market value (the number for which all assets—like fixed assets and inventory—with any value could be sold if the company were to be liquidated).   _____
4. Subtract all intangibles on the books that have no value (that is, cannot be sold separately in liquidation), such as goodwill or a covenant not to compete.   _____
5. Balance—adjusted book value. $ _____

The adjusted book value approach is important because it is one of the elements used in the valuation approaches that follow.

Book value as the sole or predominant factor also makes sense in certain special situations:

1. a relatively new business

2. a business whose earnings have been unstable

3. a business whose sole owner is disabled or has died

4. a business for which an earnings approach to valuation is highly speculative—for example, where uncertainty due to things like supply shortages, strikes, government legislation, and product obsolescence makes the future unpredictable.

FACTOR APPROACH

According to the factor approach, three major factors are considered the most significant in determining value: earnings, dividend-paying capacity, and book value.

Earnings are normally the prime interest of the investor, but their weight, of course, must be tempered by consideration of the type of business being valued. Manufacturing companies and companies that sell a product or service usually give earnings heavier weight. On the other hand, gross revenue is the main factor in the valuation of a strictly service operation.

When an investment or holding company is valued, the greatest weight, up to 100 percent if appropriate, is given to the underlying net asset values. The payment of dividends does not permit much weight in the valuation of closely held stock.

The factor approach was used in two well-known cases, Bader (*Bader* v. *U.S.*, 172 F Supp. 833-1959) and Central Trust (*Central Trust Co., Exr* v. *U.S.*, 350 F2d 393-1962). Following is a comparison of the weight and values given to each factor in those two cases. Keep in mind that the weighting process is a subjective one: the full text (of Central Trust can be found in Part III-B) should be read for the justifications behind the assumptions resulting in the actual weights assigned each factor.

	Capitalized Value	Bader		Central Trust	
		Weight	Value	Weight	Value
1. Earnings: $50 x 12.5	$625	2	$1,250	.5	$312
2. Dividends: $25 x 24	600	1	600	.3	180
3. Book value: $800 x .6	480	1	480	.2	96
4. Total			$2,330		$588
5. Average			$ 582		$588
6. Discount:					
10.00 percent			58		
12.17 percent					72
7. Per share value			$ 524		$516

EARNINGS APPROACH

The earnings approach (often called *Capitalized Earnings Approach*) rarely is ignored in the valuation of an operating privately held business. This method deals with actual past earnings (usually five years), as distinguished from the present value of the cash flow approach, which deals with estimated future earnings. However, the earnings approach can yield extremely different results depending on the purpose of the valuation and the nature of the entity to be valued. It is usually the investor's best method for calculating expected return on investment.

Judgment must be exercised at each of two significant levels when implementing the earnings approach.

At one level, the "true" earnings of the business must be determined. Adjustments must be made for such items as officers' salaries and expenses that would not be made (or if made, not in the same amount) by the usual self-serving owners of a privately held business. The number of operating years (three, four, or five) to be considered, eliminated (as not representative), or weighted (with greater weight given to the most recent years) must be selected.

At another level, after the "true earnings" have been determined, the appropriate multiple is applied, which will be higher for a low-risk business (seldom as much as ten) and lower for a high-risk business (often only one or two). The amount of the multiple is, of course, affected by the many facts, factors, and circumstances peculiar to the business.

Often an operating business is valued completely by earnings, ignoring the liquidation approach. This is true when a business is valued solely as a multiple of earnings. For example, under proper circumstances a business with average earnings over the preceding five years of $0.4 million after taxes might be valued at $2.0 million—a five times multiple of earnings.

HOW TO DETERMINE THE CAPITALIZATION RATE FOR YOUR PARTICULAR BUSINESS

Is your business worth two times earnings? Three? Six? Ten? What about some other multiple? The answer is, it all depends on the capitalization rate. The higher the capitalization rate, the lower the multiple. For example, a 20 percent capitalization rate would give you a multiple of five (100 divided by 20). A 25 percent capitalization rate would yield a multiple of four.

So where do you find this mysterious capitalization rate? The starting point is always your own industry, or better yet, your particular niche or specific type of business. Simply put, a different rate of return can be expected in a tool and die shop as opposed to a mouse trap manufacturer or a high tech company or a service business. Why? Because statistics in your particular business group (identified by your SIC code) can give you an idea of what the rate of return should be in your particular business. Put another way—those businesses are similar to your business. *They are comparable!* And that's the key.

See Valuation Example 9 for a sample of how the rate of return was determined in a real-life valuation situation. In Example 9, the Standard Industry Code (SIC) used is 3612 (see page 259). When valuing your business, look up the statistics for your business' SIC code as compiled by Dun and Bradstreet or Robert Morse. Some industries—usually through their trade associations—accumulate statistics that can be used to determine the capitalization rate. There are also other methods. See examples on pages 261 and 262.

COMBINATIONS AND VARIATIONS

This is the method by which most closely held businesses change hands between a willing buyer and a willing seller. It is also the method preferred by the courts and often employed by the IRS in practice. In most valuations of an operating business, a combination of several basic methods is employed to arrive at the final valuation. The variations used are at least equal to the number of businesses to be valued. A typical example would combine the adjusted book value and earnings approach. There is no single correct way.

Every valuation eventually has to face its alter ego. The valuation of the taxpayer must confront that of the IRS; the valuation of the seller that of the buyer. Each of the valuation approaches can be taken piecemeal, *a la carte* if you will, by a contending party to fit his or her purposes. The IRS is particularly adept at adopting whatever method generates the most tax dollars in a particular case.

Because of this fact, the courts have recognized that no one particular approach is controlling. Instead, they take the facts of each particular case, use the approach they deem appropriate to the facts, and make a judgment call in reaching a final valuation figure.

Ponder the lamentations of the Tax Court:

> Too often in valuation disputes the parties have convinced themselves of the unalterable correctness of their positions and have consequently failed successfully to conclude settlement negotiations—a process clearly more conducive to the proper disposition of disputes such as this. The result is an overzealous effort, during the course of the ensuing litigation, to infuse talismanic precision into an issue which should frankly be recognized as inherently imprecise and capable of resolution only by Solomon-like pronouncement.
>
> (*Messing* v. *Commissioner*, 48 T.C. 502)

> Indeed, each of the parties should keep in mind that, in the final analysis, the Court may find the evidence of valuation by one of the parties sufficiently more convincing than that of the other party, so that the final result will produce a significant financial defeat for one or the other, rather than a middle-of-the-road compromise which we suspect each of the parties expects the Court to reach.
>
> (*Buffalo Tool & Die Mfg. Co.* v. *Comm'r*, 74 T.C. 441, 1980)

In their effort to reach a compromise, the courts often resort to the combination approach.

CHAPTER 6

WHEN TO USE AND WHEN NOT TO USE COMPARABLES

The use of the market price of stock of comparable publicly traded corporations as a measure of valuation of the stock of closely held corporations has become a prime valuation tool. It is resorted to much too frequently in unjustifiable situations; nevertheless, in certain situations the use of comparables is not only desirable but necessary.

THE BASICS OF HOW COMPARABLES ARE USED

Problems with Comparables

There are four basic problems with the use of comparables: difficulty finding comparables, fluctuating prices of publicly held stock, missed significance of adjusted book value, and lack of real buy-to-sell experience based on comparables.

Difficulty Finding Comparables. The smaller the privately held business, the less likely that the appraiser will be able to find one or more comparable public companies. In fact, the appraiser has no duty to engage in a fruitless search when logic and experience dictate otherwise. On the other hand, when the nature and size of the company to be valued indicate the feasibility of using comparables, the appraiser has a duty to search for comparable public companies. If found, they should be used.

It is not always clear whether comparables can be found. An experienced and knowledgeable appraiser will not be stampeded into the use of comparables by such statements as "The

IRS only accepts comparables," or even, "The IRS prefers comparables." What the business owner and other interested parties want and need is the right valuation. Forced use of comparables that are "close" but not really comparable can result in a correct valuation only by accident.

Often, when the comparables are not what the appraiser would like them to be, more than one method is used to make the valuation. Then, the results of the comparable method and other method are averaged (usually by weighting) to arrive at the final valuation. [Chapter 7 contains an example (Royal Oil, Inc.) of such a valuation.]

Fluctuating Prices of Publicly Held Stock.   Publicly held stocks often have wide fluctuations in price. The value of any particular stock or group of industry stocks can and does move up and down several times during a year. When such volatile stocks are used as comparables, what price from the wide, yearly range should be used? The value of the privately held stock, when aligned with such comparables, would have a value that would jump up and down along with the price of its volatile comparable. Is this realistic?

This fluctuating price problem runs directly counter to the principle that says a valuation is a determination of the value of a business on a specific date. However, the fluctuating price problem can largely be overcome by averaging or weighting prices of the publicly held stocks. [An excellent example of how this can be accomplished is contained in Chapter 7 (Royal Oil, Inc.).]

Missed Significance of Adjusted Book Value. Comparables use earnings as a basis of comparability. How valid is the use of comparables when the privately held business shows losses or low profits? Should comparables in similar dire financial straits be used? Of course not. Comparables just won't work in such cases. Adjusted book value less a discount for the lack of profit or liquidation value are two bases for valuing an unprofitable privately held business that make much more sense.

What about profitable privately held businesses that have large adjusted book values? Consider these four companies that are identical in all respects, including profits, except their names and adjusted book values:

Name	Adjusted Book Value	After-Tax Profits
Smallest	$ 500,000	$500,000
Small	$ 2,000,000	$500,000
Big	$ 8,000,000	$500,000
Biggest	$32,000,000	$500,000

The blind use of comparables would make the value of each of the four companies equal, based on their earnings. That is clearly an absurd result. Earnings, when large in comparison to book value, rule. However, it is the appraiser's job to make sure that the book value, as adjusted, does not get swallowed by a multiple of earnings controlled by the price-earnings ratio of comparables.

The problem of the overwhelming predominance of earnings in the comparable method can be overcome by using one of the combination methods of valuation discussed in Chapter 5.

Lack of Real Buy-Sell Experience. In the real world, buyers and sellers of a privately held company do not use comparables when they sit down to negotiate the price at which the business will be bought or sold. There are two exceptions to this rule: (1) when the buyer is a publicly traded company and (2) when the privately held business approaches its publicly traded comparable counterpart in sales, size, diversification, and other factors. "Willing buyers" and "willing sellers," as used in the legal definition of fair market value (see Chapter 3) simply do not use comparables (subject to the few exceptions) when fixing the price at which a privately held business will change hands.

In the final analysis, the appraiser must ask this question: What method will duplicate the price that would be hammered out by a real buyer and a real seller? That is the method that should be used. Theory is fine, but a good appraiser thinks like a real buyer and seller hammering out a price. The theory must support real-life market conditions or the theory is plain wrong.

THE IRS AND THE USE OF COMPARABLES

The main and most important proponent of the use of comparables has been and is the IRS. As noted previously, Revenue Ruling 59-60 and various provisions of tax law endorse the use of comparables. Here is what Revenue Ruling 59-60 says:

> Section 2031(b) of the Code states that, in valuing unlisted securities, the value of the stock or the securities of corporations engaged in the same or similar line of business which are listed on an exchange should be taken into consideration along with all other factors. An important consideration is that the corporations to be used for comparisons have capital stocks which are actively traded by the public. In accordance with Section 2031(b) of the Code, stocks listed on an exchange are listed first. If sufficient comparable companies whose stocks are listed on an exchange cannot be found, other comparable companies which have stocks actively traded on the over-the-counter market also may be used. The essential factor is that, whether the stocks are sold on an exchange or over-the-counter, there is evidence of an active, free public market for the stock as of the valuation date. In selecting the corporations for comparative purposes, care should be taken to use only comparable companies. Although the only restrictive requirement as to comparable corporations specified in the statute is that their lines of business be the same or similar, yet it is obvious that consideration must be given to other relevant factors in order that the most valid comparison possible will be obtained. For illustration, a corporation having one or more issues or preferred stock, bonds, or debentures in addition to its common stock should not be considered to be directly comparable to one having only common stock outstanding. In like manner, a company with a declining business and decreasing markets is not comparable to one with a record of current progress and market expansion.

The IRS admits, then, that a comparable company must be just that—comparable. This reduces the use of the comparable approach to a search for a publicly traded corporation that closely resembles the closely held corporation to be valued. Needless to say, such a search is time-consuming and consequently very costly. Worse yet, in most cases the closely held company being valued does not have a true comparable counterpart. Close, unlike with horseshoes and hand grenades, counts for zero in comparable valuations.

What criterion should be used to measure similarity? How similar must a publicly traded corporation be to be valuable as a valuation guide? The answers to these questions are subjective, despite the objective nature of their goal. One is reminded of the Supreme Court justice who, when attempting to define pornography, stated, "You'll know it when you see it." The same could apply to the definition of a comparable. The use of comparables is not an exact science but only a method of approximation that can vary as much as the biases of individual appraisers and companies to compare and be compared to—which leads us back into the same discretionary and judgmental quandary that affects valuation in general.

Undaunted, proponents of comparables have attempted to set guidelines for determining comparability. These guidelines involve both financial and nonfinancial characteristics.

The irony of these guidelines is that instead of using facts and figures of the closely held corporation to be valued, the data of the publicly traded corporation, in effect, dictates the valuation process. This is because after the publicly traded corporation is deemed comparable, the only task that remains is to assign the price (by using the multiple of earnings) of the publicly traded corporation's stock to that of the closely held corporation's stock.

THE MOST IMPORTANT QUESTIONS

How does one go about finding a comparable publicly traded company? Consider the following. Suppose the closely held business to be sold does $10 million a year in sales in one county in a midwestern state and sells one product. The owner, who is also president and chief operating officer, has a back-up manager who is 60 years old. Before-tax profits, after subtracting the owner's compensation of $250,000, is $800,000. The owner spends three months of the year in Florida relaxing. Would a prospective buyer of such a company be well-served by determining an asking price by checking into the price-earnings ratio of comparable publicly traded companies?

Do buyers and sellers of closely held businesses use comparables? A survey of such buyers and sellers would reveal that closely held businesses are almost always bought and sold without a thought being given to the price at which any publicly traded company—comparable or otherwise—has sold for in the past or is selling for now.

THE COURTS AND THE USE OF COMPARABLES

The use of comparables is widespread, however, in the imaginary world of the estate tax. Remember the imaginary buyer and seller and the determination of an imaginary price at which a business would be bought and sold?

The use of comparables has been forced on the courts by the IRS. The word "forced" is appropriate, because the courts have used almost every opportunity presented them to refrain from using the comparable method.

In *Tallichet* v. *Comm'r* (33 T.C.M. 1133, 1974), the Tax Court put forth the following factors to be considered in determining compatibility:

1. capital structure

2. credit status

3. depth of management

4. personnel experience

5. nature of the competition

6. maturity of the business

The *Tallichet* court went on to quote itself from another case, as if uncomfortable in its comparison task:

> In short, a publicly traded stock and a privately traded stock are not . . . the same animal distinguished only by the size, frequency, or color of its spots. The essential nature of the beast is different.
> (*Messing* v. *Comm'r*, 48 T.C. 502)

This schizophrenic ambivalence exhibited by the Tax Court regarding the use of comparables is confusing to say the least. It gives the comparable approach the credibility of a methodology that compares apples and oranges simply because they are fruit.

Needless to say, quite a few courts have rejected the IRS' use of comparables out of hand. In *Bader* v. *U.S.*, 172 F.Supp. 833 (DC-Ill., 1959), the court rejected the comparable method for the good reason that there were no publicly traded corporations in the same business (grain elevator operator). In *Worthen* v. *U.S.*, 192 F.Supp. 727 (DC-Mass., 1961), the court rejected the use of a comparable because it had sales four times that of the closely held business and because it was not engaged in wholesaling, as the closely held business was (trader in coarse paper products). Another court rejected the use of a comparable with different assets and in a different geographical location (*Estate of Tompkins* v. *Comm's.* 20 TCM 1763, 1961; real estate holding and development company).

All of these cases involved the IRS advocating a comparable company that produced a higher valuation of the closely held company and the court rejecting it. In an anomalous case, in *Estate of Gallo* (TCM 1985-363), the IRS argued against the use of comparables only because the closely held corporation to be valued was itself larger than any of the publicly traded corporations in the same business (wine making).

CENTRAL TRUST REVISITED: A LESSON IN THE USE OF COMPARABLES

The court in *Central Trust Company* v. *U.S.*, 305 F.2d 393 (Ct.Cl., 1962), used the economy of scale argument to hold that giant corporations such as Continental Can Company and American Can Company were sublimely different from the closely held corporation to be valued because of their mammoth manufacturing facilities and advanced automation. (See Chapter 3 for the facts of *Central Trust*.)

After knocking the wind out of the estate's expert witnesses' valuations, the court turned to the IRS' witness and did the same thing. However, while it rejected the government's bottom-line valuation figure, it accepted the comparable approach as the proper one. It just didn't like the companies chosen as comparable. It chose its own comparables instead. Here's a summary of that court's use of the comparable approach.

IRS' Expert Witness Testimony

The expert witness for the IRS presented a comprehensive survey of eight companies in the can and glass container industries. He developed percentage ratios for profits and dividends to net worth over a five-year period for the comparables and the period 1950–1954 for Heekin, the closely held company whose stock was at issue. He considered two of those eight companies to be comparable to Heekin, arriving at a price between $18.75 and $19.75 for a share of Heekin stock. After applying a marketability discount of 20 percent, he reached a valuation of between $16 and $15.25 per share.

That value, however, was approximately equal to book value. Therefore the IRS' expert felt it was too conservative. Using the price-earnings ratios and book values of 11 comparable companies, and the dividend yields of seven comparables, the IRS' expert reached a value of between $21.85 and $21.35 for each share of Heekin.

The Court's Critique of the IRS' Expert's Testimony

While the court lauded the thoroughness of the IRS' expert's valuation, it found fault with the two selected comparable companies. One was a bottle cap and bottling machinery manufacturer, and the other declared periodic stock dividends, which was ignored by the IRS' expert. The court remarked:

> Although no two companies are ever exactly alike, it being rare to have such almost ideal comparatives . . . so that absolute comparative perfection can seldom be achieved, nevertheless the comparative appraisal method is a sound and well-accepted technique. In employing it, however, every effort should be made to select as broad a base of comparative companies as is reasonably possible, as well as to give full consideration to every possible factor in order to make the comparison more meaningful . . . the selection of such companies as American Can and Continental Can as comparatives— companies held in esteem—will obviously give an unduly high result. It is simply not fair to compare Heekin with such companies and to adopt their market ratios for application to Heekin's stock. Furthermore, defendant's (IRS) use of the comparatives is confusing. The employment of different comparatives for different purposes is unorthodox. When the comparative appraisal method is employed the comparatives should be clearly identified and consistently used for all purposes.

The Court's Own Comparative Valuation Approach

The court picked its own comparatives, which while "by no means perfect comparables" were "at least reasonably satisfactory for the purpose in question." The court, in effect, made its own opinionated value judgment. Never mind why the companies were chosen. As stated before, all appraisers worth their salt could make cases for or against any given valuation assumption.

The court used earnings, book value, and dividend yield in its comparison of the closely held business to the five publicly traded ones. It accorded the most weight to the earnings factor, 50 percent; 30 percent to dividends yield; and 20 percent to book value.

As to the weight accorded book value, the court succinctly stated:

> Book value indicates how much of a company's net assets valued as a going concern stands behind each share of its stock and is therefore an important

factor in valuing the shares. As defendant's expert pointed out, this is the factor that plays such a large part in giving a stock value during periods when earnings may vanish or be suspended. However, principally because book value is based upon valuing the assets as a going concern, which would not be realistic in the event of a liquidation of a corporation, a situation which a minority shareholder would be powerless to bring about in any event . . . this factor is, in the case of a manufacturing company with a consistent earnings and dividend record, normally not given greater weight than the other two factors.

The court then applied a marketability discount of 12.17 percent based on the costs of floating shares of the company for public trading. (As will be explained in Chapter 8, such a low discount is not common; the courts on the average have awarded discounts of 20 to 30 percent.)

As a final valuation figure, the court held that $15.50 a share was correct. Could any fault be found with the court's process and result? Of course it could. The important thing to note, however, as remarked in Chapter 3, is *how* it was reached.

The trend in these cases is not apparent. What is apparent is that a party opposed to the use of comparables need only build a case on the uniqueness of the closely held corporation in order to discredit the approach. Since all companies are unique, any competent advocate should be able to accomplish the objective: proper valuation of the particular business, with the full realization that the use of comparables will not yield the real strike price at which the business would be sold to a real buyer.

Do not, however, totally dismiss use of comparables as a means of valuation. If the comparable shoe fits, wear it! Use comparables where appropriate. The larger the closely held company, the more likely a comparable counterpart can be found in the marketplace. When one or more comparable companies can be found, not using these comparables as the only, or at least a significant, factor in the valuation opens the entire valuation to question. *Just as the use of comparables should not be forced, no other method should be forced if use of comparables is appropriate. The goal is always the same: the right valuation, by whatever method, rather than the use of any particular method.*

A good test is to use other methods being offered. If there is a wide discrepancy between two valuation amounts reached by two different methods, logic tells the appraiser that at least one of the methods must be discarded.

OTHER DRAWBACKS OF COMPARABLES

From a conceptual standpoint it is almost impossible to make valid comparisons of listed companies with privately held companies. Here's why:

- When the closely held company is small, the size differential alone makes comparison impossible.

- Closely held companies often pay large salaries and expense items that a public company would capitalize. Accounting treatment may also differ.

- Public companies have a depth of management that closely held companies often lack.

- Closely held companies usually are limited to one product, while a public company that makes the same product will usually have several other lines that may or may not be related.

- Public companies have access to credit lines unavailable to closely held companies.

- As an investor, a person might pay $100 per share for 500 shares of GM for one set of reasons; yet that same person might pay the same $500,000 (more or less) for 100 percent of the stock of a closely held manufacturing company as an investor/operator for a completely different set of reasons.

What impact do these drawbacks have on valuation in practice? Simply put, blind use of comparables often produces absurd results. The following example actually happened in the 70s. It still happens today and will happen tomorrow if you make the mistake of using comparables in the wrong circumstances.

Example

A privately held company was in the retail business, and the valuation was based on 1974 data. Earnings for 1974 were 25 percent higher than those for 1973, and book value had increased substantially. Obviously, the company could not be worth less in 1974 than it was in 1973. The average price-earnings ratios, however, for two listed comparable companies fell from 20 in 1973 to 6.7 in 1974. If the numbers produced by the mechanistic use of comparables were used as the measure of value, the forced conclusion was that in 1974 the privately held company was worth only one-third of what it was worth in 1973. This result is absurd and illustrates the danger of using comparables.

PROPER USE OF COMPARABLES

The most appropriate situation for the use of comparables is when the closely held corporation is large enough that its economies of scale are on par with the publicly traded corporations it is compared to: the *size* of the closely held corporation makes its operations and financial condition similar to the comparables.

The task of finding the most appropriate comparable with which to value a particular closely held corporation is similar to that of a police detective who gradually, through thorough investigation, narrows the list of suspects in a crime. Like the police detective who compiles a list of suspects, the appraiser of a closely held business using the comparable approach must compile a list of publicly traded corporations. This is not an easy task and involves reasoned judgment and intuition.

The Search Begins

There are many sources from which to compile such a list. Since the starting point for the search is the industry in which the closely held corporation operates, an excellent place to begin the search is the *Standard Industrial Classification Manual* published by the U.S. Office of Management and Budget (OMB). It gives Standard Industrial Classifications (SIC) codes for each particular industry.

Once the industry of the business is established, the next step is to consult one of various financial directories—such as the Securities and Exchange Commission's (SEC's) *Directory of*

Companies Required to File Annual Reports which lists companies with more than $1 million or more in assets and 500 or more shareholders.

Once a list of companies with the same financial statement characteristics as the closely held corporation is compiled from these directories, they should be contacted and their most recent financial reports for the past five years obtained. Then begins the real task.

Comparative Analysis

Needless to say, before any comparisons can be made, the financial data of the closely held corporation and the comparable must be organized in the same manner—digested and spit out in the same form so as to make similarities and differences identifiable. Otherwise the comparative analysis can be attacked for its sloppy methodology.

For example, several ratios could be used (see Part IV-A), such as these:

1. *Liquidity ratios.* These measure the ability of the corporation to meet its current obligations.

2. *Leverage ratios.* These indicate the amount of the business' operations and expenditures that are debt- rather than equity-financed.

3. *Activity ratio.* These measure the efficiency and productivity of the business in utilizing its available resources.

4. *Profitability ratio.* These measure the nitty-gritty of the business—does it make money by returns on its sales and investments?

There are many other ratios that can measure other nuances of a business that may just prove the differences between comparability and disqualification.

The Process of Elimination.   Once the data has been organized, objective criteria should be established. The data gathered has two purposes: (1) to help in the process of eliminating corporations that aren't comparable and (2) to provide guideposts in comparing the companies that are. Granted, the process, as described, is discretionary and could vary enormously depending upon who is governing it. However, the selection must still be made. It must be made with the thought in mind that no matter how thorough and logical the process of elimination and subsequent comparison, someone will find fault with it.

MAKING THE COMPARISON

Once the comparable publicly traded companies have been selected, the following steps should be used in reaching a comparative value. The first three steps should be applied to each comparable company.

1. Determine the earnings per share (EPS) by using no more than five years (or a shorter period if this will be more comparable). Often only one year—the year closest to the valuation date—is used. If the information is available, earnings should be adjusted for extraordinary and nonrecurring items that would affect the income and accounting differences between the comparable and the closely held company.

2. Determine the average price per share (APS). This is usually done by using the price on the valuation date, taking an average of the high and low prices for the year, or

using some averaging method to eliminate or reduce the impact of fluctuating stock prices.

3.   Divide the APS by the EPS to arrive at the price-earnings ratio (P/E).

4.   Determine an average P/E ratio for all the comparable companies being used. This is done by aggregating the P/E ratios of the selected companies and dividing by the total number of companies. The P/E of the individual public companies can be weighted to arrive at the average P/E ratio.

5.   Apply the average P/E ratio to the average earnings per share (usually a five-year average) of the closely held company being valued.

[See Chapter 7 for an example of a valuation using comparables (Royal Oil, Inc.).]

An errant P/E should be excluded. For example, suppose the P/E for the four selected public companies ran between 4.5 and 11.3 for each of the five years selected. If there is one anomalous year of 26.8, it should be ignored.

There it is—the comparable approach. The comparable company (or companies) has been found and the market price of its stock assigned as the value of the closely held corporation's stock. Use it carefully, and remember: anyone who uses it indiscriminately may get burned.

CHAPTER 7

VALUATION IN PRACTICE

This chapter pulls it all together. This is the chapter you want to mark up, underline, and return to as a starting point and reference. It fans out and refers to other chapters, as necessary, to organize all the elements needed to do a valuation in practice. What is most interesting is that, even in practice, the world of theory (but supported in logic by how a real buyer and a real seller would value the business) can never be left far behind.

This chapter brings into focus in one place the most important aspects of any valuation. In many respects, this chapter is like a checklist, although not every consideration for every valuation can be included.

In a nutshell, this is what the chapter covers:

- Avoiding a valuation altogether

- Making a valuation the easy, no-frills way

- Selecting the right method of valuation

- Reviewing the checklist of considerations

- Using valuations in practice

The first three of these are a sort of valuation pecking order. If the first solves the valuation problem, then the others are unnecessary. If the first can't do the job, move to the second. If the valuation can be completed there, the rest of the numbers can be ignored. Once you get to selecting a method for valuation—as is almost always necessary in practice—the valuation roller coaster ride begins. The considerations checklist and the actual practice examples, taken together, form a guide to the valuation of a privately held business.

AVOIDING VALUATION ALTOGETHER

What if the stock to be valued can be purchased for a price that has been fixed by an enforceable contract? Is another valuation, which would no doubt produce a value different from the fixed price, necessary? Of course not.

If a buy-sell agreement or other contractual arrangement exists, read it before beginning any valuation process. There are three possible results:

1. The price (value) is fixed in the contract without any doubt. Result: No valuation is necessary.

2. There is no question that the document does not set the value. Result: A valuation is necessary.

3. There is genuine doubt as to whether the document fixes the value. Result: A lawyer should be consulted to render an opinion as to whether the document does or does not fix the value. If the doubt remains, all the parties involved must decide the next step: whether an appraisal should be made. If an appraisal is ordered, the appraiser must do at least the following:

    ■   Obtain a letter from the principal stating that the valuation is to be made in spite of the possibility that it might not be necessary.

    ■   Mention the problem, accompanied by an appropriate discussion, in the appraisal report.

(See Chapter 10 for a discussion of when a document might fix the value.)

MAKING A VALUATION THE EASY, NO-FRILLS WAY

Recent Sales of Stock

Sales of stock made by a willing seller to a willing buyer, which are close in time to the valuation date and made under similar circumstances, could fix the valuation number. (See Chapter 3 for a more detailed discussion.)

If such stock sales cannot be used in lieu of a complete valuation, then the sales would be a factor to be considered along with other factors in the valuation. Another possibility is to use the stock sales price or prices as one of the factors, along with other factors, and give the stock sales an appropriate numerical weight in determining the final valuation.

Industry Standard

The appraiser must determine if there is an established industry standard or some industry rule of thumb that is used to value the type of business under consideration. Sometimes the standards vary from one geographic area to another. Find out. Ask questions. These standards can take many forms: a percentage or multiple of gross sales or billings, so many cents or dollars for each unit sold (measured in terms of per gallon, barrel, pound, or other measure), a multiple of gross profit or net profit before taxes, and many other methods.

As in the case of a recent sale of stock, if the total valuation cannot be accomplished by using the established industry standard, it would be a factor to be considered or, possibly, weighted along with other factors.

The above is the industry standard theory. But a warning is necessary: Don't use it blindly. In my opinion, you should use it as a check to determine if the valuation, using the methods discussed in this book, gives a value the same as or close to the industry standard method. If the two methods give a value in the same range, fine. If not, something is wrong.

Never, but never, let a client buy a business using the industry standard method that gives a price greater than a non-industry standard valuation method. Remember, in the end, the ability of a business to produce earnings determines its value, not some mechanical industry rule of thumb.

SELECTING THE RIGHT METHOD OF VALUATION

Review the eight basic methods of valuation described in Chapter 5. Select the method or methods to be employed.

Remember these two points:

1. If the comparable method is appropriate, use it. If it isn't, don't waste your time trying to put a square peg into a round hole.

2. The valuation must never produce a value less than liquidation value.

Since most valuations in practice use more than one method to accomplish the valuation, the examples used later in this chapter illustrate combination valuations. It is very rare indeed that an appraiser can resort to only one valuation method and not be subject to withering criticism.

REVIEWING THE CHECKLIST OF CONSIDERATIONS

The checklist is meant to be a memory jogger, not an exhaustive list of every possible consideration. Steps, procedures, and considerations that are obvious are intentionally omitted.

1. Scan the table of contents of this book noticing any subject or point that should be reviewed.

2. Review the eight factors listed in Revenue Ruling 59-60 (in Chapter 3).

3. Select the additional factors to be used from the list of 30 factors in the Valuation Factors table in Chapter 3.

4. Reread the material "The Fact-Gathering Process:—A Checklist Section" at the beginning of Chapter 4.

5. If one valuation method is not capable of producing proper valuation results, use more than one method and weight the methods.

6. After selecting the factors to be considered, determine the weight to be assigned, if any, to each factor. This is probably the most subjective part of the process—the one requiring the skill of a winning trial lawyer to justify the assumptions behind the weighting.

7. After the prediscount value has been determined, select the discount, if any, that should be taken for any of the following (see Chapter 9 for more on discounting a valuation):

- Less than 100 percent of the stock of the privately held business being valued

- A general lack of marketability of the stock

- A minority interest

USING VALUATIONS IN PRACTICE

This section of the book could go on and on with hundreds of pages of examples of hundreds of valuations for hundreds of purposes using hundreds of methods. That being the case, and since such an overload of information tends to confuse rather than instruct, now seems a good time to divide the total appraisal report (valuation report) into its natural sections: the valuation numbers, support materials, and financial data.

The Valuation Numbers.   This chapter contains examples of how these numbers are set forth to accomplish the valuation.

Support Material.   This includes everything considered essential to support the valuation conclusion and give it validity—from the history of the company to the credentials of the appraiser. Examples of this support material are included in Part II.

Financial Data.   The report should include all essential financial data. At a minimum, the financial statements—balance sheet and profit-and-loss statement—for the years reviewed should be included. Various ratios (see Part IV-A), statistics, or selected revenue or expense figures may be shown to highlight important data or indicate trends. (This book does not provide complete examples of financial statements, as they are readily available elsewhere. However, Appendix A contains examples of the type of raw financial data used in a valuation.)

Now let's examine some examples that put to work the methods discussed in this text.

A Basic Combination Approach That Works

This example employs a combination of two methods: adjusted book value and a multiple of earnings. Most privately held businesses are bought and sold using this method or some variation of the method. Essentially, this particular combination method asks two questions:

1. How much would be the total cost to a buyer to buy each of the assets now being used in the business? More simply put, how much must be invested in the operating assets of the business? (This question is answered by the adjusted book value method.)

2. How much can be earned on this investment? If the earnings produce more than a fair rate of return, a premium (goodwill) must be paid. On the other hand, if the business cannot produce a fair rate of return, it is worth less than the adjusted book value, and a discount must be allowed.

In actual negotiations, the buyer and seller discuss how each asset on the balance sheet should be valued for purposes of the potential sale. Then they hammer out the goodwill number or the discount. Often the goodwill will be recast in various ways for tax purposes: for example, assigning a specific dollar figure to a covenant not to compete, a patent, and other intangibles that might be written off over a fixed and determinable useful life. The tax consequences of buying and selling a business are not covered in this book; you should hire the best tax advisor you can to oversee the entire transaction from beginning to end.

The following six-step example is offered as *one of many* approaches that can give proper valuation results.

Sample Computation:

1. Determine the *average after-tax earnings* for the company for five years. $ 360,000
2. Determine the *averge annual net tangible assets* (this is actually adjusted book value) in the business for the five-year period. $2,000,000
3. Apply a *fair rate of return* on the average net tangible assets computed in (2). Say 15 percent x $2,000,000. $ 300,000
4. Deduct (3) from (1): equals *excess earnings attributable to goodwill*. $ 60,000
5. Capitalize the excess earnings in (4) at a selected rate to yield the *value of goodwill* (or intangibles). Say 25 percent (or a multiple of 4 x $60,000). $ 240,000
6. Add net tangible assets of the company as of the valuation date to (5)
   a. Assuming net tangible assets (adjusted book value) at the valuation date $2,500,000
   PLUS
   b. Capitalized excess earnings from (5), and 240,000
   c. the fair market value is $2,740,000

Do businesses actually change hands by use of this simple computation? The mathematical result should not be the exclusive test. Every element of the business and every factor that affects it must be taken into consideration: the nature and history of the business, quality of management, future prospects, competition, general economic and industry outlook, all the rhetoric contained in this book, plus a liberal amount of the appraiser's gut feeling, which seems to improve with age and experience.

The seductive simplicity of the above example is that it looks objective, yet any experienced appraiser could point out the many things that make the approach extremely subjective. By changing any one of the several assumptions, the results can be altered significantly.

Keep in mind these notes on this approach:

1. This method can (and often does) produce a fair market value that is less than adjusted book value. Such a result is acceptable to a point. If the valuation figures dip below liquidation value (after deducting estimated liquidation expenses), then liquidation value must be used.

2. Whatever the fair market value as determined might be (no matter what valuation approach has been used), an appropriate discount must be taken.

Now comes the key question: Could $2,740,000 truly be the value of a real operating business as determined by the method shown? The answer is an emphatic *YES*. Although it can be argued skillfully that changing any one of the assumptions would change the fair market value mathematically arrived at, that does not invalidate the method itself. As a practical matter, the ability to change the numbers (for valid reasons) in any one of the steps allows the appraiser to fine-tune the appraisal.

Actually, this particular approach can be summarized as a combination of the two basic approaches to valuation:

1. *the liquidation approach*—Step 6a is the appraisal value of the assets minus the liabilities or adjusted book value—and

2. *the earnings approach*—Step 6b is, in effect, a separate valuation of the earnings of the business in excess of a reasonable rate of return required on the investment (adjusted book value).

The job of the appraiser is to combine the factors, methods, and procedures (for convenience these will be called "methodology") discussed in this book to allow the mathematical result to produce a "correct" fair market value.

The following is an analysis of how the appraiser might use the selected methodology in the sample computation to reach a correct valuation.

Step 1. Determine the *average after-tax earnings* for the business for five years. The earnings must be analyzed and adjustments made for nonrecurring items, discretionary expenses, and so on. The task is to predict what profits will be in future years by eliminating those expenses and income items that are not likely to occur again and including anticipated future expenses and income.

What earnings should be used as average earnings if the after-tax profit of the business for the past five years has been as follows?

Year	Profit
1987	$120,000
1988	80,000
1989	50,000
1990	20,000
1991	480,000
Total	$750,000

Would a simple average be appropriate? Should more weight be given to 1991 because it is the most recent year? The 1991 figure is an anomaly. Looking at the figures alone, it should be eliminated as an extraordinary year. So you would probe. Is 1991 the breakthrough year that will produce another Xerox? Or was this a one-time windfall to be disregarded?

Step 2. Determine the *average annual net tangible assets (adjusted book value)* used in the business for a five-year period. First, convert each item on the balance sheet to its adjusted book value. (For our purposes, adjusted book value means fair market value for each asset on the balance sheet on the valuation date.)

There is not much room to manipulate the numbers, because each asset should, in fact, be stated at its appraisal (fair market) value. This average should be computed to reflect the amount actually invested in the business on the average over the past five years. Simply add the adjusted book values at the beginning of each of the five years and divide by five, as follows:

Year	Tangible Assets at Fair Market Value Less All Applicable Liabilities
1	$1,560,000
2	1,720,000
3	2,040,000
4	2,180,000
5	2,500,000
Average net tangible assets	10,000,000 ÷ 5 = $2,000,000

Note: Often only the last year is used. In the above example, this would be $2,500,000 for Year 5.

Step 3. Determine a *fair rate of return*. What constitutes a fair rate of return is dependent upon the same factors that affect financial markets in general, such as inflation and the cost of money (interest rates). If U.S. Treasury bonds are yielding 10 percent, logic dictates the rate of return for an investment must be more than 10 percent. Also, if the cost of money is 11 percent, the business must earn more to repay borrowings. One accepted rule of thumb is to use a rate-of-return that is approximately one to three points over the prime rate of interest, with adjustments made for the industry rate of return, if known, and risk factors.

Comparisons should be made with investment returns for preferred stocks, tax-free municipal bonds, industrial bonds, and other appropriate investments.

Risk is the most volatile element of a fair rate of return. It must be quantified. Factors like competition, general economy, industrial outlook, and technological advancement all come under the heading of *risk.*

In the end, a fair rate of return is made up of two elements: (1) the right rate of return according to the present investment market, and (2) the degree of risk. Add the two together and the determination is complete. For example, a fair rate of return might be determined as follows:

Return On Investment	11%
Degree of Risk	4%
Total Fair Rate of Return	15%

Step 4. Determine the *excess earnings attributable to goodwill* by deducting the number arrived at in step 3 from the number arrived at in step 1. This can also be called the *intangible value of the business.*

Step 5. Capitalize excess earnings in step 4. The real challenge here is to select a capitalization rate (multiple of earnings). The same risk considerations come into play in this step as in step 3 where a fair rate of return was determined. Should the two rates be the same? Not necessarily so, but they usually are.

The multiple will be higher for a steady line of business, and lower for a business that is new, risky, or tends to have widely fluctuating profits. Any uncertainty concerning the business usually lowers the multiple.

Step 6. Determine the *fair market value of the business* by adding the net tangible assets as of the valuation date (*not* the five-year average of step 2) to the capitalized excess earnings amount from step 5. The sum of these two numbers should not be regarded as the exact value of the business but as a median figure within a value range. Suppose the figure is $2 million. The range might be from 10 percent more ($2.2 million) to 10 percent less ($1.8 million), subject to all the literature and evidence that can be mustered in justification, together with a proper gut feeling.

A Final Important Note.   In the end, logic and common sense must prevail. Any final valuation amount must be fine-tuned to be acceptable to all parties to avoid conflict. When a business is bought and sold in the real world, sooner or later a real price (the real fair market value) is struck and the deal is made.

In my experience, more closely held businesses have changed hands at a price arrived at using something like the six-step method above than by any other method.

TWO REAL-LIFE SAMPLE VALUATIONS

The following two valuations are taken from the office files of Blackman Kallick Bartelstein (BK). All names, locations, and other data were changed to prevent identification of the client. These cases were chosen to be a guide, not to be a how-to-do-it bible. Neither is a complete formal valuation proposal, but both contain excerpts that illustrate specific concepts of valuation.

For a complete valuation proposal, see Part II (which sets out a valuation proposal, except for financial statements, as it actually appears when provided to BK clients).

Capsule Valuation for Purposes of Discussion of Proposed Offers to Purchase Company

This first valuation is not a full-fledged valuation, but was requested by a client company for discussion purposes by its board of directors who were evaluating which of two preliminary offers (one from a private investor and the other from a publicly traded company) to purchase the company might be considered further.

The formula approach was used for the purpose of considering the merits of the offer from the private investor, and the *multiple of earnings approach* (using comparable publicly traded corporations) was used for purposes of considering the merits of the offer from the publicly traded company.

This capsule valuation is set out to illustrate that there is no one valuation method that is appropriate to use in every situation. Actually, in practice, it is just the reverse: different valuation methods must be used for different purposes, even if for the same company.

Often an appraiser is called upon to develop a short presentation for discussion purposes only. This example offers a format that accomplishes this purpose. Read the material under Discussion Outline and follow each step under the Capsule Valuation.

THE SUCCESS CORPORATION
Valuation for Purpose of Sale
May, 19__

DISCUSSION OUTLINE

I.   Formula Approach

   A.   Determine adjusted book value
      1.   Book value (net assets)
      2.   Divide net assets as to:
         a.   Operations
         b.   Investments
      3.   Add (subtract) items where book value is not true value of operating assets
         a.   LIFO inventory reserve
         b.   Fair market value of building in excess of depreciated basis
         c.   Income tax effect
            i.   on above
           ii.   S Corporation status
   B.   Determine reasonable rate of return
      1.   Monetary
      2.   Risk
   C.   Determine excess profit over a reasonable rate of return (goodwill)
   D.   Capitalize goodwill
   E.   Add goodwill to adjusted book value of operating assets
   F.   Set range and price
   G.   Add investment net assets at fair market value

II.   Multiple of Earnings Approach

   A.   Determine value of earnings by reference to comparable companies
   B.   Set price and range
   C.   Add investment net assets at fair market value

CAPSULE VALUATION

I.   Formula Approach

   A.   Determine value of earnings by reference to comparable companies
      1.   Book value
         (net assets) $8,800,000
      2.   Divide net assets

	a. Operations	b. Investments
	$3,440,000	$5,360,000

      3.   Add (subtract)
         items
         a.   LIFO inventory reserve   1,400,000
         b.   Building (to increase book
            value to appraisal value)   1,000,000

(continued on next page)

  c. Tax effect
      i. Above items
          (a) LIFO   (720,000)
          (b) Building   (200,000)
      ii. S Corporation (see note 1)   (1,120,000)
          ADJUSTED BOOK VALUE $3,840,000

B. Determine reasonable rate of return (after tax)
    1. Monetary
        Tax-frees available in market from 7 1/2–9 1/2 percent. Use average
        after-tax.   8%
    2. Risk (see note 2)
        a. Unit sales decreasing
        b. Product is almost indestructible (small reorder)
        c. Cashless society
        d. Lawsuit   5%
        REASONABLE RATE OF RETURN (after-tax)   13%

C. Determine excess profit over a reasonable rate of return
    1. Adjusted book value $3,840,000
    2. Reasonable rate of return   13%
    3. Reasonable return (line 1 x 2) $ 499,200
    4. Operating income (last year-end after adjustments for tax effect) 1,004,000
    5. Excess profit (goodwill) $ 504,800

D. Capitalize goodwill
    1. Excess profit $ 504,800
    2. Reasonable monetary rate
        of return (after-tax)   8%
    3. Reasonable monetary rate
        of return (pre-tax)   16%
    4. Multiplication factor   100/16
        Capitalized goodwill $ 3,155,000

E. Adjusted book value $3,840,000
    Capitalized goodwill   3,155,000
    Total $6,995,000
    Rounded $7,000,000

F. Set price and range   –10%   +10%
    1. Price $ 7,000,000 $ 7,000,000
    2. Range – / + 10%   700,000   700,000
    Value of operating assets   6,300,000   7,700,000
    (see note 4)

G. Add investments   5,360,000   5,360,000
    (see notes 3 & 4)
    TOTAL VALUE $11,660,000 $13,060,000

II. Multiple of Earnings Approach

A. Determine value of earnings by reference to comparable companies

Price/earnings ratio
per *Wall Street Journal* on date

1.	Burrroughs	11
2.	NCR	8
3.	Sperry Rand	10
4.	Pitney Bowes	10
	AVERAGE	<u>10</u>

		–10%	+10%
B.	Set price and range		
	1. Operating income (last year-end after adjustment for tax effect)	$ 1,004,000	$ 1,004,000
	2. Above at multiple of 10	$10,040,000	$10,040,000
	3. Range – / + 10%	(1,004,000)	1,004,000
	Value of operating assets (see note 4)	9,036,000	11,044,000
C.	Add investments (see note 4)	5,360,000	5,360,000
	TOTAL VALUE	$14,396,000	$16,404,000

Note 1: Since an S corporation pays no tax, an adjustment must be made to book the tax liability that would be shown for a regular taxpaying corporation.

Note 2: The four items listed all have a negative impact on future profits, hence increase the risk.

Note 3: The business has investments with a fair market value of $5,360,000 that are not used in the operations of the business. The income from these investments is not included in the operating income at C.4.

Note 4: No matter what method is used to value an operating business that might be sold, it must be tested against what the seller will pay. Hence, only a range for discussion or negotiation purposes is established above. Investments, on the other hand, will change hands at dollar-for-dollar value based on fair market value on the date of closing.

Comparison of Comparable Valuation Approach to Capitalized Excess Earnings Approach

This valuation illustrates the pitfalls of the comparable method. As will be seen in the excerpts from the valuation that follows, the appraiser used two methods to determine the final valuation number: the comparable method and the capitalized excess earnings method. Its purpose was for valuing a minority stock interest in the company that was to be sold to the company's ESOP (see Chapter 13).

The client in this case wanted advice as to the validity of a valuation report from an appraiser that used the comparable approach. The client is founder, CEO, and chairman of the board of the company. The company is a wholesale and retail distributor of diesel, gasoline, and other petroleum products and currently has annual sales in excess of $25 million.

The client was dissatisfied with the results of the comparable valuation. He did not feel that any of the publicly traded companies used were anywhere near comparable to his closely held business.

The reasons for the client's apprehension could be found in the appraiser's report itself. In justifying its use of comparables, the report concluded that the closely held company was larger, had a stronger liquidity position, had a stronger working capital position, had a stronger leverage position, had a stronger profitability position, and stronger asset management relative to the 400 companies in the composite industry it was compared to. One can imagine the client already scratching his head in bewilderment.

The appraiser went on to state that the company was smaller than, had a comparable liquidity position to, had a comparable leverage position to, had a comparable profitability position to, had a stronger asset management than, and weaker revenue growth than four publicly traded companies selected as being comparable. The client became disturbed when the above factors led the appraiser to conclude that the closely held company was a higher investment risk than the comparables and should be sold at a discount five percent below the weighted average of the publicly traded stock.

The only criterion that directly connected the closely held company with the four publicly traded companies was that they too were engaged substantially in the sale and distribution of petroleum and petroleum products.

Was the client justified in lacking confidence in the comparability conclusions? In his eyes, the appraisal was unreliable because the appraiser had unwittingly made a case against the closely held company being comparable to any other company—publicly traded or otherwise—in the process of justifying the use of the comparable approach.

The client favored the capitalized excess earnings approach because it gave weight to the goodwill (excess earnings) attached to his particular business. He felt this approach did justice to the aspect of his business that sets it apart from others—his own ownership and management.

The final valuation figure in the appraisal was reached by weighting the results of each valuation approach. Even though the client felt strongly biased against the use of the comparable approach, we convinced him that it could not be ignored or the valuation could be subject to attack by other parties interested in the ESOP. We also pointed out to him that the final results reached by each method were close enough so that none need be regarded as far off the mark. Therefore the weighted average was close to the final result reached by the capitalized excess earnings approach alone.

Following are the exhibits to the valuation. Only names, dates and minor changes (for clarity) have been made to the material as originally presented. They are for illustration only, and the reader is reminded that they were the work of another appraiser. [This author does not favor the use of comparables for this particular valuation, but when the day comes that you must use comparables, you will turn back to these pages and relish them as pure gold.] However, the example is the work of an experienced appraiser who has excellent credentials and technique. The presentation is well done. Follow the flow of the data closely. You are the judge: based on what you have learned thus far, decide whether you agree or disagree with the logic or conclusions of the valuation.

LISTING OF EXHIBITS

*These Exhibits are not reproduced in this text. They are listed here to indicate to the reader other documents and data used in the valuation.

Exhibit 1
Royal Oil, Inc.
Conclusion of Total Fair Market Value As of September 30, 1991

Approach	Exhibit No.	Value	Weighting Factor	Weighted Value
Market comparison	A-1	$2,323,200	.4	$ 929,280
Capitalized excess earnings	B-1	$2,464,740	.6	$1,478,840

Total fair market value as of September 30, 1991	$2,408,120
Total number of common shares outstanding as of September 30, 1991	127,820
Fair market value per common share outstanding as of September 30, 1991	$ 18.85

Note: In accordance with the observations and disclosures made throughout this report with regard to the applicability, nature, and reliability of the approaches utilized to value a minority interest in the Capital Stock of Royal Oil, Inc., it is our opinion that the above weighting factors yield a fair and reasonable value for said interest in the company as of September 30, 1991.

The accompanying report is an integral part ot this Exhibit.

Author's Comment: A common and acceptable method of valuation is to use two methods (sometimes even more) of valuing a company. The results of the two methods are then averaged or weighted (as above) to arrive at the final fair market value.

A discount is not normally taken because in theory the ESOP provides a marketplace for the closely held stock.

Exhibit A-1

Royal Oil, Inc.

Market Comparison Approach Indication of Value As of September 30, 1991

	Net Income (Exhibit A-2)	Multiple (Exhibits A-3, A-4, and A-5)	Indicated Value	Weighting Factor*	Weighted Value
Current-Year Indication					
Net income for the twelve months' ended September 30, 1991, with current-year's weighed average P/E	$262,280	10.9	$2,858,850	.50	$1,429,430
Two-Year Average Indication					
Average net income for the fiscal years' ended 1990 and 1991, with two-year weighted average P/E	$192,960	8.8	$1,698,050	.25	$ 424,510
Three-Year Average Indication					
Average net income for the fiscal years' ended 1988 through 1991, with three-year weighted average P/E	$148,970	12.6	$1,877,020	.25	$ 469,260
Market comparison approach indication of value (to Exhibit 1)					$2,323,200

*Note: In accordance with the observations and disclosures made throughout this report and in consideration of the trend in net income, it is our opinion that the above weighting factors yield a realistic fair market value for Royal Oil, Inc. as of September 30, 1991.

Exhibit A-2

Royal Oil, Inc.

Calculation of Net Income Figures for the Periods Indicated

Fiscal Years Ended September 30	Last Two-Years' Net Income	Last Three-Years' Net Income
1989	—	$ 61,000
1990	$123,640	123,640
1991	262,280	262,280
	$385,920	$446,920

1990 Net income = $262,280 (To Exhibit A-1)

Two-year average net income for the period October 1, 1989 through September 30, 1991: $385,920 divided by 2 = $192,960 (To Exhibit A-1)

Three-year average net income for the period October 1, 1988 through September 30, 1991: $446,920 divided by 3 = $148,970 (To Exhibit A-1)

The accompanying report is an integral part of this Exhibit.

Author's Comment: Why are three years used rather than the usual five years? The reason is that the above income of Royal Oil, Inc. is to be compared to the income of the Public Companies and four years or more is considered to be too remote.

Exhibit A-3

Royal Oil, Inc.

Calculation of Current-Year's Weighted Average Price/Earnings (P/E) Multiple

Company	Ratio*	Weighting Factor (Exhibit A-6)	Weighted Ratio
Comparable Co. A	11.1	6	66.6
Comparable Co. B	NM	NA	NM
Comparable Co. C	13.7	4	54.8
Comparable Co. D	8.0	2	16.0
Totals	32.8	12	137.4

Range 8.0–13.7

Median 11.1

Mean 10.9

Current-year's weighted average P/E: 137.4 ÷ 12 = 11.5

Reduced multiple applied to Royal Oil, Inc.: 11.5 − 5% = 10.9 (To Exhibit A-1)

---

*The indicated price/earnings multiple for the current year's average is derived by dividing the average of each company's high market price and low market price for the nine months ended September 30, 1991 by each company's respective earnings for 1991 as reported in Standard & Poor's Corporation's *Security Owner's Stock Guide,* October 1, 1991 edition.

NM = Not Meaningful

NA = Not Applicable

The accompanying report is an integral part of this Exhibit.

Author's Comment: The note above uses two logical approaches to minimize the impact of market price fluctuations—(1) using only the last 9 months of the public companies high-low market price, and (2) averaging those 9 months. Whether the result obtained is logical is left to the reader. To help in this decision, ask and answer this question: Would the buyers and sellers of closely held businesses you know, buy or sell based on this kind of information?

Exhibit A-4
Royal Oil, Inc.
Calculation of Last Two-Years' Weighted Average Price/Earnings (P/E) Multiple

Company	Ratio*	Weighting Factor (Exhibit A-6)	Weighted Ratio
Comparable Co. A	8.5	6	51.0
Comparable Co. B	NM	NA	NM
Comparable Co. C	10.9	4	43.6
Comparable Co. D	8.7	2	17.4
Totals	28.1	12	112.0

Range   8.5–10.9

Median 8.7

Mean   9.4

Two-year weighted average P/E: 112.0 + 12 = 9.3

Reduced multiple applied to Royal Oil, Inc.: 9.3 – 5% = 8.8 (To Exhibit A-1)

*The two-year average price/earnings multiple is derived by dividing the average of each company's high market price and low market price for the years 1990 and 1991 by each company's respective earnings for each year. The two years are summed and the total is then divided by 2 to obtain the two-year average P/E multiple.

NM = Not Meaningful

NA = Not Applicable

The accompanying report is an integral part of this Exhibit.

Exhibit A-5
Royal Oil, Inc.
Calculation of Last Three-Years' Weighted Average Price/Earnings (P/E) Multiple

Company	Ratio*	Weighting Factor (Exhibit A-6)	Weighted Ratio
Comparable Co. A	6.9	6	41.4
Comparable Co. B	24.3	6	145.8
Comparable Co. C	9.0	4	36.0
Comparable Co. D	8.1	2	16.2
Totals	48.3	18	239.4

Range   6.9–24.3

Median   8.6 (9.0 + 8.1 = 17.1 + 2)

Mean   12.1

Three-year weighted average P/E: 239.4 + 18 = 13.3

Reduced multiple applied to Royal Oil, Inc.: 13.3 − 5% = 12.6 (To Exhibit A-1)

*The three-year average price/earnings multiple is derived by dividing the average of each company's high market price and low market price for the years 1989, 1990, and 1991 by each company's respective earnings for each year. The three years are summed, and the total is then divided by 3 to obtain the three-year average P/E multiple.

The accompanying report is an integral part of this Exhibit.

Author's Comment: Company B shows a ratio of 24.3, which is way out of the ratio of all the other companies. Also Company B was not used in Exhibits A-3 or A-4. Do you think the use of Company B for one year helps value Royal Oil, Inc.? Maybe this explains the 5% "Reduced Multiple Applied to Royal Oil, Inc." [13.3 x 5% = .665 (rounded to .7); 13.3 − .7 = 12.6]

Exhibit A-6
Royal Oil, Inc.
Determination of Weighting Factors Applicable to Comparable Public Companies

Comparable Public Companies	Size (A)	Financial Performance (B)	Product Line (C)	Combined Factor (A + B + C)
Comparable Co. A	1	2	3	6*
Comparable Co. B	1	2	3	6*
Comparable Co. C	2	1	1	4*
Comparable Co. D	0	1	1	2*
Totals	4	6	8	18

---

*(To Exhibits A-3, A-4, and A-5)

Note: We have identified the above listed public companies as comparable to the non-public subject entity Royal Oil, Inc. for the reasons outlined in the explanation of the Market Comparison Approach. We have further identified three key classifications of comparability in order to calculate a combined weighting factor for each of the public companies. These weighting factors, when applied to the Price/Earnings multiples of the respective public companies, enables one to accentuate those public companies most similar to Royal Oil, Inc. in terms of Size, Financial Performance, and Product Line. The public companies were weighted under each of the three comparability classifications by the following ranking: zero—not comparable, one—slightly comparable, two—comparable, or three—highly comparable. These combined weighting factors represent our opinion of each public company's relative similarity to Royal Oil, Inc. premised upon information contained primarily in Exhibits A-7 and A-8 in this report.

The accompanying report is an integral part of this Exhibit.

Exhibit A-7
Royal Oil, Inc.
Public Companies' Comparative Financial Statistics

Statistics and Ratios*	Comparable Company A	B	C	D	Range	Royal Oil, Inc.	Subject Comparability
Fiscal years ended	10/31/90	1/31/91	7/31/91	12/31/90		9/30/91	
Size ($ Million)							
Revenue	$327.2	$186.8	$61.4	$5,393.0	$61.4–5,393.0	$26.8	Smaller
Total assets	$ 60.1	$ 74.0	$25.7	$4,644.5	$25.7–4,644.5	$ 4.3	Smaller
Net worth	$ 40.4	$ 32.5	$ 7.1	$1,422.0	$ 71.–1,422.0	$ 1.5	Smaller
Liquidity ratios							
Current ratios	3.0	1.6	1.1	1.0	1.0–3.0	1.5	Low range
Working capital turnover	8.1	23.5	NM	NM	8.1–23.5	23.6	Above range
Leverage ratio							
Total liabilities to equity	0.3	1.3	2.6	2.3	0.3–2.6	1.9	Mid range
Profitability ratios							
Net profit to:							
Sales	2.3%	0.2%	0.8%	2.9%	0.2–2.9%	1.0%	Low range
Equity	18.5%	1.0%	7.0%	10.9%	1.0–18.5%	17.3%	High range
Total assets	12.5%	0.4%	2.0%	3.3%	0.4–12.5%	6.1%	High range
Activity ratio							
Asset turnover	5.4	2.5	2.4	1.2	1.2–5.4	6.2	Above range
*Growth index***							
Revenues	NA	1.1	2.3	1.8	1.1–2.3	1.1	Above range

*Based on latest available annual report.

**Most recent year's revenues divided by revenues four years prior.

NA = Not Available

NM = Not Meaningful

The accompanying report is an integral part of this Exhibit.

Exhibit A-8

Royal Oil, Inc.

Synopses of Comparable Public Companies

Comparable Co. A

The Company mainly engages in crude oil and petroleum products supply and marketing. The Company was incorporated in Bermuda in 1980, and its corporate headquarters are located in Bermuda.

Comparable Co. B

Company, through its subsidiaries, is engaged in the wholesale sale of residential fuel oil and the distribution of gasoline and petroleum products to stations, some of which are operated by the Company. These stations sell at retail company-distributed gasoline, motor oil, lubricants, etc., under the company's proprietary brand name Power Test, or under other brand names. At January 31,1990, the company distributed gasoline to 436 stations in New Jersey, Connecticut, Pennsylvania, Massachusetts, and New York. It owned 245 and leased 173 stations, 290 of which were leased or subleased to others.

Comparable Co. C

Company retails natural gas in northwest Tennessee. They obtain the natural gas from East Tennessee Natural Gas Company. Wholly owned subsidiary, Holston Oil, Inc., markets a full line of Texaco Petroleum products in its seven-county service area in northeast Tennessee.

Comparable Co. D

Company, mainly through wholly owned Texas Eastern Transmission Corp., and Transwestern Pipeline Company, transports and sells at wholesale natural gas. It also explores for and produces oil and gas, produces and sells petroleum, sells at retail and wholesale liquified petroleum gas, operates a petroleum product pipeline, performs chemical process research, development and engineering, explores for uranium, and develops commercial real estate.

Author's Comment: Elsewhere in the report, it says Royal Oil, Inc. "is a wholesale and retail distributor of diesel, gasoline, and other petroleum products in " one of the western states. "It currently has two locations . . . and revenues totaling in excess of $25 million." The appraiser did a terrific job of finding companies that are as comparable as possible given the size and business makeup fo Royal Oil, Inc. Nevertheless, none of the "Comparable Public Companies" are in fact really comparable to Royal Oil, Inc.

Exhibit B-1

Royal Oil, Inc.

Capitalized Excess Earnings Approach Indication of Value as of September 30, 1991

Average net tangible assets used in business for the period 1986–1990 (Exhibit B-3)		$1,136,890
(a) Industry rate of return at 10.0% (Exhibit B-4)	$113,690	
(b) Average net income for the period 1987–1991 (Exhibit B-2)	$208,920	
Excess earnings (b–a)		$ 95,230
Capitalized at 15% ($95,230 + .15)		$ 634,870
Add adjusted net tangible asset at September 30, 1985 (Exhibit B-5)		$1,829,870
Capitalized excess earnings indication of value (to Exhibit 1)		$2,464,740

The accompanying report is an integral part of this Exhibit.

Author's Comment: The "industry rate of return"—10% as used above—is usually the best rate to use. But beware. If the industry rate of return is much higher or lower than the return for typical closely held businesses or other typical investments (say AAA bonds and U.S. Treasuries plus 2 to 4 points for the added risk of a closely held business), then use of the rate may give a false value. Use a typical rate (as described in the preceding sentence) instead. Caution is also required when an industry rate is unusually high or low due to temporary market conditions. For example, the industry rate of return for companies like Royal Oil, Inc. is only 5.7%. See Exhibit B-4.

Exhibit B-2

Royal Oil, Inc.

Schedule of Adjustments to After-Tax Net Earnings and Calculations of Average Adjusted Earnings for the Period September 30, 1987—September 30, 1991

Fiscal Years Ended September 30	Net Income	Add (Less): LIFO Effect*	Add: Discretionary Contribution**	Adjusted Earnings
1987	$226,740	$ -0-	$ 90,420	$ 317,160
1988	90,810	42,690	59,680	193,180
1989	61,000	(5,260)	-0-	55,740
1990	123,640	(23,630)	6,670	106,680
1991	262,280	41,040	68,540	371,860
Totals	$764,470	$54,840	$225,310	$1,044,620

Average adjusted net income for the period 1981–1985: $1,044,620 ÷ 5 = $208,920 (To Exhibit B-1)

*The inventory of gasoline, oil, accessories, etc., is accounted for by the last-in, first-out (LIFO) method. When compared to the first-in, first-out (FIFO) method, the effect of LIFO is to reduce income before taxes in a year of rising prices. Conversely, in a year of falling prices, LIFO will show greater income before taxes than FIFO. In our analysis, we have adjusted net income by the after-tax effect (assumed to be 33%) of any LIFO adjustment in order to restate income on a FIFO basis.

**Adjustments to the net income of Royal Oil, Inc. were made to reflect the average after-tax effect (assumed to be equal 33%) of contributions to the Company's Employee Stock Ownership Plan, which are of a discretionary nature.

The accompanying report is an integral part of this Exhibit.

Exhibit B-3

Royal Oil, Inc.

**Average Net Tangible Assets Used in Business for the Period
September 30, 1986–September 30, 1990**

Fiscal Years Ended September 30	Total Assets	Less: Total Liabilities	Net Tangible Assets
1986	$ 2,941,500	$ 2,177,500	$ 764,000
1987	3,318,600	2,304,000	1,014,600
1988	3,717,500	2,576,700	1,140,800
1989	3,760,200	2,441,800	1,318,400
1990	3,663,480	2,216,840	1,446,640
Totals	$17,401,280	$11,716,840	$5,684,440

Average net tangible assets for the period September 30, 1986–September 30, 1990:
$5,684,440 + 5 = $1,136,890 (to Exhibit B-1)

Note: In accordance with generally accepted valuation techniques, greater weighting has been accorded the more recent net tangible assets of the Company.

The accompanying report is an integral part of this Exhibit.

Author's Comment: Note that the determination of these asset figures use the beginning of the period, as opposed to the end of the period. Why? Because this represents the net assets invested to start with. Remember, the rate of earnings are always based on the initial investment rather than the ending investment.

Exhibit B-4
Royal Oil, Inc.
Computation of Industry Median Return on Net Worth

	RMA & Profit Before Taxes to Net Worth (Notes 1 & 2)	Assumed % Tax Rate	RMA & Profit After Taxes to Net Worth	Weighting Factor (Note 2)	Weighted Average % Profit After Taxes to Net Worth	Weighting Factor (Note 1)	Weighting % Profit to Net Worth
Fuel Oil (Note 1-A)							
Upper quartile	23.9%	50%	12.0%	25%	3.0%		
Median quartile	11.1%	50%	5.6%	50%	2.8%		
Lower quartile	1.7%	50%	0.9%	25%	0.2%		
					6.0%	50%	3.0%
Petroleum Products (Note 1-B)							
Upper quartile	20.5%	50%	10.3%	25%	2.6%		
Median quartile	10.4%	50%	5.2%	50%	2.6%		
Lower quartile	1.8%	50%	0.9%	25%	0.2%		
					5.4%	50%	2.7%
							5.7%

(See Author's Comment)

Note 1: Robert Morris Associates' Annual Statement Studies, 1990 Edition; Asset Size $1,000,000–$10,000,000; Industry Classifications;

    (A) Wholesalers—Fuel Oil, SIC #5172, 168 companies reporting
    (B) Wholesalers—Petroleum Products, SIC #5171, 232 companies reporting

Note 2: The figures are not average, but depict the upper quartile, median and lower quartile figure in each case. These figures were calculated by, first, arraying all the numerical values of that ratio in order of the strongest to the weakest ratio. The figure which falls in the middle of the list of ratio values is the median. The figure halfway between median and the strongest is the upper quartile and the weakest is the third quartile. Ratios presented in this fashion preclude the undue influence of extreme ratio values which would result if merely an "average" ratio figure were presented. Also, and more importantly, they give the analyst some idea of the "spread" or range of ratio values in each case. This might be made even clearer by realizing that the total spread between its first and third quartiles by definition includes the middle 50% of the companies represented. Ratio values greter than the third quartile, and less than the first quartile, therefore, rapidly begin to approach "unusual" values. Consequently, to consider these factors appropriately, the median ratio has been weighted at 50% while the upper and lower quartiles have been weighted at 25% each for purposes of these computations.

Author's Comment: Although the "Weighting % profit to net worth" computed above is 5.7%, the rate used in Exhibit B-1 is 10%, without any additional explanation as to why. However, see author's comment on Exhibit B-1.

The accompanying report is an integral part of this Exhibit.

Exhibit B-5

Royal Oil, Inc.

Schedule of Adjusted Net Tangible Assets as of September 30, 1991

Net tangible assets as of September 30, 1991		$1,517,020
Add: independent appraisal of fair market value of the following corporate assets*	$385,000	
Total net book value of appraised assets	$ 72,150	
Total fair market value in excess of net book value as of September 30, 1991**		$ 312,850
Adjusted net tangible assets as of September 30, 1991 (to Exhibit B-1)		$1,829,870

*The independent appraisal of fair market value was made by Real Estate Appraisal, Inc. as of May 8, 1989. It is management's opinion that this appraisal is still valid.

**During the fiscal year ended September 30, 1991, the building became fully depreciated.

The accompanying report is an integral part of this Exhibit.

SECTION B

PARTICULARS OF VALUATION

CHAPTER 8

PUTTING A VALUE ON GOODWILL AND OTHER INTANGIBLES

Goodwill is one of those terms that many people use but few can define precisely. In too many sales and purchases of privately held businesses, the buyer and seller hammer out a price for the business, and almost matter-of-factly, as a last-minute string to be tied in a pretty bow, allocate a portion of the price to "goodwill." Usually, one or both of the parties do so ignorant of the disastrous tax consequences that will attach to at least one of the parties to the transaction. That's because the income tax laws usually make valuation of goodwill a zero-sum game between buyer and seller, in which one party's tax savings is the other party's tax liability.

DEFINITION OF GOODWILL

A good working definition of the term goodwill is the difference between the value of a business' net assets—both tangible and intangible, but excluding goodwill—and the price that a willing buyer would pay for the business as a whole. Generally, this difference reflects the expectation that a business will maintain customer patronage, and as a result, will generate a reasonable rate of return after the buyer assumes ownership. Also, it is a value that comes from the favorable reputation arising out of an established, well-known, and well-conducted business.

Goodwill is inseparable from the business, which means it cannot be sold separately. It is assumed that goodwill can be transferred to the buyer.

PROFESSIONAL GOODWILL

Is there really such a thing as professional goodwill? Yes. Is it different than goodwill as defined above? Again, yes, but not entirely. The real question is, is it subject to valuation and how? The answer, in most cases, depends on whether the goodwill is transferable. If not (personal goodwill)—like the expertise of a star quarterback, actor, surgeon, doctor, lawyer or indian chief—the goodwill has no specific dollar value. On the other hand, if the goodwill is transferable (enterprise goodwill)—like an entire football team, group medical or other licensed professionals that practice as a group—then it can be valued. How? By the same principles, in general, as discussed in this book.

A recent Illinois Supreme Court case deals with professional goodwill and does the best job of telling you what it is and how to value it that I have ever seen. Here are excerpts from the already famous *Zell* case.

Docket No. 70419—Agenda 22—January 1991.

In re MARRIAGE OF MYRA JOYCE ZELLS, Appellant, and MARTIN B. ZELLS, Appellee.

JUSTICE HEIPLE delivered the opinion of the court:

This case concerns the division and distribution of marital property between a lawyer and his spouse. There are two issues. The first is whether a lawyer's contingent fee contracts are subject to valuation, division and distribution as part of the marital estate. The second issue is whether professional goodwill is a marital asset and subject to division or distribution.

Our conclusion is that neither contingent fee contracts nor professional goodwill is subject to valuation, division or distribution as marital assets.

We next address the issue of the goodwill value of the law practice. Goodwill represents merely the ability to acquire future income. Consideration of goodwill as a divisible marital asset results in gross inequity.

Panels of the Illinois appellate court have similarly held that the goodwill of a professional business is not marital property subject to division. The first district adopted this position with its decision *In re Marriage of Wilder* (1988), 122 Ill. App. 3d 338.

The third district followed the reasoning of *Wilder* in *In re Marriage of Courtright* (1987), 155 Ill. App. 3d 55, holding that the goodwill value of the husband's medical practice was not a marital asset. The court stated:

> "Although many businesses possess this intangible known as good will, the concept is unique in a professional business. The concept of professional good will is the sole asset of the professional. If good will is that aspect of a business which maintains the clientele, then the good will in a professional business is the skill, the expertise, and the reputation of the professional. It is these qualities which would keep patients returning to a doctor and which would make those patients refer others to him. The bottom line is that this is reflected in the doctor's income-generating ability.

> Although good will was not considered in the court's valuation of the business itself, it was a factor in examining [the husband's] income potential. To figure good will in both facets of the practice would be to double count and reach an erroneous valuation." 155 Ill. App. 3d at 58-59.

The reasoning presented in *Courtright* is correct. Adequate attention to the relevant factors in the Dissolution Act results in an appropriate consideration of professional goodwill as an aspect of income potential. The goodwill value is then reflected in the maintenance and support awards. Any additional consideration of goodwill value is duplicative and improper.

TAX TREATMENT OF GOODWILL AND OTHER INTANGIBLES

Goodwill is a two-sided tax coin. In the purchase and sale of a business, goodwill is a capital asset to the seller and a nondepreciable asset to the buyer. Accordingly, sellers benefit by putting a larger value on goodwill, increasing their capital gains, while buyers benefit by putting a smaller value on goodwill, allowing them to allocate more of the total purchase price to depreciable assets.

The tax treatment of other intangible assets, however, can be more favorable than goodwill. If it can be determined that a particular intangible asset has a limited useful life that can be estimated with reasonable accuracy and has a cost basis separate and distinct from goodwill, a buyer can deduct this asset via depreciation or amortization.

Examples of intangible assets are patents and copyrights, trademarks and trademark names, trade secrets, contracts and licenses, and mass assets such as customer lists and subscription lists.

WHY ALLOCATION OF PRICE TO GOODWILL AND OTHER INTANGIBLES IS NECESSARY

The competing tax interests of the buyer and seller make it necessary to spell out in the sale agreement the precise portion of the purchase price that is allocable to each asset. Why? Because if it is not done, both the IRS and the courts will take it upon themselves to do so. Not only that, but once involved they will concern themselves with other matters, such as going-concern value and valuation of covenants not to compete.

Generally, the courts have respected the efforts of buyers and sellers to reconcile their competing tax interests regarding such items as recapture of prior depreciation and investment tax credits, assignments of income, and allocation of ordinary income versus capital gain regarding goodwill, covenants not to compete, and going-concern value. To be acceptable, the parties' allocation must be realistic. Also, the ultimate value assigned to the particular asset concerned should not be drastically raised or lowered in relationship to actual value to produce favorable results.

The IRS has declared that, while it is not bound by contractual allocations, it will respect them unless they are devoid of economic substance and defy the realities of the transaction. In other words, the IRS will nix the contract allocation if it thinks the parties were motivated by tax avoidance.

GOING-CONCERN VALUE

The IRS has in recent years successfully argued that an operating business possesses an asset separate from goodwill and other intangibles—*going-concern value*. Going-concern value must be recognized, goes the IRS argument, when acquired assets are assembled in an ongoing operating business. It is that element of value adhering to an assembled and established plant doing business and earning money, and does not apply to one not so established.

The courts describe going-concern value as the ability of a business to continue to function and generate income without interruption as a consequence of a change in ownership and management. Note how closely that definition corresponds with the goodwill definition of continuation of customer patronage.

Like goodwill, going-concern value is not depreciable. The significance of this is that the IRS will alternatively argue the presence of both goodwill and going-concern value in the assets of a business, hoping to score with either or both arguments. Unfortunately, this strategy has worked.

For example, in *VGS Industries* (68 TC 563; 1977), the IRS unsuccessfully argued for goodwill but was successful in arguing going-concern value. The court rejected goodwill because of the business' highly competitive industry (indicating no assurance of continued customer patronage) and lack of excess earnings.

Defining going-concern value as the ability of the business to continue to function and generate income without interruption as a consequence of a change in ownership, the court reasoned as follows:

> The combined business operations acquired by New Southland [the buyer] had in place and operational the Crupp and Rogerslacy Refineries, a terminal, a gas pipeline, six bulk plants and service stations, and various other necessary equipment in addition to a source of supply for crude oil and gasoline and the Southland trade name. Moreover, the Southland operations were able to survive and make a profit in a highly competitive industry during a time when many small refineries were unable to break even without the application of the foreign oil import quota. The business acquired by New Southland was more than a mere collection of assets. It was rather a viable, functioning, and going concern capable of generating a profit, and New Southland acquired a valuable property right as a result.

If the company was able to generate a profit, why was that not classified as goodwill? The difficulties involved in distinguishing between goodwill and going concern are illustrated by the *VGS* case. It appears that the courts treat goodwill as *demonstrated* earning power, while going-concern value is *potential* earning power. Either way, the buyer is stuck with a nondepreciable asset.

In *Concord Control, Inc.* (35 TCM 1345; 1976), the buyer purchased all of the assets of another company for $3.8 million. In order to head off a minority shareholder suit disputing the sales price, an independent appraisal of all tangible assets was made. The sales price was 89.5 percent of the appraisal value, with $1 set aside for all other assets. The buyer allocated the entire purchase price to tangible assets based upon the sales contract. The IRS allocated over $1 million of that price to goodwill.

The Tax Court rejected the goodwill contention of the IRS, mostly because the business' largest customer was lost after the sale. The buyer heaved a sigh of relief:

> A precondition to the possession of transferable goodwill is a finding that the seller's business is of such a nature as to provide the purchaser with the expectancy of both continuing excess earning capacity and competitive advantage of continued patronage. Excess earning capacity in and of itself is insufficient to demonstrate the transfer of goodwill . . . . Here K-D (the sold business) at the time of the sale was engaged in a industry fraught with a high degree of competition and little customer loyalty . . . . The loss (of K-D's largest customer) . . . amply demonstrates that the [buyer] had no reasonable expectancy of continued customer patronage flowing from its purchase of K-D.

However, the court then took off into the tax law stratosphere by fashioning a nondepreciable asset where none had existed before. To the buyer's chagrin, the court found that going-concern value of $335,000 was purchased by the buyer in the form of assets whose value was increased due to their existence as an integral part of an ongoing business.

As in the *VGS* case, the Tax Court distinguished going-concern value as potential earning capacity as opposed to goodwill as demonstrated earning power:

> Notwithstanding our conclusion that petitioner acquired no goodwill in connection with its purchase of K-D, it clearly did acquire an ongoing business that *was earning money*, had a trained staff of employees, had a product line presently ready for sale, and equipment ready for immediate use.

In the more recent case of Curtis Noll Corp. (44 TCM 288; 1982), a business was purchased for $3.2 million. The Tax Court found no going-concern value because inventory with a high turnover rate was a major part of the businesses' assets (which meant competitors could easily spring up by simply investing in inventory) and tangible operating assets were a small part of the business' total assets. But guess what?

The Tax Court found goodwill to be present because:

- the buyer succeeded to a well-established business,

- the buyer acquired the seller's favorable reputation built over 60 years of operations,

- recent profits were on the upswing,

- the buyer acquired company names, personnel, store leases, advertising and good store locations, and

- the business had been in business for 60 years, indicating a record of competitive pricing and good customer relations.

The term "going concern value" was defined by the Supreme Court in 1983 (Los Angeles Gas & Electric Corp., 289 U.S. 287). This case was referred to in a more recent case (Northern Natural Gas, 470 F2d 1107). The court said, ". . . there is an element of value in an assembled and established plant, doing business and earning money over one not thus advanced, and that this element of value is a property right which should be considered in determining the value of the property upon which the owner has a right to make a fair return."

Going-concern value, like goodwill, is an intangible asset. It may exist with a separate value for the assemblage of a business regardless of the business profitability. For valuation purposes, going-concern value must be measured separately from other assets, although it is not a property that may be sold separately. Going-concern value, like goodwill, however, cannot exist or have value unless considered as part of an operating business.

Maybe the best way to identify going-concern value is to set down the elements that are included in its identity:

1. The physical assets (and identifiable intangibles) of an assembled (and operating) business.

2. Noncapital costs directly related to the assembling of the business assets.

3. Even if there is no history of excess profits, it can exist. Goodwill, however, cannot exist if there is not current excess profit or potential for same in the immediate future.

Examples of going concern value would be:

1. Start-up expenses incurred.

2. Assembled plan, management, employees, and the like.

3. Assembled identifiable intangibles, such as patents and licenses.

4. Developed procedures, methods and systems that are in operation.

5. Financial and other relationships established to make the business operate.

6. Marketing, advertising, and promotion concepts that are in use.

7. Sources of established supply and contracts for same.

Goodwill on the other hand relates to such things as the (1) physical assets (location); (2) excess profits on invested capital; (3) the kinds of things that generate continued patronage (reputation, special skills, name, quality); and has no existence if there are no excess profits or potential for same in the near future.

What these cases concerning going-concern value illustrate is that no matter how hard the buyer and seller try to avoid it, the value of an operating business will always contain an intangible nondepreciable asset, be it goodwill or going-concern value, at least if the courts or the IRS have anything to say about it.

GOODWILL AS MEASURED BY EARNINGS POWER

Goodwill is most easily measured by excess earnings power. However, excess earnings power is *indicative* of goodwill, not goodwill itself. Excess earnings over and above a reasonable rate of return could be attributable to extraordinary efforts or talents of key employees or the owner, nonrecurring windfalls, special customer relationships (such as captive supplier situation), or extraordinary market conditions.

On the other hand, the courts rarely find goodwill without excess earnings. Excess earnings power is a signal that goodwill is probably present. The reasons for the excess earnings is then determined, and usually attributed to goodwill. And remember, a court that refuses to find goodwill because of lack of excess earnings may still find going-concern value.

What is the standard way to measure excess earnings? That depends on your perspective. If you are the IRS, the so-called *gap* or *subtraction method* is used. The advantage to this method is simplicity. Take the net fair market value of all assets and compare that to the price paid for the business. The difference is goodwill, or going-concern value, if appropriate.

However, in my experience, the average buyer and seller consider a fair rate of return in determining goodwill. Here is the more realistic and most often used method of valuing goodwill:

1. Calculate a normal rate of return for the net assets of the business.

2. Compare the normal rate of return with the actual rate of return of the business.

3. If there is an excess of the actual over the normal rate, capitalize that difference by an appropriate factor.

4. The amount determined, if any, is the goodwill of the business.

Does this formula sound familiar? Look back to Chapter 3 to the section on ARM-34. It comes from there and is now comprehensively set forth in Revenue Ruling 68-609 (see Part IIIA). The IRS says that this formula should be used only if there is no better basis for goodwill calculations. What this means is that the IRS will recognize its use only when it produces a larger value for goodwill. For the purposes of buying and selling in the real world, it is one of several good valuation methods.

The use of the earnings approach method of valuation precludes any additional calculation for goodwill. The earnings approach will determine whether excess earnings are present in a business, and whether an appropriate premium should be paid for it. That premium, however, usually includes the price tag for goodwill. The ARM-34 method is another way to calculate that same premium, and use of both methods should result in approximately the same goodwill amount.

When determining a normal rate of return and an appropriate capitalization rate, the skill and experience of the appraiser come to the forefront. In fact, resort to comparable businesses may be necessary, as well as an industry survey of reasonable rates of return.

COVENANTS NOT TO COMPETE

Often, when a buyer plans to continue a business as it is, he or she needs reassurance that the seller will not immediately set up a rival shop carrying on the same trade or business. To prevent this possibility, the buyer, as part of the sales transaction or agreement, will require the seller to covenant (promise), that he or she will not do so. A covenant not to compete is not an asset of the business, but is a condition of sale for which the seller receives consideration.

The tax consequences of such a covenant are as follows: the seller recognizes ordinary income, and the buyer can amortize the cost of the covenant over its life.

Unlike goodwill and going-concern value, where the buyer is the tax loser, here it is the seller who wishes to allocate the smallest possible amount to the covenant. Usually, where there is goodwill, a covenant not to compete is also present, to protect the buyer's investment in that goodwill. Normally, in the sales negotiations, there is a trade-off between buyer and seller concerning the tax consequences of the two items.

ALLOCATION ISSUES CONSIDERED BY THE COURTS

Several issues have arisen in the courts regarding the allocation of value in a sales price to intangibles such as goodwill, going-concern value, and covenants not to compete. There are three allocation situations that usually are considered in a court case:

1. where no allocation has been made and the IRS imposes its own allocation,

2. where an incorrect allocation is made ignorant of the tax consequences and the slighted party petitions for more favorable tax treatment, or

3. where the IRS considers the buyer and seller to have made inconsistent allocations for tax purposes.

An example of the IRS imposing its own allocation occurred in *Illinois Cereal Mills, Inc.* (46 TCM 1001; 1983). A purchase agreement did not contain an allocation of the purchase price, $240,000, among the various intangible assets acquired by the buyer. Those intangible assets included goodwill, a trademark, technical data, and customer lists. The purchase agreement also contained a five-year covenant not to compete. The buyer attempted to claim on his tax return that the entire purchase price was allocable to a covenant not to compete. The IRS claimed that the business as a whole was indivisible and that no allocation was possible.

The Tax Court made an allocation. It assigned a 20 percent value of $48,000 to the covenant not to compete (amortizable by the buyer), 10 percent applicable to the technical data, and the remaining 70 percent to goodwill and the other intangible assets (all found to be nondepreciable).

An example of an incorrect allocation being made ignorant of the tax consequences and an illustration of the court-created "strong-proof rule," occurred in *Stryker Corporation* (44 TCM 1020; 1982). There the buyer attempted to reallocate a larger portion of the purchase price of a business to a covenant not to compete. The buyer and seller had signed a separate no-competition agreement which contained a $1,000 price tag for a covenant not to compete. The buyer claimed the entire purchase price on his income tax return as paid for the covenant not to compete. Of course, the IRS disallowed all but the $1,000 evidenced in the separate agreement.

The Tax Court used the "strong-proof rule" to rule against the buyer. The strong-proof rule places heavy emphasis on the intention of the parties at the time the sales contract is entered into. That intention is best evidenced by the sales contract. Unless the party wanting to change the allocation contained in the sales contract can come up with strong proof that that allocation is not what the parties wanted, the court will not change it.

The strong-proof rule is the biggest obstacle a taxpayer faces if he or she makes a mistake in allocation in the sales contract. In the *Stryker* case, the court would not allow an allocation for the covenant not to compete over the agreed $1,000.

An example of the IRS considering the buyer and seller to have made inconsistent allocations for tax purposes usually involves the buyer and seller having hammered out a sales contract agreeable to both, including its tax consequences, and the IRS then dragging them into court for a reallocation that results in a higher overall tax on the transaction. Suppose in negotiation the buyer was unable to allocate as much as he or she wanted to depreciable assets, being stuck with a high nondepreciable goodwill amount, but in return was able to have a large amount of the purchase price allocated to an amortizable covenant not to compete. The other side of the same coin would be that the seller would realize more capital gain on the goodwill allocation but more ordinary income on the covenant not to compete.

When filing their tax returns, the temptation would be great for the buyer to assign a higher amount to the covenant than that agreed upon and a lower amount for the goodwill. The opposite would be true for the seller. The IRS would step in in such a situation and attempt to reduce the tax benefit to one or both parties. In a confusing irony, to correct taxpayers' inconsistent reporting, the IRS is allowed to take a position toward one party that is inconsistent with its position toward the other party.

This is what happened in *Jacques B. Wallach* (44 TCM 1002; 1982). In that case, buyer and seller agreed to a $330,000 purchase price for a medical laboratory business, and the sale took place. However, for tax purposes the buyer reported the transaction as a purchase of stock for $14,500 and a purchase of a covenant not to compete for $315,500. The seller reported the same transaction as a sale of his stock in the business for the $330,000 total. As reported, the buyer could maximize amortization of the purchase price, and the seller could maximize capital gains.

The IRS' inconsistent position taken towards the taxpayers' inconsistent reporting was this: It told the seller that $315,500 of the purchase price was allocable to a covenant not to compete (resulting in ordinary income) and told the buyer that none of the purchase price was allocable to the covenant not to compete (no amortization). Of course, the IRS couldn't have it both ways, but this case is a good illustration of how the IRS hedges its bets with a shotgun approach to revenue collecting.

The court nailed the buyer. First, it held that none of the purchase price was allocable to the covenant not to compete. Second, it held that $315,500 of the purchase price was allocable to goodwill. The seller had the capital gain; the buyer a nondepreciable asset in the same amount. The IRS won either way the court ruled: the court only decided whose goose was to be cooked.

What these cases teach is that in the purchase and sale of a privately held business, allocation of the purchase price to the business' nontangible assets can make or break the deal from the viewpoint of the buyer or the seller, or both. No allocation, or an incorrect allocation, can cost more in tax liability and court and attorney fees in the long run than any short-term benefits seemingly derived in sales negotiation by either party. True, the buyer and seller are natural adversaries when it comes to negotiating the total value of the business, but they would be better served to cooperate on the issue of allocation for tax purposes.

One final point: The buyer can buy insurance, in a sense, to prevent an IRS reallocation battle. How? Specify a specific dollar amount for goodwill in the sales contract and another specific amount for going-concern value. The seller won't mind; he or she will get a capital gain. Interestingly, the higher the premium paid—the more allocated to goodwill and going-concern value—the more likely the IRS will nod its approval.

CHAPTER 9

VALUATION DISCOUNTS

The first part of this book deals with determining the fair market value of a privately held business. In most cases, the final value determined by using the various valuation methods and approaches is not really the final value that will be used by the appraiser. A further adjustment is needed to reach the final real fair market value that reflects the unique position of a privately held business. This adjustment is known as a *discount*. The valuation figure determined by the appropriate valuation method usually must be discounted to reflect the fact that a stock interest in a closely held business is not as easily marketable, for a variety of reasons, as that of a publicly traded corporation.

THE REAL FAIR MARKET VALUE

In order to value any business for tax purposes two distinct steps are required:

First. Value the business using the factors and approaches set out in the first part of this book.

Second. Subtract an appropriate discount from the value determined in the first step in order to arrive at the *real fair market value*. The real fair market value is the number that will be submitted to the IRS, court, or other entity. There are two discounts that should be considered:

1. discount for general lack of marketability, and

2. discount for minority interest.

Discount for General Lack of Marketability

Here is a simple way to illustrate the concept of discounting a valuation figure because of a general lack of marketability of shares of a privately held business:

Take a stack of stock certificates representing shares in a publicly traded corporation. The morning newspaper gives yesterday's stock market value at $1 million. A call to a broker will bring $1 million, less commissions, in cold cash in four business days.

Now take $1 million worth of Close Fam Co. just valued by the appropriate methods described in this book. Is it worth $1 million? Maybe. Somebody out there, when found, will pay the million—over maybe five to seven years (plus interest at 10 percent, maybe, on the unpaid balance). But the $1 million of Close Fam Co. stock is *not* going to bring a real million dollars in cash or equivalent on the valuation data.

Intuition tells you a discount is in order. Why and how much? That is the subject of this chapter.

The justification for a discount for a lack of marketability was stated by the court in *Central Trust* as follows:

> It seems clear, . . . that an unlisted closely held stock of a corporation such as Heekin, in which trading, is infrequent and which therefore lacks marketability, is less attractive than a similar stock which is listed on an exchange and has ready access to the investing public.

Besides a general lack of marketability, shares of privately held corporations can be rendered unmarketable because of various restrictions on their sale or transfer.

Recent valuation cases provided substantial discounts to the stock's value for non-marketability and other inhibiting factors. In *Estate of Arthur F. Little, Jr.* (TCM 1982-26, CCH Dec. 38729-M), the Tax Court allowed a total discount of 60 percent for shares of restricted stock of a publicly held company. The court allowed a 35 percent discount for sales restrictions, a 15 percent discount for an irrevocable two-year voting proxy agreement, and a 0 percent discount for shares that were held in escrow.

In *William T. Piper, Sr. Est.*, (72 TC No. 88, CCH Dec. 36, 315), the court allowed a total discount of 64 percent for stock of a corporation that owned publicly traded securities and rental property. The court allowed a discount of 35 percent for lack of marketability, 17 percent for relatively unattractive investment portfolios, and another 12 percent for possible stock registration cost.

The IRS considers the discount for lack of marketability as only one factor to be considered in valuing a business. The IRS frowns upon the use of arbitrary discount percentages (see Revenue Ruling 77-287 in Part III-A).

Discount for Minority Interests

The definition of a *minority interest* is control of less than 50 percent of the shares of a corporation. What if the interest being valued is exactly 50 percent? Since this interest lacks the ability to control the corporation, for discount purposes, a 50 percent interest is a minority interest.

The discount for a minority interest in a privately held business results from the unenviable position of the minority shareholder. The holder of 15 percent (or any other minority interest) of the stock of a closely held corporation cannot determine the dividend he or she will get, cannot get hired at a salary of his or her choosing, cannot compel a sale of the corporation, and many other unfortunate "cannots." Most importantly, minority shareholders are helpless if they want to cash in their interest in the corporation. No buyer will pay the 15 percent minority shareholder 15 percent of the total value of the whole corporation for that interest, because the buyer would be under the same disability. It necessarily follows that in the marketplace, this 15 percent interest cannot be sold for a price equivalent to 15 percent of the intrinsic value of the whole corporation. Normally, it will bring only some reduced price. That reduced price represents a discount.

To summarize, minority shareholders' problems are threefold:

1. Their interest lacks liquidity. Minority shareholders can get out of their position only if (a) the company goes public, (b) the business is sold or merged, or (c) they sell their shares to either the company or to fellow stockholders.

2. Their interest lacks current yield. Most privately held businesses don't declare dividends, and minority shareholders are powerless to compel them.

3. Their interest lacks control. Minority shareholders are powerless to affect the management and operations of the business. Their interests are at the mercy of the majority shareholder.

The Internal Revenue Service's position toward minority discounts is stingy, as is to be expected. While conceding that the discount is usually appropriate, the IRS almost always attempts to reduce its size. And in Revenue Ruling 81-253 (see Part III-A) it refuses to allow minority discounts for gift tax purposes when privately held stock is gifted between family members and the family as a whole owns a controlling interest. This position is at odds with court decisions that allow minority discounts in intrafamily transfers of privately held stock.

For instance, in *Estate of Bright* (658 F.2d 999, CA-5 1981), the appellate court refused to value half interest in a controlling block of 55 percent of a privately held corporation as half of a controlling interest, ruling instead that it was a 27.5 percent minority interest.

In *Estate of Andrews* (79 TC 938; 1982), the court applied both a discount for lack of control (minority interest) and for lack of marketability despite the fact that all shares of a privately held business were held by a decedent and his brothers. Citing the *Bright* case, the *Andrews* court held that a decedent's shares should not be valued as though the only hypothetical "willing buyer" would be a family member. To say that the only market for the decedent's shares would be a family member would violate the rule of Regulation 20.2031-1b regarding hypothetical willing buyers and sellers.

Most recently, the case of *Propstra* vs. *U.S.* (82-2 USTC 13, 475, CA-9; 1982), the Ninth Circuit Court of Appeals let it be known that only legislation would change its position on intrafamily minority discounts:

> We are unwilling to impute to Congress an intent to have "ownership of unity" principles apply to property valuations for estate tax purposes.... Fair market value [is defined] as the price at which property would change hands between a willing buyer and a willing seller, neither being under any compulsion to buy or sell and both having reasonable knowledge of relevant facts. By no means is this an explicit directive from Congress to apply the unity of ownership principles to estate valuations. In comparison, Congress has made explicit its desire to have unity of ownership or family attribution principles to apply in other areas of Federal tax law. In the absence of similarly explicit directives in the estate tax area, we shall not apply these principles when computing the value of assets in the decedent's estate ....
>
> Defining fair market value with reference to hypothetical willing-buyers and willing-sellers provides an objective standard by which to measure value .... The use of an objective standard avoids the uncertainties that would otherwise be inherent if valuation methods attempted to account for the

likelihood that estates, legatees, or heirs would sell their interests together with others who hold undivided interests in the property. Executors will not have to make delicate inquiries into the feelings, attitudes, and anticipated behavior of those holding undivided interests in the property in question. Without an explicit direction from Congress we cannot require executors to make such inquiries.

Not only would these inquiries require highly subjective assessments, but they might well be boundless. In order to determine whom the legatee or heir might collaborate with when selling his or her property interest, one would have to consider all the owners.

Despite these cases, the IRS is determined to fight minority discounts in intrafamily transfers of stock of privately held family businesses. The IRS pattern in this type of behavior is to stubbornly stick to its position until the U.S. Supreme Court rules one way or another on the issue.

Minority Interest vs. Lack of Marketability

Courts have a tendency to lump the discount for lack of marketability and the discount for minority interest together, as was the case in *Central Trust* (see Part III-B). In practice, that is usually what happens when a business is bought and sold. Both discounts deal in lack of marketability, but for different reasons. The discount for minority interest is concerned with the minority shareholder's lack of control over the corporation's affairs. The discount for lack of marketability is concerned with the marketability of shares of a privately held business as compared to a comparable publicly traded corporation. However, the discount for lack of marketability applies to both minority and majority (controlling) interests in the corporation.

Some courts still make a distinction between the two discounts. The Tax Court distinguished the two as follows:

In their arguments neither petitioner [taxpayer] nor respondent [IRS] clearly focuses on the fact that two conceptually distinct discounts are involved here, one for the lack of marketability and the other for lack of control. The minority shareholder discount is designed to reflect the decreased value of shares that do not convey control of a closely held corporation. The lack of marketability discount, on the other hand, is designed to reflect the fact that there is no ready market for shares in a closely held corporation. Although there may be some overlap between these two discounts in that lack of control may reduce marketability, it should be borne in mind that even controlling shares in a non-public corporation suffer from lack of marketability because of the absence of a ready private placement market and the fact that flotation costs would have to be incurred if the corporation were to publicly offer its stock.

The IRS is wary of making a distinction between the two discounts because it thinks that multiple discounts result in a larger overall total discount percentage. It tells its appeals officers to use a lower capitalization rate in the valuation process to reflect any appropriate discount or discounts. Remember, the lower the capitalization rate, the higher the multiple; the higher the multiple, the higher the value. (See *IRS Valuation Guide for Income, Estate, and Gift Taxes,* Federal Estate and Gift Tax Reporter (CCH), no. 115, part II, October 14, 1985, p. 86.)

HOW BIG A DISCOUNT?

Once it has been determined that a discount is in order, how big should it be? When negotiating a sale, a buyer will shoot for a higher discount, and the seller a lower one, if any. In tax disputes, the IRS will attempt to downplay the discount issue, while the taxpayer might use a discount to directly reduce the valuation and taxes.

Historically, no one, including the courts, has ever questioned the validity of the theory that a minority interest, or any interest subject to a market disability, must be discounted in value. The dispute always arises over the *size* of the discount. Historically, the discounts granted by the courts have almost invariably been in a low range of 5 percent to 15 percent.

Now the courts are yielding. In the past few years, the courts have tended to recognize higher discounts. Discounts of 40 percent to 50 percent, once unheard of, have been granted. (See "Minority Discounts Beyond Fifty Percent Can Be Supported," 59 *Taxes* 97, February 1981 and "Nonmarketability Discounts Should Exceed Fifty Percent," 59 *Taxes* 25, January 1981; both articles by George Arneson.) Even an IRS valuation expert employed a discount of 50 percent for illiquidity, along with the taxpayer's valuation expert, in *Estate of Ernest E. Kirkpatrick*, 34 TCM 1490 (1975).

The size of lack-of-marketability discounts, on the average, are smaller than those for minority interests. This is because the courts feel that in many instances a lack of marketability can be remedied (through a public flotation offering, for example), while a minority interest has no way of improving itself short of conversion to a controlling interest through the purchase of additional stock.

The IRS considers the determination of the size of a discount an arbitrary process that is subject to dispute, just like the overall process of valuing the privately held business. One school of thought holds that an appraiser should expect that any discount percentage will be disputed by the IRS. To counter this, as in any bargaining position, the appraiser should aim high on the discount percentage, but no higher than reason will support. This author, on the other hand, believes in another school of thought: Take the discount that the facts and circumstances call for: then fight like a tiger for your position if the IRS dares to challenge. (See Chapter 16 for the Tax Court's position on unreasonable valuation claims.)

Generally, lack-of-marketability discounts of 15 percent to 35 percent, and minority-interest discounts of 35 percent to 50 percent can be appropriate. Total discounts of over 50 percent are becoming more prevalent. Of course, the facts and circumstances of each case will determine the amount of the discount percentage. However, the recent trend upward in discounts no longer leaves the appraiser who takes a justifiable 50 percent or more discount feeling like he or she will be attacked, and likely overwhelmed, by other parties to the valuation.

Determining the size of a lack-of-marketability discount can be a simple matter of calculating the public offering expenses or "flotation costs" necessary to creating a public market for a stock. (See discussion on flotation costs in Part II, example 4.)

Determining the value of a minority interest usually involves three steps:

1. Determine the overall value of the business.

2. Determine the value of the minority shareholder's interest by determining the percentage interest in the overall value.

3. Apply the discount percentage to the minority shareholder's value.

The sample valuations (Part II) have some recent cases and a compilation of excellent material dealing with the entire subject of discounts. Better yet, the material in the sample valuations shows you how the theory is put into practice.

CONCLUSIONS

Considering the number of plausible and possible discounts reaching 50 percent or more, getting oneself into a minority position in a privately held business makes a lot of sense for estate and gift tax purposes. And if the courts keep up their support for minority discounts in transfers of stock of privately held family corporations, obtaining a minority position through intrafamily sales can give a privately held business owner the best of both worlds—retention of control of the business within the family and maximization of tax savings.

Discounts should never be taken arbitrarily to arrive at the valuation objective of the party requesting the valuation. When the IRS is involved, such irresponsible values are subject to severe penalties. (See Chapter 16.)

CHAPTER 10

RESTRICTIVE AGREEMENTS

Like it or not, the day comes when all successful business owners must transfer their controlling interest in the fruit of their live's labors—their privately-held business. The transfer might take place because of their disability, retirement, or desire to move on to something more challenging, but let there be no doubt about it, the transfer will take place—if not during life, then certainly after death. Concerning ownership succession, restrictive agreements can kill three birds with one stone for the owners of a privately held business. If properly drafted, a restrictive agreement can do the following for owners:

1. ensure the orderly transfer of their controlling interest in the business to whomever they desire, without an interruption in the business' operations,

2. freeze the value of the owners' controlling interest for estate and gift tax purposes, avoiding the necessity to break up and sell part of the business to pay any tax liability, and

3. avoid the necessity of a valuation of the owners' interest for estate and gift tax purposes.

TYPES OF RESTRICTIVE AGREEMENTS

The commonly used methods of valuing closely held stock may go out the window wherever, by virtue of a provision in the bylaws or other agreements involving the stockholder, the owner (whether the original owner, executor or any other successor) is restricted in selecting a market for the sale of the stock. Such restrictions are found in buy-sell agreements, options and restrictive sale agreements.

Buy-Sell Agreements

This is an agreement between the corporation or an individual to buy and a stockholder to sell shares at a specified price upon death of the stockholder. Usually, the stockholder further agrees not to sell during life, except at the specified price to either the corporation or the other stockholders. Because there are mutual promises, the agreement may be enforced, and the owner cannot sell the shares except to one or more of the other contracting parties at the specified price. The courts therefore adopt the specified price as the federal estate tax value. (Estate of O.B. Littick, 31 TC 181-1958)

Options

This is where another person has an option to buy the stockholder's stock at a specified price on the happening of a contingency. In theory, this should fix the value just as a buy-sell agreement does, because if the option is still outstanding and enforceable, the stock could not be sold to anyone for more than the option price. The courts, however, make an important distinction.

1. If there was no consideration for the option, the option price is ignored for purposes of valuations. (Bensel, Edith M., 100 F2d 639-1938)

2. But where consideration does exist, making the option enforceable, the option price controls for federal estate tax purposes. (Lomb v. Sugden, 82 F2d 166-1936)

3. Note then, an option price only sets an upper limit on value. Even if the stock could be sold for more, if the option is enforceable, the option price will control. But think about this: What is the result in the case where the stock is not worth the option price? Here you argue the optionee would not exercise his option and attempt to prove a lower value by normal means.

4. Note also the importance of both buy-sell and option agreements of a provision preventing the stockholder from selling to others during life. Absence of this provision would allow the stockholder to sell at a higher price to others before the contingency (death) happens. Therefore, the agreed price does not control. (Estate of J. H. Matthews, 3 TC 525-1944)

Restrictive Sale Agreements (Right Of First Refusal)

This is where the stockholder agrees that, if the stock is to be sold during life or after death, it will first be offered at a specified price to the other stockholders or the corporation. Under such circumstances, the courts hold that the agreed price does not control. (City Bank Farmer's Trust Co., 23 BTA 663-1931)

Important Hint

One of the significant objectives of a buy-sell agreement for a closely held corporation is to fix the value of the shares owned for estate tax purposes. To attain this objective:

a. Do make the life price the same as the death price.

b. Do not use a right of the first refusal requiring a first offer to the other stockholders at a specified price (restrictive sales agreement). Why? Because, if the other stockholders refuse to buy, the stock could then be sold at a higher price to some third party prior to death of the seller. The same objective can be accomplished by (1) giving the remaining stockholders (and/or the corporation) an enforceable option to purchase during life, and (2) at death making the purchase by the remaining stockholders (and/or the corporation) mandatory.

This chapter discusses the first type of restrictive agreement—the buy-sell agreement. Only this type of agreement is capable of killing the three birds with the one stone. The option agreement and the right of first refusal agreement can serve as methods for transferring controlling interest but with less certainty for tax planning purposes. Why? Because the people who can exercise the option or who have the right of first refusal can walk away from the agreement, by not exercising their right to buy. That may leave the owner off the hook and able to sell to someone else. As a practical matter, because the owner is not locked into a fixed price, these agreements may not be recognized for tax purposes. However, it is the mutual obligation between the parties of the buy-sell agreement that locks in the price and makes it an excellent tax and financial planning tool.

TYPES OF BUY-SELL AGREEMENTS

Buy-sell agreements, as discussed in Chapter 2, can be broken down into three types:

1. The *redemption agreement* obligates the privately held corporation to buy the shareholder's interest upon the happening of any one of a list of specified events. The most commonly named events are death, disability, retirement, or termination of employment.

2. The *cross-purchase agreement* obligates the remaining shareholders to purchase the interest.

3. The *combination agreement* does one of two things. It either gives the remaining shareholders the option to buy the shares with the corporation obligated to purchase what the shareholders don't, or vice versa.

FUNCTION OF BUY-SELL AGREEMENTS

Buy-sell agreements are an excellent way to make sure that the termination of a shareholder's interest in the business does not create problems for the terminating shareholder, remaining shareholders, and the business. It creates a market for the terminating shareholder's interest, and in the case of his or her death, fixes the value of his or her interest for estate tax purposes.

The provision in the buy-sell agreement that requires the transfer of the terminating shareholder's interest to other shareholders or the corporation protects the corporation's existence as a going concern. It prevents the transfer of the interest to parties whose goals are inimical to present management or who would force a liquidation. The remaining shareholders are spared anxiety and apprehension over the business' future. Present employees are assured that there will not be wholesale or radical changes that could make their positions tenuous.

Finally, the successful drafting and implementation of a buy-sell agreement can make an appraisal of the business' value unnecessary. (See the steps in the valuation process listed in Chapter 7.)

Defeating the Estate Tax

A properly drafted and implemented buy-sell agreement can fix the estate tax value of a deceased shareholder's interest in a privately held corporation. In Chapter 2, four general requirements are listed to achieve the value freeze. Actually, they can be broken down further into six specific requirements:

1. The price stated in the agreement must be fixed or determined according to a valid valuation formula. For the deceased's estate, the fixed price will cause less trouble from an estate planning perspective. However, if the shareholders want to have appreciation in the stock considered to determine the final price—the usual case—a formula should be used. When hammering out the agreement, the interests of a deceased shareholder's estate must be weighed against those of the surviving shareholders or the corporation. When the shareholders are closely related, lower estate tax liability means lower basis for the purchasers of the stock which, in turn, means higher capital gain upon future sale, and vice versa. If the shareholders are not related, the price becomes an economic force; the selling stockholder wants the highest possible price, and the estate tax becomes a secondary consideration.

2. The estate of the deceased shareholder must be obligated, under the agreement, to sell the deceased's stock to the corporation or the shareholders at the agreement price. There does not have to be an actual purchase of the shares by either of those two parties, as in the case of an option agreement, but failure to do so may be held as evidence that the stock is not worth the agreement price.

3. The agreement must state that the deceased cannot sell his or her interest while alive to a third party without first offering the shares to the corporation or the remaining shareholders at the agreement price. The offer cannot be a right of first refusal which has the same price and terms as that offered to the third party. Such a right would be an escape hatch to lower the price for estate tax purposes. The offer must be at the agreement price.

4. The agreement price cannot be lower than the fair market value of the stock at the time the agreement is entered into. This requirement makes it mandatory for the shareholders to enter into the agreement as early as possible to avoid the IRS including appreciation in the value of the stock. An agreement entered into solely for the purpose of freezing the par or book value of a dying shareholder's interest shortly before his or her death will not do the trick.

5. The agreement must have what is called in tax parlance a *bona fide* business purpose. The courts have ruled, and the IRS reluctantly agrees, that preservation of management control, be it family or other, is a *bona fide* business purpose for a buy-sell agreement. So is a desire to prevent disruption of the business' operation.

6. The sixth requirement is that the agreement's *raison d'etre* (reason for existence) cannot be "testamentary," i.e., to beat the estate tax. In the words of the IRS, the agreement "must not be a tax avoidance device for passing a decedent's shares to the natural objects of his bounty for less than full and adequate consideration." Usually, if a *bona fide* business purpose exists, there is no tax avoidance. However, as is discussed below, this is changing. *Bona fide* business purpose is no guarantee that tax avoidance will not be found in the agreement.

IRS' Position on Buy-Sell Agreements.   The IRS doesn't say what a valid buy-sell agreement is, because it is not in the business of telling taxpayers how to beat the estate tax and lower government revenues. However, it does say what will not pass muster. For example, in Regulation 20.2031-2(h), it states:

> *Securities subject to an option or contract to purchase.*   Another person may hold an option or contract to purchase securities owned by the decedent at the time of his death. The effect, if any, that is given to the option or contract price in determining the value of the securities for estate tax purposes depends upon the circumstances of the particular case. Little weight will be accorded a price contained in an option or contract under which the decedent is free to dispose of the underlying securities at any price he chooses during his lifetime. Such is the effect, for example, of an agreement on the part of a shareholder to purchase whatever shares of stock the decedent may own at the time of his death. Even if the decedent is not free to dispose of the underlying securities at other than the option or contract price, such price will be disregarded in determining the value of the securities unless it is determined under the circumstances of the particular case that the agreement represents a bona fide business arrangement and not a device to pass the decedent's shares to the natural objects of his bounty for less than an adequate and full consideration in money or money's worth.

The IRS' position as stated above seems to say that the *bona fide* business agreement and testamentary tax avoidance device test are mutually exclusive—if an agreement is one it can't be the other.

Chapter 2 contains an explanation of a new IRS tactic: use of the gift tax to attack buy-sell agreements.

The Courts and Buy-Sell Agreements.   While the IRS has chosen to leave taxpayers guessing as to what agreements will or will not pass muster, the courts have stepped in to fill the void. The six requirements listed earlier in this chapter derive from requirements fashioned over the years by the courts.

The general rule on buy-sell agreements is as follows:

> It now seems well-established that the value of property may be limited for estate tax purposes by an enforceable agreement which fixes the price to be paid therefor, and where the seller if he desires to sell during his lifetime can receive only the price fixed by the contract and at his death his estate can receive only the price theretofore agreed on. (*Wilson v. Bowers*, 57 F.2d 682.)

Most of the litigation surrounding buy-sell agreements centers on the dichotomy between *bona fide* business purpose and testamentary device, and on whether the presence of one eliminates the possibility of the presence of the other (i.e., whether the two concepts are mutually exclusive). The IRS usually attacks buy-sell agreements as testamentary devices with the taxpayer contending that it had a *bona fide* business purpose. The courts are not in full agreement that these two positions are mutually exclusive. Here are two cases that illustrate this point.

In *Estate of Bischoff* (69 TC 32; 1977), the court followed the mutually exclusive rule. That case involved a partnership interest subject to a buy-sell agreement. The partnership held stock in a family business. Here is the court's reasoning in upholding the price set in the buy-sell agreement as the value of the decedent's stock for estate tax purposes:

> We are convinced that the members of F.B. Associates and Frank Brunckhorst Co. entered into their respective partnership agreements in order to assure their continuing ability to carry on the pork processing business without outside interference, including that of a dissident limited partner. In order to accomplish this objective, restrictive buy-sell provisions were incorporated into the partnership agreements. The F.B. Associates agreement maintained ownership and control of F.B. Associates in the Bischoff and Brunckhorst families and in turn maintained ownership and control of Boar's Head and its sister corporation within those two families, and the Frank Brunckhorst Co. in the Bischoff, Brunckhorst, and Weiler families. We therefore conclude that the buy-sell provisions were grounded on legitimate business considerations . . . Having found such a purpose for both the F.B. Associates and Frank Brunckhorst Co. partnership buy-sell provisions and since the partnership provisions provided for a lifetime and after-death restrictions, we conclude that the value of the decedents' interests in F.B. Associates and Frank Brunckhorst Co. is the amount provided for and paid under the buy-sell provisions of the partnership agreement.

The IRS raised numerous objections to the buy-sell agreement in *Bischoff*. It argued that the partnership interests did in fact pass to the natural objects of the decedents' bounty, i.e., the interests passed to their children. The four partners were almost certain to predecease the children partners. Besides that, the children were only passive partners.

The *Bischoff* court did not disagree with these IRS contentions. It merely held that the legitimate business purpose of maintaining family control of the family business negated any testamentary intent in the buy-sell agreement.

In the case of *St. Louis County Bank* (674 F.2d 1207 CA-8 1982), the appellate court held that the existence of a *bona fide* business purpose in a buy-sell agreement did not negate the need for the taxpayer to also prove that the agreement was not a testamentary device. Instead of finding the two positions mutually exclusive, the court found that the taxpayer had to prove that the agreement (1) had a *bona fide* business purpose, and (2) was not a testamentary device.

The facts of the case were these: The decedent held a majority interest in a privately held moving and storage business. All the other shareholders were members of the decedent's family. A buy-sell agreement among the shareholders and the corporation gave surviving shareholders and the corporation the option to purchase a deceased shareholder's shares under a formula price based on the company's average annual earnings. At the time the agreement was entered into, the agreement price was close to the fair market value of the shares. Subsequently, however, the company's business changed from a profitable operating company to a real estate investment company. Losses mounted yearly. Under the agreement price formula the stock's price fell to zero.

One shareholder died and the agreement was not used. Upon the death of a second shareholder, the corporation invoked the agreement and redeemed the second deceased shareholder's shares for free, at the zero-formula price.

Although the appellate court found a legitimate business purpose for the buy-sell agreement (preservation of family ownership), three disturbing facts led it to hold that the agreement was a testamentary device: (1) all of the parties to the agreement were related, (2) although the book value of the decedent's shares was $200,000, the agreement formula price was $0, and (3) the deceased had suffered two heart attacks at the time the agreement was executed.

The difference in the decisions in *Bischoff* and *St. Louis County Bank* seem to hinge on the health problems of the deceased. In *Slocum* (256 F. Supp. 753; 1966), failing health was also held as a reason for the court to find testamentary intent in an agreement. However, compare the opposite result in *Estate of O.B. Littick* (see Chapter 2) where the fact that the deceased had terminal cancer at the time of the execution of the buy-sell agreement was disregarded by the court in upholding its *bona fide* business purpose.

In summary, if the six requirements listed earlier in this chapter are satisfied, a buy-sell agreement should pass muster. Be aware, however, that the failing health of one party to the agreement, especially in a privately held family business situation, could lead to close scrutiny by the IRS and a probable attack on the value of the deceased's shares for estate tax purposes.

If the price in the agreement is set by formula, that formula should use one of the valuation methods or approaches listed in this book. For example, if a company is profitable, the earnings approach might be used. If the company is unprofitable or, as in the *St. Louis County Bank* case, has major nonoperating assets, a book value formula might be used.

A must regarding buy-sell agreements is that when a situation arises in which the agreement can be invoked (such as the death of one of the parties), it *must* be invoked. Failure by the parties to the agreement to exercise their purchase rights under the agreement (and take as a beneficiary under the will) is a red flag to the IRS that the agreement is a testamentary device and that the agreement price is below the actual value of the stock. This is again an instance when the interests of the surviving parties are pitted against those of the deceased's estate.

Finally, a bit of advice: enter into a buy-sell agreement as soon as possible, particularly when all the parties are in good health. Many of the tax problems mentioned in this chapter can then be avoided.

A Case that Shows How to Get the Job Done . . . Right

Almost uniformly the stockholders of a closely held business do not want any shares of stock to fall into strange hands. This purpose is most often accomplished by the use of a buy-sell agreement between the shareholders. The question often comes up: Does the price fixed in the agreement hold up for estate tax purposes?

The answer to this important question can be a loud "Yes" if the agreement is properly drafted. An interesting case points the way. Here's the story.

Five shareholders entered into an agreement that provided that all transfers of stock were subject to its terms. A written consent was required for all transfers. In the absence of such a consent, a selling shareholder had to give 60 days notice to the other shareholders and the corporation. All shares were to be sold to the corporation or the other shareholders at book value. The agreement was enforceable against all the shareholders and the estate of a deceased shareholder. The right of shareholders to own stock was dependent on their continuation in their position as a director, officer or employee. When this relationship was severed, a shareholder was required to sell his stock in accordance with the agreement.

One of the shareholders, Mabel, died and her shares were offered for sale to the corporation at book value, $251,800. The IRS claimed the fair market value of the shares was $460,000 and wanted that value to be reported for estate tax purposes.

The court (Estate of Mabel G. Seltzer, TCM 1985-519) turned thumbs down on the IRS' claim holding that an enforceable agreement, which fixed the price to be paid, can limit the value of the shares for estate tax purposes. After all, in this case, the estate was obligated to demand no greater value than the book value of the shares. The court pointed out that if Mabel had attempted to sell the stock on the date of her death, she would have been limited to a book value price by the terms of the agreement. The fact that the fair market value may have been higher was ruled to be immaterial.

A Look at New Chapter 14

The Omnibus Budget Reconciliation Act of 1990 (Act) has added a new, but very important, twist to family buy-sell agreements. Among the provisions in the Act is Chapter 14 which provides that a buy-sell agreement does not affect the value of property for gift and estate tax purposes (put bluntly, will be ignored by the IRS) unless the agreement:

1. is a bona fide business arrangement;

2. is not a device to transfer such property to family members for less than full consideration; and

3. has terms comparable to similar arrangements used by person in arms' length transactions.

The law, by its terms, does not limit agreements between or among family members, but be careful—the IRS will take a close look at such agreements between related parties. The penalty of a family buy-sell agreement running afoul of this provision is painfully clear. Since the value in the agreement will be disregarded, the fair market value on the date of gift or death for estate tax purposes will control.

CHAPTER 11

RECAPITALIZATIONS—
THE OLD LAW

INTRODUCTION

This particular paragraph is being written in June 1991, as I update this book, originally published in 1986. I was about to red ink most of this chapter and "Chapter 12-Preferred Stock" as that chapter was titled in 1986. Then I changed my mind. It seemed a shame to destroy all of that old and very interesting history of recapitalizations. Instead, the old 1986 Chapters 11 and 12 have been combined and renamed "Recapitalizations—The Old Law." New Chapter 12 tells you about the New Law.

Both of these old chapters remain untouched, except for (1) a few "authors comments," which you will recognize when you see them, and (2) appropriate minor cosmetic changes.

In recent years, the most popular valuation-freezing tool for estate tax purposes has been the recapitalization. Unfortunately, the effectiveness of the recapitalization has been put in doubt because its desired estate tax results have become hotly contested by the IRS. Planning in this area has become increasingly treacherous. Some practitioners have begun to look elsewhere to obtain the results previously sought from recapitalizations. However, there is still a place for the recapitalization to fulfill the needs of the privately held business owner.

THE GENIUS OF DR. SALSBURY

The history of the recapitalization as an estate planning tool begins with the ingenuity of Dr. Joseph Salsbury. In 1946, Dr. Salsbury undertook a recapitalization of his privately held business, Salsbury Laboratories. Here's what he did. The only class of common stock in the company was canceled, and the shareholders were issued instead new preferred and common stock. The preferred stock received a six-cents-a-share fixed dividend with any excess being paid to the new class of common stock. The voting structure of the company after the recapitalization was as follows: one vote per share for the 690,000 shares of preferred and 27,290 shares of common stock. The voting control of the company was fixed in the preferred stock. The preferred stock was issued to the shareholders in the same proportions as the canceled old common. Dr. Salsbury, having 54 percent of the old common, received 54 percent of the preferred and retained control of the company. The new common stock, with minimal voting power, was issued to the doctor's wife and children.

As a result, Dr. Salsbury achieved the dream of the estate planner. He retained control of the company, froze the value of the company in the preferred stock, enabled his wife and children to share in any future appreciation in the company's worth, and avoided any gift tax on the issuance of the new common to his family.

The fruits of Dr. Salsbury's planning acumen were harvested when he died in 1967. At his death, he held voting control over a privately held business worth $13 million. However, he only owned preferred stock in that company that was eventually valued by the Tax Court for estate tax purposes at $514,000. In other words, $12.5 million worth of the business was not included in his estate and therefore escaped the estate tax. Keep in mind that Dr. Salsbury also managed to avoid the gift tax during his lifetime, and the magnitude of his accomplishment can be appreciated. He saved over $7 million in taxes (See *Estate of Salsbury*, TCM 1975-333). If only it were that easy today.

DEFINITION OF A RECAPITALIZATION

Technically, a recapitalization is a reorganization or reshuffling of a corporation's capital structure under Section 368 (a)(1)(E) of the Internal Revenue Code. If properly carried out, there is no gain or loss recognized by the shareholders or the corporation. It involves the cancellation of old and the issuance of new classes of stock.

RECAPITALIZATION SCENARIO

Following is a scenario that illustrates the actual situation of thousands of closely held business owners all over the United States. This author hears the story again and again in his office: he does more valuation for recapitalizations than for all other valuation purposes combined. You should change the facts as necessary to fit your own circumstances.

One point must be kept in mind: a recapitalization always uses a second class of stock, usually preferred stock.

The Scenario

Let's illustrate the use of preferred stock in the recapitalization of a jobbership. Joe Jobber is 61 years old, married, and has two children. He owns 1,000 shares, which is 100 percent, of Rich Corporation's common stock. He acquired these shares in 1960 when he incorporated his sole proprietorship. The fair market value of the corporation is $1 million.

His wife, let's call her Mother, does not participate in management. Nor does Joe's youngest child, who we will call Daughter. Daughter is married to an engineer, who will never be active in the corporation. Joe's oldest child, who we will call Son, has been employed by Rich Corporation for about 15 years and is now almost in complete control of operations. Joe's objectives and problems can be summarized in four statements.

One

Joe doubts that his estate will have the cash to pay any substantial amount of estate tax. Most of his wealth is tied up in Rich Corporation, which has land, buildings, and equipment. The inventory and receivables seem to grow incessantly. It is doubtful whether he or the corporation could accumulate any large amount of cash. Joe would like to freeze the value of his estate at its current level.

Two

Joe wants to stay in control of the corporation as long as he lives. He would like control to pass to his son upon his death.

Three

Joe would like Mother to have adequate support, after his death, assuming that she survives him.

Four

After Mother's death, Joe would like his estate to be divided equally between his son and his daughter. It is important to Joe that Son's control of Rich Corporation not be disturbed after his death. Although Joe would like Daughter to receive the same value as Son, Joe does not want her to be able to interfere in the management of the business.

After several meetings, Joe decides upon a recapitalization. To accomplish the recapitalization, Rich Corporation will issue three classes of stock in exchange for all of Joe's old 1,000 common shares. This exchange is tax free.

After the exchange this is the way Joe's new stock holdings will look:

Stock	Shares	Value
Voting Common	90	$ 90,000
Preferred		
Nonvoting	900	900,000
Voting	1,000	10,000
TOTAL VALUE		$1,000,000

Since most of the value of the corporation is in the nonvoting preferred, Joe is free to gift the voting common without incurring any current gift taxes. Assume that Joe makes a gift of 45 shares to his son and an equal gift to his daughter. If Joe has never made any other taxable gifts before, the $90,000 would be free of any immediate tax cost.

The most important objective accomplished is that 100 percent of the future growth of Rich Corporation will belong to Joe's children. The value of the business has been frozen for estate tax purposes.

HOW RECAPITALIZATION SOLVES PROBLEMS

The nonvoting preferred stock would be retained by Joe Jobber, to provide for Mother's support after his death via dividend payments or possibly by a complete redemption. Let's examine a variation. A portion of these shares could be used to equalize Daughter's shares of Joe's estate if Son had been given all or a larger proportion of the voting common at the inception of the recapitalization.

Let's clarify this variation. Often what is done in such a recapitalization is to give the son who is active in the business all of the shares of the common growth stock with none going to the daughter. In such a case, if Joe is typical, he will want Daughter to receive an amount equal to that Son received. This can be accomplished by leaving the nonvoting preferred to Daughter following a life estate to Mother. In any event, it can be seen that a tremendous amount of flexibility is available with either Son or Daughter taking a current interest in the future growth or a delayed interest via Joe's will.

One more point should be made—a clause in Joe's will should leave the 1,000 voting preferred shares to his son. Thus, Joe has been able to maintain control during his life and, at death, pass control to his son. Since these shares are worth $10,000, an equal gift might be left to Daughter in Joe's will.

VARIATIONS

The objectives, financial goals, and family requirements are as varied as the number of business owners in the United States.

The best news about a recapitalization is its *total flexibility*. A recapitalization can be tailored to fit the financial and family needs of each particular privately held or family held business.

RECAPITALIZATION CHECKLIST

Here is a checklist of the steps to be undertaken to implement the recapitalization:

1. A plan of recapitalization should be adopted by the board of directors of the corporation and approved by the shareholders. A copy of the plan should be submitted with the corporation's tax return for the year in which the recapitalization takes place.

2. The articles of incorporation of the company should be amended to allow for the issuance of the new classes of stock and the cancellation of the old. (Reg. 1-368-3(a).)

3. Cancel the old stock and issue the new shares. This involves the valuation of the stock canceled and the stock issued because they must be approximately equal in value. The valuation issue is discussed in detail below.

4. Be able to show a legitimate business purpose for the recapitalization, such as increasing the shareholding of a younger generation, providing incentives to key employees, minimizing difficulties in transferring the business so as not to damage ongoing operations, and so on. (See Letter Ruling 8213027.)

VALUATION PROBLEMS

Three valuation problems are present in a recapitalization: valuation of the preferred stock, valuation of the common stock, and valuation of the company as a whole. Before the recapitalization, the total value of the company is usually contained in one class of old common stock. After the recapitalization, that same total value must be contained in the sum of the value of the new common and new preferred.

The IRS attacks Dr. Salsbury's invention by attempting to show a lesser value for the preferred stock at the time of the recapitalization and a higher value for the common stock. If there is substantial value assigned to the common stock, the owner of the old common is deemed to have gifted the new preferred to its recipient in the amount of its value, and a gift tax results.

For example, if the old common stock had a value of $10 million, and the value of the new preferred is determined to be $9 million, the holder of the old common is deemed to have gifted the $1 million to the recipients of the new common.

At the death of the preferred shareholder, the IRS will attempt to show that the preferred stock has all the characteristics of common stock and should be treated as such, carrying with it any appreciation in the company's value since the recapitalization. This results in a higher estate tax. The valuation experts attempting to keep intact the spirit of Dr. Salsbury must walk a minefield to avoid these dangers.

REVENUE RULING 83-120

This ruling is now the main weapon in the IRS' arsenal in attacking recapitalizations. It is reproduced in full in Appendix B. Basically, it sets out factors to be considered in valuing the preferred and common stock issued in the recapitalization. When considering these factors remember this: a decrease in the value of the preferred stock increases the value of the common stock and the gift tax liability connected with the common, and an increase in the value of the preferred stock has the opposite effect. Following is a summary of the factors listed in the ruling:

1. Preferred Stock

   a. *Yield.* What is the yearly or cumulative payout of the preferred stock? The absence of a cumulative provision on the preferred lowers its value, because dividends not paid are lost permanently. The presence of the cumulative features will increase the preferred stock's value, but it partially defeats the freeze because it increases the preferred shareholder's estate at the dividend rate. Only if the company appreciates in value above that rate is the purpose of the freeze fulfilled. Not only that, but what taxpayer is willing to incur the higher lifetime income tax liability on the cumulative dividend in order to save estate taxes after death?

b.   *Convertibility.*   Establishing a ratio for the conversion of the preferred stock to a certain number of shares of common stock can substantiate the purported value of the preferred. For example, a 1:1 conversion rate would help establish the preferred stock at its par value.

c.   *Put Option.*   Obligating the company to buy the stock at its stated par value when the shareholder exercises a put can produce the same result as the conversion factor.

d.   *Dividend Yield Rate.*   A dividend rate on the preferred stock that is lower than the rate on preferred of a comparable publicly traded company means the par value of the stock is overstated. A higher rate means it is understated.

e.   *Dividend-paying Capacity.*   The capacity of the company to pay the dividend yield provided for in the preferred stock is indicative of the stock's value. Can the company pay the preferred dividends yearly at the stated rate? The earnings history of the company is important as a determining factor of future capability. Here a regression analysis (See examples 3 and 4 in Part II) could be useful. If it is determined that the company cannot cover its dividend-paying obligation, the value of the preferred stock must be less than par. This factor makes it imperative for the company to pay the dividends in the years immediately following the recapitalization to establish a history of dividend-paying capacity. Otherwise the IRS will up the estate tax, claiming that the recapitalization plan never intended to pay the preferred dividends, making it easier to portray the preferred stock as common stock in disguise.

f.   *Liquidation Preference.*   The IRS will also look at the ability of the company to pay a full liquidation preference. This is measured at the time of the recapitalization by the ratio of the excess of the fair market value of the company's assets over liabilities.

g.   *Voting Rights.*   Voting rights increase the value of preferred stock. If the preferred shareholder has a controlling interest that value is increased even more. Most of the value of preferred stock is attained by the retention of controlling interest.

Note: The value of the preferred stock can exceed its par value when the holder of these shares has voting control (IRS Technical Advice Memorandum 8510002, 11/26/84).

2.   Common Stock

a.   *Right to Future Appreciation.*   The main factor considered by the IRS to give value to the common stock is the right to receive any future appreciation in the value of the company. Such a right "usually warrants a determination that the common stock has substantial value."

b.   *Subordinated Liquidation Preference.*   The fact that the common stock's liquidation preference is subordinated to that of the preferred may lower the value of the common if it is determined that the company does not have the capacity to cover the preferred liquidation preference.

c.   *General Valuation Factors.*   The common stock should also be valued according to the general valuation principles of Revenue Ruling 59-60.

3.   Company

The valuation of the company itself can be accomplished by the appropriate method under the principles outlined in this book. Discounts for lack of marketability and minority interests are also appropriate.

SUMMARY

As can be seen from the preceding discussion of recapitalizations, the general valuation skills described in various chapters in this book should be used to fight the IRS in its efforts to impose a gift tax at the time of the recapitalization or a larger estate tax at the death of the preferred shareholder. The recapitalization is just one valuation-freeze tool. Buy-sell agreements can fulfill the same function from a control and an estate planning viewpoint. In all likelihood, the IRS will continue its attack on recapitalizations, attempting to make an effective estate planning tool too costly to undertake in terms of time, money, and hassle. (Author's comment: And the IRS did exactly that. See Chapter 12.)

PREFERRED STOCK

Most of the valuation techniques described in this book that apply to common stock of the privately held business also apply to the valuation of preferred stock. There are no set rules, regulations, or case laws specifically applicable to preferred stock valuation. However, many of the factors listed in Revenue Ruling 83-120 (see Chapter 11 and Part III-A) for valuing preferred stock in recapitalizations have been individually used by the courts for valuation purposes.

Preferred stock issued in a recapitalization also carries with it hidden income tax traps that can result in ordinary income to the preferred stock shareholder. There problems are discussed in this chapter.

COURT CASES

A typical preferred stock valuation case is *FX Systems Corp.* (79 TC 957; 1982). The taxpayer corporation purchased assets of another corporation with cash, a promissory note, 500 shares of its series-A preferred stock, and 500 shares of its series-B preferred stock. The corporation claimed a basis in the assets equal to their fair market value. The IRS claimed that the assets should be valued according to what their cost was—the property (cash, promissory note, and preferred stock) given in exchange therefore. Since the value of the cash and promissory note was easily ascertainable, the bone of contention was the value of the preferred stock. Convertibility and the redemption price of the preferred stock was the court's benchmark in reaching its decision:

> Furthermore, the record indicates that the preferred stock that petitioner issued to Ferroxcube was worth nowhere near the amount that petitioner would have us find. The series A and series B preferred stock issued to Ferroxcube was redeemable by petitioner for a total price of $100,000. To accept

petitioner's position, we would have to find that such preferred stock had a value of $652,180. We find it difficult to believe that stock worth $652,180 would be redeemable for only $100,000. Although petitioner maintains that the conversion privilege that accompanied the series B preferred stock was of considerable value, the record clearly shows that the conversion privilege could not account for this discrepancy. At the time of the sale, 345,000 shares of the petitioner's common stock were outstanding and another 40,000 had been subscribed, while the series B preferred stock issued to Ferroxcube was only convertible into 22,500 shares of common stock. Moreover, if anything, the record indicates that at the time of the sale 22,500 shares of petitioner's common stock were worth considerably less than the $50,000 redemption price of the series B preferred stock issued to Ferroxcube.

The court found the preferred stock to be worth only $100,000 for both series, which was $147,000 less than contended by the taxpayer.

In *Estate of Von Hajke* (79-1 USTC 13,290), the court agreed with the estate's valuation because of the difficulties that would be caused by the redemption of the deceased shareholder's preferred stock. The deceased had the right to have her stock redeemed at a $1,000 par value. The estate set the value of the stock at $675. The IRS contended that the redemption price was the stock's value because the deceased shareholder held a controlling interest in the company and could have used her controlling interest to compel a redemption at that price.

The court disagreed:

In my opinion, Mr. Johnston (the IRS expert) failed to give sufficient attention to the problems (of) a redemption .... Although a majority shareholder, under the by-laws and certificates of incorporation, would have the power to elect a board of directors, it does not follow that he would have the right to demand that the board redeem the stock (*U.S.* v. *Byrum*, 408 U.S. 125; 1972) .... Moreover, I believe that the government failed to consider other difficulties that might be encountered if the redemption of the preferred stock were accomplished. The board of directors owes a fiduciary duty to the minority shareholders which precludes it from acting against the interests of the minority shareholders. A redemption of the preferred stock would likely require liquidation of a substantial portion of the corporation's assets, including some low-basis blocks of stock, which would produce a large capital gains tax liability offensive to the minority shareholders .... In addition, a recapitalization might effect a "squeeze-out" of the minority shareholders and result in litigation. Such litigation is a proper matter to consider in valuing the stock.

The *Von Hajke* case illustrates the point that valuation considerations applicable to common stock can also be used to value preferred stock.

Sometimes the attributes of preferred stock taken by itself would call for a lower value. However, if the preferred shareholder is also a common stock shareholder, certain situations require that the common and preferred holdings be valued as a block because a combination of the features of both classes of stock in the hands of the shareholder increases the combined value. For example, suppose the preferred had dividend and liquidation preference, but no voting rights, which were embodied in the common shares. This was the situation in *Estate of Lee* (69 TC 860; 1978), where the court valued the deceased shareholder's interest in a company, embodied in both preferred and common shares, as a whole. Here's the court's reasoning:

The common and preferred stock each had negative features which would detract from their fair market value if sold separately. The preferred shares entitled their owner to a claim in liquidation or redemption to all the assets then owned plus all subsequent appreciation up to $10 million. The common shareholders had no prospect of realizing any monetary return from corporation assets for some time, yet had control over their management. In combination, however, the preferred and common shares entitled their owners to all the positive benefits while negating the detriments. As experts for both respondent and petitioner testified, the normal approach would be to market the preferred and common shares as a block.

As is evident from these cases, the valuation of preferred shares is even a more arbitrary process than the valuation of the privately held business as a whole. Similar to the valuation process in recapitalization set out in Revenue Ruling 83-120, after the value of the business as a whole is reached, the capital structure of a company often requires that the two component parts of that total valuation amount be calculated in a zero-sum game. The more value to common, the less to preferred, and vice versa. Below is a list of the most common attributes of preferred stock that might affect its value:

1. Is it nonconvertible or convertible to other securities in the capital structure of the company?

2. Is it noncumulative or cumulative regarding the payment of dividends?

3. Does it possess voting rights, and if so can the exercise of those rights affect the management and operations of the company?

4. Does it possess a liquidation preference with regard to the company's assets?

5. Can it be redeemed at a set price (does it possess a *call* feature)?

6. Is it subordinate or superior to other classes of preferred stock?

7. Does it possess a right to share in the earnings and profits of the corporation?

8. Does it possess other rights contingent on the happening of some event?

These are traits that affect the value of the preferred shares, and consequently, the value of the common shares of the corporation. The same process exists for the common shares. Listing the attributes of common shares can increase or decrease the value of those shares and consequently affect the value of the preferred shares.

RECAPITALIZATION PROBLEMS

Excess Redemption Premium

Although a recapitalization is tax-free, certain features of the preferred stock can cause problems. One problem arises upon the issuance of the preferred stock and the other upon the subsequent sale of it.

Under Section 305, in a recapitalization where the corporation issues preferred stock that must be redeemed on the shareholder's death at a price that exceeds 110 percent of the issue price, the excess is treated as a distribution taxable as ordinary income that is received ratably over the life of the shareholder. For example, suppose the issue price of preferred stock is $100, and the stock must be redeemed at $140. The excess of $30 (110 percent x $100 = 110; $140 – $110 = $30) is deemed to be received by the shareholder over his or her life expectancy. Actuarial tables determine that estimated lifetime. If the shareholder had a remaining life expectancy of 20 years, he or she would be deemed to receive $1.50 a year per share as ordinary income over that 20 year period. (Reg. 1.305-5(b)(2)).

The same regulation states that redemption premiums above the 110 percent safe harbor may be nontaxable if shown to reasonable. A redemption premium is reasonable if it is in the nature of a penalty for the premature redemption of the preferred stock. For example, a shareholder receives the preferred stock in the expectation that it will provide income for a number of years. If, however, the stock is immediately redeemable at any time at the option of the corporation, the shareholder is deprived of the assurance that the income stream will continue. Therefore, if the corporation issues the preferred stock at a premium above the 110 percent in order to compensate the shareholder for the uncertainty of how long he or she will hold the preferred stock, no ordinary income will result on the distribution of the stock to the shareholder in the recapitalization. Therefore, a redemption premium in excess of 110 percent of issue price should always be accompanied by a "call" option exercisable by the corporation.

See Revenue Ruling 83-119 in Appendix B for a thorough explanation of how Section 305 affects the issuance of preferred stock redeemable at a premium above its issue price.

Section 306 Taint

A second problem that accompanies the issuance of preferred stock in a recapitalization is that it can be classified as Section 306 stock. Section 306 stock is preferred stock that is issued with respect to common stock and is received by the shareholder as a nontaxable stock dividend at the time the corporation has earnings and profits. The problem with Section 306 preferred stock arises when it is redeemed, sold, or transferred. The amount received for the Section 306 preferred stock is an ordinary income distribution to the extent that the fair market value of the stock was covered by the earnings and profits of the corporation on the date it was distributed. In this case, that would be the date of the recapitalization.

However, the Section 306 taint is removed from the stock upon the death of the shareholder. If one of the purposes of the recapitalization is to allow the owners of the business to remain in control until their death, the Section 306 taint is no problem since it will disappear when they die. In addition, as a general rule, the preferred stock received by the owner of the recapitalized corporation is free of the Section 306 taint if the owner receives only preferred stock (none of the common) in the recapitalization.

Author's Comment: It should be noted that Section 306 is not affected by the new recapitalization rules discussed in Chapter 12.

CHAPTER 12

RECAPITALIZATIONS—
THE NEW LAW

Since the last printing of this book, Congress adopted the Omnibus Budget Reconciliation Act of 1990 (Act). This chapter summarizes the law changes that affect the specific areas addressed in Chapter 11.

A SIMPLE EXPLANATION OF THE NEW LAW

Prior to 1987, recapitalizations (recaps) were the direct route to the promised land for freezing the value of your family business. Everybody did it. The IRS got fed up. The Congress got fed up. So Congress changed the law by passing the dreaded Section 2036(c) in late 1987. Recaps were dead and buried.

Small businesses complained. Trade associations complained. Tax practitioners complained. Congress listened. Congress heard. Congress killed the hated Section 2036(c) in late 1990. All hail. The wicked witch is dead! Hurrah!

But wait. This time Congress really got creative. How? Well, it created something entirely new in the Internal Revenue Code: "Chapter 14—Special Valuation Rules," complete with four new Sections (2701 through 2704).

What does the new law do to hamper freezing the value of your closely held business? In a nutshell, this is how Section 14 can hurt you. To make a recap work (freeze the value of your preferred stock for estate tax purposes), you must not only follow a host of recap rules, but you must also have your total corporation valued. The preferred stock must also be valued. The value of the preferred stock is subtracted from the value of the total corporation; and the difference is considered the value of the common stock. If the preferred stock is flawed (for example, noncumulative), its value is *ZERO*.

Let's explore the world of recaps—Chapter 14, new-law style. Suppose Joe Owner owns 100 percent of the common stock of Your Co. In April 1991 he exchanges it for 100 percent of all the new common stock and all the new preferred stock of Your Co. Joe has Your Co. appraised. The appraiser values the total company at $1,000,000, the preferred stock at $900,000 and the common at $100,000. That exchange of the old common for the new common and preferred stock is called a "recapitalization." Joe keeps the preferred stock; his two sons—who are active in the business—receive the common stock from Joe as a gift.

Now then, let's make two assumptions: First, Joe does everything right and the recap works (even the IRS agrees); second, Joe messes up and the IRS says (and is right), "the recap doesn't work."

Okay, the first assumption: Suppose the preferred stock is cumulative and pays a 10 percent dividend. Your Co. pays the 10 percent dividend of $90,000 ($900,000 times 10 percent) to Joe every year, until Joe dies in the year 2015 (25 years after the recap). Your Co. is worth $10,900,000 on the day Joe dies. What is the value of the preferred stock in Joe's estate? A measly $900,000. Great! The IRS just got shortchanged on the estate tax that would have been owed on $10 million (the value of the common stock)—a savings of about $5.5 million (assuming the estate tax rates don't change). Good move, Joe.

Now, let's take a look at the second assumption. Somehow, Joe made a mistake; for example, the preferred stock was noncumulative and Your Co. never paid Joe a dime in dividends. The IRS will ignore the attempted recap. Joe dies on the same day as in the first assumption in the year 2015 and Your Co. is worth the same $10.9 million. This time the entire $10.9 million will be taxable in Joe's estate. Ouch!

The key point you must understand: Unless you think your corporation is about to skyrocket in value, a recap is not the best way to transfer or freeze your business.

A MORE COMPLEX EXPLANATION OF THE NEW LAW

The material that follows is complicated. Tough reading. Review it with your professional advisor.

Special Valuation Rules

New Chapter 14 provides special valuation rules for certain transfers involving interests that are retained (usually preferred stock) by the transferor (usually the founder/owner of the business). The value of these retained rights is determined under these special rules. The value of the retained interest (preferred stock most likely) is then subtracted from the value of the entire corporation to arrive at the value of the transferred interest (the common stock given to the kids). Chapter 14 provides the following valuation rules for determining the value of the retained interests in corporations and partnerships:

1. The retained right to receive "qualified payments" is valued by determining the present value of the expected cash flow to the recipient (say the owner of the preferred stock). A qualified payment is a dividend payable on a regular basis on cumulative preferred stock (or a comparable payment on a partnership interest) to the extent the dividend (or a partnership payment) is at a fair market rate.

2. Retained dividend rights, other than "qualified payments" are valued at *zero*.

Example

If a corporation is recapitalized with non-cumulative preferred stock and the founder/owner makes a gift of common stock to his children, the preferred stock will be treated as having no value in determining the gift value of the common stock on the date of the gift.

3. And don't try to get fancy. For example, retained liquidation, put, call, and conversion rights are also valued at zero, unless they are held in conjunction with the right to receive "qualified payments." Such a right held in conjunction with the right to receive "qualified payments" is valued as if such liquidation, put, call or conversion right were exercised in the manner resulting in the lowest value for all such rights. A lousy tax deal!

Example

Father gives common stock to son and retains cumulative preferred stock that entitles father to "qualified payments." The cumulative dividend on the preferred stock is $100 per year and the stock may be redeemed at any time after two years for $1,000. The value of the cumulative preferred stock is the *lesser* of (1) the present value of two years of $100 dividends plus the present value of the redemption for $1,000 in year two, or (2) the present value of $100 paid every year in perpetuity.

Recapitalizations

It is now possible to engage in *a traditional preferred stock recapitalization (see Chapter 11) to freeze the value of a parent's interest*, as long as the preferred stock is entitled to a dividend at a fair market rate. If the dividend is noncumulative, the parent must elect qualified payment treatment. Otherwise, the preferred stock will be treated as having no value in determining the value of the common stock.

Special Rules

1. The common stock must have at least a value equal to 10 percent of the entire corporation.

2. And again don't try to get fancy. If the dividends are not paid in a timely fashion and the owner of the preferred stock transfers the stock or dies owning the stock, there will be an increase in the taxable gifts of the owner or in the taxable estate of the owner. The increase is the sum of all missed payments, compounded to reflect the time value of money. Outrageous!

Joint Asset Purchases

Chapter 14 also eliminates the tax advantages of most joint asset purchases. For example, if two or more members (say a father and a son) of the same family jointly purchase a term interest and a remainder interest, the person who acquires the term interest (say the father) is treated as if he purchased the entire property and then transferred the remainder interest to the family member (the son) who actually acquired the remainder interest. The subsequent transfer is treated as having been made in exchange for the actual amount paid by the family member for the remainder interest. In determining the amount of gift on the subsequent transfer, the term interest would have a zero value. This eliminates the tax advantages of most joint asset purchases.

Exception

An exception is provided for certain joint purchases such as a personal residence, works of art, and undeveloped real estate.

Liquidation Restrictions Disregarded

When an interest in a corporation or partnership is transferred to a family member, any restriction limiting the ability of the corporation or partnership from liquidation is disregarded in the valuation of the transferred interest if:

1. The restriction either lapses or can be removed, in whole or in part, after the transfer; and

2. The transferor and his family control the corporation or partnership immediately before the transfer.

One Final Point

The complex maze created by Chapter 14 has many rules, traps, and exceptions not covered in this book. Make sure you get expert help before attempting a recapitalization to freeze your corporation or partnership.

CHAPTER 13

EVERYTHING YOU EVER WANTED TO KNOW ABOUT ESOPS AND ESOTS

The valuation of stock contributed to and distributed from an Employee Stock Ownership Plan (ESOP) is of critical importance. Unfortunately, there is little guidance for the valuation process in case law or legislation. All that is stated in those sources is that if the valuation is done improperly, there will be Hades to pay by the closely held corporation sponsoring the ESOP. But before explaining that, a discussion of what an ESOP is and how it functions is in order.

DEFINITION AND OPERATION OF AN ESOP

A stock bonus plan, like any other qualified plan, is usually composed of two parts: (1) a plan called an Employee Stock Ownership Plan (ESOP) and (2) a trust agreement establishing an Employee Stock Ownership Trust (ESOT) or trust. All designations—ESOP, plan, ESOT, or trust—can be used interchangeably.

The ESOT has been touted as an important financial and estate-planning tool and as a worthwhile form of deferred employee compensation for the closely held corporation. A closely held corporation is one in which the stock is not traded on any market and for which there is no established market, except among the limited group of individuals who currently own stock in the corporation.

As ESOT is defined in Section 4975(e)(7) as a stock bonus plan, or combination stock bonus and money purchase plan, qualified under Section 401(a), which is an individual account plan designed to invest primarily in qualifying employer securities. Since every ESOT is a stock bonus plan, at least in part, the requirements applicable to stock bonus plans under Section 401(a) must be met if the ESOT is to be a qualified plan.

The term qualifying employer security means an employer security that is (1) stock (or an equity security) or (2) a bond, debenture, note, or other evidence of indebtedness (IRC Sec. 409(1)).

In the beginning, when Louis Kelso, a California attorney, fathered the ESOT concept, it was viewed as a leveraged financing vehicle. Times have changed, and many ESOT-like plans are now installed without any borrowing whatsoever. Such a plan is nothing more than a stock bonus plan, which this chapter will call SBP-NL(nonleveraged) to distinguish it from an ESOT. Stock bonus plans will be identified as:

1. ESOT (or ESOP)—a stock bonus plan designed to have the trust borrow money to acquire the employer's stock;

2. SBP-NL—a stock bonus plan that does not borrow funds (therefore it is nonleveraged);

3. Stock bonus plans—both ESOTs and SBP-NLs.

Essentially, a plan (either an ESOP or SBP-NL, or both, as the circumstances dictate) is subject to the same rules and is identical to a profit-sharing plan, with one important exception: A profit-sharing plan can make distributions either in cash or in kind, including stock of the employer. Distributions from an ESOT can be made in employer's stock or cash (IRC Sec. 409(h)(2)). However, if the securities are not readily tradeable, a participant must have a right to demand that the employer repurchase employer securities (IRC Sec. 409(h)(1)).

The following is a thumbnail description of an ESOT operation. First the trust purchases the employer's stock from the employer or shareholder. The employer or the ESOT borrows the money from a bank, pledging the stock as security. It then holds the stock for the benefit of participants, who have, in general, the same rights and privileges as any other stockholder. The stock is then distributed to the participants when they are eligible to receive it under the terms of the plan. The ESOT or the corporation can then reacquire the stock from the participant or his beneficiary. It is this flow of stock to, from, and back to the ESOT or the corporation, combined with the tax rules applicable to each transaction, that makes the entire concept an exciting tool.

FIDUCIARY DUTIES

The danger inherent in the valuation of employer securities contributed to an ESOP is that the Pension Reform Act of 1974 imposed upon the fiduciary or trustee running the ESOP a duty to run the plan solely in the interest of the plan participants and beneficiaries. This means that when buying employer securities for the ESOP or purchasing them back from plan participants, the trustee must do so with care, skill, and diligence, paying as little as possible for the contributed shares and purchasing the shares back from participants at their fair market value.

A plan fiduciary who violates this fiduciary duty is personally liable to compensate the ESOP or others for any losses suffered because of his or her mistakes in dealing in the ESOP's employer stock. In many cases, the trustee is somehow affiliated (stockholder, officer, employee) with the employer corporation, especially in the case of a privately held business.

VALUATION PROBLEMS

If the ESOT trustee causes the ESOT to purchase employer stock at a price greater than its fair market value, the purchase can be a violation of the trustee's fiduciary duties.

If the employer corporation contributes stock to the ESOT and claims a deduction for the contribution greater than the fair market value of the stock, the deduction will be disallowed by the amount of the excess claimed. Worse yet, an excise tax can be imposed upon the principal shareholder or employer who sells stock to an ESOT at greater than fair market value.

If a plan participant sell shares back to the ESOT or the employer corporation at a put option priced at less than its fair market value, the participant may have a cause of action against the ESOT or the employer.

An interesting case that illustrates these principles is *Donovan* v. *Cunningham* (716 F.2d 1455, CA-5; 1983). In that case, the issue was whether the ESOT trustees had caused the ESOT to purchase employer stock from the employer corporation's sole shareholder for more than its fair market value.

The trustees had obtained an appraisal of the value of the stock from an independent appraiser, which is a statutory requirement for ESOP purchases. The Secretary of Labor, who had brought the suit against the trustees for their alleged violation of labor laws pertaining to ESOPs, disagreed with the appraisal report.

First, he claimed in his suit that the report was not updated and was made a considerable time before the purchases took place. He claimed that the report needed to be updated to take into account the impact of the ESOP on the value of the company stock and to reflect the difference between the actual operating results of the company following the appraisal and those that had been projected in the appraisal report itself.

Second, the secretary argued that the valuation in the appraisal should have been discounted to account for the ESOP's purchasing only a minority interest in the employer corporation. It must be admitted that this conclusion is a blow. Many commentators have maintained that no discounts should be taken when valuing ESOP stock: after all, the ESOT provides a marketplace for the stock. This case punctures this time-accepted logic.

The appellate court ruled for the secretary, holding:

> Under [legislation], as well as at common law, courts have focused the inquiry under the "prudent man" rule on a review of the fiduciaries' independent investigation of the merits of a particular investment rather than on the evaluation of the merits alone. As a leading commentator has put it, the test of prudence is one of conduct and not a test of the result of the performance of the investment. The focus of the inquiry is how the fiduciary acted in his selection of the investment and not whether his investment succeeded or failed.

By this standard, the appellate court found the appraisal report to be lacking, because it failed to identify the facts and assumptions that justified its final valuation figure. Not only that, but the trustees failed to determine whether the appraisal report still had validity at the time of the purchases.

The lesson of this case is that a mistake in valuation methodology—or a failure to heed the lessons contained in this book—can be costly from a legal standpoint when valuations are done for ESOPs. As the *Donovan* court admonished, "valuations must be made in good faith and based on all relevant factors for determining the fair market value of securities." Be careful and thorough! The secretary of labor is watching you!

ADVANTAGES AND DISADVANTAGES OF ESOTs

Some ESOT advocates offer their product as a cure-all for everything from business financial woes to snakebite.

Advantages of ESOTs

1. Employers can take deductions for stock. The employer can deduct the fair market value of employer securities contributed within the applicable ceiling—15 percent if it is a stock bonus plan; 25 percent if it is a combination stock bonus plan and money purchase plan.

2. The shareholder can bail out. No cash contribution is necessary; the shareholder can sell his stock. The sale results in a capital gain. Installment reporting is available to the selling stockholders.

3. Redemption is easier. The requirements of Sections 302(b) and 303 (to avoid dividend treatment on redemption) are not applicable to trust purchases.

4. An ESOT may improve employee morale.

5. An ESOT provides a market for stock held by shareholders of a closely held corporation. In addition, if the ESOT were not used, a purchaser of such stock, whether the employer or a third party, would have to use after-tax dollars to fund the purchase.

6. An ESOT is superior to public sale of stock because it is cheaper, involves no public disclosure, and requires no SEC registration if the plan is noncontributory.

7. As a financing vehicle, an ESOT can be used to refinance an existing debt of the employer, raise capital for any purpose, or acquire a target company.

   Example

   P Corporation wants to acquire T Corporation. T forms an ESOT. The ESOT borrows the necessary funds to purchase 90 percent of T's outstanding stock. P purchases the other 10 percent and has voting control. Of course, the theory is that the 90 percent trustee-ESOT-owner will be and stay forever friendly to P, the minority stockholder.

8. An ESOT may solve a Section 531 problem: Occasionally, a corporation is backed into a Section 531 corner—unreasonable accumulation of surplus. The only alternatives are dividends or almost certain Section 531 penalties—neither choice has much to recommend it. An SBP-NL, on the other hand, allows a new choice. The corporation can contribute to the SBP-NL (eliminating or reducing the Section 531 problem) and have the SBP-NL bail out the stockholder, who now has a capital gain as opposed to a dividend. All are good strokes.

9. An ESOT may be used to accomplish antitrust-required divestitures by selling the corporation to the ESOT. Public companies may also use the ESOT to go private.

10. Contributions by a corporation to a leveraged ESOP that are used by the plan to pay loan principal and interest are allowed separately as deductions to the corporation. The deduction for contributions used to pay loan principal is limited to 25 percent of

the compensation of all employees under an ESOP. An unlimited deduction is permitted for amounts used to pay interest on the loan.

11. The owner of a closely held corporation can take advantage of a tax-free rollover. The shareholder sells stock to the ESOT, and as long as the ESOT owns at least 30 percent of the corporation after the sale, the sales proceeds may be reinvested within one year in securities of other domestic operating companies. The gain on the sale is deferred until the rolled-over securities are sold.

Example

Rick Rich owns 100 percent of Success Co. Rick sells $2.2 million of his stock to Success' ESOT. Rick reinvests the proceeds in a tax-free rollover, which he holds until death. Rick's heirs get a step-up in basis and never pay income tax on the gain.

Planning Pointer

Elderly shareholders may prefer a rollover into bonds rather than stock. They should choose bonds with a maturity well beyond their life expectancy. This move effectively locks in the gain, and in addition, gives the taxpayer assets he can hold until death to avoid income taxes on the gain entirely.

---

12. A lending institution is required to include in its taxable income only 50 percent of the interest received on an ESOP loan. As a result, the ESOP or the employer can borrow at a lower interest rate than other borrowers. Such loans are called security acquisition loans.

13. The employer can deduct dividends paid on employer securities that are used to make payments on an employer security acquisition loan.

14. An SBP-NL can obtain some of the advantages of an ESOP (leveraged) via an immediate allocation loan.

Example

With an immediate allocation loan, a company can borrow, say, $2 million and, as long as it makes a $2 million stock contribution to an SBP-NL within 60 days, the loan will be considered a securities acquisition loan. The lender may exclude from taxable income 50 percent of the interest it receives.

Disadvantages of ESOTs

1. Dilution can lead to loss of control by nontrust stockholders and can reduce the proportionate share of company equity held by pre-ESOT shareholders.

   If new stock is issued or if existing stock is sold to the trust, the problem is the same—some control is lost. If, perchance, the trust gets over 50 percent of voting stock ownership, control may be shifted away from the nontrust stockholders if the trustee becomes unfriendly, or if an Internal Revenue Code (the Code) amendment puts voting rights into the hands of employee participants.

If new stock is issued, the proportionate share of company equity held by the pre-ESOT shareholders is reduced. Once these shares leave the hands of the employer, the dilution (short of reacquisition) is permanent. Future economic benefits (increase in share value) must be shared with the owners of the stock held or distributed by the ESOT.

2. An ESOT is expensive to set up and expensive to administer.

3. At best, the annual valuation of the stock of a closely held corporation is a problem. TRA-86 requires an annual independent appraisal for employer stock held by an ESOP. Most well-run ESOPs have had an annual appraisal in the past, but now it is required.

4. The following are the current voting rules:

    Publicly traded. The voting rights on all shares allocated to individual participant accounts are passed through to the participants. Shares held in a suspense account pending repayment of an ESOP loan are generally voted by the trustee or other plan fiduciary.

    Closely held businesses. The voting rights on allocated shares must be passed through to participants only with respect to major corporate transactions such as merger, recapitalization, or sale of substantially all the company assets.

    For normal corporate matters, such as election of the board of directors, the allocated shares are voted by the trustee or other plan fiduciary. As a practical matter, this allows the non-ESOT shareholders (in general, the same shareholders who controlled the corporation before the creation of the ESOT) to maintain absolute control of the day-to-day business operations.

    Nonallocated shares held in a suspense account pending repayment of an ESOP loan are voted by the trustee or other plan fiduciary.

5. The value of employee retirement benefits depends on unknown factors in the marketplace, which could seriously jeopardize, or even wipe out, any hope of employee retirement security.

Planning Pointer

An analysis will usually indicate that ESOTs are an expensive and dilutive way to raise cash; all other available sources of funds should be explored before an ESOT is used. Direct borrowing may be better than obtaining tax deductions by giving stock away to an ESOT. Work out the numbers carefully each time an ESOT situation presents itself.

---

6. The employer has a significant repurchase liability generated as people die, leave, or retire from the company. The corporation cannot just give employees stock and say, "Pleasant retirement." The law requires that the company (or the ESOP) buy the shares back at fair market value.

7. TRA-86 creates a new diversification requirement that increases the repurchase liability. When a participant reaches age 55 and has 10 years of participation in the ESOP, he has the right to elect to diversify up to 25 percent of his account balance for a six-year period. Each plan year counts as a separate election period. At age 60, the percentage becomes 50 percent for the purpose of a one-time diversification election.

    Diversification means that a company can either distribute owned shares to the eligible participant or make available, within the ESOP, the opportunity to transfer the appropriate portion of the account to one of three investment funds. These diversification rules apply only to employer stock acquired by the ESOP after December 31, 1986. The diversification must be completed no later than 90 days after the close of the election period. This is a tough rule for the closely held business because the repurchase liability is created sooner. Since there is no market in which to turn the shares into cash, to the extent a participant elects diversification, the company must repurchase the shares to be diversified.

8. ESOP participants entitled to benefits can demand those benefits in the form of employer securities. However, participants forfeit their right to employer securities for the portion of their account that they elect to diversify.

Planning Pointer

Would the employer give this stock free to the employees covered by the plan if there were no tax benefits involved? If the answer is *Yes*, the employer should decide if a stock bonus plan is the best approach to what is clearly an employee compensation problem.

No means that the tax and ultimate economic consequences must be considered. Remember, someday the stock will have to be bought back; today, each $1.00 of stock contributed to, or purchased by, an ESOT will save the employer, even at the highest tax bracket, only a fraction of the $1.00 in taxes; tomorrow (say 10 years), the same stock could cost the employer more than $1.00 (say it tripled to a value of $3.00), with no tax deduction if purchased by the corporation because of appreciation.

To put it plainly, a lousy tax deal.

ACQUIRING THE STOCK

There are two ways to accomplish the tax-deductible contributions to an ESOT:

1. With no increase in outstanding stock.

    a. Internal Financing. The corporation contributes cash to the trust, which in turn purchases the stock from a present stockholder.

    b. External Financing. The ESOT borrows the funds with which to purchase the stock. The trust could borrow from a third party (usually a bank) and then purchase newly issued stock from the employer-corporation.

2. With an increase in outstanding stock.

    Internal Financing. The corporation could contribute cash to the trust, which would purchase newly issued shares from the corporation, or the corporation could contribute the newly issued shares directly to the trust. It is recommended that the direct contribution of stock be used because of the penalties that might be assessed if the trustee purchases the shares for more than an adequate consideration.

TYPES OF CONTRIBUTIONS

1. Contributions in Kind

    Generally, contributions in kind to a qualified plan are troublesome. The employer may deduct the fair market value of the contributed property at the date of contribution. However, the excess of this fair market value over basis is taxable as a gain to the employer. This rule does not apply when contributions are made in employer's stock. The employer can deduct the entire fair market value of the stock, while no income is taxable on the transfer. The stock is valued in accordance with the customary rules for determining fair market value. (See Example 20 in Part II of this book.)

2. Other Contributions

    Contributions to an ESOT need not be made solely in one type of stock of the employer. Contributions may be made:

    ■   All in common stock of the company;

    ■   All in some other class of stock, such as common A or preferred;

    ■   All in cash;

    ■   In any combination of the above.

    Cash contributions have several important functions. Cash can be accumulated to acquire additional stock when available, purchase life insurance, or make temporary income-producing investments.

HOLDING, DISTRIBUTING, AND REACQUIRING STOCK

Probably the most practical consideration when discussing a plan with a client is to reassure him that he will neither lose control of the corporation nor gain any significant minority shareholders.

The first fear is easily handled because the corporation itself is always in voting control of the stock held by the trustee (although, as previously pointed out, caution should be taken not to let the trust acquire more than 50 percent voting control). An advisory committee is appointed by the board of directors to administer the plan. (Technically, under the Employee Retirement Income Security Act (ERISA), an administrator would administer the plan.) The board of directors or the advisory committee may appoint a bank as trustee or the stockholders or officers of the corporation can be the trustee. Employees may be given a voice as part of the advisory committee.

The second fear—of gaining a minority stockholder—does not arise until such time as a participant is entitled to receive, and actually does receive, all or a portion of the stock that has been allocated to his account. Such distributions are made exactly in the same manner and at the same time as they would be in the usual profit-sharing plan, that is, at retirement, disability, or death, to the extent vested. The stock may be distributed at one time or in installments over a period of years. Such distributions are taxed exactly the same as distributions from a pension or profit-sharing trust with this important exception: The excess of the fair market value of the stock on the date it is distributed over the fair market value of the stock on the date it was contributed to, or purchased by, the trust is taxable only when the stock is sold. Appreciation after distribution will be taxed as a capital gain.

The ESOT documents will set forth the specific rights of the trustee and the participants once the stock has been distributed. The distributed stock may be handled with a great deal of flexibility to protect the employee, the corporation, and the trustee. The plan can adopt any one or more of the following provisions:

- The employee may retain the stock as an investment while granting the trustee a right of first refusal if the employee decides to sell or transfer any of his stock.

- The employee may be granted a put to sell the stock to the trustee immediately or within a specific time frame, usually one year.

- The trustee may reacquire the stock pursuant to a buy-and-sell agreement (but this must be strictly discretionary, giving the employee-participant the free choice to enter or not to enter into the agreement after the stock is distributed).

  When stock is reacquired by the trustee for any reason, the price must be the fair market value on the date the stock is reacquired.

CHAPTER 14

REDEMPTIONS

One of the asset-freezing tools mentioned in Chapter 2 is the redemption. Valuation methods and approaches are usually necessary in the context of a redemption of shares of a privately held business, because a price must be set at which the shares are to be redeemed. The typical valuation problems and issues are inherent in the redemption of stock of the privately held business owner. This chapter does not discuss those issues per se, but is rather an explanation of what redemptions are and how they are used. The following discussion should give the reader a better appreciation of the valuation problems discussed elsewhere in this book, which often use the redemption as an example (see the *FX Systems Corp.* and *Estate of Von Hajke* cases in Chapter 12).

THE BASICS

A redemption occurs when a corporation uses its property to acquire its own stock from one or more stockholders. It is immaterial whether the redeemed stock is canceled, retired, or held as treasury stock. The term "property" includes money, securities, and other property (Section 317).

The vital question really is this: "Will the tax treatment to the redeeming stockholder be ordinary income or capital gain?"

The Internal Revenue Code provides a clear answer—Section 302. If the redemption qualifies as a sale or exchange, the excess of the proceeds over the taxpayer's basis will be a capital gain. If the redemption does not qualify, the entire amount of the proceeds will be a dividend. Of course, the amount of the dividend is limited to the earnings and profits (usually the same as retained earnings) of the corporation at the time of the redemption. The Code provides four redemption methods of attaining capital gain treatment:

1. Complete redemption,

2. Substantially disproportionate redemption,

3. Redemptions not essentially equivalent to a dividend, and

4. Certain redemptions involving railroad stock or bankruptcy situations.

Following are examples of the results in a typical situation where the corporation redeems part or all of the controlling shareholder's stock and the remaining shareholder is unrelated:

Example 1

Joe Founder owns 70 percent of the stock; the other 30 percent is owned by an unrelated business associate. The corporation J.F. Inc. is worth $1,000,000. J.F. Inc. redeems 10 percent of Joe's stock for $100,000. Joe is hung with a $100,000 dividend. (Because it is not a "complete redemption" and flunks the complex requirements of a "substantially disproportionate redemption.")

Example 2

J.F. Inc. redeems all of Joe's stock for $700,000. Joe's profit is a capital gain.

The redemption price may be paid in a lump sum or in installments. If paid in installments (or otherwise eligible), the redeeming stockholder may elect the installment method.

COMPLETE REDEMPTION (STOCKHOLDERS RELATED)

The Rule

Section 302(b)(3) provides for capital gains treatment when a shareholder terminates *his or her entire stock interest owned* by means of redemption. This means *ALL* of the stock owned by the redeeming shareholder. That sounds easy enough. In practice, however, the rule is complex and can result in a dividend.

Examples of the Rule in Operation

Facts

The percent of stock of Corporation C owned and the relationships between stockholders are as indicated. All stock has been owned for 12 years.

Stockholders	Percent Owned
Related	
F (father)	40%
W (F's wife)	20
S (F's son)	10
D (F's daughter)	20
M (unrelated manager)	10
Total	100%

Problem

Situation 1:   F desires to have *ALL* of his shares redeemed by C, together with *ALL* the shares owned by W, S, and D. C will redeem for cash. F will stay on the payroll as president of C.

Situation 2:   Same as situation 1, except F alone will redeem.

Result: Capital Gain?

Situation 1:   Yes! Per Revenue Ruling 76-524, F has terminated his entire stock interest, actual and constructive. The word "constructive" means the shares owned by W, S, and D.

Situation 2:   Yes, no, or maybe—the answer depends on more facts. In particular, F must satisfy one of two requirements under Section 302(c) to receive capital gains treatment: (1) avoid the "attribution rules" of Section 318(a), or (2) meet the five "additional requirements."

ATTRIBUTION RULES

The attribution rules apply to both complete redemptions and substantially disproportionate redemptions [Section 302(c)].

Effect of the Rules

Complete Redemption.   Although the attribution rules are applicable, complete redemption of the stock of a particular family is not only practical but should be an integral part of the tax planning of every closely held family corporation. This is made possible by Section 302(c)(2), which allows waiver of the family attributions rules. (See following discussion under "Additional Requirements.")

Substantially Disproportionate Redemption.   As a practical matter, this type of redemption will never attain capital gain treatment when the stockholders are related by attribution. The arithmetic just does not work out, until all the interests of all the related family stockholders are redeemed.

The Rules

The attribution rules simply say that a shareholder will have attributed to his or her shares of stock owned by someone else if he or she is related to that someone else.

Example

A owns 55 percent of the stock of X Co., his wife owns 30 percent, and his 15-year-old son owns 15 percent. Since everyone is related, everyone owns 100 percent of the stock under the attribution rules.

The rules are not as complex as they appear; however, they must be precisely understood to work effectively with complete and substantially disproportionate redemptions.
All the rules are detailed in Section 318(a).
The following example illustrates the most important rules.

Example

The stock of C Co. is owned as follows:

Stockholder	Percent Owned
F (founder)	65%
W (F's wife)	15
B (F's brother)	20
Total	100%

Situation 1: B redeems all his shares.

Result: Okay for capital gains treatment; attribution rules do not apply to siblings.

Situation 2: W redeems all her shares.

Result: Yes, capital gains treatment applies. The family attribution rules can be waived, assuming all the additional requirements are met.

Situation 3: B dies. F is the sole beneficiary of B's estate. B's executor has C redeem the 20 percent owned by the estate pursuant to a buy-sell agreement between F, B, and C.

Result: Disaster! The redemption will be treated as a dividend. The shares owned by B's estate are attributed to F. Neither the estate nor F can take advantage of the waiver rule (additional requirements).

Note

The result would be the same if W died and was substituted for B in this fact situation.

ADDITIONAL REQUIREMENTS

The attribution rules are avoided if the following five conditions are met under Section 302(c)(2) (often called the "waiver rule"). The first three conditions must always be met.

1. Immediately after the redemption, the redeeming stockholder must have no interest in the corporation as an officer, employee, or director. It is okay to be a creditor.

Example

F sells all his stock to C for $250,000—$50,000 in cash, plus a series of 10 notes of $20,000 each, payable over 10 years and secured by the assets of the corporation.

Result: Capital gain.

Exception

Here's a practical exception supported by a revenue ruling. Dad and his children, Bob and Charles, own 100 percent of Big Corp. Dad retires, and Big redeems all of his shares by a cash payment equal to the value of his stock. Bob and Charles assume all responsibility for operating Big. Under an unfunded preexisting written agreement between Dad and Big, Dad starts to receive a lifetime pension of $1,000 per month. The payments are not dependent upon Big's future earnings. Nor is Dad's claim to the payments subordinated to the claims of Big's general creditors. At retirement, Dad's life expectancy was 18 years.

The pension agreement is Dad's only continuing relationship with Big. The ruling says that this relationship does not constitute a prohibited interest. In addition, the payment to Dad for his stock is a complete redemption entitled to capital gain treatment. (Revenue Ruling 84-135)

2. Within 10 years from the date of redemption, the redeeming stockholder must not acquire an interest in the corporation, other than as a creditor or by bequest or inheritance. An interest includes a position as an officer, employee, or director.

Example

F receives and accepts a gift of shares in C Co. five years after the redemption. The redemption will be considered a retroactive dividend back to the date of the redemption.

A purchase of shares by F would give the same result.

An inheritance from W would be okay.

3. An agreement is filed by the redeeming stockholder (or an executor per Revenue Ruling 77-93) agreeing to notify the IRS of any acquisition described in condition 2 above and agreeing to retain the necessary records.

Note: The agreement must be in the form of a separate signed statement attached to a timely filed return for the year in which the redemption occurred [Reg. 1.302-4(a)].

4. The redeemed stock shouldn't be acquired within the 10 years before redemption from a family member whose stock would be attributed to the redeeming stockholder under attribution rules.

Example

F, 100 percent stock owner, gives his son, S, 10 percent of his stock in 1972. S redeems his 10 percent stock interest in 1977. The redemption is a dividend.

5. No person within the scope of the attribution rules should obtain stock from the redeeming stockholder within the 10-year period prior to the redemption unless such stock was also redeemed in the same transaction.

Example

All stockholders are related under the attribution rules. Percentage of ownership and dates acquired appear below. The last three stockholders acquired their shares from F by gift. In 1985, all shares owned by F, W, and D are redeemed. S is now sole shareholder.

		Date Acquired Situation	
Stockholder	Percent Owned	A	B
F (father)	80	1950	1950
W (F's wife)	10	1965	1965
S (F's son)	5	1965	1977
D (F's daughter)	5	1978	1978

Situation 1: The redemption is a capital gain. Although D's stock does not meet the 10-year rule, it was redeemed in the same transaction with F.

Situation 2: The redemption will be treated as a dividend. S did not own his stock for 10 years.

Exception

If the redemption did not have a tax-avoidance motive, capital gains treatment will result even if the 10-year rule is violated.

Example 1: Add to situation B—in 1985, F has an unexpected disabling stroke. The doctor tells him to retire forever and move to a warmer climate.

Example 2: The corporation will redeem all of W's stock. She made gifts of stock (shortly before the redemption) to S, who will remain a shareholder and assume major management responsibility (Letter Ruling 8147169).

Example 3: A couple gave stock to their three children. Immediately following the gift, to shift control and majority ownership to one son and his immediate family, the corporation will redeem all the stock of the son's two sisters, who will each receive a 50 percent ownership in real property as tenants in common, plus interest-bearing notes (Letter Ruling 8147185).

DOES YOUR CORPORATION OWN APPRECIATED PROPERTY?

Quite often a family-controlled corporation owns property that has appreciated substantially over the years. Although the corporation may be rich in terms of appreciated property (in the form of vacant land, improved real estate, or something else), there may be no cash with which to redeem a retiring or selling founder.

A neat trick is having the redeeming stockholder (using a complete redemption) exchange stock for the appreciated property. *Result:* The corporation treats the transaction just like a sale to a stranger: the stockholder walks off with both a capital gain and the appreciated property. Where real estate is involved, the stockholder can lease the property back to the corporation.

HOW TO GET APPRECIATED PROPERTY OUT OF THE PRIVATELY HELD CORPORATION

Example

Stock redemptions can be used to take money or property out of a corporation at capital-gains rates. Consider this scenario. Assume Old Corp. owns free and clear land and a building that originally cost $300,000. Its reduced tax basis, due to depreciation, is $100,000, and because of appreciation and inflation, the property is now worth $500,000. Mother, the founder of the corporation, owns 40 percent of the stock, while the other 60 percent is owned by members of her immediate family. Mother wants to retire. Her 40 percent of the stock is worth $500,000. The corporation exchanges the real estate for Mother's stock.

Here are the tax consequences:

1. The corporation realized a $400,000 profit—$500,000 value less $100,000 basis—just as if the corporation had sold the property. Except for depreciation recapture, the entire profit gets favorable capital gains treatment.

2. Mother has a capital gain equal to the difference between the $500,000 real estate value and her tax basis for the stock.

3. Mother can now turn around and lease the real estate to the corporation at a fair rental.

4. Best of all, Mother can depreciate the real estate (the building only, but not the land) just as if she had purchased it for $500,000.

Additional Tax-Saving Hints

1. If the property is worth less than the stock being redeemed, the corporation can pay the difference in cash or in notes to be paid over a period of time.

2. An installment election may be available to the stockholder.

3. If the property to be used for the redemption is worth more than the stock, a mortgage can be put on the property sufficient to reduce its net value to the value of the stock being exchanged.

   Caution: If the property is subject to a mortgage (say $250,000) and its tax basis (say $150,000) is less than the liability, the difference ($100,000) is taxable income to the corporation [Section 311(c)].

4. If the only appreciated property available for the exchange is needed in the operation of the business, the property can still be exchanged for the stock. Simultaneously with the exchange, the corporation should lease the property back from the stockholder. The exchange must be made at fair market value (FMV) and the lease at fair rental. An expert appraiser should be used to fix the FMV—both of the stock and the real estate—and the rent.

5. Any appreciated property can be used. However, it may not be practical to use personal property subject to a large amount of depreciation recapture. Appreciated securities owned by the corporation can be used. Real estate subject to a substantial amount of depreciation recapture should not be used. Always, but always, make a projection of the tax impact on both the corporation and the stockholder.

   Comment: Not only does this method remove future growth of the family corporation's stock from the founder's estate, but the rent (or dividends or interest in the case of securities) also provides a flow of income.

   With the property out of the corporation, it is no longer subject to the claims of corporate creditors. Many founders find this last accomplishment reason enough to use this method.

How to Plan Ahead

These favorable tax results are accomplished by the tandem use of two sections of the Code plus a revenue ruling:

1. Section 302(b)(3) for a complete redemption gives the stockholder capital gains.

2. Section 311(d) gives the corporation capital gains, except for any depreciation recapture.

3. A shareholder's interest may be deemed terminated under Section 302(b)(3) despite a leaseback of the same property distributed in redemption (Revenue Ruling 70-369).

Example

The owner's wife plays no role in the corporation other than as a 20 percent shareholder. If the corporation buys her out, the gain is considered a capital gain. There is no dividend. And since the wife became a stockholder at the inception of the corporation, she does not have to wait 10 years to get capital gains treatment. The 10-year rule only applies to a transfer of stock.

SUMMARIZING WHEN AND WHY TO TAKE APPRECIATED PROPERTY OUT OF THE CORPORATION

This maneuver—distributing appreciated property—makes the most sense taxwise in two situations:

1. At the corporate level. The corporation has a large carryforward loss, and the gain to the corporation (on the appreciated property distribution) will be offset (all or in part) by the carryforward.

2. At the stockholder level.

   a. Capital loss carryforward. Just like the corporation situation outlined above, all or part of the gain on the redemption might be wiped out by the carryforward.
   b. Other reasons.
      i. The owner wants the property out of the grasp of corporate creditors.
      ii. The future depreciation (an ordinary deduction) of the property in the hands of the stockholder could provide a real estate tax shelter.

3. After retirement, the founding stockholder will have a source of income.

4. An appreciating asset is removed from the corporation for estate purposes. Assume the founder takes appreciating real estate.

   a. These are the tax goodies the family gets: income sheltered by depreciation during the founder's life, an income-tax-free raised basis (to the property's fair market value) at the founder's death, and the ability of the heirs to depreciate the property all over again using the raised basis as a new cost at the founder's death.
   b. The real estate can be left to members of the family who do not work for the family corporation.

Hint: It is important to make a projection (for each year, carried out for 10 years or more) showing the tax consequences and cash flow for the corporation and for the redeeming stockholder.

The projections will give you the information needed to determine whether taking the appreciated property out of the corporation via a complete redemption is a "go" or a "no-go."

CHAPTER 15

GIFTS AND CHARITABLE CONTRIBUTIONS

The primary advantage of an annual gift program, which is one way of freezing the value of and transferring ownership and control of a privately held business, is its simplicity. It can work very well to transfer a small business. Unfortunately, the larger the size of a privately held business, the less efficient the sole use of a gift program becomes. For larger businesses, the use of a gift program in combination with other asset-freezing transfer tools, such as redemptions and recapitalizations, is necessary. This chapter explains the important technical aspects of a combination gift-giving program and when combination plans should be used. The potential estate and gift tax liability that accompanies such freeze and transfer plans demand that the business valuation be exact.

Another form of gift-giving, the making of tax-deductible charitable contributions of closely held stock to exempt organizations, creates a reversal of the valuation game between privately held business owners and the IRS. Owners want to maximize their deductions so they push for the highest possible value for their contributed stock, while the IRS' interest is to value the stock as low as possible. These strategies are discussed in this chapter.

HOW THE GIFT TAX WORKS

Before going into the specifics of a stock-gift program, an overview of the gift tax structure as a whole is helpful in understanding the problems involved.

Before 1977, because the gift tax rates were lower than the estate tax rates, it was often tax-wise to gift the entire value of the closely held business' stock in order to escape the potentially higher estate tax liability.

But Congress slammed the door: the estate and gift taxes are now one unified transfer tax. Even though the gift tax is imposed during life, at death all transfers made during life as gifts and all transfers made at death are added up and the total is subject to one unified transfer tax (misleadingly called the estate tax) using one schedule of tax rates (see Part IV-B). There are certain tax breaks, such as the $10,000 annual exclusion for the gift tax, and the unified credit that can be used to reduce the unified transfer tax. That may sound simple, but the way it works in practice makes it appear as if the gift tax and the estate tax are two different animals. Here is a simplified explanation beginning with the $10,000 annual exclusion.

THE $10,000 ANNUAL EXCLUSION

Before going into the intricacies of how the gift tax works, let's begin with basics. First let's define the two people involved in a gift. The *donor* is the person who makes (gives) the gift. The *donee* is the person who receives it. An unmarried (single) donor can give up to $10,000 per year per donee without incurring any gift tax. In other words, as long as a donor does not give $10,000 or more to any one person, these gifts are tax-free.

If a donor is married, the annual exclusion can be doubled to $20,000 (Section 2513). This is accomplished when the spouse of the donor consents to the gifts. The result is a split gift, which means that each spouse is considered for gift tax purposes to have made half the gift. This allows each spouse individually to use the $10,000 exclusion, which results in a total $20,000 exclusion.

Example 1: Unmarried (Single) Taxpayer

Joe Bachelor makes a $9,000 gift to his nephew, Steve. Since the $9,000 gift is less than the $10,000 annual exclusion, Joe pays no gift tax.

Example 2: Married Taxpayer

Joe marries Sue. He makes an $18,000 gift to Steve, and Sue consents. Because the $18,000 split gift is less than the $20,000 combined annual exclusion for Joe and his wife, they pay no gift tax.

Any year in which a taxpayer makes more than a $10,000 gift, a gift tax return must be filed. Both Joe and Sue must file a gift tax return even though neither incurred any gift tax liability.

TAXABLE GIFTS

What happens if a donor makes a gift or gifts in one year that are more than the annual exclusion? The excess is considered a "taxable gift" on which a gift tax might have to be paid—a "gift tax payable" is created.

Example 3: Unmarried (Single) Taxpayer

Joe makes a $50,000 gift to Steve. After deducting the $10,000 annual exclusion, Joe is considered to have made a taxable gift of $40,000 ($50,000 – $10,000).

Example 4: Married Taxpayer

Joe marries Sue. With Sue's consent, they make a split gift to Steve of $50,000. The taxable gift made by each of them is determined as follows:

	Total	Split	
		Joe	**Sue**
Gift	$50,000	$25,000	$25,000
Less—annual exclusion	20,000	10,000	10,000
Taxable gift to Steve	$30,000	$15,000	$15,000

The annual exclusion is calculated on a per donee basis. In other words, Joe could give $10,000 (or $20,000 with the split-gift) each to an infinite number of people tax free. For example, if single he could give away $100,000 a year tax-free, $10,000 apiece to 10 individuals.

In examples 3 and 4, the fact that a taxable gift has been made does not necessarily mean that a gift tax must be paid in cash. However, once the gift exceeds the annual exclusion, the resulting taxable gift creates a potential gift tax liability—a gift tax payable. Fortunately, all or a portion of this liability can be snuffed out by using the unified credit. Simply put, the gift tax payable can be "paid" (up to a point) by using the unified credit instead of cash.

UNIFIED CREDIT

A gift tax payable is created for each year a taxable gift is made. The amount of the gift tax payable can be reduced dollar for dollar by the available unified credit.

For each dollar of estate or gift tax liability snuffed out, an equivalent (corresponding) amount of gifts or an equivalent amount of a taxpayer's gross estate is shielded from tax by an exemption (see the schedule on page 168). If a taxpayer makes a taxable gift of $600,000, the tax payable is $192,800. However, up to $192,800 in those taxes can be eliminated by the unified credit, which shields up to $600,000 (the equivalent amount) of taxable gifts and the estate from the single transfer tax.

The $600,000 amount applies to the sum total of lifetime and death transfers. What isn't used during a taxpayer's lifetime to shield gifts is available to shield the estate. To put it another way, the amount of the unified credit used against the gift tax payable effectively reduces the amount of the unified credit available against the estate tax.

For example, if the taxpayer makes only $300,000 in taxable gifts during his or her lifetime and shields that amount with the unified credit, enough of the credit would remain to shield $300,000 of the estate.

The taxpayer must use the unified credit to "pay" as much gift tax payable as possible. There is no choice (Rev. Rul. 79-398, 1979-2 CB 338).

During a taxpayer's lifetime, the unified credit can be used in conjunction with the annual exclusion to escape paying any cash gift tax.

Example 5: Unmarried (Single) Taxpayer

Take the same facts as Example 3, where Joe makes a $50,000 gift which resulted in a $40,000 taxable gift after the $10,000 annual exclusion. Joe can use the unified credit to negate the gift tax payable ($8,200) and shield the $40,000 taxable gift from the gift tax.

The gift-splitting provision in Section 2513 also makes it possible to double the unified credit. This allows each spouse to shield (avoid paying any gift tax payable in cash) an exemption equivalent amount of $600,000 in lifetime gifts—or $1,200,000 for a married couple.

Example 6: Married Couple

Take the facts of Example 4, in which Joe and Sue make a split gift of $50,000 to Steve. They use their combined $20,000 annual exclusion, leaving a $30,000 taxable split gift. Each is responsible for the gift tax payable on his or her $15,000 portion of the split gift. The gift tax payable on a $15,000 taxable gift is $2,800. Both can use their unified credit to pay their $2,800 gift tax payable; combined they can use their unified credits to pay $5,600 in gift taxes payable. This shields the remaining $30,000 of the gift to Steve.

In examples 5 and 6, note that if the same $50,000 gift is made by a single taxpayer and married taxpayers who split the gift, the married taxpayers pay $2,600 less in taxes and use up less of their unified credit.

HOW THE GIFT TAX IS CALCULATED

Let's recap. A taxpayer can make tax-free gifts each year up to the $10,000 annual exclusion amount. Anything above that is a taxable gift, upon which is imposed a gift tax payable. A unified credit can be used to offset ("pay") up to $192,800 in gift taxes payable, shielding an exemption equivalent of up to $600,000 in taxable gifts. If the gift exceeds the amount of the annual exclusion and the exemption equivalent of the unified credit, the gift tax payable on the excess must be paid in cash. A gift tax return must be filed whenever a taxable gift is made.

The amount of the unified credit used to "pay" the gift tax on taxable gifts (1) effectively reduces the amount of the credit that can be used to shield a taxpayer's estate from the estate tax, and (2) actually reduces the amount of the unified credit that can be used to shield future taxable gifts. Theoretically, all $192,800 of the credit could be used in one year to shield a $600,000 taxable gift. But then there would be no credit to "pay" gift taxes payable on future taxable gifts or to protect the taxpayer's estate.

With all that in mind, here's an overview of how the gift tax is calculated. The gift tax applies to all taxable gifts made during the donor's lifetime. At the end of each year in which a taxable gift is made, a gift tax is imposed. (See the tax-rate schedule in Part IV-B.) That tax is determined by four steps:

1. Add up all taxable gifts made by the donor in his or her lifetime, including the year in question, and then apply the uniform estate and gift tax rate schedule to that amount. The result is tentative tax (1); say, for example, $14,200.

2. Add up all the taxable gifts made by the donor in his or her lifetime, not including the year in question, and apply the uniform rate to that amount. The result is tentative tax (2); say $6,200.

3. Subtract tentative tax (2) from tentative tax (1). The result is the gift tax payable for the year in question, or $8,000 ($14,200 – 6,200).

4. The taxpayer cannot pay the gift tax payable in cash until he or she uses up the unified credit to "pay" the gift tax payable for the year. The amount of the unified credit available for the year is reduced by the amount of the unified credit used in previous years. Once the unified credit is exhausted, any additional gift tax payable must be paid in cash.

Example 7: Unmarried (Single) Taxpayer

In 1991, George, who has made no previous lifetime gifts, makes a $50,000 gift to his cousin, Fred. This results in a $40,000 taxable gift ($50,000 – $10,000 annual exclusion). Since there were no previous lifetime transfers, George's gift tax payable for 1991 on the $40,000 under the uniform rate schedule is $8,200, and is "paid" by using a portion of the $192,800 unified credit.

In 1992, George makes another gift of $50,000 to Fred, resulting in a taxable gift for 1992 of $40,000. George's gift tax for 1992 is determined as follows: First, George's tentative tax (1) is $18,200, determined by applying the uniform rate schedule to $80,000 (his total lifetime taxable gifts, including 1992). Second, his tentative tax (2) is $8,200, determined by applying the uniform rate schedule to $40,000 (his total lifetime gifts not including 1992). His gift tax payable for 1992 is tentative tax (1) minus tentative tax (2), or $10,000. Again, George must "pay" by using his unified credit against this amount.

What happens if George keeps making yearly gifts in the same amount? The total lifetime transfers will keep adding up, pushing subsequent gifts into higher and higher rate brackets. Once his unified credit is used up, the gift tax must be paid in cash.

HOW THE ESTATE TAX IS CALCULATED

The transfer tax is unified because when Joe dies and it comes time to figure his estate tax, (1) all taxable gifts made during his lifetime are added to his gross estate, and (2) any gift tax Joe actually paid in cash (not including those "paid" by the unified credit) in his life is subtracted from his estate tax.

Example 8: Unmarried (Single) Taxpayer

(A) Joe dies in 1996. He leaves a gross estate of $1,000,000. Taking into account the lifetime gifts he made in example 7 (on which he paid no cash gift tax), his estate tax liability is calculated as follows:

Gross estate	$1,000,000
Add: Lifetime taxable gifts	80,000
Taxable transfers	$1,080,000
Tentative tax (see Appendix E)	$ 378,600
Minus: Gift taxes paid in cash	0
Gross estate tax	$ 378,600
Minus: Unified credit	192,800
Net estate tax (to be paid in cash)	$ 185,800

(B) Suppose that Joe made lifetime taxable gifts of $1,000,000, and shielded $600,000 of that amount with the unified credit. That would mean he paid a cash gift tax of $153,000 on the $400,000 excess. (The tax of $1,000,000 is $345,800, as shown in Appendix E). After deducting the $192,800 unicredit, the cash-gift-tax payment is $153,000. If he has a gross estate of $80,000, his estate tax liability is calculated as follows:

Gross estate	$ 80,000
Add: Lifetime taxable gifts	$1,000,000
Taxable transfers	$1,080,000
Tentative tax (same as above)	$ 378,600
Minus: Gift taxes paid in cash	153,000
Gross estate tax	$ 225,600
Minus: Unified credit	192,800
Net estate tax (to be paid in cash)	$ 32,800

Add the $32,800 estate tax to the $153,000 gift tax paid in cash by Joe during his life, and you come up with the same total tax paid in cash in A as in B, $185,800. This is proof of the unified nature of the estate and gift taxes. Whether Joe transferred wealth by gift or at his death, he eventually ended up paying the same amount of tax.

PUTTING IT ALL TOGETHER

By using the annual exclusion and the unified credit, a good part of the unified transfer tax can be avoided. How? By gifting enough property during one's lifetime to reduce the remaining estate so it is protected by the unified credit.

Let's put all of this into the context of the closely held business owner. For example, if Joe Entrepreneur is single, he would want to gift enough of his stock during his lifetime, using $10,000 annual exclusions, so that the remaining value of his business in his estate would be protected by the unified credit. As noted earlier, unless Joe begins the gift program early in life, or unless his business is small, he probably can't protect his entire business and other assets from the unified estate and gift tax.

Now let's put this into the context of real life. Many privately held business owners are married, have children, and want to pass their businesses on to the next generation. Here's where a gift program can become a tax hero.

For example, within a week, Joe Entrepreneur—if he is married and has two children—could transfer $80,000 of his business tax-free. How? Suppose on December 27 of Year 1 he and his wife make split gifts of stock worth $20,000 to each of the children. Using the annual exclusion, $40,000 worth of stock gifts can be made tax-free in Year 1. Suppose also that a week later on January 3rd of Year 2, Joe and his wife make the exact same split gifts to the children. Because the gift tax is imposed on an annual basis, this second set of gifts would also be tax-free, courtesy of another $40,000 of annual exclusions. In the space of one week, Joe transferred a substantial part of his business. If Joe continued this gift-program over a 10-year period, he could transfer $400,000 of his business tax-free.

Not only that, but gift-splitting could allow Joe to shield up to $1,200,000 of his business from the gift tax, over and above the annual exclusions.

GIFTS OF APPRECIATED PROPERTY: PRIVATELY HELD STOCK

Property that is likely to appreciate over time (like stock in a privately held corporation) is the perfect gift to be made to members of a younger generation. Future appreciation is revoked from the donor's estate without any tax cost.

CONTROL OF THE CORPORATION

Although the founder would like to transfer the ownership of the stock, so that it will be removed from his or her estate, he or she might not want to transfer control to his or her children. At least three circumstances always require attention:

- The children are minors.

- Although adult children are active in the business, they are not capable of managing (or, as is often the case, the management ability of one or more of the adult children is a matter of fierce family disputes), and the founder wants to hang in there.

- Adult children are not active in the business and could not (even if given the opportunity) make intelligent voting decisions to direct management.

These problems can usually be solved by the founder

- putting the stock into a trust,

- issuing nonvoting stock, or

- always keeping enough stock to stay in control.

STOCK IN TRUST

Only gifts of a "present interest" can benefit from the $10,000 annual exclusion. A present interest is an "unrestricted right to immediate use, possession, or enjoyment of property or the income from property." [Reg. 25.2503-3(b)]. If the stock is put in trust, and represents a future interest (the beneficiary can only get benefits from the trust in future years), the $10,000 annual exclusion is lost. The goal then is to convert the gift into a gift of a present interest under Section 2503. The use of a so-called *Crummey* provision can accomplish this goal. This provision arises from the case of *Crummey* v. *Commissioner* (397 F.2d 82; CA-9, 1968). A *Crummey* trust is one in which a beneficiary has the right to demand distributions from the trust in the same year in which the gift is made to the trust. That right to demand distributions makes the gift of stock to such a trust a present interest eligible for the exclusion. The IRS has indicated in Revenue Ruling 73-405 that it will recognize the *Crummey* powers provision as creating a present interest for gift tax purposes, even if the right to demand distribution cannot be practically exercised because the minor beneficiary has no appointed guardian.

LIMITATIONS

Lifetime gifts alone can seldom fulfill the goals of the privately held business owner. This is simply a matter of the relatively small amount of the $10,000 annual exclusion and the fact that most businesses are worth more than the $600,000 exemption equivalent. Even when these amounts are doubled for a married taxpayer, many business owners still cannot escape the unified transfer tax. Because of this, gifts—in an overall financial plan to transfer the stock of a privately held business—are used in combination with other methods.

COMBINATIONS

The principal goal of using gifts in combination with other transfer tools is to shift income to lower-bracket family members and to allow the future appreciation of the privately held business to accrue to the younger shareholders, while reducing the elders' estate.

On the other hand, the owners of the business, although desiring that the transfer tools be put in place, do not want to negate their ability to control and run the business' operations during their lifetime or before their voluntary retirement.

Following are some tools, which, when properly used in conjunction with a gift program, are capable of achieving these goals of the business owner: (1) defeating the estate and gift taxes, (2) transferring control of the business, and (3) retaining control for the owner during his lifetime or until he retires. But be careful: not all of the tools are designed to achieve all of the goals.

GIFTS AND INSTALLMENT SALES

The use of an installment sale of stock in conjunction with a gift program can freeze the value of the gifted property. If the owner's stock interest in the privately held business has appreciated significantly, the use of the installment method is tax-wise, especially if the business has good future prospects or property used in the business (such as land) will continue its appreciation.

If the purchasers of the stock are cash-poor in any year, the annual gift tax exclusion can be used to allow the seller to forgive up to $10,000 per year in installment payments from the buyers (that is, the buyer would not have to pay the amount forgiven). That's because if property is exchanged for less than its full value, the deficit between its fair market value and its price is regarded as a gift from the seller to the buyer. Here's how it works:

> Joe Owner controls 100 percent, or $200,000 of Company X stock. Over a 10-year period, Joe could gift the stock to his two sons incurring no gift tax liability. Or he could sell the stock on the installment method, with $10,000 payments over 10 years, utilizing the gift tax exclusion to forgive payments in years the sons were unable to make payments. A word of caution: the forgiveness should not be assumed or evidenced in the installment note. The IRS could regard the entire sale as a gift in the year the sale is made if it is.

What is accomplished is that the property is out of the owner's estate, and the future appreciation accrues to the heirs. Keep in mind that the spousal gift-splitting provisions could allow up to $20,000 per year per donee to be transferred to the two sons, or $40,000 of stock per year. If used in combination with an installment sale without any forgiveness, a substantial amount of a business can be transferred over a couple of years while ensuring the owner an income stream from the installment sale. The individual facts and circumstances of each privately held business owner's situation will dictate what percentages of the business should be transferred either by gift or sale.

GIFTS AND REDEMPTIONS

Use of the gift and installment sale method along with a complete redemption can also effect the transfer and freeze. Part of the owner's interest can be gifted and sold, while the balance can be redeemed by the corporation, effectively putting the donee/purchasers in control of the corporation as the sole shareholders. (See Chapter 14 for the correct use of redemptions for capital gains treatment to the owner redeeming stock.) This combination is especially effective if the future owners cannot afford to buy the entire business at once.

GIFTS AND RECAPITALIZATIONS

In Chapter 11, the valuation problems of a recapitalization are discussed, particularly the valuation of the common and preferred stock issued in the recapitalization and the gift tax consequences attached to the valuation of the common stock.

VALUATION OF GIFTS OF STOCK

The valuation of gifts of privately held stock is determined by the IRS under the same principles applied to estate tax purposes (see Section 2512). However, this chapter is concerned with the gifting of minority interests in stock that eventually add up to a controlling interest. In recognition of this fact, especially in a family business setting, the IRS in Revenue Ruling 81-253 (see Appendix B) has made it clear that it will not allow discounts for gift tax purposes on gifts of minority interests, while such minority discounts are allowable for estate tax purposes. Instead, for valuation purposes in determining a gift tax liability, the entire value of the company is determined and then multiplied by the percentage of stock gifted. (See also the *Albert C. Luce* case in Part III-B for a gift tax valuation.)

IRS VICTORY AFFECTS EVERY GIFT OF CLOSELY HELD STOCK— PAST AND FUTURE

Have you ever made a gift of stock of your closely held business? Thinking of doing so? Then this is must reading. A new Tax Court case (*Smith vs. Commissioner*, 94 TC 55, 6/13/90) is sending out ominous shock waves. In a nutshell, this case allows the IRS to revalue your lifetime gifts after you die. Your estate can get ripped with more tax on those old gifts. This is a terrible blow to a basic time-honored method of transferring family businesses: the founder gifting stock to his children.

Here's the story. The decedent (Smith) made taxable gifts of corporate stock in 1982, filed a gift tax return in 1983 and paid the gift tax due in a timely manner. Smith died in 1984. The time for the IRS to assess a gift tax deficiency expired on April 15, 1986. Put another way, the statute of limitations ran out against the IRS and blocked it from getting any additional gift tax on the 1982 stock gift. Sounds like that should be the end of the story.

Unfortunately, for every family owned business in the country, it's only the beginning of the story. In 1988, the IRS went after Smith's estate, claiming that the value of the stock gifted in 1982 was $400,000 more on the date of the gift than the amount reported on the gift tax return. Get *them* apples. Here it is, six years later, and the IRS wants to revalue the gift for estate tax purposes. Remember, the IRS was out of luck for gift tax purposes because the statute of limitations had run out against them. No way could the IRS pull off such a caper—right? Wrong! The Tax Court agreed with the IRS, allowing the revaluation.

What's the impact of the court's decision? It keeps the IRS' revaluation book open on lifetime gifts until after you die. It could be five years or 50 or more years, but time will never run out on the IRS. Wow!

What should you do? All gifts of closely held business stock you make from this day forward must be backed up by a valuation done by a qualified expert. Retain the valuation report with the related gift tax return. If you didn't file a gift tax return, because the value of the stock was less than $10,000 per donee, keep the valuation report with your will.

What about prior stock gifts—whether or not a gift tax return was filed? Get a proper valuation done now to back up the old gift. Don't backdate the valuation. Backdating for a tax advantage could be criminal fraud.

This brief explanation does not attempt to cover all the aspects of the case, its widespread ramifications, and how much it can hurt you. Don't ignore it. It is urgent that to protect your family, consult with a qualified professional to determine what the best course of action is for you and your family business.

CHARITABLE CONTRIBUTIONS AND DONATING APPRECIATED PROPERTY

A corporation can deduct contributions or gifts made to or for the use of exempt organizations in an amount up to 10 percent of its taxable income.

Shareholders of a privately held corporation can make contributions of stock and arrange to have the corporation redeem the shares from the charitable organization without having the redemption proceeds taxed to the shareholders.

In the case of *Palmer* (62 TC 684; 1974), the controlling shareholder of a privately held corporation donated stock to a charitable organization and then caused the corporation to redeem the shares. The IRS claimed that the contribution was actually a redemption of the shares by the shareholder, followed by a donation of the proceeds to the charity. The Tax Court disagreed and let the transaction stand as it was. The shareholder got the charitable contribution and was not taxed on the proceeds.

Under Revenue Ruling 78-197, the IRS announced that it agreed with the *Palmer* decision and would treat the arrangement as a gift of the stock to the charitable organization. But caution is advised: the charitable organization must not be under an obligation to sell the shares back to the privately held corporation. If it is, redemption income will result to the donor.

Whether the corporation or the shareholder should make the contribution depends upon which is in the higher tax bracket and can make the best use of the deduction.

As mentioned before, gifts of appreciated property are tax-wise because they remove the appreciation from the donor's estate. Charitable contributions of appreciated property, such as stock in a privately held corporation, yield two tax benefits to the owner: (1) the estate tax reduction, and (2) an income tax deduction [see Section 170(e)]. The following example shows why this deduction has special additional income tax advantages:

> Jill Owner wants to make a $10,000 gift to charity. One share of stock in her privately held business has a basis of $2,000, but a fair market value of $10,000. Jill can make the $10,000 contribution in one of two ways:
>
> 1. She can sell the stock for $10,000 and give the proceeds to charity. If Jill is in the 50 percent tax bracket, she pays about $1,600 in capital gains tax. Her total tax savings is about $3,400—the $5,000 in taxes saved by deducting the $10,000 contribution minus the $1,600 in capital gains.
>
> 2. She can give the appreciated stock directly to the charity. The charity sells the stock and realizes a full $10,000 contribution. Jill gets a $10,000 deduc-

tion saving $5,000 in income taxes. Jill is in-pocket $1,600 more with this alternative. Why? Because the appreciated value (the $8,000 profit) escapes taxation when the stock is gifted to charity.

VALUATION OF CHARITABLE CONTRIBUTIONS

The larger the value determined for the contributed closely held stock, the larger the deduction. If this can be accomplished, fine and dandy. But be aware that the IRS could come right back with that same larger contribution valuation as past evidence of valuation for estate and gift tax purposes.

The following are recent cases in which the stock of closely held corporations were valued for the purpose of charitable contributions: *Paul W. Learner* (45 T.C.M. 922; 1983), *William E. Gatlin* (44 T.C.M. 945; 1982), and *Estate of Thomas L. Kaplin* (44 T.C.M. 660; 1982).

VALUATION OF STOCK CONTRIBUTED TO CHARITY: REPORTING REQUIREMENTS

As the example above shows, the amount of the charitable contribution deduction is equal to the fair market value of the property contributed on the date the contribution is made. In the case of stock of a privately held corporation, there are certain requirements a taxpayer must meet in order to substantiate the value of the stock claimed for the deduction. These requirements amount to a lot of paperwork.

The requirements must be met if the value claimed for the closely held stock is more than $10,000 ($5,000 in the case of all other property).

The main requirement is that the donor must obtain a formal appraisal from an independent appraiser to substantiate the value of the stock. The appraiser must submit to the taxpayer two documents: the appraisal itself and an appraisal summary. The appraisal summary must be attached to the income tax return on which the deduction is claimed.

The appraiser must be independent of the donor and the charitable organization and must be qualified to value stock in the particular closely held corporation.

The appraisal report cannot be made earlier than 60 days before the charitable contribution is made and must contain certain information describing the property contributed, the method by which the property was appraised, and the qualifications of the appraiser (see Regulation 1.170A-13T). (See Chapter 16 for penalties for incorrect appraisals.)

CHAPTER 16

OTHER THINGS YOU SHOULD KNOW

This chapter addresses a number of issues not previously discussed, but important still to the valuation process.

THE IRS AND POSSIBLE VALUATION PENALTIES

The Revenue Reconciliation Act of 1989 substantially overhauled the old penalty provisions. The Revenue Reconciliation Act of 1990 added an additional penalty provision.

These new provisions create a single penalty commonly referred to as the uniform accuracy-related penalty, which replaces five old penalties. The penalties repealed were the negligence penalty (formerly Section 6653), the substantial understatement penalty (formerly Section 6661), and the three valuation penalties (formerly Sections 6659, 6659A, and 6660).

The uniform accuracy-related penalty is coordinated with a new fraud penalty to eliminate the potential overlapping and stacking of penalties that occurred under prior law. Both penalties can be waived under a reasonable-cause exception.

The new provisions (Section 6662) impose a uniform 20-percent penalty on the portion of an underpayment of tax that results from any of the following situations:

1. Negligence or disregard of IRS rules or Regulations.

2. Substantial understatements of income tax liability.

3. Substantial estate or gift tax valuation understatements.

4. Substantial valuation overstatements.

5. Substantial overstatements of pension liability.

6. Substantial valuation misstatements.

Negligence or Disregard

If an underpayment of tax is attributable to negligence or disregard of rules or regulations, the 20 percent penalty applies only to the portion of the underpayment actually attributable to negligence, not the entire underpayment.

The term "negligence" includes any failure to make a reasonable attempt to comply with the laws. The term "disregard" includes any careless, reckless, or intentional disregard. The new law dropped the old presumption that an underpayment is attributable to negligence if it is attributable to a failure to include an amount shown on an information return (e.g., Form 1099). As a practical matter, however, evidence of such a failure is still strong evidence of negligence.

Substantial Understatement of Income Tax

A substantial understatement of income tax occurs if the amount of understatement for the tax year is more than the greater of:

1. 10 percent of the tax that should have shown on the return, or

2. $5,000 ($10,000 for regular C corporations that are not personal holding companies).

As under prior law, adequate disclosure of a position may reduce the substantial understatement penalty. Disclosure, however, does not necessarily prevent the imposition of the negligence penalty.

Example

The IRS determines that the taxpayer owes an additional $6,000 in taxes after a downward adjustment of the property value claimed as a contribution deduction. The penalty is $1,200 (20 percent of $6,000).

Substantial Estate or Gift Tax Valuation Understatement

The new law replaces the three-tier penalty structure of prior law which a two-tier structure for any substantial estate or gift tax valuation understatement. The penalty is applied when the amount of underpayment of tax exceeds $5,000. The new penalty amount is 20 percent of the underpayment of tax if the value of any property claimed is 50 percent or less of the correct value. The penalty is increased to 40 percent of the underpayment of tax if the value of any property claimed is 25 percent or less of the correct value.

Example

Jill's $42,000 valuation on a gift tax return ends up being $100,000 (less than 50 percent but more than 25 percent of correct value) after an IRS audit. This causes an additional tax of $25,000. Jill's penalty is $5,000 (20 percent of $25,000).

Substantial Valuation Overstatements

The penalty is triggered if (1) the value or adjusted basis of any property claimed on a return is 200 percent or more of the correct value or basis (for example, the value on an estate tax return for vacant land should have been $100,000, but was reported as $250,000—250 percent more); and (2) the overstatement results in a tax underpayment of at least $5,000 ($10,000 for regular C corporations that are not personal holding companies). The penalty is 20 percent of the tax underpayment, but would be increased to 40 percent when the value or adjusted basis claimed is 400 percent or more of the correct amount.

IMPLIED VALUATION PENALTIES IMPOSED BY THE COURTS

In Chapter 9 (under "How Big a Discount?"), it is stated that some appraisers take the position that since the IRS almost always will seek a higher value for the privately held business for tax purposes (except in the case of charitable contributions) it makes sense to contend a higher than justified discount in expectation that the compromise figure will be reached in negotiations with the IRS or in the courts.

But be forewarned: the Tax Court has let it be known that it is becoming increasingly fed up with this tactic, on the part of the taxpayer and the IRS. In order to stem this practice, the Tax Court sounded a warning in the case of *Buffalo Tool and Die Manufacturing Co. v. Commissioner* (74 T.C. 441; 1980), in which it stated:

> We are convinced that the valuation issued is capable of resolution by the parties themselves through an agreement which will reflect a compromise Solomon-like adjustment, thereby saving the expenditure of time, effort, and money by the parties and the Court—a process not likely to produce a better result. Indeed, each of the parties should keep in mind that, in the final analysis, the Court may find the evidence of valuation by one of the parties sufficiently more convincing than that of the other party, so that the final result will produce a significant financial defeat for one or the other, rather than a middle-of-the-road compromise which we suspect each of the parties expects the court to reach. If the parties insist on our valuing any or all of the assets, we will. We do not intend to avoid our responsibilities but instead seek to administer them more efficiently—a factor that has become increasingly important in light of the constantly expanding workload of the court.

The Tax Court's threat is clear: if the IRS and taxpayers continue jamming the courts with cases that should be resolved through negotiation, the court will make one or the other pay the total price. No compromise: one party's valuation will be thrown out, and the other's accepted as is. This either/or approach to contending valuations is not universally accepted by all the members of the Tax Court. The Tax Court in *Estate of Mark S. Gallo* (see Appendix C) reserved the right to itself to pick apart each of the contending valuations and fashion its own from their parts *a la carte*.

When contending with the IRS over valuation issues, don't count on the help of some third party, such as the courts, to reach a compromise. Be able to document and justify your valuation methods and amounts, and then fight like a wildcat for them. If you don't, you might catch the Tax Court in a foul mood and suffer the consequences.

HOW MUCH DISCOUNT CAN BE TAKEN FOR NONVOTING STOCK?

A recent valuation case is important to every owner of a closely held business. First, the result. The court held that nonvoting stock was worth less than voting stock (TCM 1989-231, Docket No. 28151-85). Now, a little background. Clara Winkler died in 1981, leaving stock in a closely held business to her children. Some of the stock was voting, some nonvoting. The estate valued all the shares at $20 per share. The IRS wanted to boost the value to $45.94 for the voting stock and $41.77 for the nonvoting stock. Notice that even the IRS was opting for a lower value (about 10 percent) for the nonvoting stock as compared to the voting stock.

The Tax Court compromised in a very interesting way, and valued the voting stock at $37.86 per share (closer to the IRS's figure) and the nonvoting stock at $25.24 per share (very close to the estate's figure). Now, make sure you keep your eye on the ball—both the IRS and the court agreed on one thing—the nonvoting stock had a lower value than the voting stock.

Why is this case so important? Because every owner of a closely held corporation who wants to transfer his business to his children can take advantage of this decision. Here's how. Step 1: Recapitalize your corporation by turning in all of your voting common stock and exchanging it for new voting common stock (say, 1,000 shares) and new nonvoting common stock (say, 9,000 shares). This transaction is tax free and works for S corporations, as well as taxpaying corporations. Step 2: Give the nonvoting stock to your children. Since it's worth less than the voting stock, you can give more shares without triggering any gift tax.

UNBOOKED ASSETS AND LIABILITIES TO BE PAID OR RECEIVED OVER TIME

Sometimes the financial statements made available to the appraiser do not contain certain assets or liabilities. As a result, the book value of the company is overstated or understated. The profit and loss statement may suffer the same disability because of the unbooked asset or liability. For the purposes of the appraisal, such items should be booked to correct both the book value and the earnings. Usually, the items not reflected on the statements are contingent assets and liabilities. These must be estimated and reflected.

What about assets or liabilities that will be paid or received over some time period in the future—either fixed (say 5, 10, or 15 years) or variable (when the president of the company dies)? The amount, as well as the time frame, can be fixed or variable. In any event, reasonable assumptions must be made when the amount or time frame is uncertain and the contingent items must be reduced to a single hard number or, if appropriate, a range of numbers.

Following are some examples of what is likely to occur in practice.

Royalty Income (An Asset)

If the company is entitled to receive royalty income, the value of the income can be determined by preparing a schedule as follows:

Licensee Name	Years Left	Anticipated Annual Royalty	Present Value Factor*	Present Value of Future Royalty
Luckey Co.	3	$100,000	2.4437	$244,370
Star Inc.	6	23,638	4.2305	100,000
Batt Co.	3	22,765	2.4437	55,630
Total present value of future royalties				$400,000
Less: taxes at 50%				(200,000)
After-tax value of future royalties				$200,000

*Select a present value factor, usually about the same percentage rate as prime or the before-tax rate of return earned by the company.

Deferred Compensation to Executives (A Liability)

A common nonbooked liability is the liability to key executives (or their heirs) that will become payable down the road, pursuant to a nonqualified deferred compensation agreement. Here is a sample of a typical schedule taken from an actual client's file covering two executives:

Details	Sam Goget	George Charger
1. Age	62	59
2. Deferred compensation per year before tax	$250,000	$100,000
3. Beginning payment date	Age 65	Age 65
4. Life expectancy for men who attain age 65	15 years	15 years
5. Number of years before executives reach age 65	3	6
6. Total number of years from present to end of life expectancy	18	21
7. Present value annuity factors for 18 and 21 years, respectively at 11%	7.7016	8.0751
8. Present value annuity factor for the number of years before executives reach age 65	2.4437	4.2305
9. Net present value annuity factor (line 7 minus line 8)	5.2579	3.8446
10. Deferred compensation per year after-tax (50% tax rate)*	125,000	50,000
11. Present value of deferred compensation liabilities (line 9 times line 10)	$657,238	$192,230
Total deferred compensation liability	$849,468	

*Always use the tax rate applicable at the time of the valuation; 50% was the tax rate when the above was prepared.

EIGHT-STEP PER-SHARE VALUATION APPROACH

Often, when two or more factors are used to value a business, it is easier to reduce each factor to a value per share. Then the factor can be weighted as desired to arrive at the final per-share fair market value. The following shows an easy and organized way to make the computations.

The eight steps summarize the case of *Skove* v. *United States*, Report of Special Commissioner to the Court of Claims, May 26, 1967. This is a *formula approach*, according to most commentators. This author calls it a *combination approach* (book value and earnings).

Step	Per Share
1. Adjusted book value	$49.18
2. Earnings—five-year average weighted in favor of most recent years	7.58
3. Dividends paid—five latest years considered. Last year used.	1.00
4. Ratios—6 principal price-earning customers used at about 11 times earnings. $7.58 x 11 =	78.00
5. Dividend yield—principal customers based on average market prices $1 capitalized at 5.4%	18.50
6. Weighting of factors	

Factor	As Above	Weight	Product
Earnings	$78.00	50%	$39.00
Dividend yield	18.50	30%	5.55
Book value	49.18	20%	9.83

Statistical fair market value   54.38

Less discounts:

7. Lack of marketability	15%	
8. Minority interest	10%	
Total	25%	

$54.38 x 25% =   13.58

Fair market value $40.80

HOW TO TEST THE VALUATION RESULT

Often, logic alone dictates that the valuation is too high or too low. The appraiser must take another look. However, it is difficult to explain unsupported logic or a gut feeling to an adversary on the other side of the table, the IRS, or the courts.

There is a practical way to test a high or low valuation. The liquidation value of a business is the floor value of any valuation. No matter what method or combination of methods is involved, if it causes the valuation to dip below liquidation value, the result can be disregarded. So the mission becomes to determine liquidation value, and that becomes fair market value.

Note: At best, liquidation value is an estimated figure. It is determined by estimating what the amount of cash in hand would be if every asset on the company's balance sheet was sold. For this purpose, cash can mean "cash and notes." All the liabilities of the company and the cost of liquidating each asset (appraiser fees, real estate fees, brokerage commissions, legal and accounting fees, and so on) then must be subtracted from the total cash received to determine the net liquidation value.

If net liquidation is the floor—the test for a low valuation—is there a way to test the ceiling—a high valuation? Yes. Something a client told this author after returning from a valuation seminar provides a crude but effective explanation of the method. He said that the seminar instructor, with tongue in cheek, said this about the buyer's viewpoint: "I don't care what the seller wants for the business. The selling price is not all that important. Just let me set the terms." And those terms will depend upon how much cash the buyer has in hand. Those "terms" determine how the balance of the price is to be paid: amount of payments, over what period of time, interest rate, and so on. The point is that if the buyer can meet the terms (i.e., make the payments), the price isn't too high.

On the other hand, if the payments cannot be made out of the cash flow of the business being bought, the price is too high, or the terms forcing the high payments are too steep, or both. When valuing a business, one way to look at the transaction is through the eyes of a willing buyer. It is a three-step process:

1. Set down the most likely price and terms.

    a. Price
    b. Terms
        i. Amount down
        ii. Number of months or years to pay
        iii. Rate of interest

2. Make a cash flow projection considering the after-tax profit of the business being bought.

3. Vary the price, terms, and cash flow projections. Usually, at least three variations are required—best, most likely, and worst case.

Each projection should be carried out for as many years as is necessary to show that the business can (or cannot) meet the required payments and pay off the balance due.

Following is a sample taken from an actual client file. The client was trying to determine whether he could meet the payments for a proposed $3,000,000 purchase price. Here are projections for the first four years:

Projections For	Year 1	Year 2	Year 3	Year 4
Operating income (A)	$1,260,000	$1,050,000	$1,196,000	$1,242,000
Interest expense				
To seller (B)	217,879	187,256	153,257	115,510
To bank (C)	315,000	295,504	287,617	273,437
Total interest	532,879	482,760	440,874	388,947
Taxable income	727,121	567,240	755,126	853,053
Less: income tax (D)*	363,560	283,620	377,563	426,526
Net income (E)	363,561	283,620	377,563	426,527
Add: depreciation	100,000	100,000	100,000	100,000
Net cash available (E)	463,561	383,620	477,563	526,527
Principal to seller (B)	277,886	308,509	342,508	380,255
Principal to bank (C)	$ 185,675	$ 75,111	$ 135,055	$ 146,272

Notes

A. Actually, six projections were made using various assumptions. The above projection was considered the most likely.

B. The buyer, our client, was buying only the assets of the seller. The purchase price was $2,200,000. The terms were no money down, 72 equal monthly payments including principal and interest with interest at 10.5 percent per annum on the unpaid balance. Our client is a leader in the industry and is very substantial; thus the no-money-down terms.

C. It was estimated that a $3,000,000 loan was needed from the bank to finance the additional sales volume. The bank agreed to renew the loan as needed at a floating prime to be adjusted every three months. The above projection was prepared using a 10.5 percent (prime was 9.5 percent at the time) per annum interest rate on the unpaid balance. The projection assumes that the "Principal to Bank" (the bottom line of the projection) would reduce the principal balance due to the bank.

D. Every cash-flow projection must arrive at net income after taxes.

E. In order to arrive at Net Cash Available, depreciation must be added back. Under ordinary circumstances, amounts required for capital expenditures (buildings, plant, equipment) would be subtracted at this point. In this case, there is no provision for capital expenditures because our client could easily absorb all of the purchased increased sales in its present plant and equipment, which is already in place, by running an additional shift.

*At the time the projection was made, the tax rate was 50%.

The preceding projections show that the $2,200,000 purchase price passed the valuation test. But take another look at the numbers and recognize that the purchase really required a $5,200,000 investment (counting the $3,000,000 bank loan). Only the willingness of the bank to go along with an old customer made this purchase possible.

The ceiling valuation amount, in the practical sense, is the highest amount that will enable the company to pay for itself over a reasonable period of time out of its available cash flow. One caveat: approximately 20 percent to 40 percent of the available cash flow should be kept as a reserve for unforeseen contingencies. This is particularly true when buyers are buying a new business that will be their one and only business. If the buyer has an existing business that can subsidize any shortfall in the cash flow of the purchased business, the contingency reserve can be narrowed and in some cases, even eliminated.

OTHER FACTORS THAT CAN AFFECT PRICE (VALUATION)

Suppose that the fair market value has been determined using the appropriate methods as detailed in this book. Here are some factors that can raise or lower the price in an actual negotiation between a real buyer and a real seller:

Leverage versus Cash

An all-cash transaction almost always produces a lower price. Installment sales should yield a higher price: the longer the term, assuming a market rate of interest, the higher the price is likely to be. Another general rule to keep in mind is that the more leveraged the transaction, the higher the purchase price.

Security to Seller

Often the seller does not want all cash. Why? All cash can cause a higher tax bill. So the seller wants two things: first, to string the payments out for a designated period of time, and, second, to have the maximum security possible to collateralize the note received for the noncash balance. The collateral might include the buyer's personal signature, the stock being purchased, or other assets of the buyer. As a rule, the greater the security, the lower the purchase price (value of the business). Put another way, the greater the amount of cash or security at the time of closing, the greater the discount on the valuation of the business.

Form of Sale

When the business is appraised for the purposes of sale, the form of the sale affects the ultimate price. There are two reasons for this: the tax effect and the assumption of liabilities. There are two basic forms (methods) of selling a corporate business: sell the stock (assume 100 percent) or sell the assets. Which method is the best way to buy a particular business for tax reasons is an important and complex subject and must be explored in-depth with the help of a tax expert.

In general, a sale of stock is preferred by sellers because (1) they simply pay capital gains tax on their profits, (2) all corporate liabilities are assumed by the buyer as the new owner of the corporation, and (3) they do not get taxed at the corporate level for depreciation recapture (ordinary income) when the corporation sells the assets.

On the other hand, buyers usually want to buy only the assets because they do not have to worry about corporate liabilities (known or unknown) and they get a new depreciation basis for the assets they purchase. Consider these facts together when there is an asset purchase: (1) sellers get stung for depreciation recapture (more taxes, reducing the after-tax profit) and (2) buyers can reduce their tax bill because of a larger depreciation deduction improving their after-tax cash flow. Both of these facts tend to increase the value of the company.

Amount of Interest

A rate of interest greater than the current market rate on the unpaid purchase price balance should lower the purchase price. The result is the opposite for a lower than market rate of interest. In general, if the interest rate charged is less than a current market rate, the tax law imputes a market rate of interest for tax purposes. This raises the interest and lowers the purchase price as far as the IRS is concerned.

The "How-Much-Can-I-Pay" Formula (or How to Test Your Valuation)

The highest price any buyer should pay for a business should be controlled by the "How-much-can-I-pay" formula. This formula tests the price according to these criteria: is it a price at which the company has the ability to pay for itself, with a reasonable cushion for a margin of error, over a reasonable length of time. The formula can be reduced to numbers by taking the following steps:

1. After the initial cash payment at closing, determine the time frame over which payments should be made (usually 5 to 10 years) to pay off the balance due. If the cash flow will not retire the debt, the price paid is too high or the terms must be renegotiated.

2. Project the net available cash for the time frame selected (see the cash-flow sample earlier in this chapter). Make sure to add back depreciation to the after-tax profit and deduct required capital expenditures.

3. Allow 60 percent to 80 percent of the net available cash for debt retirement, the balance (20 percent to 40 percent) should be considered a reserve to handle the cash needed for the unexpected.

A FINAL WORD

Now you are ready to go forth and conquer the valuation world. And as I have been telling my clients for years, "If you have any questions—call me."

Maybe it would help if you knew when to call based on when other closely held business owners (or a member of their family) call:

1. You *WANT TO SELL YOUR BUSINESS* and want to know—

    a. What's the right price, and
    b. How to best structure the deal for tax purposes.

2. You *WANT TO BUY A BUSINESS* and want to know—

    a. How much to pay (set the price);
    b. How to make a cash-flow projection (will you be able to afford the payments);

    or

    c. You need help negotiating the deal (there are many ways to skin a cat);
    d. You need help structuring the deal for tax purposes (remember, the after-tax cost in dollars is even more important than the price).

3. You *WANT TO TRANSFER YOUR BUSINESS* to your kids (a valuation is a must).

4. You're not *TALKING ABOUT DIVORCE* any more; you're getting one (again, a valuation of your business is a must).

5. Sorry, but you're now a "dearly departed" and a member of your family or his lawyer calls to ask me to value your business for *ESTATE TAX PURPOSES.*

Just call 312-207-1040—ask for Irv Blackman

PART II

Sample Real-Life/ Real-Business Valuations

For many students, professional practitioners and other readers of this book, this Part probably is and will remain the most important part. Why? It shows you by actual example how to apply the valuation theory and principles set forth elsewhere in this book. As far as we know, it is the most complete and comprehensive set of real-life sample valuations every published.

This Part is designed as both a teaching aid and a resource. If it does its job well, you will return to it again and again.

This appendix contains excerpts of valuations that the author has personally compiled in actual practice. The excerpts have been chosen to illustrate certain valuation methods and particular circumstances. They should give you the flavor of real-life valuation techniques. They also act as a reference and material for sections in the main text of the book. Only selected portions of the valuations are shown, which have been edited for book presentation and to protect the identity of the clients.

But indulge me for a moment. Before looking at the examples that follow, just let me run you through the routine used in my office, by me and the valuation staff alike, before attempting to commit a valuation to paper.

First, you eyeball the facts. Your initial goal is to decide if this particular business earns a fair rate of return on its investment. Assume it does. Say these are the facts: It earns $500,000 per year on its net assets (adjusted book value) of $1 million.

Now comes your second task: Pick a valuation method (or methods). Who cares about the precise net asset value under the above facts. You know immediately that you're going to use some kind of earnings method to value this business. Let's face it, the buyer is after that $500,000 per year in earnings. Remember, in the long run, for any business the buyer intends to continue to operate, earnings is king. That's what he's buying, and the value of those future earnings will drive the price. Whether the equipment is worth $100,000 or $200,000 in excess of book value, more or less, will rarely impact on the value of the business.

Now, turn the tables: Same business, but it only earns in the $40,000 per year range on its $1 million in net assets—definitely not a reasonable rate of return. No doubt about it, even a fool would not pay $1,000,000 for $40,000 in earnings in today's market. Your head will turn toward some kind of asset valuation approach. Now the fair market value of the equipment becomes important.

But what about this? That same $1 million net-asset business earns about $100,000 per year? Reasonable rate of return? Maybe yes, maybe no. Chances are you would want to use more than one valuation method to determine the fair market value of the business.

And remember, more often than not, you are trying to value future earnings. If the data is available, you might want to project future earnings, or cash flow, or both.

One final point of theory: The value you determine by any single method or combination of methods cannot be less than the liquidation value of the business.

Now you're ready to read the examples. Go to it.

A NOTE ABOUT THE FIRST FOUR EXAMPLES

These examples give you an overview of the most common valuation methods and types of problems seen in real-life practice situations in the author's office.

EXAMPLE 1

Valuation Methods:

1. Adjusted book value and

2. combination of book value and earning capacity.

Comment

Company earns *more* than a fair rate of return on its net operating assets.

EXAMPLE 2

Valuation Methods: combination of adjusted book value and earning capacity.

Comments

Company earns *less* than a fair rate of return on its net operating assets and has substantial nonoperating assets.

Points of Special Interest:

- Has non-operating assets, as well as net operating assets used in business operations.

- Discusses discount for general lack of marketability.

EXAMPLE 3

Valuation method: Adjusted book value—with multiple complex adjustments.

Comment

Company owns substantial real estate used in operations but does not make a fair rate of return on its net operating assets.

Points of Special Interest:

- Values a 50 percent interest.
- Values preferred stock.
- Values voting versus non-voting stock.
- Deals with a substantial contingent liability.
- Discusses real estates owned—to be kept and to be sold.

EXAMPLE 4

Valuation Methods:

1. Comparables and
2. net asset value (another name for adjusted book value).

Comment

This is a company that indeed can be valued (and, in fact, was valued) by the comparable method.

Points of Special Interest:

- Has interesting business history and industry outlook.
- Values common and preferred stock.

A NOTE ABOUT EXAMPLES 5 THROUGH 20

These examples should be considered building blocks to be used, together with all the other material in this book, to build your own real-life valuations.

EXAMPLE 5

A short-form valuation: Sometimes a client needs a valuation but the circumstances or the amounts involved dictate that a full-blown valuation, like Example 20, would simply be too expensive. This example gives you the entire valuation as actually delivered to the client, with only such changes necessary to protect the client's identity. It gets the job done—effectively, while containing the cost.

EXAMPLE 6

Valuation building blocks: Shows (1) company profile—interesting I-made-it-in-America facts, and (2) general economic and business discussions during a recession.

EXAMPLE 7

Valuation building blocks: Capitalized earnings approach showing (1) how to remove unusual items from prior year's earnings and (2) use of "Ibbotson" to determine rate of return instead of industry rate.

EXAMPLE 8

Valuation building blocks: Capitalized earnings approach showing how to use various factors—Ibbotson, industry rate, cost of debt, cost of equity—to determine rate of return.

EXAMPLE 9

Valuation building blocks: Capitalized earnings approach yields lower value than liquidation approach forcing use of *liquidation value approach.*

EXAMPLE 10

Valuation building blocks: Capitalized earnings approach using industry rate of return, yields extremely low value forcing use of *adjusted net book value approach.*

EXAMPLE 11

Valuation building blocks: Discounted cash flow approach.

EXAMPLE 12

Valuation building blocks: Uses three valuation methods. Market comparison approach shown in entirety.

EXAMPLE 13

Valuation building blocks: Valuation of a construction company that gets almost 100 percent of its business by competitive bidding. What method do you think is used? In my opinion, such a company cannot be worth more than book value unless the contracts-in-process can be separately valued or there are some other special circumstances.

EXAMPLE 14

Valuation building blocks: An unusual valuation that gathers together four separate elements of one business unit to determine the value of the entire business. The four elements are:

- Value of operations
- Value of single large contract
- Value of a pending litigation award
- Value of investment assets.

EXAMPLE 15

Valuation building blocks: An old line company falls upon hard times. Features:

- Fascinating "Business History and Outlook"
- Discounted cash flow approach (more complex than Example 11)
- Value significantly reduced because of dismal future outlook
- Investment assets from old accumulated profits exceed value of operating business.

EXAMPLE 16

Valuation building blocks: Unusual factors—almost entire value of company dependent on collectibility of one doubtful receivable.

EXAMPLE 17

Valuation building blocks: Buy-sell agreement controls valuation.

EXAMPLE 18

Valuation building blocks: Valuation of preferred stock meets requirements of Revenue Ruling 83-120 (See ruling in Part III-A).

EXAMPLE 19

Valuation building blocks: Contains logic and rich citation of supporting case law and other authorities for:

- Discount for general lack of marketability
- Discount for minority interest
- Minority discounts and intrafamily transfers.

EXAMPLE 20

An ESOP valuation: The entire valuation report is reproduced. Shows you how to put the theory, elements, and factors discussed throughout the book into a comprehensive valuation report—almost word for word as actually submitted to the client and ESOT trustee.

VALUATION EXAMPLE 1
ADJUSTED BOOK VALUE AND COMBINATION OF BOOK VALUE AND EARNING CAPACITY

(This company earns more than a fair rate of return on its net operating assets.)

Purpose of Valuation

This valuation has been requested to enable the 51 percent controlling shareholder brother of the company to buy out his 49 percent minority shareholder sister. The purpose of the valuation is to value the sister's interest to determine whether the brother's buyout offer of $2,205,000 is reasonable. The brother operates the business. The sister is a passive owner.

Brief Description of Company

The company (XYZ for our purposes), founded in the mid-1940s, is a metal stamping factory producing spare parts for radios, televisions, autos, appliances, and computers. Its largest customer, accounting for 10 percent in annual sales, is Sting computers. XYZ has four sales representatives to service its customers nationwide. It has one class of common stock (owned in the proportions stated above) and no preferred stock.

Methods of Valuation

The following two methods of valuation are used to determine the fair market value of XYZ:

Method I   Adjusted Book Value
Method II   Combination of Book Value and Earning Capacity

The higher amount produced by either Method I or Method II is the fair market value of the company as of July 31, __.
An updated version should be considered when current fiscal financial statements become available.

Method I: Adjusted Book Value. Method I considers assets that have appreciated in determining fair market value. The machine presses used by XYZ have fair market values that materially exceed their book values. Accordingly, the book value of the company is adjusted as follows:

Book value of assets as of 7/31/__	(Exhibit 1)*	$3,034,923
Add: Fair market value of machine presses	$2,660,000	
Less: Book value of machine presses	(1,298,324)	1,361,676
Total Adjusted Book Value of Assets as of 7/31/__		$4,396,599

*Exhibit 1 is the balance sheet of XYZ and is not included in this book.

Method II: Combination of Book Value and Earning Capacity. Method II combines the earning capacity and book value of XYZ to determine the fair market value. In calculating the earning power of XYZ, net income should be adjusted, net of taxes, over a five-year period ended July 31, __ to reflect the following facts:

1. Inventories are stated at cost under the last-in, first-out (LIFO) method of accounting. The LIFO method suggests that the higher-prices, current-year inventory purchases are still in ending inventory, resulting in a higher cost of goods sold. Consequently, net income should be adjusted to reflect inventory under the first-in, first-out method of accounting.

2. XYZ owns a 7 percent interest in two limited partnerships. Since the valuation is done on the earning power of *operating* assets, the losses generated by the limited partnerships should not be used in calculating net income.

3. For four years of the five years under review, the salary of John Winter, the president, remained somewhat consistent—ranging from $136,000 to $171,000. However, for year 2, his salary was $322,800. Net income for the period should be adjusted to reflect a more reasonable compensation amount.

(See Exhibit 3, which details the above three income statement adjustments.)

Method II Computation		
Weighted average after-tax earnings (Exhibit 4)		$ 557,950
Weighted average annual net assets (Exhibit 5)	$2,483,934	
Fair rate of return	× 15%	372,590
Excess earnings attributed to goodwill		185,360
Capitalization rate of excess earnings		× 4
Capitalized excess earnings		741,440
Plus: book value of XYZ assets as of 7/31/__ (Exhibit 1)		$3,034,923
Fair market value of XYZ		$3,776,363

SUMMARY

Based on using the higher fair market value between Method I and Method II, the sister's interest can be valued at $2,154,334 ($4,396,599 x 49%).

Note

This valuation excludes two limited partnership interests owned by the company. When this is taken into consideration, the offer to purchase the sister's 49 percent interest in XYZ for $2,205,000 is reasonable and fair.

It should also be pointed out that the price offered by the brother for the company's operations is viewed as a cash price (either lump sum or, more likely, a down payment and the

Exhibit 3

Adjustments to Financial Statement Net Income for Five Years

	Year 1**	Year 2	Year 3	Year 4	Year 5
Net income (loss) (Exhibit 2)*	$265,709	$544,713	$622,648	$ (59,507)	$297,910
Excess of FIFO over LIFO	212,450	239,067	262,169	226,038	351,429
Partnership loss	—	—	63,622	532,460	100,000
Salary adjustment ($322,800–$160,000)	—	162,800	—	—	—
Total adjustments	212,450	401,867	325,791	758,498	451,429
Less tax effect	50%	50%	50%	50%	50%
	106,225	200,934	162,896	379,249	225,715
Total adjustments after tax effect	106,225	200,934	162,896	379,249	225,715
Net income after adjustments	$371,934	$745,647	$785,544	$319,742	$523,625

*Exhibit 2 is XYZ's Profit and Loss Statement, and is not included in this example.

**Year 2 is the most recent year.

Exhibit 4
Weighted Average of XYZ After-Tax Earnings for Five Years

Year	Weight	Adjusted after-tax earnings (Exhibit 3)	Total
1	3	$371,934	$1,115,802
2	2	745,647	1,491,294
3	2	785,544	1,571,088
4	1	319,742	319,742
5	1	523,625	523,625
			5,021,551
			÷ 9
Weighted average after-tax earnings			$ 557,950

Exhibit 5
Weighted Average of XYZ Book-Value of Assets for Five Years

Year	Weight	Book value of assets	Total
1	3	$3,034,923	$ 9,104,769
2	2	2,769,214	5,538,428
3	2	2,224,501	4,449,002
4	1	1,601,852	1,601,852
5	1	1,661,359	1,661,359
			22,355,410
			÷ 9
Weighted average book value of assets			$ 2,483,934

balance to be paid over time plus a reasonable rate of interest on any unpaid balance). Any rate of interest lower than one point below prime would be considered a reduction of the price.

VALUATION OF GOODWILL

This valuation also contains a good example of calculating goodwill. Under the Method II computation, the weighted average of annual net assets is multiplied by a fair rate of return. The weighted average after-tax earnings of the company itself are then compared to that result and the difference is attributed to goodwill. The rate of return of XYZ was actually 22 percent ($557,950 divided by $2,483,934). The calculation for goodwill is another method of calculating the premium that should be attached to XYZ's value because it earns more than a fair rate of return on its adjusted book value.

VALUATION EXAMPLE 2
COMBINATION METHOD OF ADJUSTED BOOK VALUE
AND EARNING CAPACITY

(This company earns less than a fair rate of return on its net operating assets.)

Purpose of Valuation

This valuation determines the fair market value of 48 shares (representing an 18.25 percent interest) of J-R Tool Inc.'s common stock as of December 31, 19 __.

The 48 shares are in a trust for numerous grandchildren. The shares will be distributed to the grandchildren upon termination of the trust on December 31, 19 __. And will be paid the price determined in this valuation.

The valuation involves a small minority interest in a corporation that has a rate of return on its operating assets below a fair or industry average rate.

Brief Description of Company

J-R Tool was founded in the mid 1940s. It is a tool and die job shop producing metal parts tailored to specific customer needs.

J-R Tool has historically used a high percentage of its profits to purchase nonoperating assets such as Treasury bills, certificates of deposit, and marketable securities. Appropriate adjustments are made for these assets of the business that are not being used in operations.

There is one class of common stock and no preferred stock. A 32 percent block of the common stock (from which the 18.25 percent interest comes) is held in trust for 28 grandchildren of the owner/founder (now deceased). The owner/founder's son owns 17 percent of the stock. The remaining 51 percent of the stock of J-R Tool is owned by 12 individuals whose ownership interests range between 4 and 8 percent.

Method of Valuation

A combination of the earning capacity and adjusted book value methods is used to determine the fair market value of J-R Tool, Inc. as of December 31, 19 __. This methodology requires several steps.

Step 1. Determination of adjusted book value.

	Operating assets	Nonoperating assets	Total
Book value (Exhibit 5)	$1,033,584	$1,035,288	$2,068,872
Adjustments			
Building (Note 1)	50,000		50,000
Securities (Note 2)		(2,400)	(2,400)
Adjusted book value	$1,083,584	$1,032,088	$2,116,472

Note 1: Management estimates that the value of real estate is $50,000 greater than its book value.

Note 2: The $2,400 downward adjustment reflects management's determination that the actual market value of the marketable securities as of 12/31/__ was $2,400 less than book value. The actual market value of these non-operating assets should be redetermined for any purchase of stock after the valuation date.

Step 2. Determination of the fair market value of operating assets.

Weighted average of earnings from operating assets (Exhibit 4)		$ 107,615
Adjusted book value of operating assets	$1,083,584	
Fair rate of return including risk (Note)	× 18%	195,045
Negative earnings capacity		(87,430)
Capitalized at 25% ($87,430 × 4)		$(349,720)
Add: adjusted book value as of 12/31/—		1,083,584
Value before discounts		$ 733,864

Note: The fair rate of return is the sum of two elements—a return available in the marketplace as of December 31, 19__ without much risk in the range of 13 percent, plus an additional rate of 5 percent for the risk inherent in the business in which the operating assets are used.

An easy way to understand the theory of earnings capacity is to ask *how much would someone pay to earn $107,615 considering the type of investment that requires an 18 percent return because of the risk?* The answer would be $597,861 (because $597,861 x 18 percent equals $107,615). This valuation method is commonly used to value securities, like long-term bonds. However, the

$733,864 value is preferred because if the earnings capacity had been positive, as opposed to the negative figure, it would have been capitalized at 25 percent. This method is used to value a going business.

Step 3. Discount for general lack of marketability.

The current economic environment of the tool and die industry is not on solid ground. A company's continued earnings stream and ability to increase sales depend on whether the manufacturer can satisfy its customers' demands for state of the art products.

Many of J-R Tool's customers are, or will soon be, advanced technology companies. These high-tech companies need nonmetal products to use for computers, circuits, semiconductors, and so on.

If J-R Tool does not update and convert its equipment to facilitate plastic injection molding and powered metal processing, the company will subsequently lose business to its competition. In fact, sales to one of its major customers have already sharply declined, because J-R Tool does not have the capacity to supply parts for that customer's new typewriters.

Considering the economic environment, would a willing purchaser pay the value before discounts as shown for a tool and die/metal stamping company that has machinery and processes that are not up-to-date? It would be safe to assume that a reasonable purchaser would pay only a lesser value.

The buyer, if in fact one could be found to buy this type of business in this uncertain business climate for tool and die companies, would be able to negotiate a discount for general lack of marketability.

Value before discounts	$733,864
Discount for general lack of marketability—20%*	146,773
Fair market value of operating assets	$587,091

*It was agreed that the discount could have been larger, but management requested a 20 percent ceiling.

Comment: In some cases the fair market value of a business as an ongoing operating concern is less than its liquidating value. If the liquidating value is higher than the fair market value, it should be used. No attempt has been made herein to determine a liquidating value, which requires an extensive investigation and analysis to determine the losses that would be incurred in selling the assets and dismantling the going operations.

Operating assets (as previously noted)	$ 587,091
Nonoperating assets (as previously adjusted)	1,032,888
Total fair market value	$1,619,979
Shares to be valued	x 18.25%
Fair market value of these shares ($1,619,979 x .1825)	$ 295,646
Let's say	$ 300,000

Exhibit 3
J-R Tool, Inc.
Adjustments to Financial Statement Net Income for the Years Ending December 31, 19___

	Year 1**	Year 2	Year 3	Year 4	Year 5
Net income (Exhibit 2)*	$189,953	$76,979	$197,777	$181,153	$253,566
Nonoperating income					
Interest	56,672	70,632	96,718	43,386	39,250
Dividends	30,875	17,799	7,026	5,402	5,319
Gain on sale of marketable securities	6,749	4,288	—	—	—
Total nonoperating income	94,296	92,719	103,744	48,788	44,569
Less—dividend exclusion	(26,244)	(15,129)	(5,972)	(4,592)	(4,521)
Net taxable nonoperating income	68,052	77,590	97,772	44,196	40,048
Approximated tax rate	50%	20%	50%	50%	50%
Approximated tax on nonoperating income	34,026	15,518	48,886	22,098	20,024
Total nonoperating income after-tax effect	60,270	77,201	54,858	26,690	24,545
Net income minus nonoperating income	$129,683	$ (222)	$142,919	$154,463	$229,021

*Exhibit 2, The Profit and Loss Statement of J-R Tool, Inc., is not shown.

**Year 1 is the most recent year.

Exhibit 4

Weighted Average of J-R Tool, Inc. Net Income for the Five Years Ended December 31, 19___

Year	Weight	Net income minus nonoperating income (Exhibit 3)	Total
1	5	$129,683	$ 648,415
2	4	(222)	(888)
3	3	142,919	428,757
4	2	154,463	308,926
5	1	229,021	229,021
	15		1,614,231
			+ 15
Weighted average of net income			$ 107,615

Exhibit 5

J-R Tool, Inc.

Book Value of Operating Assets for the Year Ended December 31, 19___

December 31, 19—— book value of assets (Exhibit 1)*		$2,068,872
Less nonoperating assets:		
Cash and equivalents	601,510	
Certificates of deposit and treasury bills	205,903	
Marketable securities	276,584	
CSV of life insurance	51,291	
	1,135,288	
Cash needed for operations	(100,000)	
Total nonoperating assets	1,035,288	
		(1,035,288)
Total December 31, 19— book value of operating assets		$1,033,584

*Exhibit 1, the Balance Sheet, is not shown.

Taking into consideration the data made available and the company's general lack of marketability, a $300,000 offer to purchase an 18.25 percent interest in J-R Tool would be fair and reasonable if the entire company was being sold (100 percent of all stock). However, if only the minority interest were to be the subject of the sale, an additional substantial discount (perhaps has high as 25 percent to 33 percent of the $300,000) for such a minority interest should be considered.

VALUATION EXAMPLE 3
ADJUSTED BOOK VALUE METHOD

The following valuation is unique because it calls for the valuation of a 50-percent interest in a privately held business. Is the shareholder's controlling interest glass half empty or half full? Does he control the company? If he does, a premium attaches to his stock. If he doesn't, a discount for not having control is in order. Since the purpose of the valuation is determination of estate tax liability, the shareholder takes the position that it is not a controlling interest and is therefore entitled to a discount.

This example contains a large excerpt of the valuation text (about half) but very little of the supporting financial data. Aside from the discount issue, you should be aware of several other unusual points considered in the valuation text:

1. The method of valuation selected and the reasons therefore

2. The larger discount given to the nonvoting common stock over the voting stock, and again, the reasons therefore

3. Why the value of the common stock was reduced by the par value of the preferred stock rather than the fair market value of the preferred

4. Treatment of the contingent liability for compliance with EPS regulations

5. Treatment of the after-tax effect for various adjustments, and in particular, the difference in after-tax treatment between fixed assets to be retained in the business and fixed assets to be sold

Purpose of Valuation

The purpose of this valuation is to determine the fair market value of the 50 percent interest in two classes of common stock of Ewing Enterprises, Inc., owned by Jason Ewing at the date of his death April 15, 19__. The results of the valuation are to be used to determine the estate tax value under Section 2031 of the Internal Revenue Code.

Brief Description of Business

Ewing Enterprises was founded in the late 1920s by the father of the present owners. It began as a gasoline and heating oil wholesaler and expanded to acquiring and building service stations. Ewing Enterprises sells its products primarily through its service stations and ARCO and Shell stations. It also sells products to wholesale and commercial accounts through card-lock sales outlets identified as Gulf Goods.

The company has made numerous real estate investments for petroleum and non-petroleum use. It still owns property not being used in business operations. The deceased was co-owner with his brother, Cliff Ewing, until his death.

As of April 15, 19__, Ewing Enterprises, Inc.'s capital structure consisted of the following:

Class	Authorized shares	Outstanding shares
Class A—voting common stock	25,000	18,538
Class B—nonvoting common stock	25,000	18,538
Nonvoting preferred stock	3,000	2,596

On April 15, 19__, Jason Ewing owned 9,269 shares of Class A Voting Common Stock and 9,269 shares of Class B Nonvoting Common Stock. His brother Richard Ewing owns the remaining shares of the common stock.

Ewing Enterprises, Inc. experienced a substantial operating loss in 19__. The major oil companies have been highly price competitive in Ewing's dominant marketing areas. The outlook for the near term indicates that this competitive condition will remain unchanged.

Ewing Enterprises, Inc.'s operations may be divided into three categories:

1.   retail service stations

2.   wholesale operations

3.   convenience store operations

The bulk of its operations is in the retail service station business.

Outlook for the Oil Industry

U.S. gasoline demand is projected to fall some 1 percent per year for the rest of the century.

After the 1973 Arab oil embargo, the consumer's mind was on the availability, and marketing strategy was simply securing supplies. With current abundant supplies, the consumer is back in the driver's seat. A consumer can be selective with regard to price, product quality, service, and convenience. Accordingly, the marketing strategy has gone through a period of dramatic changes. Retailers have been forced to achieve cost-effectiveness and meet customer's needs for quality and convenience.

With price controls on gasoline and many long-term oil supply relationships gone, competition at the retail level is intense. In January 1981, President Reagan abolished price controls on domestic gasoline, allocations of crude products in time of scarcity, and the entitlement programs. This initially may have helped some independents, who turned quickly to the noncontract market for supplies to compete effectively with major integrated oil companies that were still tied to many long-established high-price contractual supply arrangements. However, with the drop in Saudi crude prices in March 1983 and with most of the other major integrated oil companies working out of their unfavorable contractual arrangements, the entire industry seems to be on an equal footing in 19__. This has hurt the independents, because some major integrated oil companies have operated their retail operations at a loss to compete with them. Major companies with oil and gas production profits can absorb these losses; the independents cannot and are vulnerable to being pushed out of business. Margins (the equivalent of gross profit in other commercial businesses) on gasoline and oil have narrowed due to this competitive pressure. As a result, cost-effectiveness has become the high priority in marketing.

In addition to cost-effectiveness, retailers are paying increased attention to customers' demand for products and convenience. Marketing techniques include self-service electronic credit using card-lock devices, multiproduct dispensers, and more convenient dispensers. Moves designed to appeal to customers' desire include the combination gas station-convenience outlet, offering such items as milk, bread, and other fast-moving convenient items. Many stations also are being remodeled to project a uniform image quickly identifiable by brand-oriented customers, and stations are being equipped to emphasize the complete car-care concept. Innovation and change has become routine.

In summary, cost-effectiveness and appeal to consumer demand for products and convenience are the keys to survival in the highly competitive oil retailing environment.

Problems of Retail Service Stations

The primary problem in the retailing service station operations for Ewing Enterprises, Inc. has been the poor profit margin in the marketplace. As the major oil companies continue to battle for market share in its operating areas, profit margins probably will remain at low levels and only the most effective marketers will survive.

In 19__ and 19__, company management took various steps to reduce operating costs. Five unprofitable units were closed in 19__. In spite of these steps, operating costs remain high in relation to the gross profit potential. In addition, the company tried to reduce the volume of petroleum products purchased on an unbranded basis. Late in 19__, efforts were made with Shell, Mobil, Chevron, and Texaco to brand many of their service outlets. However, management has not been successful in this endeavor. Management intends to continue these steps in an attempt to reduce costs and improve profit margins; in addition, it will strive to reduce general and administrative overhead costs.

The wholesale operations have not received much management attention in the past. The company lacks information on its competitive price condition in relation to its competitors. Sales volume was down by 136 percent in 19__ (compared to 19__).

Management does not anticipate any significant progress in wholesale sales growth.

Ewing Enterprises, Inc. has only one convenience store. The store has experienced inadequate sales due to poor promotional, merchandising, and marketing efforts. However, there have been positive changes in recent months because of new merchandising and promotional programs. Company management has determined that the company should not be involved in the convenience store business in the near future. Management is attempting to lease the existing store operation to an operating chain.

In summary, Ewing Enterprises, Inc.'s future plan is to control costs and to meet consumer demands for products and convenience.

Specific Valuation Methods

We have considered four basic approaches toward valuing the 50 percent common stock ownership interest of Ewing Enterprises, Inc. as follows:

- net book value approach
- adjusted book value approach

- capitalized earnings approach

- market comparison approach

Selection of Valuation Techniques. We have considered all of the foregoing approaches and have selected the appropriate method to correspond to the specific circumstances of Ewing Enterprises, Inc. as of the valuation date. For various reasons discussed later, the value of Ewing Enterprises, Inc. has been determined on a going-concern basis with primary reliance on the adjusted net asset approach. Each method and the underlying philosophies are described in the following pages and considered in relation to the circumstances of the company.

Net Book Value Approach. The net book value approach (or *net equity method*) implies that a company is worth its accumulated retained earnings or deficit plus its original capitalization. There have been litigated cases where either the Internal Revenue Service or the taxpayer contended that the fair market value of stock approximated its book value. The courts in all such cases generally rejected the contention that book value approximated the fair market value of capital stock.

The primary reason the net book value approach is not relied upon as a good method of ascertaining the fair market value of Ewing Enterprises, Inc. is the substantial real estate owned by the company. The real estate has appreciated substantially and its fair market value is substantially higher than its original cost less accumulated depreciation.

Adjusted Book Value Approach. One of the key inherent weaknesses of the net book value method, namely, that historical cost-based asset value may bear very little relationship to market value, is overcome in the adjusted net book value approach.

The adjusted book value method requires that all assets be evaluated to determine their true economic value. Fixed assets are appraised at a figure approximating their market value as opposed to depreciated cost.

This approach is used in cases (e.g., in bankruptcy proceedings) where the assets are actually to be liquidated following their acquisition. This method also is appropriate in those entities where economic goodwill is not present but whose assets are collectively employed in such a way as to produce a going concern and contain a value over and above what is recorded on the books of the business. This approach is applicable to companies having erratic or depressed earnings which are inadequate to provide a fair return on the value of the net tangible assets employed. In theory, the value of all assets, less all outstanding liabilities, provides an indication of the fair market value of ownership equity.

In Revenue Ruling 59-60, the IRS also indicates that the net asset value can be the primary consideration for valuing closely held investment or real estate holding companies.

Because of the depressed earnings of Ewing Enterprises, Inc. for the past five years ended December 31, 19__, coupled with its relatively large real estate holdings, we believe that the adjusted net book value approach should be relied upon for determining the fair market value of the company.

Capitalized Earnings Approach. Conceptually, the capitalized earnings approach determines the fair market value of an ongoing business enterprise based on its earnings capacity. This approach is based on the theory that an investment (i.e., net tangible assets) will yield a return sufficient to recover its initial cost and to justly compensate the investor for the inherent risks of ownership. This approach is often used to arrive at a value for a company that reflects the company's goodwill due to its earnings in excess of the industry norm.

What constitutes a reasonable return on net tangible assets can best be answered by referring to Revenue Ruling 68-609, which states:

> The percentage of return on the average annual value of tangible assets used should be the percentage prevailing in the industry involved at the date of valuation.

The median return on net worth for the gasoline service station industry as compiled by Dun and Bradstreet for 19__ was 5 percent for the lower industry quartile. The median return on net worth of all companies in the sample was 17.5 percent.

For the past five years, Ewing Enterprises, Inc. experienced losses. Thus its past losses tend to indicate that the company does not have goodwill (i.e., excess earnings) that can be quantified currently. Although future earnings are to be used for earnings capitalization, past earnings are usually the guide for determining future earnings. In this regard, Revenue Ruling 59-60 states, Prior earnings records usually are the most reliable guide as to the future expectancy. In view of past losses, the company's future earnings are uncertain. Accordingly, we believe that the capitalized earnings approach should not be relied upon to value the company, as the capitalization of losses would produce an unrealistic negative value.

Market Comparison Approach.   The market comparison approach involves selecting public companies that are in the same or similar businesses and using their price-earnings multiples as a guide in determining the value of the subject company. Price-earnings multiples established in active trading represent the market's fair rates of return on the investment. They are considered as being reliable indicators of the fair capitalization rates for the subject company, as appropriately adjusted for the risk factors associated with the subject company.

Finding price-earnings multiples of comparable publicly traded companies is a more difficult task than might be imagined. Often, finding even one listed company comparable to a closely held company is no easy task. In fact, such a comparable company might not exist. Moreover, Ewing Enterprises, Inc. has been experiencing losses over the past years. Applying price-earnings multiples to Ewing Enterprises, Inc. would create a negative value to the company as a whole. Accordingly, using price-earnings multiples of publicly traded companies would not be meaningful.

Computations of Adjusted Net Asset.   As indicated previously, we believe that the adjusted net asset approach should be relied upon in determining the value of Ewing Enterprises, Inc. This approach involves adjusting the company's net assets from a book value basis to an approximation of market. We made the following adjustments to the assets:

1. Convert investments and securities to approximate market value from cost. Some of the adjustments, for investments in privately held companies, are based on company management's estimations.

2. Convert inventory from LIFO to FIFO by using the shareholders' equity as computed under the FIFO method by the company's independent certified public accountants.

3. Markup fixed assets to an approximation of market value. The adjustments are based on an appraisal of these assets.

4. Incorporate the approximate after-tax loss during the period from January 1, 19__ to April 30, 19__. This adjustment is a rough approximation based on unaudited financial statements provided by company management. Such an adjustment is necessary to

account for the change in net assets from the audited financial statements as of December 31, 19__ to April 30, 19__, the month prior to the death of Jason Ewing.

5. Proceeds received by the corporation as the beneficiary of Jason Ewing's life insurance policy.

6. Company management's estimate of costs to comply with regulations of the U.S. Environmental Protection Agency (EPA) regarding protection and clean-up costs on gas pumps and underground tanks. The company has engaged a consultant to make an independent study regarding such costs.

The computations of the adjusted net assets of Ewing Enterprises, Inc. as of April 15, 19__, as shown in Exhibit D (page 212) is $3,982,969.

Valuation of Common Stock Interest. Since our purpose is to value the common stock, it is necessary to determine how much of the $3,982,969 adjusted net asset value is allocable to the common stock interest.

As of April 15, 19__, the company had 2,596 shares of outstanding nonvoting preferred stock. The preferred stock is callable at $100 par value, with a 5 percent cumulative dividend rate.

Revenue Ruling 83-120, 1983-2CB 170 provides guidance to the valuation of preferred stock. It states that the most important factors to be considered in determining the value of preferred stock are its yield, dividend coverage, and protection of its liquidation preference.

The ruling also states that the dividend yield determines whether the preferred stock has a value equal to its par value. It specifically states the following:

> Whether the yield of the preferred stock supports a valuation of the stock at par value depends in part on the adequacy of the dividend rate. The adequacy of the dividend rate should be determined by comparing its dividend rate with the dividend rate of high-grade publicly traded preferred stock. A lower yield than that of high-grade preferred stock indicates a preferred stock value of less than par. In addition, whether the preferred stock has a fixed dividend rate and is nonparticipating influences the value of the preferred stock. . . . A publicly traded preferred stock for a company having a similar business and similar assets with similar liquidation preferences, voting rights, and other similar terms would be the ideal comparable for determining yield required in arms length transactions for closely held stock. Such ideal comparables will frequently not exist. In such circumstances, the most comparable publicly-traded issues should be selected for comparison and appropriate adjustments made for differing factors.

In short, the valuation method for preferred stock is to capitalize the annual dividend at a market rate equal to the rate of returns from similar grade marketable securities and then make appropriate adjustments for variations.

The ruling is essential for the determination of the fair market value of the preferred stock. However, it is not our objective here to value the preferred stock. Our goal is to determine the portion of the adjusted net asset value that is allocable to the common stock interest. A prudent investor planning to purchase only the common stock would allocate the adjusted net asset value to the preferred stock at the par value, as the preferred stock is callable at par and has a liquidation preference at par. A preferred stock having a market value less than its par value does not necessarily mean that the value attrition would increase the portion of the adjusted net asset value allocable to the common stock. Accordingly, the adjusted net asset value allocable to the common stock should be determined by accounting for the preferred stock at its par value, as follows:

Adjusted net asset value (Exhibit D)	$3,982,969
Less: Amount allocated to preferred stock at $100 par value per share	(259,600)
Adjusted net asset value allocable to the two classes of common stock	$3,723,369
Shares of common stock outstanding	37,076
Adjusted net asset value per share of common stock	$ 100.43

DISCOUNT FOR GENERAL LACK OF MARKETABILITY AND NONCONTROLLING INTEREST

The adjusted net asset value figure of $3,723,369 allocable to common stock is a value based on intrinsic factors (i.e., the aggregate values of the underlying assets). Since Ewing Enterprises, Inc. is a closely held business, a discount for general lack of marketability is appropriate. The lack of marketability discount concept recognizes the fact that closely held stock interests are less attractive and have fewer potential purchasers than similar publicly traded stock.

Recent cases in valuation provided substantial discounts for non-marketability and other inhibiting factors. In *Estate of Arthur F. Little, Jr.* [TCM 1982-26, CCH Dec. 38729(M)], the Tax Court allowed a total discount of 60 percent for shares of restricted stock of a publicly held company. The court allowed a 35 percent discount for sales restrictions, a 15 percent discount for an irrevocable two-year voting proxy agreement, and a 10 percent discount for shares that were held in escrow.

In addition to the general lack of marketability as discussed above, the 50 percent interest in common stock owned by Jason Ewing does not represent a controlling interest in the company. An acquisition of such interest does not afford a potential purchaser the power to fully influence management and day-to-day business operations. An acquisition of a 50 percent interest may afford a greater discount than a mere discount for the general lack of marketability. Put another way, the value of a noncontrolling interest (50 percent or less) is lower than the per-share value of an interest in the same company that would have control (more than 50 percent).

The extent to which any restriction on marketability and inhibiting factors reduce the value of a specific stock is determined based on facts and circumstances. In view of the depressed earnings of Ewing Enterprises, Inc. over the recent past years, the noncontrolling block of stock, and the general lack of marketability factors, a 30 percent discount is appropriate for the valuation of the 50 percent voting common stock owned by Jason Ewing. An additional 10 percent discount is appropriate for the valuation of the other 50 percent nonvoting common stock owned by Jason Ewing. This additional 10 percent discount accounts for the nonvoting privileges of the stock. As held in *Estate of Arthur F. Little, Jr.,* the Tax Court allows a 15 percent discount for an irrevocable two-year voting proxy agreement.

Applying the discounts, the value per share of the two classes of common stock are as follows:

	Class A voting	Class B nonvoting
Adjusted net asset value per share	$100.43	$100.43
Less: discount for general lack of marketability, noncontrolling interest, and depressed earnings—30%	(30.13)	(30.13)
Discount for nonvoting privilege—10%	—	(10.04)
Adjusted net asset value per share after discount	$ 70.30	$ 60.26

Conclusion

Based on the information and analyses summarized in this report, it is our opinion that, as of April 15, 19__ , the fair market value of each of the two classes of common stock held by Jason Ewing is as follows:

	Common stock		Total
	Class A voting	Class B nonvoting	
Value per share	$ 70.30	$ 60.26	
Number of shares held	9,269	9,269	
Total value	$651,611	$558,550	$1,210,161

Exhibit D

Ewing Enterprises, Inc. Computations of Adjusted Net Assets as of April 15, 19__

Description	Amount	
1. Total stockholders' equity as of December 31, 19 — (per audited statements)		$2,312,743
2. After-tax adjustment to retained earnings from LIFO to FIFO inventory method		
a. Retained earnings under LIFO	$1,924,982	
b. Retained earnings under FIFO	1,941,867	
Adjusted increase in retained earnings		16,885
3. Investments in affiliates		
a. Westar fueling (partnership)—approximate increase in earnings from 1/1/— to 4/30/— from unadjusted statements		
Earnings as of 4/30/—	$ 80,374	
Earnings as of 12/31/—	54,173	
Increase	$ 26,201	
50% interest		13,101*
b. Atlas petroleum (corporation)—approximate increase in after-tax earnings from 11/1/— to 4/31/— as provided by management		3,526
4. Investment in securities		
a. Port of Naples—$100,000		(16,821)
b. Atlantic Resources—272 shares		1,349

Notes to Computations of Adjusted Net Assets

Investments in Affiliates.   Adjustments for investments in affiliates were based on respective affiliate management's representations that the shareholder's equity approximates the fair market value of such affiliates. We relied upon such representations without verification. The net adjustment to Westar Fueling involves the determination of the approximate after-tax earnings for the period between January 1, 19__ to April 30, 19__. Increase in capital contribution to Tri-Met Fueling during the same period is not adjusted, as it involves a mere shifting of funds.

Fixed Asset Mark-up.   Adjustments to fixed assets represent company management's appraisal of fair market value of the fixed assets. Company management represented that they are knowledgeable in the determination of market value of these types of fixed assets. Appraisals by independent appraisers usually are obtained and preferred. We relied upon management's valuation as accurate and reliable and have no reason to believe that these valuations should not be used.

Vehicles and Furniture/Fixtures. No adjustments were made to vehicles ($493,165) and furniture and fixtures ($168,667) as shown on the 12/31/__ balance sheet, as company management represented that their net book values fairly reflected the fair market value of these assets.

Other Fixed Assets.   In adjusting the net book value of other fixed assets to fair market value, we divided the fixed assets into four separate categories:

- Real properties (and improvements and equipment thereon) owned and to be kept by the company indefinitely.

- Real properties (and improvements and equipment thereon) owned by the company but which management intends to dispose of.

- Real properties leased by the company and on which the company management intends to continue to operate businesses over the lease terms.

- Real properties leased by the company and which the company management intends to abandon.

Real Properties Owned and to Be Kept.   In adjusting net book value to fair market value for real properties owned and to be kept by the company, no adjustments are provided for potential trapped-in income taxes related to the appreciation. Although such an adjustment could be proper, the courts have on various occasions rejected such an adjustment. In *Edwin A Gallum* [1974-284 TCM (CCH) p. 1320], U.S. Tax Court rejected an adjustment for potential capital gains tax. It states,

> In arriving at our determination we have rejected the argument of [taxpayer] that a discount should be allowed for a potential capital gains tax that would result if the investment portfolio were to be liquidated. The record does not establish that the management of the portfolio had any immediate plans to liquidate the investment portfolio. Furthermore, it is possible that the management at some time in the future may dispose of certain or all of the investment assets without incurring a capital gains tax. Under these circumstances, such a discount is not appropriate. See Estate of Frank A Cruikshank (Dec. 15, 1941), 9 T.C. 162 (1947); Estate of Alvin Thalheimer (Dec. 32, 714(M)), T.C. Memo. 1974-203.

The court's position seems to be based on the fact that the taxpayer had no intention to liquidate its investment holding at the time of the valuation. Although the court has denied an adjustment for capital gains tax, a trapped-in capital gains tax is a liability that arguably should be recognized. Support for this position is found in the American Institute of Certified Public Accountants official guidelines for the preparation of personal financial statements, where assets with unrealized appreciation are adjusted to market value. They unequivocally take the position that any upward adjustment to market value must be accompanied by a deduction for the related capital gains tax. The text of the AICPA position is this:

> An accrual for income taxes on net unrealized appreciation (the difference between the tax basis of the net assets and estimated value) is required in the presentation of the estimated value column in personal financial statements. This accrual is necessary because the estimated values cannot generally be realized without incurring taxes.
> —AICPA, *Audits of Personal Financial Statements* (New York, 1968), p. 5.

Real Properties Owned and to be Sold.   For real properties and related equipment to be sold by the management, we adjusted the value to account for potential income tax effects. We believe such an adjustment is proper since management's intention is to dispose of the assets. The fact that management intends to sell is distinguishable from the Edwin A. Gallum case.

Improvements and Equipment on Leased Properties to be Abandoned.   Since management's intention is to abandon such assets, a potential investor would not be willing to pay for shares of stock whose intrinsic value includes the full net book value of such assets. A payment of its full net book value would result in an inherent immediate loss in the stock investment. Accordingly, improvements and equipment are adjusted downward to reflect the after-tax losses from intended abandonment.

Other Improvements and Equipment of Leased Properties.   Company management represents that the net book value of these improvements and equipment approximates the fair market value.

Equipment in Storage.   Equipment with a total net book value of $40,509 was in storage and not being utilized. Management estimated the fair market value of these idle assets to be $25,000. No income tax effects are given to the downward adjustments since management does not intend to dispose of these assets in the near future. No income tax effect adjustment was given in accordance with the argument as suggested by the Tax Court in *Edwin A. Gallum.*

After-Tax Loss from January 1, 19__ to April 30, 19__.   The approximate tax loss is based on unaudited and unadjusted financial statements for the four months ended April 30, 19__. We did not verify the accuracy of such information.

Compliance with EPA Regulations.   The estimated after-tax costs to comply with the EPA regulations were provided by company management. The company is conducting a study on the costs for EPA compliance. Company management expects that the study will be completed in November 19__. Adjustments to the estimated compliance costs should be made if the study indicates any major differences in compliance costs.

Cumulative Income Tax Effects.   The cumulative income tax effects are computed as follows:

a.	Approximate increase in earnings from Westar Fueling	$ 13,101
b.	Increase in value on owned properties intended to be sold	1,213,641*
c.	Decrease in value on improvements and equipment on leased properties to be abandoned	(57,987)
d.	Approximate loss of Ewing Enterprises, Inc. from 1/1/__ to 4/30/__	(149,000)
e.	Estimated costs to comply with EPA regulations	(220,000)
	Cumulative increase in value subject to income tax effects	$ 799,755
	Approximate tax rate*	30%
	Cumulative Income Tax Effects	$ 239,926

*Almost all of this amount would be taxable as a long-term capital gain (the law as it existed at the time the above valuation was prepared). Always use the tax rate applicable at the time of the valuation.

VALUATION EXAMPLE 4
COMBINATION METHOD—COMPARABLES AND NET ASSET VALUE

This next valuation uses a combination method based on two approaches: comparables and net asset value. The purpose of the valuation was to value common and preferred stock to be issued under a recapitalization. Because of the size of the company being valued and to protect the identity of the client, some facts concerning the company and actual dates involved have been changed.

Business History and Industry Outlook

J.J. Bean, Inc. was founded in 1939 by J.J. Bean, the principal shareholder. It was incorporated in Massachusetts and specialized in the manufacture of tailored sportcoats. Its main production facilities are located at 15th and Fenway Street, Beantown, Massachusetts.

Over the years, J.J. Bean, Inc. branched out into other apparel under the leadership of its founder. It began to manufacture women's apparel in 1960.

J.J. Bean, Inc. presently produces men's tailored sportcoats, suits, slacks, sweaters, and assorted sportswear. Its ladies division produces women's jackets, pants, blouses, and other assorted articles. In 19__, menswear accounted for about 60 percent of the total sales, while womenswear accounted for the remaining 40 percent. Tailored clothing continues to be the solid base of the business. In menswear, it is about 70 percent; in womenswear, 45 percent.

J.J. Bean, Inc. is noted as a slacks specialist and is one of the largest slacks makers in the country in its price range. Also, it is well known for in-stock service, maintaining substantial inventories to handle customers' at-once orders.

J.J. Bean, Inc.'s various menswear divisions have approximately 50 representatives throughout the country and the womenswear division has approximately ten. Sales are made to major department stores and specialty stores throughout the country. The number of active accounts is approximately 4,500.

J.J. Bean, Inc. has four wholly-owned subsidiaries:

- Pan Am Sporting Corp.

- J.J. Spooling Co., Inc.

- J & R Clothing, Inc.

- J.J. Bean Underwear, Inc.

Total current employment by J.J. Bean, Inc. and subsidiaries is approximately 1,800 people.

Except for fiscal years ended September 19__ and 19__, the company has experienced growth under the leadership of J.J. Bean. He has been the key driving force in the business. He devotes 12 or more hours a day to operating the business. He personally manages the day-to-day operations of the sales, styling, and design offices, while Phillip Dalmas (president and shareholder) manages the production facilities.

J.J. Bean is a businessman and designer, as well as an advertising pro. He formulates the strategic plans of the company and makes all major business and personnel decisions. He directs and oversees the development and design of all new product lines, such as the company's latest additions of women's specialty wear and men's specialty merchandise. It was J.J. Bean who spearheaded the company's drive to become one of the first companies producing women's specialty clothing.

J.J. Bean also personally selects and purchases the fabric for the company's products. He also decides on the price range of the company's product lines.

J.J. Bean shapes the company's image by formulating all its marketing and promotional campaigns. He also coordinates with licensees in developing national advertising campaigns. He was instrumental in developing the new, successful plentiful and up-beat style advertising approach which greatly benefited the licensees.

J.J. Bean single-handedly builds up the company's clientele. He is the driving force in developing a binding and lasting relationship with all clients by dealing with them personally. He constantly entertains, assists, and nurtures the clients. He also maintains personal relationships with clients.

J.J. Bean, Inc. has four classes of stock authorized and outstanding. The current outstanding shares are as follows:

Class of stock	Number of shares outstanding
Common stock	
Class A voting	10.00
Class B nonvoting	124.00
Preferred stock	
Class A nonvoting	500.00
Class B nonvoting	2,375.00

J.J. Bean owns 100 percent of the outstanding voting common stock. He also owns a number of shares of nonvoting common stock and class B preferred stock.

No public sale of any stock has occurred over the past five years.

The apparel industry is considered a risky and highly volatile industry. Although apparel represents a necessity of life, both for protection against the elements and for reasons of social decency, most clothing purchases can be postponed indefinitely.

The basic analysis (dated December 19__) from Standard & Poor's *Industry Surveys* stated that 19__ was a record year for the number of bankruptcies in the apparel industry. It indicated that the number of bankruptcies was twice or even three times as high as the previous year. In addition, the unemployment rate for apparel workers hit 18.4 percent in April 19__, the highest postwar level since the record 19.3 percent registered in March 1975.

The current analysis (dated April 21, 19__) from Standard & Poor's *Industry Surveys* indicated that the apparel industry was soft in 19__ but is in a rebound. Members of the industry attributed the rebound to improved retail sales. However, they cautioned that price promoting by retailers was partly responsible for the retail sales growth.

The Value Line *Investment Survey* (dated September 9, 19__) also stated that retail clothing sales grew by 18.7 percent adjusted for inflation in the second quarter of 19__. The improved retail clothing sales in the second quarter of 19__ would have translated into improved sales for the manufacturers in subsequent quarters when retailers rebuild their inventories. This delayed effect thus should have caused an upsurge in manufacturing sales in the third quarter of 19__ since retailers had been operating with extremely lean inventories during the early part of 19__. As Value Line stated in its report, retailers have significantly stepped up their buying for the fall season, providing an additional fillup to bookings that were already on an uptrend as a result of storekeepers' need to rebuild their bare bones inventories.

Notwithstanding the encouraging industry forecast, Value Line also cautioned unforeseeable problems:

> Besides the usual caveat having to do with surprise changes in the economy, there's one particularly applicable to the apparel industry: As we move through a new year, overall industry estimates tend to be reduced. That's because in a high-style industry, some of the participants are likely to stray off the path of current fashion, thereby losing a portion of profitability, even falling into the red. There's no way our analysts can spot a backfiring fashion line until the industry is in season.

Sales volume of J.J. Bean, Inc. and subsidiaries was $69.5 million for fiscal year ended September 30, 19__ and dropped down to $65.8 million the next year. Management estimated that the sales volume for the next fiscal year would be slightly less than $60 million. Management indicated that its peak sales period is between April and September.

Despite the encouraging industry news and the improved clothing sales in the second quarter of 19__ announced by Value Line, J.J. Bean, Inc. still experienced a drop of more than $5 million in sales for fiscal year 19__ compared to the preceding year.

Management attributed the decline in sales over the past two years to increasingly keen competition. One noticeable source of competition came from overseas. In 19__, the value of apparel imports rose 9.2 percent to $7.1 billion at wholesale. Over the past few years, imports have risen at a faster rate than has overall U.S. consumption of apparel and footwear, a pattern that is not expected to change in the future. Foreign-made clothing is estimated to account for one out of every four garments sold in the United States.

In particular, imports from Mainland China grew 47 percent during 19__. Recently, China and the U.S. entered into a new five-year textile agreement which allows the Chinese an average annual growth of 3.5 percent in textile sales in the U.S. Presently, the exact details of the agreement are not available. Management indicated that the new agreement could have an adverse impact on the company, although the magnitude of any such impact cannot be ascertained at the present time.

Management stated that it does not anticipate or foresee any real growth in its sales volume. It stated that its main goal is to maintain its current market share. Management indicated that its most likely sales volume for next year would be within the range of $50–$60 million.

In summary, the industry forecast is encouraging. J.J. Bean, Inc., however, has not experienced the sales rebound mentioned in the forecast. Its sales volume for fiscal year 19__ (just ended) is the lowest over the last three years.

Seemingly, the increasingly keen competition overshadows the daylight of the industry forecast for J.J. Bean, Inc. and its subsidiaries.

Comparative Approach to Valuation

Selection of Comparable Corporations. In searching for comparable corporations for the purpose of valuing J.J. Bean, Inc. and subsidiaries (herein referred to as J.J. Bean, Inc.), both financial and nonfinancial characteristics were considered. Factors considered in the selection process included these:

- Business activities;

- Competitive standing in terms of the company's reputation, depth of management, and growth rate;

- Profitability in terms of net income to sales; and

- Corporate capital structure (i.e., long term debt to total equity).

Financial ratios were also developed to determine the operating and financial posture of J.J. Bean, Inc. in comparison to the selected comparable companies.

Five publicly held companies were initially selected as possible comparables from a candidate list of over 15 corporations that are in the apparel industry. The other corporations were not selected because their product lines are quite different from those of J.J. Bean, Inc. (Appendix A [not shown in this book] provides a partial listing of corporations.) Subsequent examination of corporate financial information resulted in further elimination of two of the five companies: Philips Van Heusen and Oxford, Inc.

Philips Van Heusen was eliminated because its overall operating performances (i.e., percent of net income to net sales and rate of return on total assets) were comparatively lower than those of J.J. Bean, Inc. and the other four public companies over the five-year period under review. Its capital structure (i.e., percentage of long term debt to total equity) was also materially different from that of J.J. Bean, Inc.

Oxford, Inc. was also excluded because of its substantial sales to two principal customers. J. C. Penney Co. and Sears, Roebuck & Co. accounted for 20 percent and 12 percent of its sales, respectively, in fiscal year 19__.

The three publicly held corporations selected as the best possible comparable corporations are (1) Hartmarx (formerly Hart, Schaffner and Marx), (2) Palm Beach, Incorporated, and (3) Cluett, Peabody.

Business Summary of Selected Comparables.   Following is a business overview of the three companies selected as comparables.

1. *Hartmarx.* Hartmarx is the leading diversified manufacturer and retailer of men's and women's apparel. Its main emphasis is on quality and fashion. Through a recent acquisition, it is expanding into the low-markup market for men's suits and sportcoats.

    Its product lines include suits, sportcoats, slacks, outercoats, rainwear, and sportswear. Men's apparel is manufactured under such high-quality labels as Hart Schaffner & Marx, Hickey Freeman, Society Brand, and Austin Reed of Regent Street.

    The company also operates specialty stores. About two-thirds of the clothing sold in the specialty stores is produced by its manufacturing division. Its manufacturing operations accounted for 74 percent of its net profit in 19__; its retailing activities accounted for the remaining profit.

2. *Palm Beach, Incorporated.* Palm Beach manufactures a diversified line of apparel with concentration on brand names. The Palm Beach name is used in men's tailored clothing, blazers for men, and tailored clothing and blazers for boys. Other clothing labels include Evan-Picone, Gant, Haspel, Pierre Cardin, and John Weitz. Palm Beach sells directly to department stores and clothing specialty stores.

    Palm Beach is the smallest of the three companies selected. However, Palm Beach has experienced relatively rapid growth over the past few years.

3. *Cluett, Peabody.* Cluett, Peabody manufactures a diversified line of apparel. It owned eight retail stores until their recent sales in July. Manufacturing accounted for 91 percent of its profit and retailing accounted for 4 percent of profit in 19__. The remaining 5 percent of its profit was derived from the licensing of trademarks and patents. Its Shoeneman division produces men's and women's suits and sportcoats and a line of designer clothing under the Halston name. Other apparel manufactured includes men's dress, sport, and knit shirts, jackets, sweaters, underwear, sportswear, and hosiery.

The three companies selected are larger and more diversified than J. J. Bean, Inc. These differences, however, should not deter them from being considered as comparable to J.J. Bean, Inc.

Rarely will two companies be identical. If unduly restrictive criteria were set for the selection of comparable companies, it would be virtually impossible to find a comparable. This would render the comparative approach to valuation virtually meaningless. In *Estate of Ethyl L. Goodrich* TCM 1978-248, CCH Dec 35250(M), taxpayer rejected certain companies as comparables of a newspaper publishing company that was being valued because these companies had (1) much smaller or larger revenues, (2) policies of growth through corporate acquisition (instead of only internal growth), or (3) revenues from activities other than newspaper publishing. The U.S. Tax Court stated that such a selection process was too selective and excluded companies that in our view are of probative value in the determination of the value of the Central Newspapers stock.

The size differential and product diversification of the comparables selected indicate that they are less risky than J.J. Bean, Inc. from the investment standpoint. These differences can be reasonably accounted for in arriving at the value of J.J. Bean, Inc. The use of larger and more diversified companies as comparables is acceptable. A case in point is *Sol Koffler*, TCM 1978-159, CCH Dec 35119(M), wherein the comparable company selected for the valuation of a luggage manufacturing company was the largest luggage manufacturer in the United States. In addition, it also manufactured and sold furniture, toys, and small computers. The company was accepted as a comparable with adjustments made to account for the dissimilarities.

The three comparables are reasonably similar to the business activities conducted by J.J. Bean, Inc., as all specialize in good quality men's clothing. They all manufacture men's suits and sportcoats. In particular, Hartmarx is the leader in quality men's suits and blazers. It is a more integrated operation than J.J. Bean, Inc., as it has its own sales outlets. Its sales outlets provide a greater visibility of its products and facilitate the marketing of its products. Being the leader in quality clothing with a well integrated operation, many potential investors would view its operations as a benchmark of excellence. Its stock value and price-earnings ratio would likely represent the starting point for a potential buyer to determine the price for a less established and less integrated apparel manufacturer like J.J. Bean, Inc.

Financial Analyses. To determine the operating and financial posture of J.J. Bean, Inc. in comparison to the three selected comparable companies, certain ratios were computed to determine growth, profitability, and financial stability.

1. *Sales Growth.* J.J. Bean, Inc. and Palm Beach, Inc. have been growing at a comparatively rapid pace. Hartmarx and Cluett, Peabody experienced comparatively less growth. This disparity is attributable to the fact that Hartmarx and Cluett, Peabody are substantially larger and have reached the point where the relative growth rate would be low.

Palm Beach's sales were about seven times that of J.J. Bean, Inc. over the past five years. The average annual growth for both over this five-year period was around 20 percent. The following table shows the growth status (Year 1 is the most recent year):

| | Annual sales growth % from previous year | | | | | |
	Year 5	Year 4	Year 3	Year 2	Year 1	Annual average
J.J. Bean, Inc.	7.5	35.5	36.3	26.1	(5.4)	20.0
Palm Beach	13.1	39.0*	25.9	21.8	(1.3)	19.7
Hartmarx	6.8	3.9	6.9	20.8*	5.7	8.8
Cluett, Peabody	(2.3)	16.6*	9.9	10.6	5.9	8.1

*Reflects mergers and acquisitions.

2. *Profitability.* Over the past five years, the percentage of net income to gross revenue of J.J. Bean, Inc. climbed from 2.3 percent in Year 5 to 3.2 percent in Year 3, but then dropped to 0.7 percent in Year 1. Palm Beach's net income percentage declined steadily from 5.9 percent in Year 5 to 1.9 percent in Year 1. Hartmarx moved steadily upward from 3.0 percent to 3.7 percent. Cluett, Peabody fluctuated between 2.1 percent and 3.3 percent.

Net income as a percentage of gross revenue shows the average rate of profit earned on each dollar of revenue received. J.J. Bean, Inc. and Palm Beach each demonstrated a relatively poor trend on this performance measure. J.J. Bean, Inc. lacked income stability; while Palm Beach was on a downward trend because of marginal or poor performance by some of its operating divisions. Hartmarx and Cluett, Peabody performed relatively better in terms of income stability. The following table shows the relationship of net income to revenue:

| | % of Net income to revenue | | | | | |
	Year 5	Year 4	Year 3	Year 2	Year 5	Average
J.J. Bean, Inc.	2.3	2.3	3.0	3.2	0.7	2.30
Palm Beach	5.9	4.2	3.5	2.7	1.9	3.64
Hartmarx	3.0	3.3	3.3	3.4	3.7	3.34
Cluett, Peabody	3.3	2.6	2.1	2.6	2.7	2.66

An analysis of rate of return (i.e., net income over average total assets) also shows that the profitability of J.J. Bean, Inc. has been unstable. Its rate of return on assets climbed from 8.6 percent in Year 4 to 11.2 percent in Year 3, but then dropped dramatically to 2.3 percent in Year 1. The following table shows the rate of return on assets:

	Rate of return (%)				
	Year 4	Year 3	Year 2	Year 1	Average
J.J. Bean, Inc.	8.6	11.2	11.2	2.2	8.3
Palm Beach	9.6	7.4	6.0	4.1	6.8
Hartmarx	6.1	6.0	6.3	7.0	6.4
Cluett, Peabody	4.8	4.7	6 0	5.4	5.2

As the table indicates, J.J. Bean, Inc. experienced a relatively high rate of return except for Year 1. A closer examination, however, reveals that its high rate of return was attributable to its low level of current assets. J.J. Bean, Inc. has been financing its accounts receivable externally by factoring, thereby reducing its asset base. The comparable companies basically financed their accounts receivable internally. Should J.J. Bean, Inc. have financed its outstanding accounts receivable internally, its rate of return on assets would be appreciably lower.

3. *Financial Position.* J.J. Bean's financial position is less secure than that of the comparable companies. The following tables show the current ratio and the quick asset ratio of the respective companies:

	Current ratio					
	Year 5	Year 4	Year 3	Year 2	Year 1	Average
J.J. Bean, Inc.	1.58	1.56	1.56	1.69	1.99	1.67
Palm Beach	2.7	2.2	1.8	1.7	2.9	2.26
Hartmarx	3.3	3.4	2.7	2.3	2.6	2.86
Cluett, Peabody	3.5	3.3	3.6	3.0	3.3	3.34

	Quick asset ratio			
	Year 3	Year 2	Year 1	Average
J.J. Bean, Inc.	.21	.11	.17	.16
Palm Beach	.70	.67	1.27	.88
Hartmarx	1.15	1.02	1.19	1.12
Cluett, Peabody	1.55	1.20	1.33	1.36

Undoubtedly, the low level of current assets was due to the external financing of accounts receivable. A review of the accounts receivable records indicates a severe cash shortage. J.J. Bean, Inc. has been continuously receiving advances from its factoring company in excess of its outstanding accounts receivable balance. In April 19__, total advances from the factoring company were $11.6 million in excess of its outstanding accounts receivable.

In summary, J.J. Bean, Inc. has experienced sales growth in most, but not all, recent years. Such growth, however, was not unique, as Palm Beach also experienced a good rate of growth. It does not now appear likely that J.J. Bean, Inc. will continue its past growth, since its sales volume stagnated in the range of $60 million in Year 2 and Year 1, and it is projected that next year sales will also be at this same level.

The profit margin (i.e., net income as a percentage of revenue) of J.J. Bean, Inc. has been fluctuating over the last few years. It moved to a high of 3.2 percent in Year 3 and then dropped down to .7 percent in Year 2. Its profit margin has been highly volatile compared to that of Hartmarx and Cluett, Peabody. Except for Year 3, its profit margin was also consistently less than that of Palm Beach.

The unstable profit margin of J.J. Bean, Inc. was partially attributable to its high level of external financing of accounts receivable. Its earnings potential is relatively sensitive to the movement of market interest rates.

The financial position of J.J. Bean, Inc. has been weak in relation to the comparables. It has experienced cash flow problems and has repeatedly required advances from its factor company (lender) in excess of its outstanding accounts receivable in order to continue to finance its production and maintain inventory levels.

Nonfinancial Analyses. Besides the financial differences (as discussed above) between J.J. Bean, Inc. and the comparables, nonfinancial characteristics must also be considered. These main nonfinancial characteristics are diversification and depth of management. The apparel industry is sometimes classified as a relatively high-risk industry. This risk can be reduced through sound management practices and broad-based diversification.

Although J.J. Bean manufactures different lines of products, its main concentration is in slacks and sweaters. Furthermore, its products are manufactured only under one brand name label. The manufacturing operations of the comparables are much more diversified in terms of product lines and name labels. For example, Hartmarx has about 19 brand-name labels for men's suits and blazers.

Having one brand name label makes J. J. Bean, Inc. more susceptible to the problems of off-price retailing. Off-price retailing has been a serious problem for J. J. Bean, Inc., as its products have continuously and unseemingly appeared in discount stores. The discount stores sell the products at off-price (i.e., at a substantially lower price). Hence, consumers would purchase the products at discount stores at substantial savings instead of paying a full price at department stores and specialty stores. Some department and specialty stores would, in turn, stop purchasing and carrying the products or would only purchase the products at a lower price. Off-price retailing thus has the effect of dissipating the value and reputation of the products. This ultimately affects the profitability of the products.

While off-price retailing is an industry-wide problem, medium-price-range products such as those of J. J. Bean, Inc. are more susceptible to the problem. With only one name label, the profitability of J. J. Bean, Inc. could be seriously impaired should its name label dissipate in value due to off-price retailing.

Although J. J. Bean, Inc. has been successful, its success is solely the result of the work of its founder, J. J. Bean. J. J. Bean is paramount to the company's success and reputation. He is personally involved in almost every facet of the company operations; he personally (1) purchases the fabrics, (2) develops advertising and promotional campaigns, (3) formulates pricing, (4) services and entertains clients, and (5) makes all major business decisions. In essence, the company is faced with thin management.

In summary, J. J. Bean, Inc. is less attractive than the selected comparables from investment and business standpoints because of thin management and the lack of diversification in products and name labels.

Price-earnings Multiples.   To establish a value for J. J. Bean, Inc., a price-earnings ration must be determined by analyzing the respective ratios of the comparables. In connection with the determination of an appropriate price-earnings ratio, the U.S. Tax Court has stated:

> In times of wide speculation and resulting fluctuations in the stock market, we are extremely doubtful that the price at which a stock is traded on the exchange on any particular day is a true reflection of what an investor would pay for the stock if he was looking primarily to the historical earnings of the corporation to determine a fair price. We believe such an investor would give more weight to price-earnings ratios of comparable stocks during each of the years under consideration in determining a multiple that he can apply to the historical earnings of a corporation whose stock he is buying to determine the price he would pay for that stock.
> —*Estate of Oakley J. Hall*, TCM 1975-141, CCH Dec. 33198(M).

The present stock market has been extremely bullish. The stock market began one of its greatest rallies in stock prices in 50 years in August 19__. The Dow Jones Industrial Average climbed from about 100 in August to 305 in June 19__.

No bull market in modern history has gotten off to as strong a start as the current one, as the following table illustrates:

Bull market	*Gain after 10 months
Aug. '21–Sep. '29	34%
June '32–Mar. '37	34
Apr. '42–May '46	47
June '49–Aug. '56	33
Oct. '57–Aug. '59	22
June '62–Feb. '66	33
Oct. '66–Nov. '68	31
May '70–Jan. '73	44
Oct. '74–Sep. '76	41
Mar. '78–Nov. '80	14
Aug. '82	59

*Based on S&P composite index of 500 stocks (402 stocks in 1921–29 calculation).

In light of the unprecedented bullishness of the market, it is inappropriate to rely entirely on the current price-earnings ratios to determine the fair market value of J. J. Bean, Inc. The proper price-earnings ratio for a buyer of a closely held business should be a normative amount free from excessive, exaggerated, or depressed price factors.

If a potential buyer relies unequivocally on the current price-earnings ratio, he could be faced with a disastrous result. As a matter of fact, the bullish sentiments had taken a disastrous toll on some unwary investors. The bullish sentiments attracted many companies to go public. Enthusiastic investors in some of these companies faced a murderous dive in their investments, as illustrated by the following table:

Stock	Offering price	High bid	Current bid	Change from offering
Fortune Systems	$22.00	$22.50	$ 9.37	– 57%
Victor Tech.	17.50	22.12	7.50	– 57
U.S. Telephone	14.00	26.62	6.50	– 53
Amgen	18.00	18.00	8.00	– 56
Kolff Medical	12.50	12.50	7.12	– 43
Micro D	16.00	16.75	9.25	– 42
Activision	12.00	12.62	8.75	– 27
Wicat	18.00	20.00	12.50	– 31
Integrated Genetics	13.00	13.00	9.00	– 31
Gtech	13.25	13.25	10.12	– 24
Damon Biotech	17.00	17.50	12.00	– 30
Biogen	23.00	24.25	14.50	– 37
Zymos	12.50	12.75	9.50	– 24

Source: New Issues Ft. Lauderdale, Fla., published in the *Chicago Tribune.*

An article in the *Chicago Tribune,* September 24, 19__, also suggested a less than bullish sentiment in the future from the chief investment officer of one of the nation's leading banks. The article stated that the investment officer thinks the Dow could tumble to the –050 range. That's about a 200–250 point drop.

As the Tax Court has articulated in *Estate of Oakley J. Hall,* a potential buyer of a closely held operating business would consider the price-earnings ratio of comparable stocks over a number of years in determining a price multiple and the price he would pay for the business. In arriving at an appropriate price-earnings ratio, the following factors deserve consideration:

1.   The unweighted average price-earnings ratio for the three comparable companies over a five-year period is 6.20. (See Schedule 1 for computations.)

2.   A weighted average of price-earnings ratios over the same period is 6.82. The weighted average approach is a form of exponential smoothing (a standard statistical procedure used for time-series data), giving greater weights to the ratios of the more recent periods. (See Schedule 2 for computations.)

3.   The June 10, 19__ issue of Value Line *Investment Survey* projected the average price-earnings ratio for the three-year period, 19__ to 19__, for the entire apparel industry to be about 9.0. This projected price-earnings ratio is close to the industry composite ratio of 8.3 in 19__, the period before the current market rally. This indicates that the current inflated price-earnings ratio is a temporary phenomenon. It also projected that the average annual price-earnings ratio for Palm Beach (a selected comparable that was relatively similar to J. J. Bean, Inc. in terms of growth rate and earnings stability) would come back down to 7.5 for the three-year period indicated above.

4. Available information on two recent acquisitions of apparel manufacturers indicates that the price-earnings multiple paid for these acquisitions was about 5.5. In April 19__, Leslie Fay, Inc. went private for approximately 5.4 times of earnings. Leslie Fay is a manufacturer of women's apparel such as sportswear, sweaters, and dresses.

    In December 19__, Hartmarx acquired Kuppenheimer Manufacturing Co., Inc. for about $28.8 million. Based on available information, it is estimated that the price-earnings ratio for the acquisition was about 5.6. Kuppenheimer manufactures men's low-price suits and sportcoats and operates 41 retail discount outlets.

No single prescribed formula or mathematical average may be applied to arrive at a price-earnings ratio. After considering the Value Line projections, the price-earnings ratios over a 5 1/2 year period, and two recent apparel acquisitions, a 7.0 earnings multiple would be a generous estimate of the price which a potential buyer would pay, given the past movement of market price-future earnings ratios and anticipation of future movement thereof.

Earnings Projections.   Once the price-earnings ratio is determined, it is necessary to determine the earnings potential of J. J. Bean, Inc. An important factor affecting the future earnings of J. J. Bean, Inc. is the prime interest rate, since its earnings are relatively sensitive to the movement of interest rates.

As of August 19__, the prime interest rate stood at 11 percent. Presently, there is a good deal of uncertainty among investors about the future behavior of interest rates. An officer of a large money-management firm indicated that there is a strong possibility that the prime rate will advance to 12 percent (*Chicago Tribune*, August 21, 19__). An August report, issued by the U.S. Congressional Budget Office, indicated that the federal deficits could total about $200 billion in each of the next several fiscal years if Congress and the Reagan administration do not agree on deficit reduction actions. The projected deficits could result in possibly higher interest rates and slower economic growth. In an article in *The Wall Street Journal* on August 22, 19__, two economists interviewed were concerned with the budget dispute and indicated that the deficit problems would put a crimp on interest-sensitive business sectors. Also, respected observers, like the Nobel Laureate Milton Friedman, have looked at the tremendous surge in the money supply that began in August 19__ and concluded that a return to rapid inflation is inevitable.

J. J. Bean, Inc. experienced good sales growth for the three-year period from 19__ to 19__. However, it is unlikely that growth pattern can be sustained. Sales volume was at $69.5 million for fiscal year 19__ and dropped down to $65.9 million for 19__. For the six months ended March 31, 19__, J. J. Bean, Inc. experienced net sales of $26 million. Although general economic forecasts for the apparel industry indicate a sales recovery for 19__, management anticipated that the sales volume would be slightly less than the $60 million level for fiscal year ended September 30, 19__. Thus, the company's sales volume has been declining two years in a row. Its sales volume has dropped by about 13.7 percent since 19__. Management attributed the sales reduction to the increasingly keen competition.

Management estimated that the most likely sales volume for next year would be around the $50–$60 million level. Management does not anticipate any real growth in the future. Management also indicated that sales reduction is possible due to the recent five-year textile agreement between China and the U.S., which allows the Chinese an average annual growth of 3.5 percent in textile sales in the U.S. Management indicated that the new agreement could have an adverse impact on the company, although the magnitude of any such impact cannot be ascertained at the present time.

Given the continuing sales reduction for the two years ended in 19__, it is management's view that future sales volume will most likely be at the $60 million level. Taking into account the uncertainty of future interest rates, annual earnings will most likely be in the range of $1.3 million.

The $1.3 million earnings are determined after considering the following analyses:

1. *Regression Analysis:* Regression analysis is a mathematical technique which expresses earnings as a function of sales volume. In the present case, this technique was used to project the earnings potential associated with the expected future sales volume.

    Operating results for six years were used as the basic data for projecting the earnings potential. (See Schedule 3 for information.) Six years of data were used so that periods of high as well as low prime interest rates are included in the data base. (In Year 6 in Schedule 3, the prime rate was only 6.8 percent). Given a projected sales volume of $60 million for the future years, earnings of about $1.3 million are computed using regression analysis. To test the reasonableness of the projection, the earnings for Year 1 in Schedule 3 were projected at $1,329,582 for the anticipated $60 million sale volume. Management's estimate of net earnings after-tax for this year was also about $1.3 million. Thus, the regression-based earnings projection compares very favorably to the actual (projected) results reported by the management, lending credibility to the regression model.

2. *Simple Average of Earnings:* Since the sales volumes for Years 2, 3, and 4 in Schedule 3 are around the $60 million level, a simple average of the earnings for these years was computed to provide insight about the future earnings at the projected sales level of $60 million. An average computation can be helpful it is applied judiciously. The simple average of the three-year's earnings is $1,302,519. (See Schedule 4 for computations.)

3. *Weighted Average of Earnings:* Instead of a simple average, a weighted average for the same three-year period would provide an average earnings of $1,301,889. The earnings for Year 1 are given twice as much weight as the previous years because the present conditions probably more closely resemble the future. (See Schedule 4 for computations.)

Comparative Value Based on Comparables. Applying a price-earnings ratio of 7.0 to a projected annual earnings of $1.3 million, the comparative value per share of common stock of J. J. Bean, Inc. is determined as follows:

Projected annual earnings		$1,300,000
Number of shares of common stock outstanding:		
Class A Voting	10	
Class B Nonvoting	124	
	134	
Projected annual earnings per share of voting or nonvoting stock		$ 9,701
Price-earnings multiple		7.0
Comparative value per share		$ 67,907

Comparative values for the voting common stock and nonvoting common stock are as follows:

	Common stock	
	Voting	Nonvoting
Comparative value per share	$ 67,907	$ 67,907
No. of shares outstanding	10	124
Total comparative value	$679,070	$8,420,468

Note: The only difference between the voting common stock and the nonvoting stock is the voting rights.

Discount Adjustments. The comparative value per share of common stock is based on the implicit assumption that ownership of the common stock of J. J. Bean, Inc. entails the same risk as ownership of the common stock of the comparables selected. However, the risk involved in investing in an actively traded corporation is less than that of purchasing a company for which there is no ready market.

As discussed in the earlier part of this report, J. J. Bean, Inc. differs from the comparables in the following respects:

■   size differential

■   less product and name label diversification

■   thin management

■   weak financial position

In addition, the stock of J. J. Bean, Inc. lacks marketability since it is not publicly traded and could not be marketed easily. To account for these differences, a reasonable discount must be provided. In an article entitled Nonmarketability Discounts Should Exceed Fifty Percent, 59 *Taxes* 25 (1981), the author suggests that a discount of 50 percent or more for closely held corporations should be applied. The author offered a reasonable basis for arriving at a 50 percent discount.

A possible step in determining a nonmarketability discount is to consider the public offering expenses or flotation costs necessary to create a hypothetical market for a closely held company. Such costs range from 5 percent for large offerings to 20 percent for smaller offerings based on aggregate offer price, as shown in the following:

Cost of flotation for offerings to general public through securities dealers

Size of issue ($ millions)	No.	Compensation (percent of gross proceeds)	Other expenses (percent of gross proceeds)
Under– .5	43	13.24	10.35
.5– .99	227	12.48	8.26
1.0– 1.99	271	10.60	5.87
2.0– 4.99	450	8.19	3.71
5.0– 9.99	287	6.70	2.03
10.0– 19.99	170	5.52	1.11
20.0– 49.99	109	4.41	.62
50.0– 99.99	30	3.94	.31
100.0–499.99	12	3.03	.16
Over –500.0	0	—	—
Total/averages	1,599	8.41	4.02

Source: "Cost of Flotation of Registered Issues, 1971–1972," Securities and Exchange Commission, December, 1974 at 9.

The SEC in its report also noted that, in addition to costs shown above, there was noncash compensation in the form of warrants or portions in many instances. It stated that such compensation has been prevalent among small equity issues, but during "hot issues" periods it has been prevalent among equity issues across all issues size strata. As a practical matter, valuation of these arrangements is not possible. Many closely held companies would most likely require such additional noncash compensation, and in appraising the cost to market such securities, these noncash items should be provided for.

While flotation costs provide a reasonable judgment of the cost of creating a public market for the stock being valued, other factors (such as size differential, business diversification, thin management, and financial position) must also be considered to give full effect of the privately held company in comparison to the publicly held companies.

An IRS study published in the IRS Valuation Guide for Income, Estate, and Gift Taxes [CCH Federal Estate and Gift Taxes, No. 264 Part II (5/11/82)], demonstrated the need for discount of size differentials. The study encompassed all manufacturing and merchandising corporations having their common stock traded or quoted on the New York Stock Exchange as of February 28, 1957. The following statistics are provided by the IRS:

Market price of outstanding stocks and long-term debts		No. of companies of this size	Price/earning ratios on basis of:	
Minimum value	Maximum value		Latest years earnings	5-Year average earnings
$ 1,000,000	$ 4,999,999	17	11.51	12.26
5,000,000	9,999,999	36	8.95	10.10
10,000,000	24,999,999	131	9.78	11.35
25,000,000	49,999,999	118	10.40	11.76
50,000,000	99,999,999	119	11.18	13.74
100,000,000	499,999,999	156	12.84	15.91
500,000,000	or more	51	16.13	18.56

The table indicates discount for size differential as much as 45 percent [i.e., 1–(8.95–16.13)] based on the latest year's earnings. The IRS states this:

> This tendency seems to be quite logical, however, in view of the practical consideration which most investors follow when making their buy and sell decisions. For one thing, the most successful companies gradually become the largest companies and in many cases become the leaders in their particular industries. Their very success and consequent size is ample evidence to the investing public that each of these enterprises has the ability to meet and survive competition and also has the ability to develop and grow either from internal expansion of its plant and products or by means of mergers. High quality management is ordinarily a prime requisite in such firms and with such the investing public is likely to place greater confidence in these corporations. Certainly, the securities of such corporations are better known to the public and become by the same fact more marketable. Any of these reasons could account for the greater interest, popularity, and consequent higher ratio of price to earnings. Regardless of the underlying causes, however, it is apparent that a genuine and easily discernible trend exists with respect to the size of the corporate enterprise and the price-earnings ratios which it displays.

Recent cases in valuation provided substantial discounts for nonmarketability and other inhibiting factors. In *Estate of Arthur F. Little, Jr.* [TCM 1982-26, CCH Dec. 38729(M)], the Tax Court allowed a total discount of 60 percent for shares of restricted stock of a publicly held company. (Restricted stock is stock of a publicly held company that is subject to certain sales restrictions.) The court allowed a 35 percent discount for sales restrictions, a 15 percent discount for an irrevocable two-year voting proxy agreement, and a 10 percent discount for shares that were held in escrow.

In *William T. Piper, Sr. Est.* [72TC No. 88, CCH Dec. 36,315], the court allowed a total discount of 64 percent for stock of a corporation which owned publicly traded securities and rental property. The court allowed a discount of 35 percent for lack of marketability, 17 percent for relatively unattractive investment portfolios, and another 12 percent for possible stock registration costs.

In *Sol Koffler* [TCM 1978-159], the taxpayer gifted common stock of a luggage manufacturing company, American Luggage Works, Inc. (ALW). The comparable selected for valuation was the largest luggage manufacturer in the U.S. It was also a diversified company engaged in the manufacture and sale of furniture, toys, and small computers, which accounted for about 25 percent of the net sales.

The dissimilarities between J. J. Bean, Inc. and its selected comparables resemble that of the *Sol Koffler* case in the following respects:

- thin management

- lack of product diversification

- failure to pay dividends to common stockholders

- nonmarketability

In *Sol Koffler*, the U.S. Tax Court provided a total discount of 60 percent or more to account for the differences between ALW and the comparable selected, as follows:

> Using Samsonite as a comparative, we think substantial discounts would be required in arriving at a price-earnings ratio for ALW: at least 15 percent for ALW's thin management; at least 30 percent for ALW's lack of diversification, its outmoded manufacturing facilities, its limit to the domestic market, its failure to pay any dividends since 1951, and its domination by a single family; and an equal discount for the fact that the ALW stock was not publicly traded and could not be easily marketed.

In view of the circumstances surrounding J. J. Bean, Inc., a discount of 35 percent is reasonable for the voting common stock. An additional 5 percent should be added to the nonvoting common stock because of its absence of voting rights. In *Estate of Arther F. Little* [TCM 1982-26, CCH Dec. 38729(M)], the U.S. Tax Court accepted a 15 percent discount for the loss of voting privilege of common stock because of an irrecoverable two-year proxy executed by the decedent.

Applying the discount as determined, the value of the common stock is as follows:

	Common Stock	
	Voting	Nonvoting
Discount for nonmarketability, thin management, weak financial position, lack of diversification, etc.	35%	35%
Discount for nonvoting privilege	—	5%
Total discount	35%	40%
Comparative value after discount	$441,400	$5,052,380
Comparative value per share	$ 44,140	$ 40,745

Net Asset Value of Underlying Assets

Revenue Ruling 59-60 states that the appraiser will accord primary consideration to earnings when valuing stocks of companies which sell products or services to the public. It states that net asset value should be a primary consideration for valuing closely held investment or real estate holding companies. According to Revenue Ruling 59-60, net asset value should be given minimum weight in the valuation of an operating company such as J. J. Bean, Inc.

The position expressed in Revenue Ruling 59-60 is fully supported by other authorities. For example, Judge Learned Hand stated in *Borg v. International Silver Co.* [11F. 2d 147, 152 (2nd Cir. 1925)] that Everyone knows that the value of shares in a commercial or manufacturing company depends chiefly on what it will earn.

Authorities on valuation also commented that earnings, not net asset value, are the ultimate factor in valuing operating businesses. In *The Financial Policy of Corporations* [5th ed., The Ronald Press, 1953], A.S. Dewing, an authority in valuation, takes the position squarely and openly that the ultimate and final controlling criterion of the value of a going business is earning power:

> The businessman, frankly, is interested neither in the engineer's appraisal of physical property, according to some arbitrary rule of unit values, nor in the accountant's report of past expenditures. He is interested primarily in the past earning capacity of the business so far as this can throw light on the future earnings in his hands. He is buying earning capacity and not physical assets.

In the *Estate of Oakley J. Hall,* the U.S. Tax Court also indicated that the net asset value approach plays a minor role in the valuation of an operating business. The court stated;

> We have not overlooked the fact that [the operating business] had a book value of $3,422,000 at September 30, 1967, but we deem it quite unlikely that such a value could have been realized if the company had been liquidated; further-more, there was no indication in the evidence that there was any intent to liquidate the company at the time of decendent's death.

In summary, the net asset value approach can be a meaningful technique for valuing an investment or real estate holding company. But it has some conceptual limitations for valuing a vigorous operating company such as J. J. Bean, Inc. Nonetheless, the net asset value of the business must be determined since courts have given this value some consideration. As the U.S. Tax Court stated in *Estate of Woodbury G. Andrews* [79 TC No. 58, CCH Dec. 39523],

> Certainly, the degree to which the corporation is actively engaged in produc-ing income rather than merely holding property for investment should influ-ence the weight to be given to the values arrived at under the different approaches but it should not dictate the use of one approach to the exclusion of all others.

Computations of Net Asset Value.   Net asset value represents the fair market value of the net assets (fair market value of all assets less liabilities) underlying the stock of the corporation. Pursuant to section 5(b) of Revenue Ruling 59-60, the net asset value (before discount adjust-ments) of J. J. Bean, Inc. as of September 30, 19__ was determined at about $9.6 million, as follows:

Shareholder's equity as of March 31, 19 —		$8,656,863
Adjustments:		
Add:	(1) After-tax LIFO reserve	850,000
	(2) Estimated after-tax earnings for the 6 months ended 9/30/8_	1,200,000
	(3) Approximated value of net assets from dormant corporation that merged into J. J. Bean, Inc.	700,000
Minus:	(1) Present value of estimated after-tax deferred compensation to officers and executives	(1,849,468)
Net asset value as of September 30, 19— before discount		$9,557,395

Valuation authorities have suggested that book value of assets shown on the balance sheet may be adjusted to reasonably reflect their market value when the net asset value approach is used. Revenue Ruling 59-60 also suggests that in computing the book value per share of stock, assets of the investment type should be revalued on the basis of their market price and the book value adjusted accordingly. This means that investment assets (i.e., assets not utilized in the trade of business of the corporation) held by either an investment or an operating company would be revalued at their market value. However, physical assets used in the trade of business (i.e., operating assets such as building and machinery) would not be revalued or adjusted. The approach advocated by the revenue ruling seems logical for an operating company, since the primary emphasis is on earnings and the actual value of operating assets could not be realized without ceasing operations and liquidating the business.

Adjustments may also be made to reflect elements that do not appear on the balance sheets. Items requiring consideration are intangible assets and deferred or contingent liabilities.

An examination of the balance sheet of J. J. Bean as of March 31, 19__ indicates that only one adjustment to the book value of assets is necessary: adjustment for the LIFO Reserve. The book value of the fixed assets should approximate their net realizable value.

As of September 30, 19__, the original costs of the land and building improvements were $2,428,145, with accumulated depreciation of only $258,005. The land and buildings are located in a deteriorated neighborhood where vandalism and crime are not an uncommon occurrence. An appraisal conducted as of October 20, 19__ indicated that the property had a remaining useful life of probably no greater than 20 years. The appraisal report also stated that the general industrial market would find the property to be somewhat limited in flexibility of use primarily because of its design, size, and age. In view of the circumstances, it is unlikely that the property would command a value substantially higher than the book value.

Examination of financial statements and other financial records also revealed that certain assets and liabilities not presented in the balance sheet must be accounted for to reflect the net asset value of the company. These undisclosed assets and liabilities are discussed below.

Corporate Merger. During fiscal year ended September 30, 19__, a corporation wholly owned by J. J. Bean was merged into J. J. Bean, Inc. The net asset value of the merged corporation was estimated by management at about $700,000.

Deferred Compensation to Officers. J. J. Bean, Inc has entered into various deferred compensation agreements with its key officers and executives. In general, the agreements state that the corporation shall pay the employee a sum of $___ yearly to commence in equal monthly installments at age 65 and continuing during the employee's lifetime.

If the employee should die after age 65 before receiving installment payments over a 10-year period, payments will continue to be made by the corporation for the remainder of the 10-year period to a beneficiary designated by the employee. The agreements are binding on the corporation and its successor.

The compensation, although deferred to the future, represents a true liability of the corporation. A. G. Cox, an actuarial consulting firm, made the determination of this liability. The after-tax deferred compensation amount is $1,849,468.

Allocation of Net Asset Value. The net asset value computed above represents the value of both common stock and preferred stock as a whole. Accordingly, the net asset value must be allocated to each class of stock outstanding. The amount of net value allocable to the preferred stock would be the liquidation preference amount. The remaining value would be allocated to the two classes of common stock. The net asset value for each share of common stock was determined to be $69,178, as follows:

Net asset value before discount	$9,557,395
Less: amount allocated to preferred stock at $100 per share of liquidation preferences	(287,500)
Net asset value allocable to common stock	$9,269,895
Net asset value per share of common stock ($9,269,895—134 shares)	$ 69,178

Net asset value for each class of common stock would be $691,780 for Class A voting stock and $8,578,072 for Class B nonvoting stock. Computations are as follows:

	Class A voting	Class B nonvoting
Net asset value per share	$ 69,178	$ 69,178
No. of shares outstanding	10	124
Total net asset value before discount	$691,780	$8,578,072

Discount Adjustments for Net Asset Value. As discussed in the Comparative Approach to Valuation section, a discount must be provided for an interest held in a closely held business. Applying the discount factors presented in the Comparative Approach to Valuation section, the total value of the common stock under the net asset value approach would be $5,596,528, as follows:

	Class A voting	Class B nonvoting
Net asset value after discount	$449,660	$5,146,868
Value per share	$ 44,966	$ 41,507

Dividend-paying Capacity

Dividend-paying capacity is identified in Revenue Ruling 59-60 as one factor to be considered in valuing a closely held business. In determining dividend-paying ability, liquidity is an important consideration. A relatively profitable company may be illiquid as funds are needed for fixed assets and working capital.

J. J. Bean, Inc. has not paid any dividends to its common stock shareholders over the years. Based on its financial history, J. J. Bean, Inc. has limited capacity to pay dividends. It has been continuously obtaining operating funds from a factoring company in excess of its outstanding accounts receivable balance. Any dividend payment to shareholders would exacerbate the present cash problems. As a practical matter, J. J. Bean, Inc. has a nominal value based on its dividend-paying capacity.

Valuation of Preferred Stock

Revenue Ruling 83-120 (IRB 1983-33, 8, August 15, 1983) provides guidance to the valuation of preferred stock. It states that the most important factors to be considered in determining the value of preferred stock are its yield, dividend coverage and protection of its liquidation preference.

The ruling also states that the dividend yield determines whether the preferred stock has a value equal to its par value. It specifically states the following:

> Whether the yield of the preferred stock supports a valuation of the stock at par value depends in part on the adequacy of the dividend rate. The adequacy of the dividend rate should be determined by comparing its dividend rate with the dividend rate of high-grade publicly traded preferred stock. A lower yield than that of high-grade preferred stock indicates a preferred stock value of less than par. In addition, whether the preferred stock has a fixed dividend rate and is nonparticipating influences the value of the preferred stock . . . A publicly traded preferred stock for a company having a similar business and similar assets with similar liquidation preferences, voting rights, and other similar terms would be the ideal comparable for determining yield required in arms length transactions for closely held stock. Such ideal comparables will frequently not exist. In such circumstances, the most comparable publicly traded issues should be selected for comparison and appropriate adjustments made for differing factors.

In short, the valuation method for preferred stock is to capitalize the annual dividend at a market rate equal to the rate of returns from similar grade marketable securities and then make appropriate adjustments for variations.

Schedule 1
J. J. Bean, Inc.
Simple Average of Price-Earnings Ratios of Selected Comparables

Company	Year 6	Year 5	Year 4	Year 3	Year 2	Year 1
Hartmarx	5.9	4.9	4.8	6.1	6.3	10.67
Palm Beach	4.1	4.6	4.9	7.4	7.7	11.73
Cluett, Peabody	5.8	5.8	5.8	5.8	6.7	9.28
Totals	15.80	15.30	15.50	19.30	20.70	31.68
Averages per period	5.26	5.10	5.16	6.43	6.90	10.56
Simple average weighted factor	1	1	1	1	1	.50
Simple average per period	5.26	5.10	5.16	6.43	6.90	5.28

Simple average over the 5 1/2
year period $(5.26 + 5.10 + 5.16 + 6.43 + 6.90 + 5.28) \div 5.5 = 6.20$

Source: The Value Line Investment Survey

Standard & Poor's Standard NYSE Stock Reports

Standard & Poor's Stock Guide

Schedule 2
J. J. Bean, Inc.
Weighted Average of Price-Earnings Ratios of Selected Comparables

Company	Year 6	Year 5	Year 4	Year 3	Year 2	Year 1
Hartmarx	5.9	4.9	4.8	6.1	6.3	10.67
Palm Beach	4.1	4.6	4.9	7.4	7.7	11.73
Cluett, Peabody	5.8	5.8	5.8	5.8	6.7	9.28
Totals	15.80	15.30	15.50	19.30	20.70	31.68
Averages per period	5.26	5.10	5.16	6.43	6.90	10.56
Weighted factor	1	2	3	4	5	3
Weighted average per period	5.26	10.20	15.48	25.72	34.50	31.68

Weighted average over the 5 1/2
year period $(5.26 + 10.20 + 15.48 + 25.72 + 34.50 + 31.68) \div 18 = 6.82$

Source: The Value Line Investment Survey

Standard & Poor's Standard NYSE Stock Reports

Standard & Poor's Stock Guide

Schedule 3
J. J. Bean, Inc.
Regression Analysis* of Earnings Potential

Year	Net sales	Net earnings
3	$65,806,459	$ 453,531
4	69,505,067	2,154,026
5	55,075,549	1,650,668
6	40,371,493	882,124
7	29,783,391	671,006
8	27,689,397	473,569

Projections	Given net sales**	Projected earnings	Index of correlation
Year 2	$60 million	$1,320,582	.35
Year 1 (including projected earnings of year 2 in the data base)	$60 million	$1,320,582	.37

*(It is not the author's wish to burden the reader with the complex mathematical formulas involved in regression analysis. Suffice it to say, regression analysis is a mathematical formula that attempts to determine the future behavior of one factor, such as earnings in Schedule 3 above, by charting its past behavior in relation to another factor, such as net sales above.

Look at the relationship between net sales and earnings from years 3 to 8, with year 3 being last year or the most recent year. During that time, a change in net sales either up or down would produce a change in net earnings in a similar direction. By using a mathematical formula to analyze the relation between net sales and earnings, a projection is made as to what earnings will be next year (Year 2), and the following year (Year 1), given a certain amount of net sales, in our case $60 million. The Index of Correlation tells what percentage of the change in projected earnings is due to the given amount of net sales—for example, from Year 3 to Year 2 it is .35 or 35%.)

**Net sales as projected by management.

Schedule 4
J. J. Bean, Inc.
Average Earnings for Three-Year Period Fiscal Years Ended 9/30/__ to 19__

Year	Net earnings	Weighted factor	Weighted earnings
1	$1,300,000*	2	$2,600,000
2	453,531	1	453,531
3	2,154,026	1	2,154,026
Totals	3,907,557		5,207,557
Simple average	$1,302,519		
Weighted average			$1,301,889

*Earnings as estimated by management for year 1.

Classes of Preferred Stock. J. J. Bean, Inc. has two classes of preferred stock outstanding. Presently, there are 500 shares of Class A preferred stock and 2,375 shares of Class B preferred stock outstanding. The features of these preferred stocks are as follows:

Stock features	Preferred stock	
	Class A	Class B
Par value	$100	$100
Annual dividend rate	8%	10%
Liquidation preferences	$100	$100
Callable amount	$100	$105

In addition, both classes of stock are nonparticipating, noncumulative, nonconvertible, and nonvoting. These classes of stock are not a particularly attractive investment because of their callable and noncumulative features.

Comparative Value After Adjustments. Cluett, Peabody is the only comparable company whose preferred stock was publicly traded in September 19__. This preferred stock was priced to yield 5.6 percent. However, this stock is far from comparable to either class of J. J. Bean, Inc.'s preferred stock. The Cluett, Peabody stock is cumulative and convertible into common stock. Because of the convertible feature, a lower yield is provided. J.J. Bean, Inc.'s preferred stock should provide a higher yield because of the nonconvertible and callable features. Adjustments to account for the nonconvertibility feature using Cluett, Peabody as a comparable, while possible, are difficult and possibly unsound. It would be more appropriate to search for other preferred stock as possible comparables.

The search for comparable preferred stock was extended to other companies in the apparel industry. However, no preferred stock that was traded to yield a rate of return of around 12–13 percent. (Appendix I [not shown in this book] provides a listing of public utility preferred stocks.)

In view of the lack of comparable preferred stock in the apparel industry, the search was extended to the public utility sector. In September, high-grade preferred stocks in selected public utility companies were traded to yield a rate of return of around 12–13 percent. (Appendix I [not shown in this book] provides a listing of public utility preferred stocks.)

Given the dividend yield from selected stock of public utility companies, the preferred stock with features similar to those of J. J. Bean, Inc. should be priced to earn a dividend yield of at least 12 percent. At a dividend yield of 12 percent, the value of the preferred stock would be as follows:

	Number of shares	Price per share to yield 12%	Total value
Class A	500.00	$66.70	$ 33,350
Class B	2,375.00	83.30	197,838
			$231,188

The value of the preferred stock as indicated above represents value of high-grade publicly traded stock. Due to J. J. Bean, Inc.'s thin management, weak financial position, and lack of marketability, the value should be discounted by at least 35 percent. Accordingly, the fair market value of the preferred stock of J. J. Bean, Inc. would be $150,286, as follows:

	Preferred stock	
	Class A	Class B
Value before discount	$33,350	$197,838
Discount	35%	35%
Value after discount	$21,680	$128,606
Value per share	$ 43.36	$ 54.15

Summary Statements

The common stock of J. J. Bean, Inc. was valued based on three approaches: comparative value, net asset value, and dividend-paying capacity. Although the dividend-paying capacity approach provides a much lower value for J. J. Bean, Inc., the comparative value approach and the net asset value approach should be given the greatest weights in determining the value of J. J. Bean, Inc. Both the comparative value approach and the net asset value approach provide approximately the same after-discounted values. The comparative value approach provides a total value of $5,493,780, while the net asset value approach gives a total value of $5,596,528. Given the close proximity of the values between the two methods, the value of the common stock as of September 30, 19__ would clearly be within the price range of $5.5 million to $5.6 million. Accordingly, the fair market value of the two classes of common stock should be $5,493,780, divided as follows:

	Common Stock	
Voting	Nonvoting	Total
$441,440	$5,052,380	$5,493,780

VALUATION EXAMPLE 5
A SHORT-FORM VALUATION

VALUATION OF ANIMAL ENTERPRISES, INC., MIDDLE ROCK FOODS, INC., AND LEASED ROCK DEPARTMENTS, INC.

1. *Purpose of Valuation.* To determine the fair market value of Animal Enterprises, Inc., Middle Rock Foods, Inc., and Leased Rock Departments, Inc. (The Companies), on or about July 31, 19__. The valuation will be used to determine, for gift tax purposes, the value of the stock of each company.

2. *Definition of Fair Market Value.* For purposes of this valuation, fair market value is defined as: "the price at which the property would change hands between a willing buyer and a willing seller, neither being under any compulsion to buy or sell and both having reasonable knowledge of relevant facts. . . ."

3. *Sources of Information.* Financial and statistical information is deemed to be reliable. However, we make no representation as to our sources' accuracy or completeness and have accepted their information without further verification. We were not engaged to review or examine the financial statements in accordance with standards established by the American Institute of Certified Public Accountants. We express no opinion on and accept no responsibility for the accuracy of the financial information provided to us by others.

4. *Corporate Structure.*

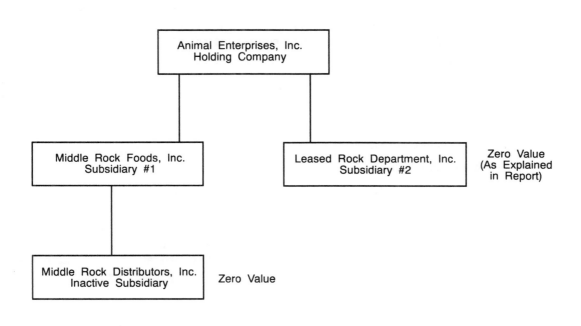

The structure of our valuation will be as follows:

    a.   Middle Rock Distributors, Inc. has zero value. It does not own any assets, nor conduct any activity and as such is worthless.

    b.   Leased Rock Departments, Inc. has a zero value, but for gift tax and transactional purposes we will assign this company a value of one dollar (see below).

    c.   Middle Rock Foods, Inc. will be valued by considering various valuation methods (see below); and

    d.   Animal Enterprises, Inc. will be assigned whatever value we determine its wholly-owned subsidiary, Middle Rock Foods, Inc., is worth. Animal Enterprises, Inc.'s only assets are (1) 100 percent of the stock of Leased Rock Departments, Inc. and (2) 100 percent of the stock of Middle Rock Foods, Inc.

5.   *Capital Structure.*

As of July 31, 19___, Animal Enterprises, Inc.'s capital structure and its ownership were as follows:

Name	Shares	Percent
Bill Animal	498	78.67%
Hill Animal	16	2.53
Will Animal	43.5	6.87
Dill Daughter	13	2.06
Phill Animal	43.5	6.87
Middle Rock Foods, Inc.	19	3.00
	633*	100.00%

*The shares held by Middle Rock Foods, Inc. will actually be treated as though they were treasury stock for valuation purposes since Animal Enterprises, Inc. owns 100 percent of this company.

6.   *Specific Valuation Methods.*

    ■   Adjusted Net Book Value

    ■   Capitalization of Earnings

    ■   Liquidation Value

7.   *Determination of Value Using the Adjusted Net Book Value Approach.* The following steps were taken to determine the value:

    a.   The adjusted net book value approach requires that all assets be evaluated to determine their true economic value. Fixed assets are appraised at a figure approximating their present market value as opposed to depreciated cost. The appraisal value used for fixed assets, as supplied by the Company's management, is assumed to be accurate.

b. Adjusted net book value represents the fair market value of the net assets (fair market value of all assets less liabilities) underlying the stock of the corporation. We determined the adjusted net book value of Middle Rock Foods, Inc. as of July 31, 19__ at about $2,175,000 as follows:

Net book value as of July 31, 19__ *		$2,173,618
Add adjustments for fixed assets from book to fair market value:		
Approximate fair market value (Fixed Assets)**	81,909	
Book value	(81,909)	0
Investments @ FMV**	740,547	
Book value	(740,547)	0
Adjusted book value		$2,173,618
Rounded		$2,175,000

*Middle Rock Foods, Inc. has a due from affiliate on their July 31, 19__ statements in the amount of $445,406. This account should have been higher because the intercompany sales are not sold at the market rates. We will not make an adjustment currently because the amount of the increase is so subjective.

**The adjusted net book value of all fixed assets approximates fair market value, according to the company's management. The fair market value of the investment assets equals the adjusted book value since all of these are cash or cash equivalents.

We determined the adjusted net book value of Leased Rock Departments, Inc. as of July 31, 19__ at about $0 as follows:

Net book value as of July 31, 19__		(54,590)
Add adjustments for fixed assets from book to fair market value:		
Approximate fair market value*	0	
Book value	(33,075)	(33,075)
Adjusted book value		(87,665)
Rounded		0

*The fixed assets of Leased Rock Departments, Inc. consist entirely of leasehold improvements in department stores. Based on the Company's management these assets have no fair market value.

This method is most appropriate in those entities where economic goodwill is not present, but whose assets, when considered as a whole, produce a going concern and contain a value over and above what is recorded on the books of the business. This approach is also most applicable to companies having erratic or depressed earnings which are inadequate to provide a fair return on the value of the net tangible assets employed. In theory, the value of all assets, less all outstanding liabilities, provides an indication of the fair market value of ownership equity.

Rev. Rul. 59-60 states that the appraiser will accord primary consideration to earnings when valuing stocks of companies which sell products or services to the public. It states that the net asset value should be a primary consideration for valuing closely held investment or real estate holding companies. According to Rev. Rul. 59-60, net asset value should be given minimum weight in the valuation of an operating company.

In summary, the net asset value approach can be a meaningful technique for valuing an investment or real estate holding company. The net asset approach is not a meaningful technique for valuing an operating company. Since Middle Rock Foods, Inc. is an operating company, the above computation only serves to provide a value to which the capitalized earnings and the liquidation value methods can compare. As we will show in the remainder of this report, the liquidation value will be the lowest value that can be assigned for comparison purposes. The adjusted net book value on the previous page would be discounted by as much as 35 percent to 45 percent for both marketability and minority discounts. These discounts would lower the value of the company's stock as follows:

Adjusted Net Book Value	$2,175,000
Less 35% Discount	(761,250)
Net Value—for comparison purposes	$1,413,750

8. *Determination of Value Using the Capitalized Earnings Approach.* The following steps were taken to determine the earnings:

   a. The figures in the yearly reviewed financial statements were assumed to have been accurate when they were provided to the board of directors and stockholders of Middle Rock Foods, Inc.

   b. Approximate Federal income tax was subtracted from net income before taxes to arrive at the after-tax net income. (See Exhibit A.)

   c. Earnings from investments have been subtracted from earnings before income tax to better reflect operations of the business. After the operating earnings are capitalized (see below) the fair market value of all investment assets will be added back to reflect the total value of the company.

   d. The income from Middle Rock Foods, Inc. for the years 1 through 5 was weighted to arrive at average expected earnings, as follows:

Year	Adjusted Net Income **	Weighted Factor	Weighted Income
1*	$154,265	5	$ 771,325
2	94,816	4	379,264
3	103,568	3	310,704
4	65,307	2	130,614
5	65,862	1	65,862
Total			1,657,769
Divided by			15
Average Expected Earnings from Operations			$ 110,518

*Most recent year
**See Exhibit A

e. The income for Leased Rock Departments, Inc. for the years 1 through 5 was weighted to arrive at average expected earnings, as follows:

Year	Adjusted Net Income	Weighted Factor	Weighted Income
1	$(57,375)	5	$ 0
2	36,446	4	145,784
3	(7,390)	3	0
4	53,887	2	107,774
5	11,118	1	11,118
Total			264,676
Divided by			15
Average Expected Earnings			$ 17,645

Since Leased Rock Departments, Inc. does not have sufficient income to support a desired return on investment (i.e., net tangible assets) the capitalized earnings approach is not an appropriate valuation method. From this point on our discussion of capitalized earnings will focus on Middle Rock Foods, Inc. and SIC 5149.

f. *Industry Rate of Return.* Industry rate of return, based on Dun & Bradstreet's *Industrial Norms and Key Business Ratios, 19__ –19__,* under SIC 5149. The median after-tax return on net worth was 14.4 percent. The median represents the midpoint of all observed results.

g. *Selection of Capitalization Rates.* In selecting the capitalization rates, we considered the rate that would constitute a reasonable rate of return. What constitutes a reasonable rate can best be answered by referring to IRS Rev. Rul. 68-609, which states:

> The percentage of return on the average annual value of tangible assets used should be the percentage prevailing in the industry involved at the date of valuation.

Because the industry's median rate of return was 14.4 percent for 1989 for the groceries and related products, not classified elsewhere, we used 14.4 percent as the capitalization rate. However, if another investment alternative provides a greater return than the industry's return, an investor would want to invest in the other investment—provided both investments carry the same degree of risk. The average yield of a 3-month U.S. Treasury bill (which is virtually risk-free) in July 1990 was 7.92 percent. Based on studies done by Ibbotson Associates, as set forth in the *Stocks, Bonds, Bills and Inflation: 19__ Yearbook,* the average annual rate of return for common stock (as based on Standard and Poor's Composite Index) in excess of the average rate of return of Treasury Bills from 1926 to 19__ was 8.4 percent. In addition, the average annual rate of return for small stock (i.e., basically stocks making up the two smallest deciles in terms of capitalization, which are traded on the New York Stock Exchange and stock listed on the American Stock Exchange and over the counter with the same or less capitalization) in excess of the S&P composite index stock was 3.8 percent for the same period.

Undoubtedly, the Company is at least as risky as the small stock traded on the NYSE. Logically, an investment in the Company must provide a return at least as great as the small stock. The return for small stock is about 20 percent, computed as follows:

Treasury Bills—October	7.92%
Premium for Equity	8.40
Premium for Small Stock	3.80
Total	20.12%
Rounded	20.00%

h.   *Computation of Value.*

Average Expected Earnings	$ 110,518
Dividend by Expected Rate of Return	20.0%
Capitalized Value	552,590
Add Fair Market Value of Investment Assets*	740,547
Total Value of Company	$1,293,137

*The Investment Assets consist entirely of cash and cash equivalents.

It is a generally accepted valuation principle that the capitalized earnings value cannot be less than the liquidation value. The next section will discuss in detail all the necessary steps needed to determine the liquidation value of Middle Rock Foods, Inc.

9.   *Determination of Value Using the Liquidation Value Approach.*   The liquidation value approach estimates the total amount that would be realized from selling or otherwise disposing of the individual assets of a business, after all liabilities and liquidating costs of the business had been paid or otherwise satisfied. It is generally accepted valuation principle that the liquidation value is the lower limit of the value of the business.

The liquidation value approach is similar to the adjusted net book value approach, as each asset is appraised at its disposal value. In the liquidation value approach, however, all the anticipated costs of liquidation must be deducted to arrive at the value of the business. In contrast, most of the liquidation costs normally would not be deducted to arrive at the adjusted net book value of an ongoing business. Some of the liquidation costs are (1) brokerage commission and professional fees for the sale of assets; (2) forfeiture of security deposits and penalty payments resulting from the cancellation of long-term leases; (3) indemnity payments for the cancellation of any outstanding contractual obligations; and (4) possible tax consequences resulting from any gain recognized from the sale or disposition of the assets.

The liquidation value for Middle Rock Foods, Inc. of $1,800,000 was computed as follows:

	Book Value	Percentage	Estimated Liquidation Value
Cash	$842,968	100%	$ 842,968
Accounts Receivable–Trade	448,620	80	358,896
Accounts Receivable–Leased Rock	445,406	–	326,028*
Interest Receivable	2,113	100	2,113
Notes Receivable–Trade	28,900	90	26,010
Notes Receivable–Other (Employee)	3,393	100	3,393
Prepaid Expenses	16,526	100	16,526
Inventory	397,801	90	358,021
Fixed Assets	81,909	100	81,909**
Cash Surrender Value–Life Insurance	21,819	100	21,819

Total Value of Assets (Liquidation Value before Expenses)			2,037,683

Less:
  Liabilities   (115,837)
  Liquidation Cost***   (125,770)

Liquidation Value @ 7/31/19__ $1,796,076

Rounded $1,800,000

*The account receivable from Leased Rock Department, Inc. has been reduced to reflect the net tangible asset value of that company. The following is a detailed liquidation value of Leased Rock Department, Inc.:

	Book Value	Percentage	Estimated Liquidation Value
Cash	$114,351	100%	$114,351
Inventory	267,107	90	240,396
Prepaid Expenses	3,000	100	3,000
Security Deposits	2,110	100	2,110
Fixed Assets	33,075	0	0
Goodwill	5,000	0	–

Liquidation Value before Expenses   359,857
Less:
  Liabilities to unrelated parties   (33,829)

Net Tangible Asset Value Available to Repay Affiliated Corporation $326,028

**The adjusted net book value of all fixed assets approximates fair market value, according to the management of the company.

***Liquidation costs are estimates of the costs that would be incurred during liquidation, including commissions for the sale, rent and other overhead costs. See following schedule:

Schedule of Estimated Liquidation Costs

	Per Month	# of Months Factor	Liquidation Cost
Overhead Costs*			
Utilities	$ 802	2	$ 1,604
Rent	1,310	2	2,620
Insurance	6,249	2	12,498
Salary			
Warehouse	7,600	2	15,200
Selling	16,540	2	33,080
Office	5,180	2	10,360
Officer	0	2	0
Delivery	3,671	2	7,342
Legal and audit	–	–	10,000
Gas & Oil	1,850	2	3,700
Telephone	1,000	2	2,000
Travel	–	2	5,000
Advertising	–	–	5,000
Repairs and maintenance	–	2	10,000
Real estate taxes	1,419	2	2,838
Payroll taxes	2,264	2	4,528
Total Overhead Costs			125,770
Other Costs			
Tax on gain from sale of improvements and equipment (sold at adjusted book value)			0
Total Estimated Liquidation Costs			$125,770

*Per discussion with management of the company.

10. *Discount for Lack of Marketability.* The rationale for a discount for lack of marketability is well accepted.

The principle of a discount for lack of marketability has been stated as follows: It seems clear . . . that an unlisted closely held stock of a corporation . . . , in which trading is infrequent and which therefore lacks marketability, is less attractive than a similar stock which is listed on an exchange and had ready access to the investing public. Central Trust Co., 305 F2d 393 (CtCl 1962). The lack of marketability discount concept recognizes the fact that closely held stock interests are less attractive and have fewer potential purchasers because they are not readily marketable.

Various studies have been done on the discount for lack of marketability. For example, Professor Steven E. Bolten investigated studies that had been done in the area of valuation discounts. In his article, Discounts for the Stocks of Closely-Held Corporations, 123 *Trusts and Estates* 22 (December 1984), he concluded that the results of previous studies indicate (1) an average of 39.86 percent for nonmarketability discount and (2) an average of 29.37 percent discount for minority position. Commenting on the studies done on the discount of nonmarketability, Professor Bolten states:

Although these studies took place over a ten-year period, each discovered an average discount of approximately the same amount. Thus, we may safely assume that the nonmarketability discount not only is appropriately applied because of its historically observed presence but also because of its relative stability.

In *Valuing a Business: The Analysis and Appraisal of Closely-Held Companies,* (Dow Jones - Irwin, 1981), Dr. Shannon P. Pratt states:

There is considerable evidence to suggest that the discount for the lack of marketability factor alone for a closely held stock compared with a publicly traded counterpart should average about 35 percent.

Since the liquidation method has provided a value greater than the adjusted net book value the capitalized earnings value, respectively, discount would not be applicable.

11. *Conclusion.* To restate our valuation procedure in valuing the subject companies: (1) Middle Rock Distributors, Inc. has a zero value and is an inactive wholly-owned subsidiary of Middle Rock Foods, Inc., (2) Leased Rock Departments, Inc. has been assigned a $1 value for transactional purposes only, the economic fair market value of this company is zero, and (3) Animal Enterprises, Inc. is the sole parent of Middle Rock Foods, Inc. and Leased Rock Departments, Inc. Animal Enterprises, Inc. does not own any other assets. Since Leased Rock Departments, Inc. has a zero economic value the only asset of value is the 100 percent interest in Middle Rock Foods, Inc. Subsequently the value of Animal Enterprises, Inc. will be the value assigned to Middle Rock Foods, Inc.

Based on the information and analyses summarized in this report it is our opinion that, on or about July 31, 19__, the fair market value of Middle Rock Foods, Inc. is the liquidation value of $1,800,000. As a result, the value of Animal Enterprises, Inc. also equals $1,800,000 or $2,932 per share computed as follows:

Total Value	$1,800,000
Number of outstanding shares	+ 614
	$ 2,932

Exhibit A
Middle Rock Foods, Inc.
Statement of Significant Numbers

	Year 1	Year 2	Year 3	Year 4	Year 5
Sales	$4,017,501	$3,786,955	$3,471,152	$3,310,774	$3,313,133
Gross Profit	$1,155,315	$1,073,170	$ 953,611	$ 874,980	$ 802,269
Net Before Tax Earnings	$ 307,865	$ 192,959	$ 207,897	$ 139,145	$ 140,128
Less Earnings from Investments	(54,971)	(37,523)	(38,113)	(32,084)	(32,158)
Net Before Tax Earnings from Operations	252,894	155,436	169,784	107,061	107,970
Less Taxes*	(98,629)	(60,620)	(66,216)	(41,754)	(42,108)
Net After Tax Earnings from Operations	$ 154,265	$ 94,816	$ 103,568	$ 65,307	$ 65,862

*Taxes were computed at a combined federal and state tax rate of 39 percent. This rate has been applied to each year to better reflect the net earnings an investor would receive.

EXAMPLE 6
VALUATION BUILDING BLOCKS

COMPANY PROFILE

Roman Foods Company's origins can be traced back to the mid-1930s, when an Italian immigrant named Michael Goodbody opened a grocery store in the street level unit of his apartment building at Bigo and Bend Avenues in Bigtown. The senior Goodbody and his son, Michael V. Goodbody, soon expanded operations to include the employment of a resurrected can fabricating machine from a Tin Can Company fire. The father and son team rebuilt the machine, set it up in the basement and formed the Little Can Company, which rapidly became a formidable supplier of cans to local oil packaging companies.

When a shortage of cooking oil developed during World War II, the Goodbodys were able to secure a source and the result was a flourishing oil packager that became know as Roman Packing Company. That packing company is where the heritage of today's Roman Foods Company was spawned.

Since a modest yet auspicious beginning, the company has moved several times to its present location; a 45,000-square-foot facility on Bigtown's west side. Management has passed through and into the capable hands of three generations of Goodbodys and currently resides with the founder's grandchildren, Michael and Penny Goodbody.

Today, the company continues to wear the Roman name well and coexists among the other leaders in the Shortening and Oil Industry. Sales have expanded to all 50 states as well as various international locations and the product line has reached approximately 100 quality items. Product options range from the highly competitive commodity oils to the most exotic specialty shortenings and oils, while packaging options range from bulk tankers to 16 oz. retail sizes.

Quality, competitive pricing, and breadth of product lines continue to be the company's strength, and service is second to none. The company has built a tradition of serving the food service and industrial industries with a complete and comprehensive line of shortening and oils.

GENERAL ECONOMICS AND BUSINESS

The December 15, 199__ issue of *Standard and Poors, Trends and Projections*, included these economic and business highlights:

1. The recession is here. The Department of Commerce's Index of leading indicators now shows four consecutive declines—one more than the number that traditionally signals a recession.

2. Consumer sentiment slid again in November, and consumers translated some of their nervousness into a slowdown in retail sales growth.

Following are annotated excerpts from *Trends and Projections*.

Given the recent economic developments and the flow of data, there is little doubt that the recession of 1990–91 is here—and the expansion that began in the ancient past of 1982 is over. The strong jump in initial unemployments claim, the flat consumer spending in October, and the fourth consecutive decline in the leading indicators all confirm the outlook. For perennial optimists, the chance remains that the situation in the Middle East could be settled far more quickly than most now expect, which could make this recession a strong contender for the brevity record held by the 1980 downturn. But for the moment, we see this one as more likely to last in the range of one year. Hopefully, that makes next summer the expected turning point.

Consumer finance is a growing concern for many. Debt levels are not rising rapidly, but concern is spreading that defaults will climb. In the housing area, activity continues to be quite slow. Lower interest rates have not yet benefitted home sales.

Even a recession has some good aspects that deserve mention. First, inflation typically declines during and shortly after a recession. The sharp drop in the early 1980s was unusually large, but some cyclical decline in price inflation is likely this time around, too. The core rate of inflation has been about 4 percent since 1983 or 1984. In 1992 this rate could dip to the 3 percent range, where it could remain even after the economy recovers and growth resumes. Hard times, and memories of hard times, tend to limit demands for higher prices and higher wages.

Second, interest rates normally decline in recessions. The Fed eases rates to minimize the damage but, more importantly, the demand for credit declines. When business is weak, usually fewer people borrow to buy a house or a car, and fewer businesses borrow to build new factories or add to inventories. The result is less borrowing and lower interest rates.

Third, exports continue to expand, although the growth may slow in the next few months. The weak dollar and continued economic expansion in much of Europe and Asia should help exports and contribute to the economy. Corporate capital spending, however, will not hold up as well in 1991 as in 1990.

At the start we noted that the optimists might still hope for a very short recession. It is the nature of recessions that people dwell more on their fears about how bad it could be than on the hopes that it could be almost painless. Can things get worse? The answer is yes.

Oil is one of the more important variables. Despite the standoff with Iraq, oil prices have been relatively well behaved in recent weeks. On a number of occasions we have seen oil trade below $30 per barrel. However, if a prolonged war were to continue in the Middle East, we could see much higher oil prices and substantial damage to the economy.

Another key factor that seems to be limiting the damage to manufacturing and the whole economy is continued export growth. If the recession spreads to Europe and Japan, exports won't grow much at all and that would mean more damage here. Also, consumer sentiment surveys continue to paint a picture much worse than the data on spending and auto sales are showing. The sentiment surveys may prove to be right and sales might slip much further.

Finally, in this catalog of nightmares is government policy. So far, policy has been only mildly troublesome—money is still too tight, and this is the wrong moment to raise taxes. But what if a dose of bad economic numbers sparks efforts to balance the budget at any price? We probably would see more tax increases and reductions in government spending.

EXAMPLE 7
VALUATION BUILDING BLOCKS

CAPITALIZED EARNINGS APPROACH

Conceptually, the capitalized earnings approach determines the fair market value of an ongoing business enterprise based on its earnings capacity. This approach is based on the theory that an investment (i.e., net tangible assets) will yield a return sufficient to recover its initial cost and to justly compensate the investor for the inherent risks of ownership. Given that Smith Brothers, Inc. is an operating company, we based the valuation on this approach pursuant to Rev. Rul. 59-60 and other valuation authority.

Under the capitalized earnings approach, we determined the normalized future earnings and capitalized such earnings based on a reasonable rate of return, as indicated by available statistics. Normalized future earnings refers to the average future annual earnings over a period of time.

Although future earnings are to be used for earnings capitalization, past earnings are usually the best guide for determining future earnings. In this regard, Rev. Rul. 59-60 states: Prior earnings records usually are the most reliable guide as to the future expectancy.

Accordingly, the past earnings records would be the starting point for determining future earnings. To determine future earnings capacity, prior earnings records are analyzed.

The normalized future earnings of $330,000 were computed as follows:

Year	Income ***	Weight**	Weighted Income
1*	$476,322	3	$1,428,966
2	(567,189)	1	(567,189)
3	885,821	1	885,821
4	200,565	1	200,565
5	358,133	1	358,133
			2,306,296
Dividend by weight factor			7
			$ 329,471
Rounded			$ 330,000

*Year 1 is the most recent year.

**Current years are weighted heavier, however, Year 2 has a low weight because it is a loss year for a company with a history of making profits.

***Income was computed as follows:

Year September 30,	1	2	3	4	5
Net profit before taxes	$1,299,473	$ 84,255	$2,053,006	$ 811,380	$1,003,301
Adjust for unusual items:					
Land sale		(646,404)			
Building sale					(32,116)
Stripper well refund		(117,821)			
50% blending profits*	(505,637)	(454,408)	(281,363)	(410,250)	(254,919)
Adjusted profit before tax	793,836	(1,134,378)	1,771,643	401,130	716,266
Less income tax	(317,534)		(885,822)	(200,565)	(358,133)
Tax benefit**		567,189			
Adjusted net profit	$ 476,302	$(567,189)	$ 885,821	$ 200,565	$ 358,133

*Blending profits are the extra profit the company earned as a result of blending the gasoline with alcohol. Although the price per gallon of blended fuel is higher than non-blended fuel, the federal and state tax credits reduce the total cost of blended fuel below the cost of non-blended fuel, as illustrated below:

	Blended		Non-Blended	
Cost per gallon	90% UL	$.4613	100% UL	$.5350
	10% ALC	.1020		
Federal & state tax		.1910		.2510
Other fees		.0325		.0325
Total cost per gallon		$.7868		$.8185

UL = Unleaded gasoline
ALC = Alcohol

This illustrates a $.0317 per gallon savings to blend. Since the continuation of federal and state credits is questionable (many states no longer allow the credit), we believe only 50 percent of the blending profits should be included.

**Tax benefit is the result of taxes which would be refunded due to the net operating loss carryback to Years 5, 4, and 3, i.e., $358,133, $200,565, and $8,491, respectively.

In selecting the capitalization rate, we considered the rate that would constitute a reasonable rate of return. What constitutes a reasonable return can best be answered by referring to IRS Rev. Rul. 68-609, which states the following:

> The percentage of return on the average annual value of tangible assets used should be the percentage prevailing in the industry involved at the date of valuation . . .

We were unable to locate any single rate of return for businesses that parallel the business activities of Smith Brothers, Inc. Accordingly, we examined the rates of return for the gasoline service station industry and convenience food stores industry as a guide for arriving at the rate of return.

The year 1 median after-tax return on net worth (i.e., percentage of after-tax profit on net worth) for the gasoline service stations under SIC 5541, as compiled by Dun and Bradstreet, was 13.8 percent. The year 1 after-tax return on net worth for the convenience food stores industry under SIC 5411 was 14.0 percent.

It is reasonable to assume that a potential investor would at least want to receive a return on his investment equal to the industry's norm (i.e., median). However, if another investment alternative provides a greater return than the industry's return, an investor would want to invest in the other investment, provided both investments carry the same degree of risk.

The median returns of both industries, 13.8 and 14.0 percent, respectively, are low in view of the company's risks and size. The average yield of a 3-month U.S. Treasury bill (which is virtually risk-free) in December year 1 was 9.17 percent. Based on studies done by Ibbotson Associates, as set forth in the *Stocks, Bonds, Bills and Inflation: 19__ Yearbook*, the average annual rate of return for common stock (as based on the Standard and Poor's Composite Index) in excess of the average rate of return of Treasury bills from 1926 to year 1 was 8.4 percent. In addition, the average annual rate of return for small stock (i.e., basically stocks making up the two smallest deciles in terms of capitalization, which are traded on the New York Stock Exchange and stock listed on the American Stock Exchange and over the counter with the same or less capitalization) in excess of the S&P composite index stock was 3.8 percent for the same period.

Undoubtedly, Smith Brothers, Inc. is at least as risky as the small stock traded on the NYSE. Logically, an investment in Smith Brothers, Inc. must provide a return at least as great as the small stock. The return for small stock is about 21 percent, computed as follows:

Treasury Bills–December Year 1	9.17
Premium for Equity	8.40
Premium for Small Stock	3.80
	21.37
Rounded	21.00

Since the median rate of return for both industries is low in view of the company's risk and size, we used the rate of return for small stock, 21 percent, as computed above. Capitalizing the normalized future earnings of $330,000 at 21 percent, the capitalized value of the Company is about $1,572,000. The value per share would be $600, computed as follows:

Capitalized value	$1,572,000
Dividend by the number of shares of stock outstanding	3,000
Value per share outstanding	$ 524
Rounded (Before Discounts)	$ 600

EXAMPLE 8
VALUATION BUILDING BLOCKS

CAPITALIZED EARNINGS APPROACH

Conceptually, the capitalized earnings approach determines the fair market value of an ongoing business enterprise based on its earnings capacity. This approach is based on the theory that an investment (i.e., net tangible assets) will yield a return sufficient to recover its initial cost and to justly compensate the investor for the inherent risks of ownership.

Under the capitalized earnings approach, we determined the normalized future earnings and capitalize such earnings based on a reasonable rate of return as indicated by available statistics. Normalized future earnings refers to the average future annual earnings over a period of time.

Although the future earnings are to be used for earnings capitalization, past earnings are usually the best guide for determining future earnings. In this regard, Revenue Ruling 59-60 states: Prior earnings records usually are the most reliable guide as to the future expectancy.

Accordingly, the past earnings records would be the starting point for determining future earnings. To determine future earnings capacity, prior earnings are analyzed.

The normalized future earnings of $347,679 were computed as follows:

Period Ended	Income	Weight	Weighted Income
December, Year 1	$442,307	3	$ 1,326,921
December, Year 2	177,921	2	355,842
December, Year 3	(226,768)	0*	—
June, Year 3	403,310	1	403,310
		6	2,086,073
Dividend by weight factor			6
Normalized future earnings			$ 347,679

*No weight was assigned to this period, since it was a short period that produced a loss for a company that has a history of making a profit.

Generally, the discount rate is the expected rate of return available on alternative investment opportunities with similar risks. We developed a discount rate based on the weighted average after-tax cost of capital. The weighted average cost of capital is made up of the after-tax returns paid to all sources of capital, weighted by the proportions of each of these sources to total capital.

Here we used two sources of capital: equity (which includes contributed capital and retained earnings on common stock) and debt. Both the risk rates and the debt/equity ratio are determined after considering the business risks. This is intended to reflect the analysis that a prudent investor might conduct to estimate the fair market value.

We estimated the cost of debt on the monthly average for the month ended December 31, 19__ yield on corporate BAA bonds of 10.43 percent with a premium adjustment of 3 percentage points for the risk involved to arrive at 13.43 percent. After adjustment for an assumed 39 percent effective tax rate, the after-tax cost of debt becomes 8.19 percent.

To arrive at the cost of equity, we estimated the (1) expected risk-free rate (RF), (2) expected return on the equity market in excess of the risk-free rate (RM) (i.e., equity market risk premium), and (3) industry/company risks (R). These inputs were incorporated into the following formula:

Ke = Rf + Rm + R
Ke = Cost of equity
Rf = Risk-free equity (see A. below)
Rm = Equity market return in excess of the risk-free rate (see B. below)
R = Industry/company risks (see C. below)

A. The risk-free rate was based on the monthly average for the month ended December 31, 19__ of 8.24 percent on 30-year Treasury bonds.

B. The difference between the return on the market and the risk-free interest rate (Rf) is termed the market risk premium (Rm). We used a risk premium of 10.6 percent based on studies done by Ibbotson Associates as set forth in the *Stocks, Bonds, Bills and Inflation: 19__ Yearbook*. The risk premium is the sum of (1) the average excess of the total returns of company stock in the S&P Composite Index over long-term Treasury bond income yield and (2) the average excess of the small company stock returns over the return of the S&P Composite Index. Small company stock return basically consists of stocks making up the two smallest deciles in terms of capitalization, which are traded on the New York Stock Exchange and stock listed on the American Stock Exchange and over the counter with the same or less capitalization.

The risk premium of 10.6 percent is computed as follows:

Excess common stock returns (S&P composite)	6.8%
Excess small stock return over common stock returns	3.8
Total Risk Premium	10.6%

C. The industry/company risk is a subjective measure to account for the relative risk of This Little Company and its industry in relation to the general stock market as a whole. We used 3 percent to account for such company risks because of its relatively small size. Applying the percentage to the formula, as stated above, provides a cost of equity of 21.84 percent as follows:

Ke = Rf + Rm + R
Ke = 8.24% + 10.6% + 3%
Ke = 21.84%

For cost of equity, no adjustment is made for income taxes because neither dividends nor redemptions are deductible by the corporation.

The weighted average cost of capital is computed using an assumed debt-to-equity ratio 40/60 based on best available industry statistics, as compiled by Dun & Bradstreet. The overall result is 16.50 percent cost of capital, computed as follows:

	Percent	Weight	Weighted Percent
Cost of debt	8.19	40%	3.28%
Cost of equity	21.84	60	13.10
Total cost of capital			16.38
Rounded			16.50

Capitalizing the normalized future earnings of $347,679 at 16.5 percent, the capitalized value of the company is $2,107,145. The value per share would be $2,100, computed as follows:

Capitalized value	$2,107,145
Number of shares of stock outstanding	1,000
Value of share outstanding	$ 2,107
Rounded	$ 2,110

EXAMPLE 9
VALUATION BUILDING BLOCKS: CAPITALIZED EARNINGS
APPROACH VS. LIQUIDATION VALUE APPROACH

CAPITALIZED EARNINGS APPROACH

Conceptually, the capitalized earnings approach determines the fair market value of an ongoing business enterprise based on its earnings capacity. This approach is based on the theory that an investment (i.e., net tangible assets) will yield a return sufficient to recover its initial cost and to justly compensate the investor for the inherent risks of ownership. Given that Radionic Industries, Inc. is an operating company, we based the valuation on this approach pursuant to Rev. Rul. 59-60 and other valuation authorities.

Under the capitalized earnings approach, we determined the normalized future earnings and capitalized such earnings based on a reasonable rate of return, as indicated by available statistics. Normalized future earnings refers to the average future annual earnings over a period of time.

Although future earnings are to be used for earnings capitalization, past earnings are usually the best guide for determining future earnings. In this regard, Rev. Rul. 59-60 states: Prior earnings records usually are the most reliable guide as to the future expectancy.

Accordingly, the past earnings records would be the starting point for determining future earnings. To determine future earnings capacity, prior earnings records are analyzed.

The normalized future earnings of $29,653 were computed as follows:

Year**	Income*	Weight	Weighted Income
1	$23,075	5	$115,375
2	22,943*	4	91,772
3	36,317	3	108,951
4	44,046	2	88,092
5	40,604	1	40,604
			444,794
Dividend by weight factor			15
			$ 29,653

*Income before extraordinary items.
**Year 1 is the most recent year.

In selecting the capitalization rate, we considered the rate that would constitute a reasonable rate of return. What constitutes a reasonable return may best be answered by referring to IRS Rev. Rul. 68-609, which states:

> The percentage of return on the average annual value of tangible assets used should be the percentage prevailing in the industry involved at the date of valuation. . . .

We examined the rate of return for the electric equipment industry as a guide for arriving at the rate of return. The 19__ median after-tax return on net worth (i.e., percentage of after-tax profit on net worth) for the electronic equipment industry under Standard Industry Code 3612 for 19__, as compiled by Dun and Bradstreet, was 12.8 percent. The upper quartile was 22.6 percent. The median represents the mid-point of all observed results, while the upper quartile represents the mid-point between the highest result and the median. It should be noted that the spread between the upper and lower quartiles represents the middle 50 percent of all the observed companies.

It is reasonable to assume that a potential investor would at least want to receive a return on his investment equal to the industry's norm (i.e., median). However, if another investment alternative provides a greater return than the industry's return, an investor would want to invest in the other investment, provided both investments carry the same degree of risks.

A median return of 12.8 percent is low in view of the company's risks and size. The average yield of the three-month U.S. Treasury bill (which is virtually risk-free) in July 19__ was 8.13 percent. Based on studies done by Ibbotson Associates as set forth in the *Stocks, Bonds, Bills and Inflation: 19__* Yearbook, the average annual rate of return for common stock (as based on the Standard and Poor's Composite Index) in excess of the average rate of return of Treasury bills from 1926 to 19__ was 8.4 percent. In addition, the average annual rate of return for small stock (i.e., basically stocks making up the two smallest deciles in terms of capitalization, which are traded on the New York Stock Exchange and stock listed on the American Stock Exchange and over the counter with the same or less capitalization) in excess of the S&P composite index stock was 3.8 percent for the same period.

Given the fact that Treasury bills were yielding an 8.13 percent rate of return in July 19__, it is clear that the median return of 12.2 percent does not adequately compensate for the risks associated with the business. As indicated above, the average annual return for common stock (i.e., S&P index stock) in excess of Treasury bills is 8.4 percent. Another additional 3.8 percent is added for small company stock traded on the NYSE. In total, the small stock traded on the NYSE has a return of 12.2 percent in excess of the Treasury bill rate. Undoubtedly, This Company, Inc. is much smaller and riskier than the small stock traded on the NYSE. Logically, an investment in This Company, Inc. must provide a greater return than the small stock. With a current rate of 8.13 percent for Treasury bills and an excess return of 12.2 percent for small stock, the rate of return for This Company, Inc. should be somewhere above the 20 percent mark.

The upper quartile of the rate of return for the electronic equipment industry is 22.6 percent. We believe this is a better indication of what an investor would accept as a return for a business with similar risks. Accordingly, we used 23 percent to capitalize the business.

Capitalizing the normalized future earnings of $29,653 at 23 percent, the capitalized value of the company is $128,926. The value of 63.8 percent interest in the company before discounts would be $82,255.

It is a generally accepted valuation principle that the capitalized earnings value cannot be less than the liquidation value.

LIQUIDATION VALUE APPROACH

The liquidation value approach estimates the total amount that would be realized from selling or otherwise disposing of the individual assets of a business, after all liabilities and liquidating costs of the business have been paid or otherwise satisfied. The liquidation value is the basis for establishing the lower limit of the value of the business.

The liquidation value approach is similar to the adjusted net book value approach, as each asset is appraised at its disposal value. In the liquidation value approach, however, all the anticipated costs of liquidation must be deducted to arrive at the value of the business. In contrast, most of the liquidation costs normally would not be deducted to arrive at the adjusted net book value of an ongoing business. Some of the liquidation costs are (1) brokerage commission and professional fees for the sale of assets, (2) forfeiture of security deposits and penalty payments resulting from the cancellation of long-term leases, (3) indemnity payments for the cancellation of any outstanding contractual obligations, and (4) possible tax consequences resulting from any gain recognized from the sale or disposition of the assets.

The liquidation value for This Company, Inc. of $171,317 was computed as follows:

Asset	Book Value	Percentage	Estimated Liquidation Value
Cash	$ 26,808	100%	$ 26,808
Accounts receivable	427,285	90	384,557
Other receivables	27,904	100	27,904
Inventory			
Raw materials	149,142	50	74,571
Work in process	100,000	10	10,000
Finished goods	25,000	75	18,750
Prepaid expenses	13,231	100	13,231
Patents and goodwill	3,146	—	—
Deposit to rebuild machine	4,000	—	—
Property and equipment	73,604	*	121,489
Automobiles	16,002	*	12,500
Total assets			689,810
Less			
Liabilities			(406,741)
Liquidation costs**			(111,752)
Liquidation Value @ 7/31/__			$171,317

The value of 63.8 percent interest in the company would be $109,300.

*See attached computation.

**Liquidation costs are estimates of the costs that would be incurred during liquidation, including commissions for the sale, rent and other overhead costs. See attached schedule.

Computation of Liquidation Value for Property and Equipment

Asset	Cost	Percentage	Estimated Liquidation Value
Furniture and fixtures (Includes computer equipment)	$ 34,112	25%	$ 8,528
Machinery and equipment	171,520	50	85,760
Dies	54,402	50	27,201
Leasehold improvements	44,570	–	–
Total Property and Equipment			$121,489
Automobiles	$ 30,144		
19__ Sterling			$ 11,000
19__ Diesel wagon			1,500
Total Automobiles			$ 12,500

Schedule of Estimated Liquidation Costs

	Year 1 Amount		Factor		Liquidation Costs
Overhead Costs					
Supervisors' salaries	$58,748	x	2/12	=	$ 9,791
Office salary	23,899	x	2/12	=	3,983
Rent*	28,997	x	10/12	=	24,164
Utilities	20,204	x	2/12	=	3,367
Telephone	8,586	x	2/12	=	1,431
Payroll service	2,946	x	2/12	=	491
Scavenger, maintenance and repair	4,593	x	2/12	=	766
Health and welfare	37,725	x	2/12	=	6,288
Insurance	26,892	x	2/12	=	4,482
Legal and accounting	10,142	x	2/12	=	1,690
Taxes and licenses	1,051	x	2/12	=	175
Payroll taxes	43,062	x	2/12	=	7,177
Interest expenses	10,733	x	2/12	=	1,789
Officer's salary	70,000	x	2/12	=	11,667
Total Overhead Costs					77,261
Estimated commissions on liquidation sale of $689,810 in assets (see preceding table) x 5%				=	34,491
Total Estimated Liquidation Costs					$111,752

*The lease runs from May 19__; therefore, we included the ten months of rent the company would have to pay.

EXAMPLE 10
VALUATION BUILDING BLOCKS: CAPITALIZED EARNINGS
APPROACH VERSUS ADJUSTED NET BOOK VALUE APPROACH

HISTORY AND NATURE OF BUSINESS

In June 1965, what if Sharkman opened the Jaw's Grill restaurant in Red Beach, Georgia? The restaurant is at the end of a boardwalk-type mall on the beach. The restaurant is constructed of driftwood and built on stilts. The location and design provides restaurant patrons with a beautiful panoramic view of the ocean. Naturally, the restaurant's menu consists of various seafood items.

Due to the changes in local law, the building may not be rebuilt if it collapses or is destroyed by a hurricane. The state has also prohibited the company from any additional efforts to prevent further erosion of the beach. Thus, if the building is destroyed, the restaurant will lose all of its ambience since it could not be rebuilt in the same location.

CAPITALIZED EARNINGS APPROACH

The normalized pretax future earnings of $64,000 were computed as follows:

Year	Income**	Weight	Weighted Income
1*	$54,315	3	$162,945
2	88,712	2	177,424
3	38,663	1	38,663
			$379,032
Divided by the weight factor			6
Normalized pretax future earnings			$ 63,172
Rounded			$ 64,000

*Year 1 is the latest year.
**Income was computed as shown below.

	Year 1	Year 2	Year 3
Net Income	$47,431	$66,391	$10,854
Add:			
Income taxes	6,884	22,321	27,809
Before tax income	$54,315	$88,712	$38,663

In selecting the capitalization rate, we considered the rate that would constitute a reasonable rate of return. What constitutes a reasonable return can best be answered by referring to IRS Rev. Rul. 68-609, which states:

> The percentage of return on the average annual value of tangible assets used should be percentage prevailing in the industry involved at the date of valuation.

We examined the rate of return for the Retail Restaurant Industry as a guide for arriving at the rate of return.

The year 1 median before-tax return on net worth (i.e., percentage of before-tax profit on net worth) for the Retail Restaurant Industry under Standard Industry Code 5812 for year 1 as compiled by Robert Morris Associates, was 21.4 percent. Since the industry median is 21.4 percent, it is reasonable to assume that a potential investor would want to obtain at least a 21.4 percent return on his investment.

Capitalizing the normalized pretax future earnings of $64,000 at 21.4 percent, the capitalized value of the company is about $300,000 computed as follows:

Normalized future earnings	$ 64,000
Dividend by the capitalization rate	21.4%
Capitalized value	$299,065
Rounded	$300,000

In view of the low capitalized value, we believe that the capitalized earnings approach should not be relied upon to value the company.

ADJUSTED NET BOOK VALUE APPROACH

The adjusted net book value requires that all assets be evaluated to determine their true economic value. Fixed assets are appraised at a figure approximating their present market value as opposed to depreciated cost.

This method is most appropriate in those entities where economic goodwill is not present, but whose assets, when considered as a whole, produce a going concern value and contain a value over and above what is recorded on the books of the business. This approach is also most applicable to companies having erratic or depressed earnings which are inadequate to provide a fair return on the value of the net tangible assets employed. In theory, the value of all assets, less all outstanding liabilities, provides an indication of the fair market value of ownership equity.

Although Jaw's Grill is an operating company, we considered the net asset value of the business, since courts have given this value some consideration. As the U.S. Tax Court stated in *Estate of Woodbury G. Andrews*, 79 TC No. 58, CCH Dec. 39523, Certainly, the degree to which the corporation is actively engaged in producing income rather than merely holding property for investment should influence the weight to be given to the values arrived at under the different approaches but it should not dictate the use of one approach to the exclusion of all others.

Adjusted net book value represents the fair market value of the net assets (fair market value of all assets less liabilities) underlying the stock of the corporation. We determined the adjusted net book value of Jaw's Grill as of May 31, 19__, at about $1,200,000, as follows:

Net book value as of May 31, 19__		$ 690,515
Adjustment		
Fixed Assets		
Fair Market Value*	$570,193	
Book Value	115,065	455,128
Liquor License		
Fair Market Value **	140,000	
Book Value	108,622	31,378
Adjusted net book value as of May 31, 19__		$1,177,021
Rounded		$1,200,000

*The fair market value was based on an appraisal provided by Fishy Business Services, Inc.

**The fair market value is based on an estimate provided by the company's attorney.

We know of no other contingent assets or liabilities that should be considered in determining the adjusted net asset value.

Because of the low earnings from its operations, as shown above, we believe that the adjusted net book value approach should be relied upon for determining the fair market value of the company.

EXAMPLE 11
VALUATION BUILDING BLOCKS

DISCOUNTED CASH FLOW APPROACH

The discounted cash flow approach is an income-based approach. It determines the fair market value of an ongoing business enterprise based on its earnings capacity and operating cash flows. This approach involves projecting operating cash flows for an extended period of time, and then discounting those amounts back to the valuation date to determine the current value.

The discounted cash flow calculations consist of two major components: (1) future cash flows, and (2) rate of return. It involves the following steps:

1. Projected operating cash flows, year by year, for an infinite period (i.e., a perpetual stream of cash flows).

2. A rate of return is selected.

3. The estimated cash flows for each of the years are discounted at the selected discount rate to arrive at their present values.

4. The present value figures for all future years' earnings are added to determine the total operating value of the company.

Depreciation is added back to earnings after taxes since it is not an additional cash expense. Additional working capital expenditures for improvements, even though they may not be an immediate expense deduction, need to be deducted since they require actual cash outlay.

The National Restaurant Association projects that the U.S. foodservice industry will have a 1990 sales increase of 6.2 percent from the amount projected for 1989. Accordingly, we have projected sales to increase 5 percent each year for Club Gene and Georgetti, Ltd. In addition, we have substituted the median average for food and beverage costs for full-menu tableservice restaurants of a similar size as reported in *Restaurant Industry Operations Report '89*. Better operating results are anticipated due to the management now in place.

In selecting the capitalization rate, we considered the rate that would constitute a reasonable rate of return. What constitutes a reasonable return can best be answered by referring to IRS Rev. Rul. 68-609, which states:

> The percentage of return on the average annual value of tangible assets used should be the percentage prevailing in the industry involved at the date of valuation . . .

We examined the rate of return for the retail restaurant business as a guide for arriving at the rate of return.

The average 1986–1989 median before-tax return on net worth (i.e., percentage of before-tax profit on net worth) for the retail restaurant business under Standard Industrial Code 5812 for 1986–1989, as compiled by Robert Morris Associates, was 20 percent. Since the industry median is 20 percent, it is reasonable to assume that a potential investor would want to obtain at least a 20 percent return on his investment. This percentage was used in calculating the present value of the projected cash flows.

The discount cash flows, as per Exhibit C, is computed as follows:

Year	Projected Available Cash Flow	Present Value Factor	Present Value Factor
1	$ 426,574	.8333	$ 355,464
2	447,902	.6944	311,023
3	470,297	.5787	272,161
4	493,812	.4823	238,166
5	518,502	.4019	208,386
Residual	2,592,510*	.4019	1,041,930
Total			2,427,130
Less total debt capital			70,000
Total Present Value of Discounted Cash Flow for the Restaurant Operation			$2,357,130

*Computation of residual

$$\frac{\text{Year 5 (\$518,502)}}{\text{Return on investment (20\%)}} = \$2,592,510$$

EXAMPLE 12
VALUATION BUILDING BLOCKS: MARKET COMPARISON APPROACH

PURPOSE OF VALUATION

The purpose of this valuation is to determine the fair market value of one share of stock in Tower Corporation d/b/a Place and Space (Tower) Homes as of May 31, 19__ . The fair market value is determined based on the premise that the share represents a minority interest.

HISTORY AND NATURE OF THE BUSINESS

The Tower Corporation began business on February 9, 19__. Its first year of operations had sales of $9,687,403 and a before-tax profit of $682,912. The primary reasons for the low profit were low volume with high interest and other fixed costs.

The principal shareholder had basically two choices, either cut fixed costs or increase volume. He chose to increase volume. Increased volume, however, meant additional land inventory with a corresponding increase in debt. The corporation, however, could not borrow solely on its own financial position. Accordingly, the principal shareholder had to guarantee all of the corporation's loans.

For 19__ and subsequent years, the corporation's operating results are as follow (see Exhibits I and II for detail—not shown here):

Year	Sales	Pre-Tax Income	Debts Outstanding
1*	$11,322,383	$ 770,595	$ 5,341,077
2	23,921,059	161,268	14,456,657
3	51,900,172	1,019,172	24,177,844
4	63,904,283	1,956,657	22,007,127
5	63,668,016	3,709,715	24,496,099

*Year 1 is the earliest year.

The major part of the company's business involves residential development. This requires skill in land acquisition, land planning, engineering, product design, construction technology, finance, sales and marketing. The most important aspect of the business is acquiring, zoning and developing land. The company's future depends on its ability to acquire land. When the land inventory is depleted, the company is out of business.

The second most important aspect of the business is financing. Without the ability to borrow with favorable terms, the company could not acquire the land that is necessary for its existence. However, debt financing or high leverage can be fatal in a down market.

It is becoming more difficult to find good land in good locations. Zoning restrictions and impact fees have increased land cost which, in some locations, will reduce the company's gross margin.

SPECIFIC VALUATION METHODS

We considered three basic approaches toward valuing the common stock of Tower Corporation:

- Market Comparison Approach
- Adjusted Net Book Value Approach
- Capitalized Earnings Approach

Market Comparison Approach

Using comparable corporations as a guide to valuation, as a practical matter, is the most appropriate technique for valuing a closely held operating business. As stated in Revenue Ruling 59-60:

> ... When a stock is closely held, ... some other measure of value must be used. In many instances, the next best measure may be found in the prices at which the stocks of companies engaged in the same or a similar line of business are selling in a free and open market.

Finding a company exactly the same as the closely held business is an impossibility. The standard should be one of reasonable similarity. A reasonable degree of latitude must be afforded in selecting comparable companies.

The use of publicly held corporations as comparable companies cannot give an exact fair market value for the closely held business, because the risk involved in investing in an actively traded corporation is less than that of purchasing a company for which there is no ready market. The purpose of comparative analysis is to arrive at a benchmark valuation amount. Appropriate adjustments are then made to give recognition to the dissimilarities between the closely held business and the comparable corporations.

In identifying a list of comparable companies, we looked at the companies under SIC 1521: General Contractors—Single-Family Houses and SIC 1531: Operative Builders as listed in Standard & Poor's Corporate Records. In total, there were over 240 such companies, of which 51 were publicly traded. In selecting the comparables, we set these criteria:

1. The company's sales must not exceed $400 million.

2. The company must be a U.S. company operating primarily in the U.S.

3. The company must have a positive after-tax earnings.

4. The company must not be principally in the development of communities and must not have substantial operations other than housing construction.

During this selection, 43 companies were eliminated for reasons detailed in Appendix A on page 277. The following eight companies (the real names) were selected as comparables: (1) Calton, Inc., (2) Continental Homes Holding Corp., (3) International American Homes, Inc., (4)

Lennar Corp., (5) J. M. Peters Co., Inc., (6) M/I Schottenstein Homes, Inc., (7) Oriole Homes Corp., and (8) Toll Brothers Inc. Following is a business overview of these comparable companies as obtained from the *Standard Stock Reports* published by Standard & Poor's Corp.:

1. *Calton, Inc.*

    The company is primarily engaged in the building and sale of residential housing units in New Jersey, Pennsylvania, and Florida. It also acquired land which is used for planning residential developments or sold to other builders. The company also participates in land and residential development through joint ventures and provides mortgage banking and brokerage services.

2. *Continental Homes Holding Corp.*

    The company commenced operations in June 1985 when it acquired the Phoenix homebuilding operations of American Continental Corp. The company designs, constructs, sells and finances single-family homes in Phoenix, Arizona and, to a lesser extent, in Denver, Colorado and San Diego, California. In fiscal 1988, it delivered 331 move-up single-family homes, 422 entry-level single-family units, 312 patio homes, and 96 townhomes.

3. *International American Homes, Inc.*

    The company is currently offering homes in 27 communities in metropolitan Washington, D.C., greater Tampa, Florida, southeastern Florida, and southern California. The company sold its Texas operations in December 1987. For the fiscal year ended March 31, 1988, the company delivered 1,100 homes at an average price per home of $134,000.

4. *Lennar Corp.*

    The company is primarily engaged in the building and sale of moderately priced single-family homes and of low-rise, multi-family residential buildings primarily sold as condominiums.

    It delivered a total of 4,131 residential units in fiscal 1988, versus 3,950 in fiscal 1987. The average price of units sold in fiscal 1988 was $81,600, 8 percent above the fiscal 1987 average, but 41 percent below the national average of $138,300.

    Its other activities include the development of shopping centers, office buildings and mobile home parks.

5. *J. M. Peters Co., Inc.*

    The company is one of the largest builders of single-family homes in southern California for upper income buyers who have previously owned a principal residence. The company was founded in 1975, and 87 percent of its stock was acquired by San Jacinto Savings Association in 1985.

    Company operations include the location, valuation and purchase of undeveloped land and improved lots, the development of land, and the design, construction, marketing and sale of homes. Its homes are noted for their innovative design, attention to detail and quality construction. They have received numerous industry design awards in recent years, and substantially all homes are under contract for sale prior to completion of construction.

6. *M/I Schottenstein Homes, Inc.*

The company is engaged in the design, construction and marketing of single-family homes in residential developments in Ohio, Florida, North Carolina and Tennessee. Units are offered at base prices ranging from $55,000 to $201,000, with an average purchase price of about $108,000. During 1987, 1,630 new contracts were written and 1,499 homes were delivered.

7. *Oriole Homes Corp.*

It primarily builds and sells single-family homes and condominium apartments in south Florida. In addition, the company acquires land for sale to independent builders, and, to a lesser extent, is engaged in the sale of developed homesites and land.

Oriole caters largely to retirees who, to a considerable degree, have available funds to buy housing outright without utilizing mortgage financing.

8. *Toll Brothers, Inc.*

The company designs, builds, markets, and finances single-family homes, townhouses and low-rise condominiums, primarily in central and northern New Jersey and south-eastern Pennsylvania. It builds homes in middle and high income residential communities, and markets them primarily to current homeowners wishing to move up in size or quality of housing.

The eight companies selected as possible comparables are larger than Tower Corporation. These differences, however, should not deter them from being considered as comparables. Rarely will two companies be identical. If unduly restrictive criteria were set for the selection of comparable companies, it would be virtually impossible to find a comparable. This would render the comparative approach to valuation virtually meaningless.

The size differential of the comparables selected indicate that they are less risky than Tower Corporation from the investment standpoint. Larger companies are viewed as less risky because they are presumably better able to financially withstand economic downturns. This difference can be reasonably accounted for in arriving at the value of Tower Corporation. The use of larger companies as comparables is acceptable.

FINANCIAL ANALYSIS

To determine the operating and financial posture of Tower Corporation in comparison to the eight selected comparable companies, certain ratios were computed to determine profitability and financial stability.

	Equity/Assets	Profit/Equity	Profit/Assets
1. Calton, Inc.	41.3%	24.8%	9.9%
2. Continental Homes Holding Corp.	21.4	11.7	2.5
3. International American Homes, Inc.	20.0	11.5	2.5
4. Lennar Corp.	45.5	12.6	5.3
5. J. M. Peters Co., Inc.	26.4	43.1	11.4
6. M/I Schottenstein Homes, Inc.	20.0	28.5	5.6
7. Oriole Homes Corp.	39.0	19.9	7.3
8. Toll Brothers, Inc.	28.4	39.6	11.0
Tower Corporation (a)	18.1	54.6	8.3

(a) Profit/equity and profit/assets are computed on an after-tax basis as if Tower Corporation is a regular C corporation (see Exhibits I and II—not shown in this example).

Tower Corporation is highly leveraged in comparison with the publicly traded companies, as it has the lowest equity to assets ratio. Although its after-tax rate of return on equity is the highest among the comparables, it is partially the result of high leverage. The after-tax rate of return would be reduced if the corporation is less leveraged. This is apparent from the fact that the company's profit to asset ratio of 8.3 times is close to the median of the return of the comparables. Its profit to asset ratio is not much higher than the average return of 6.9 percent of the comparables.

In summary, the company is highly leveraged; thus, it is financially less stable and more risky than the comparables. Its earnings performance is within the average range of the performance of the comparables.

Value Measure

To value a company, we need to determine the earnings power and the appropriate capitalization rate for the company. Price-earnings ratio is the reciprocal of the capitalization rate. By analyzing the price-earnings ratios of the comparables, we can derive an appropriate capitalization rate for the company.

In analyzing the price-earnings ratios of the eight comparables, it is apparent that the companies which experienced a substantial increase in their earnings in year 5 in relationship to their year 4 operations generally have a low price-earnings ratio. The following table shows the companies which have an earnings per share in fiscal year 5 that is at least 30 percent higher than their prior years' earnings per share:

		Earnings per Share		
Name	Year 6 P/E Ratio	Year 5	Year 4	Increase
1. International American Homes, Inc.	4	.53	.40	33%
2. J. M. Peters Co., Inc.	4	2.81	1.67	68
3. Oriole Homes Corp.	4	2.61	1.54	69
4. Toll Brothers, Inc.	8	.80	.57	40

Source: Standard & Poor's Stock Guide, June Year 6

Other than Toll Brothers, the price-earnings ratios of the companies are at a multiple of only 4. This may reflect the investors' general sentiments that the sudden increase in earnings in year 5 will not be maintained in the future years. Prior year's earnings might be more representative of the future earnings stream. Accordingly, the increased earnings in fiscal year year 5 might not have simulated an increase in stock price for these companies.

On the other hand, the companies which did not experience a significant increase in their year 5 earnings from year 4 have a higher price-earnings ratio as follows:

		Earnings per Share		
Name	Year 6 P/E Ratio	Year 5	Year 4	(Decrease) Increase
1. Calton, Inc.	6	.62	.61	2%
2. Continental Homes Holding Corp.	9	.72	1.58	(54)
3. Lennar Corp.	8	2.78	2.50	11
4. M/I Schottenstein Homes, Inc.	7	.80	.77	4

These price-earnings ratios may indicate that the investors believed that the year 5 earnings, which are slightly higher (or lower) than the prior year's earnings, are more representative of the future income stream of the company.

In regard to Tower, its earnings after tax of about $2,300,000 in year 5 (see Exhibit II, not shown) is at least two times its prior year's income of about $1,100,000, an increase of over 100 percent. This increase is much higher than the increases of the four comparable companies that had experienced substantial increase in their earnings. If we looked at the collective increase in the earnings for year 4 and year 5, both J. M. Peters Co. and Oriole Homes have experienced high growth in earnings. J. M. Peters Co.'s earnings in year 4 had increased almost three times from its year 3 earnings, while Oriole Homes' earnings in year 4 also increased almost 1 1/2 times. Tower also experienced an increase in earnings of about 1 time in year 4. Accordingly, the earnings increase experienced by Tower in year 5 and year 4 was also witnessed by J. M. Peters Co. and Oriole Homes over the two-year period. The price-earnings ratios of J. M. Peters Co. and Oriole Homes are four. Despite the increase of earnings over a two-year period, the price-earnings ratios of four may indicate that the investors were not convinced that these earnings increases will be maintained in the future to justify a substantial increase in price, and thus an increase of the price-earnings ratio.

Similarly, the increase of Tower's earnings in year 5 does not justify a presumption that the substantial year 5 earnings will prevail in future years. As a matter of fact, the company experienced an operating loss of $693,519 for the five-month period ended May 31, year 6 (see Exhibit III, not shown). Given the fact that the company will most likely not be able to maintain its year 5 earnings level, we believe that the price-earnings ratios of the corporations which experienced substantial increase in earnings in year 5 would be the best indicator of what investors would pay for the stock in Tower. We believe that the price-earnings ratio of five would be appropriate, computed as follows:

Name	P/E Ratio
1. International American Homes, Inc.	4
2. J. M. Peters Co., Inc.	4
3. Oriole Homes Corp.	4
4. Toll Brothers, Inc.	_8_
	20
Divided by	_4_
Average Ratio	_5_

A price-earnings ratio of five reflects a capitalization rate of 20 percent, as the ratio is the reciprocal of the rate. As a test to see if the derived price-earnings ratio is appropriate, we considered the capitalization rate that would constitute a reasonable rate of return. What constitutes a reasonable return may be answered by referring to IRS Rev. Rul. 68-909, which states:

> The percentage of return on the average annual value of tangible assets used should be the percentage prevailing in the industry involved at the date of valuation. . . .

We examined the rate of return for the Single-Family Housing Construction Industry as a guide for arriving at the rate of return. The year 5 median after-tax return on net worth (i.e., percentage of after-tax profit on net worth) for the Single-Family Housing Construction Industry under Standard Industry Code 1521 for year 5, as compiled by Dun and Bradstreet, was 27.5 percent. The median represents the midpoint of all observed results.

A potential investor would at least want to receive a return on his investment equal to the industry's norm (i.e., median). Accordingly, an investor would most likely want to have a rate of return of at least 25 percent for an investment in the single-family housing construction industry. With a capitalization rate of 25 percent (i.e., the reasonable rate of return), the price-earnings ratio would also be four times.

This price-earnings ratio, based on industry's rate of return, is somewhat lower than the ratio of five based on the comparables. If we would have excluded Toll Brothers, then the price-earnings ratio of the comparables would be identical to that derived from the industry's rate of return. Nonetheless, we believe that Toll Brothers should be accounted for and the price-earnings ratio of five is a reasonable and normal price-earnings ratio for the comparable companies which have experienced substantial increase in earnings in year 5.

Aside from determining a normal price-earnings ratio for the comparable companies, we must determine the direction and the extent Tower should vary from this norm. For Tower, we believe there should be a negative adjustment for the following reasons:

1. On the *negative side*, the company is smaller than the comparables and has the smallest equity-to-assets ratio.

2. On the *positive side*, the company experienced the highest rate of return on equity in comparison to the comparables, although it is partially due to its high leverage.

3. On the significantly *negative side*, the company's debts are guaranteed by its major stockholder.

In summary, we believe there should be a 10 percent downward adjustment to the normal price-earnings ratio. This gives a 4.50 price-earnings ratio for Tower.

Since the price-earnings ratio is based on the comparables' latest 12-months earnings, Tower's year 5 earnings, which are the latest available 12-months earnings, should be used. As a result, the fair market value based on comparables for the common stock is $10,312,902, or $8,882.78 per share, computed as follows:

Earnings (see Exhibit II—not shown)	$ 2,291,756
Price-Earnings Ratio	4.50
Total Value	$10,312,902
Number of Shares Outstanding	1,161
Value per Share	$ 8,882.78

This value of $8,882.78 per share represents the value of a share of stock in Tower as if it is a minority interest (i.e., not a part of a control block of stock) and is freely traded (i.e., not subject to the lack of marketability) in the market.

Since Tower is a closely held business, a discount for general lack of marketability is appropriate to arrive at the fair market value. The lack of marketability discount concept recognizes the fact that closely held stock interests are less attractive and have fewer potential purchasers because they are not readily marketable.

Accordingly, the discount for lack of marketability is about 35 percent. Given a discount of 35 percent, the value per share for a minority interest would be $5,773.81 per share.

WEIGHING THE VALUES FROM DIFFERENT APPROACHES

Consideration of the various valuation approaches helps to minimize the effects of defects in any one approach. Even if perfectly accurate values could be derived from assets and earnings, the two figures will seldom be identical.

Since the Company is an operating company and has no immediate intention to liquidate, earnings are given primary emphasis. We weighted the capitalized earnings value and the market comparison value at 40 percent each and the adjusted net book value at 20 percent. Based on the allocation of weight, the value per share of the company for a minority interest is as follows:

	Value per Share	Weight	Weighted Value
Adjusted net book value	$2,761.16	20%	$ 552.23
Capitalized earnings value	5,368.30	40	2,147.32
Market comparison value	5,773.81	40	2,309.52
Value per Share			$5,009.07
		Rounded	$ 5,009

Appendix A
Schedule of Possible Comparable Public Companies—Reasons for Rejection

1. American Pacesetter	Its real estate development operation was spin-off on June 30, year 5. Deficits earnings.
2. Amerep Corp.	32 percent of its revenue is not in real estate development.
3. April Industries, Inc.	Located in Puerto Rico.
4. Beaman Corp.	Limited information available.
5. Camponelli Industries, Inc.	Limited information available.
6. Deltona Corp.	Primarily in the development of communities.
7. Fairfield Communities, Inc.	Primarily in the development of communities.
8. Forest City Enterprises, Inc.	Primarily in real estate rental operations.
9. General Builders Corp.	Limited information available.
10. General Homes Corp.	Deficit earnings.
11. Holiday-Gulf Homes, Inc.	Limited information available.
12. Key Co.	In bankruptcy proceeds since June year 5.
13. LVI Group, Inc.	Primarily in the interior construction management and consulting business.
14. MDC Holdings, Inc.	Deficit earnings.
15. Mod-U-Kraf Homes, Inc.	Limited information available.
16. Nvryan L.P.	Limited information available.
17. PHM Corp.	Too large, sales exceed $1 billion.
18. Punta Gorda Isles, Inc.	Deficit earnings.
19. Quality Homes, Inc.	Limited information available.
20. Roberts Enterprises, Inc.	Limited information available.
21. Royal Palm Beach Colony, LP.	Limited partnership in community development.
22. Shelter Corp. of America	Limited information available.
23. UDC-Universal Development L.P.	A limited partnership primarily in the development of retirement and family communities.
24. Union Valley Corp.	Deficit earnings, primarily in the development of retirement and preretirement communities.
25. Washington Homes, Inc.	Acquired by Sonny DeCesaris & Son Development on August 2, year 5.
26. Writer Corp.	Deficit earnings.
27. American Community Development Group, Inc.	Limited information available.
28. BTR Realty, Inc.	Limited information available.
29. Consolidated Capital Corp.	Limited information available.
30. Centennial Group	Merged on December 31, year 3.
31. General Development Corp.	Only 22 percent is housing sales, primarily a developer of communities.
32. Leroy Properties & Development Corp.	Limited information available.
33. L. B. Nelson Corp.	Limited information available.
34. Centex Corp.	Too large.
35. The Ryland Group	Too large.
36. Standard Pacific L.P.	Too large.

continued

Schedule of Possible Comparable Public Companies—Reasons for Rejection
(continued)

37. Fabulous Inns of America	Mainly in motel management.
38. Hillenbrand Industries, Inc.	Primarily in health care and casket businesses.
39. Jacobs Engineering Group, Inc.	Primarily in engineering, designing and consulting services.
40. U.S. Home Corp.	Too large.
41. Beazer PLC	Located in England.
42. Coscan Development Corp.	Located in Canada.
43. Consolidated Capital Corp.	Located in Canada.

EXAMPLE 13
VALUATION BUILDING BLOCKS: VALUATION OF A COMPETITIVE BID CONSTRUCTION COMPANY

PURPOSE OF VALUATION

The purpose of this valuation is to determine the fair market value of the common stock of Punch Construction Corporation (Company) as of December 31, 19___ . The valuation will be used to determine for gift tax purposes, the value of the 5,000 shares of the company transferred from J. J. Punch to his daughter, Judy, on December 15, year 1 and also the 5,000 shares transferred on February 9, year 2.

HISTORY AND NATURE OF THE BUSINESS

The company was incorporated in September, 19___ by J. J. Punch to conduct an outside electrical contracting business, installing electrical apparatus, above ground and underground.

The company began operations May 1, 19___, billed $207,000 and had net income of $20,000 in its first fiscal year of operation.

Substantially, all of the company's business is obtained through competitive bidding on contracts let by governmental agencies. This sales environment does not lend itself to the establishment of the usual long-term business relationships but rather tends to result in instability of revenues and earnings. The company's major customers over the years have been various villages and towns in Near County, The Far Transit Authority, U.S. Department of Army and Navy, State of Illinois and AT&T. This customer list is active only when there is public funding available.

CAPITALIZED EARNINGS APPROACH

Conceptually, the capitalized earnings approach determines the fair market value of an ongoing business enterprise based on its earnings capacity. This approach is based on the theory that an investment (i.e., net tangible assets) will yield a return sufficient to recover its initial cost and to justly compensate the investor for the inherent risks of ownership.

Under the capitalized earnings approach, we determined the normalized future earnings and capitalized such earnings based on a reasonable rate of return as indicated by available statistics. Normalized future earnings refers to the average future annual earnings over a period of time.

Although future earnings are to be used for earnings capitalization, past earnings are usually the best guide for determining future earnings. In this regard, Rev. Rul. 59-60 states: Prior earnings records usually are the most reliable guide as to the future expectancy.

Usually, the past earnings records would be the starting point for determining future earnings. However, this concept does not apply to the real business world when the particular business must obtain each new job through a competitive bidding procedure unrelated to any previous job done by the bidder. Substantially all of the company's business is obtained through competitive bidding on contracts let by governmental agencies. The bidding process tends to result in instable earnings. The contracts and earnings from one year have no relationship to the contracts and earnings for any other year. The fact you won a contract in year one has no effect on the awarding of a contract in year two. In addition, the agencies (potential customers) must have money to let contracts. Therefore, a valuation method based on earnings is not an appropriate method to value Punch Construction Corporation.

ADJUSTED NET BOOK VALUE APPROACH

The adjusted net book value requires that all assets be evaluated to determine their true economic value. Fixed assets are appraised at a figure approximating their present market value as opposed to depreciated cost.

This method is most appropriate in those entities where economic goodwill is not present, but whose assets, when considered as a whole, produce a going-concern value and contain a value over and above what is recorded on the books of the business. This approach is also most applicable to companies having erratic or depressed earnings which are inadequate to provide a fair return on the value of the net tangible assets employed. In theory, the value of all assets, less all outstanding liabilities, provides an indication of the fair market value of ownership equity.

Although the Company is an operating company, we considered the net asset value of the business since courts have given this value some consideration. As the U.S. Tax Court stated in *Estate of Woodbury G. Andrews*, 79 TC No. 58, CCH Dec. 39523, Certainly, the degree to which the corporation is actively engaged in producing income rather than merely holding property for investment should influence the weight to be given to the values arrived at under the different approaches but it should not dictate the use of one approach to the exclusion of all others.

Adjusted net book value represents the fair market value of the net assets (fair market value of all assets less liabilities) underlying the stock of the corporation. We determined the adjusted net book value of the Company as of December 31, year 1 at about $1,615,880 as follows:

Net book value as of December 31, Year 1		$1,070,998
Adjustments from book value to fair market value of machinery, equipment and vehicles:		
Approximate fair market value*	$1,024,441	
Book value as of April 30, Year 1	(483,168)	541,273
Adjusted net book value as of April 30, Year 1		$1,612,271
Rounded		$1,615,000

*The fair market value was based on estimates of the fair market value as of April 30, Year 1 provided by the company's management. All fixed asset acquisitions between April 30, Year 1 and December 31, Year 1 were included at cost. No depreciation was computed for the period May 1, Year 1 to December 31, Year 1.

We made no adjustments to the office equipment or leasehold improvements since the company's management estimates the book value approximates the market value. Also, we do not know of any contingent liabilities that should be considered in determining the adjusted net asset value.

EXAMPLE 14
VALUATION BUILDING BLOCKS: SEPARATE VALUATION OF FOUR
ELEMENTS OF ONE BUSINESS

UNITED STATES POSTAL SERVICE CONTRACT

The Company (Our Client) has a $12,650,000 fixed price contract with the United States Postal Service (USPS) which commits the Company to the manufacture of 58,000 (GIZMOS) for the USPS. Shipment is currently scheduled to commence in mid-1990 and continue for fourteen months. The USPS has reimbursed the company for certain expenditures made in 19__ which relate to production of the (GIZMOS). The USPS reimbursements are reported as deferred revenue until shipment commences, on the September 30, 19__ financial statements.

We separated the USPS contract from the Company's remaining operations because the contract is the first such contract ever received by the Company. This Company was involved in bidding for and securing the contract for several years before the contract was awarded to the Company.

Similar contracts are unlikely to become part of the Company's regular business. The probability of obtaining similar contracts in the foreseeable future is almost nil, although the USPS has an option to acquire additional (GIZMOS). Because of the extraordinary nature of the contract, coupled with the unlikelihood of obtaining a similar contract in the near future, the appropriate way to account for this contract is to include the present value of the projected future earnings.

It would be inappropriate to treat the USPS contract as a recurring business activity and incorporate its potential earnings as part of the normalized future earnings for earnings capitalization. To be a part of the normalized future earnings, there must be sufficient assurance that such income will be generated on a regular basis.

The value of the government contract is based upon the projected future net earnings and is determined as follows:

1. Company management projected the pretax earnings of each shipment.

2. Corporate income tax was applied to the earnings to arrive at after-tax earnings.

3. The amounts were then discounted and added to arrive at the present value of the future after-tax earnings.

In selecting the discount rate, we used the same rate (i.e., 20 percent) as used in the capitalized earnings approach. The rationale in deriving a capitalization rate is equally applicable in selecting a discount rate.

Discounting the future after-tax earnings of the USPS contract gives a value of $1,725,322. See Exhibit G (not shown).

LITIGATION AWARD

In August, 19__ Bad Guys Services, Inc. (BGS), d/b/a GIZMO Services, John Jones, Jim Jones, and Jack Jones (Joneses) brought an action for damages and injunctive relief against the

Company. This action was brought under the antitrust laws. BGS is a competitor of Our Client. Our Client counterclaimed and included More Bad Guys Company of Florida (MBG) as a counterclaim defendant.

A judgment in favor of Our Client was entered on August 14, 19__ awarding approximately $11,000,000 in compensatory and punitive damages against all of the above named defendants. In November 19__, the Company received $1,700,000 as a settlement with BGS and the Joneses.

In May 19__, an appellate court upheld the trial court decision awarding damages. In August 19__, the appellate court allowed MBG an additional $1.7 million credit. The Company then demanded and received $6,453,872 from MBG. MBG has brought further legal action to overturn or modify the decision by applying for a writ of certiorari to the United States Supreme Court. Our client is also appealing the $1.7 million credit awarded to MBG.

If the decision is overturned by the United States Supreme Court, the Company must return the $6,453,872 received in August 19__.

To place a value on the litigation award, we considered the probability that the decision would be overturned by the Supreme Court. A person would be willing to pay at most (although highly unlikely) an amount equal to the probable value of the award. The probable value is computed by multiplying the probability that the decision will be upheld by the amount of the award. Most likely, a person would be willing to pay an amount less than the probable value since he would want to realize a profit for taking such a gamble.

To assess the probability that the decision would be overturned, we searched the *U.S. Law Week* Volume 58 covering opinions and proceedings for the U.S. Supreme Court between July 4, 19__ and June 26, 19__ (one year). We limited our search to those cases where the Court either granted or denied the writ of certiorari during this period. Our search was further limited to those cases categorized as pertaining to antitrust law as determined by the editors of The Bureau of National Affairs, Inc. Of these cases, we found that certiorari was granted three times and denied 44 times.

In addition, we reviewed the U.S. Supreme Court opinions for the period of June 1, 19__ through August 24, 19__ (21 years). We determined that six cases were decided during this period that related to antitrust law. Of these cases, three were affirmed and three were overruled on antitrust issues.

We did not compare the facts of each case with those of the Company's. Based on our search, the probability of the decision being overturned is about three percent, computed as follows:

$$\text{Probability} = \frac{\text{Number of writ of certiorari granted}}{\text{Total applications for writ of certiorari}} \times \frac{\text{Number of cases overturned}}{\text{Total Cases}}$$

$$\text{Probability} = \frac{3}{47} \times \frac{3}{6}$$

$$\text{Probability} = 3.19 \text{ percent.}$$

Based on our analysis, the probability is small that the case will be overturned. One may refine this analysis by examining each case to determine the probability of cases having similar facts to our situation. However, this would be a time-consuming and expensive process.

A probability of 3.19 percent of being overturned translates to a 96.81 percent of the case being upheld. This results in probable value of $6,247,993. It is highly unlikely that a person would pay the probable value for the award. He would be receiving only a return of three percent (i.e., $205,879 divided by $6,247,993) for taking the risk of losing $6,247,993, plus the legal fees incurred to defend the case. We do not believe that too many people would be willing to pay $6,247,993 to earn only three percent even if they are sufficiently certain that they will receive the principal. For example, the weekly average yield of the 30-year U.S. Treasury bonds (which are virtually risk-free) for the week ended July 27, 19__ was 8.54 percent. Certainly, one would require a much greater yield than 8.54 percent to accept the risk of potentially losing the entire investment of $6,247,993 plus legal fees.

The issue is how much of a return is needed for an investor to accept the risk of losing $6,247,993. In other words, how much is the discount for the probable value.

As illustrated below, businessmen usually average similar risks to determine an appropriate discount. However, each lawsuit is unique, and cannot be averaged with other lawsuits. In fact, a lawsuit is more like a bet. Therefore, a buyer would require a larger discount to accept the risks of the lawsuit.

In addition, a buyer buying stock is really interested in acquiring the operations of the company. Since the lawsuit is not the type of asset the buyer wanted, the buyer would require a greater discount for the lawsuit.

Finally, a buyer would consider the potential income taxes due on the proceeds. At the minimum, a buyer would discount the value for the potential income taxes due. For example, if the buyer was an individual or an S corporation, each $1 million recovered from the lawsuit would net only $720,000 (after Federal tax at a 28 percent bracket, without considering state income taxes). A C corporation buyer would be in an even higher bracket.

The above factors illustrate why a buyer would want a larger discount for the lawsuit, but do not quantify that discount. To assist us in quantifying the discount, we examined certain broad guidelines offered for the selection of rates of return.

Ralph E. Badger, one of the earliest and most often quoted writers on required rates of return by risk class, offers the following in his book, *Valuation of Industrial Securities* (New York: Prentice-Hall, 1925):

Class I	Low risk	12–14.99%
Class II	Medium risk	15–19.99%
Class III	High risk	20–24.99%
Class IV	Very high risk	25% and over

James H. Schilt, in his article, A Rational Approach to Capitalization Rates for Discounting the Future Income Stream of a Closely Held Company, *The Financial Planner*, January 1982, provides the following comments and risk premiums:

> As discount or capitalization rates are fairly arbitrarily determined, I have attempted to set forth guidelines for using specific risk premiums. Beginning with the risk-free rate, a premium would be added according to the risk category, and the sum would be the risk-compensated discount rate.

Risk Premiums

Category	Descriptions	Risk Premium
1	Established businesses with a strong trade position, are well financed, have depth in management, whose past earnings have been stable and whose future is highly predictable.	6–10%
2	Established businesses in a more competitive industry that are well financed, have depth in management, have stable past earnings, and whose future is fairly predictable.	11–15%
3	Businesses in a highly competitive industry that require little capital to enter, no management depth, element of risk is high, although past record may be good.	16–20%
4	Small businesses that depend upon the special skill of one or two people. Larger established businesses that are highly cyclical in nature. In both cases, future earnings may be expected to deviate widely from projections.	21–25%
5	Small "one man" businesses of a personal services nature, where the transferability of the income stream is in question.	26–30%

NOTE: "The risk premium chosen is added to the risk-free rate . . .The resulting figure is the risk-adjusted capitalization rate for use in discounting the projected income stream. Because of the wide variation in the effective tax rates among companies, these figures are designed to be used with pre-tax income."

As the above guidelines indicate, a high-risk situation would easily require a risk premium of 25 percent or more in addition to risk-free rate. With a risk-free return of 8.54 percent, we believe that a rate of return of 35 percent is a minimum return for accepting the risk. Accordingly, the probable value of the judgment is discounted by 35 percent to arrive at $4,061,195, as follows:

Probable value	$6,247,993
Less discount of 35 percent	(2,186,798)
Risk-Adjusted Value	$4,061,195

Based on the above analysis, the Company has a 3.19 percent chance of receiving the additional $1.7 million. Using the above methodology, the value of the $1.7 million would be $35,250, computed as follows:

Total	$1,700,000
Times the probability of winning	3.19%
Probable value	54,230
Less discount of 35 percent	(18,980)
Risk-Adjusted Value	$ 35,250

INVESTMENT ASSETS

When an operating company owns a substantial amount of investment assets, the investment assets are usually valued separately from the business operations. In *Edwin A. Gallum*, 33 T.C.M. 1316 (1974), the company being valued owned a leather tanning operations with related land, buildings, and equipment, plus an investment portfolio of stocks and bonds. The expert witnesses for the taxpayer and the government agreed the company was a combined operating company and investment company and, therefore, the investment portfolio should be valued separately.

With the assistance of the Company's management, certain assets are determined to be unnecessary for the business operations and represent investment assets. The costs and the fair market value of these assets follow.

Description	Cost	Fair Market Value
Cash and cash equivalents in excess necessary for operations	$ 442,729	$ 442,729
Franklin U.S. Government Securities Fund	1,462,871	1,405,370
Interest and dividend receivable	19,579	19,579
Chase Manhattan DP fd 10.50%	225,645	273,000
Consolidated Edison D $4.65	80,000	129,925
Florida Power and Light K 8.70%	96,800	148,000
Mortgage note receivable	170,000	170,000
Margin loan	28,366	28,366
	$2,525,990	$2,616,969

TOTAL VALUE OF COMPANY

In valuing the common stock of the Company, we segregated the Company into the four value attributes or elements and valued each element separately. The four value elements are:

1. The value attributable to its regular operations (operating value),[*]

2. The value of the extraordinary contract with the USPS,

3. The value of an award from the litigation, and

4. The value of its investment assets currently not needed for its operations.

[*]Not shown

To arrive at the value of the Company, the values of all elements are totaled. This gives a total value of $13,240,000, computed as follows:

Operating value	$ 4,801,100
USPS contract	1,725,322
Litigation awards	4,096,445
Investment assets	2,616,969
Total Value Before Discounts	$13,239,836
Rounded	$13,240,000

EXAMPLE 15
VALUATION BUILDING BLOCKS: OLD LINE EX-PROFITABLE
COMPANY FACES FUTURE NEGATIVE CASH FLOW

CAPITAL STRUCTURE

The outstanding common stock of the Proud Corporation, on September 30, 19__, was held as follows:

	Number of Shares	Percentage of Ownership
Rob (Father)	100	55.55%
Mary (Mom)	50	27.78%
Robby (Son)	12	6.67%
Patty (Daughter)	9	5.00%
Bonny (Daughter)	9	5.00%
Totals	180	100.00%

No other form of stock is authorized or issued by the company.

BUSINESS HISTORY AND OUTLOOK

Proud Corporation was founded by Mr. Teddy Baar, Sr. in the early 1920s as the Machine Sales Company. The Company manufactured and sold fun machines. Subsequently, the Company name was changed to American Fun Company and then again changed to Proud Corporation, its present name. Over the years, the Company's products have remained the same.

In 1946, Mr. Rob joined the Company. In 1965, Mr. Teddy Baar, Sr. died and was succeeded by his son, Teddy Baar, Jr., in managing the company. In 1971, Teddy Baar, Jr. died and Rob became the executive operating officer of the Company. In 1976, Rob purchased 100 percent of the stock of the Company from the estate and heirs.

The Company is located at the site it has occupied since the 1960s. The Company's products have not changed over the years. Proud manufactures Go-goes and sells them through independent representatives.

Although the Company is in a strong financial position, and is the largest manufacturer of Go-goes, it has various weaknesses. The market for Go-goes has been shrinking over the years, as sales dropped from $10,940,491 for the year ended September 30, 19__ to $8,830,059 for year ended September 30, 19__. Realizing the uncertain future of the Company, top management of the Company held its first strategic planning meeting recently.

Major weaknesses identified in the strategic planning process are in management, sales, and the product line. There is a lack of communication and team effort between departments at the management level; much of the product line is at the end of its life cycle; and the current sales force is not sufficiently productive.

SPECIFIC VALUATION TECHNIQUES

In valuing the common stock of the Company, we segregated the Company into the following value attributes or elements:

1. The value attributable to its regular operations (operating value).

2. The value of its investment assets currently not needed for its operations.

After determining the value of each attribute, we totalled the amounts to arrive at the tentative value of the common stock.

We considered three basic approaches in determining the operating value of the Company:

- Market Comparison Approach

- Adjusted Net Book Value Approach

- Discounted Cash Flow Approach

The methodology for determining the value of the investment assets is discussed in its respective section below.

MARKET COMPARISON APPROACH

Management of the Company does not believe that there are any publicly traded companies comparable to the Company, therefore, we did not try to locate a publicly traded company comparable to the Proud Corporation.

ADJUSTED NET BOOK VALUE APPROACH

Although the Proud Corporation is a vigorous operating company, we considered the net assets value of the business since courts have given this value some consideration. As the U.S. Tax Court stated in *Estate of Woodbury G. Andrews,* 79 TC No. 58, CCH Dec. 39523, Certainly, the degree to which the corporation is actively engaged in producing income rather than merely holding property for investment should influence the weight to be given to the values arrived at under the different approaches but it should not dictate the use of one approach to the exclusion of all others.

Adjusted net book value represents the fair market value of the net assets (i.e., fair market value of all assets less liabilities). We determined the adjusted net book value of the Proud Corporation's operations as of September 30, 19__, at $8,116,000. (Computation not shown.)

DISCOUNTED CASH FLOW APPROACH

The discounted cash flow approach is an income-based approach. It determines the fair market value of an ongoing business enterprise based on its earnings capacity and operating cash flows. This approach involves projecting cash flows for a period of time, estimating a residual value (equivalent to the continuing earnings power of the business in perpetuity) at the end-of-the-time horizon, and then discounting those amounts back to the valuation date to determine the current value.

The discounted cash flow calculations consist of three major components: (1) future cash flows, (2) residual value, and (3) discount rate. The calculation involves the following steps:

1. Projected operating cash flows, year by year, for the ten years from 19__ to 20__ were prepared. These cash flow projections were compiled by Company's management. See Exhibit C for details. (Not shown.)

2. A residual value was determined. Residual value is the assumed value of a company at the end of the projection period. Since the Company is projecting negative cash flows, we are assuming a $0 residual value.

3. A discount rate (or cost of capital) is selected.

4. The estimated cash flows for each of the projected years are discounted at the selected discount rate to arrive at their present values.

5. The present value figures are added to determine the total operating value of the Company.

6. The operating value, if any, of the Company is then adjusted by subtracting the principal of interest bearing debt service. The interest bearing debt service is subtracted because it reduces cash flow and thus the value of the Company's operations.

Generally, the discount rate is the expected rate of return available on alternative investment opportunities with similar risks. We developed a discount rate based on the weighted average after-tax cost of capital. The weighted average cost of capital is made up of the after-tax returns paid to all sources of capital, weighted by the proportions of each of these sources to total capital.

Here we used two sources of capital: equity (which includes contributed capital and retained earnings on common stock) and debt. Both the risk rates and the debt/equity ratio are determined after considering the business risks. This is intended to reflect the analysis that a prudent investor might conduct to estimate the fair market value.

We estimated the cost of debt based on the weekly average for the week ended September 28, 19__ yield on Moody Seasonal BAA bonds of 10.76 percent with a premium adjustment of 2 percentage points for the risk involved to arrive at 12.76 percent. After adjustment for an assumed 39 percent effective tax rate, the after-tax cost of debt becomes 7.78 percent.

To arrive at the cost of equity, we estimated the (1) expected risk-free rate (Rf), (2) expected return on the equity market in excess of the risk-free rate (Rm) (i.e., equity market risk premium), and (3) industry/company risks (R). These inputs were incorporated into the following formula:

$$Ke = Rf + Rm + R$$

Ke = Cost of equity

Rf = Risk-free rate (see A. below)

Rm = Equity market return in excess of the risk-free rate (see B. below)

R = Industry/company risks (see C. below)

A. The risk-free rate was based on the weekly average for the week ended September 28, 19__ of 9.10 percent on 30-year Treasury bonds.

B. The difference between the return on the market and the risk-free interest rate (Rf) is termed the market risk premium (Rm). We used a risk premium of 10.6 percent based on studies done by Ibbotson Associates as set forth in the *Stocks, Bonds, Bills and Inflation: 19___ Yearbook*. The risk premium is the sum of (1) the average excess of the total returns of company stock in the S&P Composite Index over long-term Treasury bond income yield and (2) the average excess of the small company stock returns over the return of the S&P Composite Index. Small company stock return basically consists of stocks making up the two smallest deciles in terms of capitalization, which are traded on the New York Stock Exchange and stock listed on the American Stock Exchange and over the counter with the same or less capitalization.

The risk premium of 10.6 percent is computed as follows:

Excess common stock returns (S&P composite)	6.8%
Excess small stock returns over common stock returns	3.8
Total Risk Premium	10.6%

C. The industry/company risk is a subjective measure to account for the relative risk of Proud and its industry in relation to the general stock market as a whole. We used 2 percent to account for such company risks because of its relatively small size. Applying the percentage to the formula, as stated above, provides a cost of equity of 21.70 percent as follows:

Ke = Rf + Rm + R
Ke = 9.10 + 10.6% + 2%
Ke = 21.70%

For the cost of equity, no adjustment is made for income taxes because neither dividends nor redemptions are deductible by the corporation.

The weighted average cost of capital is computed using an assumed debt-to-equity ratio of 20/80 based on industry statistics. The overall result is 19.00 percent of cost of capital, computed as follows:

	Percent	Weight	Weighted Percent
Cost of debt	7.78	20%	1.56
Cost of equity	21.70	80%	17.36
Total Cost of Capital			18.92
Rounded			19.00

We determined the discounted cash flows value of the Proud Corporation as of September 30, 19__, at about $4,486,000, as follows:

Year	Projected* Available Cash Flow	Present Value Factor	Present Value
1	$ 3,782,514	.840336	$3,178,583
2	1,464,893	.706165	1,034,456
3	1,351,046	.593416	801,732
4	1,578,177	.498669	786,988
5	442,675	.419049	185,503
6	245,582	.352143	86,480
7	(1,589,028)	.295918	(470,222)
8	(1,588,632)	.248671	(395,047)
9	(1,773,182)	.208967	(370,537)
10	(2,003,800)	.175602	(351,871)
Total			$4,486,065
Rounded			$4,486,000

*Exhibit C (Not Shown)

WEIGHING THE OPERATING VALUES FROM DIFFERENT APPROACHES

Consideration of the various valuation approaches acts as a crosscheck to any one approach. Even if perfectly accurate values could be derived from assets, market earnings, and dividends, these figures will seldom be identical. The weights assigned to each value approach are based on the facts and circumstances of the particular business.

The adjusted net book value approach relating to the Proud Corporation provides a value substantially higher than the discounted cash flow value approach. This variation is attributable to the substantial appreciation in fixed assets. A shareholder may enjoy the appreciation in the assets only if he can liquidate the corporation. However, a liquidation will incur substantial costs (e.g., corporate income taxes, professional fees, etc.) that could eliminate all or much of the adjusted book value of the operating assets and could, in certain circumstances, require utilization of nonoperating assets to pay liabilities from operations. Furthermore, the shares transferred with respect to the valuation represent a minority interest in the Company. Such interest will not be sufficient to force a liquidation of the Company. Accordingly, the adjusted net book value should not be the sole or primary criterion to determine the fair market value of the shares transferred.

In view of the Company's continued operations, and the substantial amount of appreciated fixed assets, we weighed the discounted cash flow value and the adjusted net book value equally. Based on the allocation of weight, the value of the Company's operations prior to discounting is as follows:

Valuation Method	Value	Weighing	Weighted Value
Adjusted Net Book Value	$8,116,000	x 50%	$4,058,000
Discounted Cash Flow Value	4,486,000	x 50%	2,243,000
Value of Company's Operations			$6,301,000

INVESTMENT ASSETS

When an operating company owns a substantial amount of investment assets, the investment assets are usually valued separately from the business operations. In *Edwin A. Gallum*, 33 T.C.M. 1316 (1974), the company being valued owned a leather tanning operation with related land, buildings, and equipment, plus an investment portfolio of stocks and bonds. The expert witnesses for the taxpayer and the government agreed the company was a combined operating company and investment company and, therefore, the investment portfolio should be valued separately.

With the assistance of the Company's management, certain assets were determined to be unnecessary for the business operations and represent investment assets. The costs and the fair market value of these assets follow.

Description	Cost	Fair Market Value
Cash and cash equivalents in excess of amounts necessary for operations	$6,896,601	$6,896,601
Investment in securities	1,896,534	1,975,874
Mortgage note receivable	189,852	189,852
	$8,982,987	$9,062,327

TOTAL VALUE OF COMPANY

In valuing the common stock of the Company, we segregated the Company into the two value attributes or elements and valued each element separately. The two value elements are:

1.   The value attributable to its regular operations (operating value), and

2.   The value of its investment assets currently not needed for its operations.

To arrive at the value of the Company, the values of both elements are totaled. This gives a total value of $15,365,000, computed as follows:

Operating value	$ 6,301,000
Investment assets	9,062,327
Total Value Before Discounts	$15,363,327
Rounded	$15,365,000

EXAMPLE 16
VALUATION BUILDING BLOCKS: ONE DOUBTFUL RECEIVABLE CONTROLS VALUE OF BUSINESS

PURPOSE OF VALUATION

The purpose of this valuation is to determine the fair market value of the common stock of Zim Zam Tool, Inc. (Company) as of December 28, 19__. The valuation will be used to determine for gift tax purposes, the value of the company transferred from Zelda Zam to her sons, Frick and Frack, on December 28, 19__.

HISTORY AND NATURE OF BUSINESS

The company was incorporated in 1956 as Sim Sam Precision, Inc., a tool and die shop that manufactured dies and other small parts for various customers.

In 1986 it sold the Sim Sam name together with all patents, trademarks, and customer lists to an unrelated party. It changed its name to Zim Zam Tool, Inc.

After the sale, Zim Zam Tool either manufactured or purchased dies and other small parts exclusively for Too Two, Inc., which is wholly owned by relatives of the company's stockholder. It also repaired dies currently in use by Too Two.

ADJUSTED NET BOOK VALUE APPROACH

Adjusted net book value represents the fair market value of the net assets (fair market value of all assets less liabilities) underlying the stock of the corporation. We determined the adjusted net book value of Zim Zam Tool, Inc. as of December 28, 19__ at $838,161 as follows:

Total assets as of December 28, 19__ (Schedule A—not shown)	$1,021,280
Less Liabilities (Schedule A)	(183,119)
Adjusted net book value as of December 28, 19__	$ 838,161

No adjustment was made to property and equipment since the company's management estimates the book value of the property and equipment approximates the market value.

In addition, the $927,120 receivable from Too Two, Inc. was included at face value for this computation even though the collectibility of the receivable is in doubt due to Too Two's recent financial problems. We will account for the collectibility question through the discount.

DISCOUNT FOR GENERAL LACK OF MARKETABILITY

The $838,161 value is based on intrinsic factors. It does not necessarily mean this is the fair market value of the company in question because of the general lack of marketability.

Based on case laws, as cited above (not shown) the discount for lack of marketability is applicable. In view of the studies that have been done, as cited earlier (not shown), this discount can go as high as 40 percent.

As previously discussed, the company's major asset is a receivable from Too Two, Inc. The collectibility of this receivable is very questionable due to Two Two's recent financial problems. Therefore, we believe an additional discount is necessary to account for the questionable collectibility of Two Two's receivable.

We believe a total discount of 50 percent is appropriate to account for lack of marketability and the doubtful collectibility of the receivable from Too Two.

The value of the company after the discounts would be as follows:

Value before discounts	$ 838,161
Less discounts	(419,080)
Value after discounts	$ 419,081
Rounded	$ 419,000

EXAMPLE 17
VALUATION BUILDING BLOCKS: BUY-SELL AGREEMENT
CONTROLS VALUATION

PURPOSE OF VALUATION

The purpose of this valuation is to determine the fair market value of Juicy Beef Company, Inc. (Company) at February 29, 19__. The valuation will be used to determine, for a divorce settlement, the value of Red Water's one-half interest in the company.

STOCK PURCHASE AGREEMENT

The corporation and its shareholders entered into a stock purchase agreement which essentially provides:

1. During the shareholder's lifetime, the corporation and other shareholders have the first right to acquire a proposed stock sale at the lower of (1) the purchase price offered by an outside party or (2) the formula price as specified in the agreement.

2. In the case of employment termination, other than excused leave of absence, retirement, total disability, or death, the corporation and other shareholders may exercise the option to purchase the shares at the formula price.

3. Upon the shareholder's death, the corporation *shall* acquire the stock at the formula price.

The formula price is the greater of $100 per share or the book value, as adjusted for certain items, per share (referred to as the adjusted book value hereafter). Since the adjusted book value per share is substantially higher than $100, the formula price, in effect, is the adjusted book value.

In essence, the stock purchase agreement allows the corporation and other shareholders to purchase a shareholder's stock, during his lifetime, at a price not to exceed the company's adjusted book value. This provision was provided for the benefit of the corporation and other shareholders, rather than the selling or departing shareholder. If the fair market value is greater than the adjusted book value, the corporation can exercise its right to purchase the shares from the proposed sale to a third party at the adjusted book value. The corporation and the remaining shareholders will economically benefit from the exercise. If the fair market value is lower than the adjusted book value, the corporation need not exercise its option to purchase the shares at the adjusted book value, even if the shareholder terminates his employment. If the departing shareholder plans to sell his stock to a third party at a price lower than the adjusted book value, he must first offer such terms to the corporation. At this time, the corporation may purchase the stock at a price lower than the adjusted book value.

Upon the shareholder's death, the corporation must purchase, and the estate must sell, the shares at the adjusted book value. This after-death provision benefits the corporation if the fair market value is greater than the adjusted book value, and benefits the shareholder's family if the fair market value is less than the adjusted book value.

The stock purchase agreement, in effect, creates a price ceiling on the value of the company. For a departing or selling shareholder, the company cannot have a fair market value in excess of its adjusted book value. Except for death, the agreement does not place a price floor, as the company or other shareholders are not required to purchase the shares at the adjusted book value if the actual market value is below the adjusted book value. Accordingly, the stock purchase agreement effectively limits the fair market value of the company to *not more than the adjusted book value.*

Numerous court decisions in the federal estate tax area concluded that a purchase agreement will definitely set a ceiling on the estate tax values if:

1. The price is either fixed or determinable according to a formula.

2. The estate is obligated to sell at a fixed price at death.

3. The obligation to sell at the agreed price is binding upon the decedent during his lifetime as well as upon his estate after his death.

4. The agreement is a bona fide business arrangement, and not a device to pass the decedent's shares to the natural objects of his bounty for less than adequate and full consideration in money or money's worth.

The company's stock purchase agreement possesses the four characteristics cited above and thus effectively limits the fair market value to no greater than the adjusted book value.

EXAMPLE 18
VALUATION BUILDING BLOCKS: VALUATION OF PREFERRED STOCK

Since our purpose is to value both the preferred stock and the common stock, it is necessary to determine how much of the $1,200,000 value (total value of Company) is allocable to each interest.

As of May 31, 19__, the Company had 20 shares of outstanding preferred stock—Series A and 579 shares of outstanding preferred stock—Series B. Neither series of stock is callable.

Revenue Ruling 83-120, 1983-2 CB 170, provides guidance on the valuation of preferred stock. It states that the most important factors to be considered in determining the value of preferred stock are its yield, dividend coverage, and protection of its liquidation preference.

The ruling also states that dividend yield determines whether the preferred stock has a value equal to its par value. It specifically states the following:

> Whether the yield of the preferred stock supports a valuation of the stock at par value depends in part on the adequacy of the dividend rate. The adequacy of the dividend rate should be determined by comparing its dividend rate with the dividend rate of high-grade publicly traded preferred stock. A lower yield than that of high-grade preferred stock indicates a preferred stock value of less than par. In addition, whether the preferred stock has a fixed dividend rate and is nonparticipating influences the value of the preferred stock. . . . A publicly traded preferred stock for a company having a similar business and similar assets with similar liquidation preferences, voting rights and other similar terms would be the ideal comparable for determining yield required in arms length transactions of closely held stock. Such ideal comparables will frequently not exist. In such circumstances, the most comparable publicly-traded issues should be selected for comparison and appropriate adjustments made for differing factors.

We were unable to locate a comparable publicly traded issue. Since the preferred stock is not callable, has a cumulative current market dividend rate, and the company is worth more than liquidation value, the most a preferred shareholder could get for his preferred stock would be liquidation value. Therefore, we valued the preferred stock at its liquidation value of $1,000 per share.

Adjusted net asset value	$1,200,000
Less: Amount allocated to preferred stock at $1,000 liquidation value per share	
–Series A	20,000
–Series B	579,000
Adjusted net asset value allocable to the common stock	$ 601,000

EXAMPLE 19
VALUATION BUILDING BLOCKS: DISCUSSION OF VARIOUS
DISCOUNTS

DISCOUNT FOR GENERAL LACK OF MARKETABILITY AND MINORITY INTEREST

A major difference between the Company's shares and those of publicly traded companies is their lack of marketability. All other things being equal, an investment is worth more if it is marketable, since investors prefer liquidity. Interests in closely held businesses are generally illiquid and lack marketability.

If one wishes to dispose of shares of a publicly traded company, all one has to do is call a local stockbroker. However, it's no easy task to dispose of shares in a privately held company.

The value of $13,240,000 is a value based on intrinsic factors. Intrinsic factors are those which relate to the financial condition of the company, such as earnings capacity, book value, dividend paying capacity, goodwill, or other intangible value. This value does not reflect the fact that the Company lacks marketability.

In *Valuing a Business: The Analysis and Appraisal of Closely Held Companies.* (Dow Jones-Irwin, 1981), the author states:

> All other things being equal, an interest in a business is worth more if the interest is readily marketable or, conversely, worth less if it is not. It is well known that investors prefer liquidity to lack of liquidity. Interests in closely held businesses are relatively illiquid, compared with most other investments. This problem may be compounded further by restrictions on transfer of interest found in buy-sell agreements in many companies.

Since The Success Corporation is a closely held business, a discount for general lack of marketability is appropriate to arrive at the fair value. The lack of marketability discount concept recognizes the fact that closely held stocks are less attractive and have fewer potential purchasers because they are not readily marketable.

The principle of a discount for lack of marketability has been stated as follows: It seems clear. . . that an unlisted closely held stock of a corporation. . . , in which trading is infrequent and which therefore lacks marketability, is less attractive than a similar stock which is listed on an exchange and has ready access to the investing public. *Central Trust Co.*, 305 F2d 393 (CtCl 1962). If the owners of closely held stocks tried to list a block of such securities on a stock exchange for sale to the public, they would probably have to make the offerings through underwriters. There would be costs for registering nonpublicly traded stocks with the Securities and Exchange Commission (SEC) involving, among other fees, the expense of preparing a prospectus. In addition, the underwriters themselves would receive commissions. The actual costs of such an offering can range from 10 to 25 percent of the selling price to the public.

Another support for the amount of discount for lack of marketability is provided by transactions in letter stocks. A letter stock is identical in all respects to the freely traded stock of a public company except that it is restricted from trading on the open market for some period. The duration of the restrictions varies from one situation to another. Marketability is the only difference between the letter stock transactions and open market transactions in the same stock and provides solid evidence that the market produces a price spread between a readily marketable security and its otherwise identical counterpart that is subject to certain market-ability restrictions.

In a major study done by the SEC on institutional investor actions, one of the topics was the amount of discount at which transactions in restricted stock (letter stock) took place, as compared with the prices of otherwise identical but unrestricted stock on the open market. Discounts Involved in Purchases of Common Stock in U.S. 92nd Congress, 1st Session, House. *Institutional Investor Study Report of the Securities and Exchange Commission.* Washington D.C.: U.S. Government Printing Office (March 10, 1971), 5:2444-2456. (Document No. 92-64, Part 5). The study shows the amounts of discounts on letter stock transactions by four market categories: (1) New York Stock Exchange; (2) American Stock Exchange; (3) Over-the-Counter (reporting companies); and (4) Over-the-Counter (nonreporting companies). A reporting company is a publicly traded company that must file Forms 10-K, 10-Q and other information with the SEC. A nonreporting company is publicly traded OTC but is not subject to the same reporting requirements.

The study shows that the discounts on the letter stocks were the least for NYSE listed stocks, but increased, in order, for ASE listed stocks, OTC reporting companies and OTC nonreporting companies. For OTC nonreporting companies, the largest number of restricted stock transactions fell in the 30 to 40 percent discount range. Slightly over 56 percent of the OTC nonreporting companies experienced discounts greater than 30 percent on the sale of their restricted stock. A little over 30 percent of the OTC reporting companies experienced discounts over 30 percent, and over 52 percent experienced discounts over 20 percent.

Another study on marketability discounts for closely held business interests was done by J. Michael Maher, *Discounts for Lack of Marketability for Closely Held Business Interests*, Taxes (September 1976), pg. 562–71. The study involves a comparison of prices paid for restricted stocks with the market prices of their unrestricted counterparts. The study showed that The mean discount for lack of marketability for the years 1969–73 amounted to 35.43 percent. Maher then made an interesting second computation: eliminating the top 10 percent and the bottom 10 percent of purchases to remove especially high and low risk situations. The result was almost identical with a mean discount of 34.73 percent.

Maher concludes:

> The result I have reached is that most appraisers underestimate the proper discount for lack of marketability. The results seem to indicate that this discount should be about 35 percent. Perhaps this makes sense because by committing funds to restricted common stock, the willing buyer (a) would be denied the opportunity to take advantage of other investments, and (b) would continue to have his investment at the risk of the business until the shares could be offered to the public or another buyer is found.

> The 35 percent discount would not contain elements of a discount for a minority interest because it is measured against the current fair market value of securities actively traded (other minority interest). Consequently, appraisers should also consider a discount for a minority interest in those closely held corporations where a discount is applicable.

Finally, Professor Steven E. Bolten investigated studies that had been done in the area of valuation discounts. In his article, *Discounts for the Stocks of Closely Held Corporations*, 123 Trusts and Estates 22 (December 1984), he concluded that the results of previous studies indicate (1) an average of 39.86 percent for nonmarketability discount and (2) an average of 29.37 percent discount for minority position.

Commenting on the studies done on the discount of nonmarketability, Professor Bolten states:

> Although these studies took place over a ten-year period, each discovered an average discount of approximately the same amount. Thus, we may safely assume that the nonmarketability discount not only is appropriately applied because of its historically observed presence but also because of its relative stability.

Professor Bolten also concludes:

> The growing body of studies and evidence on the issues of minority position and nonmarketable discounts sustains their presence at observed, substantial levels. The average total substantiated discount for both from a comparable public traded security is over 69 percent.

In *Valuing a Business: The Analysis and Appraisal of Closely Held Companies* (Dow Jones-Irwin, 1981), Dr. Shannon P. Pratt also states:

> There is considerable evidence to suggest that the discount for the lack of marketability factor alone for a closely held stock compared with a publicly traded counterpart should average about 35 percent.
>
> * * * * *
>
> If a minority interest in a closely held business is being valued by capitalization of earnings, book value, adjusted book value, or whatever other approach, but without comparison to daily trading prices of public stocks, then discounts must be taken to reflect both the lack of marketability and the minority interest. It is not uncommon to find a minority interest discounted at 65 percent or more below the stock's underlying net asset value.

Actual sales of minority interests in closely held businesses were compiled by a bank officer responsible for administering estates that owned closely held businesses. He compiled information on 30 actual sales of minority interests and found the average transaction price was 36 percent below book value. He stated that:

> ... only 20 percent of the sales were made at discounts less than 20 percent. A little more than half the sales (53-1/3 percent) were made at discounts that ranged from 22 percent to 48 percent, and 23-1/3 percent of the sales were made at discounts of from 54.4 percent to 78 percent.
>
> (H. Calvin Coolidge, Fixing Value of Minority Interest in a Business; Actual Sales Suggest Discount as High as 70 Percent, *Estate Planning*, Spring 1975, p. 141.)

The discounts in the surveys were based on book value. Book value does not recognize appreciation in assets above depreciated net asset value. Only in a very few cases in the survey were the discounts computed from an adjusted book value reflecting appreciation in real estate values.

An update published in 1983 indicates a trend toward even higher discounts when disposing of minority interests in closely held corporations. In the update, there was a much higher concentration of discounts from book value at the high end of the range, and the average discount of the two studies combined was about 40 percent.

In *William T. Piper, Sr. Est.*, 72 TC No. 88, CCH Dec. 36,315, the court allowed a total discount of 64 percent for stock of a corporation that owned publicly traded securities and rental property. The court allowed (1) a discount of 35 percent for lack of marketability; (2) 17 percent for relatively unattractive investment portfolios; and (3) another 12 percent for possible stock registration costs.

In *Estate of Mark S. Gallo*, TCM 1985-363, CCH Dec. 42241(M), the Tax Court allowed a discount of 36 percent for general lack of marketability.

In *Jack D. Carr*, 49 TCM 507 (1985), the Tax Court allowed a total discount of 55 percent for stock of a corporation that engaged in real estate development. The court allowed a discount of 30 percent for market absorption (i.e., a discount that parallels the marketability discount) and a 25 percent discount for minority interest.

In *The Northern Trust Company*, 87 TC 349 (1986), the Tax Court allowed a 25 percent discount for lack of marketability and a 20 percent discount for minority interest, for a total discount of 45 percent.

MINORITY DISCOUNTS AND INTRAFAMILY TRANSFERS

In Rev. Rul. 81-253, the IRS held that no minority discount is allowable for shares involved in intrafamily transfers. However, the courts have disagreed with the IRS and have held that a minority discount is allowable in an intrafamily transfer.

In *Estate of Happenstall*, 8 T.C.M. 136 (1949), the donor-taxpayer owned 2,310 of 4,233 outstanding shares of a closely held corporation and gifted 300 shares to each of four family members. He parted with control but the total gifted shares would not have constituted a controlling interest, even if aggregated. No donee acquired control as a result of the gifts. The Tax Court valued the shares as minority shares, stating by way of dictum that each 300-share gift must be valued separately.

In *Whittemore*, 127 F. Supp. 710 (D.C. Conn, 1954), the taxpayer owned all 820 outstanding shares of a corporation. He gave 600 shares to his three sons, 200 shares to each. The taxpayer argued that the value of the shares, for gift tax purposes, was to be based upon three separate gifts of 200 shares each, so that the gifts were those of minority interests. The Commissioner argued that a single gift of 600 shares had been made, so that a gift of a controlling interest was involved. The Court held that each gift should be treated as a separate gift. Accordingly, the gifts were valued as minority interests.

In *Estate of Andrews*, 79 T.C. 938 (1982), the Tax Court rejected Rev. Rul. 81-253, stating that lack of marketability and minority interest discounts are allowable under the hypothetical willing buyer-willing seller principle, even though related family members own the balance of the controlling shares and no evidence of family discord exists. The court did not apply family attribution rules.

In *Charles W. Ward*, 87 TC 6, the Tax Court again rejected Rev. Rul. 81-253, stating that the lack of marketability and minority interest discounts are allowable when the shares of stock gifted to each of the children represent minority interests in the corporation, even though related family members own the remaining shares.

The shares of The Success Corporation stock to be transferred represent a minority interest. Based on case laws, as cited above, both the discounts for lack of marketability and minority interest are applicable. In view of the studies that have been done, as cited earlier, these discounts can go as high as 65 percent. Even though the Company has a large amount of cash and cash equivalents, a minority shareholder would not be able to force the distribution of these assets. In addition, such a distribution would incur additional costs. Therefore, we believe a total discount of 40 percent is appropriate to account for lack of marketability and minority interest in the instant case.

The value per share after the discount for lack of marketability and minority interest would be as follows:

Total value before discount	$11,440,000
Discount	(4,576,000)
Total value after discount	6,864,000
Divided by the number of shares outstanding	180
Value per Share	$ 38,133
Rounded	$ 38,000

CONCLUSION

Based on the information and analyses summarized in this report, it is our opinion that, as of July 31, 19__, the fair market value of the shares of The Success Corporation to be gifted is $38,000 per share for a minority interest.

EXAMPLE 20
AN ESOP VALUATION: THE REAL THING, ALMOST WORD FOR WORD

VALUATION OF WILDWOOD CORPORATION (Not real client's name)

PURPOSE OF VALUATION

The purpose of this valuation is to determine the adequate consideration of Wildwood Corporation (Wild or Company) as of August 21, 19__. The valuation will be used as the basis for the sale of stock in the Company to a proposed Employee Stock Ownership Plan (ESOP).

Section 3(18)(B) of the Employee Retirement Income Security Act of 1974 (ERISA) and proposed regulations Section 2510.3-18(b)(l)(i) essentially provides that the term adequate consideration means, in the case of a plan asset other than a security for which there is a generally recognized market, the fair market value of the asset as determined in good faith pursuant to the terms of the plan and in accordance with regulations promulgated by the Secretary of Labor. Accordingly, two criteria—good faith and fair market value—must be met for a valid determination of adequate consideration.

DEFINITION OF FAIR MARKET VALUE

For purposes of this valuation, fair market value is defined as the price at which an asset would change hands between a willing buyer and a willing seller when the former is not under any compulsion to buy and the latter is not under any compulsion to sell, and both parties are able, as well as willing, to trade and are well-informed about the asset and the market for that asset. Proposed Regulation Section 2510.3-18(b)(2)(i).

DEFINITION OF GOOD FAITH

Proposed Section 2510.3-18(b)(3)(ii) focuses on two factors for determining if there is good faith. First, one must apply sound business principles of valuation and conduct a prudent investigation of the circumstances prevailing at the time of the valuation.

Second, the person making the valuation must be independent of all the parties to the transaction (other than the plan).

SOURCES OF DATA

The following sources of information were used and relied upon for the valuation:

1. Compiled financial statements for the five years ending December 31, 19__ to December 31, 19__.

2. A seven-month interim financial statement for the period ending July 31, 19__.

3. The projected financial statements for the five years ending December 31, 19___ to December 31, 19___.

4. *Industrial Norms and Key Business Ratios*, 19___ – 19___ , Dun and Bradstreet.

5. *Industry Surveys*, April 19___ , Standard and Poor's.

6. U.S. Industrial Outlook for 19___.

7. Information furnished by management of the company.

8. Other sources as cited in the body of this report.

Financial and statistical information from the above sources are deemed to be reliable. However, we make no representation as to our sources' accuracy or completeness and have accepted their information without further verification.

The financial statements of Wild for the periods 19___ to 19___ were prepared by independent certified public accountants, while the interim statement was prepared by the Company's management. We have assumed, without independent verification, that the financial data furnished by the Company or its representations correctly reflects the results of the operations and financial conditions of the Company in accordance with generally accepted accounting principles applied on a consistent basis.

We obtained various information from the Company's management, including the following:

1. A copy of an equipment appraisal as of August 20, 19___;

2. A list of the ten largest dollar volume suppliers and the ten largest dollar volume customers of the Company;

3. A summary of all the leases that the Company has with third parties and affiliates;

4. Copies of existing financial statements as listed above;

5. Copies of all federal and state tax returns for the past five years;

6. A statement that the Company does not have any open audits or assessments with the Internal Revenue Service or any other taxing agencies;

7. A list of all other tax returns regularly filed by the Company, such as sales, franchise, and excise tax returns; and

8. Copies of environmental reports that were prepared in 19___ and 19___ on the Company.

We also discussed with the management of the Company the following matters:

1. Its business history, markets, and competitors;

2. Business plans and projected statements of the Company; and

3. Environmental issues of the Company.

We also visited the Company's corporate headquarters.

INTRODUCTION TO VALUATION

Proposed regulations from the U.S. Department of Labor (DOL) cite Revenue Ruling 59-60 as the main guideline in the valuation of closely held businesses with respect to the meaning of adequate consideration under the ERISA. Revenue Ruling 59-60 sets forth the premise that valuation is a question of fact dependent upon the circumstances. The specific factors that Revenue Ruling 59-60 sets forth are as follows:

1. The nature of the business and the history of the enterprise from its inception;

2. The economic outlook in general and the condition and outlook of the specific industry in particular;

3. The book value of the stock and the financial condition of the business;

4. The earning capacity of the company;

5. The company's dividend-paying capacity;

6. Whether or not the enterprise has goodwill or other intangible value;

7. Sales of stock and the size of the block of stock to be valued; and

8. The market price of stock of corporations engaged in the same or similar line of business having their stock actively traded in a free and open market, either on an exchange or over the counter.

In addition, the proposed regulations from the DOL specifically require a consideration of two other factors:

1. The marketability, or lack thereof, of the business; and

2. The control premium, if any, afforded to the stock.

GENERAL ECONOMICS AND BUSINESS

The July 12, 19__ issue of Standard & Poor's, *Trends & Projections*, included these economic and business highlights:

1. Business investment is expanding, but not as fast as some hoped. Business investment is expected to continue with spending on producer's durable equipment leading the way.

2. Export sector continues to show strong reports, and with growth in foreign economies and a modest decline in the dollar, this sector should expand in the second half.

3. Retail sales have been down three months in a row, and new construction is at its lowest level since 19__.

4. The economy is inching along at around 2 percent real growth and with no indication of acceleration. An estimated 2.4 percent growth is projected for 19__.

Following are annotated excerpts from *Trends & Projections*:

> As it has been doing, the Fed will continue to adjust short-term interest rates to achieve its GNP objective of about two percent real growth. Given the economy's recent weakness, the forecasters no longer expect any Fed tightening in the second half of the year. Because of this, interest rates should stay relatively unchanged through most of 19__.

> The outlook is for inflation rates to settle down to between 4 and 4-1/2 percent, and for the unemployment rate to stay at its 19__ and early 19__ levels of around 5.4 percent.

> While only modest growth was expected in consumer spending for 19__, the weather created above-average gyrations in the first half. A warm start to the year boosted consumer spending. Subsequently, a wet spring slowed spending sharply, which wreaked havoc with year-over-year comparisons. The stage is set for a third quarter rebound and a relatively normal fourth quarter.

> No recession is expected in the near future mainly because inventories are under control. Inventories are one of the few economic phenomena that always follow the business cycle. At present, inventory-to-sales ratios are as low as they have been anytime in at least ten years. Recessions are caused in large part by excessive inventory pile-up.

> Talk of tax increases by President Bush may not be bad news. The forecasters can only hope that Bush's willingness to talk about taxes means that some progress on fiscal policy is possible. With lower deficits should come lower interest rates as well. As a matter of fact, June's interest rates were down slightly, reflecting the President's comments about accepting a tax increase as part of a budget package.

SPECIFIC INDUSTRY ANALYSIS

Household Products Industry

Household starch (not the real product of this company) is one of many household products. The household product industry is noted for its defensive investment characteristics. A defensive company is one whose earnings are fairly stable regardless of what is happening in the overall economy.

When the economy is good, people do not necessarily wash clothes or brush teeth more often. So sales of products for such use do not accelerate. Conversely, when times are bad, people generally do not cut back on such activities. So earnings for these companies are not prone to big shortfalls, even during recessions. This is an oversimplification, as some products are more defensive than others. While the frequency of clothes washing does not change in a recession, the frequency with which people buy a new set of cookware may be somewhat affected. Even so, housewares is considered a defensive business since such purchases in lean times are not as difficult to make as would be the case with automobiles, homes or major appliances. Indeed, bad times sometimes spark such purchases, in lieu of the more expensive expenditures.

The Commerce Department estimated 19__ product shipments for polishes and sanitation goods at 5.5 billion, up 10 percent (unadjusted) from those of 19__. Polishes and sanitation goods include household starch, specialty cleaners and disinfectants, and polishing preparations. Sales growth is projected at 5 percent a year through 19__.

Other products containing starch such as blue stuff may eventually replace starch. The difference between these two types of starches is that blue stuff is safe to use with cottons as well as with wools, while our stuff is not safe to use with yarn. This problem has been present in the industry for the past twenty years, but up to this date it has not made a substantial impact in the quantity of product being produced for the two types of starch. Research is being done to activate blue stuff starch effectively at low water temperatures, thus extending their use to most ironing situations. This paragraph has substantial changes.

Chemical Industry

Automotive antifreeze is a chemical product derived from ethylene. Ethylene is the largest volume organic chemical produced in the United States. In the U.S., natural gas is the primary feedstock for ethylene, while in Japan and Europe, petroleum is the main source. Natural gas is separated into ethane, propane, and butane, which are then steam-cracked to yield varying percentages of ethylene, propylene, and butane, the most important building blocks for most organic chemicals and synthetic materials.

Like the household products industry, the automotive antifreeze business basically has defensive characteristics. When the economy is good, people do not necessarily use more automotive antifreeze. Conversely, when times are bad, people generally do not cut back on the use of antifreeze.

Retail vehicle sales are expected to decline in 19__, to approximately 14.8 million (10 million passenger cars and 4.8 million trucks). However, this does not necessarily translate to less demand for antifreeze. Consumers merely keep their cars longer instead of buying new cars. After buying some 52.9 million cars and 23.6 million trucks from 19__ to 19__, U.S. consumers paused in 19__ to catch their breath and assess what was in store for the future. This resulted in a slowdown in the first half of 19__, with auto sales sliding 7.2 percent, year to year, and truck sales off 5.5 percent. Low levels of new car sales mean a longer retention of existing autos. Nonetheless, these existing autos still need antifreeze.

Low levels of new car sales in the three-year period ending in 19__ and the longer retention of existing autos increased the average age of passenger cars on the road. In 19__, 19__, 19__, and 19__, the average age was 7.6 years, up from 7.5 years in 19__, 6.6 years in 19__, 6.0 in 19__, and 5.6 in 19__. Although the aging of the car fleet adversely affects new car demand, it favors sales of replacement parts (and possibly antifreeze). In 19__, about 36 percent of all passenger cars in operation were nine years or older, and roughly 76 percent of all automobiles were three years of age or older.

Based on information published by the Federal Highway Administration, the U.S. traffic volume has steadily increased since 19__, as shown in the following:

	U. S. Traffic Volume Trends (All Motor Vehicles)	
Year	Billion Miles	% Change
19__	1,991.0	+3.5
19__	1,924.4	+3.4
19__	1,860.6	+5.4
19__	1,765.0	+2.8
19__	1,716.8	+4.1
19__	1,649.1	+4.9
19__	1,571.4	+1.1
19__	1,554.0	+3.1
19__	1,507.5	−1.2
19__	1,525.9	−1.4

With steady increase in traffic volume, it is unlikely that there will be a drop in the future use of antifreeze just because there is a drop in auto sales. Over the long term, total automobile sales will continue to mirror general economic conditions, especially changes in disposable personal income. A favorable demographic trend will be the projected increase in U.S. population in the major car buying 25- to 64-year old age bracket.

Output in 19__ was up 10 percent, according to the Federal Reserve Board (FRB) production index for industrial organic chemicals. Many products, notably ethylene, were running at full capacity. As a result of increased worldwide demand and unexpected shutdowns of several ethylene plants at mid-year, a shortage of the material was experienced. Customers then scrambled for available ethylene and derivative products, sending prices dramatically higher.

In 19__, a different picture emerged. With recent capacity additions and supply relief, ethylene prices stabilized at the beginning of the year and began to decline in the second quarter. Customers, who had built up ethylene and derivative inventories in 19__ in anticipation of continued shortages and price increases, started to work down stocks. Inventory adjustments were expected to be largely complete by late 19__, and production should have then begun to better match final demand. With a better match of supply and demand, ethylene prices should be stabilized. This could mean a stabilized price for antifreeze as well.

However, the Iraq-Kuwait conflict may increase the prices of ethylene and ultimately antifreeze. Natural gas is the primary feedstock for ethylene in the U.S. In Japan and Europe, petroleum is the main source. The Iraq-Kuwait conflict will likely increase the petroleum prices due to the shortage. The petroleum shortage may ultimately affect the U.S. and worldwide supply of ethylene.

BUSINESS HISTORY AND OUTLOOK

Wild was founded in 19__ by George Wildwood to produce and market starc'. He was a salesman for Slow & Co., a starch consumer, which he obtained as a customer · whose business he built a clientele for Wild's products.

The company continued under his ownership and direction until 19__ when it was acquired by Moe High and Joe Wide. Neither of them had any prior experience or background in the chemical industry. High was a lawyer, while Wide was a tool maker. At the time the company was acquired, it was already a tenant in its present premises.

On January 1, 19__ , Hoe Handsome became a shareholder in the company and assumed the position of vice president of sales. Handsome has spent his entire career in the starch industry, specializing in sales. Since 19__ , the three shareholders have operated the enterprise as equal owners. High has been responsible for finance and administration, Wide for production and shipping, and Handsome for sales.

The shareholders equally own the real estate occupied by Wild and a parcel of vacant land adjacent to Wild's premises. A part of the vacant land is rented on a month-to-month basis to a neighboring plant, while the rest is used by Wild for parking passenger vehicles and a truck fleet. The building is leased to Wild on a year-to-year basis on a net-net-net lease basis.

Wild is a party to union labor contracts with Local 122 of the Warehousemen's Union (a Teamster affiliate). In addition, Wild's truck drivers are members of the Independent Teamsters Union of Moeplace. Relations between the companies, their employees, and the unions are peaceful according to management.

The company operates in a competitive environment. Among its competitors are the nationally advertised brands marketed by some of the Fortune 500 companies, such as Big, Bigger, and Biggest. However, the competition is not new to Wild. It has successfully competed head-on with these giants, as well as with many small companies over the years. Wild has survived and prospered by finding its niche in (other) markets. So, as a practical matter, they do not compete against the higher priced branded competition's market segment.

The outlook for Wild seems bright. During the summer of 19__, Biggee Corp., one of the company's most effective competitors in its market niche, decided to close its plant in Moeplace and to serve its customers by shipping its product to the Moeplace market from Far Town. Since the product in which the two companies compete is starch, which contains (lot'sa) water, this strategy should help Wild gain additional business. An increase in volume was experienced in the last half of 19__, and throughout 19__. The company does not expect a new competitor to establish a plant in Moeplace in the foreseeable future. It expects to continue to enjoy this increase in volume over the next few years.

Wild has excellent relationships with its key suppliers. Wild purchases raw materials in their most cost-effective mode (i.e., barges, tank cars, etc.). Basic producers treat Wild as a volume customer and a key account in its market place. Accordingly, Wild is sought out by competitive sources as a desirable potential customer and is generally able to negotiate pricing on key products at levels below established posted market.

Labor relations have been excellent and tranquil. Many of Wild's rank-and-file employees have been with the company for more than fifteen years and some have an employment record extending back to more than twenty-five years. Wild operates under a union contract negotiated with Local 122 of the Warehousemen's Union (a Teamster affiliate). The current contract was negotiated for three years and will expire on February 28, 19__. In addition, the company employs five to six truck drivers who are members of the Independent Teamsters Union of Moeplace. These employees are covered by a separate contract negotiated between the union and an employers' bargaining council and subscribed to by Wild.

Wild sells to more than 400 customers. Not all of these customers buy all of Wild's products and no one customer accounts for more than 10 percent of the company's sales volume.

Its market for starch is primarily regional, within a two hundred-mile radius of Moeplace. Customers for these products are essentially supermarket chains, cooperatives, and service companies. Many of these companies have been customers for more than 25 years and look to Wild as a part of their private label household chemical marketing program.

The geographic area in which Wild markets some of its automotive products is national in character. The company sells its antifreeze through a combination of employees and independent representatives. Wild currently employs four salesman. One of the salesmen acts as a sales manager, coordinating the activities of the other salesmen and the sales representatives. The other sales employees act as field salesmen calling primarily upon oil jobbers in their territories.

Independent representatives cover mass merchandisers as well as oil jobbers in New England, Middle Atlantic States, the Great Lakes, Missouri, Kansas, Oklahoma, Texas, and the West Coast. Besides the company's own manufacturing facility in Moeplace, these areas are serviced by having product contract-packaged by independent companies in the Wettstown, Big City, Dallas, and Los Gopher areas.

It was 15 years ago that the company contracted with a packaging facility in southern Rhode Island to package antifreeze to service the east coast market. In 19__ it obtained a second contract with a packaging facility in Dallas, Texas to service the southwest part of the United States. During 19__ and early 19__, the company has continued to expand in this market by contracting with packaging facilities in Georgetown and Georgeville. The company intends to aggressively penetrate these markets and to establish additional contract packagers so that its sales growth may be accelerated without the prohibitively large capital outlays associated with building additional plants. The Midwest is serviced by the company's existing plant in Moeplace. The other market niche currently accounts for only a small portion of the automotive product sales.

FINANCIAL OVERVIEW

The determination of the fair market value of closely held securities requires a complete financial analysis of the subject company, including a review of historical operating results and financial condition. This financial information has been summarized as follows:

1. Exhibit A—Comparative balance sheets as of December 31, 19__ to December 31, 19__ (five years, not shown).

2. Exhibit B—Comparative statements of income and retained earnings for the years ended December 31, 19__ to December 31, 19__ (five years, not shown).

We reviewed the financial statements for the periods ended December 31, 19__ through July 31, 19__. The following observations are made concerning their historical financial performance:

■   Wild's sales volume was fairly constant until 19__ when it jumped to $18 million from $11.2 million in 19__ and $23.8 million in 19__. From 19__ to 19__ experienced growth of over 100 percent. For 19__, sales were $19,749,095. The 19__ sales were high due to market conditions in the antifreeze and related products area. The drop in 19__ sales is a reflection of these markets returning to normal operations. Sales for the first seven months of 19__ were $7,068,567. Traditionally, sales have been substantially higher in the second half of the year.

■   Gross profit margin of Wild has been around the 9–10 percent range, except for in 19__ when it jumped to 11.51 percent, followed by a drop to 7.09 percent in 19__. The average for the two-year period is 9.3 percent. Due to effective purchasing, the 19__ and 19__ (as of July 31) gross profit jumped to 15.18 percent and 23.16 percent, respectively.

■ Wild has shown an operating loss for each year, ranging from an operating loss of $48,150 to $3,335,148. This history of operating loss is partially attributable to the officers' salaries. The company has eliminated its operating profits by paying officers' salaries.

If officers' salaries had been eliminated, the operating income would have been as follows:

	Year 1*	Year 2	Year 3	Year 4	Year 5
Income (loss) from operations	$ (40,006)	$(3,335,148)	$ (48,149)	$ (51,223)	$ (61,336)
Officers' salaries	1,820,673	4,808,545	392,310	331,637	330,900
Operating income before officers' salaries	$ 1,780,667	$ 1,473,397	$ 344,161	$ 280,414	$ 269,564
Net sales	$19,749,095	$23,812,118	$18,068,613	$11,192,507	$12,963,698

*The most recent year.

The substantial increase in operating income before officers' salaries in 19__ reflects the fact that expenses have not increased at a comparable rate as the sales have increased. The operating income before officers' salaries for the seven-months ended July 31, 19__ was $1,054,396. Operating expenses, as a percentage of sales, excluding officers' salaries, were as follows:

	Year 1	Year 2	Year 3	Year 4	Year 5
Operating expenses as % of sales	15.2%	24.45%	7.35%	11.97%	10.04%
Officers' salaries as % of sales	9.2%	20.2	2.2	3.0	2.6
Net % of sales	6.0%	4.25%	5.15%	8.97%	7.44%

Accordingly, if sales volume were to maintain at the $20 million level, Wild's operating income would be substantial. Operating performances in years prior to 19__ may not be representative of current or future operating performances due to the substantial difference in sales volume.

In summary, the comparative financial analysis indicates the following:

■ Wild has experienced significant sales growth in the past 2–3 years.

■ Wild's gross profit margin was relatively stable until 19__ when it climbed by 50 percent.

- Ignoring the officers' salaries, Wild has improved its operating expenses over the last few years.

- Wild is highly leveraged, even though it has no long-term debts.

- Wild has become highly profitable in the last two years due to the substantial increase in sales volume and the improved control over expenses.

SPECIFIC VALUATION METHODS

We considered three basic approaches toward valuing the company:

- Adjusted Net Book Value Approach

- Discounted Cash Flow Approach

- Market Comparison Approach

SELECTION OF VALUATION TECHNIQUES

We considered all of the foregoing approaches and selected the appropriate method to correspond to the specific circumstances of the company as of the valuation date. For various reasons discussed later, the valuation is determined on a going-concern basis with reliance on the discounted cash flow approach. As a crosscheck, we used the market comparison approach to see if the value based on the discounted cash flows is reasonable. Each method, with its underlying philosophies, is described in the following pages and is considered in relation to the circumstances of the company.

ADJUSTED NET BOOK VALUE APPROACH

The adjusted net book value requires that all assets be evaluated to determine their true economic value. Fixed assets are appraised at a figure approximating their present market value as opposed to depreciated cost.

This method is most appropriate in those entities where economic goodwill is not present, but whose assets, when considered as a whole, produce a going concern and contain a value over and above what is recorded on the books of the business. This approach is also most applicable to companies having erratic or depressed earnings which are inadequate to provide a fair return on the value of the net tangible assets employed. In theory, the value of all assets, less all outstanding liabilities, provides an indication of the fair market value of ownership equity.

Rev. Rul. 59-60 states that the appraiser will accord primary consideration to earnings when valuing stocks of companies which sell products or services to the public. It states that the net asset value should be a primary consideration for valuing closely held investment or real estate holding companies. Accordingly, net asset value may be given minimum weight in the valuation of an operating company.

The position expressed in Rev. Rul. 59-60 is fully supported by other authorities. For example, Judge Learned Hand stated in *Borg vs. International Silver Co.* 11F. 2d 147, 152 (2nd

Cir. 1925) that: Everyone knows that the value of shares in a commercial or manufacturing company depends chiefly on what it will earn.

Authorities on valuation also commented that earnings, not net asset value, are the ultimate factor in valuing operating businesses. In *The Financial Policy of Corporations*, 5th ed. (The Ronald Press, 1953), A. S. Dewing, an authority in valuation, states:

> This chapter takes the position squarely and openly that the ultimate and final controlling criterion of the value of a going business is earning power.
>
> * * * * *
>
> The businessman, frankly, is interested neither in the engineer's appraisal of physical property, according to some arbitrary rule of unit values, nor in the accountant's report of past expenditures. He is interested primarily in the past earning capacity of the business so far as this can throw light on the future earnings in his hands. He is buying earning capacity and not physical assets.

In the *Estate of Oakley J. Hall*, the U.S. Tax Court also indicated that the net asset value approach plays a minor role in the valuation of an operating business. The court stated: ...We have not overlooked the fact that Marine had a book value of $3,442,000 at September 30, 1967, but we deem it quite unlikely that such a value could have been realized if the company had been liquidated; furthermore, there was no indication in the evidence that there was any intent to liquidate the company at the time of decedent's death.

In summary, the net asset value approach can be a meaningful technique for valuing an investment or real estate holding company. The net asset approach may not be a meaningful technique for valuing an operating company. We believe that the company's future earnings provide a greater value than the adjusted net book value. Relying on the adjusted net asset approach would fail to recognize the possible economic goodwill due to its current earnings potential. Accordingly, this approach was not relied upon, even though we considered the adjusted net asset value of the company.

DISCOUNTED CASH FLOW APPROACH

The discounted cash flow approach is an income-based approach. It determines the fair market value of an ongoing business enterprise based on its earnings capacity and operating cash flows. This approach involves projecting cash flows for a period of time, estimating a residual value (equivalent to the continuing earnings power of the business in perpetuity) at the end-of-the-time horizon, and then discounting those amounts back to the valuation date to determine the current value.

The discounted cash flow calculations consist of three major components: (1) future cash flows, (2) residual value, and (3) discount rate. The calculation involves the following steps:

1. Projected operating cash flows, year by year, for the five years from 19__ to 19__ were prepared. These cash flow projections were compiled by the company's management. See Exhibit C for details. (Eight years, not shown.)

    According to the company's management, the projections do not reflect (1) the company's anticipated sales growth in distant markets and (2) its ability to raise prices for its starch products because of the competitive advantage discussed in the Business History Section. The projections show that the company will receive a favorable lease during the five-year period in accordance with the lease agreement with the company's shareholders who also own the property.

The projections also do not show any capital expenditures or additions, although sales are projected to grow at a rate of five percent. The company's management believes that additional capital expenditures or additions are not necessary to maintain the projected growth because of excess productive capacity. Wild has three production lines, none of which run more than one shift. Expanding the hours of operation can thus effectively increase production by more than 200 percent. In addition, the company is able to take advantage of contract packagers in strategically located areas to supply new and distant markets with no capital outlays. Financial statements from 19__ to 19__ show limited capital expenditures as follows:

Year	Capital Expenditures
1	$ 26,416
2	47,814
3	21,132
4	41,428
5	134,919
Total	$271,709
Average	$ 54,342

If $55,000 of capital expenditures were incorporated into the projections, the projected cash flows would be as shown in Exhibit C-1. (Eight years, not shown.)

Finally, the projections show officers' salaries of $157,500 for 19__ with an annual increase of 5 percent. Shareholders of the company will contract with the company to provide their services and expertise and will be compensated only if the actual income is in excess of the projected income. Their compensation will be an amount equal to the lesser of (1) the excess of profits over losses realized during the year from trading chemicals as a commodity, or (2) the excess of the actual company income over the projected income. The company will employ and train an executive to succeed the shareholders upon their retirement. The officers' salaries shown in the projections reflect the compensation of such an executive.

2. A residual value was determined. Residual value is the assumed value of a company at the end of the projection period. This reflects the cash flows realized from the end of year five to the indefinite future.

We used the perpetuity with growth method for calculating the residual value at the end of the five-year projection period, as follows:

$$\text{Future Residual Value} = \frac{1}{k - g} \times c$$

Where: k = discount rate
  g = cash flow growth rate
  c = the projected cash flows for the first year after the
      projection period

We assumed that the annual cash flow growth after 19__ will be 5 percent. This future residual value is then discounted to the present to determine the present residual value. See Exhibit D (page 334) for detail of the residual value computations.

3. A discount rate is selected.

4. The estimated cash flows for each of the projected years and the future residual value are discounted at the selected discount rate to arrive at their present values.

5. The present value figures are added to determine the total operating value of the company.

6. The operating value of the company is then adjusted, if any, by subtracting the principal of long-term debt service. The long-term debt service is subtracted because it reduces cash flow and thus the value of the company. After these adjustments, the final value represents the equity value of the company.

Generally, the discount rate is the expected rate of return available on alternative investment opportunities with similar risks. We developed a discount rate based on the weighted average after-tax cost of capital. The weighted average cost of capital is made up of the after-tax returns paid to all sources of capital, weighted by the proportions of each of these sources to total capital.

Here we used two sources of capital: equity (which includes contributed capital and retained earnings on common stock) and debt. Both the risk rates and the debt/equity ratio are determined after considering the business risks. This is intended to reflect the analysis that a prudent investor might conduct to estimate the fair market value.

We estimated the cost of debt based on the weekly average for the week ended July 27, 19__ yield on corporate A bonds of 9.26 percent with a premium adjustment of 2 percentage points for the risk involved to arrive at 11.26 percent. After adjustment for an assumed 38 percent effective tax rate, the after-tax cost of debt becomes 6.98 percent.

To arrive at the cost of equity, we estimated the (1) expected risk-free rate (RF), (2) expected return on the equity market in excess of the risk-free rate (RM) (i.e., equity market risk premium), and (3) industry/company risks (R). These inputs were incorporated into the following formula:

Ke = Rf + Rm + R
Ke = Cost of equity
Rf = Risk-free rate (see A. below)
Rm = Equity market return in excess of the risk-free rate (see B. below)
R   = Industry/company risks (see C. below)

A. The risk-free rate was based on the weekly average for the week ended July 27, 19__ of 8.54 percent on 30-year Treasury bonds.

B. The difference between the return on the market and the risk-free interest rate (Rf) is termed the market risk premium (Rm). We used a risk premium of 10.6 percent based on studies done by Ibbotson Associates as set forth in the *Stocks, Bonds, Bills and Inflation: 19__ Yearbook.* The risk premium is the sum of (1) the average excess of the total returns of company stock in the S&P Composite Index over long-term Treasury bond income yield and (2) the average excess of the small company stock returns over the return of the S&P Composite Index. Small company stock return basically consists of stocks making up the two smallest deciles in terms of capitalization, which are traded on the New York Stock Exchange and stock listed on the American Stock Exchange and over the counter with the same or less capitalization.

The risk premium of 10.6 percent is computed as follows:

Excess common stock returns (S&P composite)	6.8%
Excess small stock returns over common stock returns	3.8
Total Risk Premium	10.6%

C. The industry/company risk is a subjective measure to account for the relative risk of Wild and its industry in relation to the general stock market as a whole. We used 2 percent to account for such company risks because of its relatively small size. Applying the percentage to the formula, as stated above, provides a cost of equity of 21.14 percent as follows:

Ke = Rf + Rm + R
Ke = .54% + 10.6% + 2%
Ke = 21.14%

For cost of equity, no adjustment is made for income taxes because neither dividends nor redemptions are deductible by the corporation.

The weighted average cost of capital is computed using an assumed debt-to-equity ratio of 20/80 based on industry statistics. The overall result is 18.00 percent of cost of capital, computed as follows:

	Percent	Weight	Weighted Percent
Cost of debt	6.89	20%	1.40
Cost of equity	21.14	80%	16.91
Total Cost of Capital			18.30
Rounded			18.00%

In selecting the discount rate, we also considered the rates that would constitute reasonable rates of return for businesses engaged in specialty cleaning, polishing and sanitation preparations under Standard Industry Code (SIC) 2842 and businesses engaged in chemicals and chemical preparations under SIC 2899. The SIC 2842 category includes manufacture of starch (may or may not be true) while the 2899 code includes manufacture of antifreeze compounds. What constitutes a reasonable return can best be answered by referring to IRS Rev. Rul. 68-609, which states:

> The percentage of return on the average annual value of tangible assets used should be the percentage prevailing in the industry involved at the date of valuation. . .

The following industry statistics regarding 19__ after-tax return on net worth under SIC 2842 and 2899, as compiled by Dun and Bradstreet, are helpful in determining whether an 18 percent discount rate is reasonable:

	2842	2899
Median	13.9%	12.2%
Upper Quartile	26.4%	25.8%

As shown above, the 19__ median after-tax return on net worth (i.e., percentage of after-tax profit on net worth) for businesses under SIC 2842 was 13.9 percent, while the median for businesses under SIC 2899 was 12.2 percent. The median represents the midpoint of the entire observations.

The upper quartile was 26.4 percent for SIC 2842 and 25.8 percent for SIC 2899. The upper quartile represents the midpoint between the highest result and the median. It should be noted that the spread between the upper and lower quartiles represents the middle 50 percent of all observed businesses.

It is reasonable to assume that a potential investor would at least want to receive a return on his investment that approximates the industry's median (i.e., middle). Preferably, the investor would like to receive a return as close as possible to the upper quartile. Most likely, an investor would be satisfied with a return that is somewhere between the median and the upper quartile.

In determining a reasonable rate of return for Wild, we computed a blended rate since Wild is involved in businesses under both SIC 2842 and 2899. Since about 30 percent of Barton's sales (excluding the sale of various chemicals which accounted for about 5 percent of the total volume) is in starch as listed under SIC 2842 and about 70 percent is in antifreeze compounds under SIC 2899, we weighted the rates of return from the two industries in proportion to the sales proportion of the two businesses to arrive at a blended rate of return, computed as follows:

	Rate of Return	Sales Proportion	Weighted Rate of Return
Median			
Starch	13.9%	30%	4.2%
Antifreeze Compounds	12.2%	70%	8.5%
Blended Rate of Return			<u>12.7</u>%
Upper Quartile			
Starch	26.4%	30%	7.9%
Antifreeze Compounds	25.8%	70%	<u>18.1</u>%
Blended Rate of Return			<u>26.0</u>%

The blended median rate of return is 12.7 percent, and the blended upper quartile is 26.0 percent. As indicated earlier, an investor would like to receive a return close to the upper quartile, although he probably would be willing to accept the median return as a minimum return. A compromise would be a rate of return somewhere between the median and the upper quartile, possibly the midpoint between them. A midpoint would be a rate of return of about 18–19 percent.

The weighted average after-tax cost of capital, discussed earlier, is 18 percent. The blended rate of return ranges from a median of 12.7 percent and an upper quartile of 26.0 percent, with a midpoint of about 18–19 percent. In view of this data, a discount rate of 18 percent is reasonable.

Discounting the future cash flows at 18 percent, the operating value of the company is about $4,500,000. See Exhibit D (shown) for the computations. Since the company has no long-term debt, no adjustment is necessary to arrive at the equity value of the company. If $55,000 of capital expenditures were incorporated into the cash flow projections, the operating value of the company would be about $4,200,000. (See Exhibit D.)

MARKET COMPARABLES APPROACH

As a cross-check to the values derived from the discounted cash flow valuation approach, we examined market prices and resulting valuation multiples for public companies engaged in businesses which may be considered comparable to that of the subject company. We found four publicly traded firms: (1) Big Co., (2) Bigger Co., (3) Biggest Co., and (4) Biggerest Co. A brief synopsis of each company is in Exhibit E-1, as excerpted from *Standard & Poor's Corporation Records*. While the selected firms do not exactly match the line of business, size, operating performance or financial condition of the company, they do provide a market measure of value.

The use of publicly held corporations as comparable companies cannot give an exact fair market value for the closely held business, because the risk involved in investing in an actively traded corporation is less than that of purchasing a company for which there is no ready market. The purpose of comparative analysis is to arrive at a benchmark valuation amount. Appropriate adjustments are then made to give recognition to the dissimilarities between the closely held business and the comparable corporations.

Comparison with Wild

Analysis of the size, financial condition, and operating performance of the comparative public companies (Exhibit E-1, shown) indicates the following:

1. *Wild is Smaller in Size.*

   The latest statistics indicate that revenues earned for the public companies ranged from $31.9 million to $1.35 billion versus $19.8 million for the year ended December 31, 19__ for Wild. Total assets ranged from $25.8 million to $1.21 billion for the public companies versus $4.4 million as of December 31, 19__ for Wild.

2. *Wild has a Weaker Liquidity Position.*

   Liquidity is generally measured by the current ratio (which is current assets divided by current liabilities). The ratio measures the short-term liquidity available to meet current debt. Generally, the lower the ratios, the higher the risk for short-term creditors.

   Wild's current ratio, as of December 31, 19__, of 1.16 is weaker than all of the public companies' current ratios which range from 1.5 to 2.2.

3. *Wild Has a Weaker Leverage Position.*

   A company's leverage position is normally measured by the ratio of total liabilities to shareholders' equity. The ratio measures the leverage factor, or capital derived from creditors, versus the capital derived from the owners of the business. The higher the ratio, the greater the risk for the creditors and the owners.

   Wild has extremely high leverage relative to the comparative public companies in terms of total liabilities to net worth. Its total liabilities to net worth ratio of 8.99 as of December 31, 19__ is much higher than the public companies' range of .54 to 1.97.

4. *Wild has Lower Profitability.*

   Wild's net income to sales ratio of 4.6 percent (after adjusting for officers' compensation to $150,000) lies near the lower end of the comparative public companies' range of 4.1 percent to 10.7 percent.

In summary, Wild is smaller than the comparative public companies in terms of size and weaker in terms of liquidity and profitability. Furthermore, it is highly leveraged. Given these factors, we would consider Wild to be a substantially greater investment risk than the public companies as a group.

In determining a value based upon comparable companies, six different valuation techniques have been adopted. In the first, we multiply the appropriate market to book value ratio, based on the comparables, by the book value of the company. The second approach is similar to the first, except the market to sales ratio was used. The third and fourth involve the application of a price to earnings multiple, both on a current and historical basis, based upon the comparables, to the respective earnings of the company. The fifth and sixth analyses compare the current and historical cash flows of the comparables with that of the company. For details on the derivation of the comparables companies multiples, see Exhibit E, (shown).

Nonoperating income and nonrecurring expense items have been removed from the historical performance of the comparable companies and the company.

Since the company is much smaller and less diversified than the comparable companies, we believe that an adjustment is necessary to arrive at the multiples. In Sol Koffler TCM 1978–159, the U.S. Tax Court provided a total discount of 60% or more to account for the differences between ALW (the taxpayer) and the comparable selected, as follows:

> Using Samsonite as a comparative, we think substantial discounts would be required in arriving at a price-earnings ratio for ALW: at least 15 percent for ALW's thin management; at least 30 percent for ALW's lack of diversification, its outmoded manufacturing facilities, its limit to the domestic market, its failure to pay any dividends since 1951, and its domination by a single family; and an equal discount for the fact that the ALW stock was not publicly traded and could not be easily marketed.

In view of the circumstances surrounding Wild and the comparables used, we believe that a downward adjustment of 50 percent is reasonable. This adjustment is reflected in the multiples used below (see Exhibit E, shown)

Market to Book Method (See Exhibit E-2)

The market value to book value ratio of the common of the comparable companies ranged from 217.97 to 353.26. The adjusted average market to book value ratio was 142.74 percent. The value, after adjustment is $976,082:

$$\begin{array}{r} \$683,818 \\ \underline{\times\ 142.74\%} \\ \underline{\$976,082} \end{array}$$

Market to Sales Method (See Exhibit E-3)

The market to sales value calculation is very similar to the market to book calculation. The ratio of market price per share to sales per share ranged from 42.498 to 158.770. Since the adjusted average ratio for the comparables was 32.934 percent, the value using this method is $6,504,167:

$$\begin{array}{r} \$19,749,095 \\ \underline{\times\ 32.934\%} \\ \underline{\$\ 6,504,167} \end{array}$$

Price to Current Earnings Ratio (See Exhibit E-4)

The market price of stock is compared to the earnings per share figure in this analysis. For the four comparables, P/E's ranged from 10.000 to 29.792. The adjusted average PE is 6.671, giving a value of $6,888,461:

$$\begin{array}{r} \$1,032,598 \\ \underline{\times\ 6.671} \\ \underline{\$6,888,461} \end{array}$$

Price to Historical Earnings Method (See Exhibit E-5)

In determining the value based upon its historical earning capacity, we multiplied a two-year weighted average earnings by the respective price/earnings multiple, as adjusted and derived from the comparable companies.

Two Year Weighted Average Earnings:

Two Year Weighted Average Earnings (FYE 12/31/__ – 12/31/__) =	$ 998,321
Price to Current Earnings Multiple from Comparables =	x 5.956
	$5,946,000

Price to Current Cash Flow (See Exhibit E-6)

The market price per share is compared with the current cash flow earned per share. Price to cash flow multiples had a range from 5.541 to 14.075. The adjusted average is 4.875. Multiplying this number by the cash flows generated by the company in 19__ results in the following value:

$1,092,153
x 4.875
$5,324,246

Price to Historical Cash Flow Method (See Exhibit E-7)

The historical cash flow method is very similar to the historical earnings based method in that we have selected the two year weighted average multiple derived from our comparable companies. The only difference between the earnings and cash flow methods are that the cash flow method incorporates depreciation and amortization. We used the adjusted average cash flow multiplier of 5.07.

Two Year Weighted Average Cash Flow:

Two Year Weighted Average Cash Flow (FYE 12/31/__ – 12/31/__) =	$1,062,315
Price to Current Earnings Multiple from Comparables =	x 5.07
	$5,385,937

Summary of Comparable Company Valuation Approaches

Method	Indicated Value
Market to Book	$ 976,082*
Market to Sales	6,504,167
Price to Current P/E	6,888,461
Two Year Weighted Average P/E	5,946,000
Price to Current Cash Flow	5,324,246
Two Year Weighted Average Price to Cash Flow	5,385,937
Total	31,024,893
Less (Market to Book)	-976,082*
	30,048,811
	5
Divided by	$ 6,009,762

*Market to Book does not approach the range that represents the fair market value of the Company, as shown by the other five methods. Since to leave it in would distort the valuation, it is removed.

We have taken an average of the different techniques highlighted above to arrive at our estimate of value based upon comparable companies. Market to book has been excluded from the average since that technique did not produce a value estimate which is consistent with the other methods. The average value is $6,009,762.

The indicated value derived from the comparables is based on transactions of minority interest in public markets. To determine the amount of premium on a control interest, premiums over minority value paid for control in merger and acquisitions transactions may be used. Mergerstat Review for 1989, published by W. T. Grimm & Company, indicates that the median premium paid for control was 29.0 percent. In over one-third of the transactions where a premium over market was paid, the premium was 20 percent or less.

We believe that a control premium for a small firm such as Wild would be lower than the average premiums cited by W.T. Grimm & Company. It is our opinion that a 10 percent premium over the freely traded minority price would be a reasonable premium for such a small company. After the 10 percent control premium, the average value, based on market comparables, would be $6,610,738.

Based on the performance of the company relative to the comparable companies, we are able to conclude from the comparable company analysis that the consideration of $4,500,000 to be paid by the ESOP is not above its fair market value.

ENVIRONMENTAL AND LITIGATION ISSUES

Environmental Issues

The premises occupied by the company at 1111 West Luck Street, Love Park, Indiana was inspected by B. Tough Engineering, Inc., on December 22, 19___. The purpose of the inspection was to determine the presence of potential on-site contamination due to possible surface spills of hazardous materials stored on-site or landfilled foundry sands from past operations. No current environmental audit has been done.

The B. Tough report is written in engineering and technical language. The report does not appear to provide any recommendation. The company's management informed us that B. Tough suggested additional tests to determine if near-surface contaminants present a real problem.

Apparently there may be potential environmental concerns regarding possible contamination from hazardous materials. We are not engaged or qualified to evaluate the extent of the potential environmental issues; however, an environmental attorney of the company's outside counsel, in response to an August 7, 19___ memorandum regarding environmental conditions at the company, concluded the following:

> . . . Any release of hazardous materials is to the MWRD sewer pursuant to a permit. Further investigation of possible lead contamination does not appear warranted until the party principally responsible for any release can be notified and a plan developed for putting any liability for a release onto such party.

According to the attorney, the party principally liable for the releases of lead and foundry sand would be the prior owner of the property. The attorney recommends that the company demand the prior owner to remedy any hazardous materials in the sand.

An environmental issue such as contamination can affect the fair market value of a property, including stock of a company. We examined the proposed stock purchase agreement (Agreement) of Wild's common stock. The Agreement provides the sellers of the stock shall indemnify, defend and hold the ESOP and the company harmless against (1) all fines or penalties hereafter incurred by reason of present violations of Environmental Laws, and (2) clean-up costs hereafter incurred by reason of the present condition of the property presently leased by the company. The Agreement also provides indemnification for breach of any of the sellers' representations and warranties. The indemnification becomes operative only if the aggregate liabilities are in excess of $200,000, in which event the sellers are liable only for the amount in excess of the $200,000 threshold. Accordingly, the ESOP, as potential buyer, may bear a maximum potential, contingent cost of $200,000 for possible environmental problems as well as other breach of the sellers' warranties.

The contingent costs of $200,000, if translated into current dollars, may be substantially less due to its contingent nature. How much less is a question of the time and the likelihood of the occurrence of these contingent costs. Without trying to quantify these contingent costs, we believe that the consideration of $4,500,000 to be paid by the ESOP is still not above its fair market value because of the following reasons:

1.   The average value based on market comparables, even after adjusting for the $200,000 contingent costs, is still much higher than purchase price of $4,500,000.

2.   The discount rate for the discounted cash flow approach of valuation is developed in view of the company's risks. Accordingly, the discount rate implicitly accounts for the potential risks of operating a business facing possible environmental issues.

Litigation Issues

On its December 31, 19__ financial statements, Wild identified a lawsuit pending with a chemical company regarding an open purchase order. In this regard, the chemical company has countersued. The company's management feels that the parties will settle the matter without any material liability to either party.

The company also has the following lawsuits pending:

1.   *Pretty Big Corporation v. Wild Corporation and Pretty Small, Inc.*, Case No. 93Q03179, Circuit Court of That County, Indiana, Law Division.

2.   *Big Oil Company v. Wild Corporation and Texas Slim Individually*, Case No. PU9-0255, United States District Court for the Northern District of Ohio Dayton Division.

3.   *Booze Industries, Inc. (US) v. Wild Corporation*, Case No. 94-414, United States District Court for the District of Colorado.

4.   *United States Round Company v. American Flat Products, Inc., et al. v. Wild Corporation*, Case No. B4U-00087, United States District Court for the Northern District of Florida, Roll Division.

The company's management represented that any liabilities arising out of actual or potential claims relating to these lawsuits will not have a material impact on the financial condition of the company.

In addition, the Agreement provides that the sellers of the stock shall indemnify the ESOP and the company against any liability *(other than legal fees)* arising out of the settlement or judgment of these lawsuits. This indemnification is part of the same indemnification referred to in the Environmental Issues section (see above).

DISCOUNT FOR GENERAL LACK OF MARKETABILITY

The value of $4,500,000 is a value based on intrinsic factors. It does not necessarily mean this is the fair market value of the shares in question because of the general lack of marketability. This is because shares in a privately held company lack the marketability of shares in comparison with the publicly traded shares. The proposed regulations from the DOL specifically require an assessment of the effect of the lack of marketability upon shares of any nonpublicly traded company.

If one wishes to dispose of shares of a publicly traded company, all one has to do is call a local stockbroker. However, it's no easy task to dispose of shares in a privately held company.

In *Valuing a Business: The Analysis and Appraisal of Closely Held Companies*, Dow Jones-Irwin, 1981, the author states:

All other things being equal, an interest in a business is worth more if the interest is readily marketable or, conversely, worth less if it is not. It is well known that investors prefer liquidity to lack of liquidity. Interests in closely held businesses are relatively illiquid, compared with most other investments. This problem may be compounded further by restrictions on transfer of interest found in buy-sell agreements in many companies.

Since Wild is a closely held business, a discount for general lack of marketability may be appropriate. The lack of marketability discount concept recognizes the fact that closely held stock interests are less attractive and have fewer potential purchasers than similar publicly traded stock.

The principle of a discount for lack of marketability has been stated as follows: It seems clear . . . that an unlisted closely held stock of a corporation. . . , in which trading is infrequent and which therefore lacks marketability, is less attractive than a similar stock which is listed on an exchange and has ready access to the investing public. *Central Trust Co.*, 305 F2d 393 [CtCl] 1962. If the owners of closely held stocks should try to list a block of such securities on a stock exchange for sale to the public, they would probably have to make the offerings through underwriters. There would be costs for registering nonpublicly traded stocks with the Securities and Exchange Commission (SEC) involving, among other fees, the expense of preparing a prospectus. In addition, the underwriters themselves would receive commissions. The actual costs of such an offering can range from 10 to 25 percent of the selling price to the public.

Another support for the amount of discount for lack of marketability is provided by transactions in letter stocks. A letter stock is identical in all respects to the freely traded stock of a public company except that it is restricted from trading on the open market for some period. The duration of the restrictions varies from one situation to another. Since marketability is the only difference between the letter stock and its freely tradable counterpart, the differences in the same stock provide solid evidence that the market produces a price spread between a readily marketable security and its otherwise identical counterpart that is subject to certain marketability restrictions.

In a major study done by the SEC on institutional investor actions, one of the topics was the amount of discount at which transactions in restricted stock (letter stock) took place, as compared with the prices of otherwise identical but unrestricted stock on the open market. Discounts Involved in Purchases of Common Stock in U.S. 92nd Congress, 1st Session, House. *Institutional Investor Study Report of the Securities and Exchange Commission.* Washington, D.C.: U.S. Government Printing Office (March 10, 1971), 5:2444-2456. (Document No. 92-64, Part 5). The study shows the amounts of discounts on letter stock transactions by four market categories: (1) New York Stock Exchange; (2) American Stock Exchange; (3) Over the Counter (reporting companies); and (4) Over the Counter (nonreporting companies). A reporting company is a publicly traded company that must file Forms 10-K, 10-Q and other information with the SEC. A nonreporting company is a company that is publicly traded OTC but is not subject to the same reporting requirements.

The study shows that the discounts on the letter stocks were the least for NYSE-listed stocks, but increased, in order, for ASE-listed stocks, OTC reporting companies and OTC nonreporting companies. For OTC nonreporting companies, the largest number of restricted stock transactions fell in the 30 to 40 percent discount range. Slightly over 56 percent of the OTC nonreporting companies experienced discounts greater than 30 percent on the sale of their restricted stock. A little over 30 percent of the OTC reporting companies experienced discounts over 30 percent, and over 52 percent experienced discounts over 20 percent.

Another study on marketability discounts for closely held business interests was done by J. Michael Maher, *Discounts for Lack of Marketability for Closely Held Business Interests*, Taxes (September 1976), pg. 562–71. The study involves a comparison of prices paid for restricted stocks with the market prices of their unrestricted counterparts. The study showed that The mean discount for lack of marketability for the years 1969–73 amounted to 35.43 percent. Maher then made an interesting second computation: eliminating the top 10 percent and the bottom 10 percent of purchases to remove especially high and low risk situations. The result was almost identical with a mean discount of 34.73 percent.

Maher concludes:

> The result I have reached is that most appraisers underestimate the proper discount for lack of marketability. The results seem to indicate that this discount should be about 35 percent. Perhaps this makes sense because by committing funds to restricted common stock, the willing buyer (a) would be denied the opportunity to take advantage of other investments, and (b) would continue to have his investment at the risk of the business until the shares could be offered to the public or another buyer is found.

> The 35 percent discount would not contain elements of a discount for a minority interest because it is measured against the current fair market value of securities actively traded (other minority interest). Consequently, appraisers should also consider a discount for a minority interest in those closely held companies where a discount is applicable.

Finally, Professor Steven E. Bolten investigated studies that had been done in the area of valuation discounts. In his article, *Discounts for the Stocks of Closely Held Corporations*, 123 Trusts and Estates 22 (December 1984), he concluded that the results of previous studies indicate (1) an average of 39.86 percent for nonmarketability discount, and (2) an average of 29.37 percent discount for minority position. Commenting on the studies done on the discount of nonmarketability, Professor Bolten states:

> Although these studies took place over a ten-year period, each discovered an average discount of approximately the same amount. Thus, we may safely assume that the nonmarketability discount not only is appropriately applied because of its historically observed presence but also because of its relative stability.

Professor Bolten also concludes:

> The growing body of studies and evidence on the issues of minority position and nonmarketable discounts sustains their presence at observed, substantial levels. The average total substantiated discount for both from a comparable public traded security is over 69 percent.

In *Valuing a Business: The Analysis and Appraisal of Closely Held Companies* (Dow Jones-Irwin, 1981), Dr. Shannon P. Pratt also states:

> There is considerable evidence to suggest that the discount for the lack of marketability factor alone for a closely held stock compared with a publicly traded counterpart should average about 35 percent.

Since we are valuing the entire company, a discount for minority interest would be inappropriate. However, a discount for nonmarketability may remain applicable. In the case of an ESOP, a willing buyer of the shares is usually referenced in the ESOP agreement. Depending on the terms of the plan and the financial position of the company, a marketability discount may be minimal or inappropriate.

An ESOP generally must make a distribution of the employer stock within one year of a participant's termination of employment. Furthermore, an employee is entitled to demand that the company or the ESOP repurchase the stock that was distributed to him (a put option). However, a leveraged ESOP may defer distributions (and the consequent cash demands imposed by the put option) until the ESOP loan has been repaid. In the case of the Company, it is our understanding that the proposed plan will incorporate such distribution deferral provisions. Furthermore, the ESOP will be designed so that no distributions of stock will be made until an employee attains his tenth anniversary of participation in the ESOP. Accordingly, this would alleviate the potential cash demands of the put option during the loan repayment period.

Questions arise as to whether the distribution deferral rule has priority over the mandatory distribution rules which require mandatory distributions at age 70-1/2 or within five years of death. If the mandatory distribution rules take precedence, then a potential cash demand may result during the loan repayment period. It is our understanding that only two of the company's 72 current employees are above age 60 (one is 62 and another is 63). The average age of Company's employees is 37. Accordingly, only two of the company's current employees will attain age 70-1/2 in the next ten years. Also, mortality tables published by the Pension Benefit Guaranty Corporation indicate that less than 2 percent of the company's current employees would be expected to die in the next ten years.

Therefore, with the possible de minimis exception that those who die or attain age 70-1/2 within that period might become entitled to earlier distributions, the company expects that the ESOP put options will not impose cash demands upon the ESOP or the company before the ESOP loan is repaid.

Given a willing buyer as provided in the proposed ESOP agreement, a discount for lack of marketability is necessary if the willing buyer will likely be financially incapable of redeeming the shares. Based on the projections used for the valuation, it is highly unlikely that the company will not be able to redeem shares tendered by an employee. Furthermore, the likelihood that any employee will be redeeming any shares within the loan repayment period is minimal. Accordingly, we believe that a discount for lack of marketability is not necessary since the company will most likely be financially capable to redeem any shares tendered by an employee.

CONTROL PREMIUM

When more than 50 percent of the stock of a company is transferred, the concept of control premium may be relevant in determining the value of the stock transferred. The proposed regulations from the DOL specifically require a discussion on control premium.

The purpose of a control premium is to provide for common benefits such as:

1. Elect directors and appoint management.
2. Determine management compensation and perquisites.
3. Declare and pay dividends.
4. Sell or acquire treasury shares.

5.   Acquire or liquidate asset.

6.   Set policy and change the course of business.

7.   Make acquisitions.

8.   Select people with whom to do business and award contracts.

9.   Change the articles of incorporation or by-laws.

10. Liquidate, dissolve, sell out, or recapitalize the company.

In analyzing the control premium, it is relevant to determine whether the value to which the premium might be applied was based principally on sales of minority interests or intrinsic factors. If the value is based on sales of minority shares, a control premium should be applied. In *Estate of Ruben Rodriguez*, 56 TCM 1033 (1988), the U.S. Tax Court stated that:

> ... A 'control premium' should be added to value determined from sales of minority interests . . .

The control premium, in essence, is applied to the market price of a minority interest. However, if the value is based on intrinsic factors, no control premium should be applied. Intrinsic factors are those which relate to the financial condition of the company, such as earning capacity, book value, dividend paying capacity, goodwill, or other intangible value. See Krahmer, 221-2nd T.M., *Valuation of Shares of Closely Held Corporations*, A-36. The author commented as follows:

> It is difficult to see how control of a family holding company would make each share of the control block more valuable than the underlying net asset value per share. The net asset value per share is the most that could be realized by liquidation and it might be that the income tax liability which liquidation would create would be substantial. A similar situation would be present if the corporation was a manufacturer and the valuation were initially based primarily upon earning power. Even if it is assumed that the controlling shareholder can siphon off earnings as salary, he is principally penalizing the value of his own shares.

It has been stated that the discounted cash flow approach is based on evidence of rates of return on what are for the most part minority interest transactions in public markets. Accordingly, control premium should be applicable. Even if the argument (that the rates of return are based for the most part on minority interest transactions) prevails, the benefits of control should have already been reflected in the future cash flow projections. The future operating cash flow projections show the likely operating results based on decisions which are subject to the management/owner's control. Accordingly, the benefits of control should not again be provided through the use of control premium. A control premium is valid only if the cash flow projections do not account for such control influences.

In summary, a control premium should be provided if the value is based on sales of minority shares from comparables. The control premium should not be provided if the company's value is based on projected cash flows.

CONCLUSION

Based upon our investigation and analysis and subject to the assumptions, qualifications and limitations set forth within this report, it is our opinion that the purchase price of $4,500,000 for the planned acquisition of the company's common stock as of August 21, 19__ is an adequate consideration. The purchase price, based on its financial performance through July 31, 19__, does not exceed the fair market value of the stock. The value of $4,500,000 is determined based on the projected cash flow approach. Neither marketability discount nor control premium was applied to the value. No marketability discount was provided since the company should have no problem in redeeming any shares tendered by employees. No control premium was provided since the projected cash flows have accounted for the benefits derived from owning a control interest.

It is also our opinion that the proposed purchase is fair to the ESOP, its potential participants, and its beneficiaries.

LOAN AMORTIZATION ANALYSIS

As a check to see if the company generated sufficient cash flows to support the indicated fair market value of $4.5 million based on the discounted cash flow approach, a loan amortization schedule based on the projected cash flows from 19__ to 19__ (five years) was prepared. See Exhibit I (pages 342–343). The loan amortization schedule indicates that the outstanding loan balance of a $4.5 million loan would be $1,854,331 at the end of 19__. The analysis indicates that the loan should be completely paid-off by the end of the eighth year.

The loan amortization schedule was prepared based on the following assumptions:

1. Same assumptions as used in the projected cash flows except that federal and state income taxes were computed at income after the deduction for ESOP contributions.

2. The company's contributions to the ESOP are limited to the sum of:

   a. Twenty-five percent of ESOP participant's wages,

   b. Interest on the ESOP's loan, and

   c. A reasonable dividend on the cost of the shares ($123,000 is used in this case).

3. Interest rate for the ESOP's loan is estimated at 8 percent per year.

A key assumption in the loan amortization schedule is that the contributions to the ESOP will be fully deductible for regular federal income tax. The following are comments regarding the deductibility of dividends:

1. Dividends can be paid only out of earnings and profits, a tax concept. To the extent that a dividend distribution to the ESOP exceeds earnings and profits, the distribution is not deductible. The loan amortization analysis assumes that the earnings and profits will be equal or greater than the projected income before the dividend distribution.

2. Dividends paid with respect to ESOP stock will not give rise to deductions to the extent that the IRS determines that the dividend constitutes, in substance, an evasion of taxation. This subjective facts-and-circumstances requirement inputs a reasonableness standard to the dividends that can be deducted, notwithstanding the existence of earnings and profits from which the dividends can be paid.

    In the loan amortization analysis, it is assumed that the dividends are reasonable, and therefore deductible.

3. Deductions for dividends that are used to repay ESOP debt are allowed only in the year when the debt is repaid. The declaration of dividends and the record date are irrelevant to the timing of deductions. Even though it may take a period of time after the close of the year to determine the total amount of the company's earnings and profits, the dividend must be declared and paid prior to the close of the fiscal year in order to obtain the deduction for that year. The loan analysis assumes that the dividends are paid prior to the respective year-end.

4. A dividend paid with respect to stock that is allocated to a participant's account may be deducted only if the ESOP account to which the dividend would have otherwise been paid receives stock of a fair market value at least equal to the dividend. It is assumed that this requirement is met.

5. Finally, there is an uncertainty regarding how the dividends would be treated for AMT purposes. For taxable years beginning after December 31, 1989, the Alternative Minimum Taxable Income (AMTI) of a corporation is increased by 75 percent of the excess of the corporation's adjusted current earnings (ACE) over its AMTI. In proposed regulations, the IRS treats the ESOP dividends as being an add-back for ACE tax basis, on the theory that dividends are not deductible for computing earnings and profits. The present law does not appear to require that dividends paid to an ESOP be added back for AMT purposes. The loan amortization analysis assumes that the dividends would be an add-back, which could result in an AMT tax, even though there may be no regular income tax.

The loan amortization analysis is a projection based on numerous assumptions. As indicated, the income from the company can amortize the loan within eight years. If any of the assumptions varies from the actual happenings, however, the actual amortization of the bank loan may also vary.

STATEMENT OF LIMITING CONDITIONS

In accordance with recognized professional ethics, the fee for this service is not contingent upon our conclusion of value, and neither Blackman Kallick Bartelstein nor any of its employees has a present or intended financial interest in the company.

Financial and statistical information is from sources we deem reliable. However, we make no representation as to our sources' accuracy or completeness. The value of the company may change in the future due to uncertainty or unforeseen economic or competitive conditions. In addition, any future price actually received may also vary from the value due to unique circumstances of a particular purchaser or to the vagaries of negotiation.

The opinion of value expressed herein is valid only for the date of the appraisal and is prepared exclusively for the intended purpose of our client who is completely familiar with the business.

Future services regarding the subject matter of this report, including, but not limited to, testimony or attendance in court shall not be required of Blackman Kallick Bartelstein unless previous arrangements have been made in writing.

Neither all nor any part of the contents of this report shall be conveyed to the public through advertising, public relations, news, sales, mail, direct transmittal or other media without the prior written consent and approval of Blackman Kallick Bartelstein.

APPRAISER'S QUALIFICATIONS

Irving L. Blackman, C.P.A. and J.D., is a senior tax partner with the public accounting firm of Blackman Kallick Bartelstein.

Mr. Blackman has extensive experience in the valuation of closely held businesses. He has given expert testimony in the valuation areas in various courts of law.

Irving L. Blackman has written extensively in the tax area, including the following publications relating to valuation:

- How to Value Your Oil Jobbership for Tax Purposes

- How to Value Your Business for Tax Purposes—and Win the Tax Game

- How to Value the Family Business—Breaking the Tax Barrier

- How to Value Your Restaurant

- How to Value Your Tooling and Manufacturing Business

Mr. Blackman's most comprehensive valuation book was published in 1986 and is entitled *The Valuation of Privately-Held Businesses—State-of-the-Art Techniques for Buyers, Sellers, and Their Advisors*. The book is published by Probus Publishing Company.

Mr. Blackman has lectured to owners of closely held businesses from coast to coast in about 40 states, covering such subjects as Business Valuation and How to Save Taxes. These seminars are usually sponsored by trade associations. He also writes a monthly tax column for over 100 trade journals.

Exhibit D

Wildwood Corporation

Statement of Discounted Cash Flow Analysis
Income Projected @ A Growth Rate of 5%

Analysis without Capital Expenditures

Future Year	Cash Flow Before ESOP	Discount Factor @ 18%	=	Present Value per Year
1*	$ 579,202	0.8475	=	$ 490,874
2	607,319	0.7182	=	436,177
3	640,951	0.6086	=	390,083
4	676,926	0.5158	=	349,158
5	714,219	0.4371	=	312,185
Residual Value	749,928			
	$5,768,677	0.4371	=	2,521,489
	Discounted Cash Flow			$4,499,966

*First full year following valuation date.

Analysis with Capital Expenditures

Future Year	Cash Flow Before ESOP	Discount Factor @ 18%	=	Present Value per Year
1*	$ 527,189	0.8475	=	$ 446,793
2	557,823	0.7182	=	400,628
3	596,088	0.6086	=	362,779
4	634,900	0.5158	=	327,481
5	666,452	0.4371	=	291,306
Residual Value	699,776			
	$5,382,887	0.4371	=	2,352,860
	Discounted Cash Flow			$4,181,847

Residual Value Computation

1. The Capitalized Earnings Rate   0.18
2. The Growth Rate   0.05

Cash Flow Year Six $ 749,928
Residual Multiplier = 1/(.18−.05)   7.6923

Residual Value $5,768,677

Residual Value Computation

1. The Cap. Earnings Rate   0.18
2. The Growth Rate   0.05

Cash Flow Year Six $ 699,776
Residual Multiplier = 1/(.18−.05)   7.6923

Residual Value $5,382,887

Exhibit E-1

1. COMPANY A

Company makes specialty cleaning and maintenance compounds, cutting fluids, dishwashing compounds, and kitchen and laundry and household products for use in a wide variety of industries, such as hotel, restaurant, education, and health care. Company also provides laundry detergents and related specialties or use in large on-premise laundries, and the uniform rental and linen supply agencies. Company also owns 61 percent of Roto-Rooter, a plumbing service.

2. COMPANY B

Company and subsidiaries make and sell sodium bicarbonate-based consumer products sold mainly under the Arm & Hammer name. Products include Arm & Hammer baking soda, liquid and powder laundry detergent, fabric softener dryer sheets, all fabric bleach, dental care products, washing soda, and rum and room deodorizers and cleaners. Company also makes sodium bicarbonate for industrial customers in various industries. In 1988 consumer products accounted for 72 percent of net sales.

3. COMPANY C

(Any information given about this public company probably would identify the real client.)

4. COMPANY D

Company blends, formulates, packages, and distributes specialty chemicals; blends and packages anti-freeze; and makes plastic containers. Facilities are located in Chicago, Illinois and Montgomery, Alabama. Company also performs hot-dip galvanizing services. Chemical formulating and packaging accounted for 44.4 percent of 1988 operating income.

Exhibit E-2
Comparable Company Analysis
Market to Book Ratio

Company	Latest Year End	Market	Market Price (A)	Book Value (B)	MV/BV %
A	31–Dec–__	NYSE	24.500	11.24	217.97
B	31–Dec–__	NYSE	17.875	5.06	353.26
C	30–Jun–__	NYSE	39.375	14.47	272.11
D	31–Dec–__	ASE	5.375	1.80	298.61

Average					285.49
Adjustment (50%)					(142.75)
•					142.74%

Wildwood	31–Dec__			$683,818	

Price from Average ($683,818 x 142.74%) $976,082

Exhibit E-3
Comparable Company Analysis
Market to Sales Ratio

Company	Latest Year End	Market	Market Price (A)	Sales Per Share (B)	MV/Sales %
A	31–Dec–__	NYSE	24.500	57.650	42.498
B	31–Dec–__	NYSE	17.875	18.740	95.384
C	30–Jun–__	NYSE	39.375	24.800	158.770*
D	31–Dec–__	ASE	5.375	9.000	59.722
Average					65.868
Adjustment (50%)					(32.934)
Adjusted Market Average					32.934%
Wildwood	31–Dec__			$19,749,095	

Price from Average ($19,749,095 x 32.934%) $6,504,167

*Excluded from average

Exhibit E-4
Comparable Company Analysis
Price to Current Earnings Ratio

Company	Latest Year End	Market	Market Price (A)	Last 12 Months Earnings (D)	Current P/E
A	31–Dec–__	NYSE	24.500	2.450	10.000
B	31–Dec–__	NYSE	17.875	0.600	29.792*
C	31–Dec–__	NYSE	39.375	2.360	16.684
D	31–Dec–__	ASE	5.375	(1.230)	N/M

Average	13.342
Adjustment (50%)	(6.671)
	6.671%

Wildwood	31–Dec__	$1,032,598 (E)

Price from Average ($1,032,598 x 6.671%) $6,888,461

*Excluded from average

Net Income Before Tax 19__	$ (5,193)
Add Officer Salary	1,820,673
Deduct Agreed Salary	(150,000)
	1,665,480
Less Tax @ 3%	(632,882)
Wildwood's Earnings	$ 1,032,598

Exhibit E-5
Comparable Company Analysis
Price to Historical Earnings

Company	Latest Year End	Market	Market Price	2 Year Weighted Average EPS	2 Year Weighted Average P/E
A	31–Dec–__	NYSE	24,500	2.480	9.879
B	31–Dec–__	NYSE	17,875	0.680	26.287*
C	30–Jun–__	NYSE	39,375	2.570	15.321
D	31–Dec–__	ASE	5,375	0.510	10.539

Average					11.913
Adjustment (50%)					(5.957)
Adjusted Market Average					5.956

Wildwood	31–Dec__		$998,321 (F)

Price from Average ($998,321 x 5.956)   5,946,000

*Excluded from average

Net before Tax–19__	$ 864,268
Other Income	2,088
Add Officer Salary	4,808,545
Deduct Agreed Salary	(150,000)
Deduct Extraordinary Income	(4,025,279)
	1,499,622
Tax @ 38%	569,856
Adjusted Earnings	929,766
	929,766
Current Earnings (See Ex. E-4)	1,032,598
Current Earnings (See Ex. E-4)	1,032,598
	2,994,962
Weighted Average	$ 998,321

Exhibit E-6
Comparable Company Analysis
Price to Cash Flow

Company	Latest Year End	Market	Market Price (A)	Last CF (B)	Current P/CF
A	31–Dec–__	NYSE	24.500	3.100	7.903
B	31–Dec–__	NYSE	17.875	1.270	14.075
C	30–Jun–__	NYSE	39.375	3.430	11.480
D	31–Dec–__	ASE	5.375	0.970	5.541

Average					9.750
Adjustment (50%)					(4.875)
Adjusted Market Average					4.875

Wildwood	31–Dec__		$1,092,153	

Price from Average ($1,092,153 x 4.875) $5,324,246

Current Earnings (See Ex. E-4)	$1,032,598
Add Back Depreciation	59,555
	$1,092,153

Exhibit E-7
Comparable Company Analysis
Price to Historical Cash Flow

Company	Latest Year End	Market	Market Price (A)	2 Year Weighted Average CF (B)	2 Year Weighted Average P/CF
A	31–Dec–__	NYSE	24.500	2.96	8.28
B	31–Dec–__	NYSE	17.875	1.22	14.65
C	30–Jun–__	NYSE	39.375	3.32	11.86
D	31–Dec–__	ASE	5.375	0.93	5.78

Average	10.14
Adjustment (50%)	(5.07)
Adjusted Market Average	5.07

Wildwood	31–Dec__	$1,062,315

Price from Average ($1,062,315 x 5.07) $5,385,937

19__ Current Earnings (Ex. E-4)	$1,032,598
19__ Current Earnings (Ex. E-4)	1,032,598
19__ Earnings (Ex. E-5)	929,765
Add Back Depreciation:	
19__ + 2	119,110
19__	72,875
	3,186,946
Average	$1,062,315

Exhibit I
Wildwood Corporation
Statement of ESOP Loan Amoritization Projected

Future Years	1	2	3	4	5	6	7	8
Sales	$21,000,000	$22,050,000	$23,152,500	$24,310,125	$25,525,631	$26,801,913	$28,142,009	$29,549,109
Cost of Sales:								
Material	17,430,000	18,301,500	19,216,575	20,177,404	21,186,274	22,245,588	23,357,867	24,525,760
Labor	472,500	496,125	520,931	546,978	574,327	603,043	633,195	664,855
Overhead	1,112,107	1,156,230	1,207,799	1,261,822	1,318,418	1,384,339	1,453,556	1,526,234
Total Cost of Sales	19,014,607	19,953,855	20,945,305	21,986,204	23,079,019	24,232,970	25,444,619	26,716,850
Gross Profit	1,985,393	2,096,145	2,207,195	2,323,921	2,446,612	2,568,943	2,697,390	2,832,260
Operating Expenses	1,087,562	1,131,809	1,183,525	1,239,356	1,296,511	1,361,337	1,429,404	1,500,874
Income (Loss) B/4 ESOP & Taxes	897,831	964,336	1,023,670	1,084,565	1,150,101	1,207,606	1,267,986	1,331,386
ESOP Deduction*	(850,500)	(829,635)	(808,219)	(786,224)	(763,621)	(740,380)	(716,469)	(698,556)
Income (Loss) B/4 Income Taxes	47,331	134,701	215,451	298,341	386,480	467,226	551,517	632,830
Tax Provision—Illinois	3,327	9,600	15,398	21,349	27,677	33,475	39,527	45,365
Tax Provision—Federal	6,601	32,039	61,271	91,277	121,993	147,475	174,077	199,738
Alternative Min. Tax	12,650	6,799	0	0	0	0	0	0
Income (Loss) After Tax	$ 24,753	$ 86,263	$ 138,782	$ 185,715	$ 236,810	$ 286,276	$ 337,913	$ 387,727

*Contribution, which is deductible, to be made to Employee Stock Option Trust and used to amortize loan.

continued

Exhibit I (continued)

Schedule of Loan Amortization

Beginning Loan Balance	$4,500,000	$4,009,500	$3,500,625	$2,972,456	$2,424,029	$1,854,331	$1,262,297	$ 646,812
Payment (25% of Salaries)	(367,500)	(385,875)	(405,169)	(425,428)	(446,699)	(469,034)	(492,485)	(517,110)
Dividend Payment	(123,000)	(123,000)	(123,000)	(123,000)	(123,000)	(123,000)	(123,000)	(129,702)
Ending Loan Balance	4,009,500	3,500,625	2,972,456	2,424,029	1,854,331	1,262,298	646,812	1

Schedule of ESOP Contribution

25% of Total Salaries	**367,500	385,875	405,169	425,428	446,699	469,034	492,485	517,110
8% of Beg. Loan Bal.	360,000	320,760	280,050	237,796	193,922	148,346	100,984	51,745
Dividend—$123,000 Per Year	123,000	123,000	123,000	123,000	123,000	123,000	123,000	129,702
Total ESOP Contribution	850,500	829,635	808,219	786,224	763,621	740,380	716,469	698,556

**Schedule of Salaries

Direct Labor	472,500	496,125	520,931	546,978	574,327	603,043	633,195	664,855
Salaries—Officers	157,500	165,375	173,644	182,326	191,442	201,014	211,065	221,618
Salaries—Office	105,000	110,250	115,763	121,551	127,628	134,010	140,710	147,746
Salaries—Drivers	210,000	220,500	231,525	243,101	255,256	268,019	281,420	295,491
Salaries—Salesmen	105,000	110,250	115,763	121,551	127,628	134,010	140,710	147,746
Total Barton Salaries	1,050,000	1,102,500	1,157,626	1,215,507	1,276,281	1,340,096	1,407,100	1,477,456
Salaries—Midway	420,000	441,000	463,050	486,203	510,513	536,038	562,840	590,982
Total Salaries—Both Corporations	$1,470,000	$1,543,500	$1,620,676	$1,701,710	$1,786,794	$1,876,134	$1,969,940	$2,068,438

**For example in Year 1 "Total Salaries—Both Corporations" are $1,470,000 x 25% = $367,500.

PART III

IRS REVENUE RULINGS

Contents

*Contains full text of A.R.M. 34, C.B. 2, 31 (1920)

Rev. Rul. 68-609, 1968-2 C.B. 327   363

This ruling summarizes and updates the changes made to Rev. Rul. 59-60 regarding the use of the formula approach contained in A.R.M. 34 in valuing the intangibles assets of a privately-held business.

This ruling makes the methods and approaches of Rev. Rul. 59-60 applicable to the valuation of business interests of any and all types, including partnerships and proprietorships.

Rev. Rul. 77-287, 1977-2 C.B. 319   365

This ruling provides guidelines for valuation of shares of stock (to determine the appropriate discount) of a privately-held business where the shares are subject to some restriction under the Federal securities laws.

Rev. Rul. 78-367, 1978-2 C.B. 249   370

This ruling involves the valuation of stock of a privately-held business for purposes of the gift tax. It states that the valuation should take into account the effects of a public announcement of a merger of the privately-held business into a larger publicly-traded corporation.

Rev. Rul. 79-7, 1979-1 C.B. 294   372

This ruling states that when a person transfers a minority interest of stock in a privately-held business while retaining a majority interest, and the transferred minority interest is includible in his estate upon death, the minority interest and the retained majority interest are valued as one block of stock for estate tax purposes.

Rev. Rul. 81-15, 1981-1 C.B. 457   374

This ruling was issued in reaction to the Supreme Court decision in *Byrum*, 408 U.S. 125 (1972). That case concluded that where a decedent transferred in trust the stock of a privately-held business, the retention of certain rights by the decedent over the disposition of the stock did not make the stock includible in his estate.

The IRS in Rev. Rul. 67-54 had come to the opposite conclusion under circumstances similar to *Byrum*. Rev. Rul. 67-54 is revoked.

Rev. Rul. 81-253, 1981-2 C.B. 187   376

This ruling disallows minority discounts for gifts of all the stock of a privately-held business given by the controlling shareholder to members of his family. Each family member received a minority interest. Each minority interest must be valued the same as if it were part of a controlling interest held by one member of the family.

Rev. Rul. 83-119, 1983-2 C.B. 57   380

This ruling says that where preferred stock issued as part of a recapitalization must be redeemed in excess of 110% of its issue price when the holder dies, the amount in excess of 110% can be treated as a distribution, which could be a taxable dividend, deemed to be received ratably over the life of the shareholder receiving the preferred stock in the recapitalization.

Rev. Rul. 83-120, 1983-2 C.B. 170   385

This ruling sets forth guidelines for the valuation of common and preferred stock issued in a recapitalization (see Chapter Eleven).

Revenue Ruling 59-60

SECTION 2031.—DEFINITION OF GROSS ESTATE

26 CFR 20.2031–2: Valuation of stocks and   Rev. Rul. 59–60
bonds.
(Also Section 2512.)
(Also Part II, Sections 811 (k), 1005, Regulations
105, Section 81.10.)

> In valuing the stock of closely held corporations, or the stock of
> corporations where market quotations are not available, all other
> available financial data, as well as all relevant factors affecting the
> fair market value must be considered for estate tax and gift tax
> purposes. No general formula may be given that is applicable to
> the many different valuation situations arising in the valuation of
> such stock. However, the general approach, methods, and factors
> which must be considered in valuing such securities are outlined.
> Revenue Ruling 54–77, C.B. 1954–1, 187, superseded.

Section 1. Purpose.

The purpose of this Revenue Ruling is to outline and review in
general the approach, methods and factors to be considered in valuing
shares of the capital stock of closely held corporations for estate tax
and gift tax purposes. The methods discussed herein will apply likewise to the valuation of corporate stocks on which market quotations
are either unavailable or are of such scarcity that they do not reflect
the fair market value.

Sec. 2. Background and Definitions.

.01 All valuations must be made in accordance with the applicable
provisions of the Internal Revenue Code of 1954 and the Federal
Estate Tax and Gift Tax Regulations. Sections 2031(a), 2032 and
2512(a) of the 1954 Code (sections 811 and 1005 of the 1939 Code)
require that the property to be included in the gross estate, or made
the subject of a gift, shall be taxed on the basis of the value of the
property at the time of death of the decedent, the alternate date if
so elected, or the date of gift.

.02 Section 20.2031–1(b) of the Estate Tax Regulations (section
81.10 of the Estate Tax Regulations 105) and section 25.2512–1 of
the Gift Tax Regulations (section 86.19 of Gift Tax Regulations 108)
define fair market value, in effect, as the price at which the property
would change hands between a willing buyer and a willing seller
when the former is not under any compulsion to buy and the latter
is not under any compulsion to sell, both parties having reasonable
knowledge of relevant facts. Court decisions frequently state in addition that the hypothetical buyer and seller are assumed to be able,
as well as willing, to trade and to be well informed about the property
and concerning the market for such property.

.03 Closely held corporations are those corporations the shares of
which are owned by a relatively limited number of stockholders.
Often the entire stock issue is held by one family. The result of this

Revenue Ruling 59-60

situation is that little, if any, trading in the shares takes place. There is, therefore, no established market for the stock and such sales as occur at irregular intervals seldom reflect all of the elements of a representative transaction as defined by the term "fair market value."

SEC. 3. APPROACH TO VALUATION.

.01 A determination of fair market value, being a question of fact, will depend upon the circumstances in each case. No formula can be devised that will be generally applicable to the multitude of different valuation issues arising in estate and gift tax cases. Often, an appraiser will find wide differences of opinion as to the fair market value of a particular stock. In resolving such differences, he should maintain a reasonable attitude in recognition of the fact that valuation is not an exact science. A sound valuation will be based upon all the relevant facts, but the elements of common sense, informed judgment and reasonableness must enter into the process of weighing those facts and determining their aggregate significance.

.02 The fair market value of specific shares of stock will vary as general economic conditions change from "normal" to "boom" or "depression," that is, according to the degree of optimism or pessimism with which the investing public regards the future at the required date of appraisal. Uncertainty as to the stability or continuity of the future income from a property decreases its value by increasing the risk of loss of earnings and value in the future. The value of shares of stock of a company with very uncertain future prospects is highly speculative. The appraiser must exercise his judgment as to the degree of risk attaching to the business of the corporation which issued the stock, but that judgment must be related to all of the other factors affecting value.

.03 Valuation of securities is, in essence, a prophesy as to the future and must be based on facts available at the required date of appraisal. As a generalization, the prices of stocks which are traded in volume in a free and active market by informed persons best reflect the consensus of the investing public as to what the future holds for the corporations and industries represented. When a stock is closely held, is traded infrequently, or is traded in an erratic market, some other measure of value must be used. In many instances, the next best measure may be found in the prices at which the stocks of companies engaged in the same or a similar line of business are selling in a free and open market.

SEC. 4. FACTORS TO CONSIDER.

.01 It is advisable to emphasize that in the valuation of the stock of closely held corporations or the stock of corporations where market quotations are either lacking or too scarce to be recognized, all available financial data, as well as all relevant factors affecting the fair market value, should be considered. The following factors, although not all-inclusive are fundamental and require careful analysis in each case:

(a) The nature of the business and the history of the enterprise from its inception.

Revenue Ruling 59-60

(b) The economic outlook in general and the condition and outlook of the specific industry in particular.

(c) The book value of the stock and the financial condition of the business.

(d) The earning capacity of the company.

(e) The dividend-paying capacity.

(f) Whether or not the enterprise has goodwill or other intangible value.

(g) Sales of the stock and the size of the block of stock to be valued.

(h) The market price of stocks of corporations engaged in the same or a similar line of business having their stocks actively traded in a free and open market, either on an exchange or over-the-counter.

.02 The following is a brief discussion of each of the foregoing factors:

(a) The history of a corporate enterprise will show its past stability or instability, its growth or lack of growth, the diversity or lack of diversity of its operations, and other facts needed to form an opinion of the degree of risk involved in the business. For an enterprise which changed its form of organization but carried on the same or closely similar operations of its predecessor, the history of the former enterprise should be considered. The detail to be considered should increase with approach to the required date of appraisal, since recent events are of greatest help in predicting the future; but a study of gross and net income, and of dividends covering a long prior period, is highly desirable. The history to be studied should include, but need not be limited to, the nature of the business, its products or services, its operating and investment assets, capital structure, plant facilities, sales records and management, all of which should be considered as of the date of the appraisal, with due regard for recent significant changes. Events of the past that are unlikely to recur in the future should be discounted, since value has a close relation to future expectancy.

(b) A sound appraisal of a closely held stock must consider current and prospective economic conditions as of the date of appraisal, both in the national economy and in the industry or industries with which the corporation is allied. It is important to know that the company is more or less successful than its competitors in the same industry, or that it is maintaining a stable position with respect to competitors. Equal or even greater significance may attach to the ability of the industry with which the company is allied to compete with other industries. Prospective competition which has not been a factor in prior years should be given careful attention. For example, high profits due to the novelty of its product and the lack of competition often lead to increasing competition. The public's appraisal of the future prospects of competitive industries or of competitors within an industry may be indicated by price trends in the markets for commodities and for securities. The loss of the manager of a so-called "one-man" business may have a depressing effect upon the value of the stock of such business, particularly if there is a lack of trained personnel capable of succeeding to the management of the enterprise. In

Revenue Ruling 59-60

valuing the stock of this type of business, therefore, the effect of the loss of the manager on the future expectancy of the business, and the absence of management-succession potentialities are pertinent factors to be taken into consideration. On the other hand, there may be factors which offset, in whole or in part, the loss of the manager's services. For instance, the nature of the business and of its assets may be such that they will not be impaired by the loss of the manager. Furthermore, the loss may be adequately covered by life insurance, or competent management might be employed on the basis of the consideration paid for the former manager's services. These, or other offsetting factors, if found to exist, should be carefully weighed against the loss of the manager's services in valuing the stock of the enterprise.

(c) Balance sheets should be obtained, preferably in the form of comparative annual statements for two or more years immediately preceding the date of appraisal, together with a balance sheet at the end of the month preceding that date, if corporate accounting will permit. Any balance sheet descriptions that are not self-explanatory, and balance sheet items comprehending diverse assets or liabilities, should be clarified in essential detail by supporting supplemental schedules. These statements usually will disclose to the appraiser (1) liquid position (ratio of current assets to current liabilities) ; (2) gross and net book value of principal classes of fixed assets; (3) working capital; (4) long-term indebtedness; (5) capital structure; and (6) net worth. Consideration also should be given to any assets not essential to the operation of the business, such as investments in securities, real estate, etc. In general, such nonoperating assets will command a lower rate of return than do the operating assets, although in exceptional cases the reverse may be true. In computing the book value per share of stock, assets of the investment type should be revalued on the basis of their market price and the book value adjusted accordingly. Comparison of the company's balance sheets over several years may reveal, among other facts, such developments as the acquisition of additional production facilities or subsidiary companies, improvement in financial position, and details as to recapitalizations and other changes in the capital structure of the corporation. If the corporation has more than one class of stock outstanding, the charter or certificate of incorporation should be examined to ascertain the explicit rights and privileges of the various stock issues including: (1) voting powers, (2) preference as to dividends, and (3) preference as to assets in the event of liquidation.

(d) Detailed profit-and-loss statements should be obtained and considered for a representative period immediately prior to the required date of appraisal, preferably five or more years. Such statements should show (1) gross income by principal items; (2) principal deductions from gross income including major prior items of operating expenses, interest and other expense on each item of long-term debt, depreciation and depletion if such deductions are made, officers' salaries, in total if they appear to be reasonable or in detail if they

Revenue Ruling 59-60

seem to be excessive, contributions (whether or not deductible for tax purposes) that the nature of its business and its community position require the corporation to make, and taxes by principal items, including income and excess profits taxes; (3) net income available for dividends; (4) rates and amounts of dividends paid on each class of stock; (5) remaining amount carried to surplus; and (6) adjustments to, and reconciliation with, surplus as stated on the balance sheet. With profit and loss statements of this character available, the appraiser should be able to separate recurrent from nonrecurrent items of income and expense, to distinguish between operating income and investment income, and to ascertain whether or not any line of business in which the company is engaged is operated consistently at a loss and might be abandoned with benefit to the company. The percentage of earnings retained for business expansion should be noted when dividend-paying capacity is considered. Potential future income is a major factor in many valuations of closely-held stocks, and all information concerning past income which will be helpful in predicting the future should be secured. Prior earnings records usually are the most reliable guide as to the future expectancy, but resort to arbitrary five-or-ten-year averages without regard to current trends or future prospects will not produce a realistic valuation. If, for instance, a record of progressively increasing or decreasing net income is found, then greater weight may be accorded the most recent years' profits in estimating earning power. It will be helpful, in judging risk and the extent to which a business is a marginal operator, to consider deductions from income and net income in terms of percentage of sales. Major categories of cost and expense to be so analyzed include the consumption of raw materials and supplies in the case of manufacturers, processors and fabricators; the cost of purchased merchandise in the case of merchants; utility services; insurance; taxes; depletion or depreciation; and interest.

(e) Primary consideration should be given to the dividend-paying capacity of the company rather than to dividends actually paid in the past. Recognition must be given to the necessity of retaining a reasonable portion of profits in a company to meet competition. Dividend-paying capacity is a factor that must be considered in an appraisal, but dividends actually paid in the past may not have any relation to dividend-paying capacity. Specifically, the dividends paid by a closely held family company may be measured by the income needs of the stockholders or by their desire to avoid taxes on dividend receipts, instead of by the ability of the company to pay dividends. Where an actual or effective controlling interest in a corporation is to be valued, the dividend factor is not a material element, since the payment of such dividends is discretionary with the controlling stockholders. The individual or group in control can substitute salaries and bonuses for dividends, thus reducing net income and understating the dividend-paying capacity of the company. It follows, therefore, that dividends are less reliable criteria of fair market value than other applicable factors.

(f) In the final analysis, goodwill is based upon earning capacity.

Revenue Ruling 59-60

The presence of goodwill and its value, therefore, rests upon the excess of net earnings over and above a fair return on the net tangible assets. While the element of goodwill may be based primarily on earnings, such factors as the prestige and renown of the business, the ownership of a trade or brand name, and a record of successful operation over a prolonged period in a particular locality, also may furnish support for the inclusion of intangible value. In some instances it may not be possible to make a separate appraisal of the tangible and intangible assets of the business. The enterprise has a value as an entity. Whatever intangible value there is, which is supportable by the facts, may be measured by the amount by which the appraised value of the tangible assets exceeds the net book value of such assets.

(g) Sales of stock of a closely held corporation should be carefully investigated to determine whether they represent transactions at arm's length. Forced or distress sales do not ordinarily reflect fair market value nor do isolated sales in small amounts necessarily control as the measure of value. This is especially true in the valuation of a controlling interest in a corporation. Since, in the case of closely held stocks, no prevailing market prices are available, there is no basis for making an adjustment for blockage. It follows, therefore, that such stocks should be valued upon a consideration of all the evidence affecting the fair market value. The size of the block of stock itself is a relevant factor to be considered. Although it is true that a minority interest in an unlisted corporation's stock is more difficult to sell than a similar block of listed stock, it is equally true that control of a corporation, either actual or in effect, representing as it does an added element of value, may justify a higher value for a specific block of stock.

(h) Section 2031(b) of the Code states, in effect, that in valuing unlisted securities the value of stock or securities of corporations engaged in the same or a similar line of business which are listed on an exchange should be taken into consideration along with all other factors. An important consideration is that the corporations to be used for comparisons have capital stocks which are actively traded by the public. In accordance with section 2031(b) of the Code, stocks listed on an exchange are to be considered first. However, if sufficient comparable companies whose stocks are listed on an exchange cannot be found, other comparable companies which have stocks actively traded in on the over-the-counter market also may be used. The essential factor is that whether the stocks are sold on an exchange or over-the-counter there is evidence of an active, free public market for the stock as of the valuation date. In selecting corporations for comparative purposes, care should be taken to use only comparable companies. Although the only restrictive requirement as to comparable corporations specified in the statute is that their lines of business be the same or similar, yet it is obvious that consideration must be given to other relevant factors in order that the most valid comparison possible will be obtained. For illustration, a corporation having one or more issues of preferred stock,

Revenue Ruling 59-60

bonds or debentures in addition to its common stock should not be considered to be directly comparable to one having only common stock outstanding. In like manner, a company with a declining business and decreasing markets is not comparable to one with a record of current progress and market expansion.

SEC. 5. WEIGHT TO BE ACCORDED VARIOUS FACTORS.

The valuation of closely held corporate stock entails the consideration of all relevant factors as stated in section 4. Depending upon the circumstances in each case, certain factors may carry more weight than others because of the nature of the company's business. To illustrate:

(a) Earnings may be the most important criterion of value in some cases whereas asset value will receive primary consideration in others. In general, the appraiser will accord primary consideration to earnings when valuing stocks of companies which sell products or services to the public; conversely, in the investment or holding type of company, the appraiser may accord the greatest weight to the assets underlying the security to be valued.

(b) The value of the stock of a closely held investment or real estate holding company, whether or not family owned, is closely related to the value of the assets underlying the stock. For companies of this type the appraiser should determine the fair market values of the assets of the company. Operating expenses of such a company and the cost of liquidating it, if any, merit consideration when appraising the relative values of the stock and the underlying assets. The market values of the underlying assets give due weight to potential earnings and dividends of the particular items of property underlying the stock, capitalized at rates deemed proper by the investing public at the date of appraisal. A current appraisal by the investing public should be superior to the retrospective opinion of an individual. For these reasons, adjusted net worth should be accorded greater weight in valuing the stock of a closely held investment or real estate holding company, whether or not family owned, than any of the other customary yardsticks of appraisal, such as earnings and dividend paying capacity.

SEC. 6. CAPITALIZATION RATES.

In the application of certain fundamental valuation factors, such as earnings and dividends, it is necessary to capitalize the average or current results at some appropriate rate. A determination of the proper capitalization rate presents one of the most difficult problems in valuation. That there is no ready or simple solution will become apparent by a cursory check of the rates of return and dividend yields in terms of the selling prices of corporate shares listed on the major exchanges of the country. Wide variations will be found even for companies in the same industry. Moreover, the ratio will fluctuate from year to year depending upon economic conditions. Thus, no standard tables of capitalization rates applicable to closely held corporations can be formulated. Among the more important factors to

Revenue Ruling 59-60

be taken into consideration in deciding upon a capitalization rate in a particular case are: (1) the nature of the business; (2) the risk involved; and (3) the stability or irregularity of earnings.

SEC. 7. AVERAGE OF FACTORS.

Because valuations cannot be made on the basis of a prescribed formula, there is no means whereby the various applicable factors in a particular case can be assigned mathematical weights in deriving the fair market value. For this reason, no useful purpose is served by taking an average of several factors (for example, book value, capitalized earnings and capitalized dividends) and basing the valuation on the result. Such a process excludes active consideration of other pertinent factors, and the end result cannot be supported by a realistic application of the significant facts in the case except by mere chance.

SEC. 8. RESTRICTIVE AGREEMENTS.

Frequently, in the valuation of closely held stock for estate and gift tax purposes, it will be found that the stock is subject to an agreement restricting its sale or transfer. Where shares of stock were acquired by a decedent subject to an option reserved by the issuing corporation to repurchase at a certain price, the option price is usually accepted as the fair market value for estate tax purposes. See Rev. Rul. 54-76, C.B. 1954-1, 194. However, in such case the option price is not determinative of fair market value for gift tax purposes. Where the option, or buy and sell agreement, is the result of voluntary action by the stockholders and is binding during the life as well as at the death of the stockholders, such agreement may or may not, depending upon the circumstances of each case, fix the value for estate tax purposes. However, such agreement is a factor to be considered, with other relevant factors, in determining fair market value. Where the stockholder is free to dispose of his shares during life and the option is to become effective only upon his death, the fair market value is not limited to the option price. It is always necessary to consider the relationship of the parties, the relative number of shares held by the decedent, and other material facts, to determine whether the agreement represents a bonafide business arrangement or is a device to pass the decedent's shares to the natural objects of his bounty for less than an adequate and full consideration in money or money's worth. In this connection see Rev. Rul. 157 C.B. 1953-2, 255, and Rev. Rul. 189, C.B. 1953-2, 294.

SEC. 9. EFFECT ON OTHER DOCUMENTS.

Revenue Ruling 54-77, C.B. 1954-1, 187, is hereby superseded.

Revenue Ruling 65-192

SECTION 1001.—DETERMINATION OF AMOUNT OF AND RECOGNITION OF GAIN OR LOSS

26 CFR 1.1001-1: Computation of gain or loss.   Rev. Rul. 65–192

> The general approach, methods and factors outlined in Revenue Ruling 59–60, C.B. 1959–1, 237, for use in valuing closely-held corporate stocks for estate and gift tax purposes are equally applicable to valuations thereof for income and other tax purposes and also in determinations of the fair market values of business interests of any type and of intangible assets for all tax purposes.
>
> The formula approach set forth in A.R.M. 34, C.B. 2, 31 (1920), and A.R.M. 68, C.B. 3, 43 (1920), has no valid application in determinations of the fair market values of corporate stocks or of business interests, unless it is necessary to value the intangible assets of the corporation or the intangible assets included in the business interest. The formula approach may be used in determining the fair market values of intangible assets only if there is no better basis therefor available. In applying the formula, the average earnings period and the capitalization rates are dependent upon the facts and circumstances pertinent thereto in such case.

SECTION 1. PURPOSE.

The purpose of this Revenue Ruling is to furnish information and guidance as to the usage to be made of suggested methods for determining the value as of March 1, 1913, or of any other date, of intangible assets and to identify those areas where a valuation formula set forth in A.R.M. 34, C.B. 2, 31 (1920), as modified by A.R.M. 68, C.B. 3, 43 (1920), both quoted in full below should and should not be applied. Since it appears that such formula has been applied to many valuation issues for which it was never intended, the Internal Revenue Service reindicates its limited application.

SEC. 2. BACKGROUND.

A.R.M. 34 was issued in 1920 for the purpose of providing suggested formulas for determining the amount of March 1, 1913, intangible asset value lost by breweries and other businesses connected with the distilling industry, as a result of the passage of the 18th Amendment to the Constitution of the United States. A.R.M. 68 was issued later in the same year and contained a minor revision of the original ruling so that its third formula would be applied in accordance with its purpose and intent.

SEC. 3. STATEMENT OF POSITION.

.01 Although the formulas and approach contained in A.R.M. 34, were specifically aimed at the valuation of intangible assets of distilling and related companies as of March 1, 1913, the last two paragraphs of the ruling seemingly broaden it to make its third formula applicable to almost any kind of enterprise. The final sentences, however, limit the purpose of such formula by stating that "In * * * all of the cases

Revenue Ruling 65-192

the effort should be to determine what net earnings a purchaser of a business on March 1, 1913, might reasonably have expected to receive from it, * * *, "and by providing certain checks and alternatives. Also, both A.R.M. 34 and A.R.M. 68 expressly stated that such formula was merely a rule for guidance and not controlling in the presence of "better evidence" in determining the value of intangible assets. Furthermore, T.B.R. 57, C.B. 1, 40 (1919), relating to the meaning of "fair market value" of property received in exchange for other property, which was published before A.R.M. 34 and A.R.M. 68 and has not been revoked, set forth general principles of valuation that are consistent with Revenue Ruling 59–60, C.B. 1959–1, 237. Moreover, in S.M. 1609, C.B. III–1, 48 (1924) it was stated that "The method suggested in A.R.M. 34 for determining the value of intangibles is * * * controlling only in the absence of better evidence." As said in *North American Service Co., Inc.* v. *Commissioner*, 33 T.C. 677, 694 (1960), acquiescence, C.B. 1960–2, 6, "an A.R.M. 34 computation would not be conclusive of the existence and value of good will if better evidence were available * * *."

.02   Revenue Ruling 59–60 sets forth the proper approach to use in the valuation of closely-held corporate stocks for estate and gift tax purposes. That ruling contains the statement that no formula can be devised that will be generally applicable to the multitude of different valuation issues. It also contains a discussion of intangible value in closely-held corporations and some of the elements which may support such value in a given business.

SEC. 4. DELINEATION OF AREAS IN WHICH SUGGESTED METHODS WILL BE EFFECTIVE.

.01   The general approach, methods, and factors outlined in Revenue Ruling 59–60 are equally applicable to valuations of corporate stocks for income and other tax purposes as well as for estate and gift tax purposes. They apply also to problems involving the determination of the fair market value of business interests of any type, including partnerships, proprietorships, etc., and of intangible assets for all tax purposes.

.02   Valuation, especially where earning power is an important factor, is in essence a process requiring the exercise of informed judgment and common sense. Thus, the suggested formula approach set forth in A.R.M. 34, has no valid application in determinations of the fair market value of corporate stocks or of business interests unless it is necessary to value the intangible assets of the corporation or the intangible assets included in the business interest. The formula approach may be used in determining the fair market values of intangible assets only if there is no better basis therefor available. In applying the formula, the average earnings period and the capitalization rates are dependent upon the facts and circumstances pertinent thereto in each case. See *John Q. Shunk et al.* v. *Commissioner*, 10 T.C. 293, 304–5 (1948), acquiescence, C.B. 1948–1, 3, affirmed 173 Fed. (2d) 747 (1949) ; *Ushco Manufacturing Co., Inc.* v. *Commissioner*, Tax Court Memorandum Opinion entered March 10, 1945,

Revenue Ruling 65-192

affirmed 175 Fed. (2d) 821 (1945); and *White & Wells Co.* v. *Commissioner*, 19 B.T.A. 416, nonacquiescence C.B. IX–2, 87 (1930), reversed and remanded 50 Fed. (2d) 120 (1931).

SEC. 5. QUOTATION OF A.R.M. 34.

For convenience, A.R.M. 34 reads as follows:

The Committee has considered the question of providing some practical formula for determining value as of March 1, 1913, or of any other date, which might be considered as applying to intangible assets, but finds itself unable to lay down any specific rule of guidance for determing the value of intangibles which would be applicable in all cases and under all circumstances. Where there is no established market to serve as a guide the question of value, even of tangible assets, is one largely of judgment and opinion, and the same thing is even more true of intangible assets such as good will, trade-marks, trade brands, etc. However, there are several methods of reaching a conclusion as to the value of intangibles which the Committee suggests may be utilized broadly in passing upon questions of valuation, not to be regarded as controlling, however, if better evidence is presented in any specific case.

Where deduction is claimed for obsolescence or loss of good will or trade-marks, the burden of proof is primarily upon the taxpayer to show the value of such good will or trade-marks on March 1, 1913. Of course, if good will or trade-marks have been acquired for cash or other valuable considerations subsequent to March 1, 1913, the measure of loss will be determined by the amount of cash or value of other considerations paid therefor, and no deduction will be allowed for the value of good will or trade-marks built up by the taxpayer since March 1, 1913. The following suggestions are made, therefore, merely as suggestions for checks upon the soundness and validity of the taxpayers' claims. No obsolescence or loss with respect to good will should be allowed except in cases of actual disposition of the asset or abandonment of the business.

In the first place, it is recognized that in numerous instances it has been the practice of distillers and wholesale liquor dealers to put out under well-known and popular brands only so much goods as could be marketed without affecting the established market price therefor and to sell other goods of the same identical manufacture, age, and character under other brands, or under no brand at all, at figures very much below those which the well-known brands commanded. In such cases the difference between the price at which whisky was sold under a given brand name and also under another brand name, or under no brand, multiplied by the number of units sold during a given year gives an accurate determination of the amount of profit attributable to that brand during that year, and where this practice is continued for a long enough period to show that this amount was fairly constant and regular and might be expected to yield annually that average profit, by capitalizing this earning at the rate, say, of 20 per cent, the value of the brand is fairly well established.

Another method is to compare the volume of business done under the trademark or brand under consideration and profits made, or by the business whose good will is under consideration, with the similar volume of business and profit made in other cases where good will or trade-marks have been actually sold for cash, recognizing as the value of the first the same proportion of the selling price of the second, as the profits of the first attributable to brands or good will, is of the similar profits of the second.

The third method and possibly the one which will most frequently have to be applied as a check in the absence of data necessary for the application of the preceding ones, is to allow out of average earnings over a period of years prior to March 1, 1913, preferably not less than five years, a return of 10 per cent upon the average tangible assets for the period. The surplus earnings will then be the average amount available for return upon the value of the intangible assets, and it is the opinion of the Committee that this return should be capitalized upon the basis of not more than five years' purchase—that is to say, five times the amount available as return from intangibles should be the value of the intangibles.

In view of the hazards of the business, the changes in popular tastes, and the

Revenue Ruling 65-192

difficulties in preventing imitation or counterfeiting of popular brands affecting the sales of the genuine goods, the Committee is of the opinion that the figure given of 20 per cent return on intangibles is not unreasonable, and it recommends that no higher figure than that be attached in any case to intangibles without a very clear and adequate showing that the value of the intangibles was in fact greater than would be reached by applying this formula.

The foregoing is intended to apply particularly to businesses put out of existence by the prohibition law, but will be equally applicable so far as the third formula is concerned, to other businesses of a more or less hazardous nature.   In the case, however, of valuation of good will of a business which consists of the manufacture or sale of standard articles of every-day necessity not subject to violent fluctuations and where the hazard is not so great, the Committee is of the opinion that the figure for determination of the return on tangible assets might be reduced from 10 to 8 or 9 per cent, and that the percentage for capitalization of the return upon intangibles might be reduced from 20 to 15 per cent.

In any or all of the cases the effort should be to determine what net earnings a purchaser of a business on March 1, 1943, might reasonably have expected to receive from it, and therefore a representative period should be used for averaging actual earnings, eliminating any year in which there were extraordinary factors affecting earnings either way.   Also, in the case of the sale of good will of a going business the percentage rate of capitalization of earnings applicable to good will shown by the amount actually paid for the business should be used as a check against the determination of good will value as of March 1, 1913, and if the good will is sold upon the basis of capitalization of earnings less than the figures above indicated as the ones ordinarily to be adopted, the same percentage should be used in figuring value as of March 1, 1913.

Sec. 6. Quotation of A.R.M. 68.

Also for convenience, A.R.M. 68 reads as follows:

The Committee is in receipt of a request for advice as to whether under A.R.M. 34 the 10 per cent upon tangible assets is to be applied only to the net tangible assets or to all tangible assets on the books of the corporation, regardless of any outstanding obligations.

The Committee, in the memorandum in question, undertook to lay down a rule for guidance in the absence of better evidence in determining the value as of March 1, 1913, of good will, and held that in determining such value, income over an average period in excess of an amount sufficient to return 10 per cent upon tangible assets should be capitalized at 20 per cent.   Manifestly, since the effort is to determine the value of the good will, and therefore the true net worth of the taxpayer as of March 1, 1913, the 10 per cent should be applied only to the tangible assets entering into net worth, including accounts and bills receivable in excess of accounts and bills payable.

In other words, the purpose and intent are to provide for a return to the taxpayer of 10 per cent upon so much of his investment as is represented by tangible assets and to capitalize the excess of earnings over the amount necessary to provide such return, at 20 per cent.

Sec. 7. Effect on Other Documents.

Although the limited application of A.R.M. 34 and A.R.M. 68 is reindicated in this Revenue Ruling, the principles enunciated in those rulings are not thereby affected.

Valuation of intangible assets of a business where separate appraisal of tangible and intangible assets may not be possible.   See Rev. Rul. 65-193.

Revenue Ruling 65-193

26 CFR 20.2031–2: Valuation of   Rev. Rul. 65–193
   stocks and bonds.
(Also Sections 1001, 2512; 1.1001–1, 25.2512–2.)

Revenue Ruling 59–60, C.B. 1959–1, 237, is hereby modified to delete the statements, contained therein at section 4.02(f), that "In some instances it may not be possible to make a separate appraisal of the tangible and intangible assets of the business. The enterprise has a value as an entity. Whatever intangible value there is, which is supportable by the facts, may be measured by the amount by which the appraised value of the tangible assets exceeds the net book value of such assets."

The instances where it is not possible to make a separate appraisal of the tangible and intangible assets of a business are rare and each case varies from the other. No rule can be devised which will be generally applicable to such cases.

Other than this modification, Revenue Ruling 59–60 continues in full force and effect. See Rev. Rul. 65–192.

Revenue Ruling 68-609

SECTION 1001.—DETERMINATION OF AMOUNT OF AND RECOGNITION OF GAIN OR LOSS

26 CFR 1.1001–1: Computation of gain or loss.   Rev. Rul. 68–609 [1]
(Also Section 167; 1.167(a)–3.)

The purpose of this Revenue Ruling is to update and restate, under the current statute and regulations, the currently outstanding portions of A.R.M. 34, C.B. 2, 31 (1920), A.R.M. 68, C.B. 3, 43 (1920), and O.D. 937, C.B. 4, 43 (1921).

The question presented is whether the "formula" approach, the capitalization of earnings in excess of a fair rate of return on net tangible assets, may be used to determine the fair market value of the intangible assets of a business

The "formula" approach may be stated as follows:

A percentage return on the average annual value of the tangible assets used in a business is determined, using a period of years (preferably not less than five) immediately prior to the valuation date. The amount of the percentage return on tangible assets, thus determined, is deducted from the average earnings of the business for such period and the remainder, if any, is considered to be the amount of the average annual earnings from the intangible assets of the business for the period. This amount (considered as the average annual earnings from intangibles), capitalized at a percentage of, say, 15 to 20 percent, is the value of the intangible assets of the business determined under the "formula" approach.

The percentage of return on the average annual value of the tangible assets used should be the percentage prevailing in the industry involved at the date of valuation, or (when the industry percentage is not available) a percentage of 8 to 10 percent may be used.

The 8 percent rate of return and the 15 percent rate of capitalization are applied to tangibles and intangibles, respectively, of businesses with a small risk factor and stable and regular earnings; the 10 percent rate of return and 20 percent rate of capitalization are applied to businesses in which the hazards of business are relatively high.

The above rates are used as examples and are not appropriate in all cases. In applying the "formula" approach, the average earnings period and the capitalization rates are dependent upon the facts pertinent thereto in each case.

The past earnings to which the formula is applied should fairly reflect the probable future earnings. Ordinarily, the period should not be less than five years, and abnormal years, whether above or below the average, should be eliminated. If the business is a sole proprietorship or partnership, there should be deducted from the earnings of the business a reasonable amount for services performed by the owner or partners engaged in the business. See *Lloyd B. Sanderson Estate* v. *Commissioner*, 42 F. 2d 160 (1930). Further, only the tangible assets entering into net worth, including accounts and bills receivable in

[1] Prepared pursuant to Rev. Proc. 67–6, C.B. 1967–1, 576.

Revenue Ruling 68-609

excess of accounts and bills payable, are used for determining earnings on the tangible assets. Factors that influence the capitalization rate include (1) the nature of the business, (2) the risk involved, and (3) the stability or irregularity of earnings.

The "formula" approach should not be used if there is better evidence available from which the value of intangibles can be determined. If the assets of a going business are sold upon the basis of a rate of capitalization that can be substantiated as being realistic, though it is not within the range of figures indicated here as the ones ordinarily to be adopted, the same rate of capitalization should be used in determining the value of intangibles.

Accordingly, the "formula" approach may be used for determining the fair market value of intangible assets of a business only if there is no better basis therefor available.

See also Revenue Ruling 59-60, C.B. 1959-1, 237, as modified by Revenue Ruling 65-193, C.B. 1965-2, 370, which sets forth the proper approach to use in the valuation of closely-held corporate stocks for estate and gift tax purposes. The general approach, methods, and factors, outlined in Revenue Ruling 59-60, as modified, are equally applicable to valuations of corporate stocks for income and other tax purposes as well as for estate and gift tax purposes. They apply also to problems involving the determination of the fair market value of business interests of any type, including partnerships and proprietorships, and of intangible assets for all tax purposes.

A.R.M. 34, A.R.M. 68, and O.D. 937 are superseded, since the positions set forth therein are restated to the extent applicable under current law in this Revenue Ruling. Revenue Ruling 65-192, C.B. 1965-2, 259, which contained restatements of A.R.M. 34 and A.R.M. 68, is also superseded.

Revenue Ruling 77-287

Section 2031.—Definition of Gross Estate

26 CFR 20.2031-2: Valuation of stocks and bonds.
(Also Sections 170, 2032, 2512; 1.170A-1, 20.2032-1, 25.2512-2.)

Valuation of securities restricted from immediate resale. Guidelines are set forth for the valuation, for Federal tax purposes, of securities that cannot be immediately resold because they are restricted from resale pursuant to Federal securities laws; Rev. Rul. 59-60 amplified.

Rev. Rul. 77-287

Section 1. Purpose.

The purpose of this Revenue Ruling is to amplify Rev. Rul. 59-60, 1959-1 C.B. 237, as modified by Rev. Rul. 65-193, 1965-2 C.B. 370, and to provide information and guidance to taxpayers, Internal Revenue Service personnel, and others concerned with the valuation, for Federal tax purposes, of securities that cannot be immediately resold because they are restricted from resale pursuant to Federal securities laws. This guidance is applicable only in cases where it is not inconsistent with valuation requirements of the Internal Revenue Code of 1954 or the regulations thereunder. Further, this ruling does not establish the time at which property shall be valued.

Sec. 2. Nature of the Problem.

It frequently becomes necessary to establish the fair market value of stock that has not been registered for public trading when the issuing company has stock of the same class that is actively traded in one or more securities markets. The problem is to determine the difference in fair market value between the registered shares that are actively traded and the unregistered shares. This problem is often encountered in estate and gift tax cases. However, it is sometimes encountered when unregistered shares are issued in exchange for assets or the stock of an acquired company.

Sec. 3. Background and Definitions.

.01 The Service outlined and reviewed in general the approach, methods, and factors to be considered in valuing shares of closely held corporate stock for estate and gift tax purposes in Rev. Rul. 59-60, as modified by Rev. Rul. 65-193. The provisions of Rev. Rul. 59-60, as modified, were extended to the valuation of corporate securities for income and other tax purposes by Rev. Rul. 68-609, 1968-2 C.B. 327.

.02 There are several terms currently in use in the securities industry that denote restrictions imposed on the resale and transfer of certain securities. The term frequently used to describe these securities is "restricted securities," but they are sometimes referred to as "unregistered securities," "investment letter stock," "control stock," or "private placement stock." Frequently these terms are used interchangeably. They all indicate that these particular securities cannot lawfully be distributed to the general pub-

Revenue Ruling 77-287

lic until a registration statement relating to the corporation underlying the securities has been filed, and has also become effective under the rules promulgated and enforced by the United States Securities & Exchange Commission (SEC) pursuant to the Federal securities laws. The following represents a more refined definition of each of the following terms along with two other terms—"exempted securities" and "exempted transactions."

(a) The term "restricted securities" is defined in Rule 144 adopted by the SEC as "securities acquired directly or indirectly from the issuer thereof, or from an affiliate of such issuer, in a transaction or chain of transactions not involving any public offering."

(b) The term "unregistered securities" refers to those securities with respect to which a registration statement, providing full disclosure by the issuing corporation, has not been filed with the SEC pursuant to the Securities Act of 1933. The registration statement is a condition precedent to a public distribution of securities in interstate commerce and is aimed at providing the prospective investor with a factual basis for sound judgment in making investment decisions.

(c) The terms "investment letter stock" and "letter stock" denote shares of stock that have been issued by a corporation without the benefit of filing a registration statement with the SEC. Such stock is subject to resale and transfer restrictions set forth in a letter agreement requested by the issuer and signed by the buyer of the stock when the stock is delivered. Such stock may be found in the hands of either individual investors or institutional investors.

(d) The term "control stock" indicates that the shares of stock have been held or are being held by an officer, director, or other person close to the management of the corporation. These persons are subject to certain requirements pursuant to SEC rules upon resale of shares they own in such corporations.

(e) The term "private placement stock" indicates that the stock has been placed with an institution or other investor who will presumably hold it for a long period and ultimately arrange to have the stock registered if it is to be offered to the general public. Such stock may or may not be subject to a letter agreement. Private placements of stock are exempted from the registration and prospectus provisions of the Securities Act of 1933.

(f) The term "exempted securities" refers to those classes of securities that are expressly excluded from the registration provisions of the Securities Act of 1933 and the distribution provisions of the Securities Exchange Act of 1934.

(g) The term "exempted transactions" refers to certain sales or distributions of securities that do not involve a public offering and are excluded from the registration and prospectus provisions of the Securities Act of 1933 and distribution provisions of the Securities Exchange Act of 1934. The exempted status makes it unnecessary for issuers of securities to go through the registration process.

SEC. 4. SECURITIES INDUSTRY PRACTICE IN VALUING RESTRICTED SECURITIES.

.01 *Investment Company Valuation Practices.* The Investment Company Act of 1940 requires open-end

Revenue Ruling 77-287

investment companies to publish the valuation of their portfolio securities daily. Some of these companies have portfolios containing restricted securities, but also have unrestricted securities of the same class traded on a securities exchange. In recent years the number of restricted securities in such portfolios has increased. The following methods have been used by investment companies in the valuation of such restricted securities:

(a) Current market price of the unrestricted stock less a constant percentage discount based on purchase discount;

(b) Current market price of unrestricted stock less a constant percentage discount different from purchase discount;

(c) Current market price of the unrestricted stock less a discount amortized over a fixed period;

(d) Current market price of the unrestricted stock; and

(e) Cost of the restricted stock until it is registered.

The SEC ruled in its Investment Company Act Release No. 5847, dated October 21, 1969, that there can be no automatic formula by which an investment company can value the restricted securities in its portfolios. Rather, the SEC has determined that it is the responsibility of the board of directors of the particular investment company to determine the "fair value" of each issue of restricted securities in good faith.

.02 *Institutional Investors Study.* Pursuant to Congressional direction, the SEC undertook an analysis of the purchases, sales, and holding of securities by financial institutions, in order to determine the effect of institutional activity upon the securities market.

The study report was published in eight volumes in March 1971. The fifth volume provides an analysis of restricted securities and deals with such items as the characteristics of the restricted securities purchasers and issuers, the size of transactions (dollars and shares), the marketability discounts on different trading markets, and the resale provisions. This research project provides some guidance for measuring the discount in that it contains information, based on the actual experience of the marketplace, showing that, during the period surveyed (January 1, 1966, through June 30, 1969), the amount of discount allowed for restricted securities from the trading price of the unrestricted securities was generally related to the following four factors.

(a) *Earnings.* Earnings and sales consistently have a significant influence on the size of restricted securities discounts according to the study. Earnings played the major part in establishing the ultimate discounts at which these stocks were sold from the current market price. Apparently earnings patterns, rather than sales patterns, determine the degree of risk of an investment.

(b) *Sales.* The dollar amount of sales of issuers' securities also has a major influence on the amount of discount at which restricted securities sell from the current market price. The results of the study generally indicate that the companies with the lowest dollar amount of sales during the test period accounted for most of the transactions involving the highest discount rates, while they accounted for only a small portion of all transactions involving the lowest discount rates.

(c) *Trading Market.* The market

Revenue Ruling 77-287

in which publicly held securities are traded also reflects variances in the amount of discount that is applied to restricted securities purchases. According to the study, discount rates were greatest on restricted stocks with unrestricted counterparts traded over-the-counter, followed by those with unrestricted counterparts listed on the American Stock Exchange, while the discount rates for those stocks with unrestricted counterparts listed on the New York Stock Exchange were the smallest.

(d) *Resale Agreement Provisions.* Resale agreement provisions often affect the size of the discount. The discount from the market price provides the main incentive for a potential buyer to acquire restricted securities. In judging the opportunity cost of freezing funds, the purchaser is analyzing two separate factors. The first factor is the risk that underlying value of the stock will change in a way that, absent the restrictive provisions, would have prompted a decision to sell. The second factor is the risk that the contemplated means of legally disposing of the stock may not materialize. From the seller's point of view, a discount is justified where the seller is relieved of the expenses of registration and public distribution, as well as of the risk that the market will adversely change before the offering is completed. The ultimate agreement between buyer and seller is a reflection of these and other considerations. Relative bargaining strengths of the parties to the agreement are major considerations that influence the resale terms and consequently the size of discounts in restricted securities transactions. Certain provisions are often found in agreements between buyers and sellers that

affect the size of discounts at which restricted stocks are sold. Several such provisions follow, all of which, other than number (3), would tend to reduce the size of the discount:

(1) A provision giving the buyer an option to "piggyback", that is, to register restricted stock with the next registration statement, if any, filed by the issuer with the SEC;

(2) A provision giving the buyer an option to require registration at the seller's expense;

(3) A provision giving the buyer an option to require registration, but only at the buyer's own expense;

(4) A provision giving the buyer a right to receive continuous disclosure of information about the issuer from the seller;

(5) A provision giving the buyer a right to select one or more directors of the issuer;

(6) A provision giving the buyer an option to purchase additional shares of the issuer's stock; and

(7) A provision giving the buyer the right to have a greater voice in operations of the issuer, if the issuer does not meet previously agreed upon operating standards.

Institutional buyers can and often do obtain many of these rights and options from the sellers of restricted securities, and naturally, the more rights the buyer can acquire, the lower the buyer's risk is going to be, thereby reducing the buyer's discount as well. Smaller buyers may not be able to negotiate the large discounts or the rights and options that volume buyers are able to negotiate.

.03 *Summary.* A variety of methods have been used by the securities industry to value restricted securities. The SEC rejects all automatic or me-

Revenue Ruling 77-287

chanical solutions to the valuation of restricted securities, and prefers, in the case of the valuation of investment company portfolio stocks, to rely upon good faith valuations by the board of directors of each company. The study made by the SEC found that restricted securities *generally* are issued at a discount from the market value of freely tradable securities.

SEC. 5. FACTS AND CIRCUMSTANCES MATERIAL TO VALUATION OF RESTRICTED SECURITIES.

.01 Frequently, a company has a class of stock that cannot be traded publicly. The reason such stock cannot be traded may arise from the securities statutes, as in the case of an "investment letter" restriction; it may arise from a corporate charter restriction, or perhaps from a trust agreement restriction. In such cases, certain documents and facts should be obtained for analysis.

.02 The following documents and facts, when used in conjunction with those discussed in Section 4 of Rev. Rul. 59-60, will be useful in the valuation of restricted securities:

(a) A copy of any declaration of trust, trust agreement, and any other agreements relating to the shares of restricted stock;

(b) A copy of any document showing any offers to buy or sell or indications of interest in buying or selling the restricted shares;

(c) The latest prospectus of the company;

(d) Annual reports of the company for 3 to 5 years preceding the valuation date;

(e) The trading prices and trading volume of the related class of traded securities 1 month preceding the valuation date, if they are traded on a stock exchange (if traded over-the-counter, prices may be obtained from the National Quotations Bureau, the National Association of Securities Dealers Automated Quotations (NASDAQ), or sometimes from broker-dealers making markets in the shares);

(f) The relationship of the parties to the agreements concerning the restricted stock, such as whether they are members of the immediate family or perhaps whether they are officers or directors of the company; and

(g) Whether the interest being valued represents a majority or minority ownership.

SEC. 6. WEIGHING FACTS AND CIRCUMSTANCES MATERIAL TO RESTRICTED STOCK VALUATION.

All relevant facts and circumstances that bear upon the worth of restricted stock, including those set forth above in the preceding Sections 4 and 5, and those set forth in Section 4 of Rev. Rul. 59-60, must be taken into account in arriving at the fair market value of such securities. Depending on the circumstances of each case, certain factors may carry more weight than others. To illustrate:

.01 Earnings, net assets, and net sales must be given primary consideration in arriving at an appropriate discount for restricted securities from the freely traded shares. These are the elements of value that are always used by investors in making investment decisions. In some cases, one element may be more important than in other cases. In the case of manufacturing, producing, or distributing companies, primary weight must be accorded earnings and net sales; but in the case

Section 2512.—Valuation of Gifts

26 CFR 25.2512-2: Stocks and bonds.

Valuation; closely held securities. The valuation, for purposes of section 2512 of the Code, of stock in a closely held company should take into account a proposed merger of the company with a publicly owned corporation.

Rev. Rul. 78-367

Advice has been requested concerning the value of corporate stock for purposes of section 2512 of the Internal Revenue Code of 1954, under the circumstances described below.

Three shareholders, *A*, *B*, and *C*, each owned a one-third interest in *X* corporation. These same individuals each owned a 20 percent interest in *Y* corporation, a publicly owned company. Their shares in *Y* corporation, taken together, were a majority interest.

In January 1975 the two companies publicly announced an intention to merge *X* corporation with *Y* corporation. The merger was subject to the formulation of a detailed agreement regarding the consideration to be exchanged, and subject to the approval of the stockholders of both corporations.

Two months after the announcement, *A* made a gift of some of the *X* corporation stock to *D*. In March 1976, all details concerning the merger were finally completed and the merger effected shortly thereafter. The shareholders of *X* corporation received one share of *Y* corporation stock in exchange for each share in *X* that they held. Prior to the merger, there had been no sales of *X* corporation stock.

The question presented is whether the proposed merger should be considered in the valuation of the gift of the *X* stock.

Section 2512 of the Code provides that a gift shall be taxed on the basis of the value of the property on the date of the transfer. Section 25.2512-1 of the Gift Tax Regulations states the following general rules:

> * * * The value of the property is the price at which such property would change hands between a willing buyer and a willing seller, neither being under any compulsion to buy or to sell, and both having reasonable knowledge of relevant facts. . . . All relevant facts and elements of value as of the time of the gift shall be considered. * * *

Section 25.2512-2(f) of the regulations provides the following guidelines for valuation of corporate securities for which actual sales are lacking:

> (f) *Where selling prices or bid and asked prices are unavailable.* If the provisions of paragraphs (b), (c), and (d) of this section are inapplicable because actual sale prices and bona fide bid and asked prices are lacking, then the fair market value is to be determined by taking the following factors into consideration:
> (1) In the case of corporate or other bonds, the soundness of the security, the interest yield, the date of maturity, and other relevant factors; and
> (2) In the case of shares of stock, the company's net worth, prospective earning power and dividend-paying capacity, and other relevant factors.

Some of the "other relevant factors" referred to in subparagraphs (1) and (2) of this paragraph are: the good will of the business; the economic outlook in the particular industry; the company's position in the industry and its management; the degree of control of the business represented

Revenue Ruling 78-367

of investment or holding companies, primary weight must be given to the net assets of the company underlying the stock. In the former type of companies, value is more closely linked to past, present, and future earnings while in the latter type of companies, value is more closely linked to the existing net assets of the company. See the discussion in Section 5 of Rev. Rul. 59-60.

.02 Resale provisions found in the restriction agreements must be scrutinized and weighed to determine the amount of discount to apply to the preliminary fair market value of the company. The two elements of time and expense bear upon this discount; the longer the buyer of the shares must wait to liquidate the shares, the greater the discount. Moreover, if the provisions make it necessary for the buyer to bear the expense of registration, the greater the discount. However, if the provisions of the restricted stock agreement make it possible for the buyer to "piggyback" shares at the next offering, the discount would be smaller.

.03 The relative negotiation strengths of the buyer and seller of restricted stock may have a profound effect on the amount of discount. For example, a tight money situation may cause the buyer to have the greater balance of negotiation strength in a transaction. However, in some cases the relative strengths may tend to cancel each other out.

.04 The market experience of freely tradable securities of the same class as the restricted securities is also significant in determining the amount of discount. Whether the shares are privately held or publicly traded affects the worth of the shares to the holder. Securities traded on a public market generally are worth more to investors than those that are not traded on a public market. Moreover, the type of public market in which the unrestricted securities are traded is to be given consideration.

Sec. 7. Effect on Other Documents.

Rev. Rul. 59-60, as modified by Rev. Rul. 65-193, is amplified.

Revenue Ruling 79-7

by the block of stock to be valued; and the values of securities of corporations engaged in the same or similar lines of business which are listed on a stock exchange. However, the weight to be accorded such comparisons or any other evidentiary factors considered in the determination of a value depends upon the facts of each case. * * *

Rev. Rul. 59-60, 1959-1 C.B. 237, as modified by Rev. Rul. 65-193, 1965-2 C.B. 370, and as amplified by Rev. Rul. 77-287, 1977-2 C.B. 319, outlines some methods and factors to be considered when valuing shares of stock on which market quotations are unavailable. Although nine representative factors are discussed, the ruling advises that *all* relevant factors affecting fair market value should be considered.

In the present case, no share of *X* corporation stock had been sold prior to the date of the gift. The announcement of the merger two months before, as well as the preliminary decision to merge, did not attempt to fix the consideration to be exchanged. The value of the stock, for purposes of the merger, was not finally agreed upon until one year after the gift.

The concept of "fair market value" is premised on a hypothetical sale in which both the prospective buyer and seller have reasonable knowledge of the facts. See *Estate of Reynolds v. Commissioner,* 55 T.C. 172, 195 (1970), acq., 1971-2 C.B. 2.

The standards set by the regulations and Rev. Rul. 59-60, as modified and amplified, reflect the reality of the market place. A prospective seller would inform a prospective buyer of all favorable facts in an effort to obtain the best possible price, and a prospective buyer would elicit all the negative information in order to obtain the lowest possible price. In this arm's length negotiation, all relevant factors available to either buyer or seller, known to both, provide a basis on which the buyer and seller make a decision to buy or sell and come to an agreement on the price.

Accordingly, the valuation of the stock of *X* as of the date of the gift should take into account the effects of the public announcement of the merger and all information covering the status of the merger negotiations available to the buyer and seller.

Revenue Ruling 79-7

Section 2035.—Transactions in Contemplation of Death [As in Effect Prior to 1977]

26 CFR 20.2035-1: Transactions in contemplation of death.
(Also Section 2031; 20.2031-1.)

Valuation; transfer in contemplation of death; stock of closely held corporation. An individual who owned a controlling stock interest in a closely held corporation transferred a minority stock interest that was included in the individual's gross estate as a transfer in contemplation of death. The minority interest transferred and the stock retained by the individual until death are treated as one block of shares in determining the value of the stock interest includible in the gross estate.

Rev. Rul. 79-7

ISSUE

Whether the interest in a closely held corporation that is includible in the decedent's gross estate under section 2035 of the Code should be valued as a minority interest in the corporation, under the circumstances described below.

FACTS

The decedent, *A*, owned 600 shares of the common stock of *X* corporation, a closely held corporation. The 600 shares represented sixty percent of the outstanding stock of *X* corporation. In 1974, two years prior to death, *A* transferred 300 shares to *B*, *A*'s child, in a transfer that was determined to have been made in contemplation of death.

The stock transferred by *A* was therefore includible in *A*'s gross estate under section 2035 of the Code. In addition, the 300 shares *A* owned outright at the time of death were included in the gross estate under section 2033 of the Code.

LAW AND ANALYSIS

Section 20.2031-2(f) of the regulations provides that in determining the value of a decedent's stock interest in a closely held corporation for purposes of the federal estate tax, consideration should be given to the degree of control of the corporation represented by the block of stock to be valued. The question presented in the instant case is whether the 300 shares of *X* corporation stock included in the decedent's gross estate under section 2035 of the Code is to be valued as a minority interest in the corporation, without reference to the stock interest included in the decedent's gross estate under section 2033.

Rev. Rul. 59-60, 1959-1 C.B. 237, sets forth guidelines for the valuation of shares of capital stock of a closely-held corporation. Both section 20.2031-2(f) of the regulations and Rev. Rul. 59-60, state that the determination of value of such closely-held stock is to be made with reference to a range of factors in the absence of an established "market" in the shares. It is assumed that there is no established "market" for closely-held corporate stocks. See Rev. Rul. 59-60, cited above.

At the time of *A*'s death, section 2035(a) of the Code provided that the gross estate shall include the value of any interest in property transferred by the decedent (except in the case of a bona fide sale for an adequate and full consideration in money or money's worth) in contemplation of death. Sec-

Revenue Ruling 81-15

Section 2036.—Transfers With Retained Life Estate

26 CFR 20.2036-1: Transfers with retained life estate.

Stock transferred in trust; retained power. In view of the *Byrum* decision and the enactment of section 2036(b) of the Code, Rev. Rul. 67-54 is revoked.

Rev. Rul. 81-15

ISSUE

The Internal Revenue Service has been asked to reconsider Rev. Rul. 67-54, 1967-1 C.B. 269, in view of the Supreme Court decision in *United States v. Byrum,* 408 U.S. 125 (1972), 1972-2 C.B. 518, and the enactment of section 2036(b) of the Internal Revenue Code.

FACTS

In Rev. Rul. 67-54, the decedent transferred assets to a corporation which issued nonvoting preferred stock and debentures, for the full current value of the assets transferred. The corporation also issued 10 shares of voting and 990 shares of nonvoting common stock. The decedent transferred the 990 shares of nonvoting stock in trust for the benefit of his children. The trust owned the 990 shares at the date of decedent's death. Under the terms of the trust, the trustee could not dispose of the stock without the consent of the decedent. Under an alternative fact situation, the grantor designated himself as trustee.

Rev. Rul. 67-54 concludes that the decedent has retained control of the corporate dividend policy through retention of the voting stock and, thus, has retained the right to determine the income from the nonvoting stock. The decedent has also retained control over the disposition of the nonvoting stock, either as trustee or as a result of the restrictions on the trustee's power to dispose of the stock. The ruling holds that the decedent's retention of the right to control income and the restriction on disposition amount to a transfer whereby the decedent has retained for life or for a period which in fact did not end before death the right to designate the persons who shall enjoy the transferred property or income therefrom. Therefore, the property is includible in decedent's gross estate under section 2036(a)(2) of the Code.

Rev. Rul. 67-54 also holds that, pursuant to section 2031 of the Code, the value of the nonvoting shares included in the gross estate should reflect the additional value inherent in the closely held voting shares by reason of control of company policies.

LAW AND ANALYSIS

Section 2036(a)(2) of the Code provides that the value of the gross estate shall include the value of any interest in property transferred by a decedent if the decedent has retained for life the right, alone or in conjunction with any person, to designate the persons who shall possess or enjoy the property or the income therefrom.

In *United States v. Byrum,* the Supreme Court addressed the issue of includibility of transferred stock where

Revenue Ruling 81-15

tion 20.2035-1(e) of the Estate Tax Regulations provides that the value of an interest in transferred property includible in a decedent's gross estate under section 2035 is the value of the interest as of the applicable valuation date, determined in accordance with section 2031 of the Code and the regulations thereunder.

Underlying the provisions of section 2035 of the Code is the intent to prevent the avoidance of the estate tax by taxing inter vivos gifts made as substitutes for testamentary transfers as if they were testamentary transfers. *Milliken v. United States,* 283 U.S. 15 (1931). Consequently, the value of property included in the decedent's gross estate under section 2035 should be treated, for purposes of the estate tax, in the same manner as it would have been if the transfer had not been made and the property had been owned by the decedent at the time of death. *Humphrey's Estate v. Commissioner,* 162 F. 2d 1 (5th Cir. 1947). *Ingleheart v. Commissioner,* 77 F. 2d 704 (5th Cir. 1935); Rev. Rul 76-235, 1976-1 C.B. 277.

In the situation presented here, the stock interest in *X* corporation transferred by *A* to *B* represented a minority interest in the corporation. However, pursuant to the court's decisions in *Humphrey's Estate* and *Ingleheart,* the value of the stock included in the gross estate under section 2035 of the Code should be taxed as if the decedent had retained the stock until death. If *A* had not transferred the 300 shares, then a total of 600 shares of stock would have been included in *A*'s gross estate under section 2033. That block of shares would represent a controlling interest in *X* corporation and would be valued, in accordance with Rev. Rul. 59-60, cited above, taking into account the controlling interest the shares represent.

HOLDING

The 300 shares of *X* corporation stock includible in *A*'s gross estate under section 2033 of the Code, and the 300 shares includible under section 2035, are to be treated as 1 block of 600 shares of stock for purposes of determining whether the stock includible in *A*'s gross estate represents a minority or majority interest in *X* corporation. Under these circumstances, the inclusion of the 300 shares of stock under section 2035 of the Code will have the same tax effect as if the decedent had retained the 300 shares until death.

The conclusion of this ruling would be the same under section 2035 of the Code as amended by the Tax Reform Act of 1976 for that amendment merely eliminated the requirement that the transfer be in contemplation of death. The purpose of the statute, as amended, remains the same as it was prior to modification.

Revenue Ruling 81-253

26 CFR 25.2512-1: Valuation of property; in general.

Valuation; stock; intrafamily transfers; minority discounts. Simultaneous gifts of one-third of the stock of a family controlled corporation to each of the donor's three children are not valued as minority interests for purposes of section 2512 of the Code.

Rev. Rul. 81-253

ISSUE

Whether minority discounts should be allowed in valuing for federal gift tax purposes three simultaneous transfers of all of the stock in a closely held family corporation to the donor's three children.

FACTS

The donor, *A*, owned all of the 90 outstanding shares of stock in corporation *X*, the sole asset of which is a parcel of real estate. On December 30, 1978, *A* made simultaneous gifts of one-third (30 shares) of the stock in *X* to each of *A*'s three children. On that date, the established fair market value of each share of *X* stock, if all the stock were sold together, was $100x per share.

At the time the gifts were made, there were no corporate bylaws or other instruments restricting the voting or disposition of corporate shares by any shareholder, and there were no negotiations underway for the disposition of the corporation's assets or the disposition of the shares in question before or subsequent to the date of the gifts. In addition there is no evidence of the kind of family discord or other factor that would indicate that the family would not act as a unit in controlling the corporation. The corporation still owns the parcel of real estate and *A*'s children still own the corporate shares.

LAW AND ANALYSIS

Section 2501(a)(1) of the Internal Revenue Code provides that a tax is imposed for each calendar quarter on the transfer of property by gift during such calendar quarter. Section 2512(a) provides that the value of the property at the date of the gift shall be considered the amount of the gift.

Section 25.2512-1 of the Gift Tax Regulations defines the value of property as the price at which such property would change hands between a willing buyer and willing seller, neither being under compulsion to buy or sell, and both having reasonable knowledge of relevant facts. The regulations provide that the value of a particular kind of property is not the price that a forced sale of the property would produce, and that all relevant facts and elements of value as of the time of the gift shall be considered.

Section 25.2512-2(a) of the regulations provides that the value of stocks and bonds is the fair market value per share or bond on the date of the gift. Section 25.2512-2(f) provides that the degree of control of the business represented by the block of stock to be valued is among the factors to be considered in valuing stock where there are not sales prices or bona fide bid and asked prices. See also Rev. Rul. 59-60, sections 4.01(g), 4.02(g), 1959-

Revenue Ruling 81-253

the decedent had transferred the stock in trust, retaining the right to vote the transferred shares, the right to veto the sale or acquisition of trust property and the right to replace the trustee.

The court concluded that because of the fiduciary constraints imposed on corporate directors and controlling shareholders, the decedent "did not have an unconstrained *de facto* power to regulate the flow of dividends, much less the right to designate who was to enjoy the income." See *Byrum, supra* at 143.

Thus, *Byrum* overruled the proposition on which Rev. Rul. 67-54 was based; that is, that a decedent's retention of voting control of a corporation, coupled with restrictions on the disposition of the stock, is equivalent to the right to designate the person who shall enjoy the income.

Section 2036(b)(1), added by the Tax Reform Act of 1976, 1976-3 C.B. (Vol. 1) 1, as amended by the Revenue Act of 1978, section 702(i), 1978-3 C.B. (Vol. 1) 1, 165, provides that for purposes of section 2036(a)(1), the direct or indirect retention of voting rights in transferred stock of a controlled corporation shall be considered to be a retention of the enjoyment of transferred property.

The Senate Finance Committee Report relating to section 2036(b)(1) provides as follows:

The rule would not apply to the transfer of stock in a controlled corporation where the decedent could not vote the transferred stock. For example, where a decedent transfers stock in a controlled corporation to his son and does not have the power to vote the stock any time during the 3-year period before his death, the rule does not apply even where the decedent owned, or could vote, a majority of the stock. Similarly, where the decedent owned both voting and nonvoting stock and transferred the nonvoting stock to another person, the rule does not apply to the nonvoting stock simply because of the decedent's ownership of the voting stock. S. Rep. No. 95-745, 95th Cong., 2d Sess. 91 (1978).

The legislative history of section 2036(b) demonstrates that the rule of that section will not apply to the transfer of stock in a controlled corporation where the decedent could not vote the transferred stock. Thus, the effect of *Byrum* on Rev. Rul. 67-54 is not changed by the enactment of section 2036(b) of the Code.

HOLDING

In view of *United States v. Byrum,* and the enactment of section 2036(b) of the Code, Rev. Rul. 67-54 is revoked. However, the Service will continue to apply the general principles of valuation under section 2031, noted in the revenue ruling.

EFFECT ON OTHER REVENUE RULINGS

Rev. Rul. 67-54 is revoked.

Revenue Ruling 81-253

1 C.B. 237.

The fair market value of a piece of property depends on the facts and circumstances. Section 3.01, Rev. Rul. 59-60, 1959-1 C.B. 237, *Messing v. Commissioner*, 48 T.C. 505, 512 (1967), *acq.* 1968-1 C.B. 2. Thus questions of valuation cannot be resolved by mechanical application of formulae and cases involving valuation can often be distinguished. Nonetheless, certain overriding legal principles to which each set of facts is applied govern valuation. *Powers. v. Commissioner*, 312 U.S. 259 (1941); *Maytag v. Commissioner*, 187 F.2d 962 (10th Cir. 1951).

Judicial authority is inconsistent regarding the correct legal principle governing the availability of a minority discount in the instant case. Therefore, this ruling is intended to state the Service's position.

Several cases have held or implied that no minority discount is available when the transferred stock is part of a family controlling interest. *Driver v. United States*, No. 73C 260 (W.D. Wis., Sept. 13, 1976); *Blanchard v. United States*, 291 F. Supp. 248 (S.D. Iowa, 1968); *Richardson v. Commissioner*, No. 95770 (T.C.M. 1943), *aff'd*, 151 F. 2d 102 (2d Cir. 1945), *cert. denied*, 326 U.S. 796 (1946); *Hamm v. Commissioner*, T.C.M. 1961-347, *aff'd*, 325 F.2d 934 (8th Cir. 1963), *cert. denied*, 377 U.S. 993 (1964). The Service will follow these decisions. Other cases have allowed a minority discount on similar facts. *Whittemore v. Fitzpatrick*, 127 F. Supp. 710 (D. Conn. 1954); *Obermer v. United States*, 238 F. Supp. 29, 34 (D. Hawaii, 1964); *Estate of Piper v. Commissioner*, 72 T.C. 1062 (1979); *Clark v. United States*, Civil Nos. 1308, 1309 (E.D.N.C., May 16, 1975); *Bartram v. Graham*, 157 F. Supp. 757 (D. Conn. 1957); *Estate of Lee v. Commissioner*, 69 T.C. 860 (1978), *nonacq.* 1980-2 C.B. 2; *Estate of Bright v. United States*, No. 78-2221 (5th Cir., Oct. 1, 1981). The Service will not follow these and similar cases.

It is the position of the Service that ordinarily no minority discount will be allowed with respect to transfers of shares of stock among family members where, at the time of the transfer, control (either majority voting control or de facto control) of the corporation exists in the family, *Dattel v. United States*, No. D.C. 73-107-S, (N.D. Miss., Oct. 29, 1975), *Cutbirth v. United States*, Civil No. CA-6-75-1 (N.D. Tex., June 16, 1976). However, when there is evidence of family discord or other factors indicating that the family would not act as a unit in controlling the corporation, a minority discount may be allowed. Although courts have recognized that where a shareholder is unrelated to other shareholders a minority discount may be available because of absence of control, *Estate of Schroeder v. Commissioner*, 13 T.C. 259 (1949), *acq.* 1949-2 C.B. 3, where a controlling interest in stock is owned by family members, there is a unity of ownership and interest, and the shares owned by family members should be valued as part of that controlling interest. This conclusion is based on an evaluation of the facts and circumstances that would affect the price received for the shares in a hypothetical sale. It is unlikely that under circumstances such as exist in the instant case, shares that are part of a controlling interest would be sold other than as a unit except to a family member in whose hands the shares

Revenue Ruling 81-253

would retain their control value because of the family relationship. Thus, where a controlling interest in stock is owned by a family, the value per share of stock owned by one family member is the same as stock owned by any other family member and is the same value that would exist if all the stock were held by one person.

HOLDING

No minority discount is allowable and the value of each share of stock for federal gift tax purposes is $100x.

Revenue Ruling 83-119

Section 305.—Distributions of Stock and Stock Rights

26 CFR 1.305-5: Distributions on preferred stock.

Recapitalization; excess redemption premium; preferred stock. In a recapitalization where a corporation issues preferred stock that must be redeemed at the time of the holder's death at a price in excess of one hundred and ten percent of the issue price, the amount of the excess redemption premium is treated under section 305(c) of the Code as a distribution of stock within the meaning of section 305(b)(4). The redemption amount will be constructively received ratably over the holder's life expectancy.

Rev. Rul. 83-119

ISSUE

In a recapitalization where a corporation issues preferred stock that must be redeemed on the holder's death at the price in excess of one hundred and ten percent of the issue price, is the amount of the excess redemption premium treated, by reason of section 305(c) of the Internal Revenue Code, as a distribution with respect to preferred stock within the meaning of section 305(b)(4)? If so, when is this distribution deemed to be received?

FACTS

A domestic corporation, X, had outstanding 100 shares of common stock. A owned 80 shares of the X common stock and B, A's child, owned the other 20 shares. A was actively engaged in X's business as its president, and B was a key employee. A retired from the business and resigned as a director, officer, and employee of X with no intention to take part in the future activities of X. Pursuant to a plan of recapitalization for the purpose of transferring control and ownership of the common stock to B in conjunction with A's retirement, a single class of nonvoting, dividend paying preferred stock (as defined in section 1.305-5(a) of the Income Tax Regulations) was authorized. There are no redemption provisions with regard to the preferred stock, except that on the death of a shareholder of the preferred stock, X is required to redeem the preferred stock from the shareholder's estate or beneficiaries at its par value of 1,000x dollars per share. On January 1, 1981, A had a life expectancy of 24 years determined by using the actuarial tables provided in section 1.72-9 of the regulations. On January 1, 1981, A exchanged 80 shares of common stock for 80 shares of preferred stock. Following this exchange, A held all of the preferred stock, and B held all of the common stock that X then had outstanding.

On the date of the exchange the X common stock surrendered had a fair market value of $1,000$x$ dollars per share, and the X preferred stock had a par value of $1,000$x$ dollars per share. The one-for-one exchange ratio resulted because the par value of the preferred stock was presumed to represent its fair market value. However, the fair market value of the pre-

Revenue Ruling 83-119

ferred stock was only 600*x* dollars per share. See Rev. Rul. 83-120, page 170, this Bulletin, for factors taken into account in valuing common and preferred stock. Thus, *A* surrendered *X* common stock with a fair market value of 80,000*x* dollars (80 × 1,000*x* dollars) in exchange for *X* preferred stock with a fair market value of 48,000*x* dollars (80 × 600*x* dollars).

The exchange of all of *A*'s *X* common stock for *X* preferred stock is a recapitalization within the meaning of section 368(a)(1)(E) of the Code. Under section 354, no gain or loss will be recognized to *A* with regard to the receipt of the preferred stock to the extent of its 48,000*x* dollars fair market value. However, the 32,000*x* dollars excess in the fair market value of the *X* common stock surrendered by *A* as compared to the fair market value of the preferred stock *A* received will be treated as having been used to make a gift, pay compensation, satisfy obligations of any kind, or for whatever purposes the facts indicate. Section 356(f) of the Code and Rev. Rul. 74-269, 1974-1 C.B. 87.

LAW AND ANALYSIS

Section 305(a) of the Code provides generally that gross income does not include the amount of any distribution of the stock of a corporation made by such corporation to its shareholders with respect to its stock, except as otherwise provided in section 305(b) or (c).

Section 305(b)(4) of the Code provides, in part, that section 305(a) will not apply to a distribution by a corporation of its stock, and the distribution will be treated as a distribution of property to which section 301 applies, if the distribution is with re-

spect to preferred stock.

Section 305(c) of the Code provides, in part, that the Secretary shall prescribe regulations under which a difference between issue price and redemption price will be treated as a distribution with respect to any shareholder whose proportionate interest in the earnings and profits or assets of the corporation is increased by the transaction. Section 1.305-7(a) of the regulations provides, under the authority of section 305(c), that an unreasonable redemption premium on preferred stock will be treated in accordance with section 1.305-5.

Section 1.305-5(b)(1) of the regulations provides that if a corporation issues preferred stock which may be redeemed after a specific period of time at a price higher than the issue price, the difference will be considered under the authority of section 305(c) of the Code to be distribution of additional stock on preferred stock (section 305(b)(4)) constructively received by the shareholder over the period of time during which the preferred stock cannot be called for redemption. However, section 1.305-5(b)(2) states that section 1.305-5(b)(1) will not apply to the extent that the difference between issue price and redemption price is a reasonable redemption premium, and that a redemption premium will be considered reasonable if it is in the nature of a penalty for the premature redemption of the preferred stock and if such premium does not exceed the amount the corporation would be required to pay for the right to make such premature redemption under market conditions existing at the time of issuance. Section 1.305-5(b)(2) also states that a redemption premium not in excess of 10

Revenue Ruling 83-119

percent of the issue price on stock which is not redeemable for five years from the date of issuance shall be considered reasonable.

Section 1.305-7(a) of the regulations provides, in part, that a change in conversion ratio, a change in redemption price, a difference between redemption price and issue price, a redemption which is treated as a distribution to which section 301 applies, or any transaction (including a recapitalization) having a similar effect on the interest of any shareholder will be treated as a distribution to which sections 305(b) and 301 apply if (1) the proportionate interest of any shareholder in the earnings and profits or assets of the corporation deemed to have made such distribution is increased by such transaction, and (2) such distribution has the result described in paragraph (2), (3), (4), or (5) of section 305(b).

Section 1.305-3(e), Example (12), of the regulations illustrates a situation where section 305 does not apply to exchanges of stock in a recapitalization that is a "single and isolated transaction". However, section 1.305-7(c)(1) of the regulations provides that a recapitalization, whether or not an isolated transaction, will be deemed to result in a distribution to which section 305(c) of the Code and section 1.305-7 of the regulations apply, if, among other things, it is pursuant to a plan to periodically increase a shareholder's proportionate interest in the assets or earnings and profits of the corporation.

One element which is necessary to taxability under sections 305(b) and (c) is that there must be a distribution. Regarding this requirement, section 305(b) deals with actual distributions, and section 305(c) deems certain transactions which are not actual distributions to be distributions for section 305 purposes. Certain recapitalizations, even if isolated, are treated as distributions under regulations section 1.305-7(c). That is, an actual exchange of stock, even though clearly isolated, can be treated as a distribution if the exchange is pursuant to a larger plan to periodically increase a shareholder's proportionate interest. Section 1.305-5(c) of the regulations provides, "For rules for applying sections 305(b)(4) and 305(c) to recapitalizations, see section 1.305-7(c)". This means that section 1.305-7(c) of the regulations is the rule used to impose section 305(b)(4) and (c) of the Code on an exchange of stock which qualifies as a recapitalization. However, it does not mean that section 1.305-7(c) must be found to be applicable to a transaction in order for any deemed distribution which may result from the transaction to be subject to section 305(b)(4) and (c) and the regulations thereunder.

Although an exchange of stock in an isolated recapitalization would not in itself result in section 305(b) and (c) applicability, the terms of the preferred stock used in the exchange may result in this applicability. The difference between issue price and redemption price (section 1.305-7(a) of the regulations) and the fact that the stock cannot be called for redemption for a specific period of time (section 1.305-5(b) of the regulations) are the factors which combine to produce a deemed distribution. The imposition of tax results from the deemed distribution of additional preferred stock over the period the stock cannot be called or presented for redemption.

Revenue Ruling 83-119

Section 1.305-5(d), Example (7), of the regulations describes the proper treatment of preferred stock issued pro rata to the holders of a corporation's common stock. The fair market value of the preferred stock immediately after its issuance was 50x dollars. The preferred stock is redeemable at the end of five years for 105x dollars per share. There is no evidence that a call premium in excess of 5x dollars per share is reasonable. The 50x dollars excess of the call premium (55x dollars) minus the deemed reasonable premium (5x dollars) is considered to be a distribution of additional stock on preferred stock to which sections 305(b)(4) and 301 of the Code apply. This 50x dollar excess is considered to be distributed to the shareholders ratably over the five year period.

In the present situation, X common stock was exchanged by A for X preferred stock. Since the exchange was not part of a plan to periodically increase a shareholder's proportionate interest, the recapitalization itself did not result in a deemed distribution. However, the preferred stock will be redeemed by X on the death of a shareholder at a price of 1,000x dollars per share. Since the preferred stock had a fair market value of 600x dollars per share on the date of issuance, the preferred stock has a redemption premium of 400x dollars per share. There is no evidence that a call premium in excess of 60x dollars was reasonable. Because (1) the X stock is closely held, (2) no public offerings are planned, (3) the X stock is held by members of a family group within the meaning of section 318(a), and (4) the stock is not readily marketable, it is presumed that, at the time of the exchange, the shareholders intended that A would not transfer the preferred stock, and, therefore, redemption would occur upon A's death. Although the exact duration of A's life is not yet known, A's life is "a specified period of time" within the meaning of section 1.305-5(b)(1) of the regulations. Because A has a life expectancy of 24 years, the 400x dollar redemption premium on the X preferred stock has substantially the same effect as a 400x dollar redemption premium payable at the end of a fixed term of 24 years.

HOLDING

The recapitalization in which X issues X preferred stock that must be redeemed on the shareholder's death at a price (1,000x dollars) which exceeds the issue price (600x dollars) results in the recipient, A, being deemed to receive a distribution of additional stock with respect to preferred stock, within the meaning of section 305(b)(4) of the Code, by reason of section 305(c), in the amount of 340x dollars (400x dollars less a deemed reasonable redemption premium of 60x dollars) on each share of preferred stock. This amount will be constructively received ratably (14.16x dollars per share per year) over A's life expectancy of 24 years, and will be treated as a distribution to which section 301 applies. If A should die earlier, any part of the 340x dollars per share not yet constructively received by A would be deemed received at the time of A's death.

26 CFR 1.305-5: Distributions on preferred stock.

Significant factors in deriving the fair market value of preferred and common stock received in certain corporate reorganizations. See Rev. Rul. 83-120, page 170.

Revenue Ruling 83-119

26 CFR 5c.305-1: Special rules of application for dividend reinvestment in stock of public utilities.

T.D. 7897

TITLE 26.—INTERNAL
REVENUE.—CHAPTER 1, SUB-
CHAPTER A, PART 5c—TEMPO-
RARY INCOME TAX REGULA-
TIONS UNDER THE ECONOMIC
RECOVERY TAX ACT OF 1981

Revenue Ruling 83-120

Section 2512.—Valuation of Gifts

26 CFR 25.2512-2: Stocks and bonds.
(Also Sections 305, 351, 354, 368, 2031; 1.305-5, 1.351-1, 1.354-1, 1.368-1, 20.2031-2.)

Valuation; stock; closely held business. The significant factors in deriving the fair market value of preferred and common stock received in certain corporate reorganizations are discussed. Rev. Rul. 59-60 amplified.

Rev. Rul. 83-120

SECTION 1. PURPOSE

The purpose of this Revenue Ruling is to amplify Rev. Rul. 59-60, 1959-1 C.B. 237, by specifying additional factors to be considered in valuing common and preferred stock of a closely held corporation for gift tax and other purposes in a recapitalization of closely held businesses. This type of valuation problem frequently arises with respect to estate planning transactions wherein an individual receives preferred stock with a stated par value equal to all or a large portion of the fair market value of the individual's former stock interest in a corporation. The individual also receives common stock which is then transferred, usually as a gift, to a relative.

Sec. 2. BACKGROUND

.01 One of the frequent objectives of the type of transaction mentioned above is the transfer of the potential appreciation of an individual's stock interest in a corporation to relatives at a nominal or small gift tax cost. Achievement of this objective requires preferred stock having a fair market value equal to a large part of the fair market value of the individual's former stock interest and common stock having a nominal or small fair market value. The approach and factors described in this Revenue Ruling are directed toward ascertaining the true fair market value of the common and preferred stock and will usually result in the determination of a substantial fair market value for the common stock and a fair market value for the preferred stock which is substantially less than its par value.

.02 The type of transaction referred to above can arise in many different contexts. Some examples are:

(a) *A* owns 100% of the common stock (the only outstanding stock) of *Z* Corporation which has a fair market value of 10,500x. In a recapitalization described in section 368(a)(1)(E), *A* receives preferred stock with a par value of 10,000x and new common stock, which *A* then transfers to *A*'s son *B*.

(b) *A* owns some of the common stock of *Z* Corporation (or the stock of several corporations) the fair market value of which stock is 10,500x. *A* transfers this stock to a new corporation *X* in exchange for preferred stock of *X* corporation with a par value of 10,000x and common stock of corporation, which *A* then transfers to *A*'s son *B*.

(c) *A* owns 80 shares and his son *B* owns 20 shares of the common stock (the only stock outstanding) of *Z* Corporation. In a recapitalization described in section 368(a)(1)(E), *A* exchanges his 80 shares of common stock for 80 shares of new preferred stock of *Z* Corporation with a par value of 10,000x. *A*'s common stock had a fair market value of 10,000x.

SEC. 3. GENERAL APPROACH TO VALUATION

Under section 25.2512-2(f)(2) of the Gift Tax Regulations, the fair market value of stock in a closely held corporation depends upon numerous factors, including the corporation's net worth, its prospective earning

Revenue Ruling 83-120

power, and its capacity to pay dividends. In addition, other relevant factors must be taken into account. *See* Rev. Rul. 59-60. The weight to be accorded any evidentiary factor depends on the circumstances of each case. *See* section 25.2512-2(f) of the Gift Tax Regulations.

SEC. 4. APPROACH TO VALUATION—PREFERRED STOCK

.01 In general the most important factors to be considered in determining the value of preferred stock are its yield, dividend coverage and protection of its liquidation preference.

.02 Whether the yield of the preferred stock supports a valuation of the stock at par value depends in part on the adequacy of the dividend rate. The adequacy of the dividend rate should be determined by comparing its dividend rate with the dividend rate of high-grade publicly traded preferred stock. A lower yield than that of high-grade preferred stock indicates a preferred stock value of less than par. If the rate of interest charged by independent creditors to the corporation on loans is higher than the rate such independent creditors charge their most credit worthy borrowers, then the yield on the preferred stock should be correspondingly higher than the yield on high quality preferred stock. A yield which is not correspondingly higher reduces the value of the preferred stock. In addition, whether the preferred stock has a fixed dividend rate and is non-participating influences the value of the preferred stock. A publicly traded preferred stock for a company having a similar business and similar assets with similar liquidation preferences,

voting rights and other similar terms would be the ideal comparable for determining yield required in arms length transactions for closely held stock. Such ideal comparables will frequently not exist. In such circumstances, the most comparable publicly-traded issues should be selected for comparison and appropriate adjustments made for differing factors.

.03 The actual dividend rate on a preferred stock can be assumed to be its stated rate if the issuing corporation will be able to pay its stated dividends in a timely manner and will, in fact, pay such dividends. The risk that the corporation may be unable to timely pay the stated dividends on the preferred stock can be measured by the coverage of such stated dividends by the corporation's earnings. Coverage of the dividend is measured by the ratio of the sum of pre-tax and pre-interest earnings to the sum of the total interest to be paid and the pre-tax earnings needed to pay the after-tax dividends. *Standard & Poor's Ratings Guide*, 58 (1979). Inadequate coverage exists where a decline in corporate profits would be likely to jeopardize the corporation's ability to pay dividends on the preferred stock. The ratio for the preferred stock in question should be compared with the ratios for high quality preferred stock to determine whether the preferred stock has adequate coverage. Prior earnings history is important in this determination. Inadequate coverage indicates that the value of preferred stock is lower than its par value. Moreover, the absence of a provision that preferred dividends are cumulative raises substantial questions concerning whether the stated dividend rate will, in fact, be paid. According-

Revenue Ruling 83-120

ly, preferred stock with noncumulative dividend features will normally have a value substantially lower than a cumulative preferred stock with the same yield, liquidation preference and dividend coverage.

.04 Whether the issuing corporation will be able to pay the full liquidation preference at liquidation must be taken into account in determining fair market value. This risk can be measured by the protection afforded by the corporation's net assets. Such protection can be measured by the ratio of the excess of the current market value of the corporation's assets over its liabilities to the aggregate liquidation preference. The protection ratio should be compared with the ratios for high quality preferred stock to determine adequacy of coverage. Inadequate asset protection exists where any unforeseen business reverses would be likely to jeopardize the corporation's ability to pay the full liquidation preference to the holders of the preferred stock.

.05 Another factor to be considered in valuing the preferred stock is whether it has voting rights and, if so, whether the preferred stock has voting control. See, however, Section 5.02 below.

.06 Peculiar covenants or provisions of the preferred stock of a type not ordinarily found in publicly traded preferred stock should be carefully evaluated to determine the effects of such covenants on the value of the preferred stock. In general, if covenants would inhibit the marketability of the stock or the power of the holder to enforce dividend or liquidation rights, such provisions will reduce the value of the preferred stock by comparison to the value of preferred stock not containing such covenants or provisions.

.07 Whether the preferred stock contains a redemption privilege is another factor to be considered in determining the value of the preferred stock. The value of a redemption privilege triggered by death of the preferred shareholder will not exceed the present value of the redemption premium payable at the preferred shareholder's death (i.e., the present value of the excess of the redemption price over the fair market value of the preferred stock upon its issuance). The value of the redemption privilege should be reduced to reflect any risk that the corporation may not possess sufficient assets to redeem its preferred stock at the stated redemption price. See .03 above.

SEC. 5. APPROACH TO VALUATION— COMMON STOCK

.01 If the preferred stock has a fixed rate of dividend and is nonparticipating, the common stock has the exclusive right to the benefits of future appreciation of the value of the corporation. This right is valuable and usually warrants a determination that the common stock has substantial value. The actual value of this right depends upon the corporation's past growth experience, the economic condition of the industry in which the corporation operates, and general economic conditions. The factor to be used in capitalizing the corporation's prospective earnings must be determined after an analysis of numerous factors concerning the corporation and the economy as a whole. *See* Rev. Rul. 59-60, at page 243. In addition, after-tax earnings of the corporation at the time the preferred stock is issued in excess of the stated

Revenue Ruling 83-120

dividends on the preferred stock will increase the value of the common stock. Furthermore, a corporate policy of reinvesting earnings will also increase the value of the common stock.

.02 A factor to be considered in determining the value of the common stock is whether the preferred stock also has voting rights. Voting rights of the preferred stock, especially if the preferred stock has voting control, could under certain circumstances increase the value of the preferred stock and reduce the value of the common stock. This factor may be reduced in significance where the rights of common stockholders as a class are protected under state law from actions by another class of shareholders, *see Singer v. Magnavox Co.*, 380 A.2d 969 (Del. 1977), particularly where the common shareholders, as a class, are given the power to disapprove a proposal to allow preferred stock to be converted into common stock. See ABA-ALI Model Bus. Corp. Act, Section 60 (1969).

SEC. 6. EFFECT ON OTHER REVENUE RULINGS

Rev. Rul. 59-60, as modified by Rev. Rul. 65-193, 1965-2 C.B. 370 and as amplified by Rev. Rul. 77-287, 1977-2 C.B. 319, and Rev. Rul. 80-213, 1980-2 C.B. 101, is further amplified.

SECTION B

COURT CASES

Contents

Estate of Mark S. Gallo, **TC Memo 1985-363, 50 TCM 470**   **427**

Jug table wine lovers will appreciate this valuation case. It is also a good example of how a court sets itself up as an independent arbitrating appraiser to settle a valuation dispute.

Estate of Murphy, **60 TCM 645 (1990)**   **431**

The Tax Court refused to allow a minority discount on either the gift of 1.76 percent interest in a corporation or the decedent's 49.65 percent interest in the corporation's voting stock. The gift of stock was made 18 days before the decedent's death. The Court held that the gift of stock to relinquish control "lacked substance and economic effect." Accordingly, the Court did not allow a minority discount. The Tax Court specifically stated that it reached its decision without having to rely on a family attribution theory.

Estate of Mildred Herschede Jung, **58 TCM 1127 (1990)**   **440**

The Tax Court held that a sale of the corporation's assets more than two years after the decedent's death may be relevant in determining the fair market value of the stock at the date of death. Accordingly, the sales information is discoverable by the IRS.

Estate of Clara S. Roeder Winkler, **57 TCM 373 (1989)**   **441**

The Tax Court held that a 10 percent interest in the voting common stock of a company, in which one family owned 50 percent and another family owned 40 percent, could be valued with a premium because of its "swing vote" characteristic. No minority discount was allowed due to the swing vote characteristics.

Estate of Ruben Rodriguez, **56 TCM 1033 (1989)**   **443**

The Tax Court adjusted the value of a decedent's 70 percent interest in the stock of a closely held corporation for the loss of the decedent's expertise and the lack of marketability. The decedent was the president and dominant force behind the company. Accordingly, his absence was relevant to the valuation.

Estate of Dean A. Chenoweth, **88 TC 1577 (1987)**   **445**

The Tax Court held that a 51 percent interest in the decedent's wholly owned corporation that passes to a surviving spouse may be valued with a control premium for the marital deduction.

Victor I. Minahan, 88 TC 492 (1987)   449

The Tax Court awarded attorney's fees to the taxpayer because the IRS' reliance on family attribution in valuing minority interests was seen as unreasonable. The Court stated that there has been a long-standing line of Tax Court cases repudiating the family attribution argument.

Estate of Davis Jephson, 87 TC 297 (1986)   451

The Tax Court held that the stock of a wholly owned investment company is its net asset value less the cost of liquidation.

The Northern Trust Company, 87 TC 349 (1986)   452

The Tax Court rejected the use of comparables because either they were involved in more businesses than the valued company or they were not in similar lines of business. The Court accepted the discounted cash flow analysis as a reasonable estimate of the company's intrinsic value. In addition, the Court applied a 25 percent minority discount and a 20 percent discount for lack of marketability.

Estate of Curry, 83-USTC 13,518 (7th Cir).   458

This case held that the nonvoting stock in a corporation is worth as much per share as the voting stock if the decedent held a voting controlling interest in the corporation.

The portions of the court cases contained in this appendix were not selected to illustrate a certain valuation method or approach. They are here to give a feeling for the thought processes by which a court reaches its final valuation decision. It should be noted that the valuation area is like a wild, tropical forest . . . growing all the time. This appendix contains some of the best specimens.

The cases contain good examples of the issues that this book discusses concerning the valuation of privately-held business. However, rather than compartmentalize those specific topics, the reader should read the portions of each case as a whole from beginning to end to get an idea of the role that the courts reluctantly assume as final arbiters in valuation disputes between the IRS and the taxpayer.

The cases also should give the reader an idea of the multitudinous diversity of facts and law involved in each valuation dispute. No two cases are alike. And despite the huge body of case law upon which the courts can draw principles to justify their decisions, each case comes down to the court acting as an appraiser and giving its own opinion as to a proper valuation amount.

A final word: Remember the parable about the six blind men and the elephant? Each went up to an elephant and felt a different piece of the animal's anatomy, and each, based on his own separate exploration, described a completely different animal. They all were right in their conflicting descriptions, even though they failed to realize that their restricted observations were based upon the same beast. Just substitute the privately-held business for the elephant, and appraisers for the blind men, and you get an idea of how a court can disregard the opinions of some experts and accept those of others, even though each appraiser is valuing the same business, to come up with a valuation figure that is essentially a hybrid.

If a particular case is of great interest to you, it is suggested that you read the entire case. However, enough of each case is included in the pages that follow so that you will understand the points of law involved and the court's reasoning in reaching its conclusion.

Central Trust Co. *vs.* U.S.

[Testimony of Experts]

Where, as in the present cases, the problem is the difficult one of ascertaining the fair market value of the stock of an unlisted closely held corporation, it is not surprising that, in assisting the court to arrive at an "informed judgment," the parties offer the testimony of experts. In such a situation, the opinions of experts are peculiarly appropriate. *Bader v. United States,* [59-1 USTC ¶ 11,865] 172 F. Supp. 833 (D. C. S. D. Ill). At the trial, the taxpayers produced three experts, and the Government one.

[Criticisms of Experts' Appraisals]

Various major criticisms can fairly be made of these three appraisals offered by plaintiffs. First, they all give undue weight as a factor to the $7.50 price of the prior stock sales. Almost all of these sales occurred in the relatively remote period of 1951 and early 1952. Only one small transaction occurred in each of the more recent years of 1953 and 1954. Such isolated sales of closely held corporations in a restricted market offer little guide to true value. *Wood, Adm. v. United States,* 89 Ct. Cl. 442; *First Trust Co. v. United States,* [59-1 USTC ¶ 11,843] 3 Am. Fed. Tax R. 2d 1726 (D. C. W. D. Mo.); *Drayton Cochran v. Commissioner,* 7 CCH Tax Ct. Mem. 325; *Schnorbach v. Kavanagh,* [52-1 USTC ¶ 10,836] 102 F. Supp. 828 (D. C. W. D. Mich.). In an evaluation issue, this court recently even gave little weight to the sale of shares on a stock exchange when the amount sold was "relatively insignificant." *American Steel Foundries v. United States,* Ct. Cl. No. 197-54, decided April 7, 1961 (slip opinion, p. 4). To the same effect is *Heiner v. Crosby,* [1 USTC ¶ 276] 24 F. 2d 191 (C. C. A. 3d) in which the court rejected stock exchange sales as being determinative and upheld the resort to "evidence of intrinsic value" (p. 194). Furthermore, the $7.50 price of the 1951 and 1952 sales evolved in early 1951 during a period when the Company was experiencing rather severe financial difficulties due to an unfortunate experience with a subsidiary which caused a loss of around $1,000,000, and when, consequently, the Company found itself in a depleted working capital position and was paying no dividends. Further, there is no indication that the $7.50 sales price evolved as a result of the usual factors taken into consideration by informed sellers and buyers dealing at arm's length. Fair market value presupposes not only hypothetical willing buyers and sellers, but buyers and sellers who are informed and have "adequate knowledge of the material facts affecting the value." *Robertson v. Routzahn,* [35-1 USTC ¶ 9124] 75 F. 2d 537, 539 (C. C. A. 6th); Paul, *Studies in Federal Taxation* (1937), pp. 193-4. The sales were all made at a pre-arranged price to Heekin employees and family friends. The artificiality of the price is indicated by its being the same in 1951, 1952, 1953 and 1954, despite the varying fortunes of the Company during these years and with the price failing to reflect, as would normally be expected, such differences in any way.

Secondly, in using the Company's full 1954 financial data, and then working back from December 31, 1954, to the respective gift dates, data were being used which would not have been available to a prospective purchaser as of the gift dates. "The valuation of the stock must be made as of the relevant dates without regard to events occurring subsequent to the crucial dates." *Bader v. United States, supra,* at p. 840. Furthermore, in the working-back procedure, general market data were used although it is evident that the stocks of a particular industry may at times run counter to the general trend. This was actually the situation here. Although the market generally advanced after August 3, 1954, container industry stocks did not.

Thirdly, the converse situation applies with respect to the data used by the third expert. His financial data only went to December 31, 1953, since the Company's last annual report prior to the gift dates was issued for the year 1953. But the Company also issued quarterly interim financial statements, and by the second gift date, the results of three-quarters of 1954 operations were available. In evaluating a stock, it is essential to obtain as recent data as is possible, as section 4 of the Revenue Ruling makes plain. Naturally, an investor would be more interested in how a corporation is currently performing then what it did last year or in even more remote periods. Although the use of interim reports reflecting only a part of a year's performance may not be satisfactory in a seasonal operation such

Central Trust Co. *vs.* U.S.

as canning, it is possible here to obtain a full year's operation ending on either June 30 or September 30, 1954, which would bring the financial data up closer to the valuation dates.

Fourth, it is accepted valuation practice, in ascertaining a company's past earnings, to attempt to detect abnormal or nonrecurring items and to make appropriate eliminations or adjustments. As shown, only the plaintiffs' expert who came out with the highest August 3 valuation attempted to do this by adjusting the excessive Korean war earnings and by eliminating the unusual losses suffered in 1950, 1951 and 1952 arising from the operations of a financing subsidiary (Canners Exchange, Inc.) that had been liquidated in 1952. The reason this is important is that past earnings are significant only insofar as they reasonably forecast future earnings. The only sound basis upon which to ground such a forecast is the company's normal operation, which requires the elimination or adjustment of abnormal items which will not recur. *Plaut v. Smith*, [49-1 USTC ¶ 9145] 82 F. Supp. 42 (D. C. Conn.), *aff'd, sub nom. Plaut v. Munford*, [51-1 USTC ¶ 9254] 188 F. 2d 543 (Ct. App. 2d Cir.). In *American Steel Foundries v. United States, supra*, the court similarly viewed the "earning prospects" of the company whose stock was being evaluated in light of its past earnings "as constructed by the accountants, eliminating or adjusting losses due to strikes or other nonrecurring events." And the court in *White & Wells Co. v. Commissioner*, 50 F. 2d 120 (C. C. A. 2d), also held that: "* * * past earnings * * * should be such as fairly reflect the probable future earnings" and that to this end "abnormal years" may even be entirely disregarded. The Revenue Ruling (sec. 4.02(d)) specifically points out the necessity of separating "recurrent from nonrecurrent items of income and expense."

Fifth, in deriving a past earnings figure which could be used as a reasonable basis of forecasting future earnings, none of plaintiffs' experts gave any consideration to the trend of such past earnings. They simply used the earnings of prior years and averaged them. But such averages may be deceiving. Two corporations with 5-year earnings going from the past to the present represented by the figures in one case of 5, 4, 3, 2, and 1, and in the other by the same figures of 1, 2, 3, 4, and 5, will have the same 5-year averages, but investors will quite naturally prefer the stock of the latter whose earnings are consistently moving upward. The Revenue Ruling specifically recognizes this in providing (sec. 4.02(d)) that: "Prior earnings records usually are the most reliable guide as to the future expectancy, but resort to arbitrary five-or-ten-year averages without regard to current trends or future prospects will not produce a realistic valuation. If, for instance, a record of progressively increasing or decreasing net income is found, then greater weight may be accorded the most recent years' profits in estimating earning power."

And further, since the most recent years' earnings are to be accorded the greatest weight, care must be taken to make certain that the earnings figures for such years are realistically set forth. For instance, in Heekin's case, profits for 1952-54 were understated because a noncontributory retirement plan for hourly employees was established in 1951 for which the costs attributable to 1950 and 1951 were borne in the later years of 1952-54. Similarly, 1954 profits were further understated because they reflected (1) a renegotiation refund arising out of excess profits made in 1951, and (2) they were subjected to a charge of $174,203.54 ($83,617.70 after taxes) as a result of a deduction from 1954 profits only of certain expenses attributable to both 1954 and 1955. This abnormal doubling up of 2 years' expenses in one year was permitted by a change in the tax laws which became effective in 1954 (and which was later revoked retroactively) which allowed taxpayers such as Heekin to change their methods of accounting so as to effect the accrual in 1954 of these 1955 expenses. If proper adjustments are made in Heekin's 1954 statements for these items, the earnings for the 1954 period prior to the gift dates would be realistically increased and given due weight insofar as earning trends are concerned.

None of plaintiffs' experts made any of these adjustments in connection with a trend study or otherwise.

Sixth, it is generally conceded that, as stated by the Revenue Ruling, in evaluating stocks of manufacturing corporations such as Heekin, earnings are the most important factor to be considered. *Badar v. United*

Central Trust Co. *vs.* U.S.

States, supra. Yet only one of plaintiffs' experts, who assigned double value to this factor, gave it such weight. As shown, the other two assigned the dividend factor equal weight. Some investors may indeed depend upon dividends. In their own investment programs, they may therefore stress yield and even compare common stocks with bonds or other forms of investment to obtain the greatest yields. However others, for various reasons, may care little about dividends and may invest in common stocks for the primary purpose of seeking capital appreciation. All investors, however, are primarily concerned with earnings, which are normally a prerequisite to dividends. In addition, the declaration of dividends is sometimes simply a matter of the policy of a particular company. It may bear no relationship to dividend-paying capacity. Many investors actually prefer companies paying little or no dividends and which reinvest their earnings, for that may be the key to future growth and capital appreciation.

And further, in capitalizing the dividend at 6 and 7 percent, as did two of the experts, rates of return were used which well exceeded those being paid at the time by comparable container company stocks. And still further, one of the experts used a 35-cent dividend rate as the basis for his capitalization because that was the average paid for the 5 years ended December 31, 1954. However, it seems clear that an annual dividend rate of 50 cents a share would be the proper rate to capitalize since that was the dividend paid by Heekin every year since 1945 except for the year 1950 and the first half of 1951 when, as shown, dividends were temporarily suspended. By the end of 1951 the Company had recovered from the situation causing the suspension and the normal dividend (quarterly payments of 12½ cents per share) was then resumed. By August and October 1954, Heekin's demonstrated earning capability and financial position were such that there was little doubt it would at least continue its 50-cent annual dividend, which represented only about 25 percent of its current earnings per share. To dip back into this 1950-51 atypical period to compute an "average" of dividends paid for the past 5 years is unrealistic.

Finally, the record indicates that all three experts took too great a discount for lack of marketability. Defendant disputes the propriety of taking this factor into consideration at all. It seems clear, however, that an unlisted closely held stock of a corporation such as Heekin, in which trading is infrequent and which therefore lacks marketability, is less attractive than a similar stock which is listed on an exchange and has ready access to the investing public. This factor would naturally affect the market value of the stock. This is not to say that the market value of any unlisted stock in which trading is infrequent would automatically be reduced by a lack of marketability factor. The stock of a well-known leader in its field with a preeminent reputation might not be at all affected by such a consideration, as was the situation with Ford Motor Company stock before it was listed. *Couzens v. Commissioner,* [CCH Dec. 3931] 11 B. T. A. 1040. But the stock of a less well-known company like Heekin which is a comparatively small factor in its industry is obviously in a different position. In such a situation, a consideration of this factor is appropriate, especially where, as here, only a minority interest is involved. *Bader v. United States, supra; Baltimore National Bank v. United States,* [56-1 USTC ¶ 11,576] 136 F. Supp. 642 (D. C. Md.); *Schnorbach v. Kavanagh, supra; Cochran v. Commissioner, supra; First Trust Co. v. United States, supra.* But see *Couzens v. Commissioner, supra; Estate of Katharine H. Daily v. Commissioner,* 6 CCH Tax Ct. Mem. 114.

Defendant concedes that if such a factor is appropriate in these cases, a reasonable method of determining the diminution in value attributable to lack of marketability is to determine how much it would cost to create marketability for the block of stock in question. This was the method used by the court in *First Trust Co. v. United States, supra.* The record shows that for a company of Heekin's size, and for blocks of 30,000 and 40,000 shares, which would appear to be the appropriate considerations, flotation costs would amount to about 12.17 percent of the gross sales prices. However, as shown, the discounts taken by plaintiffs' experts for this factor ranged from 15 to 25 percent.

For all the above reasons, the opinions of plaintiffs' experts are not wholly acceptable.

Central Trust Co. *vs.* U.S.

[Decedent's Expert Witness]

Defendant produced one expert, an employee of a recognized appraisal company. His primary work over may years was the valuation of intangibles, including closely held stock. His opinion was that the value of the Heekin stock in question on August 3 and October 25, 1954, was $16 and $15.25 per share, respectively. This witness also used the comparative appraisal method, considering a group of stock in the can and glass container industries. As part of a very comprehensive study, he selected eight container companies, six engaged in can production and two in glass container production, glass container enterprises being similar to those engaged in can production. He considered net assets as a key factor in the determination of a stock price, and one which keeps a stock price from declining to zero when earnings become zero or even when losses are suffered and when a price-to-earnings ratio would therefore become meaningless. He therefore developed for the comparative companies percentage ratios of profits and dividends to net worth as well as market value to net worth. In developing figures for the profits and dividends of the comparative companies for the past 5 years, he gave weight to the trends thereof. He then developed Heekin's profits over the period 1950 through September 1954, making adjustments for the retirement plan costs, the losses from subsidiaries, the renegotiation refund, and the abnormal 1951 profits, in order to reflect the more nearly normal operations over the period. Adjusted profits were developed for the 12-month periods ending June 30 and September 30, 1954. Before correlating the percentages developed for the comparative companies to Heekin, however, he concluded that only two of such companies, United Can and Glass Company and Crown Cork & Seal Company, Inc., could be considered conformable to Heekin. The others, including the giants of their industries, such as American Can, Continental Can, and Owens Illinois Glass Company which, because of acquisitions, diversification, premium investment quality position, and mere size, were not considered fairly comparable, were eliminated. Correlating the data developed with respect to such two companies, he concluded that, as of August 3, Heekin

would be worth 59.5 percent of net worth, or $19.72 per share, a stock exchange equivalent of 19¾ per share. The similar method produced $18.78 per share as the value as of October 25, 1954, or a trading equivalent of 18¾.

This witness too felt that the correlation process resulted in comparing Heekin with seasoned listed stocks enjoying marketability, and that an adjustment should be made for the closely held nature of the Heekin stock with its resultant lack of marketability, especially where only a minority interest was involved. Similarly equating this adjustment to deductions a seller would experience through floating the shares through an underwriter, which he calculated to be almost 20 percent, resulted in net valuations of 16 and 15¼ as of August 3 and October 25, 1954, respectively. Since these values approximate Heekin's current assets (including inventories) less all of its liabilities, without giving any value at all to any of its plants, equipment, or other noncurrent assets, he concluded they were extremely conservative. Employing the common tests of price-to-earnings ratio and yield on the basis of the current 50-cent dividend, these values would result in a price-to-earnings ratio of 7.24:1 as of August 3, based on $2.21 adjusted net profit per share for the 12 months ending June 30, as well as a 3.13 percent dividend yield, and a ratio of 8.29:1 as of October 25, based on $1.84 adjusted net profit per share for the 12 months ending September 30, as well as a 3.28 percent dividend yield.

This witness' study has certain meritorious features. It is based on justifiable adjustments in Heekin's earnings records to eliminate abnormal and nonrecurring items (although he made no adjustment for the 1954 doubling up of certain expenses). It considers earnings trend. It disregards the prior $7.50 sales prices as a major factor. And in employing the Company's financial data going up to June 30 and September 30, 1954, it is based on its most recent performance. However, it has certain weaknesses too, the principal one being the limitation of the comparative companies to two, one of which, Crown Cork & Seal, leaves much to be desired as a comparative because its principal business is the manufacture of bottle caps and bottling machinery, an entirely different business. Only 40 percent of

Central Trust Co. *vs.* U.S.

its business is in can production. On the basis of size too there are great differences. At that time, Crown, including its foreign subsidiaries, was doing about $115,000,000 worth of business as against Heekin's $17,000,000. And the other comparative, United Can and Glass, presents the complication that it declared periodic stock dividends to which the witness gave no consideration, although it seems that some element of value should fairly be attributed to them.* Although no two companies are ever exactly alike, it being rare to have such almost ideal comparatives as were present in *Cochran v. Commissioner, supra,* so that absolute comparative perfection can seldom be achieved, nevertheless the comparative appraisal method is a sound and well-accepted technique. In employing it, however, every effort should be made to select as broad a base of comparative companies as is reasonably possible, as well as to give full consideration to every possible factor in order to make the comparison more meaningful.

Further, in compiling Heekin's financial data for correlation purposes, this witness used Heekin's average dividends for the 4½ years preceding the valuation dates, thus including the atypical period when no dividends were paid.

Defendant, considering its own expert's valuations to be unduly conservative, and disagreeing as a matter of law with any deduction for lack of marketability (and in any event with the amount deducted by its expert for such factor), now offers valuations on what it claims to be a more realistic basis. It also adjusts and redistributes Heekin's profits, including the "doubling up" expenses in 1954, the renegotiation refund, and the retirement plan. As comparatives, it uses for the purpose of developing a price-earnings ratio 11 can and glass container manufacturing companies, including American Can and Continental Can (although it concedes that with respect to the stock of such companies in this field, the investing public affords "some extra value coincident with size"), as well as Crown Cork & Seal and United Can. The dividend yield of seven comparative companies, based on their 1954 dividend payments, was 3.77 percent. Defendant too gives no cognizance to United Can's stock dividends, although it concedes that "stock dividends have some effect on market value." On Heekin's 50-cent dividend, the market price of Heekin stock would be $13.33, based solely on a 3.75 (the figure used by defendant) percent dividend yield.

Defendant then computes representative earnings for Heekin as $1.89 per share, based on 1953 and 1954 adjusted earnings. The average price to current earnings ratio of the 11 comparative companies in 1954 was 13 to 1. On this formula, Heekin's stock would sell for $24.57 per share if earnings were the sole factor. However, defendant reduces this figure to $22.50 for the purpose in question.

On the basis of the book value of Heekin stock being $33.15 as of June 30, 1954, and comparing the market prices of various alleged comparable companies to their book value (i. e., the stocks of 11 unidentified comparatives used by the Commissioner of Internal Revenue in making his valuation sold for 1.4 times book value), defendant concludes that Heekin stock would not sell for less than $33 per share.

The three factors of earnings, dividend yield, and book value are then weighted, earnings, considering their recognized importance for valuation purposes and the upward trend thereof, being assigned 50 percent weight, and dividend yield and book value receiving 30 percent and 20 percent respectively. On this basis, defendant arrives at a fair market value figure of $21.85 as of August 3, 1954.¹

---

* "In theory, of course, the additional stock certificate gives him [the stockholder] nothing that he would not own without it * * *. But in actuality the payment of periodic stock dividends produces important advantages. Among them are the following: * * * 4. Issues paying periodic stock dividends enjoy a higher market value than similar common stocks not paying such dividends." Graham & Dodd, *Security Analysis, Principles and Technique* (3d ed. 1951) pp. 444-5.

¹ Earnings .... $22.50 × .5 = $11.25
Dividend yield .... 13.33 × .3 =   4.00
Book value .... 33.00 × .2 =   6.60

$21.85

Central Trust Co. *vs.* U.S.

Since there was a slight drop in the market price of can manufacturing stocks between August 3 and October 25, 1954, defendant concludes the fair market value on the latter date would be about 50 cents less per share, or $21.35.

Thus, defendant now seeks a fair market value determination as of the gift dates of $21.85 and $21.35 respectively, in lieu of the $24 value fixed by the Commissioner of Internal Revenue.[*]

In its selection of the three basic factors to be considered in determining fair market value, the weights to be assigned to these factors, the earnings adjustments, and the use of 50 cents per annum as the proper dividend basis, this estimate has merit. However, the selection of such companies as American Can and Continental Can as comparatives—companies held in esteem in the investment world—will obviously give an unduly high result. It simply is not fair to compare Heekin with such companies and to adopt their market ratios for application to Heekin's stock. Furthermore, defendant's use of the comparatives is confusing. The employment of different comparatives for different purposes is unorthodox. When the comparative appraisal method is employed the comparatives should be clearly identified and consistently used for all purposes. And the refusal to make any allowance for lack of marketability contributes further to the unrealistic nature of defendant's fair market value estimate.

To summarize, Heekin's stock has been valued as of August 3 and October 25, 1954,

in blocks of 30,000 and 40,002 shares respectively, as follows: $10, originally, by two donors and the executor of the third; $7.50, in amended returns; $7.88 by one expert of plaintiffs (upon which valuation plaintiffs now stand); $9.50 and $9.65 respectively by plaintiffs' second expert; $11.76 and $9.47 respectively by plaintiffs' third expert; $16 and $15.25 respectively by defendant's expert; $21.85 and $21.35 respectively by defendant in these proceedings; and $24 by the Commissioner of Internal Revenue.

[*Three Valuation Factors*]

The proper use of the comparative appraisal method, applying the principles already indicated, should provide a reasonably satisfactory valuation guide in these cases.[*] In its application, it would under all the circumstances herein involved appear appropriate to select the three factors of (1) earnings, (2) dividends and dividend-paying capacity, and (3) book value, as being the important and significant ones to apply. *First Trust Co. v. United States, supra; Cochran v. Commissioner, supra; Bader v. United States, supra.*

As to earnings, an examination of them for the periods from 1950 to June 30 and September 30, 1954, which are the most recent periods in relation to the gift dates, would be most representative. For this purpose, the annual profit and loss statements, plus the Company's interim balance sheets, from which can be derived with reasonable accuracy the Company's earnings for the 12-month periods ending June

---

[*] This $24 value resulted from a study by the Commissioner of 11 comparatives. Their price to book value ratio was 1.4; price to average earnings, 14.3; price to current earnings, 13; and price to current dividends, 31.1.
Applying these ratios to Heekin, 1.4 times book value of $33.23 as of December 31, 1954, equals $46.52 per share. Average earnings for a 5-year period of $1.68 per share times 14.3 equals $24.02 per share. Current earnings times 13 equals $17.16 a share. Price to current dividend equals $15.55 per share.
In addition, in 1954 National Can purchased Pacific Can and the Commissioner analyzed the sale price for comparative purposes. The sales price came to 12.5 times Pacific's earnings. Application of that ratio to Heekin's 1953 earnings would price Heekin's stock at $24.38 per share. Pacific's price also represented 17 times its average 1949-1953 earnings. Application of such

ratio to Heekin would price its stock at $28.39 per share. Further, Pacific's price bore a ratio of 1.6 to book value. Application of such ratio to Heekin's stock would price it at $53.17 per share.

[*] In the related estate tax area, § 2031(b) of the Internal Revenue Code of 1954 specifically provides that: "In the case of stock and securities of a corporation the value of which, by reason of their not being listed on an exchange and by reason of the absence of sales thereof, cannot be determined with reference to bid and asked prices or with reference to sales prices, the value thereof shall be determined by taking into consideration, in addition to all other factors, the value of stock or securities of corporations engaged in the same or a similar line of business which are listed on an exchange." 26 U. S. C. (1958 Ed.) § 2031(b).

Central Trust Co. *vs.* U.S.

30 and September 30, 1954 (thus eliminating distortions due to seasonal factors), are the starting points. As stated, it would then be proper to make such adjustments therein as would be necessary to eliminate abnormal and nonrecurring items and to redistribute items of expense to their proper periods. In these cases, this normalizing process would require (a) the elimination from the years 1950 to 1952 of the abnormal, non-recurring losses incident to its financing subsidiary, which had been completely liquidated by 1952; (b) the elimination of the abnormally large 1951 profits due to the Korean war; (c) the redistribution of the expenses attributable to the establishment subsequent to 1951 of a retirement plan, which expenses, although borne in later years, were also applicable to 1950 and 1951, thereby overstating 1950 and 1951 profits and similarly depressing 1953 and 1954 profits; (d) the shift from 1954 to 1951 of a renegotiation refund paid with respect to excessive 1951 profits; (e) the elimination from 1954 of the abnormally large charge relating to the accrual in 1954 of certain expenses actually attributable to 1955, as hereinabove explained, and which resulted in the doubling up of 2 years of such expenses in 1954, as permitted by a then recent change in the tax laws. The method adopted in making these adjustments, and the adjusted profit figures resulting therefrom, are set forth in detail in finding 47.

As indicated, it would then be appropriate to give due consideration and weight to the trend of such earnings. Greater weight should fairly be given to the most recent years and periods. The method adopted in finding 48 of assigning greater weight to the later periods is a reasonably accurate one, and indicates that as of June 30 and September 30, 1954, Heekin's reasonably expected annual earnings per share would be $1.93 and $1.79, based on average annual earnings of $491,460.86 and $454,492.82, respectively.

As to dividends and dividend-paying capacity, it has already been indicated that as of the gift dates, it could reasonably be expected that Heekin would continue to pay in the foreseeable future its usual 50-cent annual dividend. Indeed, on its aforesaid earnings basis, this would appear to be a conservative distribution. However,

while the declaration by the board of directors of a small increase might have been considered a possibility—a 10-cent increase would, for instance, result in a corporate outlay of only $25,412 on the 254,125 shares outstanding—it seems clear, nevertheless, that no substantially larger payment, at least for some time to come, could reasonably have been anticipated. Heekin's equipment was, as shown, not modern and the Company was in need of relatively large sums for equipment and plant modernization if it hoped to continue to be a competitive factor in the industry. For such a program, the Company would have to depend almost entirely on retained earnings. A further limitation on the Company's dividend-paying capacity was its repayment obligations on its long-term debt. Annual installments on principal of $150,000 had to be made through 1965, plus 20 percent of the net income (less $150,000) for the preceding year.

As to book value, the Company's balance sheets showed the book value per share to be, conservatively, $33.15 and $33.54 as of June 30 and September 30, 1954, respectively (findings 51-53). These statements also showed the Company to be in a current sound financial condition. As of June 30, 1954, current assets alone, amounting to almost $8,700,000, far exceeded its total liabilities of approximately $4,700,000, including its long-term debt. Its ratio of current assets to current liabilities was 3.17 to 1.

With the above basic data applicable to Heekin, it is then appropriate to select as closely comparable companies as is possible whose stocks are actively traded on an exchange, and to ascertain what ratios their market prices bear to their earnings, dividends, and book values. The application of such ratios to Heekin would then give a reasonable approximation of what Heekin's stock would sell for if it too were actively traded on an exchange.

[Proper Comparatives]

A study of all the numerous companies considered by the experts as proper comparatives indicates that five of them, i.e., Pacific Can Company, United Can and Glass Company, National Can Corporation, Brockway Glass Co., Inc., and Thatcher Glass Manufacturing Co., Inc., are, while

Central Trust Co. *vs.* U.S.

by no means perfect comparables, certainly at least reasonably satisfactory for the purpose in question. The detailed reasons for their selection are set forth in finding 57. In size they all fall generally into Heekin's class, and the nature of their operations is also comparable. In addition, five companies give a sufficiently broad base. Such companies as American Can, Continental Can, and Crown Cork & Seal, for the reasons already indicated, are eliminated (finding 56).

After similarly computing the earnings, as adjusted, of the comparatives for the same periods as for Heekin (finding 58), and similarly weighting them to give effect to the trend factor (finding 59), the average ratio of their market prices to their adjusted earnings as of August 3 and October 25, 1954 (the "price-earnings" ratio), was 9.45 and 9.84 to 1, respectively (finding 62). Thus, on the basis only of earnings, Heekin's stock would similarly sell for $18.24 and $17.61 per share on such dates.

Similarly, the comparatives' dividend payments for the 12 months ending June 30 and September 30, 1954, after making some allowance for United's stock dividend, show an average percent yield of 3.50 and 3.56 respectively (finding 64). Thus, on the basis only of dividend yield, Heekin's stock would similarly sell for $14.29 and $14.05 per share on August 3 and October 25, 1954, respectively (finding 65).

As to book value, the average market prices of the comparatives were 83.96 and 86.39 percent, respectively, of the book values of their common stocks on said dates (finding 66). Thus, on the sole basis of the average relationship between such book values and market prices, Heekin's comparable market prices on said dates would be $27.83 and $28.98 (finding 67).

[Weight Accorded Factors]

However, since the three factors of earnings, dividends, and book value are not entitled to equal weight, it becomes necessary to consider their relative importance in the case of a company such as Heekin. In this connection, plaintiffs' contention that in these cases no factor is to be considered of greater importance than dividend yield and that no investor would reasonably be expected to buy Heekin stock at a price which would afford a yield of less than 7 percent, cannot be accepted, not only for the reasons set forth above concerning the general relative importance of this factor but also because it is not supported by the specific data relating to the container industry as shown by the comparatives' yields. Investors were purchasing the stocks of comparable container companies which were yielding much less return than 7 percent. As shown, the average dividend yield of the five comparative companies was only around 3½ percent. Investors were purchasing Pacific Can at a price which afforded a yield of less than 3 percent. Indeed, they were purchasing National Can at more than $13 a share although it was paying no dividend at all.

Considering all the circumstances, it would appear appropriate to accept defendant's proposals in this respect and to consider earnings as entitled to 50 percent of the contribution to total value, and to give dividend yield (which in this case would appear to be substantially equivalent to dividend-paying capacity) 30 percent, and book value 20 percent, thereof. Cf. *Bader v. United States, supra,* in which the court gave 50 percent weight to earnings, and divided the remaining 50 percent equally between the dividend yield and book value factors. Book value indicates how much of a company's net assets valued as a going concern stands behind each share of its stock and is therefore an important factor in valuing the shares. As defendant's expert pointed out, this is the factor that plays such a large part in giving a stock value during periods when earnings may vanish and dividends may be suspended. However, principally because book value is based upon valuing the assets as a going concern, which would not be realistic in the event of a liquidation of the corporation, a situation which a minority stockholder would be powerless to bring about in any event, and for the additional reasons set forth in finding 50, this factor is, in the case of a manufacturing company with a consistent earnings and dividend record, normally not given greater weight than the other two factors.

On the above percentage bases, the fair market value of Heekin's stock on August 3 and October 25, 1954, would be $18.98 and $18.83 respectively (finding 69).

Central Trust Co. *vs.* U.S.

[Lack of Marketability]

These prices, however, assume active trading for Heekin's stock on an exchange, as was the situation with the comparatives. As shown, the closely held nature of, and the infrequent trading in, Heekin's stock resulted in a lack of marketability which would affect its market value. Equating the proper discount to be taken for this factor with the costs that would be involved in creating a market for the stock, a method which defendant concedes is reasonable, results in a deduction of approximately 12.17 percent for a company of Heekin's size and for blocks of 30,000 and 40,000 shares. On this basis, the fair market values of the Heekin stock as of August 3 and October 25, 1954, would be $16.67 and $16.54 respectively.

These are the values resulting largely from strictly formula and statistical applications. While such use of figures and formulas produces, of course, results which are of important significance, and may in certain instances be given conclusive weight, it is nevertheless recognized that determinations of fair market value can not be reduced to formula alone, but depend "upon all the relevant facts," including "the elements of common sense, informed judgment and reasonableness." Revenue Ruling, sec. 3.01. The question of fair market value of a stock "is ever one of fact and not of formula" and evidence which gives "life to [the] figures" is essential. *Estate of James Smith v. Commissioner*, 46 B. T. A. 337, 341-2. The selection of comparatives has been a particularly troublesome problem in these cases. National Can's erratic earnings record, even though adjustments are attempted to normalize its situation (findings 57-58), and its nonpayment of dividends (finding 64), certainly weaken its position as a comparative, and suggest the desirability of an adjustment in the final market value figures set forth above. Pacific Can's sharp rise in price after August 3, 1954, justifies a similar adjustment for the October 25, 1954, valuation. While the inclusion of the glass container manufacturers with their higher dividend yields tends to neutralize somewhat the National Can situation, an adjustment downward would, in fairness to plaintiffs, nevertheless guard against their being prejudiced by the aforementioned selections of comparatives.

Furthermore, while the sales of Heekin stock at $7.50 warrant, as hereinabove pointed out, only minimal consideration, the figures derived from the above formula give them no cognizance whatsoever.

[Adjustment for Comparison]

Giving important weight to the figure of $16.67 produced by the application of the comparative appraisal method as applied herein, but viewing it in light of all the facts and circumstances involved in these cases, it is concluded that the fair market value of the 30,000 shares given on August 3, 1954, was $15.50 per share.

The market for stocks of the can and glass container manufacturing companies fell somewhat between August 3 and October 25, 1954, so that ordinarily on that basis as well as on the basis of Heekin's own financial and operating positions on October 25 as compared with August 3, a slightly lower value would be justified as of October 25 (although one of plaintiffs' experts felt that, insofar as Heekin stock is concerned, the same value should be applied to both dates, and another came out with a higher value for the second date). It seems clear, however, that the brightened prospects for increased business and profits resulting from the Company's decision in August 1954 to embark upon the beer can business and to satisfy further the demands of its largest customer for new products would, in Heekin's instance, tend to neutralize the market decline and to make its stock at least as valuable on October 25 as it had been on August 3. Accordingly, it is concluded that the fair market value of the 40,002 shares given on October 25, 1954, was also $15.50 per share.

A $15.50 valuation represents a price to adjusted earnings ratio on the gift dates of between 8 and 9 percent (somewhat less than the 9-10 percent average of the comparatives (finding 62)), a dividend yield of 3.23 percent (slightly less than the 3.5 percent average of the comparatives (finding 64)), and only 46 percent of book value (considerably less than the approximately 85 percent of the comparatives (finding 66)). On these bases, it is a figure that is fair to both sides.

Plaintiffs should consider that such a valuation prices the stock only at an amount

Central Trust Co. *vs.* U.S.

representing the difference between current assets and total liabilities, including its long-term debt, as shown by its June 30, 1954, balance sheet. Thus, at such price, the value of the stock would be represented in whole by current assets, with no consideration whatsoever given to plant, equipment, or any other assets. As such, it would appear to be a conservative price indeed. Despite the difficulties under which it is laboring in a highly competitive industry, Heekin was, as of the valuation dates, a profitable, dividend-paying company, in sound financial condition, in an industry in which demand was at record levels, and in which it was forging ahead with relatively large investments in new fields holding bright prospects. Only a disregard of these favorable factors would warrant any lower valuation.

On the other hand, defendant should consider that such a valuation would give an investor a dividend yield of less than 3.5 percent on his investment, with little prospect of any significant increase in the foreseeable future. The fact that the Company was, on the gift dates, a relatively small one competing, with a comparatively old plant, against the giants of the industry operating at high efficiency with the most modern equipment, makes unwarranted a valuation of this closely held stock representing only a minority interest on any significantly higher basis. For these reasons also the $15.50 valuation is considered to be fair and just to both plaintiffs and defendant.

On this valuation basis, plaintiffs are entitled to recover, the amount of the recovery to be determined in accordance with Rule 38(c).

Estate of Andrews *vs.* Commissioner

Fair market value has long been defined as the price at which property would change hands between a willing buyer and a willing seller, neither being under any compulsion to buy or to sell and both having reasonable knowledge of relevant facts. Sec. 20.2031–1(b), Estate Tax Regs.; *United States v. Cartwright*, 411 U.S. 546, 551 (1973). This is a question of fact, with the trier of fact having the duty to weigh all relevant evidence of value and to draw appropriate inferences. *Hamm v. Commissioner*, 325 F.2d 934, 938 (8th Cir. 1963), affg. a Memorandum Opinion of this Court.

In determining the value of unlisted stocks, actual arm's-length sales of such stock in the normal course of business within a reasonable time before or after the valuation date are the best criteria of market value. *Duncan Industries, Inc. v. Commissioner*, 73 T.C. 266, 276 (1979). However, the stock of these four corporations has never been publicly traded, and there is no evidence of any sales of stock in these corporations at any time near the date of decedent's death. In the absence of arm's-length sales, the value of closely held stock must be determined indirectly by weighing the corporation's net worth, prospective earning power, dividend-paying capacity, and other relevant factors. *Estate of Leyman v. Commissioner*, 40 T.C. 100, 119 (1963), remanded on other grounds 344 F.2d 763 (6th Cir. 1965); sec. 20.2031–2(f), Estate Tax Regs.[3] These

---

[3] Sec. 20.2031–2(f), Estate Tax Regs., provides:

(f) *Where selling prices or bid and asked prices are unavailable.* If the provisions of paragraphs (b), (c), and (d) of this section are inapplicable because actual sale prices and bona fide bid and asked prices are lacking, then the fair market value is to be determined by taking the following factors into consideration:

(1) In the case of corporate or other bonds, the soundness of the security, the interest yield, the date of maturity, and other relevant factors; and

(2) In the case of shares of stock, the company's net worth, prospective earning power and dividend-paying capacity, and other relevant factors.

Some of the "other relevant factors" referred to in subparagraphs (1) and (2) of this paragraph are: the good will of the business; the economic outlook in the particular industry; the company's position in the industry and its management; the degree of control of the business represented by the block of stock to be valued; and the values of securities of corporations engaged in the same or similar lines of business which are listed on a stock exchange. However, the weight to be accorded such comparisons or any other evidentiary factors considered in the determination of a value depends upon the facts of each case. In addition to the relevant factors described above, consideration shall also be given to nonoperating assets, * * *

Estate of Andrews *vs.* Commissioner

factors cannot be applied with mathematical precision. Rather, the weight to be given to each factor must be tailored to account for the particular facts of each case. See *Messing v. Commissioner*, 48 T.C. 502, 512 (1967).

We believe, however, the corporations here cannot be characterized for valuation purposes as solely investment companies or solely operating companies. The cases cited by respondent,[10] which involved corporations holding only cash, commercial paper, or marketable securities, are readily distinguishable on the ground that the corporations involved here were actively engaged in the real estate management business. But cases dealing with corporations owning factories and other industrial or commercial operations are also not directly on point.[11] Unlike many industrial companies, where the value of the manufacturing equipment and plant is tied to the nature of the manufacturing operation, here, the value of the underlying real estate will retain most of its inherent value even if the corporation is not efficient in securing a stream of rental income. It seems reasonable to assume, as we did in *Estate of Heckscher v. Commissioner*, 63 T.C. 485, 493 (1975), that a—

potential buyer would have to forego some current return on his investment in exchange for an interest in a net worth much more valuable than the price he pays for the stock, and the seller would have to be willing to part with an equity interest in the company for much less than its indicated value in return for something that would produce a greater yield on his investment. * * *

---

[10]The following cases were cited by respondent: *Estate of Cruikshank v. Commissioner*, 9 T.C. 162 (1947); *Gallun v. Commissioner, supra*; *Estate of Thalheimer v. Commissioner, supra*; *Estate of Cotchett v. Commissioner*, T.C. Memo. 1974–31; and *Richardson v. Commissioner*, a Memorandum Opinion of this Court dated Nov. 30, 1943, affd. 151 F.2d 102 (2d Cir. 1945). *Estate of Lee v. Commissioner*, 69 T.C. 860 (1978), in which we used net asset values in arriving at the value of a close corporation that held primarily real estate is likewise distinguishable because the real estate was not rental property but rather undeveloped property that offered no immediate prospects for taxable income to the corporation.

[11]See *Waterman v. Commissioner*, T.C. Memo. 1961–225, in which we rejected both respondent's valuation based solely on net asset values and petitioner's valuation based solely on earning capacity as inappropriate for a corporation holding improved rental property; and *Estate of Tompkins v. Commissioner*, T.C. Memo. 1961–338, in which we rejected similar contentions with respect to a corporation holding unimproved real estate.

Estate of Andrews *vs.* Commissioner

Furthermore, regardless of whether the corporation is seen as primarily an operating company, as opposed to an investment company, courts should not restrict consideration to only one approach to valuation, such as capitalization of earnings or net asset values. See *Hamm v. Commissioner*, 325 F.2d 934 (8th Cir. 1963), affg. a Memorandum Opinion of this Court; *Portland Manufacturing Co. v. Commissioner*, 56 T.C. 58, 80 (1971); *Estate of Schroeder v. Commissioner*, 13 T.C. 259 (1949); *Hooper v. Commissioner*, 41 B.T.A. 114 (1940).[12] Certainly, the degree to which the corporation is actively engaged in producing income rather than merely holding property for investment should influence the weight to be given to the values arrived at under the different approaches but it should not dictate the use of one approach to the exclusion of all others.

The regulations[13] call for all relevant factors to be examined and, in a case such as this, we believe values arrived at under all the accepted valuation methods should be considered. We therefore believe respondent's expert was incorrect to simply reject earnings and dividend-paying capacity valuations because they produced too low a result. Certainly, a prospective buyer would not so reject one particular type of valuation. A buyer of stock in these corporations would necessarily look to the earning capacity for part of his return on his investment. Nevertheless, this would not be the only factor that he would consider. Undoubtedly, he would also give substantial weight to each corporation's underlying net asset value even though he would have no ability to directly realize this value by forcing liquidation.

---

[12] See also *Estate of Dooly v. Commissioner*, T.C. Memo. 1972–164; *Lippman v. Commissioner*, T.C. Memo. 1965–73; and *Wallace v. United States*, an unpublished opinion (D. Mass. 1981, 49 AFTR 2d 82–1482, 82–1 USTC par. 13,442), in which the court stated:

"The 'willing buyer' and 'willing seller' * * * test the experts' advice, and the formulas the experts advance to bolster their advice, against common sense. The willing buyer and willing seller are not limited to choosing one formula or another among competing formulas advanced by experts. [49 AFTR 2d 82–1482.]"

[13] See sec. 20.2031–2(f), Estate Tax Regs.

Estate of Andrews *vs.* Commissioner

Lack of Control and Marketability Discounts

In Mr. Bard's valuation report and in computing the amount of deficiency, the net asset values of the four corporations were each reduced first by a 25-percent discount based on a comparison with publicly traded closed end mutual fund shares, and then by discounts ranging from 11.9 percent to 20.74 percent based on Securities Exchange Commission flotation rates. These discounts were designed to reflect the shares' restricted marketability and lack of control.

Rev. Rul. 81–253, 1981–2 C.B. 187, was published by respondent after the statutory notice was issued, and it sets forth respondent's current position concerning the allowance of minority discounts in valuing stock of closely held family corporations. Based on Rev. Rul. 81–253, respondent now argues that no discounts for lack of control or restricted marketability should be applied, although he has not asserted a deficiency greater than that asserted in the statutory notice. Thus, respondent argues that discounts should not be applied to the extent they would result in reducing the values below those asserted in the notice of deficiency.

Petitioner has questioned whether it is proper for respondent to now argue against allowing a minority discount even though he allowed a discount in computing the deficiency in the statutory notice. However, this is not a case where petitioner was surprised at trial by respondent's introduction of a new issue. It is clear that petitioner was prepared for the minority discount question being raised at trial, and has devoted large portions of its briefs to rebutting respondent's position that no minority discount should be allowed. Therefore, we find no merit to petitioner's claim that the minority discount issue has been improperly raised by respondent. See *Llorente v. Commissioner*, 74 T.C. 260, 269 (1980), modified on other grounds 649 F.2d 152 (2d Cir. 1981).

Respondent argues that no discounts should be allowed because all the shareholders in the four corporations, including decedent, shared in control. According to respondent's argument, the hypothetical "willing seller" used in arriving at

Estate of Andrews *vs.* Commissioner

valuation of the stock must be presumed to be one of the five family members, including decedent, who held stock in the corporations and shared an element of control. Respondent reasons further that such a willing seller would not have sold his shares except as part of the controlling family interest, unless to another family member or the corporations, themselves. If the shares were sold in this way, respondent contends they would retain their control value, and no minority discount would be justified.

In their arguments, neither petitioner nor respondent clearly focuses on the fact that two conceptually distinct discounts are involved here, one for lack of marketability and the other for lack of control.[18] The minority shareholder discount is designed to reflect the decreased value of shares that do not convey control of a closely held corporation. The lack of marketability discount, on the other hand, is designed to reflect the fact that there is no ready market for shares in a closely held corporation. Although there may be some overlap between these two discounts in that lack of control may reduce marketability, it should be borne in mind that even controlling shares in a nonpublic corporation suffer from lack of marketability because of the absence of a ready private placement market and the fact that flotation costs would have to be incurred if the corporation were to publicly offer its stock. However, the distinction between the two discounts is not crucial for purposes of this case. Because respondent's basis for opposing both discounts is the same—that the hypothetical willing buyer must be seen as a family member—our subsequent discussion, like the parties' briefs, will consider the two discounts together.

The leading case dealing with this question is *Estate of Bright v. United States*, 658 F.2d 999 (5th Cir. 1981) (en banc), in which the court recognized that a minority interest in a corporation should not be seen as having any control value,

---

[18]See Fellows & Painter, "Valuing Close Corporations for Federal Wealth Transfer Taxes: A Statutory Solution to the Disappearing Wealth Syndrome," 30 Stan. L. Rev. 895, 920 (1978).

Estate of Andrews *vs.* Commissioner

even though the family unit had control of the corporation. The case involved whether a minority discount should be allowed in valuing a decedent's undivided one-half interest in the control block of 55 percent of the stock of a corporation, where the other one-half interest in the control block was owned by the husband of the decedent (who was also executor of the estate and subsequently trustee of the testamentary trust that received the stock in issue). Two major bases for its decision were explained by the court. First, it found that established case law did not support any type of "family attribution" in which the control of the corporation was attributed among family members. The Fifth Circuit noted that the Tax Court, since at least 1940, has uniformly valued a decedent's stock for estate tax purposes as a minority interest when the decedent, himself, owned less than 50 percent of the stock regardless of whether control of the corporation was in the decedent's family.[19] The court also cited two District Court opinions that took the same position,[20] and it stated that it had found no estate tax cases supporting respondent's position. The court found further that case authority in the analogous gift tax area also supported the taxpayer's position, although not unanimously.[21]

---

[19]The following Tax Court cases were cited by the Fifth Circuit for this proposition: *Estate of Zaiger v. Commissioner*, 64 T.C. 927 (1975); *Estate of Leyman v. Commissioner*, 40 T.C. 100, 119 (1963); *Estate of DeGuebriant v. Commissioner*, 14 T.C. 611 (1950), revd. on other grounds 186 F.2d 307 (2d Cir. 1951); *Hooper v. Commissioner*, 41 B.T.A. 114 (1940); *Estate of Kirkpatrick v. Commissioner*, T.C. Memo. 1975–344; *Estate of Stoddard v. Commissioner*, T.C. Memo. 1975–207; *Estate of Thalheimer v. Commissioner, supra*; *Estate of Maxcy v. Commissioner*, T.C. Memo. 1969–158, revd. on other grounds 441 F.2d 192 (5th Cir. 1971); *Estate of Katz v. Commissioner*, T.C. Memo. 1968–171. We agree with the Fifth Circuit that these cases show our established view that a decedent's stock in a family controlled corporation should be seen as a minority interest whenever the decedent individually did not have control.

[20]The two District Court opinions cited by the court were *Obermer v. United States*, 238 F. Supp. 29 (D. Hawaii 1964); and *Sundquist v. United States*, an unpublished opinion (E.D. Wash. 1974, 34 AFTR 2d 74–6337, 74–2 USTC par. 13,035).

[21]Cases cited by the court for the proposition that minority discounts were allowed for gifts of stock in family controlled corporations included *Meijer v. Commissioner*, T.C. Memo. 1979–344; *Koffler v. Commissioner*, T.C. Memo. 1978–159; *Estate of Heppenstal v. Commissioner*, a Memorandum Opinion of this Court dated Jan. 31, 1949; *Whittemore v. Fitzpatrick*, 127 F. Supp. 710 (D. Conn. 1954); *Clark v. United States*, an unpublished opinion (E.D. N.C. 1975, 36 AFTR 2d 75–6417, 75–1 USTC par. 13,076).

Estate of Andrews *vs.* Commissioner

The second major reason cited in the *Estate of Bright* opinion for applying a minority discount was based upon the concept of the hypothetical willing-buyer, willing-seller rule. Section 20.2031–1(b), Estate Tax Regs., sets forth the following rule, which has been universally applied by the courts and respondent:

The fair market value is the price at which the property would change hands between a willing buyer and a willing seller, neither being under any compulsion to buy or to sell and both having reasonable knowledge of relevant facts. • • •

The Fifth Circuit saw this language from the regulation as indicating that the "willing seller" is a hypothetical seller rather than the particular estate. Thus, the willing seller should not be identified with the decedent, and the decedent's stock should not be included as part of a family unit for valuation purposes. Nor was it proper, according to the Fifth Circuit, to place any weight upon the identity of the parties that actually received the stock after distribution from the estate. For purposes of valuation, one should construct a hypothetical sale from a hypothetical willing seller to a similarly hypothetical willing buyer.

In *Propstra v. United States*, 680 F.2d 1248 (9th Cir. 1982), the Ninth Circuit followed *Estate of Bright* and discounted the value of an undivided one-half interest in real estate held by the decedent and his wife as community property at the time of death. The Ninth Circuit noted that Congress has explicitly directed that family attribution or unity of ownership principles be applied in other areas of Federal taxation, and felt that in the absence of any legislative directive, it should not judicially require such principles to be applied in the estate tax area. Furthermore, the court emphasized the advantage of using an objective hypothetical willing-buyer, willing-seller standard, instead of a subjective inquiry into the feelings, attitudes, and anticipated behavior of heirs and legatees, which might well be boundless.

Respondent argues that the Fifth Circuit misinterpreted the concept of the hypothetical willing seller and willing buyer. In his briefs, he relies primarily upon three cases to support his

Estate of Andrews *vs.* Commissioner

proposition that a minority discount should not be applied if family members control a corporation. *Richardson v. Commissioner*, a Memorandum Opinion of this Court dated November 30, 1943, affd. 151 F.2d 102 (2d Cir. 1945), involved a family holding company whose assets were readily marketable securities. On appeal, the Second Circuit upheld the value established by us but questioned whether we had used the correct standard of valuation. Our *Richardson* opinion must be read narrowly in view of the long series of subsequent cases in which we have allowed discounts in valuing shares of family corporations that held operating as well as investment assets. *Blanchard v. United States*, 291 F. Supp. 348 (S.D. Iowa 1968), contains language supportive of respondent's position. But the court stressed that it was dealing with a unique situation involving a planned sale of all the family's shares of stock in the corporation. At first blush, *Rothgery v. United States*, 201 Ct. Cl. 183, 475 F.2d 591 (1973), seems to support respondent. But even though its valuation was phrased in terms of seeing the willing buyer as a particular person (the family member who already held almost 50 percent of the shares of the corporation), the court also explicitly found that there would have been other potential buyers for the decedent's shares of the stock at the same price if the stock had been offered for sale to persons outside the Rothgery family. Thus, despite analyzing the hypothetical sale in terms of the sale to a particular person, the court evidently attributed no premium to the fact that the family member would assure himself of control by obtaining these shares.

Three cases provide at best weak support for respondent's position that no discounts should be applied here. Opposed to this meager case law in favor of respondent is the large number of cases allowing such discounts, which were discussed in the *Estate of Bright* opinion. We see no reason to depart from such established precedent but follow the Fifth Circuit's well-reasoned and thoroughly researched opinion. Respondent's approach would have us tailor "hypothetical" so that the willing seller and willing buyer were seen as the particular persons who would most likely undertake the transaction. However, the case law and regulations require a truly hypo-

Estate of Andrews *vs.* Commissioner

thetical willing seller and willing buyer. We must assume these hypothetical parties exist even though the reality of the situation may be that the stock will most probably be sold to a particular party or type of person. Certainly, the hypothetical sale should not be constructed in a vacuum isolated from the actual facts that affect the value of the stock in the hands of decedent, but we do not see any actual facts in this case that require the stock to be valued as anything other than minority interests in each corporation.

Overall Valuation

We have pointed out above the defects of the approaches used by both parties' experts. Having taken diametrically opposed views as to the factors to be weighed in valuing the stock involved in this case, the parties "failed successfully to conclude settlement negotiations—a process clearly more conducive to the proper disposition of disputes such as this." *Messing v. Commissioner*, 48 T.C. 502, 512 (1967). Because we have concluded that none of the experts gave appropriate weight to net assets as well as earning and dividend-paying capacity, we must necessarily make our own best judgments of value. While we have considered the valuation reports of Messrs. Wendin, Lefko, and Bard, we have also weighed all other relevant factors such as the extremely conservative business attitudes and practices of the management, the nature of the real estate holdings, the amount of cash and other liquid assets held by the corporations, and the business climate on the valuation date, both overall and for these corporations in particular. We have discounted the values because of the restricted marketability of the shares and the lack of control a hypothetical willing buyer of these minority

Estate of Andrews *vs.* Commissioner

shares would be able to exercise. Based on all these factors and on the entire record, we conclude and find as a fact the following date-of-death fair market values for the stock held by decedent:

Andrews, Inc	$302,400
St. Anthony	158,000
Green Mountain	56,000
W.F. & H.H	64,800

Decision will be entered under Rule 155.

Righter *vs.* U.S.

[*Companies Not Comparable*]

Plaintiff attacks the valuation of such experts on various grounds. She says the companies they selected as comparatives are not truly comparable since they manufacture such items as toys and dolls, which appeal to a younger class of consumer than does Scrabble. She further argues that not enough consideration was given to certain unfavorable factors, such as (1) the company's being, as of the valuation date, in effect only a two-product business (Scrabble and Parcheesi), with over 60 percent of its sales in one product; (2) the company's relatively small size as compared with its closest competitor (the Milton Bradley Company); (3) the loss, during the six-month period preceding the valuation date, of its two top sales executives who had long been associated with the company; (4) the nonownership by the company of the Scrabble trademarks and copyrights and its position as only a licensee; (5) the legal ability of the licensor to enter into the business of manufacturing the same type of Scrabble games as S & R was licensed to manufacture; (6) the highly seasonal nature of its business, with a substantial part of its annual volume of sales being accounted for around the Christmas season, thus making it most vulnerable to strikes both within its unionized factory, and by such outside unions as those in the trucking and shipping industries, including the longshoremen;[17] and (7) considering the type of business it is in, its peculiar vulnerability to the public's fancy.[18]

We agree with the plaintiff that the companies used by the expert witnesses of defendant as comparables were not in fact truly comparable to S & R. Our trial judge found that there are no other publicly traded companies that are comparable to S & R in terms of game manufacture and that for this reason S & R was compared by such witnesses with other companies "which are essentially in the business of manufacturing toys." We do not think a company that manufactures toys or toys and games can be accurately compared to a company like S & R that manufactures only games. Their products appeal to and are used by different age groups. They are different in many other respects as shown herein. Therefore, since the basis for the opinions of defendant's expert witnesses was grounded on the comparison of companies that were not truly comparable, their analyses based on the comparative appraisal method have but little, if any, weight in establishing the fair market value of the S & R stock. This court dealt with the principle of comparables in *Jones Bros. Bakery v. United States* [69-2 USTC ¶ 9474], 188 Ct. Cl. 226, 411 F. 2d 1282 (1969). There the problem was whether or not the company had paid its officers more than reasonable salaries and deducted the same as an expense on their income tax returns. The government offered evidence of salaries of executives of another company that it contended was comparable to the plaintiff company to show plaintiff's salaries were too high. The court held that while the two companies were similar in many respects, they were also quite different in other ways, and were not truly comparables. The court proceeded by a jury verdict on the whole record to fix proper salaries for plaintiff's officers that were lower than the amounts deducted by the plaintiff but higher than those contended for by the government.

In the case before us, the government relied on the testimony of its expert witnesses to establish the fair market value of the stock by the comparative appraisal method. Since the companies used by such witnesses for comparison were not true comparables, it becomes necessary for the court to review the whole record and consider all the evidence to arrive at the correct value of the stock.

---

[17] Most of the titles, one of the components of the Scrabble game, are imported. S & R ships its products primarily by truck.

[18] Plaintiff points to the upsurge in its 1954 and 1955 sales and profits after S & R first began marketing Scrabble, followed by the drastic drops therein in 1956, when Scrabble's initial flurry of popularity receded. From approximately $1,900,000 in 1953, sales jumped to over $5,000,000 and $4,000,000 in 1954 and 1955, respectively. They then dropped to $1,800,000 in 1956. Similarly, gross profits went from $733,000 in 1953 to $2,300,000 and $1,700,000 in 1954 and 1955, respectively, falling back to $710,000 in 1956. Plaintiff says the experts' going back only five years resulted in their failing to consider this particular period in S & R's life.

Righter vs. U.S.

We held in *Penn Yan Agway Cooperative v. United States* [69-2 USTC ¶ 9719], 189 Ct. Cl. 434, 417 F. 2d 1372 (1969):

It is a well established rule of law, carefully analyzed and stated in *Drybrough v. United States* [62-2 USTC ¶ 12,098], 208 F. Supp. 279 (W. D. Ky. 1962), that *the market value of common stock* in a closely held corporation, there being no market sales of such stock, *must be determined upon consideration of all relevant factors*, such as earning capacity, anticipated profits, book value, and dividend yield. * * * [Emphasis supplied.] [*Id.* at 446, 417 F. 2d at 1378.]

We find a similar statement in *Arc Realty Co. v. C. I. R.* [61-2 USTC ¶ 9689], 295 F. 2d 98 (8th Cir. 1961) as follows:

The question of "fair market value," defined to be "the price at which property would change hands in a transaction between a willing buyer and a willing seller, neither being under compulsion to buy nor to sell and both being informed," *O'Malley v. Ames* [52-1 USTC ¶ 9361], 8 Cir., 197 F. 2d 256, at page 257; *Fitts' Estate v. Commissioner of Internal Revenue* [56-2 USTC ¶ 11,648], 8 Cir., 237 F. 2d 729, 731, is one of fact and cannot be established on the basis of fixed rules or formulae. Among the factors properly to be considered in making the determination are corporate assets, earnings, dividend policy, earning power of the corporation, prospects of the corporation, book value, character of the management, competition and other factors which an informed purchaser and informed seller would take into account. *O'Malley v. Ames, supra; Fitts' Estate v. Commissioner of Internal Revenue, supra.* [*Id.* at 103.]

The defendant contends that we should accept the evidence of its expert witnesses because they were experts in the field of market value analysis and were the only experts who testified. We are not required to do so. This was made clear by our decision in *United States v. Northern Paiute Nation,* 183 Ct. Cl. 321, 346, 393 F. 2d 786, 800 (1968) where we said:

The Indians' other complaint about the findings is that the Commission rejected its expert appraisers' views, and did not spell out why in detailed findings. In legal appraisement, however, widely divergent opinion testimony is the rule rather than the exception. The trier of fact must

decide first, of course, if such testimony is competent and and admissible. Before us, no party claims that this case was decided with respect to any issue on inadmissible testimony. The Indians wanted the Commission to take up the reasoning of its appraisers step by step, and either accept each step or show reasons for rejecting it. Having competent testimony before it, the Commission was not restricted to swallowing it whole or rejecting it utterly. It did not have to refute what it did not accept as controlling. It could, and apparently did, synthesize in its mind the immense record before it, determine to what extent opinion evidence rested on facts, consider and weigh it all, and come up with figures supported by all the evidence, perhaps, though not identified with any of it. * * *

In addition to the other circumstances favorable to the plaintiff's view in this case, as set forth above, there is the significant fact that the stock involved here was a minority interest of only 17 percent in a closely held corporation. It is logical to assume that this would adversely affect its value if it were offered for sale on the open market, as few people would be interested in buying it under these circumstances. The decided cases support this view. In *Drybrough v. United States* [62-2 USTC ¶ 12,098], 208 F. Supp. 279 (W. D. Ky. 1962), the court discounted by 35 percent the value of minority interests in a corporation. In that case the court cited with approval the decision in *Whittemore v. Fitzpatrick* [54-2 USTC ¶ 10,976], 127 F. Supp. 710 (D. C. Conn., 1954), where the court allowed a 50 percent discount for a minority interest in stock of a corporation, and stated further:

Other cases holding that minority stock interests in closed corporations are usually worth much less than the proportionate share of the assets to which they attach are *Andrew B. C. Dohrmann* [CCH Dec. 5942], (1930) 19 B. T. A. 507; *Cravens v. Welch* [35-1 USTC ¶ 9181], (D. C. Cal., 1935) 10 F. Supp. 94; *Estate of Irene De-Guebriant* [CCH Dec. 17,600], (1950) 14 T. C. 611, reversed on other grounds *Claflin v. Commissioner of Internal Revenue* [51-1 USTC ¶ 10,791], 2 Cir., 186 F. 2d 307; *Mathilde B. Hooper* [CCH Dec. 10,965], (1940) 41 B. T. A. 114, 129; *Bartram v. Graham* [57-2 USTC ¶ 11,721], (D. C. Conn., 1957) 157 F. Supp. 757; *Bader v. United*

Righter *vs.* U.S.

States [59-1 USTC ¶ 11,865], (D. C. Ill., 1959) 172 F. Supp. 833, and *Snyder's Estate v. United States* [61-1 USTC ¶ 11,987], (4 Cir., 1961) 285 F. 2d 857. [208 F. Supp. at 287.]

The problem before us is always a difficult one. It is never possible to fix the value of corporate stock in a closely held corporation which is not sold on the open market with mathematical exactness, and we are not required to do so. This was aptly stated by the court in *Arc Realty Co. v. C. I. R., supra,* when it said:

* * * The matter of fixing the fair market value of corporate stock for capital gains treatment, with numerous factors entering the picture, obviously cannot be accomplished with exactness or complete accuracy. * * * [295 F. 2d at 103.]

Many times courts solve problems like the one before us by considering all the evidence and the whole record and then deciding what is right and just under all the facts and circumstances. We did this as to officers' salaries in *Jones Bros. Bakery v. United States, supra,* and again in *Meredith Broadcasting Co. v. United States* [69-1 USTC ¶ 9126], 186 Ct. Cl. 1, 405 F. 2d 1214 (1968) in arriving at the value of certain intangibles. We think we are justified in following this procedure in the instant case. It appears to be fair and right and in accordance with justice to both parties that we do so.

Based on all the evidence and the whole record, we conclude that the fair market value of the 337 shares of S & R stock as of April 24, 1961, was $700 per share.

Luce, Jr. *vs.* U.S.

Opinion *

MILLER, Judge: This is a suit for refund of gift taxes paid with respect to gifts of stock of the Blue Bird Body Company, made in 1976 by the three Luce brothers, Albert L., Jr., George E. and Joseph P., who are the controlling stockholders of that company. On September 30, 1976, Albert gave 19,000 shares to a trust for his daughter. Thereafter, on October 29, 1976, Albert gave 2,000 additional shares directly to his daughter, and George and Joseph each gave 38,000 shares both directly to members of their families and to trusts for their benefit. There were a total of 16 gifts, consisting of 97,000 shares, 83,000 of which were in nine trusts with a common trustee, the Citizens and Southern National Bank of Macon, Georgia. The 97,000 shares represented 17 percent of the total of 582,000 shares which were outstanding.

Each donor filed a gift tax return valuing the shares at $39.31, which is equal to their book value as of September 30, 1975, the end of the prior fiscal year.

After filing appropriate claims for refund, plaintiffs [1] brought timely suit and now claim that the fair value of the gifts should more properly have been computed at $26 per share.

The Blue Bird Body Company was founded in 1927 by A. L. Luce, Sr., plaintiffs' father. By 1947 its shares were owned one-fourth by A. L. Luce, Sr., and his wife, and one-fourth by each of the three plaintiffs. Plaintiffs' father died in 1962, and by 1966 the three plaintiffs had acquired 100 percent of the shares.

Starting in 1969 Blue Bird initiated a policy of selling some of its stock to executive employees and officers other than members of the Luce family. In March 1969 it sold 10 shares to Corbin J. Davis, an officer. Preliminary to such sale it amended its by-laws to provide that no stockholder or his heirs, personal representatives or assigns may sell, pledge or otherwise dispose of any shares until he first offers to sell them to the corporation at their book value as of the end of the next preceding fiscal year. If the corporation fails to repurchase the shares within 45 days, he is to offer them to the other stockholders pro rata at the same price. If any of the other stockholders fails to exercise his purchase rights, he is to assign them to the remaining stockholders. Only if the other stockholders fail to make the purchase, may the stock be sold to outsiders.

Thereafter, from 1969 through the corporation's fiscal year ending October 30, 1976, sixteen managerial and executive employees acquired a total of 33,429 shares of Blue Bird at book values as of the end of the fiscal years preceding their acquisitions. Some shares were sold to such employees for cash; others were issued as additional compensation. Blue Bird has bought back shares from the estate of one such employee and from two others who left its employment—always at book value as of the end of the preceding fiscal year.

In 1972 the three plaintiffs gave 139,320 shares of Blue Bird stock to eight trusts for their children and grandchildren, naming themselves as co-trustees with the Citizens and Southern National Bank of the trusts of which they were grantors.

Following the 1976 gifts, Blue Bird's stock was owned:

Owner	Shares	Percentage
Plaintiffs	312,251	53.6
Plaintiffs' children ...	14,000	2.4
Citizens and Southern National Bank as trustee or as co-trustee with plaintiffs..	222,320	38.2
Non-family executives	33,429	5.8
	582,000	100.0

Section 2512(a) of the Internal Revenue Code of 1954 provides that for gift tax purposes, "If the gift is made in property, the value thereof at the date of the gift shall be considered the amount of the gift."

---

* Since all of the pertinent findings of fact are contained in this opinion, pursuant to Rule 52(a) no separate findings will be filed.

[1] Although the wives are necessary parties to the suit by virtue of their election to treat the gifts as made by both husbands and wives, the term plaintiffs will be used hereinafter to refer exclusively to the husbands because they paid the taxes.

Luce, Jr. *vs.* U.S.

Treasury Regulations on Gift Tax (1954 Code) § 25.2512-1, (26 C. F. R.)), states that such value is "the price at which such property would change hands between a willing buyer and a willing seller, neither being under any compulsion to buy or sell, and both having reasonable knowledge of relevant facts."

One of the more difficult property valuation problems is the appropriate method and measure of valuation of the shares of the stock of a closely held corporation, which are not ordinarily traded on an open market. See *Righter v. United States* [71-1 USTC ¶ 12,758], 194 Ct. Cl. 400, 407, 439 F. 2d 1204, 1207 (1971). Section 2031 of the Code, relating to the estate tax, provides:

(b) Valuation of unlisted stock and securities.—In the case of stock and securities of a corporation the value of which, by reason of their not being listed on an exchange and by reason of the absence of sales thereof, cannot be determined with reference to bid and asked prices or with reference to sales prices, the value thereof shall be determined by taking into consideration, in addition to all other factors, the value of stock or securities of corporations engaged in the same or a similar line of business which are listed on an exchange.

While no similar provision appears in the gift tax sections of the Code, gift tax Regulations § 25.2512-2(f) provides that where selling prices or bid and asked prices are unavailable, the valuation of shares of stock is to be determined by taking into consideration the company's net worth, prospective earning power, dividend-paying capacity, goodwill, economic outlook in the industry, the company's position in the industry, its management, the degree of control of the business represented by the block of stock, the value of securities of corporations engaged in similar lines of business which are listed in a stock exchange, and other relevant factors. See also *Penn Yan Agway Cooperative, Inc. v. United States* [69-2 USTC ¶ 9719], 189 Ct. Cl. 434, 446, 417 F. 2d 1372, 1378 (1969); *Arc Realty Co. v. Commissioner* [61-2 USTC ¶ 9689], 295 F. 2d 98, 103 (8th Cir. 1961).

In 1976 Blue Bird was primarily a manufacturer and seller of school bus type vehicles, plus a limited number of small urban transit buses and luxury motor homes. As previously noted, the enterprise had been founded in 1927 by Mr. A. L. Luce, Sr. After their return from military service in World War II, his three sons, the plaintiffs, entered the business with him and have been in control of the business since their father's death in 1962. The business has grown steadily. In 1945 Blue Bird manufactured 750 bus bodies, in 1946, 1,000. By 1976 Blue Bird was producing 10,000 buses per year.

Approximately 56 percent of Blue Bird's 1976 sales revenue were derived from the sale of buses for which the chassis and engines were provided by the truck manufacturers, such as Ford, GM or International Harvester. The manufacturers inventoried their trucks on Blue Bird property, and Blue Bird's only obligation was to maintain insurance on them. Blue Bird built the bodies, including seats, electrical wiring and all other appurtenances, installed chassis and engines and shipped the finished buses to the customers. An additional 30 percent of Blue Bird's revenues came from the sale of buses for which Blue Bird manufactured the chassis as well as the bodies, installing, however, engines manufactured by such engine manufacturers as Ford, GM, Cummins or Caterpillar. The remaining 14 percent of sales volume was about evenly divided between urban transit buses and the motor homes.

Blue Bird's domestic sales are generated primarily through corporate or distributor competitive bidding for state, county, and local government sales. Approximately 20 to 30 percent of Blue Bird's revenues result from state purchases by competitive bid. The other source of domestic sales for Blue Bird comes from its distributor network. In 1976, this network was comprised of 54 distributors and five direct factory representatives. A distributor may sell on the basis of competitive bids or through negotiations with school boards or with contractors to school boards at the county level. In 1975 and 1976, Blue Bird was also very active in the export market, and, during that time, the export market was very strong. Large orders from Middle Eastern countries contributed to the 1975-76 growth in export sales.

Luce, Jr. *vs.* U.S.

Many of Blue Bird's distributors have been with the Company from 20 to 30 years. Many distribute solely Blue Bird products; however, some sell, in addition, trucks, autos, or other school equipment.

Although the school bus industry is highly competitive and school bus manufacturers generally have had the capacity to produce twice as many buses as the market demand, in 1976 Blue Bird was one of the top two or three companies in unit sales in the industry. It supplied 22.4 percent of the school buses sold in the United States, 45 percent of the school buses sold in Canada and approximately 25 percent of the school buses used for such purpose in all the other countries. It was a half-century old well-established company with a good, solid, basic market. Its facilities and machinery and equipment were in good condition and well maintained. Its principal executives had been with the company for substantial periods of time, its employees were well paid, and its labor relations were good. It had no significant long term debt and it had a good line of credit. It had a network of franchises and qualified salesmen selling its products in the United States, Canada, and in the international markets. Its sales, production, and profits were on the rise, and its competitors had a difficult time competing with it. It had generally and consistently been a successful and profitable business; and its management had plans and expectations for boosting its profits by increasing its unit sales

to 25 percent of the domestic maket by 1980, which would give it the number one spot. In fact, it achieved this goal by 1978 or 1979.

Plaintiff produced, as an expert witness to testify with respect to the fair market value of the gifts of stock at issue, Mr. Charles B. Shelton, III, First Vice President in the corporate finance department of The Robinson-Humphrey Company, Inc., a member of the New York, American and Midwest Stock Exchanges and a full-service investment banking and brokerage house.

He determined that, based on information provided by management and a review of market conditions in the fall of 1976, the difference in the values of Blue Bird's common stock on September 30 and October 29, 1976, when the two sets of gifts were made, was negligible, and accordingly valued them both as of the latter date.

He accepted as correct and without further investigation the financial information concerning the company provided by Blue Bird's management. Included were audited financial statements of Blue Bird for the fiscal years ended in October 1971 through 1975, but not for 1976. Because the financial statement for October 30, 1976, was not yet available on October 29, 1976, he substituted the company's earnings projection for the fiscal year ending October 30, 1976, made by the company in the summer of 1976. And he added a forecast for fiscal 1977, also made in the summer of 1976. He summarized the earnings record for 1971-75 as follows:

(000's omitted)	1971	1972	1973	1974	1975
Net Sales	$32,008	$36,888	$40,649	$55,123	$78,886
Earnings	2,125	2,520	2,507	2,071	6,381
Earnings Per Share	3.75	4.45	4.38	3.56	10.98
Net Profit Margin	7%	7%	6%	4%	8%

Luce, Jr. *vs.* U.S.

He set forth the 1976 and 1977 estimates comparatively with the actual results for 1974 and 1975 as follows:

	1974	1975	1976 Est.	1977 Est.
Units Sold	7,701	9,566	8,995	10,221
% Increase (Decease) in Units Sold...		24.2%	(6.0)%	13.6%
Earnings (000's omitted)	$2,071	$6,381	$5,932	$3,670
% Increase (Decrease) in Earnings ...		208%	(7.0)%	(38.1)%

He also noted that the company's net worth as of November 1, 1975, was $22,839,000 (or $39.24 per share), and, after subtracting goodwill, that tangible net worth was $22,503,000 (or $38.73 per share).

In order to determine the value of the 97,000 shares which were the subject of the gift, he first found it necessary to value 100 percent of the equity in the company, which was represented by 582,000 shares of stock.

Mr. Shelton's report and testimony discussed various measure[s] of value for the stock of the entire company but he ultimately relied on only one.

He rejected the market comparison approach, which arrives at the value of a closely held company by applying to it the ratios which the market price of the stock of a publicly owned company in the same industry bears to its earnings, dividends and net book value, on the ground that he was unaware of any publicly traded company whose business was similar to that of Blue Bird in product, size and scope.

He rejected an asset appraisal approach to value on the ground that Blue Bird was a going concern and its management had no intention of liquidating the assets.

He found the book value of Blue Bird's net assets, or net worth, was $22,838,818 or $39.24 per share on November 1, 1975, and an estimated $28,189,000, or $48.43 per share on October 29, 1976 (after giving effect to a $1.00 per share dividend declared October 25, 1976), but rejected that too.

The only method he discussed to arrive at value on the basis of objective comparative data with respect to other companies was the capitalized excess earnings method of valuation. Under this method the average return of a company on its tangible net worth (the book value of tangible assets less liabilities) over a number of years is compared to that of its industry. To the extent that the company's average return on its tangible net worth is at a rate in excess of that prevailing in the industry generally, it is assumed that such excess earnings indicate it has intangible value (or goodwill) in excess of the value of its tangible net worth. To ascertain what that value is, that portion of the earnings is capitalized at a suitable rate commensurate with the investment risk. The product is then added to the value of the tangibles to determine total value.

In making this comparison, Mr. Shelton used the average net book value of Blue Bird's tangible assets for the years 1972-76 and the average earnings for the same years. For the industry comparisons for return on net worth, he used Annual Statement Studies for 1977, by Robert Morris Associates, covering eleven companies of similar asset size as Blue Bird, primarily engaged in manufacturing automobile bodies, or assembling complete passenger cars, trucks, commercial cars, buses and special purpose vehicles, with fiscal years ending in 1976; Standard & Poor's Automobile Index; Standard & Poor's Automobile Index excluding General Motors; Standard & Poor's Automobiles-Trucks & Parts Index and Standard & Poor's 400 Industrial Index. The comparison was as follows:

BLUE BIRD BODY COMPANY
COMPARISON OF RETURNS ON
NET WORTH RATIOS
(Using Tangible Net Worth,
Net of Goodwill)

Blue Bird Body Company Return on Net Worth	
1976	20.9% Est.
1975	28.4%
1974	12.2%
1973	16.1%
1972	18.4%
Average 1972-1976	19.2%

Luce, Jr. *vs.* U.S.

Robert Morris Associates
Industry Median Return
On Net Worth

1976	15.40%
1975	9.13%
1974	7.98%
1973	11.72%
1972	N.A.
Average 1973-1976	11.06%

Standard & Poor's
Automobile Index

1976	17.33%
1975	5.74%
1974	6.05%
1973	16.94%
1972	16.61%
Average 1972-1976	12.53%

Standard & Poor's Automobile
Index Excluding GM

1976	12.78%
1975	Def.
1974	3.82%
1973	12.89%
1972	12.86%
Average 1972-1976	8.47%

Standard & Poor's Automobiles-
Trucks & Parts Index

1976	14.28%
1975	Def.
1974	8.60%
1973	11.07%
1972	6.57%
Average 1972-1976	8.10%

Standard & Poor's 400
Industrial Index

1976	14.02%
1975	12.11%
1974	14.17%
1973	14.15%
1972	11.71%
Average 1972-1976	13.23%

Although over the preceding 5 years Blue Bird had earned a rate of return on tangible net worth substantially in excess of that earned by each group of comparables, nevertheless he applied a relatively low multiple, five times earnings, to the excess yield. Despite the low multiple, however, this method resulted in a total value of $32,373,000 for the whole company, equivalent to $55.62 per share.

All of the foregoing, however, appears to have been mere padding. Mr. Shelton disregarded the $39.24 and $48.43 book values, for the stated reason that the shares of some publicly held companies in the automotive industry in some years sold at prices below their book values and because he was of the opinion that earnings are generally the most important factor bearing on the value of a going concern. Also, after having gone to the trouble of making all of the foregoing calculations and comparisons, Shelton then repudiated the $55.62 value he determined by the capitalized excess earnings method of valuation because the industries whose rates of return were used were broader than Blue Bird and not largely confined to school buses, because Blue Bird's average rate of return was inflated by its 1975 high earnings level, and because the method did not consider all relevant factors.

Mr. Shelton arrived at his valuation of the company by a modified capitalization of earnings method. He averaged Blue Bird's reported earnings for 1972-75 together with the estimate for 1976 and the projection for 1977, and obtained an average earnings base of $3,847,000. Dividing this earnings base by the 20 percent capitalization rate (or applying a multiple of five times earnings) resulted in a total value for the company under this approach of $19,235,000. He then added to that figure a sum sufficient to increase the $19,235,000 to $21,500,000, without explanation other than that it was a matter of judgment. Dividing this figure by the 582,000 outstanding shares arrives at a per share value of $37 for the whole company.

Shelton then reduced the $37 per share by 30 percent to $26, for the 97,000 shares which were the subject of the gifts, because they represented in the aggregate only a 17 percent minority interest, which lacked an established market for sale to the public, and absent such a sale they were subject to the will of the controlling stockholders, who could use the corporation to benefit themselves at the expense of other stockholders.

Mr. Shelton's method of valuation is subject to criticism in several respects. First, the earnings he used are not necessarily representative of the earning capacity of the business. As the court stated in *Central Trust Co. v. United States* [62-2 USTC ¶ 12,092], 158 Ct. Cl. 504, 530, 305 F. 2d 393, 409 (1962), in using reported earnings as a

Luce, Jr. *vs.* U.S.

basis for stock valuation, it is "proper to make such adjustments therein as would be necessary to eliminate abnormal and nonrecurring items and to redistribute items of expense to their proper periods."

Blue Bird's 1974 earnings had been reduced by approximately $787,000 as a result of a one time change in the company's method of accounting. By converting from first-in first-out to last-in first-out inventory accounting in that year, Blue Bird decreased its closing inventory and pre-tax income by $1,430,800. Restoration of this sum less the offsetting tax savings attributable thereto (at the 45 percent rate used by Shelton) results in additional representative after-tax earnings of $787,000 for the year. Applying this increase to Shelton's capitalized average earnings computation results in a $1.13 per share increase in his valuation of the company.

The 1976 earnings estimate used in Mr. Shelton's earning's base, $5,932,000, was short of the earnings reported for that year, $6,381,000, by $449,000. The estimate relied on was made during the summer of 1976. However, monthly financial statements were available, and Mr. Pennington, Blue Bird's independent auditor, testified that by the end of September 1976 they would have enabled determination of the annual income with 80-90 percent accuracy. Plaintiffs have not shown that as the valuation date at issue, October 29, 1976, only one day prior to the close of the fiscal year, Blue Bird's auditors could not have furnished Mr. Shelton a closer approximation of actual earnings for the year than that made during the summer. Adjustment of the earnings base for this increase results in an additional increase of $0.64 per share in Mr. Shelton's valuation for the whole company.

The reported earnings were after reduction each year by approximately 10 percent for contributions to a private charitable trust (The Rainbow Fund) of which the three Luce brothers were the trustees. In 1976 the contribution was $575,000. It is difficult to understand why the earnings base for valuation of a company should be reduced by such a voluntary diversion of earnings which was not shown to benefit the corporation. Mr. Shelton argued that since the siphoning off of earnings by con-

trolling stockholders was adverse to a minority interest, an adjustment for this annual sum should not increase the value of the gift shares. However, it is a proper item for adjustment of the earnings base in determining the value of the entire corporation prior to computing the value of a minority interest; otherwise the witness' discount for a minority interest is duplicated. More important, once there is a significant unrelated minority interest, a serious question arises as to the right of the controlling stockholders to continue to divert a substantial share of the corporate earnings to their private charitable foundation without the consent of all of the stockholders. See *A. P. Smith Manufacturing Co. v. Barlow*, 13 N. J. 145, 98 A. 2d 581 (1953); Annot. 39 A. L. R. 2d 1192 (1955); 19 Am. Jur., Corporations § 1015; and H. Ballantine on Corporations (Rev. Ed.) § 85 at 228.

Mr. Shelton included in his earnings base a forecast of earnings for 1977, which had been prepared by the company in the summer of 1976. Although the forecast was for $3,670,100 in earnings and the actual 1977 earnings turned out to be $3,883,600, the propinquity of the forecast to the actual results (6 percent below) does not necessarily show the soundness of the forecast. It actually appears to be happenstance. The forecast was made in the summer of 1976, up to 5 months before the beginning of the 1977 fiscal year. The projection was for substantially increased sales, both in units and dollars, over prior years. The forecast of reduced earnings was based on projections of increased inflation rates and correspondingly higher material and labor costs generally, and was thought by Albert Luce to be a single year's break in the trend of increased earnings. The June 1980 report of a company official responsible for the forecast explains that the 1977 results were close to the forecast because "cost increases were not quite as great as anticipated", but "On the other hand price increases were not as great as anticipated."

The use of an earnings forecast made months prior to the start of the year, and which is based on predictions of the general inflation rate with respect to raw material and labor costs generally, as a base for

Luce, Jr. *vs.* U.S.

capitalization of earnings is subject to great error. The unreliability of such an initial estimate may be inferred from the fact that the corresponding initial forecast for 1976 was for $2,985,800 in earnings, while actual earnings turned out to be $6,189,000, more than 100 percent higher. The risks associated with such forecasts of future earnings are more properly a function of the capitalization rate than the earnings base. To reflect a forecast of a possible earnings decrease for a single future year in both the base and the rate results in an exaggeration of the effect of such a forecast.

On November 5, 1981, Mr. Shelton prepared another valuation report for the plaintiff on the entire Blue Bird stock as of August 10, 1981, for purposes of a proposed recapitalization of the company. This did not involve a tax problem. In it he followed the same general method of valuation.

However, for the average earnings base he used the results of the 1976 through 1980 years and the estimate for 1981. The latter he derived from the results for the 7 months ending in May 1981. He did not include any forecast for 1982.

In addition, in constructing the earnings base in the 1981 valuation report, Mr. Shelton used a method of averaging which emphasizes the importance of the most recent experience. He used the sum of the digits method, which places greatest weight on the most recent years, to arrive at average earnings for 1976 to 1980, and then weighed that at 40 percent and the estimated whole year 1981 earnings at 60 percent to arrive at the average for 1976-81. Had he applied that method to his 1972-76 earnings the earnings base would have been much higher, to wit:

Year	Earnings	Weight Factor	Weighted Earnings
1972	2,519,845	× 1/10	251,984
1973	2,507,003	× 2/10	501,401
1974	2,071,386	× 3/10	621,416
1975	6,381,385	× 4/10	2,552,554
		10/10	3,927,355
		× weight factor of	40%
			1,570,942
1976	5,931,800 × weight factor of 60% =		3,559,140
Weighted Earnings Base			$5,130,082

This compares to the average earnings base of $3,847,000 he actually used to value the entire company as of October 29, 1976.

In *Central Trust Co. v. United States* [62-2 USTC ¶ 12,092], 158 Ct. Cl. at 522, 305 F. 2d at 404, the court pointed out that mere averages may be deceiving since they equate both increasing and decreasing earnings without regard to their trend, and that "the most recent years' earnings are to be accorded the greatest weight."

For the foregoing reasons, Mr. Shelton's average earnings were not a wholly reliable base for the capitalization of earnings method of valuation.

Second, Mr. Shelton's valuation of Blue Bird at $37 per share as of October 29, 1976, is unacceptable because it is almost a

fourth less than the book value of its net assets less liabilities, $48.98, as of October 30, 1976, even though all but one percent of that book value was represented by tangible assets, cash and receivables. Indeed, an appraisal of the tangible assets at Blue Bird's main plants, made for insurance purposes as of December 12, 1975, established that the replacement cost of such assets less sustained depreciation was far in excess of their book value and that had it been substituted for the book figures the book value per share would have been increased to $61.65.

If a company's net worth consists of substantial write-ups of intangible value acquired in mergers or corporate acquisitions, if it has paid inflated prices for its assets, or if

Luce, Jr. *vs.* U.S.

its machinery and equipment are obsolete, and it has consistently been unable to obtain a fair return on its investment, then the fair market value of the company may understandably be less than its book value. But the undisputed evidence here is that as of the valuation date Blue Bird's ownership had been in the same family since it was organized, its net worth was not inflated by any substantial intangible value, and its plant and equipment were in good condition and enabled it to be a dominant company in its industry. Moreover, Mr. Shelton's own computations showed that the company's returns on its tangible net worth ranged between 16.1 and 28.4 percent, with an average of 19.2 percent, over the preceding 5 years, returns far in excess of those earned in the closest comparable industries Mr. Shelton could find. A seller could hardly have been expected to be willing to accept 25 percent less for the company than the cost of duplicating the net depreciated tangible assets alone, without regard to its value as a going concern with goodwill, qaufied personnel, an established national distributors' organization and high earning capacity; and a hypothetical buyer could also hardly have expected that he could obtain it for that price.[2] In such circumstances, it is reasonable to conclude that book value is at the least a floor under fair market value, which an appraiser may not properly ignore. *Cf. Schwartz v. C. I. R.* [77-2 USTC ¶ 13,201], 560 F. 2d 311, 316-17 (8th Cir. 1977); *Hamm v. C. I. R.* [64-1 USTC ¶ 12,206], 325 F. 2d 934, 937, 941 (8th Cir. 1963), *cert. denied,* 377 U. S. 993 (1964); *City Bank Farmers Trust Co. v. Commissioner* [CCH Dec. 7024], 23 B. T. A. 663, 669 (1931).

Third, the most serious weakness in Mr. Shelton's valuation of the company lies is in his failure to supply a rational objective basis for the key element thereof, the capitalization rate he applied to Blue Bird's average earnings. He testified that in his judgment "a buyer of such securities of the risks inherent in Blue Bird would look for a 20 percent return." However, he was unable to furnish any objective data with respect to any comparable situations underlying that judgment, so as to enable the court to determine whether it was soundly based. Nor could he supply any objective data which would tend to to support a judgment that a knowledgeable seller would be willing to dispose of the Blue Bird stock at a price so low as to be no more than he would have received in just 5 years of its average earnings or 3 years of its most recent earnings. When pressed, Mr. Shelton fell back on his "experience"; but he conceded he was not an expert on the market for school buses and had never sold stock of any company which manufactured or sold buses, and could not identify a single contemporaneous purchase or sale of the stock of any company in his experience which was the basis of his judgment. Nor, even omitting the names of the participants, could he described the circumstances of any comparative purchase or sale. Assuming (without necessarily deciding) the good faith of Mr. Shelton's testimony, it must be concluded that his judgment in this regard was merely intuitive and the basis therefor was not susceptible of rational or objective examination or evaluation by the court.[4]

Nor is Mr. Shelton's judgment that $2,265,000 should be added to the capitalized earnings base any more rationally founded. It is self-evident that it was added to raise the $19,235,000 to $21,500,000 in order to reach a predetermined round figure. It may also be inferred that it is in recognition that the other methods of valuation reached considerably higher figures. But why $21,500,000 rather than some other figure? It must be concluded that the wit-

---

[2] This is also supported by the fact that the controlling stockholders contemporaneously sold shares of stock and gave bonuses to executive employees at book value as of the end of the prior year and deemed the price to be at least fair to the employees.

[3] In support of the 20 percent capitalization rate, plaintiff argues that the government's expert witness used a 5.3 multiple of earnings which is not very far from Shelton's. The fact is, however, that the government's witness used a multiple of 7.7 times the 5 year average for 1972-76 and 5.3 times 1976 earnings, to arrive at a value of $54 per share. As noted hereinafter, the court finds it unnecessary to rely on the government's expert testimony.

[4] Also quoted with approval in *Continental Water Co. v. United States,* 49 A.F.T.R. 2d 82-1070, 1080 (1982), (Trial Judge, Court of Claims), adopted *per curiam* 231 Ct. Cl. —, 50 A.F.T.R. 82-5128 (1982).

Luce, Jr. *vs.* U.S.

ness' judgment in this regard is equally intuitive and not based on objective facts or reasoning susceptible of objective examination or evaluation.

Plaintiffs argue in their brief that "The value of expert opinion testimony lies in the qualifications of the witness" and that it is not the court's role to reason why. But however difficult, the law has never deemed the valuation of the stock of a closely held company to be an arcane or accult craft beyond the ken of courts, which must be content to evaluate only the credibility of the expert witness. "[L]ike any other judgments, those of an expert can be no better than the soundness of the reasons that stand in support of them." (*Fehrs v. United States* [80-1 USTC ¶ 13,348], 223 Ct. Cl. 488, 508, 620 F. 2d, 255, 265 (1980).) The opinion of an expert witness is "no better than the convincing nature of the reasons offered in support of his testimony." (*Potts, Davis & Company v. C. I. R.* [70-2 USTC ¶ 9635], 431 F. 2d 1222, 1226 (9th Cir. 1970).) "Opinion evidence, to be of any value, should be based either upon admitted facts or upon facts, within the knowledge of the witness, disclosed in the record. Opinion evidence that does not appear to be based upon disclosed facts is of little or no value." (*Baliban & Katz Corp. v. Commissioner*, 30 F. 2d 807, 808 (7th Cir. 1929).)ª "[I]n order for the opinion to have any value it must be based on assumptions which the trier of facts can find to have been proved." (*Rewis v. United States*, 369 F. 2d 595, 602 (5th Cir. 1966).) A court "is not required to surrender its judgment to the judgment of experts." (*Hamm v. Commissioner* [64-1 USTC ¶ 12,206], 325 F. 2d 934, 941 (8th Cir. 1963).) And see also *The Conqueror*, 166 U. S. 110, 131-33 (1897); *Pumice Supply Co. v. C. I. R.*, 308 F. 2d 766, 769 (9th Cir. 1962); and *Gloyd v. Commissioner* [58-1 USTC ¶ 9251], 63 F. 2d 649, 650 (8th Cir.), *cert. denied*, 290 U. S. 633 (1933).

Finally, plaintiff's reliance upon Shelton's determination that the fair market value of the 97,000 shares which were the subject of the gifts should be reduced by 30 percent, to $26 per share, because as a minority interest without an established market they could not be sold to the public except at a substantial discount, is based

on a misconception of both the law and the facts. First, under the law, the applicable market in which the hypothetical willing buyer may be found need not be one which includes the general public. It is sufficient if there are potential buyers among those closely connected with the corporation.

In *Rothgery v. United States* [73-1 USTC ¶ 12,911], 201 Ct. Cl. 183, 189, 475 F. 2d 591, 594 (1973), there was at issue the valuation for estate tax purposes of 50 percent of the stock of an automobile dealership, the remaining 50 percent being owned by the decedent's son. Since there was no public market for the shares, the court found the value of the entire stock from the book value and appraisals of the underlying assets less the liabilities, and then allocated that value on a per share basis. The court responded to the estate's argument that the pro rata allocation was excessive because there was no public market for the decedent's shares and because the 50 percent interest of the estate was not a controlling interest, by finding that the decedent's son would have been a willing buyer of the shares from any hypothetical seller; that the son intended to continue the corporate business after his father's death; that he wished to have control of the corporation, so that his own son might have a place in the business; that this objective required the acquisition of the decedent's stock interest in the corporation; and that the evidence warranted the inference that the son would have been willing to pay —and from a business standpoint would have been justified in paying—for the decedent's half-interest in the corporation an amount equal to half the value of the corporation's assets. This was a market sufficient to negate any need for a discount to sell the shares.

In *Couzens v. Commissioner* [CCH Dec. 3931], 11 B. T. A. 1040 (1928), the Board of Tax Appeals was required to find the value of the Ford Motor Company stock on March 1, 1913, in order to determine the late Senator Couzen's gain on the sale of his stock in 1920. Prior to the 1920 sale only ten individuals were the sole stockholders, there was no public market for the stock, and there was a restriction on the certificates giving existing share-

Luce, Jr. *vs.* U.S.

holders the prior right to purchase the stock at the price at which it was offered to an outsider. The Commissioner argued that the limited market for the shares under such circumstances depressed the value of a minority interest below the fair market value of the shares as a whole and would have necessitated a substantial discount to make them saleable to a willing buyer. In rejecting this contention, the court stated (11 B. T. A. at 1164):

> We do not construe a fair market as meaning that the whole world must be a potential buyer, but only that there are sufficient available persons able to buy to assure a fair and reasonable price in the light of the circumstances affecting value.*

On cross-examination, Mr. Shelton likewise concurred that if the company or its controlling stockholders pursued a policy of buying back shares from persons who were not family members or executive employees, that fact could put a greater value on the shares by providing a potential market for them.

The record in this case establishes that there was indeed an available market for the shares at issue within the company or among persons associated with the company. Plaintiff Albert L. Luce testified that it was company and Luce policy that all shares of Blue Bird's stock remain in the ownership of members of the Luce family, of trusts for their benefit, and of executive employee. This purpose motivated the adoption of the by-law in 1969, when shares were first offered to executive employee Corbin Davis, requiring any stockholder desiring to dispose of his shares to offer them first to the corporation and then to the remaining stockholders at book value. Thereafter, whenever shares were offered to an employee, Albert Luce personally told him that the company would repurchase the shares at book value if he left the company, died or desired to dispose of the shares for any other reason, and the company has in fact followed this practice.

The company's purpose for the by-law and commitment was explained by Albert as follows:

> As we offered the stock to other members, other than the Luce family, and to some of our top executives, we did not want them to dispose of their stock to our competitors or someone we would not want to know more details about our operation or our business.

He elaborated on this theme that they wanted control of the company to remain in the family and that it was their intent that no shares be held by strangers generally. Accordingly, no shares have ever been sold to outsiders.

The same intent prevailed with respect to the shares given to the trustee for the benefit of other members of their family. Luce testified that had the trustee desired to sell any of the shares on the open market he would not have allowed it, but would have bought it back, because, as a major stockholder, he wanted to retain control of the block of stock, he wanted it to remain in the family, and he had no intention of allowing it to go to outsiders. Furthermore, he conceded he would even have paid "a premium over whatever the fair market value might be not to let any Blue Bird shares get outside the Luce family and the executives or corporate management."

Even without regard to the personal funds of the Luce brothers and their families, it is clear that as of October 29, 1976, Blue Bird had the financial resources to pay for the 97,000 shares at the $39.31 1975 book value at which they were reported on the gift tax returns if they were offered to it by the trustee or by a willing buyer from the trustee. The cost of such a purchase would have been $3,813,070. The company's financial report as of October 30, 1976, shows it had net current assets (less current liabilities) of $13,375,405, of which cash and receivables were $4,697,151, and, in addition, it owned $3,480,597 in cash

---

* Accord: *Estate of Goldstein v. Commissioner* [CCH Dec. 24,086], 33 T. C. 1032, 1037 (1960), affirmed on another issue, 340 F. 2d 24 (2d Cir. 1965); *Smith v. Commissioner*, 46 B. T. A. 340-41 (1942), mod., *sub nom.*, *Worcester County Trust Co. v. Commissioner* [43-1 ustc ¶ 10,029], 134 F. 2d 578 (1st Cir. 1943).

* Neither of the other plaintiffs testified. Joseph Luce was hospitalized at the time of trial, but no explanation was given for George's absence, nor was any effort made to obtain Joseph's testimony at another time. It is assumed therefore that there was no divergence as to the facts and Albert spoke for all three.

Luce, Jr. *vs.* U.S.

value of life insurance on the lives of its officers, against which it could borrow at will. It also had a good line of credit and substantial borrowing capacity, its long term liabilities being no more than $1.7 million, which was less than 6 percent of equity.

In addition to the corporation itself and its controlling stockholders there was a further market for the shares among the other managerial employees of Blue Bird. Corbin Davis, the company's vice-president for marketing, testified without contradiction that since 1976 fifteen to twenty other managerial employees who were offered stock in the corporation at book value took the opportunity to purchase it and that there were 200 other employees in the management team, every one of whom would have been eager to purchase shares at the same price if it had been offered to him.

Thus, there was no occasion for a 30 percent discount in order for the hypothetical seller to find a willing buyer.

Estate of Mark S. Gallo

Opinion

Property includible in the gross estate is generally included at its fair market value on the date of the decedent's death. Sec. 2031(a);[*] sec. 20.2031-1(b), Estate Tax Regs. Fair market value is the price at which the property would change hands between a willing buyer and a willing seller, neither being under any compulsion to buy or to sell and both having reasonable knowledge of all relevant facts. *United States v. Cartwright* [73-1 USTC ¶ 12,926], 411 U. S. 546, 551 (1973); sec. 20.2031-1(b), Estate Tax Regs. Determining fair market value is a question of fact, and the trier of fact must weigh all relevant evidence and draw appropriate inferences. *Hamm v. Commissioner* [64-1 USTC ¶ 12,206], 325 F. 2d 934, 938 (8th Cir. 1963), affg. a Memorandum Opinion of this Court; *Estate of Andrews v. Commissioner* [Dec. 39,523], 79 T. C. 938, 940 (1982).

Where the value of unlisted stock cannot be determined by reference to bid and ask or sales prices,[*] the value thereof should be based upon, in addition to all other factors, the value of listed stock of corporations engaged in the same or a similar line of business. Sec. 2031(b). Section 20.2031-2(f), Estate Tax Regs., provides that the company's net worth, prospective earnings power, and dividend-paying capacity should be considered, along with "other relevant factors." These other relevant factors include the goodwill of the business, the economic outlook in the particular industry, the company's position in the industry and its management, and the degree of control represented by the block of stock to be valued. Sec. 20.2031-2(f), Estate Tax Regs.

The relative weight accorded to the various factors depends upon the facts of each case. *Messing v. Commissioner* [Dec. 28,532], 48 T. C. 502, 512 (1967); sec. 20.2031-2(f), Estate Tax Regs. Earnings are relatively more important for valuing the stock of operating companies, whereas asset value is relatively more important for investment companies. *Levenson's Estate v. Commissioner* [60-2 USTC ¶ 11,969], 282 F. 2d 581,

586 (3d Cir. 1960); *Central Trust Co. v. United States* [62-2 USTC ¶ 12,092], 305 F. 2d 393, 404 (Ct. Cl. 1962). See also *Estate of Andrews v. Commissioner, supra.* "Financial data is important only to the extent it furnishes a basis for an informed judgment of the future performance of the particular company." *Snyder's Estate v. United States* [61-1 USTC ¶ 11,987], 285 F. 2d 857, 861 (4th Cir. 1961). Thus, for operating companies, the proper focus is typically upon earnings trends, if such trends are representative of future expectations. *Snyder's Estate v. United States, supra; Central Trust Co. v. United States, supra.*

Reliance on Expert Opinions

Opinion testimony of an expert is admissible if and because it will assist the trier of fact to understand evidence that will determine a fact in issue. See Fed. R. Evid. 702. Such evidence must be weighed in light of the demonstrated qualifications of the expert and all other evidence of value. *Estate of Christ v. Commissioner* [73-1 USTC ¶ 9454], 480 F. 2d 171, 174 (9th Cir. 1973), affg. [Dec. 30,011] 54 T. C. 493 (1970); *Anderson v. Commissioner* [58-1 USTC ¶ 9117], 250 F. 2d 242, 249 (5th Cir. 1957), affg. a Memorandum Opinion of this Court [Dec. 21,874(M)]. We are not bound by the opinion of any expert witness when that opinion is contrary to our judgment. *Kreis' Estate v. Commissioner* [56-1 USTC ¶ 9137], 227 F. 2d 753, 755 (6th Cir. 1955); *Tripp v. Commissioner* [64-2 USTC ¶ 9804], 337 F. 2d 432 (7th Cir. 1964), affg. a Memorandum Opinion of this Court [Dec. 26,298(M.)]. We may embrace or reject expert testimony, whichever, in our best judgment, is appropriate. *Helvering v. Nat. Grocery Co.* [38-2 USTC ¶ 9312], 304 U. S. 282 (1938); *Silverman v. Commissioner* [76-2 USTC ¶ 13,148], 538 F. 2d 927, 933 (2d Cir. 1976), aff'g. a Memorandum Opinion of this Court [Dec. 32,831(M)]; *In Re Williams' Estate* [58-1 USTC ¶ 9252], 256 F. 2d 217, 219 (9th Cir. 1958), affg. a Memorandum Opinion of this Court [Dec. 21,990(M)]. Thus we have rejected expert testimony where the witness' opinion of value was so exaggerated that his testimony

---

[*] Neither petitioner nor respondent attributes any significance to the sales between the trusts for decedent.

Estate of Mark S. Gallo

was incredible. See *Chiu v. Commissioner* [Dec. 42,027], 84 T. C. 722 (1985); *Dean v. Commissioner* [Dec. 41,348], 83 T. C. 56, 75 (1984); *Fuchs v. Commissioner* [Dec. 41,349], 83 T. C. 79, 99 (1984).

Both petitioner and respondent rely primarily upon the valuations prepared by their respective experts. Petitioner asks us to implement "the policy adopted in *Buffalo Tool & Die Manufacturing Co. v. Commissioner* [Dec. 36,977], 74 T. C. 441, 452 (1980), * * * that in proper cases the Court should adopt the value put forward by the most credible party." In that case we stated:

> We are convinced that the valuation issue is capable of resolution by the parties themselves through an agreement which will reflect a compromise Solomon-like adjustment, thereby saving the expenditure of time, effort, and money by the parties and the Court—a process not likely to produce a better result. Indeed, each of the parties should keep in mind that, in the final analysis, the Court may find the evidence of valuation by one of the parties sufficiently more convincing than that of the other party, so that the final result will produce a significant financial defeat for one or the other, rather than a middle-of-the-road compromise which we suspect each of the parties expects the Court to reach. If the parties insist on our valuing any or all of the assets, we will. We do not intend to avoid our responsibilities but instead seek to administer to them more efficiently—a factor which has become increasingly important in light of the constantly expanding workload of the Court. [74 T. C. at 452.]

That language should not be misinterpreted, as some litigants apparently have, as expressing an intention of the Court to sanction a party who takes an unreasonable position. See, e. g., the argument of the taxpayer in *Estate of Kaplin v. Commissioner* [85-1 USTC ¶ 9127], 748 F. 2d 1109, 1111-1112 (6th Cir. 1984), revg. on another ground a Memorandum Opinion of this Court [Dec. 39,235(M)].

Nothing in *Buffalo Tool & Die* requires us to accept any opinion that does not withstand careful analysis. If expert testimony is to serve its intended purpose, however, we should not and will not reject it without objective reasons for doing so. *Buffalo Tool & Die* simply indicates that an objective reason for doing so is that another expert's opinion is more persuasive. In addition *Buffalo Tool & Die* does not require that we find that an expert's report is more persuasive in its entirety. We can find one such report more persuasive on one ultimate element of valuation and another more persuasive on another ultimate element.

Respondent's primary argument is that Lehman Brothers focused excessively upon earnings in its valuation. Respondent does not dispute that earnings were more important than assets in valuing Gallo, but he argues that Lehman Brothers incorrectly ignored asset value. See *Estate of Andrews v. Commissioner* [Dec. 39,523], 79 T. C. 938, 945 (1982).

Lehman Brothers did not ignore asset value but concluded, after considering Gallo's assets, that Gallo did not possess sufficient asset value to sustain a value for Dry Creek stock exceeding the price-earnings valuation. Lehman Brothers admittedly did not appraise Gallo's assets, but, with the exception of land, nor did Desmond. Unlike *Estate of Andrews*, the current case does not present a situation where net asset value per share demonstrably exceeded an earnings-based valuation. See also *Hamm v. Commissioner* [64-1 USTC ¶ 12,206], 325 F. 2d 934 (8th Cir. 1963), affg. a Memorandum Opinion of this Court; *Portland Manufacturing Co. v. Commissioner* [Dec. 30,729], 56 T. C. 58 (1971), affd. by unpublished opinion on another issue 35 AFTR 2d 75-1439, 75-1 USTC ¶ 9449 (9th Cir. 1975). Desmond's report contains the only evidence of the value of Gallo's assets. As previously indicated, we are quite skeptical of the asset values determined by Desmond. Indeed, even Desmond apparently gave little weight to his adjusted book value computation. As he stated at trial:

> But, the value could not be placed heavily, in light of the higher tangible net worth, merely because it was—they were valuable assets. Those assets are worth what they'll earn. And, if they're not producing wine, those assets aren't worth anything at all.

We need only consider asset value; we need not attribute any weight to it, if to do so

Estate of Mark S. Gallo

would be unreasonable. As the Ninth Circuit Court of Appeals, to which this case is appealable (barring stipulation to the contrary), stated:

> [T]he statutory standard for evaluating closely held stock incorporates a number of alternative methods of valuation, and merely directs the trial court to consider all relevant methods. The applicable case law directs the trial court to consider all relevant information, but grants it broad discretion in determining what method of valuation most fairly represents the fair market value of the stock in issue in light of the facts presented at trial. In light of * * * the wide discretion given the trial court to weigh the credibility of witnesses at trial and to determine the appropriate weight to give various methods of valuation, we do not believe the Tax Court erred in its choice of a method other than net asset value. [Citations omitted.] [*Estate of O'Connell v. Commissioner* [81-1 USTC ¶ 13,395], 640 F. 2d 249, 251-252 (9th Cir. 1981), affg. a Memorandum Opinion of this Court [Dec. 35,173(M)].]

Considering the entire record, we do not believe that the value of Gallo's assets justified a higher valuation for the Dry Creek stock than that determined by Lehman Brothers.

In sum, respondent's objections are unsupported by any evidence from which we could conclude that the methods and calculations used by Lehman Brothers were incorrect. Respondent is, in effect, merely asking us to substitute numbers that would achieve a higher valuation and to reject Lehman Brothers' approach because it produced a relatively low valuation. If we were to do so, we would be merely substituting our guess for the expert opinion, when the original purpose of the expert opinion is to provide us with the assistance of persons specially qualified in the areas in issue.

Discount for Lack of Marketability

Both parties agree that the fair market value of 1,178 shares of Dry Creek Class J common was less than the publicly traded value of the stock. The only issue is the proper amount of the discount to reflect the absence of a public market for the stock.

Desmond concluded in his report that a relatively low discount of 10 percent was appropriate, primarily for the following reasons:

1. The popularity and opportunity associated with the wine industry during this period (as reflected by the multitude of acquisitions that took 'place).

2. Gallo's dominant position within the industry.

3. Ernest and Julio Gallo's unique value to the company's operations, which could enhance the possibility of a merger, acquisition or public offering, due to their respective ages.

Desmond testified at trial that, because of the above factors, a sophisticated and well-financed investor might consider the purchase of the 1,178 Class J shares an opportunity to establish a position from which he could later acquire a larger, perhaps controlling, interest in Dry Creek. Desmond believed that the hypothetical investor could not reasonably foresee a public market for the stock but would instead make the purchase "[j]ust to get on the inside to see what * * * [he] could see."

We have found as facts that Dry Creek intended to remain closely held by the Gallo family and that none of the common shareholders intended to sell any shares to outsiders, as of the valuation date. These findings were supported by substantial evidence, including the extensive and uncontradicted testimony by two members of the second generation of Gallos. A rational investor would not assume that the purchase of the 1,178 Class J shares would lead to the acquisition of a larger interest in Dry Creek.

The hypothetical purchaser would acquire only a very small interest in a family-dominated corporation, for which there existed no ready market and little reasonable expectation for significant dividend income.* Dry Creek's capital structure and voting provisions, which required a majority vote of both classes of common shares for shareholder action, exacerbated the problems facing an outside investor in Dry Creek.

Citing *Luce v. United States* [84-1 USTC ¶ 13,549], 4 Cl. Ct. 212 (1983), respondent

Estate of Mark S. Gallo

implies in his brief that we should presume the purchaser of the 1,178 Class J shares to be a member of the Gallo family.[10] Respondent is desperately reaching for some support for the unsupportable. As respondent admits, such a presumption would be inconsistent with the holding of *Estate of Bright v. United States* [81-2 USTC ¶ 13,436], 658 F. 2d 999 (5th Cir. 1981) (en banc), expressly adopted by both the Ninth Circuit Court of Appeals and this Court. See *Propstra v. United States* [82-2 USTC ¶ 13,475], 680 F. 2d 1248, 1251-1253 (9th Cir. 1982); *Estate of Andrews v. Commissioner* [Dec. 39,523], 79 T. C. 938, 953-956 (1982). See also *Estate of Lee v. Commissioner* [Dec. 35,017], 69 T. C. 860 (1978). For our purposes, the assumed purchaser of the shares in issue must be hypothetical, not a Gallo family member.

Respondent further argues that a published empirical study, considered by both Desmond and petitioner's experts, supports the 10 percent discount determined by Desmond. The study relied upon by respondent concerned discounts applicable to restricted stock of publicly traded companies. Although such shares were typically issued in private placements and were not immediately tradeable, a purchaser of the shares could reasonably expect them to be publicly traded in the future. The purchaser of Dry Creek shares, by contrast, could foresee no reasonable prospect of his shares becoming freely traded.

We thus reject Desmond's 10 percent discount figure as too low. Considering the entire record, we believe that the 36 percent figure determined by Lehman Brothers, which was substantially equal to that used by Cadenasso, was a reasonable discount to reflect the illiquidity of the 1,178 Class J shares. Although Pratt concluded that 50 percent was an appropriate discount, we believe that the conclusions of Cadenasso and Lehman Brothers, as integral **portions of comprehensive analyses, were more reliable in the present case.**

Estate of Murphy

B. *MINORITY DISCOUNTS*

1. *Introduction*

Petitioner's argument for application of a minority discount here is simple enough. Petitioner argues the following. On July 29, 1982, before her death, decedent made a gift of .88 percent of the stock to each of her two children. Those are minority blocks, and should be allowed a minority discount. At her death on August 16, 1982, she exercised a power of appointment for 49.65 percent of the stock to a trust for her children. That is a minority block. The estate tax applies to that which passes at death, not what was owned before death, or what the legatee receives after death. *Estate of Bright v. United States*, 658 F.2d at 1002; *Estate of Chenoweth v. Commissioner* [Dec. 44,012], 88 T.C. 1577, 1582 (1987). Decedent should be taxed on assets that were in her gross estate on her estate tax valuation date, August 16, 1982, and not on assets she no longer owned. *United States v. Land* [62-1 USTC ¶ 12,078], 303 F.2d 170, 171-172 (5th Cir. 1962), cert. denied 371 U.S. 862 (1962); see also *Ithaca Trust Co. v. United States* [1 USTC ¶ 386], 279 U.S. 151 (1929). Decedent no longer owned the two .88 percent blocks of stock given before her death to her children, and so, petitioner concludes, a minority discount should be applied to the block transferred at her death.

The question is whether petitioner's reasoning applies here.

As simple as petitioner's approach appears, we pause before accepting it. That is because the facts in this case are extreme. Briefly, control was kept in and exercised continuously by the Murphy family, including decedent, followed by her children. Decedent implemented a plan 18 days before her death with the sole and explicit purpose to obtain a minority discount. We are aware of no case where a court has allowed a minority discount in this situation. [1]

We hold that a minority discount is not applicable to the Evening Telegram Company and Television Wisconsin, Inc. stock in these cases. Courts have rejected attempts to avoid taxation of the control value of stock holdings through bifurcation of the blocks. *Hamm v. Commissioner* [64-1 USTC ¶ 12,206], 325 F.2d 934 (8th Cir. 1963), affg. a Memorandum Opinion of this Court [Dec. 25,193(M)]; *Driver v. United States*, 38 AFTR 2d 76-6315, 76-2 USTC ¶ 13,155 (W.D. Wis 1976); *Blanchard v. United States* [68-2 USTC ¶ 12,567], 291 F. Supp. 348 (S.D.

Iowa, 1968); *Richardson v. Commissioner* [Dec. 13,610(M)], a Memorandum Opinion of this Court dated Nov. 30, 1943, affd. [45-2 USTC ¶ 10,225] 151 F.2d 102 (2d Cir. 1945), cert. denied, 326 U.S. 796 (1945); see also *Ahmanson Foundation v. United States* [81-2 USTC ¶ 13,438], 674 F.2d 761 (9th Cir. 1981); *Estate of Curry v. United States* [83-1 USTC ¶ 13,518], 706 F.2d 1424 (7th Cir. 1981); *Northern Trust Co. v. Commissioner* [Dec. 43,261], 87 T.C. 349 (1986), affd. sub nom. *Citizens Bank & Trust Co. v. Commissioner* [88-1 USTC ¶ 13,755], 839 F.2d 1249 (7th Cir. 1988); *Estate of Pudim v. Commissioner* [Dec. 39,430(M)], T.C. Memo. 1982-606. The rationale for allowing a minority discount does not apply because decedent and her children continuously exercised control powers. For example, decedent remained as chairman of the board after the transfer of stock to her children. A minority discount should not be applied if the explicit purpose and effect of fragmenting the control block of stock was solely to reduce Federal tax. *Knetsch v. United States* [60-2 USTC ¶ 9785], 364 U.S. 361, 367 (1960); *Gregory v. Helvering* [35-1 USTC ¶ 9043], 293 U.S. 465, 469 (1935).

Cases which allow minority discounts and reject family attribution, such as *Estate of Bright v. United States, supra,* have involved markedly different circumstances, and we believe they are fairly distinguished from this case. We do not apply family attribution in reaching this result, and we believe our result is fully consistent with the 1981 amendments to section 2035. Finally, we believe petitioner's theory, if extended by us to the circumstances here, would be contrary to the policy upon which estate and gift tax unification in 1976 was based.

2. *Decedent and Her Children Had Continuous Control Powers*

A minority discount is appropriate if the block of stock does not enjoy the variety of rights associated with control. *Estate of Chenoweth v. Commissioner* [Dec. 44,012], 88 T.C. 1577, 1582 (1987); *Estate of Andrews v. Commissioner*, 79 T.C. at 953; see *Harwood v. Commissioner*, 82 T.C. at 267. To decide whether to apply a minority discount here, we will compare the rights usually associated with control with the rights enjoyed by decedent and passed to her children.

In *Estate of Newhouse v. Commissioner* [Dec. 46,411], 94 T.C. 193, 251(1990), we said:

---

[1] Commentators writing about the potential for abuse of transfer of control of a closely held corporation without paying Federal transfer taxes have noted, "No court has considered whether a minority discount is permissible when the transfer of the minority interest gives the donee a majority interest in and control of the corporation." Fellows and Painter, "Valuing Close Corporations for Federal Wealth Transfer Taxes: A Statutory Solution to the Disappearing Wealth Syndrome," 30 Stan. L. Rev. 895, 898 n.13 (1978).

Estate of Murphy

Control means that, because of the interest owned, the shareholder can unilatarally direct corporate action, select management, decide the amount of distribution, rearrange the corporation's capital structure, and decide whether to liquidate, merge, or sell assets. * * *

Minority shareholders do not have control power if they are outsiders. See *Schroeder v. Commissioner* [Dec. 17,146], 13 T.C. 259 (1949). The holder of a minority interest who is an outsider lacks control over corporate policy, cannot direct the payment of dividends, and cannot compel a liquidation of corporate assets. See *Harwood v. Commissioner*, 82 T.C. at 267; *Estate of Andrews v. Commissioner*, 79 T.C. at 953.

The rights associated with control have been more particularly stated as follows:

1. Elect directors and appoint management.

2. Determine management compensation and perquisites.

3. Set policy and change the course of business.

4. Acquire or liquidate assets.

5. Select people with whom to do business and award contracts.

6. Make acquisitions.

7. Liquidate, dissolve, sell out, or recapitalize the company.

8. Sell or acquire treasury shares.

9. Register the company's stock for a public offering.

10. Declare and pay dividends.

11. Change the articles of incorporation or bylaws.

S. Pratt, Valuing a Business: The Analysis and Appraisal of Closely Held Companies, 55-56 (1989).

Other than the power to liquidate or sell assets, decedent, and her children thereafter, enjoyed the powers of control.

Actual control of stock of the Evening Telegram Company has always been with the Murphy family. Decedent's father-in-law started the business. Decedent's husband inherited and carried on the business holding all shares. Decedent was given a general power of appointment over the marital trust with a control block of Evening Telegram Company stock. She was chairman of the board from 1980 until her death in 1982.

In 1975, decedent established a trust for the benefit of her two children with First Bank-North as trustee. She transferred 6.64 percent of the voting stock from the marital trust to each of the trusts for her children. Immediately prior to her two lifetime gifts of .88 percent of the stock (100 shares) to each child, the marital trust had 51.41 percent of the voting stock, the residuary trust had 35.31 percent, and the trusts established by decedent for her children had the remaining 13.28 percent. The trust officer for First Bank-North testified that he intended to follow the intentions of the trustors and keep the Evening Telegram stock with the Murphy family. Until the two .88 percent of stock lifetime gifts, the marital trust never had less than 51 percent of the outstanding voting stock.

Upon decedent's death, 49.65 percent of stock in the marital trust passed by power of appointment to the two trusts she had established for the children. Each child also held 100 shares (.88 percent) outright and was beneficiary under decedent's husband's residual trust, with 35.31 percent of the stock.

During the 18-day period between the lifetime gifts of the stock to decedent's two children and her death, decedent continued to be chairman of the board and her two children held the two top management positions. We believe that all concerned intended nothing of substance to change between the time of transfer and the time of her death, and that nothing of substance did change.

3. Application of a Minority Discount Where a Control Block is Briefly Fragmented for Tax Avoidance Purposes

Numerous cases have denied application of a minority discount where stock is transferred between family members through bifurcated transfers. E.g., *Hamm v. Commissioner* [64-1 USTC ¶ 12,206], 325 F.2d 934 (8th Cir. 1963); *Luce v. Commissioner* [84-1 USTC ¶ 13,549], 4 Cl. Ct. 212 (1983); *Blanchard v. United States* [68-2 USTC ¶ 12,567], 291 F. Supp. 348 (S.D. Iowa, 1968). This is consistent with the established principle that transactions with no purpose or effect other than to reduce taxes are disregarded for Federal tax purposes. *Knetsch v. United States, supra* at 365; *Gregory v. Helvering, supra* at 469. Many other cases apply a minority discount, but we believe they are distinguishable as discussed below.

In a case involving valuation of stock in a closely held corporation, the taxpayer, for tax avoidance purposes, attempted to fragment a controlling interest into six minority interest blocks. *Blanchard v. United States, supra*. The taxpayer in *Blanchard* made six gifts of stock to her grandchildren which she testified were for tax avoidance purposes. *Blanchard v. United States, supra* at 351. The court found an informal family agreement to sell the stock together. Less than six weeks later, all of the family stock

Estate of Murphy

and control of the corporation was sold to a single buyer. The Government valued the gifted stock as a part of a controlling interest. In an action for refund of gift tax, the taxpayer argued that the gift tax was required to be computed with a per-share minority interest applied to the fractional shares. The court held that a fair construction of the applicable section of the Internal Revenue Code "requires that the stock be valued as part of a controlling interest." *Blanchard v. United States, supra* at 352. The court said:

> Both before and after the transfers in trust the controlling interest was owned by the family. * * * It is a necessary inference from these facts that so long as the gifted stock was controlled by the family, it had to be valued as a part of a majority interest in the bank. * * * Had it not been sold then, still would certainly have been held as part of the controlling interest and must be valued as such. * * *

Blanchard v. United States, supra at 352.

Although the stock was not sold in this case before us, it remains a part of the controlling interest. There was a lifelong commitment and understanding by Morgan and Elizabeth Murphy, and their children, to keep control of the business in the family.

The court in *Blanchard* recognized that the family had an informal agreement to (1) retain control, and (2) to sell the stock only as a controlling block. In this case there was a similar implicit understanding among all concerned to retain control of the business.

A minority discount may also be rejected where stock of a closely held corporation is given by the controlling shareholders to their children. *Luce v. Commissioner,* 4 Cl. Ct. 212 (1983). In Luce, a refund suit for gift taxes paid for gifts by the controlling shareholders of a closely held corporation, the court rejected the application of a minority discount because the applicable market in which the hypothetical willing buyer may be found need not be one which includes the general public. In *Luce* the taxpayers wanted control of the company to remain in the family and it was their intent that no shares be held by strangers.

Minority discounts need not be applied when the transferred stock is part of a family controlling interest. *Driver v. United States,* 38 AFTR 2d 76-6315, 76-2 USTC ¶ 13,155 (W.D. Wis 1976); *Richardson v. Commissioner,* a Memorandum Opinion of this Court dated Nov. 30, 1943.

In *Driver v. United States, supra,* the donor owned all the stock of a family corporation. On December 31, 1968, and January 2, 1969, the donor gave 66 percent of the stock to her nephew and his wife and children. On both days less than 50 percent was given. No one was given as much as 50 percent of the stock. She also gave 14 percent to her sister, and 4 percent to a longtime employee and his wife. She retained 16 percent of the stock for herself. The court treated the gifts made over the two days as consisting of a single gift.

In *Hamm v. Commissioner* [64-1 USTC ¶ 12,206], 325 F.2d 934 (8th Cir. 1963), affg. a Memorandum Opinion of this Court [Dec. 25,193(M)], the taxpayers sought to fragment a 100-percent control block of stock and apply a minority discount. Respondent's aggregated valuation was sustained at trial.

On appeal, *Hamm* was decided by the Court of Appeals for the Eighth Circuit, the circuit to which the instant case is appealable. The Eighth Circuit noted that the Tax Court considered a large number of factors in deciding the value of the stock in *Hamm,* including "the number of outstanding shares of each class of the company's capital stock, and the identity of the shareholders." *Hamm v. Commissioner, supra* at 938-939 n.1.

The Eighth Circuit expressed doubts about the validity of valuing stock as a minority interest when the controlling interest was owned by the family. As noted by Judge (now Justice) Blackmun:

> If, in view of the over-all complete ownership of the common [stock] by the Hamm family, this minority interest point has any real validity, the foregoing [explanation of the Tax Court's basis for its findings] convincingly demonstrates that the minority interest aspect was considered by the court and that its determination was made as to that specific interest.

Hamm v. Commissioner, supra at 941.

Minority blocks of stock have been aggregated as components of a single control block where tax avoidance motives exist. *Ahmanson Foundation v. United States* [81-2 USTC ¶ 13,438], 674 F.2d 761 (9th Cir. 1981); *Estate of Curry v. United States* [83-1 USTC ¶ 13,518], 706 F.2d 1424 (7th Cir. 1983); *Northern Trust Co. v. Commissioner* [Dec. 43,261], 87 T.C. 349 (1986). See also *Estate of Pudim v. Commissioner* [Dec. 39,430(M)], T.C. Memo. 1982-606.

Ahmanson Foundation and *Estate of Curry* address the potential for abuse if decedent's controlling interests could be fragmented for valuation purposes. In *Ahmanson Foundation,* decedent owned a controlling interest in a trust that held 100 percent of a corporation, consisting of 100 shares of stock. One share was voting stock while the remaining 99 shares were nonvoting stock. The 99 nonvoting shares were bequeathed to a charitable organization. The

Estate of Murphy

sole remaining voting share was bequeathed to a trust in favor of decedent's son. The charitable organization argued that decedent's stock should be bifurcated and valued separately. The Court of Appeals for the Ninth Circuit rejected this approach and held that the stock must be valued as one unit as held in the hands of the estate. *Ahmanson Foundation v. United States, supra* at 769.

Ahmanson Foundation is similar to the case at bar because, in both instances, the plan to transfer control was designed solely to avoid transfer taxation of the controlling interest. Decedents also attempted to obtain a discount for the vast majority of their control block by separating it from a small portion of the control stock.

Citing *Ahmanson Foundation* with approval, the Seventh Circuit Court of Appeals also rejected a fragmentation theory. In *Estate of Curry v. United States, supra,* an estate valuation refund jury trial case, a taxpayer valued a closely held corporation with the assumption that the voting and the nonvoting stock would be sold separately, even though the estate had 53-percent voting control. The trial court allowed the taxpayer's fragmentation theory to be presented to the jury. It refused to give two jury instructions requested by the Government: (1) the jury must value decedent's nonvoting stock at the same level as voting stock; and (2) the jury may not find a value less than a value that the estate conceded was liquidation value. The court held that fair market value is assessed as the property exists in the hands of the estate rather than fragmented or as it may exist if fragmented through a chain of post-death transactions. *Estate of Curry v. United States, supra* at 1427. The court stated:

> Additionally, to permit the hypothetical bifurcation of an otherwise integrated bundle of property for valuation purposes would severely undermine the estate tax system and permit abusive manipulation by inviting an executor to invent elaborate scenarios of disaggregated disposition in order to minimize total value. For example, an estate in possession of all shares of a corporation, voting and non-voting, could, under the regime urged by the estate here, arbitrarily slice the voting share block so thinly as to deny attribution of a control premium to any resulting block.
> * * *

Estate of Curry v. United States, supra at 1428.

In *Northern Trust Co. v. Commissioner, supra,* a gift tax valuation case where the taxpayers had a tax avoidance motive for the transfer of stock in a closely held corporation, we applied a rationale against fragmentation, stating:

Given petitioners' concerted estate freeze plan put in place by the simultaneous gifts in trust, we find their attempt to discredit respondent's reliance on *Estate of Curry* and *Ahmanson Foundation* to be, with all due respect, disingenuous. Petitioners attempt to draw a distinction based upon the fact that the two cited cases involved the stock of a single majority stockholder, whereas here none were in control. In the context of this case, this is a distinction without a difference, because even petitioners cannot deny that in creating the estate freeze plan they marched in lockstep. So marching, their position was no different than that of a single majority stockholder.

Northern Trust Co. v. Commissioner, 87 T.C. at 388. Relying on *Ahmanson Foundation v. United States, supra,* and *Estate of Curry v. United States, supra,* we held that value was not affected by the actual transfer of the stock to the trusts.

A taxpayer may decrease his taxes, or avoid them altogether by means which the law permits; however, this right is limited by the requirement for some substance to a transaction to support its form. *Commissioner v. Estate of Church* [49-1 USTC ¶ 10,702], 335 U.S. 632 (1949); *Helvering v. Hallock* [40-1 USTC ¶ 9208], 309 U.S. 106 (1940); *Gregory v. Helvering* [35-1 USTC ¶ 9043], 293 U.S. 465, 469-470 (1935).

The substance over form doctrine was applied in a nonbusiness setting where a taxpayer seeking tax benefits from a personal investment was required to demonstrate that the transaction had some nontax purpose. *Knetsch v. United States* [60-2 USTC ¶ 9785], 364 U.S. 361, 365 (1960). In *Knetsch,* the Supreme Court cited Judge Learned Hand's test that a deduction will be disallowed if it does "not appreciably affect [the taxpayer's] beneficial interest except to reduce his tax." *Knetsch v. United States, supra* at 366 (citing the dissent in *Gilbert v. Commissioner* [57-2 USTC ¶ 9929], 248 F.2d 399, 411 (2d Cir. 1957)).

The same rationale applies in the cases before us. Here, we conclude that decedent's two small lifetime gifts of Evening Telegram Company stock to her children do not appreciably affect decedent's beneficial interest except to reduce Federal transfer taxes. *Knetsch v. United States, supra* at 367.

Although decedent actually transferred two blocks of .88 percent of the stock and reduced her interest to 49.65 percent, we believe that it did not appreciably affect her interest.

4. Minority Discount Cases Distinguished

Cases allowing a minority discount where a family owned a controlling interest generally

Estate of Murphy

fall under one or more of the following categories: (1) the transferor did not have control prior to the transfers, *Estate of Bright v. United States* [81-2 USTC ¶ 13,436], 658 F.2d 999 (5th Cir. 1981); *Ward v. Commissioner* [Dec. 43,178], 87 T.C. 78 (1986); *Estate of Andrews v. Commissioner* [Dec. 39,523], 79 T.C. 938 (1982); *Estate of Lee v. Commissioner* [Dec. 35,017], 69 T.C. 860 (1978); *Gallun v. Commissioner* [Dec. 32,830(M)], T.C. Memo. 1974-284; (2) the parties agreed that a minority discount was applicable, *Harwood v. Commissioner* [Dec. 40,985], 82 T.C. 239 (1984); *Estate of Piper v. Commissioner* [Dec. 36,315], 72 T.C. 1062 (1979); *Estate of Heckscher v. Commissioner* [Dec. 33,023], 63 T.C. 485, 497 (1975); *Martin v. Commissioner* [Dec. 42,311(M)], T.C. Memo. 1985-424; (3) tax-motivated transactions were not found; or (4) the transaction preceded gift and estate tax unification in 1976. *E.g., Estate of Bright v. United States, supra; Estate of Lee v. Commissioner, supra.*

a. *Estate of Bright v. United States Distinguished*

The instant cases are distinguishable from *Estate of Bright v. United States, supra.* The issue in *Estate of Bright* was whether decedent's husband's stock should be attributable to decedent for purposes of determining if the decedent owned a controlling interest. We will first describe *Estate of Bright* and then explain our grounds for distinguishing it.

Mary Bright died in Texas in 1971. Before her death, she held 27.5 percent (an undivided one-half interest of 55 percent) of several closely held corporations as her half of the community property under Texas law. The remaining 45 percent was held by unrelated third parties. Her death terminated the community and the community property was divided. Under her will, her 27.5-percent interest was conveyed to a trust for the benefit of her four children with her husband as trustee.

The estate valued her 27.5-percent interest with a minority discount applied. The Government determined that for estate tax purposes, family attribution should apply before the transfer of shares, thereby valuing her share as half of a controlling interest.

Under Texas law, either the estate or the surviving spouse had the right to partition the stock. The trial court ordered that family attribution would not apply to decedent's share as a matter of law and that decedent's interest was 27.5 percent. The parties prepared for trial complying with the order. The Government appealed the validity of the trial court's pretrial order relating to control. The Fifth Circuit panel reversed and remanded. The estate's petition for rehearing en banc was granted. The Fifth Circuit en banc vacated the panel opinion and the

District Court affirmed, noting that partition would be freely granted due to fungible shares, concluding:

> Thus, the estate has no means to prevent the conversion of its interest into shares representing a 27½% block, and we conclude that the estate's interest is the equivalent of a 27½% block of the stock. Accordingly, we reject the government's approach of valuing the 55% control block, with its control premium, and then taking one-half thereof. [Citation omitted.]

Estate of Bright v. United States, supra at 1001. since a 27.5-percent block is not a controlling interest, a minority discount was allowed for its stock.

The court in *Estate of Bright* also held that the pre-death relationship between Mr. and Mrs. Bright was irrelevant. *Estate of Bright v. United States, supra* at 1006. The court affirmed the trial court's ruling

> to the extent that it defined the interest to be valued as equivalent to 27½% of the stock, to the extent that it excluded as evidence of value the fact that the estate's stock had, prior to decedent's death, been held jointly with Mr. Bright's interest as community property, and the fact that, after death, the particular executor (Mr. Bright) and legatee (Mr. Bright as trustee) was related to another stock holder [sic] (Mr. Bright individually), and to the extent that it excluded any evidence that Mr. Bright, as executor or trustee, would have refused to sell the estate's 27½% block except in conjunction with his own stock and as part of a 55% control block. We hold that family attribution cannot be applied to lump the estate's stock to that of any related party, but rather that the stock is deemed to be held by a hypothetical seller who is related to no one.

Estate of Bright v. United States, supra at 1006-1007.

Estate of Bright v. United States, supra, is distinguishable from the instant case.

i. *Estate of Bright Preceded Unification of Transfer Taxes.* Mrs. Bright died in 1971, before unification of gift and estate taxes. Thus, the case did not involve a year in which there was a unified transfer tax system, unlike the instant case. See *infra* paragraph B-5.

ii. *Minority Interest.* In *Estate of Bright,* decedent's interest was a minority interest. There is no indication Mrs. Bright ever owned more. In contrast, in the instant case, decedent owned a controlling interest almost all of her life following her husband's death.

Estate of Murphy

Since Mrs. Bright always had a minority interest, the Commissioner, to oppose a minority discount, needed to attribute Mr. Bright's holdings to Mrs. Bright. In the instant case petitioner argues that respondent must also apply attribution of stock between family members to prevail.

We disagree. We do not apply a family attribution theory to reach our result. There is no dispute that decedent had control up until 18 days before her death. We have found that decedent's plan to appear to relinquish control for that brief period lacked substance and economic effect. Accordingly, we disregard the plan to appear to relinquish control for transfer tax purposes, and treat the gift and transfer at death as part of one plan transferring control to decedent's children. This analysis does not rely on family attribution.

Attribution is treating stock owned by different persons as if it were owned by one person. It is not necessary to use attribution here because here the transfer of control to decedent's children in two steps in substance is one transaction. Using this analysis, decedent is subject to transfer tax on the control premium without attribution from family members. Accordingly, the Court does not apply a family attribution theory.

iii. *Lack of Control.* The rationale given by courts for allowing a minority discount applies to the *Estate of Bright* case, but does not apply to the instant case.

In *Estate of Bright*, there is no indication that any member of the Bright family was employed in the business. The Fifth Circuit did not indicate whether the Bright family exercised powers of control, such as possessing key management positions, in contrast with the instant case. In the instant case, there was also a clear understanding between decedent, her children, and the trustee to maintain family control of the corporation.

In *Estate of Bright*, control of the corporation did not disappear for Federal transfer tax purposes, then reappear in the hands of target parties. At issue in *Estate of Bright* was the characterization and value of property following death.

iv. *No Tax Avoidance Purpose.* The sole purpose of the transaction in the instant case was tax avoidance. That advice was given by Mr. Randy, and implemented.

The explicit plan was to transfer .88 percent of the stock to each of the children to make it appear that control had temporarily disappeared. This had no intended effect or purpose other than the anticipated tax savings. There was no comparable tax avoidance plan described by the court in *Estate of Bright.*

b. *Other Cases Distinguished*

Several other cases follow *Estate of Bright v. United States, supra,* or are consistent with it and are distinguished from the instant cases on one or more of the same grounds.

The court in *Estate of Bright* agreed with our holding in *Estate of Lee v. Commissioner* [Dec. 35,017], 69 T.C. 860 (1978). *Estate of Lee* was also a community property case where the Government argued that decedent's spouse's stock should be attributed to decedent for purposes of determining if decedent owned a controlling interest. Mrs. Lee died in the State of Washington in 1971 survived by her husband and three adult children. We held that decedent's interest was 40 percent of the common stock and 50 percent of the preferred stock of the corporation. Respondent argued family attribution under Washington community property laws. Mrs. Lee did not have control of the closely held corporation before the transfer.

Estate of Lee is inapplicable to the instant case for the same reasons that *Estate of Bright* does not apply. The taxpayer in *Estate of Lee* did not have control in her own right. Also, the court did not find any tax avoidance motive. The case also involved a year before transfer tax unification.

In *Estate of Andrews v. Commissioner* [Dec. 39,523], 79 T.C. 938 (1982), the taxpayer never owned control in his own right. Mr. Andrews died in 1975 owning about 20 percent of four closely held corporations with his two brothers and two sisters owning the remaining 80 percent. The Government argued that no minority discount should apply because "all shareholders in the four corporations, including decedent, shared in control." We rejected the pre-death family attribution theory and applied a minority discount.

In *Ward v. Commissioner* [Dec. 43,178], 87 T.C. 78 (1986), a gift tax valuation case, the husband and wife never separately owned control of a closely held corporation. The Government sought to attribute stock of one spouse to the other and to deny a minority discount. In *Ward,* the taxpayer husband purchased a ranch in Florida and deeded it in 1978 to a newly formed closely held corporation. Husband and wife each received 43.7 percent of the stock. Their three sons each received 4.2 percent of the stock in exchange for cattle and depreciable assets contributed to the corporation. In each of three subsequent years, husband and wife made gifts of minority stock interests to each of their three sons as a part of their estate plan. The taxpayers intended that the ranch continue operating as a single economic unit after their deaths. We rejected the Government's attempt to apply family attribution.

Estate of Murphy

In *Ward,* the taxpayers did not begin with individual control. Only when viewed together did the husband and wife have control. Thus, *Ward* is distinguishable from the instant case because the taxpayers in *Ward* did not fragment a controlling block of stock with an anticipated result of complete avoidance of Federal transfer tax liability on the premium associated with control.

In *Minihan v. Commissioner* [Dec. 43,746], 88 T.C. 492 (1987) (Court reviewed), four parties apparently owned a 33.6-percent, 29.4-percent, 25.2-percent, and 11.8-percent proportionate interest, respectively, in a corporation. In 1981, they sold the stock to separate trusts for their families. The Commissioner apparently characterized the transactions as gifts and valued the gifts with a control premium by aggregating the holdings of the four parties. The Government conceded all issues, and the taxpayers sought reasonable litigation costs. We concluded that the Commissioner's reliance on aggregation was unreasonable. *Minihan v. Commissioner, supra* at 500.

As stated, all of the cases following *Estate of Bright* are distinguishable from the instant case for the same reasons that *Estate of Bright* is distinguishable, except that *Ward* and *Minihan* involve post transfer tax unification years.

A few pre-1976 cases do not squarely fit into the three general areas for applying minority discounts. *Drybrough v. United States* [62-2 USTC ¶ 12,098], 208 F.Supp. 279 (W.D. Ky. 1962); *Whittemore v. Fitzpatrick* [54-2 USTC ¶ 10,976], 127 F.Supp. 710 (D. Conn. 1954); *Obermer v. United States* [65-1 USTC ¶ 12,280], 238 F.Supp. 29, 34 (D. Hawaii 1964). These cases were decided before unification of gift and estate taxes in 1976. As discussed *supra* at paragraph 5(a), we believe gift and estate tax unification showed congressional intent that all property be subject to relatively uniform transfer taxes, which may be undermined if owners of control may pass it to their relatives by using transactions structured to avoid transfer taxation of the control premium.

5. *Legislative History of the Gift and Estate Tax*

Petitioner and respondent both make arguments based on the legislative history of the gift and estate tax.

Petitioner argues that valuing the stock for estate and gift tax purposes with the premium associated with control of the business would constitute reenactment of section 2035.

Petitioner also points out that Congress has considered and rejected provisions that would restrict application of minority discounts, and argues that should be taken as a rejection of respondent's position by Congress.

Respondent argues that allowance of a minority discount to petitioner is contrary to congressional intent in enacting unification of estate and gift taxes in 1976.

The Federal estate tax was enacted in 1916, and a permanent gift tax was enacted in 1932. Prior to 1976, the burden imposed on most lifetime gifts was substantially less than the burden imposed on transfers at death. Rules to discourage "gifts in contemplation of death" arose as a by-product, and are discussed below.

(a) *Unification of Gift and Estate Taxes in 1976.* The Tax Reform Act of 1976 "unified" estate and gift taxes. Pub. L. 94-455, secs. 2001-2010, 90 Stat. 1520. Congress intended to largely eliminate the disparity between gift tax and estate tax, and to unify them into a fully integrated system by "elimina[ting] ways by which estate planners can reduce the estate and gift tax burden through special patterns of transferring their property." H. Rept. 94-1380 (1976), 1976-3 C.B. (Vol. 3) 735, 741. The unified system imposes Federal estate and gift taxes based on a single unified rate schedule applied to a donor/decedent's cumulative inter vivos transfers and transfers at death (secs. 2001, 2012, 2501, and 2502), and a unified credit applicable to a donor/decedent's cumulative gift tax and estate tax liabilities. Secs. 2010 and 2505.

Some limited advantages to lifetime giving remained, such as (1) the availability of an annual gift tax exclusion of $3,000 per donee (raised to $10,000 in 1981), sec. 2503(b), and (2) the fact that appreciation of property from the time the gift is made to the date of death is removed from the transfer tax base.

We discussed the legislative history of the unified transfer tax system enacted by the Tax Reform Act of 1976 in *Estate of Sachs v. Commissioner* [Dec. 43,823], 88 T.C. 769 (1987), affd. in part and revd. in part [88-2 USTC ¶ 13,781] 856 F.2d 1158 (8th Cir. 1988). The issue in *Estate of Sachs* was whether a gift tax paid by a donee on a gift made within three years of the donor/decedent's death was includable in the donor/decedent's gross estate under the "gross up" provisions of section 2035(c). The literal language of section 2035(c) did not require the inclusion of gift taxes paid by a donee. Nonetheless, we held that the gift tax was includable in the donor's gross estate. This holding was based upon the intent of Congress to equalize the treatment of deathbed transfers and transfers at death. We explained:

Insistence on the literal language of section 2035(c) would distort the framework erected by the Tax Reform Act of 1976. The act retained some of the prior law's preferences for lifetime gifts; however, these preferences were not made available to deathbed gifts.

Estate of Murphy

Petitioners' construction of section 2035(c) extends the benefit of one such preference to deathbed net gifts. Mechanical application of section 2035(c) would completely remove from the transfer tax base all funds used to pay gift tax on such gifts. This interpretation of the statute is wholly inconsistent with Congress' goal of sharply distinguishing deathbed gifts from other gifts and eliminating the disparity of treatment between deathbed gifts and transfers at death.

Estate of Sachs v. Commissioner, supra at 777.

Decedent owned and enjoyed control of the Evening Telegram Company. She did not transfer the stock that brought her below 50 percent of the outstanding stock until shortly before her death. The two lifetime gifts of .88 percent of stock (100 shares each) shortly before her death were an attempt to keep from being taxed on the value of the controlling interest in the corporation which she owned for a significant part of her life. Decedent's design was to appear to relinquish control of the corporation for Federal transfer tax purposes, but never in fact to have it leave the hands of her family. We believe that decedent's plan is inconsistent with the unified transfer tax enacted in 1976. *Gregory v. Helvering* [35-1 USTC ¶ 9043], 293 U.S. 465, 469 (1935).

(b) *Effect of 1981 Amendments to Gift in Contemplation of Death Rule.* We next consider petitioner's argument that disallowance of a minority discount is inconsistent with changes made to section 2035 in 1981. As indicated above, prior to 1976 the burden imposed on most lifetime gifts was lower than on transfers at death. As a result, rules were enacted to discourage estate tax avoidance by making gifts shortly before death.

Prior to 1977, gifts made within three years of death were rebuttably presumed to have been made in contemplation of death. These gifts were said to be "in contemplation of death," and were included in decedent's estate if the presumption was not overcome. Sec. 2035.

In 1976, Congress removed the rebuttable presumption and provided for automatic inclusion in decedent's estate of all gifts made within three years of death, regardless of motivation. Tax Reform Act of 1976, Pub. L. 94-455, tit. XX, sec. 2001(a)(5), 90 Stat. 1520, 1848.

Overall, however, as a result of unification of gift and estate taxes in 1976, there was much less need for a gift in contemplation of death rule. As a result, in 1981, the three-year gift in contemplation of death rule was sharply narrowed.

Petitioner concedes that, but for the 1981 amendments, the stock transferred to decedent's children would have been automatically included in her estate. Petitioner's position here, however, is that the 1981 amendments to section 2035 make petitioner eligible for a minority discount—and to escape transfer taxation of the control value—by allowing decedent to split the gift of control into a lifetime gift and a testamentary bequest. We disagree.

The Ways and Means Committee in its report on Economic Recovery Tax Act, stated that:

Under the unified transfer tax system adopted in the Tax Reform Act of 1976, the inclusion in the gross estate of gifts made within 3 years of death generally has the effect of including only the property's post-gift appreciation in the gross estate * * *. The committee believes that inclusion of such appreciation [187] generally is unnecessary except for gifts of life insurance and certain property included in the gross estate pursuant to certain of the so-called transfer sections (secs. 2036, 2037, 2038, 2041, and 2042). * * *

H. Rept. 97-201, 186-187 (1981), 1981-2 C.B. 352, 390; *Estate of Slater v. Commissioner* [Dec. 46,114], 93 T.C. 513, 519 (1989).

This shows that the Ways and Means Committee intended to no longer tax the post-gift appreciation. However, we see no basis in the statute or legislative history for petitioner's view that Congress intended the control premium to escape transfer taxation because of the 1981 amendments to section 2035.

The three-year gift in contemplation of death rule was retained for property included in the gross estate pursuant to the transfer sections, such as section 2036. Under section 2036(a)(1), property is included in decedent's estate to the extent decedent retained the actual possession or enjoyment thereof. This applies even though decedent had no enforceable right to such possession or enjoyment. *Guynn v. United States* [71-1 USTC ¶ 12,742], 437 F.2d 1148 (4th Cir. 1971); *Estate of McNichol v. Commissioner* [59-1 USTC ¶ 11,868], 265 F.2d 667 (3d Cir. 1959), affg. [Dec. 22,903] 29 T.C. 1179 (1958), cert. denied 361 U.S. 829 (1959); *Estate of Honigman v. Commissioner* [Dec. 34,039], 66 T.C. 1080, 1082 (1976); *Estate of Linderme v. Commissioner* [Dec. 29,591], 52 T.C. 305, 308 (1969).

Here, we have found that decedent enjoyed the power of control until her death. At the time of the lifetime gifts to her children, decedent and her children did not want anything to change. Decedent and the children kept the same corporate positions. Both children, the trustee, and Mr. Randy testified that they would follow decedent's desire to keep all stock

Estate of Murphy

within the family. Decedent was told that she would own only 49 percent; however, an estate planning memo provided, "Under the first alternative even though she will have a minority interest at the level of 49% she and the bank or she and the children will have control of the corporation." However, neither party raised the section 2036(a)(1) issue, and we do not reach it.

(c) *Prior Legislative Consideration of Minority Discounts.* Petitioner argues that legislative proposals dealing with attribution of stock ownership and minority discounts have been considered, but not enacted; and that we should infer from this that respondent's position has been rejected by the Congress.

In November 1984, the Treasury Department submitted a report to the President entitled "Tax Reform for Fairness, Simplicity, and Economic Growth." It stated that transfer tax saving opportunities continue to be available for lifetime gifts, and that "Minority or fractional share discounts enable taxpayers to structure transfers so as to reduce the aggregate value of property brought within the transfer tax base." Tax Reform for Fairness, Simplicity, and Economic Growth, Vol. 2 at 376, 381. The following was proposed to the President:

The value for transfer tax purposes of a fractional interest in any asset owned, in whole or in part, by a donor or decedent would be a pro rata share of the fair market value of that portion of the asset owned by the donor or decedent. Prior gifts of fractional interests in the asset, as well as any fractional interests in the asset held by the transferor's spouse, would be attributed to the donor or decedent for purposes of determining the value of the fractional interest transferred. * * *

Tax Reform for Fairness, Simplicity, and Economic Growth, Vol. 2 at 387.

The President's tax reform proposals to the Congress for Fairness, Growth and Simplicity, made in May 1985, did not include this proposal.

In 1987 the House of Representatives passed a variation of this proposal as part of the Omnibus Budget Reconciliation Act (OBRA), H. Rept. 100-391 (II), at 1041-1042 (1987). In describing its provision, the Ways and Means Committee said, "numerous courts have found that * * * minority blocks of stock are worth less than a proportionate share of the value of corporate assets," citing *Ward v. Commissioner* [Dec. 43,178], 87 T.C. 78 (1986), as an example. H. Rept. 100-391 (II), *supra* at 1042. The Committee also said, "Courts have allowed a minority discount even where related persons together own a majority interest," citing *Estate of Bright v. United States, supra.* H. Rept. 100-391 (II), *supra* at 1042. As its reasons for change, the Ways and Means Committee said:

The assignment of a discount to minority ownership of an enterprise assumes that the owners of that enterprise have adverse interests. The Committee believes that such an

assumption is less defensible incorrect [sic] when the owners are related.

H. Rept. 100-391 (II), *supra* at 1042.

The House Bill included a provision that—

(1) The value of stock in a corporation is deemed to be equal to its pro rata share of all the stock of the same class in the corporation, unless a different value is established by clear and convincing evidence. * * *

H. Rept. 100-391 (II), *supra* at 1043.

The Committee believed that this change in the burden of proof would reduce the number of situations in which the value of corporate stock is found to be different than its pro rata share of the underlying assets. H. Rept. 100-391 (II), *supra* at 1043.

In determining whether a different value can be established under the clear and convincing evidence standard, all stock held, directly or indirectly, by an individual or by members of such individual's family is treated as held by one person. Thus, a minority discount will not be appropriate for transfers between family members unless all the stock held by that person or the person's family would qualify for the discount.

H. Rept. 100-391 (II), *supra* 1043.

The above proposals passed the House of Representatives in 1987, but were not included in the Senate Bill or the conference report for OBRA. H. Rept. 100-495 (Conf.), at 994-995 (1987), 1987-3 C.B. 193, 247-248.

The House proposal would have reversed the line of cases it cites, such as *Estate of Ward v. Commissioner, supra,* and *Estate of Bright v. United States, supra.* Petitioner asks us to read Congress' failure to enact the proposal as Congress' blessing of that line of cases. Even if we did that, it does not dispose of the issue before us because our holding is not inconsistent with those cases, which we have distinguished above.

Failure to enact a proposal is speculative at best as a guide to interpretation of law. We do not read these developments as a showing that Congress would want the extreme cases before us to be decided differently.

6. Valuation of Nonvoting Stock

Petitioner seeks to value the voting and nonvoting stock of the Evening Telegram Company differently by applying a discount to the nonvoting stock. Because we have treated decedent's holdings as a control block for valuation purposes, we apply the rule stated in *Estate of Curry v. United States* [83-1 USTC ¶ 13,518], 706 F.2d 1424 (7th Cir. 1983), that where the voting and nonvoting stock are enhanced by being held together, they are to be valued together for Federal estate tax purposes. *Estate of Curry v. United States, supra* at 1429-1430. Thus, the voting and nonvoting common stock are valued the same. Accordingly, the value of 16,240 shares of nonvoting stock on August 16, 1982, was $660 per share as discounted for lack of marketability and liquidation.

Estate of Mildred Herschede Jung

Respondent contends that evidence related to the sale of the assets of Jung Corporation as a going concern is relevant to valuation of the stock held by decedent at her death and relies on *Estate of Hillebrandt v. Commissioner* [Dec. 43,508(M)], T.C. Memo. 1986-560. In *Hillebrandt*, we held that a sale of property after the date of death may be considered evidence of the property's value at the date of death so long as it occurs within a reasonable time after death and intervening events have not changed the value of the property.

Sales occurring after the date of decedent's death are relevant and do not fall within the normal proscription against consideration of events subsequent to the valuation date. *First Nat. Bank of Kenosha v. United* States [85-2 USTC ¶ 13,620], 763 F.2d 891 (7th Cir. 1985). * * * [*Estate of Hillebrandt v. Commissioner, supra.*] [2]

Petitioner urges us to distinguish *Hillebrandt* and similar cases on the ground that the property to be valued was real property, which is "unique." We are not persuaded that the type of property being valued, stock in a closely held corporation as opposed to real estate, requires us to reach a different result. This Court has previously held that:

In determining the value of unlisted stocks, actual sales made in reasonable amounts at arm's length, in the normal course of business within a reasonable time before *or after* the valuation date are the best criteria of market value. *Fitts' Estate v. Commissioner* [56-2 USTC ¶ 11,648], 237 F.2d 729 (8th Cir. 1956). [Emphasis added.]

Duncan Industries, Inc. v. Commissioner [Dec. 36,431], 73 T.C. 266, 276 (1979). Thus, evidence related to a sale of corporate stock is not inadmissible simply because the sale occurred after the valuation date. Rather, the remoteness of the sale from the valuation date may be a factor in determining what weight to give the evidence.

Although this case involves a sale of all the assets of a corporation as a going concern, and not a sale of corporate stock, the value of the underlying assets is relevant to a determination of the value of shares of stock of a closely held corporation. See *Hamm v. Commissioner* [64-1 USTC ¶ 12,206], 325 F.2d 934, 938 (8th Cir.

1963), affg. a Memorandum Opinion of this Court [Dec. 25,193(M)]. While there are obvious distinctions between a sale of a corporation's stock and a sale of its assets as a going concern, we are satisfied that either transaction could be relevant to a determination of the value of the corporation's stock.

The cases discussed above permitted the introduction of evidence *at trial* of sales of property subsequent to the valuation date. It follows, then, that the documents related to the sale of the business assets of Jung Corporation as a going concern satisfy the less stringent standard of relevancy applicable to discovery and must be produced by petitioner.

Petitioner also objected to the production of any documents related to the Jung Corporation, its subsidiaries, and shareholders created after decedent's date of death, whether or not related to the post-valuation date sale of the corporation's assets. According to petitioner, such documents are "irrelevant to the current controversy and are not reasonably calculated to lead to the discovery of admissible evidence." As noted above, the standard of relevancy where discovery is concerned is liberal. "Rule 70(b) permits discovery of information relevant not only to the issues of the pending case, but to the entire 'subject matter' of the case." *Zaentz v. Commissioner, supra* at 471. Furthermore, material which would be helpful to the discovering party in understanding relevant material is also discoverable. *P.T. & L. Construction Co. v. Commissioner, supra* at 413-414.

The value of the stock in Jung Corporation held by decedent at her death is a central issue in this proceeding. Since Jung Corporation was a closely held corporation with a limited market for its stock, valuation of the stock held by decedent will likely involve valuation of the corporation's assets. The financial statements, corporate minutes, and other documents requested by respondent are all calculated to provide insight into the business of the Jung Corporation and will aid respondent in understanding other information relevant to the value of the corporation's stock. Accordingly, we are of the opinion that the Jung Corporation qualifies as part of the "subject matter" of this case, and the documents related to Jung Corporation requested by respondent, even those created after decedent's death, are discoverable as within the broad scope of Rule 70(b).

---

[2] The U.S. Court of Appeals for the Sixth Circuit, the court of appeals to which this case is appealable, held in *Estate of Kaplin v. Commissioner* [85-1 USTC ¶ 9127], 748 F.2d 1109 (6th Cir. 1984), revg. and remanding a Memorandum Opinion of this Court [Dec. 43,017(M)], that the Tax Court erred in determining the fair market value of real

property for gift tax purposes by not taking into account a sale of the property by the donee 2 years after the valuation date. We note that we are bound by the law of the circuit to which a case is appealable under *Golsen v. Commissioner* [71-2 USTC ¶ 9497], 445 F.2d 985 (10th Cir. 1971), affg. [Dec. 30,049], 54 T.C. 742 (1970).

Estate of Clara S. Roeder Winkler

This 10 percent block of voting stock could become pivotal in this closely held corporation, where members of one family held 50 percent and members of another family held 40 percent. By joining with the Simmons family, a minority shareholder could effect control over the corporation and by joining the Winkler family, such a minority shareholder could block action. Petitioner seems to place too much emphasis on the fact that the two families had had 50-50 control for some 40 years and that neither family had ever tried to wrest control from the other. Under the willing seller-willing buyer definition of fair market value, one cannot consider the willing seller or willing buyer as a member of either family. Petitioner improperly suggests that no member of the Winkler family would sell the shares to a member of the Simmons family. Petitioner also fails to consider a sale to an unrelated outsider. Looking at this even split between the two families, the 10 percent block of voting stock, in the hands of a third party unrelated to either family, could indeed become critical. While it is difficult to put a value on this factor, we think it increases the value of the Class A voting stock by at least the 10 percent that Mr. Kramer found. The Court thinks this factor might well increase the value of the voting stock even more, but respondent has suggested no basis for a higher percentage increase. However, this factor becomes important in the matter of any minority discount below.

The experts for both parties discounted their valuation of a 100 percent ownership interest in the corporation for the fact that the decedent held a minority interest in the company and for the lack of marketability of the shares. Courts have long recognized that the shares of stock of a corporation that represent a minority interest are usually worth less than a proportionate share of the value of the assets of the corporation or a 100 percent ownership interest in a company. *Ward v. Commissioner, supra,* 87 T.C. at 106; *Estate of Andrews v. Commissioner, supra,* 79 T.C. at 953. The minority discount is recognized because the holder of a minority interest lacks control over corporate policy, cannot direct the payment of dividends, and cannot compel a liquidation of corporate assets. *Ward v. Commissioner, supra; Harwood v. Commissioner* [Dec. 40,985], 82 T.C. 239, 267 (1984), affd. without published opinion 786 F.2d 1174 (9th Cir. 1986).

A discount for lack of marketability, on the other hand, reflects the fact that there is no ready market for shares in a closely held corporation. *Ward v. Commissioner, supra,* 87 T.C. at 106-107; *Estate of Andrew v. Commissioner, supra,* 79 T.C. at 953. When determining this discount, this Court has also considered the corporation's history of paying dividends and the amount of these dividends, as well as the future

of the company and its dividend-paying capacity. *Northern Trust Co. v. Commissioner, supra,* 87 T.C. at 388-389.

In this case the decedent held 10 percent of the Class A voting stock and approximately one percent of Class B non-voting stock. Petitioner's expert, Mr. Goelzer, applied a 45 percent discount to account for the decedent's minority interest and the lack of marketability of the shares. Mr. Kramer refused to apply such a large discount, applying only a 25 percent discount for the minority interest and lack of marketability.

Mr. Kramer applied only a 25 percent discount, because he thought that the stock had swing characteristics. Mr. Kramer stated that the two families, the Winklers and the Simmons, might compete for the decedent's shares to either seek control in the case of the Simmons or prevent the Simmons from obtaining control in the case of the Winklers. When Mr. Kramer did the appraisal, he was under the impression that the Simmons' interest was owned or controlled by one individual. Thus, Mr. Kramer thought that this one individual would attempt to outbid any other willing buyers to acquire the shares and thus control the company.

While petitioner's counsel suggested that Mr. Kramer was in error and that the stock was owned by the Simmons family, not by one member of the Simmons family, petitioner has failed to prove that such is the fact, particularly as to the Class A voting stock. The record is singularly lacking in information as to exactly who holds the Rock Island stock and in what size blocks. Petitioner's expert report states that:

> The common stock is very closely held by members of seven families. It is our understanding that the Class A (Voting) stock is owned 50% by various members of the Winkler family and the other 50% by members of the Simmons family. The shareholders of Class A common consist of 3 individuals, a trust and a corporation.

* * *

The Court has assumed that the trust mentioned therein is the Clara S. Roeder Winkler Living Trust that held the 8,000 shares of voting stock involved in this case. There is simply no evidence as to the identity of the three individuals or the corporation (and its shareholders) who own the remaining Class A voting, common stock of Rock Island, or as to how many shares each held. Thus, the Class A voting, common stock held by the Simmons family may or may not be held by a single individual. If the fact is important, petitioner has failed to carry its burden of proof.

In determining how much of a minority discount to apply, we may not assume that the

Estate of Clara S. Roeder Winkler

purchaser of stock is a member of the decedent's family. *Propstra v. United States* [82-2 USTC ¶ 13,475], 680 F.2d 1248, 1251-1252 (9th Cir. 1982); *Estate of Hall v. Commissioner, supra; Minahan v. Commissioner* [Dec. 43,746], 88 T.C. 492, 499 (1987). This Court has held that a minority interest in a corporation should not be assumed to have any controlling value, even though the shareholder's family controls the corporation. *Estate of Bright v. United States, supra,* 658 F.2d at 1002-1003; *Estate of Andrews v. Commissioner, supra,* 79 T.C. at 953. The transfer must be analyzed from the point of view of a hypothetical seller and a hypothetical buyer rather than a particular person or family member. *Estate of Bright v. Commissioner, supra,* 658 F.2d at 1005-1006, *Estate of Andrews v. Commissioner, supra,* 79 T.C. at 956. This is regardless of the fact that the reality of the situation may be that the stock will probably be sold to a certain party or person. *Estate of Andrews v. Commissioner, supra.* However, the hypothetical sale should not be construed in a vacuum isolated from the actual facts that affect the value of the stock in the decedent's hands. *Estate of Andrews v. Commissioner, supra.* If there is an established or ready market for the shares, the hypothetical willing buyer need not be part of the general public. *Luce v. United States* [84-1 USTC ¶ 13,549], 4 Cl. Ct. 212 (1983). No minority discount is then applied to those shares of stock if there is a market, for example, among the existing shareholders of a closely held corporation. *Luce v. United States, supra.*

Respondent includes a discount of only 25 percent for the minority interest and lack of marketability of petitioner's shares, arguing that the decedent's shares provide leverage for the families to either maintain the status quo or gain control of Rock Island. Mr. Kramer also included only a 25 percent discount based on his impression that the Simmons' stock was owned by one individual rather than by a family. When valuing shares of a closely held corporation one cannot assume that a particular family member or other individual will purchase the stock.

The Court concludes that here both parties have placed entirely too much emphasis on the potential seller or buyer as either a member of the Winkler family or a member of the Simmons family. The willing buyer could be an unrelated third party who rather than demanding a minority discount would be willing to pay a premium for a 10 percent block of voting stock that could be pivotal as between the two families.

Mr. Kramer only labeled the stock as "swing" stock when he assumed that the Simmons' 50 percent interest was owned and controlled by one individual. Whether or not that is the fact, we conclude that a 10 percent block of voting stock has "swing vote characteristics" and that a minority discount would be inappropriate here. As to the non-voting stock, we conclude otherwise, because there would be no swing factor there in any event. Thus, we will not consider any swing characteristics when determining the discounts to apply to the Class B non-voting, common stock.

With regard to the discounts for the minority interest, the courts vary as to the actual discount to apply. Mr. Kramer testified that without the swing characteristic of the stock, a 40 to 45 percent minority and lack of marketability discount would not be unusual for this stock. We find that the value of the Class B non-voting, common stock should be discounted by 20 percent for the minority interest in the Rock Island Company. This is a moderate discount and within a range that this Court has applied many times before in cases such as this. See *Northern Trust Co. v. Commissioner, supra,* 87 T.C. at 385.

With regard to the discount for the lack of marketability of the Rock Island stock, we will apply a discount of 25 percent to both voting and non-voting stock. In applying this discount we are considering the fact that the stock of an unlisted, closely held corporation is generally difficult to sell. Again that may not be the case for the voting stock. However, since we have already disallowed the minority discount for the voting stock, we find no basis for disregarding the fact that all of the stock would probably be difficult to sell. We also are taking into account the fact that, due to the dismal outlook for the refining industry in 1981, the future of the company did not appear to be optimistic at that time.

While the factors we have considered are not readily quantifiable and any quantification of the same may give an unwarranted appearance of precision and exactitude, we nonetheless will retrace the path where our holdings lead us. We hold that the value of the Rock Island corporation as a whole was $36,712,800 which is to be apportioned among the total 800,000 shares for a value of $45.89 per share. The value of the block of Class A voting stock in this case is then to be increased by 10 percent for the fact that it is voting stock and decreased by 25 percent for lack of marketability. Thus the value of this Class A voting stock is $37.86 per share or $302,880 for the 8,000 shares. The block of Class B non-voting stock in this case is to be reduced by 20 percent for the minority discount and 25 percent for lack of marketability, for a total decrease of 45 percent. Thus the value of this Class B non-voting stock is $25.24 per share or $191,824 for the 7,600 shares.

Estate of Ruben Rodriguez

Petitioners and respondent each presented one expert witness at trial who valued decedent's 70 percent interest in Los Amigos. Petitioners' expert witness, Glen A. Hultquist, concluded the stock was worth $332,700.[3] Respondent's expert witness, Philip J. Schneider, appraised the stock at $823,000.

Both experts considered the following factors from Revenue Ruling 59-60, 1959-1 C.B. 237, 238, in determining the fair market value of Los Amigos:

(a) The nature of the business and the history of the enterprise from its inception. (b) The economic outlook in general and the condition and outlook of the specific industry in particular. (c) The book value of the stock and the financial condition of the business. (d) The earning capacity of the company. (e) The dividend-paying capacity. (f) Whether or not the enterprise has goodwill or other intangible value.

Expert witnesses' opinions are supposed to aid the court in understanding an area requiring specialized training, knowledge or judgment. As the trier of fact, we are not, however, bound by the experts' opinions. *Silverman v. Commissioner* [76-2 USTC ¶ 13,148], 538 F.2d 927, 933 (2d Cir. 1976), affg. a Memorandum Opinion of this Court [Dec. 32,831(M)]; *Chiu v. Commissioner* [Dec. 42,027], 84 T.C. 722, 734 (1985). One expert may be persuasive on one particular element of valuation while another expert may provide more incisive help on some other element of valuation. *Parker v. Commissioner* [Dec. 42,966], 86 T.C. 547, 562 (1986); *Estate of Gallo v. Commissioner* [Dec. 42,241(M)], T.C. Memo. 1985-363. Consequently, using our best judgment, we may adopt some portions and reject other portions of expert testimony. *Helvering v. National Grocery Co.* [38-2 USTC ¶ 9312], 304 U.S. 282 (1938).

In valuing the Los Amigos stock for trial, Hultquist combined an income and a book value approach. Under the income approach, Hultquist adjusted pre-tax income to account for the loss of the decedent, the key man in the business. The earnings as adjusted were $210,000. He capitalized the adjusted earnings using a 30 percent capitalization rate.[4] Hultquist next determined the book value of Los Amigos. He used the book value method because thirteen companies he examined in the food industry were sold at a percentage of book value. He adjusted the book value based on one of the thirteen sales, the only company he found truly comparable, at 80 percent of book value. Hultquist used a weighted average of the resulting amounts from the income and book value approaches, 40 percent for the income approach and 60 percent for the book value approach. Hultquist discounted the weighted average by 35 percent for lack of marketability. Seventy percent of the result was the value of decedent's 70 percent stock interest, $332,700.

Respondent's expert witness, Schneider, used only an income approach. Schneider first adjusted Los Amigos' income as if decedent owned the Armour Drive property rather than Los Amigos. He then used a 28.46 percent capitalization rate to determine the value of the corporation. Schneider noted that although normally he would adjust the capitalization rate to account for the loss of a key man, he did not adjust the rate here because of the $250,000 life insurance policy on decedent. Also, he testified that decedent's salary would pay for a replacement. Seventy percent of the corporation's value, $823,000, was the value respondent used in his deficiency notice.

Both experts used a capitalization of earnings method in determining their appraised value of Los Amigos. We accept as appropriate the use of the capitalization of earnings method. See *Central Trust Co. v. United States* [62-2 USTC ¶ 12,092], 305 F.2d 393, 404 (Ct. Cl. 1962); *Estate of Huntsman v. Commissioner* [Dec. 33,976], 66 T.C. 861, 876 (1976).

We reject, however, Hultquist's adjustment to value based on a percentage of book value. The businesses that were sold at a percentage of book value, as petitioners' expert found, were not comparable with one exception. We find that petitioners have not shown that using the book value method to adjust the value determined by the capitalized earnings method is appropriate in this case. We agree with respondent's expert that the appropriate valuation approach to use in this case is the capitalization of earnings unadjusted by book value. We also believe the capitalization rate of 28.46 percent used by respondent's expert was appropriate.

Nevertheless, we do not agree with respondent's expert that no adjustment for the loss of a key man is necessary in this case. Respondent argues that an adjustment is inappropriate because Los Amigos maintained $250,000 of insurance on decedent's life. Also, respondent's expert witness testified that he did not make any allowance for the value of decedent as a key man because his replacement cost was equal to his salary. These arguments understate the importance of decedent to Los Amigos and the adverse effect his death had on business. We agree with petitioners that an adjustment is necessary to account for the loss of decedent.

The evidence shows that decedent was the dominant force behind Los Amigos. He worked

---

[3] Hultquist initially valued the stock at $500,000 in a two-page report used on decedent's estate tax return.

[4] Both Hultquist and respondent's expert used a study by Ibottson and Sinquefield to arrive at a capitalization rate of 28.46 percent. Hultquist rounded the 28.46 percent rate up to 30 percent "because of the unique business conditions" of Los Amigos.

Estate of Ruben Rodriguez

long hours supervising every aspect of the business. At the time of his death, Los Amigos' customers and suppliers were genuinely and understandably concerned about the future of the business without decedent. In fact, Los Amigos soon lost one of its largest accounts due to an inability to maintain quality. The failure was due to decedent's absence from operations. Profits fell dramatically without decedent to run the business. No one was trained to take decedent's place.

Capitalizing earnings is a sound valuation method requiring no adjustment only in a case where the earning power of the business can reasonably be projected to continue as in the past. Where, as in this case, a traumatic event shakes the business so that its earning power is demonstrably diminished, earnings should properly be adjusted. See *Central Trust Co. v. United States*, 305 F.2d at 403. An adjustment to earnings before capitalizing them to determine the company's value rather than a discount at the end of the computation is appropriate to reflect the diminished earnings capacity of the business. We adopt petitioners' expert's adjustment to earnings for the loss of the key man.

The final adjustment to value remaining in issue is a discount for lack of marketability. Respondent contends that any discount for lack of marketability is offset by a control premium for decedent's 70 percent interest. Petitioners, on the other hand, discounted the value by 35 percent for lack of marketability.

Respondent has confused the discount for lack of marketability with a discount for minority interest. A discount for lack of marketability is warranted in this case because no established market exists for unlisted, closely held stock. *Estate of Piper v. Commissioner* [Dec. 36,315], 72 T.C. 1062, 1085 (1979).

Respondent's argument that a control premium offsets the discount for lack of marketability is unfounded in the present case. Both parties valued decedent's 70 percent interest beginning with the value of 100 percent of the company. A "control premium" should be added to value determined from sales of minority interests.

Petitioners, however, have not met their burden of proof that the appropriate discount is 35 percent. Based on the facts and circumstances in this case, we find that the proper discount for lack of marketability is 10 percent. Consequently, the value of decedent's interest in Los Amigos at the date of his death was $465,000 ($378,000 (capitalized $210,000 earnings at 28.46 percent) × 90 percent (10 percent discount for lack of marketability) × 70 percent (ownership interest) = 465,000).

Estate of Dean A. Chenoweth

Decedent died on July 31, 1982. A timely Federal estate tax return was thereafter filed for his estate by the personal representative. The principal asset of decedent's gross estate was all of the outstanding common voting stock of Chenoweth Distributing Company, Inc. (hereinafter the "company"), which was owned by decedent at the date of his death and which was valued in the Federal estate tax return at $2,834,033. For purposes of arriving at the value of the gross estate under section 2031, respondent has accepted this valuation.

Under decedent's will, duly probated, decedent left 255 shares, or 51 percent, of the company's stock to his surviving wife, Jenny, and 245 shares, or 49 percent, of the company's stock to his daughter by a prior marriage, Kelli Chenoweth. So far as the bequest to Jenny is concerned, there is no dispute between the parties that the bequest was outright and qualifies for the marital deduction provided by section 2056. The parties are likewise in agreement that under Florida law, which governs here, the 51 percent stock interest passing to Jenny gives her complete control of the company.

As filed with respondent, decedent's estate tax return claimed a marital deduction with respect to the stock interest in the company passing to Jenny in the amount of $1,445,356, which was precisely 51 percent of the date of death value of $2,834,033 for all the stock. In the petition filed herein, however, petitioner now claims that the value of the company's stock passing to Jenny for marital deduction purposes should be $1,996,038, arrived at by adding a "control premium" of 38.1 percent to the value of such stock as originally reported.

Respondent contests this claim, and, in his motion for summary judgment, takes the position that, as a matter of law, petitioner is not entitled to increase the value of the controlling interest in the company, and claimed as a marital deduction, above a strict 51 percent share of the value of all the stock of the company, as reported in the gross estate. Petitioner, opposing respondent's motion, contends that there is no such prohibition as a matter of law. The parties are in agreement that if respondent is correct as to his legal proposition, there are no remaining material facts in dispute, and that summary judgment may be granted in his favor. On the other hand, the parties agree that if petitioner is correct on the legal issue presented, then there is a remaining major material fact which is still in dispute, viz, the additional amount of value or control premium which is to be added to the majority block of shares passing to Jenny and for which marital deduction is claimed herein, so that respondent's motion for summary judgment should be denied.

The issue presented here is a novel one, and does not seem to have been directly addressed until now, at least by this Court. It requires us to consider the fundamental nature of the Federal estate tax, as a basis for how assets are to be valued for purposes of inclusion in the gross estate under section 2031. At the same time, we must also consider the nature of the marital deduction provided by section 2056, the valuation of assets qualifying for deduction under that section, and the moment in time when such assets are to be valued.

In the instant case, there is no dispute between the parties as to the value of all the stock of the company. It was all owned by decedent at the moment of his death, and the value of that 100 percent interest was included in decedent's gross estate at a value which respondent has accepted. Certainly ownership of 100 percent of the outstanding stock of the company constitutes control. Whether the value used in this case for purposes of section 2031 included an element of value because of the control factor is not clear from this record, but we assume that it did.

It has been generally held and is now accepted that the estate tax is laid only on that which passes at death, not what was owned before death or what the legatee receives after death, *Estate of Bright v. United States,* [81-2 USTC ¶ 13,436], 658 F.2d 999 (5th Cir. 1981); see and compare *Estate of Curry v. United States,* [83-1 USTC ¶ 13,518], 706 F.2d 1424 (7th Cir. 1983). Since the tax is laid upon the decedent's estate as a whole, and not upon the property which is received by the various legatees, the valuation of decedent's assets, *at least for purposes of computing his gross taxable estate under section 2031,* can usually be made without reference to the destination of those assets.

At this point, the focus of our inquiry has changed. For purposes of section 2031, we were concerned only with the value of the assets to be included in the decedent's gross estate as a whole, and without reference to the destination of those assets under decedent's will or through the laws of descent and distribution. Under section 2056, however, a somewhat different question is presented: What is the asset that passes to the decedent's surviving spouse, and what is the value of it? Here, for the first time, we *are* concerned with the destination of the asset[2] and the nature and value of that interest which passes.

Under decedent's will, 255 shares of the company's stock, representing a controlling interest in the company, was broken off from the total stock ownership of decedent, as reflected for

Estate of Dean A. Chenoweth

gross estate purposes under section 2031, and was bequeathed to his surviving spouse Jenny. That 51 percent share of the stock of the company carried with it the element of control and the additional element of value which inheres in such a controlling interest. For the first time, then, we must consider the total stock interest of decedent as composed of two pieces: the 51 percent share passing to decedent's surviving spouse, including the control element, and the 49 percent interest representing a minority share of the company which passed to decedent's child Kelli. As we have indicated above herein, it is clear to us that these two blocks of stock have different values. As we said in *Estate of Salsbury v. Commissioner, supra:*

> The payment of a premium for control is based on the principle that the per share value of minority interests is less than the per share value of a controlling interest. * * * A premium for control is generally expressed as the percentage by which the amount paid for a controlling block of shares exceeds the amount which would have otherwise been paid for the shares if sold as minority interests and is not based on a percentage of the value of the stock held by all or a particular class of minority shareholders. * * *

This leads us to the consideration of two cases which appear to bear most closely on the persent problem.

In *Provident National Bank v. United States* [78-2 USTC ¶ 13,255], 581 F.2d 1081 (3rd Cir. 1978), decedent owned a majority of both the common stock and the Class A stock of a closely held family corporation. Under his will, a portion of the Class A stock was bequeathed to a marital trust for decedent's surviving spouse, with instructions to exchange such stock for new preferred stock of the company under a plan of recapitalization provided in decedent's will. All remaining stock of the company which decedent owned or controlled, of both classes, was bequeathed to a nonmarital trust for the benefit of decedent's children, and such stock was not subject to the mandated recapitalization exchange. As the result of the recapitalization provided in decedent's will, the Class A stock bequeathed to the marital trust would be transmuted into stock which would arguably be more valuable than such Class A stock prior to the exchange.

Upon audit of decedent's Federal estate tax return, the Commissioner determined that decedent's holdings of both classes of stock were includible in his gross estate at a uniform value of $157 per share. He further allowed a marital deduction for the Class A stock bequeathed to the marital trust at the same rate of $157 per share. Deficiencies of Federal estate tax resulting from this determination were paid.

Decedent's executor, while not contesting respondent's determination of the value of both classes of stock for purposes of section 2031 and 2056(c) (the gross estate and the adjusted gross estate), claimed that the Class A stock passing to the marital trust, as the result of the prospective recapitalization exchange, was worth more than it was prior to decedent's death, and accordingly brought a refund suit based upon an increased marital deduction with respect to such stock.

Upon cross-motions for summary judgment, the district court, 436 F. Supp. 587 (E.D. Pa. 1977), granted the government's motion and dismissed the case, holding, inter alia, (a) that the Class A stock passing to the marital trust was to be valued without consideration of the will-mandated recapitalization exchange; and (b) that the value of the stock passing to the marital trust must be valued at the same figure for purposes of both section 2031 and 2056.

On appeal, the Third Circuit reversed. As relevant to the instant case, the court held that:

(1) The interest which decedent bequeathed to the marital trust was an interest passing from decedent to the trust within the meaning of section 2056(a), and included the new stock to be exchanged for the old stock, with all its characteristics, including the possibility of increased value in such interest, and the corresponding possibility of lesser value in decedent's other shares which were not bequeathed to the marital trust and were not subject to the recapitalization exchange. Material issues of fact were thus presented valuation and required a trial on the merits.

(2) The values of decedent's assets must be computed in the same manner and at the same values both for purposes of section 2031 and section 2056. Thus, decedent's entire equity interest in the stock must be revalued, to give effect to the increased value which might pertain to the stock passing to the marital trust, as well as the lower value which might be found for the remaining "nonmarital" stock. The increase in the value of the marital stock would not necessarily decrease the value of the nonmarital stock by the same amount.[3]

---

[3] On remand, the district court held that decedent's estate, after trial, had failed to provide that the stock bequeathed to the marital trust had a value greater than that assigned to it by the Commissioner. *Provident National Bank v. United States* [80-2 USTC ¶ 13,371], 502 F. Supp. 908 (E. D. Pa. 1980).

Estate of Dean A. Chenoweth

The second case which interests us here is *Ahmanson Foundation v. United States* [81-2 USTC ¶ 13,438], 674 F.2d 761 (9th Cir. 1981). In that case, at the time of decedent's death, he owned a controlling interest in the stock of HFA Co., as well as 99 nonvoting shares and one voting share (being all the outstanding stock) of another company, Ahmanco, both through a revocable trust. Under his will, Ahmanco received the controlling stock interest HFA, but at the same time, the 99 shares of Ahmanco passed to a charitable foundation. The sole voting share of Ahmanco remained in the trust, with the right to vote it vested in decedent's son. The issues presented, inter alia, involved the correct valuation of the HFA and Ahmanco stock for purposes of section 2031, and the valuation of the 99 shares of Ahmanco for purposes of the charitable deduction under section 2055.[4]

The Ninth Circuit first held that:

(1) The value of assets is to be determined at the moment of death, but in doing so, valuation must take into account any changes in values brought about by the testator's distribution plan which will take effect prior to distribution. Thus, the value of the Ahmanco stock should be established so as to include the value of the controlling interest in HFA which Ahmanco acquired at the moment of death.

(2) The court went on to say and hold:

We must distinguish, however, the effect of "predistribution" transformations and changes in value brought about by the testator's death, from changes in value resulting from the fact that under the decedent's estate plan the assets in the gross estate ultimately come to rest in the hands of different beneficiaries. The estate tax is a tax upon a transfer as the Foundation contends. However it is a tax on the privilege of passing on property, not a tax on the privilege of receiving property. "The tax is on the act of the testator not on the receipt of the property by the legatees." * * * There is nothing in the statutes or in the case law that suggests that valuation of the *gross estate* [emphasis added] should take into account that the assets would come to rest in several hands rather than one.

* * *

We therefore conclude that *for purposes of valuing the gross estate* [emphasis added] of decedent, the 100 shares of Ahmanco stock (representing the value of the 600 HFA shares that constitute the sole asset of Ahmanco) should not be viewed for valuation purposes as two separate marketable assets as they would be viewed in the hands of their respective recipients under the terms of the will. Rather, the 100 shares of Ahmanco stock should be viewed in the hands of the testator and thus given a value equal to the price which the 600 shares of HFA stock would have in an exchange between a willing buyer and seller. [674 F.2d at 768-769.]

(3) Finally, the court held that in valuing the 99 nonvoting shares of stock passing to the charity for the charitable deduction purposes of section 2055, however, different considerations control. Such value may be different from the value of the shares considered as part of the larger block for gross estate tax purposes under section 2031. The court said:

The Foundation argues that inconsistent valuations, for these two purposes, would be incompatible with the orderly administration and application of the estate tax law. There is, certainly, an initial plausibility to the suggestion that fairness dictates that the same method of valuation be used in computing the gross estate and the charitable deduction. This initial plausibility, however, does not survive a close second look.

The statute does not ordain equal valuation as between an item in the gross estate and the same item under the charitable deduction. Instead, it states that the value of the charitable deduction "shall not exceed the value of the transferred property required to be included in the gross estate". * * *

* * *

Thus there are compelling considerations in conflict with the initially plausible suggestion that valuation for purposes of the gross estate must always be the same as valuation for purposes of the charitable deduction. When the valuation would be different depending on whether an asset is held in conjunction with other assets, the gross estate must be computed considering the assets in the estate as a block. * * * The valuation of these same sorts of assets for the purpose of the charitable deduction, however, is subject to the principle that the testator may only be allowed a deduction for estate tax purposes for what is actually received by the charity—a principle required by the purpose of the charitable deduction. [674 F.2d at 772.]

Thus, since the nonvoting shares which the charity received were separated from the voting power, the court held that a lower valuation of

---

[4] There were also issues regarding the effect of state community property law upon a claimed marital deduction, which do not concern us here.

Estate of Dean A. Chenoweth

such shares for purposes of the charitable deduction was proper.

In the context of the problem presented in the instant case, both *Provident* and *Ahmanson* deserve our close consideration. As relevant here, both cases considered two closely interrelated matters:

A. Both cases agree on the proposition that changes can be wrought in the nature and value of an asset in a decedent's gross estate by the provisions of decedent's will, which may change the nature of that asset by changing some of its characteristics, and hence its value, by splitting it off from other similar assets and sending it to a different destination. Thus, in the *Provident* case, the value of the stock which decedent bequeathed to the marital trust had engrafted upon it the new stock into which it was to be converted pursuant to decedent's will, and thus arguably acquired a new and greater value. In *Ahmanson*, taking away from the stock passing to the charity the voting power, and lodging that in a different person, arguably changed the quality and value of the stock passing to the charity, and therefore had a depressing effect on its value for purposes of the charitable deduction. The parallel to the instant case is clear: that decedent, in breaking his 100 percent ownership of the company into two unequal shares, and in giving the majority interest to his surviving spouse, created a new and different asset, which carried with it the control premium for valuation purposes, and (probably) reduced the value of the minority block of stock remaining in the gross estate by some amount also, although not necessarily by the same amount. See *Estate of Salsbury v. Commissioner, supra.*

B. As to the second closely interrelated point, the two cases diverge. In *Provident*, the court held that the values of decedent's assets must be computed in the same manner and at the same values both for purposes of section 2031 and section 2056. In *Ahmanson*, on the contrary, the Court held that perfect symmetry was not required.

We are in agreement with both *Provident* and *Ahmanson* with regard to A above. In the instant case, it is clear to us that the block of the company's stock passing under decedent's will to his surviving widow was the controlling interest in the company, and was entitled to be valued for purposes of section 2056 so as to include an additional element of value because of that control. Thus, simply valuing the 51 percent share of the company's stock qualifying for the marital deduction at a mechanical 51 percent of the total value ascribed to the stock for purposes of inclusion in the gross estate would not give effect to the additional element of value for control which inheres in that block

of stock. The amount of such control premium presents a material issue of fact which is not resolved in the present record and therefore requires that respondent's motion for summary judgment be denied.

As to point B above, we think the reasoning of the *Ahmanson* court is more persuasive. While we would tend to agree that the sum of the parts cannot equal more than the whole—that is, that the majority block together with the control premium, when added to the minority block of the company's stock with an appropriate discount for minority interest, should not equal more than the total 100 percent interest of the decedent, as reported for purposes of section 2031—it might well turn out that the sum of the parts can equal less than the whole—that is, that the control premium which is added to the majority block passing to decedent's surviving spouse might be less than the proper minority discount to be attributed to the shares passing to decedent's daughter Kelli.[5]

In any event, this question is not before us at this time. We are not required to determine at this point whether the minority block of shares passing to Kelli requires that a discount be assigned to it, nor the amount of such discount, nor that such discount must precisely equal the amount of control premium which is properly assignable to the majority block of shares qualifying for marital deduction under section 2056. All we decide here is that such majority block may be entitled to an extra element of value because of the control over the company which such block possesses; that such additional element of value can properly be considered in computing the amount of the marital deduction; and that this presents a material question of fact which has not been resolved between the parties and as to which petitioner must have an opportunity to present its proof.

Victor I. Minahan

The next focus of our inquiry is whether the position of the United States in the instant cases was unreasonable within the meaning of section 7430(c)(2)(A)(i). The statute imposes on petitioners the burden of establishing such unreasonableness. This Court and the Courts of Appeals of several circuits have previously determined that any award of costs under section 7430 is to be based on a determination of the reasonableness of respondent's position from the date the petition was filed. *Ewing and Thomas, P.A. v. Heye*, 803 F.2d 613 (CA11 1986); *Baker v. Commissioner* [86-1 USTC ¶ 9311], 787 F.2d 637 (CADC 1986), affg. on this issue [Dec. 41,636] 83 T.C. 822, 827 (1984); *Wasie v. Commissioner* [Dec. 43,046], 86 T.C. 962, 967 (1986). Other courts have held that fees and costs and the measure of the reasonableness of respondent's position extends to the administrative level. *Powell v. Commissioner* [86-2 USTC ¶ 9486], 791 F.2d 385 (CA5 1986), revg. a Memorandum Opinion of this Court [Dec. 41,831(M)];[9] *Kaufman v. Egger* [85-1 USTC ¶ 9278], 758 F.2d 1 (CA1 1985). The Court of Appeals for the Seventh Circuit, to which the instant cases are appealable, has not ruled as to whether the prepetition factors are relevant to the determination of whether respondent's position is reasonable. The fact that respondent ultimately is unsuccessful at litigation or concedes the case is not necessarily determinative that his position was unreasonable. *Wasie v. Commissioner*, 86 T.C. at 969, and cases cited therein.

Respondent asserts that his position in the instant cases was not unreasonable because valuation is a factual question and the determinations in the notices of deficiency were based on expert opinion. Respondent merely states that reliance upon expert appraisal in valuation cases is reasonable. Respondent cites no authority for the legal position upon which the valuation was made. Respondent aggregated and valued as a control block of common stock all 357,124 shares of unregistered Post common stock sold by petitioners to separate trusts each of which was established for the primary benefit of an offspring.

Petitioners assert that respondent has disregarded the regulations and case authorities in the determination that the value of the unregistered Post common stock sold to the separate trusts under the agreements at issue embodied a control premium by virtue of aggregation. Section 25.2512-2(e), Gift Tax Regs.; *Propstra v. United States* [82-2 USTC ¶ 13,475], 680 F.2d 1248 (CA9 1982); *Estate of Bright v. United States* [81-2 USTC ¶ 13,436], 658 F.2d 999 (CA5 1981); *Estate of Andrews v. Commissioner* [Dec. 39,523], 79 T.C. 938 (1982). In *Estate of Bright*, the Court of Appeals for the Fifth Circuit held,

en banc, that the estate's stock was to be valued as though held by a hypothetical seller who is related to no one. *Estate of Bright v. United States*, 658 F.2d at 1007. In *Estate of Andrews*, we stated that "For purposes of valuation, one should construct a hypothetical sale from a hypothetical willing seller to a similarly hypothetical willing buyer", without regard to the fact "that the stock will most probably be sold to a particular party or type of person." *Estate of Andrews v. Commissioner*, 79 T.C. at 955, 956. Respondent's determination of a control premium by virtue of aggregation assumes that trustees of the separate trusts would sell or otherwise hold their interests together with sufficient others so as to exercise control of Post. As stated in *Propstra*, the use of an objective standard without aggregation avoids the uncertainties that would otherwise be inherent if valuation methods attempted to account for the likelihood that estates, legatees, or heirs would sell their interests together with others who hold interests in the property, and avoids an examination of anticipated behavior of those holding such interests. *Propstra v. United States*, 680 F.2d at 1252. It has been noted that the Congress has explicitly directed that family attribution or unit of ownership principles be applied in certain aspects of Federal taxation, and in the absence of legislative directives, judicial forums should not extend such principles beyond those areas specifically designated by Congress. Furthermore, the subjective inquiry into feelings, attitudes, and anticipated behavior might well be boundless. *Propstra v. United States*, 680 F.2d at 1252; *Estate of Andrews v. Commissioner*, 79 T.C. at 955.

We conclude that petitioners have established that respondent's litigation position was unreasonable. Petitioners filed their petitions in this Court on February 11, 1985. Respondent filed his answers on April 5, 1985. Petitioners participated in Appeals office conferences while the case was in docketed status. On December 24, 1985, the Court served on the parties notices of trial scheduled for March 17, 1986. Respondent agreed to concede the cases on February 17, 1986. In our view respondent simply capitulated rather than litigate the valuation theory upon which the notices of deficiency are founded. Respondent has not cited any legal authority or presented any argument to indicate that his valuation was reasonable. Respondent's assertion that the litigation position was reasonable solely because valuation is a factual inquiry and that the valuation herein was based on an expert appraisal is woefully inadequate to establish that his position is reasonable. In the context of the instant cases, petitioners have carried their burden (see *Frisch v. Commissioner*

---

[9] T.C. Memo. 1985-27.

Victor I. Minahan

[Dec. 43,459], 87 T.C. 838 (1986)) of establishing that respondent's legal position was unreasonable within the meaning of section 7430(c)(2)(A)(i).

In so holding, we emphasize that we find respondent's position unreasonable only because, by espousing a family attribution approach, he seeks to repudiate a well-established line of cases of long and reputable ancestry, going back as far as 1940. This line of cases is catalogued in the en banc opinion of the Court of Appeals for the Fifth Circuit in *Estate of Bright v. United States,* 658 F.2d at 1002-1003, and is repeated in footnote 19 of our opinion in *Estate of Andrews v. Commissioner,* 79 T.C. at 954 (discounts applied for lack of control and marketability even though decedent and his siblings held all stock in several corporations). As we pointed out there, respondent's litigating position on this issue was announced in Rev. Rul. 81-253, 1981-2 C.B. 187. In response, we said in *Estate of Andrews* that "We see no reason to depart from such established precedent but follow the Fifth Circuit's well-reasoned and thoroughly researched [*Estate of Bright*] opinion." 79 T.C. at 956. In the instant cases, respondent persists in the face of *Estate of Andrews* and its progenitors; in these cases, the persistence is unreasonable.

We note that we are not required, in the instant cases, to confront the question of when an attempt to create a conflict among the circuits might or might not be enough to save respondent from a charge of unreasonableness. See, e.g. *Keasler v. United States* [85-2 USTC ¶ 16,440], 766 F.2d 1227, 1234-1238 (CA-8 1985). We can leave that question to another day because, in respondent's memorandum in the instant cases there is not even a hint that he is attempting to create a conflict among the circuits; there is only a contention that "In valuation cases, it is certainly reasonable for respondent to rely on an expert's appraisal". Where the valuation element in dispute is essentially a point of law that respondent has lost for more than 40 years, respondent may not extricate himself from a holding of unreasonableness merely because his valuation expert is also unreasoanble. See *Frisch v. Commissioner, supra.*

Estate of Davis Jephson

Valuing stock of a closely held corporation is a factual determination for which there is no talismanic formula. A weighing of all relevant facts and circumstances is required. In determining such value, section 2031(b) requires that consideration be given, in addition to all relevant factors, to the price of stock of corporations engaged in the same or similar line of business which are listed on an exchange.

After considering all relevant facts and circumstances, we find that the date of death values of R.B. Davis and Jephson Finance Company are their respective net asset values, less the cost of liquidation. The factors that persuaded us in reaching this finding are: (1) all the assets of both investment companies were liquid assets, i.e., cash and marketable securities; (2) neither corporation had any liabilities which had to be seriously considered in valuing the companies; (3) the decedent's 100 percent ownership of both companies gave her (or her estate) the unqualified right to liquidate both companies at any time. In our opinion, neither the decent nor her estate nor a hypothetical seller would have sold the stock of either company for less than that which could have been realized through liquidation. We further believe that a hypothetical purchaser would be willing to pay such an amount.[3]

We recognize that the value of an interest in an investment company is not always equal to its proportionate share of the company's net asset value. For example, we have applied a discount where a minority interest was being valued. *Harwood v. Commissioner* [Dec. 40,985], 82 T.C. 239, 264-269 (1984), affd. 786 F.2d 1174 (9th Cir. 1986); *Estate of Piper v. Commissioner* [Dec. 36,315], 72 T.C. 1062 (1979); *Estate of DeGuebriant v. Commissioner* [Dec. 17,600], 14 T.C. 611 (1950), reversed on another issue sub nom. *Claflin v. Commissioner* [51-1 USTC ¶ 10,791], 186 F.2d 307 (2d Cir. 1951). We have also allowed a discount for the nonmarketability of an investment company's stock, particularly where its assets consist of real estate or other non-liquid assets. *Estate of Piper v. Commissioner* [Dec. 36,315], 72 T.C. 1062 (1979); *Estate of Andrews v. Commissioner* [Dec. 39,523], 79 T.C. 938 (1982). Here, however, there is neither a minority interest nor any non-liquid assets.

Petitioner does not argue that it is entitled to a minority interest discount, since it owns all of the stock of both companies. Nevertheless, petitioner indirectly seeks to obtain a minority interest discount by analogizing R.B. Davis and Jephson Finance to publicly traded closed-end investment companies. We agree that in many respects R.B. Davis and Jephson Finance are comparable to closed-end investment companies. Also, we recognize that stock in closed-end investment companies often sells for less than net asset value. However, an investor in a closed-end investment company has little or no say in the selection of the company's investment advisor or the company's portfolio and cannot easily force the liquidation of the company. Petitioner did not present any evidence of sales of controlling interests in closed-end investment companies. The sale of a controlling interest in a closed-end investment company might well command a premium, rather than be subject to discount. In any event, we find inapposite petitioner's comparison of the sale of 100 percent interests in R.B. Davis and Jephson Finance to sales of minority interests in publicly traded closed-end investment companies.

Petitioner next argues that a discount for nonmarketability is warranted. Petitioner contends that marketable securities and cash, when held in corporate solution, are not readily marketable. This argument ignores the fact that complete ownership of each corporation enables petitioner to obtain, at any time, direct ownership of the corporate assets either through a partial or complete liquidation or through a dividend in kind.

Lastly, petitioner argues that a purchaser of the stock of R.B. Davis and Jephson Finance would demand a discount for the existence of unknown liabilities. Only R.B. Davis was an operating company[4]—it manufactured baking powder prior to 1955. The potentially hazardous substance allegedly included in the baking powder manufactured by R.B. Davis is alum, which around 1905 was thought to be hazardous to health. Petitioner submitted no evidence that alum is hazardous to health or that any liability for its use was ever imposed on R.B. Davis or any other manufacturer of baking powder, or that any hazardous effects of alum had remained undetected for the 24 years which had elapsed between the date R.B. Davis ceased to manufacture baking powder and the date of decedent's death. In any event, any claim brought against R.B. Davis would probably have been time-barred. In short, we are not persuaded by this argument and believe that here no discount is warranted for unknown liabilities.

Respondent conceded that there should be a reduction for the transactional costs which the owner of R.B. Davis and Jephson Finance stock would incur in obtaining direct ownership of the corporate assets through a liquidation. We have accordingly taken these costs into account in valuing both companies.

---

[3] The hypothetical purchaser, by purchasing the companies, would save brokerage fees that otherwise would have to be paid to acquire approximately $9 million of marketable securities.

[4] As previously noted, Jephson Finance was at all times an investment company.

The Northern Trust Company

At issue in this case is the value for gift tax purposes of CCC's Class A and Class B common stock held by John Curran and William Curran on May 27, 1976,[21] the date of the gifts in issue and the value for estate tax purposes of CCC's Class A and Class B common stock held by Cecilia Simon on May 11, 1976, the date of her death.

Under section 2035(a) the value of the gross estate includes (with certain exceptions not here applicable) the value of all property transferred by the decedent within three years of death. Since the executor of Mrs. Simon's estate did not elect alternative valuation under section 2032, the date of death (May 11, 1976) value applies as to the stock in her estate. Under section 2512(a) the value of property for gift tax purposes is determined on the date of the gift.

For both estate and gift tax purposes, fair market value is defined as "the price at which such property would change hands between a willing buyer and a willing seller, neither being under any compulsion to buy or to sell, and both having reasonable knowledge or relevant facts." Section 20.2031-1(b), Estate Tax Regs.; section 25.2512-1, Gift Tax Regs. The valuation of stock presents a question of fact, and the trier of fact has the duty to weigh all relevant evidence and to draw appropriate inferences therefrom. *Hamm v. Commissioner* [64-1 USTC ¶ 12,206], 325 F.2d 934, 938 (8th Cir. 1963), affg. [Dec. 25,193(M)] T.C. Memo. 1961-347.

Section 20.2031-2(f), Estate Tax Regs., and section 25.2512-2(f), Gift Tax Regs., set forth some of the relevant factors to be considered in determining the value of stock in a closely held corporation in the absence of actual sale prices and bona fide bid and asked prices. Those factors include the company's net worth, prospective earning power, dividend-paying capacity and other relevant factors. The regulation states that "other relevant factors" include:

[T]he good will of the business; the economic outlook in the particular industry; the company's position in the industry and its management; the degree of control of the business represented by the block of stock to be valued; and the values of securities of corporations engaged in the same or similar lines of business which are listed on a stock exchange. However, the weight to be accorded such comparisons or any other evidentiary factors considered in the determination of a value depends upon the facts of each case. * * *

At trial, petitioners and respondent each presented the testimony of an expert to establish the value of CCC's common stock. Petitioners' expert valued CCC's Class A voting common stock at $470.33 per share and CCC's Class B non-voting common stock at $58.80 per share. Respondent's expert valued both the Class A and Class B stock at $454.99 per share. We recognize that expert testimony is peculiarly appropriate in cases dealing with the value of stock of unlisted closely held corporations. *Central Trust Company v. United States* [62-2 USTC ¶ 12,092], 305 F.2d 393 (Ct. Cl. 1962). Nevertheless, for the reasons stated below, we do not fully agree with either expert's valuation determination.

To summarize briefly, petitioners' expert, Grabowski, relied on the market comparable approach and the discounted cash flow approach to value CCC, Stahl, Kaneland and Holland. He relied on the liquidation values of the remaining subsidiaries as evidence of their intrinsic values. Respondent's expert, Lerner, used a modified market comparable approach to value CCC and its subsidiaries as one consolidated company as well as to individually value CCC, Stahl and Kaneland. After valuing CCC, Stahl and Kaneland by using a modified market comparable approach, Lerner valued Suburban based on its book value and Holland based on its 1974 purchase price increased by its post-acquisition earnings.

First, we cannot accept Grabowski's market comparable valuation of CCC, Stahl, Kaneland and Holland. Section 2031(b) provides that "the value of stock or securities of corporations engaged in the same or a similar line of business which are listed on an exchange" is a factor to be considered in valuing the stock of an unlisted corporation. In valuing CCC, Stahl and Kaneland, Grabowski relied on market multiples based on the financial statistics of McDowell, Rexco and Sukut, publicly traded companies engaged in the construction of highways, residential buildings, commercial buildings and industrial plants. CCC, Stahl and Kaneland, however, were Illinois companies engaged solely in the asphalt paving business. If the "other relevant factors" concept of section 20.2031-2(f) is to be meaningfully applied, then companies engaged in diversified construction are not sufficiently similar to companies engaged solely in asphalt paving to provide reliable comparisons for valuation purposes. This is particularly true in the instant case since the record contains no evidence of the percentage of revenues earned by the comparable companies from highway construction. Such revenues may be insignificant in relation to the total revenues of the companies compared.

---

[21] On brief, both petitioners and respondent treat the appropriate valuation date as May 7, 1976, the date on which the trusts in issue were created. These trusts, however, were revocable until the earlier of May 27, 1976, or the death of the grantor. Consequently, the gifts were not complete for Federal gift tax purposes until May 27, 1976, when the trusts became irrevocable. Section 25.2511-2(c), Gift Tax Regs.

The Northern Trust Company

We also point out that Grabowski's expert report shows that sales for CCC, Stahl and Kaneland increased 21 percent per year during the period 1971 through 1975, while sales for the comparable companies increased only 5 to 11 percent during this same period. Moreover, the capital structures of the comparable companies differed significantly from the capital structures of CCC, Stahl and Kaneland.

We are similarly unpersuaded by the comparable companies which Grabowski relied upon to value Holland. At the time of the transfers, a substantial portion of Holland's business consisted of the manufacture, assembly and sale of rail welding equipment. Holland also provided welding services on a contract basis. The comparable companies which Grabowski relied upon were publicly traded companies engaged in the sale of various types of railroad equipment. These businesses were in no way similar to the rail welding business engaged in by Holland. Moreover, in his report Grabowski stated that these companies were also engaged in numerous other businesses in addition to the railroad supply business. The record, however, does not disclose the nature of these businesses. Consequently, we conclude that Grabowski's comparable companies were not essentially engaged in the same or similar line of business as Holland. We therefore reject his market comparable valuation of Holland. We do not, of course, question that Grabowski used the best "comparables" he could find. We simply find that the market comparable approach is not available in this case in the absence of more reliable yardsticks.

We are similarly unable to accept Lerner's use of a modified market comparable approach to value CCC and its subsidiaries. Because he was unable to locate publicly traded companies engaged in the same or similar lines of business as CCC and its subsidiaries, Lerner relied on publicly traded companies with financial statistics similar to those of CCC. In choosing these comparable companies, Lerner did not look at the particular businesses in which they were engaged. Rather, he believed that investors would similarly value companies with comparable sales, returns on equity and debt to equity ratios, regardless of the type of business in which they were engaged. We, however, are unable to agree with this theory.

It seems self-evident that every industry is characterized by its own peculiar risks and expectations. As a result, financial statistics which may be considered outstanding for one industry may be considered disastrous for another. For example, a large debt to equity ratio might be very acceptable to a willing buyer of stock in a company engaged in a business characterized by stable earnings while a similar debt to equity ratio might be unacceptable to that investor if the company were engaged in a business subject to volatile earnings. For the same reason, an investor cannot determine what constitutes a reasonable return on equity or adequate sales volume without considering the particular business of the company. We also point out that a company's total sales volume provides little evidence of the attractiveness of an investment in the absence of evidence of the company's overall profitability. Consequently, we do not believe that Lerner's modified market comparable approach provides an adequate indication of the intrinsic value of CCC and its subsidiaries.

On the record before us, we think that Grabowski's discounted cash flow analysis provides a reasonable estimate of the intrinsic value of CCC, Stahl, Kaneland and Holland. In Rev. Rul. 59-60, 1959-1 C.B. 237 (which is applied by both Grabowski and Lerner), it is stated that earnings are the most important factor to be considered in valuing stocks of manufacturing or service corporations. In this revenue ruling and the above-quoted estate and gift tax regulations, the following factors are listed as also relevant in determining stock values: 1) the economic outlook in general and the condition and outlook of the specific industry in general; 2) the financial condition of the business; and 3) its dividend-paying capacity. Because Grabowski's discounted cash flow analysis takes into account all of these factors, we think that such analysis provides an appropriate method to use in valuing the common stock of CCC.

Grabowski's discounted cash flow analysis is based upon the theory that the price which an investor will pay for a share of stock is equal to the present value of the future stream of income which he expects to receive from the investment. Thus, as applied here, this valuation method relies primarily on the earnings of CCC and its subsidiaries, which, as Rev. Rul. 59-60 itself provides, is the most important factor to consider in valuing manufacturing and service companies like CCC, Stahl, Kaneland and Holland. Moreover, in projecting the future income stream of these companies, Grabowski considered general economic conditions as well as the condition of the construction industry and railroad supply industry, the companies' financial conditions and their dividend-paying capacity. Consequently, because Grabowski's discounted cash flow analysis emphasizes the companies' past and future earnings as well as other relevant factors listed in respondent's regulations and revenue rulings, we think that this valuation method is an appropriate method to use in

The Northern Trust Company

determining the intrinsic value of CCC, Stahl, Kaneland and Holland.[22]

Respondent, nevertheless, attacks Grabowski's discounted cash flow analysis on the ground that the projections of operating income are based on pure speculation. We demur. Rev. Rul. 59-60 states that:

Potential future income is a major factor in many valuations of closely-held stocks, and all information concerning past income which will be helpful in predicting the future should be secured. Prior earnings records usually are the most reliable guide as to the future expectancy, but resort to arbitrary five-or-ten-year averages without regard to current trends or future prospects will not produce a realistic valuation. If, for instance, a record of progressively increasing or decreasing net income is found, then greater weight may be accorded the most recent years' profits in estimating earning power. It will be helpful, in judging risk and the extent to which a business is a marginal operator, to consider deductions from income and net income in terms of percentage of sales. * * * [1959-1 C.B. 237, 241.]

Thus, Rev. Rul. 59-60 itself provides that potential future income is a major factor to consider in valuing the stock of a closely held corporation even though this factor cannot be established with certainty, but rather must be projected on the basis of prior earnings records. In the instant case, Grabowski made reasonable estimates of the future income of CCC, Stahl, Kaneland and Holland based on their prior earnings. He also projected future expenses as a percentage of sales based on the companies' prior operating experience. Consequently, because projected future income is an essential factor to consider in valuing stock and because Grabowski's method of projecting future income satisfies the guidelines set forth in Rev. Rul. 59-60, we think that Grabowski's use of the discounted cash flow method was appropriate in the instant case.

Respondent also attacks Grabowski's use of the Capital Asset Pricing Method (CAPM) to determine the cost of capital for CCC, Stahl, Kaneland, and Holland, maintaining that this formula is based on speculation and conjecture. We are, however, satisfied that the CAPM pro-vides an acceptable formula to use in calculating the cost of capital for CCC and its subsidiaries.

The CAPM used by Grabowski is not based on unfounded speculation and conjecture, but rather requires the application of the appraiser's common sense and informed judgment in weighing all the facts and circumstances in determining the cost of capital for a particular company. This approach to valuation is consistent with the statement in Rev. Rul. 59-60 that "[a] sound valuation will be based upon all the relevant facts, but the elements of common sense, informed judgment and reasonableness must enter into the process of weighing those facts and determining their aggregate significance." Indeed, we have repeatedly recognized that stock valuation is not an exact science, but rather is "inherently imprecise and capable of resolution only by a Salomon-like pronouncement." *Messing v. Commissioner* [Dec. 28,532], 48 T.C. 502, 512 (1967). We also note that respondent's expert, Lerner, described the CAPM as a "formal statistical measure of risk" whose use has flowered since 1951. Although Lerner further stated that the CAPM is presently on the wane because of the instability of the so-called "beta coefficient" (see below), he nevertheless also stated that numerous companies presently use the CAPM to estimate their cost of capital when making investment decisions.

Respondent also criticized the CAPM on the ground that the appraiser's risk added by Grabowski is simply a different estimate of the same risk quantified by the beta coefficient. We disagree.

The beta coefficient is a ratio which compares the movement of stock prices for publicly traded companies deemed comparable to the company in issue with the movement of stock prices in general. In the instant case, had CCC been a large publicly traded company, the beta coefficients relied on by Grabowski would have accurately reflected the company's perceived risk. However, because CCC is an unlisted closely held corporation, an additional premium is needed to reflect the fact that investors view such corporations as being more risky than large publicly traded companies. Thus, Grabowski's

---

[22] In *Weinberger v. UOP, Inc.*, 457 A.2d 701 (Del. 1983), the Delaware Supreme Court recognized the validity of the discounted cash flow method in reversing a lower court's decision not to use the discounted cash flow method in appraisal and other stock valuation proceedings. The Court stated:

[T]he standard "Delaware block" or weighted average method of valuation, formerly employed in appraisal and other stock valuation cases, shall no longer exclusively control such proceedings. We believe that a more liberal approach must include proof of value by any techniques or methods which are generally considered acceptable in the financial community and otherwise admissible in court * * *. [457 A.2d at 712-713.]

The Northern Trust Company

appraiser's risk reflects the additional risk inherent in CCC, Stahl, Kaneland and Holland because they are unlisted closely held corporations.

In conclusion, after consideration of the entire record before us, we are satisfied that Grabowski's discounted cash flow analysis accurately reflects the fair market value of the common equity of CCC, Stahl, Kaneland and Holland before applying discounts for lack of control and lack of marketability. Consequently, based on Grabowski's discounted cash flow analysis, we find that the total common equity of CCC had a value of $4,490,000 on the applicable valuation dates.

As to the remaining subsidiaries, Grabowski valued Suburban's real estate holdings and other assets, together with the investment real estate owned by CCC and Curran Development, at $2,665,000, which represented the liquidation value of those assets. Lerner, on the other hand, valued Suburban at $1,625,095, which represented the book value of its assets. Lerner did not individually value the investment real estate owned by CCC and Curran Development.

Although a company's liquidation value on occasion has been found to be an appropriate indication of that company's value, see *Estate of Lee v. Commissioner* [Dec. 35,017], 69 T.C. 860 (1978), on the record before us we find it more appropriate to rely on Lerner's valuation of Suburban based on the book value of its assets. At trial, Grabowski stated that a substantial portion of his liquidation value determination was based on the assessed value of Suburban's real estate holdings as adjusted to reflect fair market value. Grabowski explained that he relied on the opinion of several local real estate appraisers to properly adjust the properties' assessed values to reflect their fair market value. Grabowski admitted, however, that the appraisers never viewed the property prior to determining the appropriate adjustments. Indeed, the record contains no evidence explaining the basis of these adjustments. Section 20.2031-1(b), Estate Tax Regs., states that "[p]roperty shall not be returned at the value at which it is assessed for local tax purposes unless that value represents the fair market value as of the applicable valuation date."

We have recently held that assessed value may be considered when the relationship between assessed value and fair market value is demonstrated, but basically as a corroboration of fair market value determined by a more reliable method. *Estate of Kaplin v. Commissioner* [Dec. 43,017(M)], T.C. Memo. 1986-167. We apply this rule here. Since Grabowski has not shown the relationship between assessed value and fair market value, we think assessed values must be disregarded. We consequently rely on Suburban's book value of $1,625,095 as the fair market value of its stock.

Respondent, however, failed to provide any estimate of the fair market value of the real estate held by CCC and Curran Development. In the absence of other evidence indicative of the properties' value, we accept these properties' liquidation values as determined by Grabowski. Consequently, we find that the investment real estate owned by CCC and Curran Development had a fair market value of $415,000 on the applicable valuation dates.

For the reasons stated above, we conclude that the total fair market value of the common stock of CCC and its subsidiaries, before applying discounts for minority blocks and lack of marketability, was $6,530,095 on the applicable valuation dates. Our calculations may be summarized as follows:

Curran, Stahl, Kaneland and Holland	$4,490,000
Suburban	1,625,095
Investment Real Estate	415,000
TOTAL	$6,530,095

We must next allocate $6,530,095 between CCC's Class A voting common stock and Class B non-voting common stock. Petitioners and respondent agree that because the blocks of Class A voting common represent minority positions, the Class A voting shares are not more valuable than the Class B non-voting shares. Both parties therefore agree upon a pro rata allocation between the two classes of common stock. Consequently, we find that each share of CCC's Class A voting common stock and Class B non-voting common stock had a value of $707.95 before applying a minority position discount and discount for lack of marketability.[23]

We now reach the point upon which the parties most strongly disagree. We must determine the appropriate discounts to apply for lack of control and lack of marketability. Petitioners contend that each 25 percent block of CCC's Class A and Class B common stock should be discounted 35 percent for lack of control. Petitioners rely on a study conducted by one Douglas Austin to support this figure. (The Austin study is not part of the record and we have not been asked to take judicial notice of its existence or contents.) Petitioners also maintain that the value of the Class A and Class B shares should be further reduced by discounts of 20 percent and 90 percent, respectively, for lack of market-

---

[23] We determined this value as follows: total common equity of $6,530,095 divided by 9,224, the number of outstanding shares.

The Northern Trust Company

ability. They contend that a willing buyer of one 25 percent block of Class A stock would discount the stock by 20 percent because the remaining 75 percent of the Class A stock will be held by irrevocable voting trusts with an actuarially determined duration of 97 years. Petitioners also contend that a willing buyer would discount the Class A stock because of CCC's failure to pay dividends in the past. Petitioners further maintain that the difference in size between each 25 percent block of Class A stock (6 shares) and each 25 percent block of Class B stock (2,300 shares) supports their contention that the Class B shares should be discounted 90 percent.

Respondent disagrees, maintaining that because CCC was a financially strong old-line company with excellent and aggressive management and the capacity to pay dividends, both classes of stock should be discounted by no more than 15 percent for lack of control and 20 percent for lack of marketability. Respondent contends that the restrictions on transferability placed on 75 percent of the outstanding shares of the Class A and Class B stock by the terms of the trusts should not be considered in determining the value of each 25 percent block of stock in issue. Respondent further argues that no additional discount should be applied to the Class B shares based on the difference in size between each 25 percent block of the Class A shares and the Class B shares. After a careful review of the record, we think that a minority position discount of 25 percent and a discount of 20 percent for lack of marketability are appropriate for both classes of stock.

First, we point out that we can give little weight to Grabowski's reliance on the so-called Austin study, which is said to find that investors on average pay a premium of 35 percent in cash tender offers for stock representing a controlling interest in a company, to support a minority position discount of 35 percent in the instant case. The valuation of a closely held corporation, including the appropriate discount to apply to stock representing a minority position, must take into account all of the relevant facts and circumstances of the particular corporation under scrutiny. Grabowski, by relying on a study based on a sample of various corporations, has failed to consider the particular facts and circumstances a willing buyer would consider when discounting a block of stock representing a minority position in CCC.

We are similarly not convinced by respondent's assertion that a minority position discount of 15 percent is appropriate in this case. We do not think that this discount factor adequately reflects the amount a willing buyer

would reduce the value of each 25 percent block of common stock for lack of control. Rather, based on all of the facts and circumstances contained in the record before us, we believe that a minority position discount of 25 percent would be appropriate in the instant case. In so holding, we have considered the fact that a purchaser of a 25 percent interest in CCC would not have sufficient voting power to elect members to CCC's board of directors and therefore would not be able to participate in the management of the company.[24] We have also considered, however, that under Delaware law, corporate officers and directors owe their corporation and its minority shareholders a fiduciary obligation of honesty, loyalty, good faith and fairness. *Singer v. Magnavox Co.,* 380 A.2d 969, 977 (Del. 1977). Moreover, we point out that a willing buyer would be aware of the history of success experienced by CCC's past and present management and the dividend paying capacity of the company. Thus, although we believe that a potential investor would apply some discount to a 25 percent stock interest in CCC for lack of control, we do not think that his minority position would unduly deter a prospective investor from buying the 25 percent block of stock, given an appropriate discount in his purchase price.

Petitioners also contend that each 25 percent block of CCC's outstanding Class B common stock must be discounted 90 percent for lack of marketability. They argue that a willing buyer of a 25 percent interest in the Class B stock would discount that stock by 90 percent given the fact that the remaining 75 percent of the shares would be held in irrevocable trusts with an actuarially determined life of 97 years.

We agree with respondent that Grabowski's 90 percent discount figure is based upon a misconception of the law. In his testimony Grabowski stated:

Well, for example, valuing the Jack Curran block of stock I would be presented with the—I was presented with the necessity of placing myself as a hypothetical investor as of May 7, 1976, presented with the opportunity to buy this stock. Looking at the form I see a very good historically sound financially stable firm. I also see though that we have a situation of 18 other shares of Class A common stock being held by three other trusts, the trustees of which are Curran Management. I also see 2,300 shares of Class B common stock held in another similar trust, two different trusts, Cecilia Simon's 76-2 trust, and for example, placing myself looking at the Jack Curran block of stock, Bill Simon's 76-2 trust. So I could—I would analyze what are the

---

[24] CCC's charter does not provide for cumulative voting, nor does Delaware corporation law mandate cumulative voting.

The Northern Trust Company

types of returns that I might anticipate at that point buying a block of six shares of common stock that provides some—the opportunity to vote, and 2,300 shares of Class B common stock not providing the opportunity to vote. Given this circumstance that the other shares are housed in these trusts, given that, I would have to look at well, what are the likely scenarios, or what are the likely returns I might receive from making this investment.

Grabowski was viewing each block of stock as a separate gift on the one hand and hypothetically valuing each block before the gift. On the other hand, he was assuming that the other gifts were a fait accompli. Grabowski perceived the trusts as a restriction on the stock when in fact the trusts were not in existence until the making of the gifts. The trusts were, of course, created simultaneously and in concert by the stockholders pursuant to the estate freeze plan. Respondent's expert, Lerner, with whom we agree on this point, considered the trusts irrelevant for valuation purposes because he looked at the value of the stock from the point of view of what the donor had given.

Section 2511(a) states that the gift tax shall apply whether the transfer is in trust or otherwise, whether the gift is direct or indirect, and whether the property is real or personal, tangible or intangible. Section 25.2511-1(a), Gift Tax Regs., explains further that the gift tax is an excise tax on the transfer, and is not a tax on the subject of the gift. Section 25.2511-2(a), Gift Tax Regs. (entitled "Cessation of donor's dominion and control"), provides:

The gift tax is not imposed upon the receipt of the property by the donee, nor is it necessarily determined by the measure of enrichment resulting to the donee from the transfer, nor is it conditioned upon ability to identify the donee at the time of the transfer. On the contrary, the tax is a primary and personal liability of the donor, is an excise upon his act of making the transfer, *is measured by the value of the property passing from the donor,* and attaches regardless of the fact that the identity of the donee may not then be known or ascertainable. [Emphasis supplied.]

With respect to the critical date for valuation purposes, section 2512 states that if the gift is made in property, the value thereof as the date of the gift shall be considered the amount of the gift. Section 25.2512-2(a) of the regulations addresses the method for determining the value of stocks and bonds. It states that the value of the stocks and bonds is the fair market value per share on the date of the gift.

Ahmanson Foundation v. United States [81-2 USTC ¶ 13,438], 674 F.2d 761 (9th Cir. 1981), addressed this issue in the estate tax context.

The Court was faced with the question of the valuation of stock includable in the decedent's gross estate at his death. The taxpayer had argued that shares of stock should be partitioned into two blocks prior to valuation, that the 99 shares which went to a charitable foundation should be valued separately from the one share which had a private destination. The taxpayer argued that because the estate tax is a tax on the transfer of property, the valuation of the property in the gross estate must take into account any changes in value brought about by the fact of the distribution itself. The Court acknowledged that valuation may take into account changes brought about by the death of the testator. Usually death itself does not alter the value of property owned by the decedent, although in exceptional cases, such as when a small business loses the services of a valuable partner, death does change the value of property. See *United States v. Land* [62-1 USTC ¶ 12,078], 303 F.2d 170 (5th Cir. 1962). The Court in *Ahmanson* stated:

We must distinguish, however, the effect of "predistribution" transformations and changes in value brought about by the testator's death, from changes in value resulting from the fact that under the decedent's estate plan the assets in the gross estate ultimately come to rest in the hands of different beneficiaries. The estate tax is a tax upon a transfer as the Foundation contends. However, *it is a tax on the privilege of passing on property, not a tax on the privilege of receiving property.* * * * [Emphasis supplied.] *[Ahmanson Foundation v. United States, supra at 768.]*

In *Ahmanson* the Court concluded that a hypothetical bifurcation of stock would be contrary to the policy underlying the Federal estate tax. This is because it would be easy to implement a tax avoidance scheme whenever an asset in the gross estate would have a diminished value if divided among two or more beneficiaries.

Citing *Ahmanson* with approval, the Seventh Circuit Court of Appeals, in *Estate of Curry v. United States,* dealt with the post-transfer bifurcation theory in the following language:

[T]o permit the hypothetical bifurcation of an otherwise integrated bundle of property for valuation purposes would severely undermine the estate tax system and permit abusive manipulation by inviting an executor to invent elaborate scenarios of disaggregated disposition in order to minimize total value. For example, an estate in possession of all shares of a corporation, voting and non-voting, could, under the regime urged by the estate here, arbitrarily slice the voting share block so thinly as to deny attribution of a control premium to any resulting block. * * *

Estate of Curry

[*Estate of Curry v. United States* [83-1 USTC ¶ 13,518], 706 F.2d 1424, 1428 (7th Cir. 1983).]

See also *Estate of Pudim v. Commissioner* [Dec. 39,430(M)], T. C. Memo. 1982-606, affd. without published opinion 742 F.2d 1433 (2d Cir. 1983).

We think the anti-bifurcation rationale explained in the estate tax context by the Seventh Circuit in *Estate of Curry* and by the Ninth Circuit in *Ahmanson Foundation* applies equally here in the gift tax context. The estate tax and the gift tax, both being excise taxes on transfers, are to be construed in pari materia. *Sanford's Estate v. Commissioner* [39-2 USTC ¶ 9745], 308 U.S. 39, 44 (1939); *Carson v. Commissioner* [Dec. 35,536], 71 T.C. 252 (1978), affd. [81-1 USTC ¶ 13,396] 641 F.2d 864 (10th Cir. 1981). This case presents a paradigmatic example of the appropriateness of that rule of construction.

Given petitioners' concerted estate freeze plan put in place by the simultaneous gifts in trust, we find their attempt to discredit respondent's reliance on *Estate of Curry* and *Ahmanson Foundation* to be, with all due respect, disingenuous. Petitioners attempt to draw a distinction based upon the fact that the two cited cases involved the stock of a single majority stockholder, whereas here none were in control. In the context of this case this is a distinction without a difference, because even petitioners cannot deny that in creating the estate freeze plan they marched in lockstep. So marching, their position was no different than that of a single majority stockholder.

After a careful review of all relevant facts and circumstances, we also find a discount of 20 percent for lack of marketability for both classes of common stock to be appropriate. In determining this discount factor, we recognize that the stock of unlisted closely held corporations is generally difficult to sell. We also recognize that CCC had a history of paying little if any dividends. We believe, however, that these negative factors are substantially offset by the following positive factors: 1) the Curran companies had a stable or upward trend in earnings during the five-year period 1971 through 1975, which trend was expected to continue in the future; 2) CCC was financially strong with excellent and aggressive management; and 3) CCC had a substantial dividend-paying capacity.

In conclusion, after applying a minority position discount of 25 percent and a discount of 20 percent for lack of marketability, we find that each share of CCC's Class A voting common stock and Class B non-voting common stock had a value of $389.37.

The government first assigns as error the court's refusal to instruct the jury, as the government requested, that "[b]ecause the decedent had voting control of the company, I instruct you that in valuing [decedent's] interest in the company the non-voting stock was worth as much per share as the voting stock." In support of its instruction, the government argues that, for estate tax purposes, the property transferred must be valued as the decedent held it, not in the form it could conceivably take in a subsequent transfer, and that, in the hands of the estate, the absence of voting control appurtenant to some of the shares of stock would not diminish their value, as voting control still resided in the decedent's power. The estate, by contrast, argues that the decedent's stock holdings were more properly split into separate voting and non-voting blocks prior to valuation, and that the non-voting stock could possess a lesser value even if considered as part of a single bundle including its voting counterpart. In our view both the law and common sense compel the conclusion that the fair market value of the non-voting stock in the hands of an estate with sufficient shares of voting stock to ensure the estate's control of a corporation cannot be less than the value of the estate's voting stock. Therefore, we conclude, in rejecting the government's instruction, the district court erred as a matter of law to the substantial prejudice of the rights of the government.[1]

Section 2001 of the Internal Revenue Code of 1954, 26 U. S. C. § 2031(a) provides that the value of the gross estate of the decedent is determined by including "all property" therein. The corresponding Treasury Regulations provide that the value of includible property is its "fair market value" at the time of decedent's death. Section 20.2031-1(b), Treasury Regulations on Estate Tax (1954 Code). That regula-

---

[1] The estate has put forth numerous arguments supporting its contention that the government has "waived" its argument with respect to this and other alleged errors because, *inter alia,* the government failed to include separate texts of the refused instructions on appeal, failed to cite controlling authority in its brief on appeal, and failed to object with "sufficient clarity" to the offending instruc-

tions. We have examined these arguments and find them to be without merit. With respect to the particular instruction examined here, the record reveals that the government's objection alerted the court to each step of its argument: that the stock be valued as part of the estate's entire interest, and that such a perspective requires a finding of equal valuation for both classes of stock. Tr. 465-66.

Estate of Curry

tion states further that the "fair market value is the price at which the property would change hands between a willing buyer and a willing seller, neither being under any compulsion to buy or to sell and both having reasonable knowledge of the relevant facts." *Id.* The first question for our purposes thus becomes whether the property of which the fair market value is to be assessed should be viewed as it exists in the hands of the estate, or as it may exist if fortuitously balkanized through a chain of post-death transactions.

We believe that the first perspective comports more fully with the nature of the estate tax. As the Supreme Court has explained, the estate tax was not conceived as "a tax upon succession and receipt of benefits under the law or the will. It was death duties as distinguished from a legacy or succession tax. What this law taxes is not the interest to which the legatees and devisees succeeded on death, but the interest which ceased by reason of the death." *YMCA v. Davis* [1 USTC ¶ 89], 264 U. S. 47, 50 (1924). Other courts have emphasized that the resultant "valuation is determined by *the interest that passes,* and the value of the interest before or after death is pertinent only as it serves to indicate the value *at death.*" *United States v. Land* [71-2 USTC ¶ 9771] 303 F. 2d 170 (5th Cir. 1962) (emphasis in original); *see also Estate of Bright v. United States* [81-2 USTC ¶ 13,436], 658 F. 2d 999 (5th Cir. 1981).[2] The interest that passed in this case was the decedent's interest in an 1160-share bundle of stock, the 800 voting shares of which assured complete corporate control. Plainly, then, to meet the mandate of the Code, those shares are to be valued as part and parcel of the *interest,* not as arbitrarily disaggregated under one possible subsequent transaction scenario.

Although, surprisingly, this precise issue has not been widely addressed, our interpretation has been embraced by the Ninth Circuit in *Ahmanson Foundation v. United States* [81-2 USTC ¶ 13,438], 674 F. 2d 761 (9th Cir. 1981). In *Ahmanson* the estate argued, as here, that the estate's non-voting stock shares should be valued separately from the estate's sole and controlling voting share.[3] The Ninth Circuit rejected this argument, noting that the estate tax "is a tax on the privilege of passing on property, not a tax on the privilege of receiving property. . . . There is nothing in the statutes or in the case law that suggests that valuation of the gross estate should take into account that the assets will come to rest in several hands rather than one." *Ahmanson,* 674 F. 2d at 768. Likewise, we hold that the interest in the integrated estate forms the only basis for valuation which rationally comports with the purpose of the tax at issue.

Additionally, to permit the hypothetical bifurcation of an otherwise integrated bundle of property for valuation purposes would severely undermine the estate tax system and permit abusive manipulation by inviting an executor to invent elaborate scenarios of disaggregated disposition in order to minimize total value. For example, an estate in possession of all shares of a corporation, voting and non-voting, could, under the regime urged by the estate here, arbitrarily slice the voting share block so thinly as to deny attribution of a control premium to any resulting block. Similarly, as the *Ahmanson* court noted, under the theory professed by the estate here, a testator with two equally valuable pieces of real property could designate equal undivided shares in each to two separate beneficiaries. The resultant valuation of the estate would be diminished by an amount representing the combined discount attrib-

---

[2] It is only in rare cases that the event of death will be held to have, for estate tax purposes, any impact upon the fair market value of the interest that passes from decedent, as when, for example, a small business thereby loses the services of a key partner, *United States v. Land* [71-2 USTC ¶ 9771], 303 F. 2d 170, 172, or the will provides for a recapitalization of the stock package owned by the estate, *Provident National Bank v. United States* [78-2 USTC ¶ 13,255], 581 F. 2d 1081, 1086-87 (3d Cir. 1978); in such cases, it should be noted, the attendant revaluations occur as a result of conditions internal to the integrated estate and are not based upon any hypothetical piecemeal dissolution of the estate.

[3] Indeed, *Ahmanson* posed a case even more conclusive to the disaggregation principle proffered by the estate here, for the evidence there indicated that the non-voting and voting shares had *in fact* devolved into separate hands. *Ahmanson,* 674 F. 2d at 768. A *fortiori,* the principles applied in *Ahmanson* are applicable here, where only conclusory testimony suggested that the non-voting shares might be sold separately. See note 4, *infra.*

Estate of Curry

uted to undivided shares, even though the two recipients could later exchange their undivided shares and thus reverse the artificial division of the properties, a purely paper maneuver resulting in great loss to the treasury. As the *Ahmanson* court noted,

> Estate planners would implement such a tax-avoidance scheme whenever at least one of the assets in the gross estate had a diminished value if divided among two or more beneficiaries. As there is nothing in either the language of the statute or the underlying theory of the estate tax that requires the existence of this loophole, we shall not impute it to Congress.

Ahmanson, 674 F. 2d at 768. We likewise decline to permit such a speculative and manipulable division of property to serve as the basis for valuation.

Thirdly, permitting the estate's argued hypothetical scenario of separate disposition of voting and non-voting shares to form the basis of a proposed valuation would defy common sense and the requirements of the "fair market value" standard, at least in the present case, where the stock of a small, closely held corporation is at issue. The relevant Treasury regulations provide that "fair market value" is the "price at which the property would change hands between a willing buyer and a willing seller . . . both having reasonable knowledge of relevant facts." It is well established that the willing buyer-willing seller rule presumes that the potential transaction is to be analyzed from the viewpoint of a hypothetical buyer whose only goal is to maximize his advantage. See, e. g., Revenue Ruling 59-60, 1959-1 C. B. 237; *Estate of Bright v. United States* [81-2 USTC ¶ 13,436], 658 F. 2d 999, 1006 (5th Cir. 1981). And it does not comport with common sense that a willing buyer would be likely to purchase non-voting shares in a small, family-held business, without concomitantly purchasing a controlling voting interest.[4] Such a purchase would put the outside purchaser at the mercy of the voting insiders on matters such as dividend declaration and other important corporate policies, without affording, as in the case of most publicly-traded corporate stock, a ready "exit" remedy of disposing of the purchased stock, or the "voice" remedy of joining with voting *non*-insiders to protect the minority interest. In applying the willing buyer-willing seller rule, courts may not permit the positing of transactions which are unlikely and plainly contrary to the economic interest of a hypothetical buyer as a basis for the valuation. Thus, even apart from considerations of estate tax policy, there is logical reason to reject the estate's proposed separate fair market valuation of voting and non-voting stock.

Once it is determined that the property is to be valued as it exists in the hands of the estate rather than as it might exist if subsequently divided, the court's error in refusing the government's proffered instruction becomes clear. The sole reason for assigning a lesser value to the non-voting shares in this case is their lack of voting rights which would, the estate argues, make them less attractive to a prospective pur-

---

[4] On cross-examination, the estate's valuation witness testified in conclusory fashion as to the hypothetical existence of a willing buyer for non-voting shares in the instant case, but he was unresponsive to the government's query as to whether such a peculiarly risky investment could in fact ever attract a willing buyer; instead, the witness asserted woodenly that such a purchase is "exactly what you do when you buy General Motors or any other stock. . .", Tr. 258, thus eliding the crucial differences, noted in the text *infra*, between a publicly-held and a closely-held corporation.

Estate of Curry

chaser.[5] But that defect disappears where, as here, the non-voting stock is an integral part of the larger estate which retains a controlling equity interest. Here, when viewed in the hands of the estate, the non-voting stock would simply not be subject to the disadvantages of an isolated non-voting interest.

Like this court, the Ninth Circuit in *Ahmanson* rejected the argument, made by the estate here, that non-voting shares could be assigned a lesser value than controlling voting shares even where both comprised a single block, noting, "The record simply does not contain support for the proposition that non-voting shares are sold at a discount when sold together in a package with sufficient voting stock to give control." *Ahmanson Foundation v. United States* [81-2 USTC ¶ 13,438], 674 F. 2d 761, 769 (9th Cir. 1981). The *Ahmanson* court went on to note the logical *impossibility* of such a discount, given the block purchaser's power to fully guard the interests of his non-voting stock through control of corporate policy. *Id.*[6] In short, when viewed as part of the estate's integrated stock holdings, as they must be, the non-voting shares simply do not suffer any strategic disadvantage.[7] To view the matter otherwise would be to permit an estate to arbitrarily divide even a one hundred percent block of voting stock into units so small as to avoid the attribution of a control premium to any unit. We do not think that the "fair market value" rule may be so absurdly and abstractly parsed.

In sum, we hold that the district court erred in refusing to instruct the jury that the non-voting and voting shares held in decedent's estate were of equal value. Since the jury found, without the benefit of this instruction, a nearly $100 differential between the two classes of shares, the court's failure to give the instruction was obviously prejudicial to the government's interest and would alone warrant a new trial.

---

[5] Holders of non-voting stock in this case also did not enjoy the right to inspect the company's books and records. The estate, however, has at no point argued that this disability could form the basis for a valuation differential.

[6] The estate attempts to distinguish *Ahmanson* on two grounds. First, it argues the estate in *Ahmanson* controlled *all* of the voting shares, rather than merely a majority, as here. This fact, however, does not affect the basic *Ahmanson* principle that no discount may properly attach to non-voting shares when considered as part of a package "with sufficient voting shares *to give control*." *Ahmanson*, 674 F. 2d at 769. (Emphasis added). It is uncontested here that the estate's possession of fifty-three percent of the voting shares was sufficient to "give control."

Second, the estate argues that the *Ahmanson* court held specifically that the record did not contain support for the proposition that non-voting shares are sold at a discount when part of a package conferring voting control, while in the instant case, the estate's witness testified in support of this proposition. However, the estate offered no direct evidence on this point. Its chief witness on cross-examination expressed support for this theory in entirely conclusory and speculative terms and appeared to premise this support on a mis-apprehension as to the decedent-focused framework of valuation, despite the government's repeated attempts to educe an answer to the question which respected that framework. See Tr. 254-60, 280. A plaintiff, of course, is not entitled to inferences which rest on mere specu-lation. *Carlson v. American Safety Equipment Corp.*, 528 F. 2d 384, 386 (1st Cir. 1976).

Moreover, the following colloquy suggests that, when guided by the appropriate valuation standard, the estate's valuation witness con-ceded the logical impossibility of a discount for non-voting shares:

Q. . . . In the hands of Bernard L. Curry, his nonvoting stock cannot be adversely af-fected for purpose of dividends because he owned voting control, isn't that correct?

A. I didn't appraise the stock in his hands. But to continue your question, I would pre-sume *that would be correct, in his hands*.

Q. Okay. And in his hands—

A. He wouldn't do anything against himself, what we are saying.

Tr. 254-55 (emphasis added).

Finally, even if the estate had arguably pre-sented some specific record evidence on this point, we would agree with the *Ahmanson* court's alternative holding that a finding of a value differential between the two classes of shares when situated in a control bundle is illogical and impermissible as a matter of estate tax law and policy. See *Ahmanson*, 674 F. 2d at 761.

[7] The estate cites *Korslin v. United States* [73-1 USTC ¶ 12,907], 31 A. F. T. R. 2d (P-H) 1390 (E. D. Wis. 1973), to buttress its conten-tion that a lesser valuation for non-voting shares is permissible, even when those shares are part of a larger block including voting shares. *Korslin* is, however, distinguishable, for in that case the voting shares comprised only a minority interest. *Id.* at 1390.

PART IV

KEY RATIOS USED IN VALUATION

TYPES OF KEY RATIOS

A number of key ratios are considered primary valuation tools and are often used in valuing a privately held business. An example of the raw data used in compiling these ratios and complete ratios is provided in this appendix.

Key ratios can be divided into three groups:

1. *Liquidity ratios* measure (a) the ability of the business to meet its current obligations or (b) the efficiency and productivity of the business in utilizing its available resources and expenditures (ratios that fall into category (b) are also referred to as "activity ratios").

2. *Leverage ratios* indicate the amount of the business' operations that are debt rather than equity financed.

3. *Profitability ratios* measure the nitty gritty of the business—does it make money (rate of return) on its sales, equity, and investments?

LIQUIDITY RATIOS

Liquidity ratios measure a company's ability to meet all of its current financial obligations. If necessary, how much cash could the company come up with at short notice? Could the company sell enough of its assets to meet its current liabilities without endangering its ongoing operations? A high liquidity ratio indicates that the company not only has a cushion against capricious creditors, but is also able to take advantage of windfall business opportunities.

$$\text{Current ratio} = \frac{\text{Current assets}}{\text{Current liabilities}}$$

This measures the extent to which short-term debt can be distinguished by current assets—cash, net trade receivables, inventories, prepaid expenses, and other current assets.

$$\text{Quick ratio} = \frac{\text{Quick assets}}{\text{Current liabilities}}$$

This measures the extent to which short-term debt can be extinguished by quick assets—cash, net trade receivables, and other current assets easily convertible to cash.

$$\text{Collection period} = \frac{\text{Accounts receivable}}{\text{Average daily sales}}$$

This measures the average period of time (days) between a sale and payment. The shorter the period, the larger the company's cash flow. Average daily sales are net yearly sales divided by 360.

$$\text{Inventory turnover} = \frac{\text{Cost of goods sold}}{\text{Year–end inventory}}$$

This measures the number of times inventory is replenished during the year. A good inventory turnover is a high one. For example, if cost of goods sold is $1 million, the lower the year-end inventory, the higher the inventory turnover. What this means is that the investment needed to carry inventory is lower, freeing more working capital for other needs.

$$\text{Fixed assets to net worth} = \frac{\text{Depreciable assets}}{\text{Net worth}}$$

This measures the amount of working capital tied up in depreciable assets. A high percentage, common for capital-intensive industries, indicates that a substantial amount of working capital will have to be expended each year in renewing fixed assets, and hence, represent a significant drain on working capital.

$$\text{Sale to net working capital} = \frac{\text{Sale (receipts)}}{\text{Current assets} - \text{Current liabilities}}$$

This measures the turnover of working capital in a given period. The higher the turnover, the more efficient the use of working capital, allowing more of it to be used for other current needs.

LEVERAGE RATIOS

Leverage ratios show the degree to which a business' operations and capital expenditures are funded by borrowed funds or the owner's equity. The higher the degree of debt involved, the higher the risk an investment in such a business entails. Debt is a fixed charge that must be met yearly regardless of profitability of a business. If the business can earn a higher return on investment on borrowed funds than the cost of borrowing those funds, the difference increases shareholder equity. For example, if the cost of borrowing funds used to finance operations is 12 percent and the operations are returning 25 percent, the 13 percent difference represents an incremental increase in equity. This is called trading on equity.

Lenders use leverage ratios to determine the ability of a business to not only pay back borrowed funds but make a respectable profit at the same time. The owners of the business have little incentive to continue operations if all the profits will be eaten up by debt service. On the other hand, these ratios are the birthing tools for the current craze of leveraged buyouts.

$$\text{Long–term debt to net worth} = \frac{\text{Long–term liabilities}}{\text{Owner's equity}}$$

Who really owns the company? The shareholders or the business' long-term lenders? Creditors have priority upon liquidation. What is the liquidation value to a shareholder of a highly-leveraged business? Not much. If this ratio is more than 1 (i.e., the lenders have more long-term capital than the shareholders), the degree of risk in investing in such a business can become prohibitively high.

$$\text{Total debt to worth} = \frac{\text{Total liabilities}}{\text{Owner's equity}}$$

Similar to the immediately preceding ratio, this measures the overall position of the shareholders versus the business' creditors. The larger the percentage of all creditors in the assets of the business, the smaller the cushion the business has against adverse operating periods. A trend that shows an increase in this percentage could indicate that shareholder's equity in the business' assets eventually may be reduced to zero.

$$\text{Total debt to total assets} = \frac{\text{Total liabilities}}{\text{Total assets}}$$

This represents the percentage of assets supplied by the creditors. The same principals discussed in the previous two leverage ratios apply.

$$\text{Times interest earned} = \frac{\text{Earnings before interest and taxes}}{\text{Interest expense}}$$

How capable is a business of paying its interest obligations? Put another way, can it shoulder the burden of its debt service and make a reasonable profit? That question is answered by this ratio, which measures the number of extra times that fixed interest has been earned in a year. The more times earned, the larger the cushion the business has and the smaller the effect of debt service on the ability of the business to turn a profit.

A decision must be made when calculating this ratio about whether to use pre-tax or after-tax earnings. It is wise to make both calculations because the difference between the two reveals the extent to which taxes affect the cash earnings of the business.

PROFITABILITY RATIOS

These are the most important ratios. Does the business make money? Can it generate the profits for continued growth or survival? These ratios also reflect directly on management's abilities and decisions and how well it has used the business' resources to benefit the shareholders.

$$\text{Pre-tax return on investment} = \frac{\text{Pre-tax profit}}{\text{Owner's equity}} \times 100$$

$$\text{After-tax return on investment} = \frac{\text{After-tax profit}}{\text{Owner's equity}} \times 100$$

These two ratios are literally the bottom line. How much of the owner's or shareholder's money was returned in profit? Again it is wise to compare the results to determine if taxes in the particular geographical area or industry make investing in the company unwise, or whether a discount is necessary to compensate.

$$\text{Turnover of owner's equity} = \frac{\text{Sales (receipts)}}{\text{Owner's equity}}$$

This ratio measures the amount of sales generated by the capital employed. It is another type of ratio indicating the efficiency of management in utilizing shareholder's equity. Caution should be used with this ratio: a very high ratio could indicate inadequate capitalization as well as efficient use of capital.

$$\text{Sales to fixed assets} = \frac{\text{Sales (receipts)}}{\text{Fixed assets}}$$

This ratio measures the amount of sales generated by the depreciable assets of the business. It also indicates the ability of management to use available operating resources. A decision to invest more in plant and equipment as a way of boosting sales can often hinge on this ratio.

$$\text{Sales to total assets} = \frac{\text{Sales (receipts)}}{\text{Total assets}}$$

This ratio indicates how much in sales one dollar of assets generates. It is also an overall measure of management capability. When compared to the immediately preceding ratio, it reveals the relative importance of plant and equipment to revenue generation.

Example

Key Ratios of Astro Electronics. The following example is taken from the software package put out by Aardvark/McGraw-Hill entitled *Business Valuation.* It uses the same 15 key ratios explained in the preceding pages. The ratios cover a five-year period and are based on historical and adjusted balance sheet and income statement date.

Also included with the financial statements and key ratios is an Income Statement Percentages. This statement takes items from the income statement, and lists all debits as a percentage of sales/receipts. It covers a five-year period and is based on historical and adjusted income statement data. The income statement percentages give a good idea of what expense items are the greatest depressers of the business' bottom-line profit margin.

Astro Electronics
Valuation Date: January 15, 19____
Key Ratios

	Year 5*		Year 4		Year 3		Year 2		Year 1	
	Hist	Adj	Hist	Adj	Hist	Adj	Hist	Adj	Hist	Adj
Liquidity ratios										
Current	2.15	2.67	2.11	2.43	1.99	2.30	1.94	2.24	1.89	2.19
Quick	1.26	1.53	1.25	1.39	1.15	1.26	1.10	1.24	1.07	1.20
Collection per	81	77	81	79	84	79	84	81	90	86
Inventory turn	3.26	3.21	3.37	3.11	3.28	2.93	3.24	3.17	3.11	2.96
Fixed assets to worth	0.35	0.43	0.34	0.42	0.38	0.44	0.44	0.49	0.47	0.51
Sales to net working capital	3.84	3.34	3.87	3.40	4.00	3.48	4.06	3.59	3.86	3.38
Debt ratios										
Long-term debt to worth	0.06	0.05	0.06	0.05	0.05	0.04	0.05	0.04	0.05	0.04
Total debt to worth	0.43	0.28	0.42	0.31	0.42	0.30	0.39	0.28	0.39	0.28
Total debt to total assets	0.29	0.22	0.28	0.24	0.28	0.23	0.27	0.22	0.27	0.22
Times interest earned	12.22	12.62	9.39	10.00	7.04	7.99	5.10	5.49	3.50	4.00
Profitability ratios										
Pretax profit to worth (%)	34.77	29.10	28.75	25.21	21.94	20.53	15.52	13.88	9.84	9.55
After-tax profit to worth (%)	18.78	15.71	15.53	13.61	11.85	11.08	8.38	7.49	5.31	5.16
Worth turnover	1.63	1.31	1.56	1.28	1.44	1.17	1.31	1.07	1.18	0.95
Sales to fixed assets	4.70	3.07	4.67	3.06	3.82	2.62	2.96	2.19	2.53	1.87
Sales to total assets	1.10	1.03	1.05	0.98	0.97	0.90	0.90	0.83	0.80	0.75

*Year 5 is the most recent year

Astro Electronics
Valuation Date: January 15, 19__
Key Ratios

Estate of John Smith
Minority shareholder

Income Statement Percentages

	Year 5		Year 4		Year 3		Year 2		Year 1	
	Hist	*Adj*	*Hist*	*Adj*	*Hist*	*Adj*	*Hist*	*Adj*	*Hist*	*Adj*
Sales/receipts	100.0	100.0	100.0	100.0	100.0	100.0	100.0	100.0	100.0	100.0
Cost goods sold	63.0	62.7	64.7	63.9	66.4	64.6	68.2	67.8	70.0	69.2
Gross profit	37.0	37.3	35.3	36.1	33.6	35.4	31.8	32.2	30.0	30.8
Operating exp	13.7	13.3	14.8	14.2	15.9	15.2	17.1	16.3	18.3	17.5
Operating prof	23.3	24.0	20.5	21.9	17.7	20.2	14.7	15.9	11.7	13.3
Interest exp	1.9	1.9	2.2	2.2	2.5	2.5	2.9	2.9	3.3	3.3
Pretax profit	21.4	22.1	18.3	19.7	15.2	17.7	11.8	13.0	8.4	10.0
Income taxes	9.8	10.2	8.5	9.1	7.0	8.1	5.5	6.0	3.8	4.6
After-tax prof	11.6	11.9	9.8	10.6	8.2	9.6	6.3	7.0	4.6	5.4

Astro Electronics
Valuation Date: January 15, 19__
Key Ratios

Estate of John Smith
Minority shareholder

Adjusted Balance Sheet

	Year 5	Year 4	Year 3	Year 2	Year 1
Cash	50,540	55,750	55,000	50,245	51,550
Net trade receiv	450,000	400,000	350,000	310,500	285,000
Inventories	410,500	375,000	350,000	295,000	280,000
Prepaid expenses	16,596	15,660	15,481	15,075	14,950
Other current	75,000	65,000	35,000	24,000	24,000
TOT CURR ASSETS	1,002,636	911,410	805,481	694,820	655,500
Land	265,000	255,000	245,000	235,000	225,000
Fixed assets	682,875	595,900	605,490	629,310	641,250
Econ intangibles	40,000	50,000	60,000	70,000	60,000
Other intang	0	0	0	0	0
Other long-term	56,259	56,259	56,259	25,000	25,000
TOTAL ASSETS	2,046,770	1,868,569	1,772,230	1,654,130	1,606,750
Current liab	375,000	375,000	350,000	310,000	300,000
Long-term liab	75,000	65,000	60,000	50,000	50,000
Deferred taxes	0	0	0	0	0
TOT LIABILITIES	450,000	440,000	410,000	360,000	350,000
TOTAL CAPITAL	1,596,770	1,428,569	1,362,230	1,294,130	1,256,750
TOTAL LIABILITIES AND CAPITAL	2,046,770	1,868,569	1,772,230	1,654,130	1,606,750

Astro Electronics   **Estate of John Smith**
Valuation Date: January 15, 19__   **Minority shareholder**
Key Ratios

	Historical Balance Sheet				
	Year 5	Year 4	Year 3	Year 2	Year 1
Cash	50,540	55,750	55,000	50,245	51,550
Net trade receiv	475,000	410,000	370,000	320,560	300,150
Inventories	405,100	350,000	321,500	290,100	270,000
Prepaid expenses	16,596	15,660	15,481	15,075	14,950
Other current	75,000	65,000	35,000	24,000	24,000
TOT CURR ASSETS	1,022,236	896,410	796,981	699,980	660,650
Land	195,600	195,600	195,600	195,600	195,600
Fixed assets	446,300	390,888	415,208	466,156	475,000
Econ intangibles	120,000	117,266	96,506	78,396	60,000
Other intang	76,000	76,000	76,000	76,000	76,000
Other long-term	56,259	56,259	56,259	25,000	25,000
TOTAL ASSETS	1,916,395	1,732,423	1,636,554	1,541,132	1,492,250
Current liab	475,000	425,000	400,000	360,000	350,000
Long-term liab	75,000	65,000	60,000	50,000	50,000
Deferred taxes	0	0	0	0	0
TOT LIABILITIES	550,000	490,000	460,000	410,000	400,000
TOTAL CAPITAL	1,366,395	1,242,423	1,176,554	1,131,132	1,092,250
TOTAL LIABILITIES AND CAPITAL	1,916,395	1,732,423	1,636,554	1,541,132	1,492,250

Astro Electronics

Estate of John Smith

Valuation Date: January 15, 19__

Minority shareholder

Key Ratios

	Historical Income Statement				
	Year 5	Year 4	Year 3	Year 2	Year 1
Sales/receipts	2,098,808	1,825,050	1,587,000	1,380,000	1,200,000
Cost goods sold	1,321,756	1,180,140	1,053,696	940,800	840,000
GROSS PROFIT	777,052	644,910	533,304	439,200	360,000
Operating exp	288,375	269,509	251,878	235,400	220,000
OPERATING PROF	488,677	375,401	281,426	203,800	140,000
Interest exp	40,000	40,000	40,000	40,000	40,000
PRETAX PROFIT	448,677	335,401	241,426	163,800	100,000
Income taxes	206,391	154,284	111,056	75,348	46,000
NET PROFIT AFTER TAXES	242,286	181,117	130,370	88,452	54,000

	Adjusted Income Statement				
	Year 5	Year 4	Year 3	Year 2	Year 1
Sales/receipts	2,098,808	1,825,050	1,587,000	1,380,000	1,200,000
Cost goods sold	1,315,750	1,165,430	1,025,500	935,000	830,000
GROSS PROFIT	783,058	659,620	561,500	445,000	370,000
Operating exp	278,375	259,509	241,878	225,400	210,000
OPERATING PROF	504,683	400,111	319,622	219,600	160,000
Interest exp	40,000	40,000	40,000	40,000	40,000
PRETAX PROFIT	464,683	360,111	279,622	179,600	120,000
Income taxes	213,754	165,651	128,626	82,616	55,200
NET PROFIT AFTER TAXES	250,929	194,460	150,996	96,984	64,800

Astro Electronics
Valuation Date: January 15, 19__
Key Ratios

Estate of John Smith
Minority shareholder

Balance Sheet Percentages

	Year 5		Year 4		Year 3		Year 2		Year 1	
	Hist	*Adj*	*Hist*	*Adj*	*Hist*	*Adj*	*Hist*	*Adj*	*Hist*	*Adj*
Cash	2.6	2.5	3.2	3.0	3.4	3.1	3.3	3.0	3.5	3.2
Net trade rec	24.8	22.0	23.7	21.4	22.6	19.7	20.8	18.8	20.1	17.8
Inventories	21.1	20.1	20.2	20.1	19.6	19.7	18.8	17.8	18.1	17.4
Prepaid exp	0.9	0.8	0.9	0.8	1.0	0.9	1.0	0.9	1.0	0.9
Other current	3.9	3.7	3.7	3.5	2.1	2.0	1.6	1.5	1.6	1.5
Tot curr assets	53.3	49.1	51.7	48.8	48.7	45.4	45.5	42.0	44.3	40.8
Land	10.2	12.9	11.3	13.6	12.0	13.8	12.7	14.2	13.1	14.0
Fixed assets	23.3	33.4	22.6	31.9	25.4	34.2	30.2	38.1	31.8	39.9
Econ intang	6.3	1.9	6.8	2.7	5.9	3.4	5.1	4.2	4.0	3.7
Other intang	4.0	0.0	4.4	0.0	4.6	0.0	4.9	0.0	5.1	0.0
Other long-term	2.9	2.7	3.2	3.0	3.4	3.2	1.6	1.5	1.7	1.6
TOTAL ASSETS	100.0	100.0	100.0	100.0	100.0	100.0	100.0	100.0	100.0	100.0
Current liab	24.8	18.3	24.5	20.1	24.4	19.7	23.4	18.7	23.5	18.7
Long-term liab	3.9	3.7	3.8	3.5	3.7	3.4	3.2	3.0	3.4	3.1
Deferred taxes	0.0	0.0	0.0	0.0	0.0	0.0	0.0	0.0	0.0	0.0
Tot liabilities	28.7	22.0	28.3	23.6	28.1	23.1	26.6	21.7	26.9	21.8
Total capital	71.3	78.0	71.7	76.4	71.9	76.9	73.4	78.3	73.1	78.2
TOTAL LIABILITIES AND CAPITAL	100.0	100.0	100.0	100.0	100.0	100.0	100.0	100.0	100.0	100.0

SECTION B

UNIFIED GIFT AND ESTATE TAX

Taxable amount ($)	Tax ($)	Percentage on excess (%)
0	0	18
10,000	1,800	20
20,000	3,800	22
40,000	8,200	24
60,000	13,000	26
80,000	18,200	28
100,000	23,800	30
150,000	38,800	32
250,000	70,800	34
500,000	155,800	37
750,000	248,300	39
1,000,000	345,800	41
1,250,000	448,300	43
1,500,000	555,800	45
2,000,000	780,800	49
2,500,000*	1,025,800*	50*

*Note: For years after 1983 and before 1993, substitute the following in the above schedule:

Taxable amount ($)	Tax ($)	Percentage on excess (%)
2,500,000	1,025,800	53
3,000,000	1,290,800	55

Also, special rules apply for transfers exceeding $10,000,000.

INDEX

ABOUT THE **A**UTHOR

Irving L. Blackman is well known to thousands of business people throughout the United States. His practical, clearly written articles on taxation, accounting, and management problems are published in over 140 trade journals. Mr. Blackman also has written several books, including *The CPAs Guide to Tax Savings for Businessmen, Winning the Tax Game, The Book of Tax Knowledge,* and *How to Value Your Oil Jobbership for Tax Purposes.* An enthusiastic communicator, Blackman offers seminars for executives on various aspects of taxation.

Irving L. Blackman CPA, J.D., is a founding partner of Blackman Kallick Bartelstein, a leading Chicago-based CPA firm specializing in closely held businesses. He actively practices accounting and is a sought-after consultant by business owners from coast to coast.

His most recent book, *How the Wealthy Win the Tax Game* (self-published), is available by calling (312) 207-1040.